S0-BXF-041

The media's watching Vault!
Here's a sampling of our coverage.

"For those hoping to climb the ladder of success, [Vault's] insights are priceless."
– *Money magazine*

"The best place on the web to prepare for a job search."
– *Fortune*

"[Vault guides] make for excellent starting points for job hunters and should be purchased by academic libraries for their career sections [and] university career centers."
– *Library Journal*

"The granddaddy of worker sites."
– *US News and World Report*

"A killer app."
– *New York Times*One of Forbes' 33 "Favorite Sites"

– *Forbes*

"To get the unvarnished scoop, check out Vault."
– *Smart Money Magazine*

"Vault has a wealth of information about major employers and job-searching strategies as well as comments from workers about their experiences at specific companies."
– *The Washington Post*

"A key reference for those who want to know what it takes to get hired by a law firm and what to expect once they get there."
– *New York Law Journal*

"Vault [provides] the skinny on working conditions at all kinds of companies from current and former employees."
– *USA Today*

VAULT GUIDE TO
TOP
INTERNSHIPS

SAMER HAMADEH, MARK OLDMAN AND THE STAFF OF VAULT

All information in this book is subject to change without notice. Vault makes no claims as to the accuracy and reliability of the information contained within and disclaims all warranties. No part of this book may be reproduced or transmitted in any form or by any means, electronic or mechanical, for any purpose, without the express written permission of Vault Inc. Vault, the Vault logo, and "the most trusted name in career information™" are trademarks of Vault Inc.

For information about permission to reproduce selections from this book, contact Vault Inc.150 W. 22nd St. New York, New York 10011-1772, (212) 366-4212.

Library of Congress CIP Data is available.

ISBN 1-58131-423-x

Printed in the United States of America

Acknowledgments

Thanks to everyone who had a hand in making this book possible. We are extremely grateful to Vault's entire staff for all their help in the editorial, production and marketing processes. Vault also would like to acknowledge the support of our investors, clients, employees, family, and friends. Finally, we could not have done this guide without the help of organizations that offer top internships. Special thanks to Rebecca Rosen for her contributions to the Guide.

TO BUILD BEAUTY, WE NEED TALENT.

"AT L'ORÉAL, SUCCESS STARTS WITH PEOPLE. OUR PEOPLE ARE OUR MOST PRECIOUS ASSET. RESPECT FOR PEOPLE, THEIR IDEAS AND DIFFERENCES, IS THE ONLY PATH TO OUR SUSTAINABLE LONG-TERM GROWTH."

LAURENT ATTAL, PRESIDENT AND CEO, L'ORÉAL USA

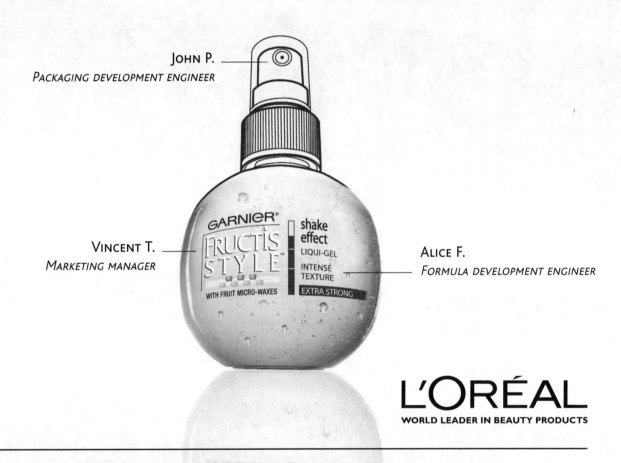

JOHN P.
PACKAGING DEVELOPMENT ENGINEER

VINCENT T.
MARKETING MANAGER

ALICE F.
FORMULA DEVELOPMENT ENGINEER

L'ORÉAL
WORLD LEADER IN BEAUTY PRODUCTS

JOIN US. WITH $4 BILLION IN ANNUAL SALES AND ACCOLADES THAT INCLUDE "AMERICA'S A-LIST INTERNSHIPS" BY THE WALL STREET JOURNAL, L'ORÉAL USA IS A COMPANY WHERE YOUR UNIQUE TALENTS CAN LEAD THE WAY TO A GREAT CAREER.

L'ORÉAL USA INTERNSHIP PROGRAM
MARKETING ▪ SALES ▪ FINANCE ▪ INFORMATION SYSTEMS ▪ LOGISTICS ▪ MANUFACTURING ▪ RESEARCH & DEVELOPMENT

IF YOU ARE AN IMAGINATIVE, RESULTS-FOCUSED AND FORWARD THINKING INDIVIDUAL WITH AN ENTREPRENEURIAL SPIRIT AND A COMMITMENT TO EXCELLENCE, THEN AN INTERNSHIP AT L'ORÉAL USA MAY BE FOR YOU. DESIGNED TO EXPOSE UNDERGRADUATE STUDENTS TO OUR DYNAMIC AND FAST-PACED BUSINESS, OUR PROGRAM OFFERS CHALLENGING ASSIGNMENTS, IMMEDIATE RESPONSIBILITY, PROFESSIONAL DEVELOPMENT TRAINING, AND CULMINATES WITH A PRESENTATION OF A STRATEGIC INDIVIDUAL PROJECT TO SENIOR MANAGEMENT. LEARN MORE ABOUT THIS EXCITING OPPORTUNITY AND APPLY AT **WWW.LOREALUSA.COM**. EQUAL OPPORTUNITY EMPLOYER.

Table of Contents

INTERNSHIP PROFILES: A 5

Academic Study Associates • Academy of Television Arts & Sciences Foundation • Accuracy in Academia • Accuracy in Media • ACNielsen • Actors Theatre of Louisville • Adler Planetarium & Astronomy Museum • The Advertising Club of New York • Advocates for Children of New York • Aetna Inc. • Africa Action • Africare • AFS Intercultural Programs • Agora Publishing • AIESEC • Aigner Associates • AIM for the Handicapped, Inc. • Alaska State Parks • Albertson's • Alliance of Resident Theatres • ALLTEL • Alticor • Amelia Island Plantation • America West Airlines • American Association for the Advancement of Science • American Association of Advertising Agencies • American Association of University Women • American Bar Association • American Cancer Society • American Civil Liberties Union • American Conservatory Theater • American Dance Festival • American Electric Power • American Enterprise Institute • American Family Insurance • American Federation of Teachers • American Forests • American Friends Service Committee • American Geographical Society • American Heart Association • American Hockey League • American Indian Science and Engineering Society • American & International Designs • American Israel Public Affairs Committee • American Management Association • American Place Theatre • The American Press • American Red Cross • American Repertory Theatre • American Rivers • American School for the Deaf • American Society of Magazine Editors • American Symphony Orchestra League • American University in Moscow • American Woman's Economic Development Corp. • American Youth Work Center • American-Arab Anti-Discrimination Committee • AMIDEAST • Amnesty International • The Anasazi Heritage Center • Anchorage Daily News • The Andy Warhol Museum • Anheuser-Busch Adventure Parks • The Antarctic and Southern Ocean Coalition • Aperture Foundation • Appalachian Mountain Club • Apple Computer • Arab American Institute • ARAMARK • Arden Theatre Company • Arena Stage • Argonne National Laboratory • Arms Control Association • Arnold Arboretum of Harvard University, The • Arthritis Foundation • Artists Space • Arup • Ashburn Institute • Ashoka • Asian American Arts Centre • Asian American Journalists Association • Asian American Justice Center • Aspen Center for Environmental Studies • Assistant Directors Training Program • Association of Trial Lawyers in America • AT&T Finance • AT&T Labs • AT&T Summer Management Program • Atlanta Ballet • Atlanta Braves • Atlanta Spirit, LLC • Atlantic Council of the United States • Atlantic Monthly • Australian Embassy • Avaya Inc

INTERNSHIP PROFILES: B 61

BAE Systems • Bain & Company • BalletMet Columbus • Baltimore Zoo • Bank of America • Barrington Stage Company • Baxter Healthcare Corporation • Beach Associates • Beacon Press • The Bear Stearns Companies, Inc. • Bechtel • Benetton • Berkeley Repertory Theatre • Bermuda Institute of Ocean Sciences • Bernstein-Rein • Bertelsmann AG • Best Buddies • BET • Bet Tzedek • Betsey Johnson • Biltmore Estate • Black & Veatch • Black Enterprise • The Blackstone Group • BMW Group • BMW of Manhattan, Inc./Mini of Manhattan • Boeing • Bonhams & Butterfields • Booz Allen Hamilton • Boston Consulting Group • The Boston Globe • Boston Magazine • Boston University International Programs • Boys Hope Girls Hope • BP • Breakthrough Collaborative • Breckenridge Outdoor Education Center • Brethren Volunteer Service • Brick Wall Management • Brookfield Zoo • Brookhaven National Laboratory • The Brookings Institution • Brooklyn Botanic Garden • Brooklyn Museum • Bucks County Courier Times • Buffalo Bill Historical Center • Bunim/Murray Productions • Burson-Marsteller • Business Executives for National Security

INTERNSHIP PROFILES: C 89

Cabrillo National Monument • California Governor's Office • California Museum of Photography • California Senate Fellows • California State Assembly • Callaway Engineering • Campbell Soup Company • Camphill Soltane • Canadian Embassy • Canoe & Kayak Magazine • CARE USA • Carnegie Endowment for International Peace • Carolyn Ray • The Carter Center • Catholic University of America • Caux Scholars Program • Cavaliers/Gund Arena

Visit Vault at **www.vault.com** for insider company profiles, expert advice, career message boards, expert resume reviews, the Vault Job Board and more.

VAULT CAREER LIBRARY   vii

Company • CBS News • CCUSA • CDS International, Inc., Internship Program in Argentina • CDS International, Inc., Internship Program in Germany • CDS International, Inc., Summer Internship Program in Spain • Center for Investigative Reporting • Center for Strategic and International Studies • Center for Talented Youth • Center for the Study of Conflict • Center for an Urban Future • Central Intelligence Agency • Centro para los Adolescentes de San Miguel de Allende • CH2M Hill • Chamber Music America • Charlesbridge Publishing • The Charlie Rose Show • Chevron • Chicago Botanic Garden • Chicago Bulls • Chicago Children's Museum • Children's Defense Fund • Children's Museum of Indianapolis • Child's Play Touring Theatre • Chincoteague National Wildlife Refuge • Choate Rosemary Hall • Christian Dior Couture • Christie's • Chronicle of the Horse • CIGNA • CIIT Centers for Health Research • Citigroup Corporate and Investment Banking • Citizens for Global Solutions

INTERNSHIP PROFILES: D

D.C. Booth Historic National Fish Hatchery • The Daily Press • DaimlerChrysler • Dallas Cowboys • Decatur House Museum • Dell • Deloitte & Touche • DesignTech International • Deutsche Bank • Deutsche Post World Net/DHL • Discovery Communications • Disney Theme Parks and Resorts College Program • Donna Karan • Dow Chemical Company • Dow Jones & Company • The Dow Jones Newspaper Fund • The Drawing Center • Dublin City Internships • Duke University Talent Identification • DuPont • Dykeman Associates

INTERNSHIP PROFILES: E

E/The Environmental Magazine • E! Entertainment Television • Eastman Kodak Company • Ecco Press • EchoStar Communications Corporation • Economic Research Service • The Economist • Edelman Public Relations • Educational Programmes Abroad • EdVenture Partners/General Motors Marketing Internship • Electronic Arts • Elite Model Management Corporation • Elizabeth Dow • Elizabeth Gillett, Ltd. • Elizabeth Glaser Pediatric AIDS Foundation • Emerson Electric • EMI Records Group North America • EMILY's List • The Emma L. Bowen Foundation • Emory University • Entertainment Weekly • Environmental Careers Organization • Ernst & Young • ESPN • Essence • ExxonMobil

INTERNSHIP PROFILES: F

Fairness and Accuracy in Reporting • Families USA • Fantagraphics • FAO Schwarz • Farm Sanctuary • Farrar, Straus & Giroux • Federal Bureau of Investigation • Federal Bureau of Prisons • Federal Emergency Management Agency • Federal Reserve Bank of New York • Federal Reserve Board • Fellowship of Reconciliation • Feminist Majority Foundation • Fenton Communications • Florida Grand Opera • Food for the Hungry • Food Network • Forbes • The Ford Foundation • Ford Models • Ford Motor Company • Foreign Affairs • Foreign Policy Research Institute • Forty Acres and a Mule • Fourth World Movement • Fox Cable Networks • Franconia Sculpture Park • Franklin D. Roosevelt Library • Freedom Theatre • French Embassy Press Office • Friends Committee on National Legislation • Frito Lay • Frontier Nursing Service

INTERNSHIP PROFILES: G

Gap • Gazette Communications • GE • GEICO • Genentech • General Mills • Gensler • Georgetown University Law Center Criminal Justice Clinic • Georgia Governor's Intern Program • Glen Helen Outdoor Education Center • Global Exchange • Global Volunteers • Goldman Sachs • Good Morning America • Goodman Theatre • Gould Farm • Government Affairs Institute • Graduate Public Service Internship at the University of Illinois at Springfield • Great Projects Film Company • Grubb & Ellis • Guggenheim Museum

INTERNSHIP PROFILES: H

H.O.M.E. • Habitat for Humanity International • Hallmark • Halstead Communications • HALT – An Organization of Americans for Legal Reform • Hansard Society for Parliamentary Government • HarperCollins • Harper's Magazine

Visit Vault at **www.vault.com** for insider company profiles, expert advice, career message boards, expert resume reviews, the Vault Job Board and more.

VAULT CAREER LIBRARY   ix

Visit Vault at **www.vault.com** for insider company profiles, expert advice, career message boards, expert resume reviews, the Vault Job Board and more.

V/ULT CAREER LIBRARY   **xi**

Introduction

What is an internship?

An internship is a sort of trial run at a company – and one of the best ways to test out a potential career field or employer. Internships vary in length – they can last two weeks or a full year – though most of them are for a three-month period. Many internships take place over the summer, while others may occur over the fall or spring semester, or of a duration of your choosing. Similarly, the majority of internships are full-time, though some are part-time.

Why do an internship?

You may be tempted just to take a job to earn money. There's nothing wrong with that – but there's so much more right with doing an internship. For example, if you want to break into a field that's tough to crack, like entertainment or advertising or politics, the very best way to get a job in the field is to have interned in it. Not only will you have great experience on your resume, but you'll meet plenty of contacts and potential mentors. Similarly, interning at a top company puts you on the fast track to getting a full-time offer from that firm – or one of its competitors! Most large companies are much more likely to hire a former intern than someone "right off the street." Even if you don't end up working for your employer, you'll have gained some invaluable and difficult-to-obtain experience.

But I need to get paid!

Don't think that doing an internship means giving up on pay altogether. It's true that many internships are unpaid or offer only academic credit – at the same time, these are often small, interesting organizations or companies in glamorous industries. But many others offer some kind of payment, from a stipend or travel allowance to a very generous salary. Others offer interesting perks, including travel and the chance to attend exclusive industry events.

Tips for applying to internships

Let's say you've found an internship that interests you. The first thing you should do is follow all the instructions. Here's a short checklist of things you need to do when applying for internships.

- Apply by the deadline. A few months before the deadline is even better – a small organization might just take the first qualified intern who applies.

- Follow the instructions! If you're asked to provide a writing sample, don't send your photo portfolio. If you're asked to provide a reference, start canvassing your teachers and professors.

- Make sure your resume is up-to-date and thoroughly spell-checked. If you've never written a resume, go to your school's career guidance center and ask for help. And ask an experienced professional or two whom you trust to review your resume. If you are applying for internships in different fields, you may need to have more than one version of your resume highlighting different experiences. Ensure that your most current contact information is on the resume.

- Don't ignore the cover letter. Make a persuasive case in your cover letter, which should be tailored to each internship, that you really want to intern at the company. Do your research and be specific – and honest – about why the opportunity is right for you. Again, make sure you carefully proofread the cover letter. Let a trusted friend or teacher read it as well.

- Follow up. If you're really interested in an internship, there's nothing wrong with a quick call or e-mail a few weeks after sending the application to let the organization know how interested you are. But don't pepper them with phone calls every day.

- Carpe diem. If you're really interested in an internship, but your qualifications aren't quite right, apply anyway and stress your real interest. Many organizations would rather have a truly excited and motivated intern than one who just meets the qualifications on paper.

- Take experience over money. You can always earn money; however, the window of opportunity for internships isn't open eternally. If you're really broke, consider taking a part-time job in order to work at the internship you really want.

Visit Vault at **www.vault.com** for insider company profiles, expert advice, career message boards, expert resume reviews, the Vault Job Board and more.

VAULT CAREER LIBRARY   1

Internships aren't just for college students. You'll be surprised at the number of companies and organizations willing to open their doors to smart and eager high school students, college grads and grad students. If your career isn't getting off to as fast a start as you might like, take a look – you might be able to intern at a company that interests you, which is an ideal way to network your way into a full-time job.

Making the most of your internship

Congratulations. You've gotten the internship you want. Here are some tips to make the most of your experience.

• Be a happy camper. Even if you're given work that you think is below you or not what you expected, do it and do it happily. A great attitude and a willingness to pitch in will impress your co-workers – and you might learn a lot more than you anticipated. Once you've proven your value, you may get projects and tasks more to your liking.

• Network, network, network. An internship is a great way to meet insiders in the industry of your choice. Don't limit yourself to your immediate co-workers or supervisors. Introduce yourself to others at the organization. Ask them to spend some time talking with you about their jobs and careers. You'll learn a lot about potential jobs and career paths, and potentially meet mentors and friends who can help you in the future.

• Talk about your expectations for the internship with your contact or supervisor. This will help your internship employer know what you want to do and give you the sort of experience that you want from your internship.

• Don't burn bridges. One thing you'll learn in the working world is that there is no such thing as an unimportant person. Everyone at your internship is a potential source of advice, contacts and career growth.

• Take full advantage of perks. If you're given the opportunity to attend a lecture from the CEO or go to a conference, go!

• Stay in touch. Make sure you get the contact information of everyone you've met at your internship and keep them posted on your career and educational progress.

A Guide to this Guide

Wondering how we've organized these internship entries? Well, read on. Here's a handy guide to the information you need in your search for the perfect internship.

The Buzz

A lighthearted look at first impressions of the employer, and at what makes this particular internship different. May include bad puns. It's a great way to take a fast look at an internship and see if you're interested in reading further.

The Stats

Industry(ies): The employer's specialties. Some employers may be listed in multiple industries or concentrations.

Location(s): The offices where the company accepts interns, alphabetized by city and state.

Number of interns: How many intern positions the company fills per time of year, if applicable. For example, some employers may accept 20 interns in the summer, but only five in the fall and two in the spring. If not applicable, internships are listed as number per year.

Pay: The salary an intern will earn, if any. Academic credit may be offered for unpaid internships, and indeed some internships require that you receive academic (or college) credit. This section also lists any perks included in the internship – which can be anything from free T-shirts to subsidized housing.

Length of internship: The typical length of an internship. Sometimes internship length will vary depending on time of year.

The Scoop

A brief look at the employer, including its history, organization, current activities and notable accomplishments.

On the Job

A description of the internship program, including the departments accepting interns, intern responsibilities and any special intern activities or projects.

Getting Hired

Apply by: Deadlines for applications, including links to online application forms, if available. This section also lists any special application requirements, such as essays or letters of reference.

Qualifications: Requirements for interns, including year of school (and if the internship is open to high school students, college graduates, grad students and/or international applicants) and required major and GPA, if applicable.

Contact: Contact information for internships can be found in this section. We list a specific name whenever possible, as well as direct phone numbers and e-mail addresses. If the employer has an internship section on its web site, the address will be listed here.

This is our second edition of this guide, and there are other great internships out there. If your organization sponsors an internship that you'd like us to cover, or if you've had an internship and want to tell the world about it, send us an e-mail at internshipbook@vault.com. If we cover the internship, you'll receive a FREE copy of next year's guide.

Visit Vault at **www.vault.com** for insider company profiles, expert advice, career message boards, expert resume reviews, the Vault Job Board and more.

VAULT CAREER LIBRARY   3

THE TOP 10 INTERNSHIPS IN AMERICA FOR 2007

BROUGHT TO YOU BY:

ACADEMY OF TELEVISION ARTS & SCIENCES

AT&T FINANCE

BOSTON CONSULTING GROUP

FEDERAL BUREAU OF INVESTIGATION

HAWK MOUNTAIN SANCTUARY

INROADS

JPMORGAN

THE LATE SHOW WITH DAVID LETTERMAN

NORTHWESTERN MUTUAL FINANCIAL NETWORK

SMITHSONIAN INSTITUTION

INTERNSHIP PROFILES: A

20/20

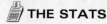

THE BUZZ

- "Find out who's 'most fascinating' before everybody else"
- "Maybe Barbara will put you on *The View*"
- "One of America's most-watched news magazine shows"

THE STATS

Industry(ies): Broadcast & Entertainment; Journalism

Location(s): New York, NY

Number of interns: Varies

Pay: None; academic credit

Length of internship: *Summer/spring:* 12 weeks each

THE SCOOP

20/20 is a long-running weekly television news magazine airing on ABC (which is owned by Disney) and hosted by John Stossel and TV news veteran Barbara Walters. Topics focus on current political and news-worthy events, celebrity profiles and interviews, and general interest pieces.

ON THE JOB

Interns learn about everything involved in putting together a news magazine television show, including production, editing, reporting and story development, working with the show's professional journalists. Interns also attend organized seminars hosted by ABC professionals (producers, on-air reporters and editors). Some interns work specifically with the "Stossel Unit," a small group producing John Stossel's one-hour news specials, as well as his weekly segments for *20/20*.

GETTING HIRED

Apply by: *Summer:* March 15; *spring:* December 1. Send resume and cover letter to the address below.

Qualifications:
Open to college juniors and seniors of all majors; not limited to journalism students. Must be able to receive academic credit for the internship.

Contact:
Nissa Walton Booker
ABC News Recruitment Coordinator
47 West 66th Street, 6th Floor
New York, NY 10023
E-mail: Nissa.Walton-booker@abc.com
abcnews.go.com/service/DailyNews/internships.html

3M

THE BUZZ

- "Find out who really invented Post-its"
- "Not just for tech-geeks"

THE STATS

Industry(ies): Consumer Products; Manufacturing; Science/Research

Location(s): St. Paul, MN

Number of interns: Varies

Pay: Varies

Length of internship: Varies

THE SCOOP

Formerly known as the Minnesota Mining and Manufacturing Company, 3M was created from a quest to perfect sandpaper in 1901 in a tiny town in northern Minnesota. The firm is now a diversified technology company boasting an operation worth $18 million annually and employing over 30,000 staff in 60 countries. It's also one of the 30 stocks that make up the Dow Jones Industrial Average. The company's collection of famous products and inventions includes Scotch tape, the Post-it Note and Thinsulate.

ON THE JOB

Many of 3M's departments accept interns, including research and development, IT, manufacturing, engineering, finance, marketing/sales/communications, logistics, human resources and administrative services. Duties vary between departments, but may include computer servicing, assisting sales staff or clerical tasks. Interns work closely with professional staff in all areas. The company often hires from its intern pool.

GETTING HIRED

Apply by: Rolling. The firm only accepts applications from the schools where it actively recruits. Check with your career office to see if your school is on the list.

Qualifications:
Open to college freshmen, sophomores, juniors and seniors and grad students studying at schools where 3M actively recruits (the list changes, so check with your career office).

Contact:
Internship Coordinator
3M Corporate Headquarters
3M Center
St. Paul, MN 55144-1000
Phone: (800) 364-3577
www.3m.com/profile/careers/areas.jhtml

A&E Television Network

 THE BUZZ
- "At the forefront of cable programming since the 1980's cable revolution!"
- "Home to *Biography*, *Cold Case Files*, *Airline* and *Family Plots*"

 THE STATS

Industry(ies): Art/Museum; Broadcast & Entertainment; Education; Internet; Journalism; Publishing

Location(s): Atlanta, GA; Chicago, IL; Detroit, MI; Los Angeles, CA; New York, NY

Number of interns: *Summer*: 10

Pay: Paid; $420-$525/week

Length of internship: *Summer*: 10 weeks

 THE SCOOP

A&E Television Network, a joint venture of the Hearst Corporation, ABC Inc. and NBC, is an award-winning international media company offering consumers a diverse communications environment including television programming, magazine publishing, web sites, music and home videos, as well as supporting nationwide educational efforts.

 ON THE JOB

A&E's internship program offers different opportunities each summer. Interns may work behind the scenes in areas involving marketing, sales, programming or promotions, or they can be on the "set" if working in production. Each department working with an intern is required to host a lunch, providing the interns with a chance to learn about the various departments within the company.

$ GETTING HIRED

Apply by: Rolling. E-mail a resume and cover letter indicating your area of interest. There will be an interview with HR and with the specific department.

Qualifications:
Open to college juniors and seniors, as well as students enrolled in graduate school. Minimum 3.0 GPA required.

Contact:
Internship Coordinator
A&E Network Television
235 East 45th Street
New York, NY 10017
Phone: (212) 210-1400
Fax: (212) 907-9402
E-mail: recruiterhj@aetn.com
www.aetv.com/global/corporate/index.jsp?NetwCode=AEN
&content_file=faq.html

A.E. Schwartz & Associates

 THE BUZZ
- "A growing firm that values its people"
- "Offers hands on practical experience"
- "Coach without breaking a sweat"

 THE STATS

Industry(ies): Management & Strategy Consulting

Location(s): Boston, MA

Number of interns: *Annual*: 30

Pay: None

Length of internship: Varies; available year-round

 **THE SCOOP**

Andrew E. Schwartz founded his namesake training company in Boston in 1982 and still serves as its CEO today. A.E. Schwartz & Associates delivers management-training programs nationally for clients in a wide range of industries and offers over 20 on-site training programs, executive coaching, a management series and a mentor/protégé program.

 ON THE JOB

Each department accepts three to five interns. Sales and marketing interns handle online and traditional promotion projects. Business technology interns work primarily on web site development. Graphic design interns create promotional flyers, web pages and printed products for the company. Writer/editor interns develop and create training products, Web text, press releases and marketing campaigns.

 GETTING HIRED

Apply by: Rolling. Send resume and cover letter to the address or e-mail below with the subject title: "Internship Application."

Qualifications:
Open to all college freshmen, sophomores, juniors and seniors, recent college graduates and grad students.

Contact:
Internship Coordinator
A.E. Schwartz & Associates
P.O. Box 79228
Waverly, MA 02479-0228
E-mail: internships@aeschwartz.com
www.aeschwartz.com/aboutuscareerinternship.htm

Visit Vault at **www.vault.com** for insider company profiles, expert advice, career message boards, expert resume reviews, the Vault Job Board and more.

VAULT CAREER LIBRARY 7

Abbott

 THE BUZZ
- "Work with Abbott to improve today's health care"

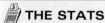 **THE STATS**

Industry(ies): Health Care; Pharmaceuticals; Science/Research

Location(s): Chicago, IL (corporate HQ); major facilities in Arizona; California; Massachusetts; Michigan; Ohio; Texas; Virginia; Germany; Japan; Puerto Rico; sales/marketing operations worldwide

Number of interns: *Summer*: 250

Pay: Paid; competitive salary. Varies based on internship assignment and location

Length of internship: *Summer*: 10-16 weeks

 **THE SCOOP**

Founded over 100 years ago by Chicago physician Dr. Wallace C. Abbott, Abbott has emerged as one of the world's top health care companies, with industry-leading pharmaceutical brands such as Biaxin XL, Humira® and Kaletra®, nutritional brands Similac, Ensure, EAS, Glucerna, and medical devices and diagnostics. Abbott's influence is apparent in a wide range of industries, including nutritional products, cardiovascular and spinal devices, and advanced instrument systems and tests for diagnosing infectious diseases, cancer, diabetes and genetic conditions. A global leader, Abbott provides innovative health care products and solutions in over 130 countries with sales at $19.7 billion.

ON THE JOB

The Abbott internship program provides undergraduate and graduate students with supervised practical work experience that is directly related to their education and career goals. The primary benefit of the program is to provide hiring managers with an opportunity to select and train high-potential students for future employment at Abbott. Students are placed within the fields of science, finance/accounting, information technology, production/operations, research and development, engineering and marketing/business related areas, with future plans to launch intern assignments globally. The primary objective of the internship program is to develop future talent for the company.

GETTING HIRED

Apply by: *Summer*: March 1 to be considered for that calendar year's internship program. Check if Abbott is recruiting at your college. If not, submit your resume through the web site: abbott.com/career/campus_internship.htm.

Qualifications:
Open to sophomore, junior and senior undergraduates who have completed at least one year of study and are registered for classes the following fall.

Contact:
College Relations
Abbott
200 Abbott Park Road
Abbott Park, IL 60064
Phone: (847) 937-6347
Fax: (847) 937-9646
abbott.com/career/Internships.htm

ABC News

 THE BUZZ
- "Think you're better than Peter Jennings? Prove it"
- "The ins-and-outs of network news"

THE STATS

Industry(ies): Broadcast & Entertainment; Journalism

Location(s): New York, NY

Number of interns: Varies

Pay: None; academic credit

Length of internship: *Summer/spring*: 12 weeks each

THE SCOOP

ABC News is one of the nation's three leading network news companies. Beside its flagship program, *World News Tonight*, ABC produces other news shows including *Good Morning America*, *Primetime*, *Nightline*, *This Week* and *World News Now*. The network also manages a 24-hour news web site, affiliates and radio news stations. ABC anchors include Peter Jennings, Barbara Walters, John Stossel and Diane Sawyer, and is owned by the Disney Corporation.

ON THE JOB

Interns are placed in several different "units," including news operations (liaisons between all news shows), graphics (assisting art directors), long-form (working on longer documentaries), film/tape library (screening and dubbing tapes), ABC News Radio, law and justice, NewsOne (affiliate feed service), news production, ABCNEWS.com, *World News Tonight with Peter Jennings*, *Weekend News*, the Brian Ross unit (the investigative team for ABC News), rights, clearances and permissions (working with outside sources), special events, *Primetime*, advertising and promotion, and ABC News VideoSource (selling stock footage). Duties vary depending on the unit.

GETTING HIRED

Apply by: *Summer*: March 15; *spring*: December 1. Send resume and cover letter to the address below.

Qualifications:
Open to junior and senior undergraduates, recent grads and grad students. Applicants must have at least college junior standing and must receive academic credit for the internship.

Contact:
Nissa Walton Booker
ABC News Recruitment Coordinator
47 West 66th Street, 6th Floor
New York, NY 10023
E-mail: nissa.Walton-booker@abc.com
abcnews.go.com/service/DailyNews/internships.html

Academic Study Associates

 THE BUZZ
- "Like summer camp, but with books"
- "For those who love campus life"

 THE STATS

Industry(ies): Education

Location(s): Amherst, MA; Berkeley, CA; Cambridge; Florence; Oxford; Barcelona; Nice

Number of interns: *Annual*: 100

Pay: $1,200 stipend plus room and board. Partial travel stipend for non-U.S. programs

Length of internship: *Summer*: 4 weeks

 THE SCOOP

For 21 years, Academic Study Associates has been running summer programs that prepare middle school and high school students for the transition into college. Usually based on a college campus, the programs – language and cultural studies, college prep, middle school and college admissions prep – are a combination of summer camp and school.

ON THE JOB:

ASA hires undergrads for positions in its pre-college and cultural immersion programs. Each residential advisor (RA) lives with a group of students and is responsible for student supervision and activities programming. Teachers and graduate students with teaching experience may apply for a faculty position at ASA's domestic programs. Others may apply for senior staff positions as Residential Life or Recreation Directors.

GETTING HIRED:

Apply by: Rolling.

Qualifications:

Qualifications vary depending on position. *RA*: open to undergraduates who have complete at least three years of college, including one year in residence; international staff must be fluent in the target language. *Senior staff*: open to college graduates only. See www.asaprograms.com/jobs/ jobs.asp for more details.

Contact:
ASA Programs
375 West Broadway, Ste 200
New York, NY 10012
Phone: (212) 786-8340
Toll free: (800) 752-2250
E-mail: summerstaff@asaprograms.com
www.asaprograms.com

Academy of Television Arts & Sciences Foundation

 THE BUZZ
- "The preeminent springboard to television careers"

 THE STATS

Industry(ies): Broadcast & Entertainment

Location(s): Los Angeles, CA

Number of interns: *Summer*: 35

Pay: Stipend provided to chosen interns

Length of internship: 8 weeks, starting in late June or early July; music interns normally start in August

 THE SCOOP

You know the Academy of Television Arts & Sciences from its role in administering the Emmy® Awards. The Academy also offers workshops, seminars and conferences on the broadcast industry, as well as "behind the scenes" evenings for members with the producers and stars of television's most innovative programs. The Television Academy Foundation Student Internship Program is a good way to start a career in the television industry.

ON THE JOB

The Academy Foundation offers internships in 29 different programs in areas such as agency, animation, commercials, casting, production, publicity and many more (log on to www.emmys.tv/foundationfor a complete list). Interns can work on game shows, made-for-TV movies, series and documentaries, learning sound, scriptwriting, editing and more. Many interns stay in touch with their summer mentors or accept job offers from their summer employers.

GETTING HIRED

Apply by: March 15. Mail cover letter, professional statement, resume, three letters of recommendation and any transcripts (check site for details). No fax or e-mail entries will be accepted.

Qualifications:
Open to current full-time college sophomores, juniors and seniors and graduate students in the U.S. Must have a car (needed for transportation in Los Angeles). See site for further information. Students who have completed college or graduate school prior to January 1, 2006, are not eligible.

Contact:
Nancy Robinson
Academy of Television Arts & Sciences Foundation – Internships
5220 Lankershim Boulevard
North Hollywood, CA 91601-3109
Phone: (818) 754-2800
www.emmys.tv/foundation

Visit Vault at **www.vault.com** for insider company profiles, expert advice, career message boards, expert resume reviews, the Vault Job Board and more.

 **VAULT** CAREER LIBRARY   **9**

Accuracy in Academia

 THE BUZZ
- "Assail ivory tower indoctrination and practice your editorial skills simultaneously"
- "A haven for conservative campus activists and writers"

 THE STATS

Industry(ies): Education; Journalism; Nonprofit

Location(s): Washington, DC

Number of interns: *Annual*: 2-10

Pay: $50/day stipend

Length of internship: *Spring/summer/fall*: Flexible; average 12 weeks, but will work with student's schedule

 THE SCOOP

Accuracy in Academia (AIA), a nonprofit group, aims to bring traditional academic ethics back into U.S. universities. The organization publishes a monthly newsletter, *Campus Report*, focusing articles on classroom course content, as well as free libertarian and conservative speech on campus (current issue available online). AIA also organizes speeches and events on campuses throughout the country, including the "Conservative University" conferences. AIA works closely with its sister organization, Accuracy in Media.

 ON THE JOB

Interns work closely with the small team making up AIA with tasks fitting the intern's particular skills. The program is great for those with keen editorial skills – interns write articles for AIA's web site, contribute to the summer issues of *Campus Report*, and edit and proofread work for both. Interns can also help organize and run AIA's annual summer conference and other events.

GETTING HIRED

Apply by: *Spring/summer/fall*: rolling. Send a cover letter, resume, application form and one or two short writing samples.

Qualifications:
Open to high school students and college freshmen, sophomores, juniors and seniors, as well as graduate students.

Contact:
Mal Kline
Accuracy in Academia
4455 Connecticut Avenue, NW, Suite 330
Washington, DC 20008
Phone: (202) 364-3085
E-mail: mal.kline@academia.org
www.academia.org/
www.campusreportonline.net/main/internships.php
www.aimajc.org

Accuracy in Media

 THE BUZZ
- "Help make the media meaningful"
- "Keep your eye on media bias"

 THE STATS

Industry(ies): Journalism; Nonprofit

Location(s): Washington, DC

Number of interns: *Annual*: 6-12

Pay: $50/day stipend

Length of internship: *Spring/summer/fall*: Flexible; average 12 weeks, but will work with student's schedule

 **THE SCOOP**

Accuracy in Media (AIM) is a small nonprofit focusing on media bias in television news, radio shows, newspapers and print magazines. The organization publishes the *AIM Report*, a bi-monthly newsletter for its members, produces a weekly syndicated column, airs radio bites regarding media bias, and runs a speaker's bureau, which sends a variety of orators to conferences, conventions and meetings around the United States. Accuracy in Media works closely with its sister nonprofit, Accuracy in Academia.

 ON THE JOB

AIM interns work in journalism, public relations, and marketing and advertising. The staff is small, so interns work closely alongside experienced professionals.

 GETTING HIRED

Apply by: *Summer*: March 31; *fall*: July 31; *spring*: December 31. Applicants should include a cover letter, resume, two references and a writing sample of two to six pages in length. An application form is available on the web site at www.aim.org/join_us/Internship.pdf or www.aimajc.org.

Qualifications:
Open to high school, college and graduate students, as well as recent college grads.

Contact:
Accuracy in Media
Attention: Carisa Bergen
4455 Connecticut Avenue, NW, Suite 330
Washington, DC 20008
Phone: (202) 364-4401 ext. 110
Fax: (202) 364-4098
E-mail: intern@aim.org
www.aim.org
www.aim.org/join_us/internships_app.html
www.aimajc.org

Actors Theatre of Louisville

 THE BUZZ
- "Further Arthur Miller's legacy"

 **THE STATS**

Industry(ies): Theater/Performing Arts

Location(s): Louisville, KY

Number of interns: *Annual*: 10-25

Pay: None; possible academic credit

Length of internship: Varies according to department

THE SCOOP

Founded in 1964, the Actors Theatre of Louisville was renamed the State Theatre of Kentucky in 1974. Now back to its original name, the nonprofit's goals have remained the same throughout – to revitalize American playwriting. Its Humana Festival, dubbed "The center of the theater world" by *Time* magazine, has long been a showcase for American drama. What began as a small theater company with a few hundred subscribers has grown to provide 30 productions and 600 performances with an annual attendance of over 200,000 audience members.

ON THE JOB

Interns work closely with the professional staff throughout the regular season, learning about arts administration or technical theater. Interns can apply to work in a variety of departments, including administration, management, communications, costumes, development, education, festival management, lighting design, literary management, properties, scenic artistry, sound design, stage management and technical direction.

GETTING HIRED

Apply by: Rolling. Download the online application from http://www.actorstheatre.org/about_a_i.htm and mail the completed form to the address below.

Qualifications:
Open to all college freshmen, sophomores, juniors and seniors, grad students and recent college graduates.

Contact:
Monica Francisco
Apprentice/Intern Company
Actors Theatre of Louisville
316 West Main Street
Louisville, KY 40202-4218
Phone: (502) 584-1265
Fax: (502) 561-3300
E-mail: mfrancisco@actorstheatre.org
www.actorstheatre.org/about_a_i.htm

Visit Vault at **www.vault.com** for insider company profiles, expert advice, career message boards, expert resume reviews, the Vault Job Board and more.

V\ULT CAREER LIBRARY   **11**

Adler Planetarium & Astronomy Museum

 THE BUZZ
- "Not just for Hubble fans"
- "Keep your eyes on the skies with this flexible internship"

 THE STATS

Industry(ies): Art/Museum; Education; Science/Research

Location(s): Chicago, IL

Number of interns: *Annual*: 2-5

Pay: None. Free or reduced admission to many of Chicago's museums and cultural institutions

Length of internship: Flexible

 **THE SCOOP**

The Adler Planetarium claimed new ground for Chicago in 1930 as the first planetarium in the Western hemisphere. Today, the Adler is ready to take on the entire world – according to its web site, it's current goal is "to be the world's leading public center for interpreting the exploration of the Universe." It's certainly on its way, with a recently completed $40-million renovation project that added 60,000 square feet to the original building. The Adler runs an extensive education series, maintains a collection of items on the history of astronomy and hosts an astronomy department with several members holding joint appointments at the University of Chicago and Northwestern University.

 ON THE JOB

The Adler offers volunteer positions to anyone 16 years of age or over. Past positions have included working with the Adler's education programs and some volunteers have also handled its information systems, membership and publicity.

 GETTING HIRED

Apply by: Rolling. Interns are accepted through online application. Log on to: www.adlerplanetarium.org/volunteer/vol_app.shtml. Interns will be called in for an interview.

Qualifications:
Open to high school students 16 years of age and older, college freshmen, sophomores, juniors and seniors, as well as recent grads and grad students.

Contact:
Alisun Dekock
Adler Planetarium & Astronomy Museum
1300 South Lake Shore Drive
Chicago, IL 60605
Phone: (312) 322-0514
E-mail: volunteer@adlernet.org
www.adlerplanetarium.org/volunteer/index.shtml

The Advertising Club of New York

 THE BUZZ
- "Network with top advertising and PR managers"
- "Find out what it's really like to get ahead in advertising"

 THE STATS

Industry(ies): Advertising

Location(s): New York, NY

Number of interns: *Summer*: 15-20

Pay: Paid; $3,000/summer

Length of internship: *Summer*: 10 weeks

 **THE SCOOP**

Founded in 1896, the Advertising Club is an organization for marketing and advertising professionals in the communications field. Members are able to network with others in the advertising, marketing and publishing fields at regular events such as luncheons and symposiums, as well as monthly young professionals socials. The Club places a special focus on nurturing the next generation of young ad professionals and has recently placed an emphasis on giving back through educational initiatives, grants and scholarships.

 ON THE JOB

The Ad Club calls itself a "mentor" for its interns, and the description is apt. The Ad Club places interns in various participating advertising agencies, marketing and publishing companies in New York City. Interns conduct their day-to-day work at an assigned agency and meet weekly at the Ad Club for seminars. Areas of possible internships include account management, creative, media, publishing and account planning. The Ad Club also welcomes interns to its regular series of discussions and events.

 GETTING HIRED

Apply by: March 1.

Qualifications:
Open to college junior and seniors. Include an essay, transcript and two recommendations, along with a completed application available on the web site.

Contact:
The Advertising Club
Attention: Internship Coordinator
235 Park Avenue South, 6th Floor
New York, NY 10003
Phone: (212) 533-8080
www.theadvertisingclub.org/pdfs/adclub_internships.pdf

Advocates for Children of New York

THE BUZZ
- "Save the children!"
- "Perfect training for education, law, JDs or undergrads looking for nonprofit experience"

THE STATS
Industry(ies): Education; Law; Nonprofit

Location(s): New York, NY

Number of interns: *Summer*: 10; *fall/spring*: 5 each

Pay: Varies

Length of internship: *Summer*: 10 weeks; *fall/spring*: 12-16 weeks each

THE SCOOP

Advocates for Children works with needy New York families to ensure that their children receive adequate and equal public education services. AFC offers case advocacy, technical assistance and outreach programs to educate teachers, students and parents about students' rights. AFC also works to improve existing education legislation and conducts long-term research and policy analysis.

ON THE JOB

Legal interns at AFC are often law school students or undergrads considering law school. The organization's summer internship program gives law students the opportunity to work directly with attorneys on individual cases. During the year, AFC offer several internships: legal internships working on its class-action litigation; development and special event fundraising; and policy research.

GETTING HIRED

Apply by: Rolling. Send a resume and cover letter to the address below.

Qualifications:
Open to college students, all graduate students and recent grads, as well as volunteers.

Contact:
Lisa Kung
Advocates for Children of New York
151 West 30th Street, 5th Floor
New York, NY 10001
E-mail: lkung@advocatesforchildren.org
No phone calls, please.

Aetna Inc.

THE BUZZ
- "Learn about the benefits business"
- "Ensure yourself a great internship in the insurance industry"

THE STATS
Industry(ies): Financial Services; Health Care; Insurance

Location(s): Hartford, CT (corporate HQ); regional offices in Blue Bell, PA; Middletown, CT; field offices in most states

Number of interns: *Annual*: 75

Pay: Paid; highly competitive hourly rates. Access to on-site fitness center

Length of internship: *Summer*: full-time employment during the summer; *co-op*: minimum of 5 months with weekly minimum of 20 hours

THE SCOOP

Aetna, which recently celebrated its 150th anniversary, is a Fortune 100 company focused (since the 2000 sale of its global health and financial service businesses) on "building the premier employee benefits company in the industry." With over 28,000 employees, the company serves a whopping 10 million medical, dental and group insurance customers in all 50 U.S. states and boasts revenues of nearly $20 billion a year. President Ron Williams was recently named one of *Fortune* magazine's 50 Most Powerful Black Executives in America.

ON THE JOB

Aetna offers a summer internship and a year-round co-op program. Interns can choose from fields including, but not limited to, information technology, marketing, sales, communications, finance, underwriting and actuarial science. The job search section of the web site is designed to acquaint potential interns with the full breadth of available opportunities.

GETTING HIRED

Apply by: Late March for summer positions. Apply for all opportunities online.

Qualifications:
All internships are open to students who have completed at least 45 credits (sophomore status or higher). A GPA of at least 3.0 is preferred. Aetna favors computer science, computer engineering, management information systems, business administration or related majors and requires strong communication, interpersonal and problem-solving skills.

Contact:
Internship Coordinator
Aetna
151 Farmington Avenue
Hartford, CT 06156
Phone: (800) 238-6247
aetna.recruitmax.com/ENG/candidates/default.cfm?szCategory=JobList&szFormat=search

Visit Vault at **www.vault.com** for insider company profiles, expert advice, career message boards, expert resume reviews, the Vault Job Board and more.

VAULT CAREER LIBRARY 13

Africa Action

 THE BUZZ
- "Advocate for Africa"

THE STATS

Industry(ies): Nonprofit

Location(s): Washington, DC

Number of interns: Varies with need

Pay: None

Length of internship: Varies. Usually, *spring*: 10-12 weeks; *summer*: 8-10 weeks; *fall*: 10-12 weeks

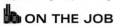 **THE SCOOP**

Africa Action, America's oldest organization addressing issues in Africa, has a long history of analysis and activism on African affairs. The organization's aim is to share accurate information about Africa with the American public and mobilize people to change policy for the better. Founded in 1953, the current organization was renamed Africa Action in 2001, when three separate groups merged.

ON THE JOB

Interns are divided into two groups: public education and policy analysis. Those who work in public education and the mobilization team support the field operations staff on mobilization strategy, work on public education efforts and campaign materials, and meet with other civil society groups dealing with similar issues. The other interns work with the policy analysis and communications staff monitoring key issues and legislative changes relating to Africa, researching organizational priorities concerning African issues (such as HIV/AIDS), and helping with media strategy and public relations.

GETTING HIRED

Apply by: *Spring*: December 15; *summer*: April 14; *fall*: July 15. Send resume, writing sample (three to five pages), references and a cover letter to the e-mail address below.

Qualifications:
Open to all college freshmen, sophomores, juniors and seniors, and grad students.

Contact:
Africa Action
Internship Program
1634 Eye Street, NW, Suite 810
Washington, DC 20006
Phone: (202) 546-7961
Fax: (202) 546-1545
E-mail: Africaaction@igc.org
www.africaaction.org/about/jobs.php

Africare

THE BUZZ
- "For those serious about their commitment to fighting AIDS and aiding Africa"
- "Help developing nations develop"

THE STATS

Industry(ies): Nonprofit

Location(s): Washington, DC

Number of interns: *Annual*: 10-15

Pay: None. Interns are expected to obtain funding through their educational institutions

Length of internship: Up to a year; most are summer internships from May-August

THE SCOOP

Africare is the oldest and largest in a collection of private, charitable U.S. organizations focusing on African issues. Concentrating its efforts on agriculture and health care (especially HIV/AIDS prevention and management), Africare also works with water resource development, environmental management, basic education, microenterprise development, governance initiatives and emergency humanitarian aid.

ON THE JOB

Internships are varied and specific to current needs, taking place either in the DC office or any of 26 countries in Africa. As positions become available, Africare contacts individuals who have sent in a resume with appropriate skills and/or experience for the position.

GETTING HIRED

Apply by: Mid-spring. Send a resume and cover letter by U.S. mail by the middle of the spring semester.

Qualifications:
Open to high school graduates, college freshmen, sophomores, juniors and seniors, college graduates and grad students. International experience and/or travel preferred, but not required.

Contact:
Charmaine Turner
Africare House
440 R Street, NW
Washington, DC 20001
Phone: (202) 462-3614
Fax: (202) 387-1034
E-mail: resumes@africare.org
www.africare.org

AFS Intercultural Programs

 THE BUZZ
- "Indulge your travel bug"
- "Get a taste of a different culture"

 **THE STATS**

Industry(ies): Education; Nonprofit

Location(s): New York, NY

Number of interns: *Summer/spring/fall*: 4-6 each

Pay: Paid; varies

Length of internship: 3-9 months; available year-round

THE SCOOP

Dedicated to building a more peaceful world through international student exchange, AFS (American Field Service) is one of the largest community-based volunteer organizations in the world. Every year, more than 10,000 students, young adults and teachers participate in AFS programs, of which there are three. Students under the age of 18 are placed with host families and schools for semesters or years abroad. Teachers are sent to live and work in a foreign community (with a host family) and school. Participants over the age of 18 can work in a community-service organization or business abroad while learning language skills. AFS started as an ambulance program during World War I. In 1947 the organization began bringing high school students from foreign countries to the U.S.

ON THE JOB

According to the internship coordinator at AFS, the organization tries to expose its interns to a diverse combination of activities. However, most interns specialize by working with a specific department (usually chosen by the intern). Departments that have taken interns in the past have been the communications/ design department, finance, programs and service evaluation (working with AFS partners). Some interns also do international work.

GETTING HIRED

Apply by: Rolling. Send resume and cover letter (explaining areas in which you want to work) to the e-mail address below.

Qualifications:
Open to college freshmen, sophomores, juniors and seniors, as well as recent college graduates and grad students.

Contact:
Emma Kalonzo
71 West 23rd Street, 17th Floor
New York, NY 10010
Phone: (212) 807-8686, ext. 140
Fax: (212) 807-1001
E-mail: human.resources@afs.org
www.afs.org

Agora Publishing

 THE BUZZ
- "Work in an historic mansion"
- "Pretend you're Socrates"
- "Columns and columns"

 **THE STATS**

Industry(ies): Publishing

Location(s): Baltimore, MD

Number of interns: *Annual*: 25-30

Pay: Paid; varies. Housing; free parking

Length of internship: *Spring/summer/fall*: flexible

THE SCOOP

Agora Publishing is a rather unusual international company that produces newsletters for the financial, travel and health industries, but also publishes special interest books. These are no run-of-the-mill publications. Rather than concentrating on the media, Agora likes to focus on the ideas within each product. After all, the name of the company – which was founded in 1979 – is the ancient Greek word for "community center," or the place where new ideas are exchanged. Agora's offices are located in a cluster of 19th-century mansions in Baltimore.

ON THE JOB

Agora's interns spend most of their time researching, but the work itself varies greatly. Some are placed in the editorial department, while others work in graphic design, advertising, marketing or human resources, completing needed research as well as other administrative duties. Interns should be prepared to work quickly and accurately.

GETTING HIRED

Apply by: Rolling. Send a resume and cover letter to the address below.

Qualifications:
Open to college freshmen, sophomores, juniors and seniors, grad students and recent college graduates.

Contact:
Elizabeth Zepp
Agora Publishing
14 West Mount Vernon Place
Baltimore, MD 21201
E-mail: ezepp@agorapublishinggroup.com
www.agora-inc.com

Visit Vault at **www.vault.com** for insider company profiles, expert advice, career message boards, expert resume reviews, the Vault Job Board and more.

V/\ULT CAREER LIBRARY   **15**

AIESEC

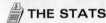 **THE BUZZ**
- "Get an internship in China – or Cameroon"
- "See the world for a minimal fee"

THE STATS

Industry(ies): All industries

Location(s): New York, NY; various other U.S. offices and 90 countries worldwide

Number of interns: *Annual:* Varies, but can be as many as 4,000

Pay: Paid; salary (at least minimum wage of host country). Participants pay program administration fee (about $500) and transportation/relocation costs

Length of internship: 8 weeks-18 months

THE SCOOP

Spanning over 90 countries and 800 universities, AIESEC is the world's largest student-based organization. It acts as an international platform for leadership development by placing students and young professionals in short-term internships around the world. Founded by seven students in France as the Association Internationale des Etudiants en Sciences Economiques et Commerciales in 1948, the organization is dedicated to helping individuals build their global network, expand their worldview and gain leadership skills to increase international understanding and cooperation.

ON THE JOB

AIESEC U.S. exchange participants will be provided with a practical traineeship experience in a company, educational institution, or nonprofit organization. Interns will be able to experience life in another country, as well as have the chance to learn practical skills in the workplace. Participants will be able to apply for positions in a wide range of fields, including marketing, finance, accounting, management, education, IT and development.

GETTING HIRED

Apply by: Rolling. Apply by registering online to join one of AIESEC's local communities at www.aiesecus.org/register.

Qualifications:
Open to college freshmen, sophomores, juniors and seniors, as well as recent graduates and grad students.

Contact:
AIESEC United States
127 West 26 Street, 10th floor
New York, NY 10001
Phone: (212) 757-3774
E-mail: Aiesec@aiesecus.org
www.aieseconline.net

Aigner Associates

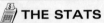 **THE BUZZ**
- "A trendy communications firm"
- "PR, marketing, image development and event production – all rolled into one"

THE STATS

Industry(ies): Public Relations; Management & Strategy Consulting

Location(s): Allston, MA

Number of interns: *Summer/fall/spring:* 1 each

Pay: None. Free parking

Length of internship: 8 weeks minimum

THE SCOOP

Aigner Associates is a strategic marketing and public relations firm based in the Allston section of Boston. The company is a management consulting and public relations firm and does not offer advertising services. Aigner also plans special events. Clients have included Panera Bread, Mount Auburn Hospital, iParty, the American Camping Association and Filen's .

ON THE JOB

Interns work with account executives, assisting with specific clients. They learn basic public relations and marketing skills by drafting press releases and pitch letters, doing research to compile fact sheets, creating press kits, maintaining media contact lists and pitching story ideas to the media. They also provide ongoing administrative support to all Aigner departments. Supervisors evaluate interns at the end of the program.

GETTING HIRED

Apply by: Rolling. Send a resume and cover letter to the address below.

Qualifications:
Open to college sophomores, juniors and seniors.

Contact:
Internship Coordinator
Aigner Associates, Inc.
250 Everett Street
Allston, MA 02134-1198
Phone: (617) 254-9500
E-mail: jobs@aignerassoc.com
www.aignerassoc.com

AIM for the Handicapped, Inc.

THE BUZZ
- "Help others help themselves"

THE STATS
Industry(ies): Education; Nonprofit

Location(s): Dayton, OH

Number of interns: *Annual*: 3

Pay: None

Length of internship: Varies based on need (usually 3 months)

THE SCOOP
Adventures in Movement (AIM) is a nonprofit organization that assists individuals with disabilities in reaching their highest potential. AIM works with any and all ages and disablties to improve a vast area of gross and fine motor skills, as well as speech and concentration issues. The organization's free movement program, called the AIM Method, focuses on improving motor skills through movement and rehabilitation techniques, and is set to rhythmic music. Several celebrities have supported the program, including the late Gene Kelly and pro golfer Nancy Lopez.

ON THE JOB
AIM has a large network of volunteers with which interns work on a water program and other activities. More often, interns work with the professional staff, mostly in classroom activities surrounding the AIM Method. Interns learn the method in a workshop and must be certified before teaching on their own.

GETTING HIRED
Apply by: Rolling. Send a resume and cover letter to the address below.

Qualifications:
Open to high school students 16 or older, college freshmen, sophomores, juniors and seniors, grad students and recent college graduates.

Contact:
AIM for the Handicapped, Inc.
Intern/Volunteer Program
945 Danbury Road
Dayton, OH 45420
Phone: (937) 294-4611
Fax: (937) 294-3782
E-mail: aimeducation@hotmail.com
aimforthehandicapped.org

Alaska State Parks

THE BUZZ
- "See how big Alaska really is"
- "Rustic, but bustling with outdoor opportunities"

THE STATS
Industry(ies): Government

Location(s): Alaska

Number of interns: *Annual*: 30

Pay: None. Most interns are provided with uniforms, a small expense allowance and rustic housing; allowance amount varies between $100-$300 per month; some positions provide food instead of an allowance

Length of internship: *Summer/winter*: minimum 6-8 week commitment

THE SCOOP
The Alaska State Parks Volunteer Program is run by the Alaska Department of Natural Resources and offers 90 full-time volunteer positions every year. A handful of these positions qualify as internships and can be applied toward academic credit. Work locations include the Kenai River Special Management Area, Chugach State Park and the Alaska Chilkat Bald Eagle Preserve, among others.

ON THE JOB
Available internships include archaeological assistant, backcountry ranger assistant, museum assistant, natural history interpreter, park caretaker, program coordinator, ranger assistant, trail crew, winter natural history interpreter, winter park caretaker and winter ranger assistant. These positions are full time and located throughout Alaska.

GETTING HIRED
Apply by: April 1, but no earlier than October 1. You may apply for as many positions as you like, filling out a different application for each internship (apply online at www.dnr.state.ak.us/parks/vip/apps.htm or call to request application).

Qualifications:
Open to freshman, sophomore, junior and senior undergrads, and college graduates who are U.S. citizens over 18 years of age. Preferred and required experience varies by internship. Check web site for details.

Contact:
Lynn Wibbenmeyer
Volunteer Coordinator
Alaska State Parks
550 West 7th Avenue, Suite 1380
Anchorage, AK 99501-3561
Phone: (907) 269-8708
Fax: (907) 269-8907
E-mail: volunteer@dnr.state.ak.us
www.dnr.state.ak.us/parks/vip/index.htm

Visit Vault at **www.vault.com** for insider company profiles, expert advice, career message boards, expert resume reviews, the Vault Job Board and more.

VAULT CAREER LIBRARY   17

Albertson's

 THE BUZZ

- "Start your career working with one of the largest conglomerates in the world"

 THE STATS

Industry(ies): Consumer Products; Food & Beverage; Pharmaceuticals; Retail

Location(s): Nationwide

Number of interns: Varies

Pay: Varies

Length of internship: Varies by department; usually 10 weeks

 THE SCOOP

Joe Albertson opened his first grocery store in 1939; today, the supermarket conglomerate is the second-largest chain in the U.S. – operating over 2,300 stores throughout the country, including Acme Markets, Jewel, Sav-on and Shaw's. Albertson stores are a combination of grocery stores and pharmacies; about a third also have onsite gas stations. The company is headquartered in Boise, Idaho, and has over 230,000 employees. Annual sales are over $35 million.

 ON THE JOB

Albertson's offers internships in a variety of departments. Food Store Management internships are offered over the summer in local Jewel and Acme stores. These programs offer experience in management, inventory control and marketing. Albertson's also has a Drug Store Management program, which gives interns a chance to learn the management procedures and policies of a pharmacy. Additionally, Pharmacy Student and Summer Intern positions are available, allowing students to assist pharmacists with filling orders and interacting with clients and medical professionals. These positions are full-time and structured to focus on disease management. Accounting and finance internships are also available at the Corporate Store Support Center in Boise.

 GETTING HIRED

Apply by: Rolling. *Food Store Management*: E-mail resume to the appropriate store (Albertsons: Employment@albertsons.com; Jewel: JJ.jobsatjewelosco@albertsons.co; Acme: acmeresumes @albertsons.com); *Drug Store Management*: apply at drug recruiting@albertsons.com. For more information on Albertson's programs, or to apply online, visit: www.albertsons.com/ abs_careers/default.asp.

Qualifications:
Drug Store Management: applicants must be enrolled in a professional pharmacy program. *Pharmacy Student/Summer Intern*: applicants must have completed at least one year of a professional pharmacy program.

Contact:
Albertson's Corporate Headquarters
250 Parkcenter Blvd.
Boise, ID 83726
Phone: (208) 395-6200 or toll free: (888) 746-7252
Fax: (208) 395-6349
www.albertsons.com

Alliance of Resident Theatres

 THE BUZZ

- "Theater buffs look no further"
- "Learn the business side of theater"

 THE STATS

Industry(ies): Theater/Performing Arts

Location(s): New York, NY

Number of interns: *Summer/winter*: 1-2 each

Pay: None. Occasional complimentary theater tickets

Length of internship: Varies depending on availability

 THE SCOOP

Founded in 1972, A.R.T./NY calls itself "the service organization for the nation's largest, most artistically influential, and most culturally diverse theater community: Off Broadway." A.R.T./NY provides low-cost office space and management-related technical assistance, makes grants to small and emerging theaters, produces audience development initiatives and serves as an advocate for state and local arts.

 ON THE JOB

A.R.T./NY hires interns in accordance with upcoming projects. There is generally a position available in the summer and another during the rest of the year. Interns have the opportunity to meet with prominent directors and actors.

 GETTING HIRED

Apply by: Rolling. Submit resume to contact below.

Qualifications:
Open to all college students.

Contact:
Jewell Campbell
575 Eighth Avenue, Suite 17 South
New York, NY 10018
Phone: (212) 244-6667
Fax: (212) 714-1918
E-mail: artnewyork@aol.com
www.offbroadwayonline.com

ALLTEL

 THE BUZZ
- "A hands-on, mentor-based internship in telecommunications"

 THE STATS

Industry(ies): Accounting; Communications; Engineering; Public Relations; Publishing

Location(s): Atlanta, GA; Charlotte, NC; Cleveland, OH; Jacksonville, FL; Little Rock, AR

Number of interns: *Annual:* 10-20

Pay: Paid; varies depending on education. Living expenses

Length of Internship: 10-12 weeks

 THE SCOOP

ALLTEL Communications Products is one of the nation's largest providers of communications products and services, with more than 50 years of experience. Thanks to relationships with hundreds of equipment manufacturers worldwide, the company is able to offer its customers thousands of high-demand items through a nationwide network of regional distribution and communications products centers. ALLTEL is a customer-focused communications company with more than 13 million customers and $8 billion in annual revenues. Alltel provides wireless, local telephone, long-distance, Internet and broadband services to residential and business customers in 27 states.

ON THE JOB

Internship and co-op programs at ALLTEL are highly-structured programs that allow students to prepare the framework for their individual program, ensuring that the experience is tailored to each intern's unique learning objectives. Interns gain work experience in a professional, fast-paced, change-oriented business environment. ALLTEL provides interns with chances to network with professionals in their field of interest and earn a competitive salary while they learn.

GETTING HIRED

Apply by: *Summer:* May 30; *spring:* December 1. Interested applicants can view current internship opportunities and apply online at http://alltel.com/career/search/index.html.

Qualifications:
Open to undergraduate and graduate students with high academic achievement and enthusiasm. Interns should have a background in extracurricular activities, possess solid communication and community-related skills. Salary is commensurate with educational status.

Contact:
Alltel Corporate Headquarters
One Allied Drive
Building 4, Second Floor
Little Rock, AR 72202-2099
www.alltel.com

Alticor

 THE BUZZ
- "Be part of a top selling machine"

 **THE STATS**

Industry(ies): Consumer Products

Location(s): Ada, MI; Bueana Park, CA; Lakeview, CA

Number of interns: *Summer:* approximately 70

Pay: Paid; $13-$18/hour. Housing allowance for interns who live over 50 miles from the office location; discount at on-site health club; discounts at company store

Length of internship: *Summer:* 3 months; *co-op:* 3-6 months

 THE SCOOP

Alticor Inc. the parent company of Amway, Access Business Group and its subsidary Nutrilite, and Quixtar, operates in over 80 countries and territories and has nearly 13,000 employees worldwide. Their services range from providing personal care products and direct selling (Amway) to facilitating e-commerce (Quixtar). Alticor supports more than 3 million independent business owners and generates sales of over $6 billion through its global network.

 ON THE JOB

Alticor accepts interns through all of its companies. Interns work in business, manufacturing, supply chain, research and development, IT, finance, engineering, logistics, protection services, to name a few. Visit the company web site for more details on available positions.

GETTING HIRED

Apply by: *Summer:* February 1; *co-op:* rolling. Apply online at www.alticor.com/careers/internship.html, or attend an on-campus career fair to discuss available opportunities. The career fair schedule may be found online.

Qualifications:
Open to college sophomores, juniors, and seniors enrolled in a BS program in a relevant discipline. Applicants must have a 3.0 GPA or higher and be authorized to work full-time in the U.S.

Contact:
Kevin Douglas, Internship Program Manager
Alticor Inc.
7575 Fulton Street East
Ada, MI 49355
Phone: (616) 787-1463
E-mail: Kevin.Douglas@Alticor.com
www.alticor.com/careers/internship.html
www.amway.com
www.accessbusinessgroup.com
www.nutrilite.com
www.quixtar.com

Visit Vault at **www.vault.com** for insider company profiles, expert advice, career message boards, expert resume reviews, the Vault Job Board and more.

V\ULT CAREER LIBRARY **19**

Amelia Island Plantation

 THE BUZZ
- "Interpret nature or clean cabanas – it's up to you"
- "Cater to Florida's vacation crowd"

 THE STATS

Industry(ies): Hospitality; Tourism/Recreation

Location(s): Amelia Island, FL

Number of interns: *Annual*: 75

Pay: Varies. Recreation, housekeeping, front desk, food and beverage, retail, aquatics/rental, marketing, graphics, conference sales, health and fitness, human resources, and environmental interpretation are considered "stipend internships" and students working in these areas are provided with a housing stipend of $250/week plus two meals per scheduled day. Golf, turf management, tennis, pastry and culinary interns are considered "seasonal" employees and earn an hourly wage. Visit the web site for a complete list of perks

Length of internship: 4-18 months; a 16-week minimum commitment is preferred

 **THE SCOOP**

Boasting 1,350 acres, four golf courses, 23 tennis courts, and a nature center, Amelia Island Plantation aptly labels itself "Florida's Premier Island Resort." Located less than 30 miles from the Jacksonville airport, the resort provides guests with a variety of accommodation options and leisure activities.

ON THE JOB

Internships are available in recreation, environmental interpretation, housekeeping, turf management, culinary, pastry, conference sales, fron desk, health and fitness, human resources, graphics, marketing, golf, tennis, food and beverage, aquatics/rentals and real estate.

GETTING HIRED

Apply by: Rolling. Apply online at http://www.aipfl.com.

Qualifications:
Open to freshman, sophomore, junior and senior undergrads. International applicants welcome. Students compensated with a stipend must have their internships recognized as part of an academic program. Preference is given to those expressing the desire to seek a permanent position with the company after their internship. Most positions require applicants to have a good driving record and they must be fluent in conversational English.

Contact:
Jennifer Lo, Internship Coordinator
Amelia Island Plantation
P.O. Box 3000
Amelia Island, FL 32035-3000
Phone: (904) 277-5904
Fax: (904) 491-4345
E-mail: intern@aipfl.com
www.aipfl.com/aboutamelia/Employment/internships.htm

America West Airlines

 THE BUZZ
- "Help your career take off"
- "Earn your wings here"

 THE STATS

Industry(ies): Transportation

Location(s): Phoenix, AZ

Number of interns: *Spring/summer/fall*: 10-15 each

Pay: None. The company strongly suggests that students go through their school to get academic credit for their time

Length of internship: *Spring/summer/fall*: 12-16 weeks each

 **THE SCOOP**

Phoenix, Arizona-based America West Airlines first launched on August 1, 1983, with just three planes and 280 employees. The airline "took off" quickly and boasted over $1 billion in revenues by 1990. Today, AWA employs over 13,000 staff with a fleet of over 142 planes and over 800 departures daily to 93 destinations, including major cities in the U.S., Mexico, Canada and Costa Rica.

 ON THE JOB

Interns are placed in various departments including marketing, finance, safety engineering and many others. Responsibilities vary with department placement, but may include assisting marketing staff with client service and promotional material, crunching numbers for finance or administrative tasks that enhance interns' real world experience.

 GETTING HIRED

Apply by: Rolling. Send a resume and cover letter, noting areas of interest, to the address below.

Qualifications:
Open to college freshmen, sophomores, juniors and seniors, and grad students. International applicants are welcome.

Contact:
Internship Coordinator
America West Airlines
Attention: CH-EMP-INT
Sky Harbor International Airport
4000 East Sky Harbor Boulevard
Phoenix, AZ 85034
Fax: (480) 693-8813
E-mail: employment@americawest.com
www.americawest.com

American Association for the Advancement of Science

 THE BUZZ
- "Experiment with this career option"
- "All the science news that's fit to write"

 THE STATS

Industry(ies): Journalism; Science/Research

Location(s): Washington, DC

Number of interns: *Annual*: approximately 10

Pay: None for most; modest salary for science news writing internship

Length of internship: Varies; available year-round

 **THE SCOOP**

The world's largest general scientific society, the American Association for the Advancement of Science (AAAS) serves over 10 million professionals and science enthusiasts. AAAS was founded in 1848 and its mission remains remarkably similar today: the organization promotes science and technological breakthroughs to benefit society.

 ON THE JOB

There are five different internship programs available: the Scientific Freedom, Responsibility and Law Program; Science and Human Rights Program; Science and Technology Policy Fellowship Programs; Program of the Dialogue on Science, Ethics and Religion (DoSER); and the Science News Writing Internship (at *Science* magazine). In each, interns work closely with professional staff conducting research, planning seminars and conferences, and assisting in other departmental duties. *Science* interns work with the news writing staff contributing to the magazine and the online publication, ScienceNow.

 GETTING HIRED

Apply by: Varies by program, see web site or contact human resources for individual internship information. Send completed application, along with current resume, brief writing samples, as directed, transcripts of undergraduate and graduate work to date, and three letters of recommendation, to the address below.

Qualifications:
Open to college freshmen, sophomores, juniors and seniors, graduate students and recent grads.

Contact:
AAAS Human Resources Department
Phone: (202) 326-6470

Visit Vault at **www.vault.com** for insider company profiles, expert advice, career message boards, expert resume reviews, the Vault Job Board and more.

V/\ULT CAREER LIBRARY   **21**

American Association of Advertising Agencies

 THE BUZZ
- "Find out how commercials are created"
- "Learn advertising all over the country"

 THE STATS

Industry(ies): Advertising

Location(s): Possible locations include: Boston, MA; Chicago, IL; Detroit, MI; Minneapolis, MN; New York, NY; San Francisco, CA; Seattle, WA; Warren, MI

Number of interns: *Summer*: approximately 100

Pay: Paid; taxable salary of $350/week. Subsidized travel; subsidized housing (30 percent of cost paid by intern)

Length of internship: *Summer*: 10 weeks

 **THE SCOOP**

The American Association of Advertising Agencies (AAAA) was founded in 1917 as the national trade organization representing advertising agencies in the U.S. AAAA offers its members the most up-to-date local, state and federal news regarding their business. With a wide variety of services and resources for its members, the organization also works with all levels of government advocating for issues pertaining to the advertising industry.

**ON THE JOB**

The AAAA Multicultural Agency Intern Program (MAIP) is designed to offer African-Americans, Asians, Hispanics and Native Americans incentives to explore the world of advertising as a career option. Interns are placed at participating member agencies around the country where they can gain practical work experience, establish contacts and prepare for entry-level positions in the industry. Internships are available in several departments, including account management, creative (art direction or copywriting), broadcast production, interactive technologies, media buying/planning, account/strategic planning, print production and traffic.

GETTING HIRED

Apply by: *Summer*: December 8. Include an application form downloaded from the web site (www.aaaa-maip.org), two letters of recommendation, transcript(s), creative samples (if applying for creative departments) and essays. Prospective interns will be interviewed thereafter.

Qualifications:
Open to undergraduate juniors and seniors, as well as graduate students and students attending participating AAAA portfolio schools. A minimum 3.0 GPA is preferred. (Applicants with a GPA between 2.7 and 2.9 are encouraged to apply, but they must complete an additional essay question found in the application).

Contact:
Angela Johnson Meadows, Manager, Diversity Programs
Multicultural Advertising Intern Program
c/o American Association of Advertising Agencies
405 Lexington Avenue, 18th Floor
New York, NY 10174-1801
Phone: (800) 676-9333
Fax: (212) 682-2028
E-mail: maip@aaaa.org
www.aaaa-maip.org

American Association of University Women

THE BUZZ
- "For everyone interested in gender equality in education"

THE STATS

Industry(ies): Education; Law; Nonprofit

Location(s): Washington, DC

Number of interns: *Annual*: 10-15

Pay: None

Length of internship: Varies

THE SCOOP

Established in 1881, the American Association of University Women's (AAUW) is a leading voice for equity and education for women and girls. AAUW is comprised of three corporations: The Association a 501(c)(4)100,000-member organization with more than 1,300 branches nationwide that lobbies and advocates for education and equity, with a 501(c)(3) Leadership and Training Institute; and the AAUW Educational Foundation, a 501(c)(3) public foundation established in 1958 to provide support andadvancement for women in higher education, to conduct research on equity in education for women and girls, and to provide funds and a support system for women seeking judicial redress for sex discrimination in higher education.

ON THE JOB

All three AAUW entities accept interns, though the specialized departments vastly differ in their internship offerings. (See the full list online at aauw.org/about/aauwjobs.cfm). Some past positions have included assisting the membership department, planning AAUW's international symposium, working on an e-zine for female college students and serving as the legal intern for the advocacy fund.

GETTING HIRED

Apply by: Rolling. E-mail a cover letter, resume and writing sample to the address below.

Qualifications:
Open to college juniors and seniors, as well as recent grads and grad students.

Contact:
Subject Line: AAUW Internships
E-mail: aauwjobs@aauw.org
aauw.org/about/aauwjobs.cfm

American Bar Association

THE BUZZ
- "Rub elbows with praticing lawyers"
- "A dream job for aspiring legal eagles"

THE STATS

Industry(ies): Law

Location(s): Chicago, IL; Washington, DC

Number of interns: Over 50 per academic term

Pay: Most internships unpaid

Length of internship: Varies; available year-round

 THE SCOOP

The American Bar Association is the professional organization for the legal profession, by the legal profession. Boasting roughly half of the lawyers in America as its members, it can also boast of being the world's largest voluntary professional association. The ABA "provides law school accreditation, continuing legal education, information about the law, programs to assist lawyers and judges in their work, and initiatives to improve the legal system for the public."

ON THE JOB

A plethora of internships is available in Washington, DC, including positions with the Juvenile Justice Center, Section of Dispute Resolution, Standing Committee on Election Law, and Asia Law Initiative Council, to name a few. The Chicago office offers two or three positions per academic term.

GETTING HIRED

Apply by: Deadline varies depending on internship desired.

Qualifications:
Varies depending on internship desired.

Contact:
Internship Coordinator
American Bar Association
740 Fifteenth Street, NW
Washington, DC 20005-1022

Chicago office
Jack Gedge
American Bar Association
321 N. Clark Street
Chicago, IL 60610
Phone: (312) 988-5193
Fax: (312) 988-5177
E-mail: gedgej@staff.abanet.org
www.abanet.org/hr/interns/home.html

Visit Vault at **www.vault.com** for insider company profiles, expert advice, career message boards, expert resume reviews, the Vault Job Board and more.

V∧ULT CAREER LIBRARY   **23**

American Cancer Society

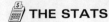 **THE BUZZ**
- "The most important nonprofit of its kind"
- "Great resume name for pre-meds"

THE STATS

Industry(ies): Health Care; Nonprofit

Location(s): Washington, DC; all 50 states (see www.cancer.org for details)

Number of interns: *Annual*: 50-60

Pay: Stipend of up to $2,500 (for some positions)

Length of internship: *Summer/fall/spring*: 8 weeks each

 **THE SCOOP**

The American Cancer Society is one of the oldest and largest health agencies in the U.S. Headquartered in Atlanta, ACS has 17 regional chartered divisions, over 3,400 local offices and some 2 million volunteers. Since it began in 1913, the organization has chartered and maintained cancer prevention programs, as well as promoting early detection guidelines, research and treatments.

ON THE JOB

Internship positions are available in cancer control, income development, advocacy, marketing, communications, human resources, public health and law. Interns also assist with ACS's "Relay for Life" fundraiser, held in about 3,000 communities around the country.

GETTING HIRED

Apply by: *Spring*: January 20; *summer*: May 2; *fall*: September 9. View available positions on the group's web site (www.cancer.org) and apply directly to your office of interest. Candidates must submit an online application, a resume that includes honors and awards, and a one-page, double-spaced essay on your reasons for applying. Those "pre-selected" from the applicant pool are then asked for a transcript and three letters of recommendation from faculty members.

Qualifications:

Open to college sophomores, juniors and seniors. A minimum 3.0 GPA is required. Applicants should be strongly interested in pursuing a nonprofit career.

Contact:

Attention: Manager of Student Programs
American Cancer Society
1599 Clifton Road NE
Atlanta, GA 30329
Phone: (800) 227-2345
Fax: (404) 982-3677
E-mail: internships@cancer.org
www.cancer.org/docroot/AA/content/AA_5_1x_Internship_Program.asp

American Civil Liberties Union

THE BUZZ
- "Become a card-carrying intern"
- "First Amendment bliss"

THE STATS

Industry(ies): Law; Nonprofit

Location(s): New York, NY; Washington, DC; numerous affiliate offices throughout the nation

Number of interns: *Spring/summer/fall*: 2-3 each

Pay: None

Length of internship: *Spring/fall*: 12-16 weeks; *summer*: 10-12 weeks

THE SCOOP

With more than 400,000 members and supporters, and offices in almost every U.S. state, the American Civil Liberties Union (ACLU) is dedicated to defending and preserving the individual rights and liberties guaranteed to every person in this country by the Constitution and laws in the United States. The ACLU challenges civil liberty violations, alerting the public through court battles and media coverage. Annual dues and contributions from members, as well as grants from private foundations and individuals, keep the ACLU in fighting form.

ON THE JOB

Internships with the National Legal Department of the ACLU provide individuals with the chance to work on racial justice, poverty, privacy and First Amendment issues. In addition to these traditional concerns, newer areas of interest, including technology and liberty, and national security and Internet censorship, are currently taking center stage.

GETTING HIRED

Apply by: *Fall*: August 1; *spring*: January 1; *summer*: April 15. Send a cover letter, resume, short nonfiction writing sample (three to five pages) and three references.

Qualifications:

Open to undergraduate students and recent grads. Applicants should have a strong interest in social and legal issues, excellent writing and communication skills, and the initiative and energy necessary to see projects to completion.

Contact:

If you are interested in working for your local affiliate, please contact them directly. If you would like to apply for an internship with the National Legal Department, contact:

Julia Otis
Undergraduate Internship Coordinator
ACLU National Legal Department
125 Broad Street, 18th Floor
New York, NY 10004
Phone: (212) 549-2694
www.aclu.org/About/Aboutlist.cfm?c=189

American Conservatory Theater

 THE BUZZ
- "Learn about theater from the best"
- "It worked for Danny Glover"

 **THE STATS**

Industry(ies): Theater/Performing Arts

Location(s): San Francisco, CA

Number of interns: *Annual*: 7-9

Pay: Paid

Length of internship: Administrative and production internships run concurrent with the Geary Theatre production performance season, typically August-June

 **THE SCOOP**

The American Conservatory Theater aims to fill the need, renew and reinvent traditional theater and theatrical writing for the modern public, and to create a new community of perfomers and audiences. It does this, in part, by teaching nearly 3,000 aspiring actors annually. Some alumni – think Winona and Denzel – are successful enough to be recognized by first name only.

ON THE JOB

ACT places interns in theater production and administration. Interns in either department get intense training, ample opportunity to meet celebrated professionals and a springboard to a theater career. Tasks can be largely clerical, but some recent interns have gone on to prominent positions within the organization and without, including placement at Yale and The Academy of Art.

GETTING HIRED

Apply by: April 15. Application must include personal statement, resume, writing sample, three letters of recommendation and a $15 nonrefundable application fee.

Qualifications:
Open to college graduates. Demonstrated training, skills or experience in the field; enthusiasm and attention to detail; PC and/or Mac computer skills; and a full-time commitment are required.

Contact:
Vinny Eng, Producing Associate
American Conservatory Theater
30 Grant Avenue
San Francisco, CA 94108
Phone: (415) 439-2410
E-mail: veng@act-sf.org
www.act-sf.org

American Dance Festival

 **THE BUZZ**
- "Like summer camp for dance fans"
- "Gain experience in arts administration"

THE STATS

Industry(ies): Theater/Performing Arts

Location(s): Durham, NC

Number of interns: *Summer*: 15-20

Pay: Paid; $950-$1,100/summer. Free program tickets; free program class

Length of internship: *Summer*: 8 weeks

THE SCOOP

The American Dance Festival was established in 1934 to promote appreciation and understanding for modern dance. Through education and community outreach, ADF brings students and dance professionals from around the world together every year for six-week sessions at Duke University. During its annual summer season, ADF produces over 40 modern dance performances. Internationally renowned dance manager Charles L. Reinhart has been its director since 1968.

ON THE JOB

ADF offers several different internships: in the box office, working with executive and development associates, coordinating studio and performance technical needs, in food and housing, running the ADF store and theater concessions, dealing with administrative and community outreach aspects of the professional performances, handling the press, working on the production crew for performances, working with the international student body and faculty on ADF workshops, and coordinating the technical needs for school.

GETTING HIRED

Apply by: *Summer*: February 15. Submit resume, cover letter and two letters of recommendation (work-related preferred) via U.S. mail to the address below. Be sure to fill out and include the application form found on the organization's web site, www.americandancefestival.org.

Qualifications:
Open to college freshmen, sophomores, juniors and seniors, as well as recent graduates.

Contact:
Cayte Connell, Intern Coordinator
Intern Program
American Dance Festival
Box 90772
Durham, NC 27708-0772
Phone: (919) 684-6402
Fax: (919) 684-5459
E-mail (for questions only): adf@americandancefestival.org
www.americandancefestival.org

Visit Vault at **www.vault.com** for insider company profiles, expert advice, career message boards, expert resume reviews, the Vault Job Board and more.

V∧ULT CAREER LIBRARY **25**

American Electric Power

 ## THE BUZZ

- "Spotlight your resume"

 ## THE STATS

Industry(ies): Energy/Utilities

Location(s): Columbus, OH (HQ); Nationwide

Number of interns: Varies

Pay: Paid; competitive. Some departments offer a monthly housing allowance

Length of internship: 1 quarter/semester

THE SCOOP

American Electric Power is the largest electricity generator and one of the largest utilities in the country. Eleven states are linked to its distribution grid, which generates more than 36,000 megawatts. The company employs 20,000 people and has over 5 million customers. AEP also has interests in telecommunication services, natural gas and barge transportation. AEP is based in Columbus, Ohio.

 ## ON THE JOB

Co-ops enrolled in the computer science tract receive practical experience in Web development, script writing, programming, database development and more. Business interns get hands-on experience in risk and market analysis, control procedures and marketing energy supplies. Engineering co-op students work with analyzed work flow, interpreted air permits and benchmarked data. Interns majoring in accounting have the opportunity to reconcile accounts, assist in capital improvement and prepare journal entries.

GETTING HIRED

Apply by: Rolling. Apply online at www.aep.com/careers/default.htm.

Qualifications:
Open to full-time college students with at least a 3.0 GPA. Engineering students must have their programs accredited by the Accreditation Board for Engineering and Technology (ABET). Students must be U.S. citizens or permanent residents.

Co-ops are open to sophomores who are able to commit to two nonsequential assignments, including one summer assignment. Co-op positions are currently only available for IT positions and some engineering positions. Programs at AEP are competitive due to the limited amount of available positions.

Contact:
American Electric Power
College Relations
1 Riverside Plaza
Columbus, OH 43215-2373
Phone: (614) 716-1856
Fax: (614) 716-1864
www.aep.com/careers/default.htm

American Enterprise Institute

 ## THE BUZZ

- "Because even Newt needs an intern"
- "Your portal into public policy"

THE STATS

Industry(ies): Government; Journalism; Law; Nonprofit

Location(s): Washington, DC

Number of interns: *Spring, summer, fall:* approximately 50 each

Pay: None. Free breakfast and gourmet lunch

Length of internship: *Spring summer, fall:* 12-16 weeks each; part-time or full-time with flexible start and end dates

THE SCOOP

One of America's oldest think tanks, the American Enterprise Institute (AEI) for Public Policy Research was founded in 1943 to preserve and bolster the federal government, American political and cultural associations, and private enterprise, as well as a strong national defense. AEI hosts a rotating group of 65 scholars, mostly professors, writers and politicians, (Newt Gingrich came aboard in 1999) who focus on public issues pertaining to the economy, law, politics and foreign policy. Though officially nonpartisan, AEI scholars consult for the government, testify before congress and are quoted in the media more than any other American think tank.

 ## ON THE JOB

Interns are usually paired with AEI scholars for research support and other assistance on various projects. Others work with business directors in various administrative departments and duties vary within each. Interns can be placed in economic policy, foreign and defense studies, social and political studies, public relations, *The American Enterprise* magazine, communications, seminars and conferences, publications, publications marketing, information systems, marketing and accounting.

 ## GETTING HIRED

Apply by: *Summer*: April 1; *fall*: September 1; *winter/spring*: December 1. Application must include a cover letter, resume, a writing sample (five pages or less) and transcripts.

Qualifications:
Open to college freshmen and sophomores, but the organization prefers juniors, seniors and graduate students. Minimum GPA is 3.0, but successful applicants tend to have a GPA of 3.5 or above.

Contact:
Ruth Smith, Intern Coordinator
American Enterprise Institute
1150 17th Street, NW
Washington, DC 20036
Phone: (202) 862-7166
Fax: (202) 862-7178
www.aei.org/internships

American Family Insurance

 THE BUZZ
- "Get personalized experience in making a large insurance company operate"

 THE STATS

Industry(ies): Insurance

Location(s): Madison, WI (HQ); Nationwide

Number of interns: *Annual*: 80-100

Pay: Paid

Length of internship: *Summer/semester*: varies by position and student availability

 THE SCOOP

In 1927, American Family Insurance began with three employees and 346 charter member policyholders. Today, the company offers multiple insurance and financial product lines in 17 states. AFI is the nation's third-largest mutual property and casualty insurer and the 16th-largest property and casualty insurance company group. AFI employs a network of approximately 4,000 independent contractor agents and more than 8,100 employees.

 ON THE JOB

Student interns at American Family are placed in paid positions related to their majors or career goals. AFI offers internships through out the company in areas including IT, actuarial, claims, marketing, finance, office administration and others. Interns are provided "real life" projects that are critical to their departments and the company. They are assigned mentors to provide guidance through their projects and to assist them in their professional development. AFI rounds out the experience by including interns in social/networking events. Interns are provided feedback on their performance and have the opportunity to provide feedback to American Family on their experience. Most interns work at AFI during summers between academic sessions, but in some cases these summer opportunities can turn into a continuous engagement during the school year, based on manager needs and intern availability.

GETTING HIRED

Apply by: Rolling. All internship positions are posted on the AFI web site. Students can apply online (www.amfam.com/careers) and have their resume routed directly to the recruiter.

Qualifications:

Open to students at any point in their academic careers who are pursuing a degree, advanced degree, or a certificate program at a two- or four-year institution. Qualifications and requirements will vary with each internship opportunity and will be specified on the individual internship job postings on www.americanfamily insurance.jobs.

Contact:
American Family Insurance Corporate Office
6000 American Parkway
Madison, WI 53783-0001
Phone: (608) 249-2111
www.americanfamilyinsurance.jobs

American Federation of Teachers

 THE BUZZ
- "Intern for a prominent labor union"
- "Perfect your research skills on behalf of teachers"

 THE STATS

Industry(ies): Education; Government

Location(s): Washington, DC

Number of interns: *Summer/fall/spring*: varies

Pay: Paid; $280-$325/week

Length of internship: *Spring/summer/fall*: 16 weeks each

 THE SCOOP

As a labor union with 1.2 million members, the American Federation of Teachers has been supporting public school staff members, from pre-kindergarten to university-level since it was started in 1916. The membership has now grown to include teachers, school and university employees, state and local government employees, and nurse and health professionals.

ON THE JOB

Interns research worker and professional issues pertaining to AFT constituents. Tasks usually involve one or two longer projects and several shorter assignments. Interns also represent AFT at education events and conferences in the DC area. Each department offers its own personalized internship program. Duties can involve research, writing (possibly for publication), and attending meetings and conferences. Departments accepting interns include financial services, educational issues, human rights and community relations, the legislative action center, research and the Union Leadership Institute.

GETTING HIRED

Apply by: *Summer*: March 1; *fall*: June 1; *spring*: November1. Applicants must send a cover letter responding to several points listed online (see www.aft.org/about/jobs/intern.htm for more details), a resume, a letter of recommendation and a writing sample (if available).

Qualifications:
Open to college freshmen, sophomores, juniors and seniors, as well as recent grads and grad students.

Contact:
Jodie Fingland
Internship Coordinator
American Federation of Teachers
555 New Jersey Avenue, NW
Washington, DC 20001
Phone: (202) 879-4400, ext. 3443
E-mail: intern@aft.org
www.aft.org/about/jobs/intern.htm

Visit Vault at www.vault.com for insider company profiles, expert advice, career message boards, expert resume reviews, the Vault Job Board and more.

VAULT CAREER LIBRARY   27

American Forests

 THE BUZZ

- "It's not easy being green"
- "Good for both the earth and your resume"

 THE STATS

Industry(ies): Environmental; Nonprofit

Location(s): Washington, DC

Number of interns: *Annual:* 12-15

Pay: None; academic credit or a small stipend

Length of internship: 3-6 months

THE SCOOP

American Forests' number one goal is "to grow a healthier world" – a lofty aim for a nonprofit organization, but then again, American Forests is America's oldest nonprofit citizens' conservation organization, dating back all the way to 1875. "Citizen conservation" is what makes American Forests unique – American Forests strives to enable communities, corporations, individuals, schools and government groups to apply strategic environmental solutions. Your community may have been "releafed" through their recent campaigns, "Tree Planting for Environmental Restoration" and "Reversing the National Urban Tree Deficit."

 ON THE JOB

American Forests offers internships in many different departments – communications, development and marketing, forest policy, global reLeaf and urban forestry. See the American Forest web site for specific descriptions of various internships. Intern tasks may include writing press releases, planning events, developing material on the importance of urban greenery, establishing tree planting partnerships with schools and businesses and helping to plan workshops.

GETTING HIRED

Apply by: Rolling. Applicants are encouraged to apply at least two months prior to the fall, spring or summer terms. Submit a cover letter, resume and one-page writing sample.

Qualifications:

Open to college sophomores, juniors and seniors, as well as recent grads and grad students.

Contact:
Lu Rose
American Forests
P.O. Box 2000
Washington, DC 20013
Fax: (202) 955-4588
E-mail: Jobs@amfor.org
www.americanforests.org/about_us/jobs.php

American Friends Service Committee

 THE BUZZ

- "Peace, social justice, and humanitarian service"
- "Help this international committee give peace a chance"

 THE STATS

Industry(ies): Nonprofit; Religious

Location(s): Philadelphia, PA (HQ); Over 40 regional offices around the U.S.

Number of interns: Varies

Pay: None; small stipend in AZ

Length of internship: Varies

THE SCOOP

The American Friends Service Committee (AFSC) began and still functions as a Quaker organization. But the group also includes people of various faiths who are committed to social justice, peace and humanitarian service. Its work is based on the Quaker belief in the worth of every person, and faith in the power of love to overcome violence and injustice.

 ON THE JOB

AFSC offers a wide range of internships in the Community Relations Unit, the International Programs unit, the Nationwide Women's Program, the Peacebuilding Unit and the Third World Coalition. Most positions are based in AFSC's national office in Philadelphia, Pa., but there are some offered in regional offices across the country.

GETTING HIRED

Apply by: Rolling. See web site for application details. Requirements vary with position.

Qualifications:

Open to high school students, college freshmen, sophomores, juniors and seniors, as well as others interested in the work of AFSC. Fellowships are offered to recent college graduates.

Contact:
www.afsc.org/volunteering/internships_fellowships.htm

American Geographical Society

 THE BUZZ

- "For the future Indiana Jones"

 THE STATS

Industry(ies): Environmental; Science/Research

Location(s): New York, NY

Number of interns: *Annual*: 2-4

Pay: None. Recommendations given for future employment and graduate school

Length of internship: 10 weeks minimum

 THE SCOOP

Founded in 1851, the American Geographical Society is the oldest of its kind in America. Made up of both professional geographers and everyday mapping fans, the society is perhaps most known for making the world of geography accessible to laymen. AGS boasts a renowned geographical research library, publishes two magazines, *Geographical Review* and *FOCUS on Geography*, and sponsors exploration, cartographic research and international travel programs.

ON THE JOB

Interns in the small AGS office work closely with permanent staff, fulfilling office needs as they arise. Duties vary according to interns' personal strengths and area of study. Past interns have worked extensively with AGS' many databases, researched funding opportunities for the society, drafted press releases on articles in AGS magazines, organized the AGS library and researched for upcoming society exhibits.

GETTING HIRED

Apply by: Rolling. See the website's internship section, www.amergeog.org/internships_program.htm, for more details.

Qualifications:
Open to college juniors and seniors, as well as grad students. International applicants are welcome.

Contact:
Mary Lynne Bird
The American Geographical Society
120 Wall Street, Suite 100
New York, NY 10005
Phone: (212) 422-5456
E-mail: ags@amergeog.org
www.amergeog.org/internships_program.htm

American Heart Association

 THE BUZZ

- "A great cause to put your heart into"
- "Learn the inner workings of a nonprofit"

THE STATS

Industry(ies): Health Care; Nonprofit

Location(s): Austin, TX; Burlingame, CA; Columbus, OH; Dallas, TX; Framingham, MA; Glen Allen, VA; Grand Rapids, MI; Marietta, GA; North Brunswick, NJ; Seattle, WA; St. Louis, MO; St. Petersburg, FL; Wormleysburg, PA

Number of interns: Varies

Pay: None

Length of internship: Varies with student availability; available year-round

 THE SCOOP

The American Heart Association traces its roots back to New York City in 1915 when a group of concerned physicians formed the Association for the Prevention and Relief of Heart Disease to educate citizens about the disease, which was quickly becoming a leading cause of death. Similar groups began to crop up in Boston, Philadelphia and Chicago in the 1920s. As national interest grew, six doctors from the associations came together in 1924 to found the American Heart Association. Today, the organization is a leading health advocate, taking on such titans as the tobacco industry and disbursing its research publicly.

 ON THE JOB

Interns can work in the editorial department, co-writing promotional and informational material, web site information, advertisements, fliers, posters and more. They also help with the association's administrative activities. Responsibilities vary with need and location, but may include handling phone inquiries, proofreading pamphlets and mailings, and clerical tasks.

GETTING HIRED

Apply by: Rolling. Send a resume and writing samples with a cover letter disclosing which office you'd like to work in.

Qualifications:
Open to college freshmen, sophomores, juniors and seniors as well as grad students.

Contact:
Internship Coordinator, Human Resources
American Heart Association
7272 Greenville Avenue
Dallas, TX 75231
Fax: (214) 706-1191
E-mail: aharesume@heart.org
www.americanheart.org/presenter.jhtml?identifier=3276

Other offices
www.americanheart.org/presenter.jhtml?identifier=3253

Visit Vault at **www.vault.com** for insider company profiles, expert advice, career message boards, expert resume reviews, the Vault Job Board and more.

V/\ULT CAREER LIBRARY   **29**

American Hockey League

 THE BUZZ
- "Work in the hockey world without having to wear a mouthguard"

 THE STATS

Industry(ies): Sports

Location(s): Springfield, MA

Number of interns: *Summer/fall/spring*: 1-2 each

Pay: None

Length of internship: *Summer/fall/spring*: 12-15 weeks each

 **THE SCOOP**

The American Hockey League is hockey's answer to baseball's minor leagues. The company manages special projects, media relations and marketing for all 27 teams in its four divisions (U.S. and Canada). These teams include the Manitoba Moose, the Manchester Monarchs, the Albany River Rats, the Chicago Wolves and the Portland Pirates.

 ON THE JOB

Most interns work in the marketing department. They also assist with hockey operations and media relations. Depending on the time of year, interns may also work on other projects. Full- and part-time applicants are considered.

 GETTING HIRED

Apply by: *Summer*: April 1; *fall*: August 1; *spring*: November 1. Send a resume and cover letter to the contact below.

Qualifications:

Open to college juniors and seniors, as well as recent grads and grad students.

Contact:
Sean Lavoine
American Hockey League
One Monarch Place, Suite 2400
Springfield, MA 01144
Phone: (413) 781-2030
Fax: (413) 733-4767
E-mail: slavoine@theahl.com
www.theahl.com

American Indian Science and Engineering Society

 THE BUZZ
- "Highly targeted engineering internship"

 THE STATS

Industry(ies): Education; Engineering; Nonprofit; Science/Research

Location(s): Atlanta, GA; Greenbelt, MD; Washington, DC; multiple additional locations throughout the U.S.

Number of interns: *Summer*: 20

Pay: None; weekly stipend. Round-trip travel; dormitory lodging; local transportation allowance

Length of internship: *Summer*: 10 weeks

 **THE SCOOP**

The American Indian Science and Engineering Society (AISES) is a nonprofit group helping and encouraging Native Americans and Native Alaskans to study science, engineering and technology. The organization provides financial and academic support to students and teachers, and works directly with tribes, schools and fellow nonprofit groups.

 ON THE JOB

AISES exposes interns to various careers in federal agencies. Positions are arranged in tandem with the U.S. Department of Commerce in Washington, DC, the Centers for Disease Control and Prevention in Atlanta, Georgia, and the U.S. State Department at its offices around the world.

 GETTING HIRED

Apply by: *Summer*: U.S. State Department and CIA by November 1; all other agencies by mid-March. Send resume, transcript, essay and two letters of recommendation to the address below. See The Society's web site (www.aises.org/highered/internships/index.html) for details.

Qualifications:

Open to college sophomores, juniors and seniors, as well as grad students. Minimum 3.0 GPA required. Must be a member of AISES and a U.S. citizen.

Contact:
Sarayl Yellowhorse
Higher Education Coordinator
American Indian Science and Engineering Society
P.O. Box 9828
Albuquerque, NM 87119
Phone: (505) 765-1052, ext. 105
Fax: (505) 765-5608
E-mail: sarayl@aises.org
www.aises.org/highered/internships/index.html

American & International Designs

 THE BUZZ

- "Fed up with your boring bank lobby? Do something about it"
- "A strong name in interior design"

 THE STATS

Industry(ies): Architecture

Location(s): Staten Island, NY

Number of interns: *Summer*: 1-2; *fall/winter/spring*: 1 each

Pay: None. Travel stipend (amount depends on location)

Length of internship: *Summer/fall/winter/spring:* 8-12 weeks each

 THE SCOOP

Opened in 1980, American & International Designs is a "multi-disciplinary" interior design firm specializing in large, public projects such as hospitals and corporations. The company is run by native-New Yorker Susan Arann, a former fashion boutique owner who has designed over 45 restaurant interiors, made bank lobbies more "people-friendly" and has worked on several health care facilities, redesigning birthing centers, patient and emergency rooms.

 ON THE JOB

According to Arann, her interns do "anything and everything." Interns are involved in every step of project management, from initial client meetings and job site visits to process consultations. It's a good program for someone looking to break into the field of interior design, and the company hires many of its interns for full-time employment.

💲 **GETTING HIRED**

Apply by: Rolling. Depending on background, applicant may have to submit work/design samples.

Qualifications:
Open to college seniors, recent grads and grad students.

Contact:
Susan Arann
American & International Designs
1110 South Avenue, Suite 2
Staten Island, NY 10314
E-mail: susan@designamericanyc.com
www.designamericanyc.com

American Israel Public Affairs Committee

 THE BUZZ

- "America's primary pro-Israel lobby group"
- "Dedicated to working with students"

 THE STATS

Industry(ies): Government; Law

Location(s): Boston, MA; Chicago, IL; Houston, TX; Los Angeles, CA; New York, NY; Newark, NJ; Philadelphia, PA; Phoenix, AZ; San Francisco, CA; Washington, DC

Number of interns: *Summer*: 38; *fall/winter/spring*: 5

Pay: Paid in summer (amount varies); no pay during academic year

Length of internship: 8 weeks

 THE SCOOP

According to *The New York Times*, the American Israel Public Affairs Committee (AIPAC) is "the most important organization affecting America's relationship with Israel." Founded in the 1950s, AIPAC has 65,000 members today in all 50 states. AIPAC works to address all issues facing Israel and to make sure that Israel is strong enough to meet the many challenges it encounters (financially and politically), usually through lobby meetings with U.S. Congress. AIPAC has many student members to whom it offers scholarships to AIPAC events and support for campus pro-Israel groups.

🏢 **ON THE JOB**

Internships are available at the Washington, DC, headquarters and all nine regional offices (however more interns work in the main DC office than elsewhere). Intern duties vary greatly between offices. In the DC office, for instance, interns can work in any one of the six departments, where tasks range from communications and finance to programming and operations. Interns work closely with the professional staff.

💲 **GETTING HIRED**

Apply by: *Summer*: March 26; *fall*: September 1; *winter*: December 15; *spring*: February 15. Contact the internship coordinator (information below) for specifics on how to apply.

Qualifications:
Open to college freshmen, sophomores, juniors and seniors, as well as recent college graduates and grad students.

Contact:
Havi Arbeter
American Israel Public Affairs Committee
440 First Street, NW, Suite 600
Washington, DC 20001
Phone: (202) 369-6924
Fax: (202) 347-6760
E-mail: harbeter@aipac.org
www.aipac.org

Visit Vault at **www.vault.com** for insider company profiles, expert advice, career message boards, expert resume reviews, the Vault Job Board and more.

VAULT CAREER LIBRARY **31**

American Management Association

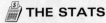 THE BUZZ
- "Training ground for future managers"
- "Good for MBAs"

THE STATS

Industry(ies): Education; Management & Strategy Consulting

Location(s): New York, NY

Number of interns: *Annual:* 60

Pay: Paid; $8/hour

Length of internship: Varies; available year-round

THE SCOOP

Now a global nonprofit, the American Management Association started in 1923 to provide practical training tools to the international business community. It provides educational and developmental services to individuals and members of governmental agencies and companies, 486 of which are Fortune 500 companies. The organization also publishes research and study guides, and sponsors several training seminars every year.

ON THE JOB

AMA hires interns on a request-basis only. Therefore, applicants are free to choose the department in which they want to work. This list includes the human resources department, information technology, the seminars department and marketing. In every department, interns work closely with trained professionals. See the AMA Career Opportunities web site at www.amanet.org/aboutama/hr/index.htm for open internship positions and detailed descriptions.

GETTING HIRED

Apply by: Rolling. Send resume and cover letter to the address below.

Qualifications:
Open to college freshmen, sophomores, juniors and seniors, as well as recent college graduates and grad students.

Contact:
Barbara Zung
Manager, Organizational Development
American Management Association
1601 Broadway, 11th Floor
New York, NY 10019
Phone: (212) 903-8018
Fax: (212) 903-8163
E-mail: Bzung@amanet.org
www.amanet.org

American Place Theatre

THE BUZZ
- "Work behind the scenes on cutting-edge, Off-Broadway productions"
- "Bring literacy on stage"

THE STATS

Industry(ies): Theater/Performing Arts

Location(s): New York, NY

Number of interns: *Spring/summer/fall:* 5 each

Pay: None

Length of internship: Varies; available year-round

THE SCOOP

Current artistic director, Wynn Handman, founded The American Place Theatre in 1963. Located near New York City's famed Times Square, the company has long been devoted to "groundbreaking" off-Broadway theater. It focuses on new works by a diverse selection of American writers, with an emphasis on pluralism. Its performance-based literacy program, "Literature to Life," is a highly regarded educational theater program.

ON THE JOB

APT hires five interns at a time, each with a different concentration. The literary intern works with the artistic director to develop new projects. The education intern stage-manages educational theater productions, alongside the director of education. The administrative intern works with all aspects of the theater, from assisting the management to marketing the theater. The technical intern works with the production manager to operate the building and all technical aspects of the performances. Finally, the development intern assists the director of development with grant writing and fundraising efforts.

GETTING HIRED

Apply by: Rolling. Send resume and cover letter to the address below.

Qualifications:
Open to college freshmen, sophomores, juniors and seniors, grad students and recent college graduates.

Contact:
Internship Coordinator
The American Place Theatre
266 West 37th Street
New York, NY 10018
Phone: (212) 594-4482
Fax: (212) 594-4208
E-mail: contact@americanplacetheatre.org
www.americanplacetheatre.org

The American Press

 THE BUZZ
- "The journalism internship where you actually get a byline"
- "The name recognition of American Press isn't huge, but your file of clips will be"

 THE STATS

Industry(ies): Journalism

Location(s): Lake Charles, LA

Number of interns: *Annual:* 7

Pay: Paid; starts at $7.50 for high school students

Length of internship: *Summer:* 14 weeks

 THE SCOOP

Southwest Louisiana's first daily newspaper, *The American Press*, has been around for more than a century. Among its successes, the paper counts the crusade against illegal gambling it launched the 1950s, but it has received Pulitzer Prize nominations for writing and photography and regularly garners regional acclaim. The newsroom consists of about 20 reporters who cover mostly news local to Southwestern Louisiana.

 ON THE JOB

The American Press truly wants its interns to report. The first couple of weeks of the internship are spent under the wing of a staff reporter, whom interns shadow throughout the day as the reporter researches and writes pieces. During this time, they are also matched with a separate writing coach who critiques and edits the interns' own work. After that, though, interns are shooed out of the nest and assigned their own stories to cover.

 GETTING HIRED

Apply by: *Summer:* March 30; *fall/winter/spring:* rolling. Send resume, cover letter and clips to the address below.

Qualifications:
Open to high school students, college freshmen, sophomores, juniors and seniors, recent college graduates and grad students.

Contact:
Brett Downer
American Press
P.O. Box 2893
Lake Charles, LA 70602
Phone: (337) 494-4080
E-mail: bdowner@americanpress.com
www.americanpress.com

American Red Cross

 THE BUZZ
- "Start a career in disaster preparedness"
- "Help others while advancing your career"

 THE STATS

Industry(ies): Nonprofit

Location(s): Washington, DC (HQ)

Number of interns: Varies; usually at least 20

Pay: Paid and unpaid; $10/hour, 40 hours/week

Length of internship: *Summer:* 10 weeks

 THE SCOOP

The American Red Cross is a humanitarian organization providing relief to victims of disasters and helping people prevent, prepare for and respond to emergencies. In addition to international disaster and humanitarian efforts, the Red Cross operates over 900 chapters and "blood regions" across the U.S. These grassroots groups help communities through blood drives, latchkey programs and food assistance services.

 ON THE JOB

Students participating in the American Red Cross internship program are paired with a staff member and are involved in professional projects, assignments and activities. Internship assignments are related to the student's academic program. Internships are available in any facet of the company, including information technology, editorial, government relations, finance and corporate diversity. Available positions include research assistant, International Services project manager or historical resource assistant.

GETTING HIRED

Apply by: March 1. Submit resume and cover letter via mail, fax or e-mail.

Qualifications:
Open to all undergraduate, graduate students and recent graduates (who graduated the semester prior to start of internship) eligible to work in the U.S. Must be able to work at headquarters in Washington, DC. Housing is the responsibility of the student.

Contact:
Jennifer Cariño
Internship Manager, Corporate Diversity Department
American Red Cross, National Headquarters
2025 E Street, NW
Washington, DC 20006
Fax: (202) 303-0200
E-mail: Carinoj@usa.redcross.org

Visit Vault at **www.vault.com** for insider company profiles, expert advice, career message boards, expert resume reviews, the Vault Job Board and more.

VAULT CAREER LIBRARY **33**

American Repertory Theatre

THE BUZZ

- "One of the three best theaters in the country"
- "A theater program for non-actors"

THE STATS

Industry(ies): Theater/Performing Arts

Location(s): Cambridge, MA

Number of interns: *Annual*: 10-20

Pay: None

Length of internship: Varies; available year-round

THE SCOOP

The American Repertory Theatre is a professional, residential theater company based at Harvard University's Loeb Drama Center. Its permanent ensemble concentrates on three repertory categories: classic texts reformatted for contemporary audiences, neglected works of the past, and new (primarily American) works. The company produces many works throughout the year and tours nationally and internationally. ART also runs a professional theater training program with a similar school in Moscow.

ON THE JOB

Interns are closely supervised in this program that focuses on production and/or management. Production internships (which are not available during the summer) are offered in stage management, production management, lighting, sound, scenery, costumes, properties and running crew. Management internships work in artistic management (not offered in the summer), box office, financial management, fundraising/ development, house management, literary management and marketing and public relations. (Detailed descriptions of each internship are available on the theater's web site at www.amrep.org/intern/index.html.)

GETTING HIRED

Apply by: Rolling. Applications are available online at www.amrep.org/intern/index.html#Application. They should be typed and mailed, along with a cover letter (indicating area of interest), resume and two letters of recommendation.

Qualifications:
Open to college freshmen, sophomores, juniors and seniors, grad students and college graduates.

Contact:
Internship Coordinator
American Repertory Theatre
64 Brattle Street
Phone: (617) 495-2668
Fax: (617) 495-1705
www.amrep.org/intern/index.html

American Rivers

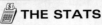 THE BUZZ

- "Restore, protect, enjoy"

THE STATS

Industry(ies): Environmental; Nonprofit; Science/Research

Location(s): Portland, OR; Seattle, WA; Washington, DC

Number of interns: *Annual*: 16

Pay: None

Length of internship: Flexible but usually 3 months; 25 hours/week

THE SCOOP

Founded in 1973, the national nonprofit American Rivers is dedicated to protecting and restoring natural U.S. rivers and wildlife. Leading the national river movement, AR is a membership-driven organization providing creative and practical solutions to problems plaguing America's river system, as well as promoting clean and healthy rivers. AR has worked with over 367 local, state and regional conservation groups to establish a list of the most endangered rivers in the U.S.

ON THE JOB

Interns work as part of the conservation staff when placed in conservation/policy positions. Duties include legislative research, grassroots organization (working with other national environmental groups), responding to requests from "river activists," researching American river issues, preparing written materials, and other long-term projects. Some interns work with the communications department on media affairs, publications (online and printed) and an annual report of the nation's rivers. Interns are separated into general communications and online community development groups.

GETTING HIRED

Apply by: Rolling. Send completed application (available online at www.amrivers.org/index.php?module = HyperContent&func = dis play&cid = 45) with a cover letter, resume, three references and a brief writing sample to the address below.

Qualifications:
Open to college freshmen, sophomores, juniors and seniors, recent college graduates and grad students.

Contact:
Office Manager
American Rivers
1101 14th Street NW, Suite 1400
Washington DC 20005
Phone: (202) 347-7550
Fax: (202) 347-9240
E-mail: americanrivers@americanrivers.org
www.amrivers.org

American School for the Deaf

 THE BUZZ
- "Learn to sign, and more..."

 **THE STATS**

Industry(ies): Education

Location(s): Hartford, CT

Number of interns: *Annual*: approximately 6

Pay: None. Room and board

Length of internship: *Summer/fall/spring*: 8 weeks

THE SCOOP

The American School for the Deaf works to "provide a comprehensive program for the development of the intellect and the enhancement of the quality of life for the deaf community by serving as a multi-purpose institution furnishing educational and vocational programs for deaf and hard-of-hearing children, youth, adults and their families." The idea for the school was planted in 1807 by a prominent Hartford physician, Mason Fitch Cogswell, who wanted to do something for his young deaf daughter, Alice. The school was officially founded 10 years later. It is the country's oldest educational organization committed to serving the deaf community.

ON THE JOB

ASD usually receives over 3,000 hours of volunteer assistance each year, which adds to the quality of life and education for students and employees. Interns and volunteers may work in all departments on everyday classroom activities, after-school tutoring and special events such as the school's annual golf tournament. All interns receive "practical experience with deaf education and deaf culture," through both classroom and dorm work. Sign language is used constantly, so interns must be prepared to learn it fast.

GETTING HIRED

Apply by: Rolling. Download the application at www.asd-1817.org/intern/index.html and send it to the address below.

Qualifications:
Open to high school students, college freshmen, sophomores, juniors and seniors, grad students and recent college graduates.

Contact:
Mary Anne Coffey
American School for the Deaf
139 North Main Street
West Hartford, CT 06107
Phone: (860) 570-2211
TTY: (860) 570-2229
E-mail: maryann.coffey@asd-1817.org
www.asd-1817.org

American Society of Magazine Editors

 THE BUZZ
- "Get your foot in the publishing door"
- "An opportunity for some real hands-on experience"
- "A dream internship for a journalism major"

 **THE STATS**

Industry(ies): Journalism; Publishing

Location(s): New York, NY; Washington, DC

Number of interns: *Summer*: 35

Pay: Paid; $325/week (undergrads)

Length of internship: *Summer*: 10 weeks

THE SCOOP

The American Society of Magazine Editors (ASME) was founded in 1963 and is headquartered in New York City, the publishing capital of the world. ASME is the professional organization for editors of consumer magazines and business publications edited, published and sold in the U.S.

ON THE JOB

ASME arranges internships with participating member magazines for college juniors majoring in journalism. The publications range from business to consumer titles. Interns work in the editorial offices and some duties may include proofreading or copyediting. ASME has arranged internships for 40 years and, to date, over 200 magazines and 1,627 students have participated in the program.

GETTING HIRED

Apply by: November 15 (a hard deadline with no exceptions). Send in a completed application (available October 2006) with a personal letter from yourself (addressed to Andrew Rhodes, Assistant Director, ASME) that details campus journalism projects, extracurricular activities, previous summer activity, magazines you regularly read, if you can work in Washington, DC, and why you want to be an intern. Also send a letter from your college dean, writing samples, a recent portrait photograph, a $25 application fee (non-refundable) payable to Magazine Publishers of America/ASME, and (if possible) a letter from a former ASME intern. See the organization's web site (www.asme.magazine.org) for more detailed information.

Qualifications:
Open to college juniors who are journalism majors or liberal arts majors actively involved in campus news writing.

Contact:
Andrew Rhodes, Assistant Director
American Society of Magazine Editors
810 Seventh Avenue, 24th Floor
New York, NY 10019
Phone: (212) 872-3700
E-mail: asme@magazine.org
www.magazine.org/Editorial/Internships

Visit Vault at **www.vault.com** for insider company profiles, expert advice, career message boards, expert resume reviews, the Vault Job Board and more.

VAULT CAREER LIBRARY   35

American Symphony Orchestra League

 THE BUZZ
- "Learn about careers in the world of symphonic music"
- "Develop your business skills here"

 THE STATS

Industry(ies): Music/Records; Theater/Performing Arts

Location(s): New York, NY

Number of interns: *Annual*: varies

Pay: None

Length of internship: Varies

 THE SCOOP

As a service and advocacy organization, the American Symphony Orchestra League assists nearly 1,000 symphony, chamber and youth orchestras financially, administratively and organizationally. Founded in 1942, and chartered by Congress in 1962, The League provides training programs, technical assistance, communications and transfer of Best Practice for its constituents. The League also sponsors fellowship programs in Orchestra Management and Conducting. League membership is open to orchestras of all types and levels, students, individuals, volunteer organizations, libraries, career centers and businesses which serve orchestras. The League is an IRS 501(c)3 tax exempt organization.

 ON THE JOB

Interns are accepted on an as-needed basis in various departments, including development, artistic services, marketing, orchestra leadership academy and publications. Tasks vary with department placement. All interns work very closely with the organization's full-time professionals.

 GETTING HIRED

Apply by: Rolling. Send a cover letter and resume to the address below indicating areas of interest.

Qualifications:

Open to college freshmen, sophomores, juniors and seniors, recent college graduates and grad students.

Contact:
Human Resources
American Symphony Orchestra League
New York Headquarters
33 West 60th Street, 5th Floor
New York, NY 10023
Phone: (212) 262-5161
www.symphony.org

American University in Moscow

 THE BUZZ
- "Get a post-Soviet education"
- "Strengthen ties between Russia and America"

 THE STATS

Industry(ies): Education; Government

Location(s): Washington, DC; Moscow

Number of interns: *Annual*: approximately 10

Pay: None

Length of internship: *Spring/fall*: 12-15 weeks each; *summer*: 10-12 weeks

 THE SCOOP

Boasting endorsements from former Soviet Premier Mikhail Gorbachev and former U.S. President George H.W. Bush, the American University in Moscow was founded to strengthen fragile U.S.-Russian ties using education. When it opened in 1990, AUM became the first private business school in Russia and offered hundreds of Russian grad students the equivalent of an American MBA. In 2002, AUM launched its graduate school, which offers master's programs and soon, PhD studies in American-Russian relations concentrating in social sciences. Students work closely with Russian and American professors, who train Russian foreign affairs experts in U.S.-Russian relations.

 ON THE JOB

Interns work in the school's DC office. Departments accepting interns include research, journalism, office, and web site support. AUM's Russia House, a consulting firm based in DC assisting Western companies investing and working in the newly free markets of the former Soviet Union, accepts interns as well.

 GETTING HIRED

Apply by: Rolling. Send a resume and cover letter to the address below.

Qualifications:

Open to college freshmen, sophomores, juniors and seniors, recent college graduates and grad students.

Contact:
Washington Office, American University in Moscow
1800 Connecticut Avenue, NW
Washington, DC 20009
Phone: (202) 986-6010
Fax: (202) 667-4244
E-mail: Russia@russiahouse.org
www.russiahouse.org

American Woman's Economic Development Corp.

 THE BUZZ

- "Help women gain equal footing in the business world"

 **THE STATS**

Industry(ies): Education; Nonprofit

Location(s): New York, NY

Number of interns: *Annual*: 8-10

Pay: None

Length of internship: Flexible; generally 6-12 weeks year-round. Time involved varies with need of the organization

THE SCOOP

The American Woman's Economic Development Corp. (AWED) began in 1976 to help new female business owners get their ventures off the ground. Using seasoned business executives to run seminars and counseling sessions, AWED trains its clientele to start and run their companies. AWED was the first organization of its kind in the United States, and over 100,000 female business owners have benefited from its services to date.

ON THE JOB

Intern tasks may involve researching economic development, working on databases, working in training program arrangement and business counseling sessions, and marketing and public relations work. Interns are also invited to attend classes and seminars on topics that interest them. In the development area, work may include researching corporations and foundations that support causes similar to AWED, working on the organization's annual fundraiser, updating the database and working on grants and proposals.

GETTING HIRED

Apply by: Rolling. Mail or e-mail a resume and cover letter to the contact below.

Qualifications:
Open to college freshmen, sophomores, juniors and seniors, as well as recent college graduates and grad students. International applicants are welcome.

Contact:
Michael Culoso, Chief Financial Officer
American Woman's Economic Development Corporation
216 East 45th Street, 10th Floor
New York, NY 10017
Phone: (917) 368-6140
Fax: (212) 986-7114
E-mail: mculoso@awed.org
www.awed.org/supporter.htm

American Youth Work Center

 THE BUZZ

- "A nonprofit that aims to make the lives of youngsters better"

THE STATS

Industry(ies): Education; Journalism; Nonprofit

Location(s): Washington, DC

Number of interns: *Spring/summer/fall*: 2 each

Pay: Paid; approximately $7/hour

Length of internship: *Spring*: 10-12 weeks; *summer*: 8-12 weeks; *fall*: 10-12 weeks

THE SCOOP

A nonprofit formed in 1984, the American Youth Work Center (AYWC) helps young Americans and assists other organizations that also work to better the lives of young people in the U.S. AYWC's activities are largely concentrated in two primary areas: the practical training program and its newspaper, *Youth Today*. The training program brings foreign social service workers into the U.S. for 18 months of training in an American social service agency. *Youth Today* is the only independent newspaper in the nation aimed at individuals and organizations specifically working with youth.

ON THE JOB

Interns contribute to all facets of the nonprofit's activities. Because AYWC has a small staff, interns get real work experience. Applicants should be interested in communications, because they will work on all aspects of *Youth Today*, their central project. Interns work from initial story planning to writing, layout and circulation. They also perform administrative tasks, public relations and general program duties (many relating to the practical training program).

GETTING HIRED

Apply by: Rolling. Send resume, cover letter, a writing sample, and three references to the address below.

Qualifications:
Open to college freshmen, sophomores, juniors and seniors, grad students and recent college graduates.

Contact:
Internship Coordinator
American Youth Work Center
1200 17th Street, NW, 4th floor
Washington, DC 20036
Phone: (202) 785-0764
E-mail: info@youthtoday.org
www.youthtoday.org

Visit Vault at **www.vault.com** for insider company profiles, expert advice, career message boards, expert resume reviews, the Vault Job Board and more.

V\ULT CAREER LIBRARY **37**

American-Arab Anti-Discrimination Committee

 THE BUZZ
- "Defend Arab culture and people against misunderstanding"

 THE STATS

Industry(ies): Government; Law; Nonprofit

Location(s): Washington, DC

Number of interns: *Summer/fall/spring:* 15 each

Pay: Must choose pay or academic credit. *Summer:* $1,250/summer for undergrads; $2,000/summer for graduate students. *Spring/fall:* $400/month for undergrads; $500/month for graduate students

Length of internship: *Summer:* 11 weeks; *spring/fall:* varies

 THE SCOOP

The American-Arab Anti-Discrimination Committee (ADC) was founded in 1980 to help defend and protect Americans of Arab descent against discrimination, hate crimes and stereotyping. The organization also promotes Arab culture and offers information about Arab affairs around the world to the American public.

 ON THE JOB

Interns work with ADC's research institute, the charitable and educational arm of the organization. They can be placed in organizing, education, government affairs, information systems, legal, media and the ADC president's office. On a weekly basis, interns visit governmental offices, various DC organizations and embassies to discuss policymaking and policy issues concerning Arab-Americans. Interns also write and publish the newsletter, *Intern Perspectives.*

GETTING HIRED

Apply by: *Summer:* March 15 (*legal department applicants:* January 15); *fall/spring:* rolling. Students can download the application (log on to www.adc.org/education/application.PDF), complete and send it with a resume, transcript, two letters of recommendation and a two-page personal statement.

Qualifications:
Open to all college freshmen, sophomores, juniors and seniors, graduate students and recent graduates.

Contact:
Intern Coordinator
American-Arab Anti-Discrimination Committee
Research Institute
4201 Connecticut Avenue, NW, Suite 300
Washington, DC 20008
Phone: (202) 244-2990
Fax: (202) 244-3196
www.adc.org

AMIDEAST

 THE BUZZ
- "Help bridge the gap betwen the U.S. and the Middle East"

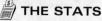 **THE STATS**

Industry(ies): Education; Government; Nonprofit

Location(s): Washington, DC

Number of interns: *Annual:* 4-6

Pay: Paid; varies

Length of internship: Varies; available year-round

 THE SCOOP

Under the motto "bridging cultures, building understanding," America-Mideast Educational and Training Services (AMIDEAST) is a private nonprofit dedicated to improving relations between the U.S. and countries in the Middle East. Founded in 1951 and headquartered in Washington, DC, the organization also has field offices in Egypt, Iraq, Jordan, Kuwait, Lebanon, Morocco, Syria, Tunisia, United Arab Emirates, West Bank/Gaza and Yemen. AMIDEAST provides educational support, advising and testing, English-language training and scholarship administration services for Arabs, as well as professional training programs and institutional development. The organization also has several programs for Americans.

ON THE JOB

AMIDEAST often hires individuals to work as interns. In the past, interns have worked on U.S. educational and training programs for foreigners, producing publications for public outreach, and advising Arab students on U.S. higher education. All positions are administrative/support level only and interns work closely with full-time professionals.

GETTING HIRED

Apply by: Rolling. Send a resume, cover letter and two references to the address below.

Qualifications:
Open to college freshmen, sophomores, juniors and seniors, grad students and recent college graduates. French and/or Arabic skills are very helpful, but not necessary.

Contact:
Director of Human Resources
AMIDEAST
1730 M Street, NW, Suite 1100
Washington, DC 20036
Phone: (202) 776-9690
Fax: (202) 776-7090
E-mail: personnel@amideast.org
www.amideast.org/employment/internships

Amnesty International

 THE BUZZ
- "Do your part to keep the flame of freedom burning bright"

 **THE STATS**

Industry(ies): Nonprofit

Location(s): New York, NY; London; Geneva

Number of interns: *Annual*: 910

Pay: None. Travel reimbursements; lunch

Length of internship: Preferably 6 months, 5 days/week; available year-round

 **THE SCOOP**

Amnesty International is a nonprofit organization whose mission is to undertake research and action focused on preventing and ending grave abuses of the rights to physical and mental integrity, freedom of conscience and expression, and freedom from discrimination, within the context of its work to promote all human rights. As one of the most internationally recognized groups of its kind, AI is independent of any government, political ideology, religion or economic interest. It is a democratic, self-governing body; all policy decisions are made by a voting international council. At the latest count, there were more than 1.8 million members, supporters and subscribers in over 150 countries and territories in every region of the world. AI's national sections and local volunteer groups are primarily responsible for funding the movement. The organization does not seek or accept funds from governments for work investigating and campaigning against human rights violations.

ON THE JOB

The International Law and Organizations Program of Amnesty International offers 5 internships: 3 in the London office, 1 in AI's UN office in Geneva, and 1 in AI's UN office in New York. These internships are for a six month period, from January to June and from July to December. Other Programs in the London office offer internships on an as needed basis, therefore the timing of open positions varies greatly. Two past internships were connected with the International Secretariat (IS) Media and Audiovisual Program: one dealt with audiovisual aid, while the other was anchored directly in the press office. Other Programs that have offered internship positions in the past include the Office of the Secretary General, Policy and Evaluation Program and Campaigns Program. Various Programs at the IS in London offer other volunteering opportunities in addition to the internships, on an as needed basis. Most AI field offices offer volunteer opportunities, and offices are located all over the world.

GETTING HIRED

Apply by: Rolling. Check the web site (web.amnesty.org/jobs/internships) for current openings and application specifics. For other volunteering opportunities at the IS check the website (web.amnesty.org/jobs/volvacancies) For volunteering opportunities in AI field offices please check the relevant local AI website.

Qualifications:

Open to college freshmen, sophomores, juniors and seniors, graduate students, and college graduates of all ages. However, requirements do vary among positions (see web.amnesty.org/jobs/internships for specifics). Language skills are necessary for several positions, including ther Geneva internships.

Contact:

Internship Coordinator
Amnesty International, International Secretariat
1 Easton Street
London, WC1X ODW, UK
Phone: 011 44-20-7413-5500
Fax: 011 44-20-7956-1157
www.amnesty.org

Visit Vault at **www.vault.com** for insider company profiles, expert advice, career message boards, expert resume reviews, the Vault Job Board and more.

VAULT CAREER LIBRARY   **39**

The Anasazi Heritage Center

 THE BUZZ
- "Honor America's Native American heritage"

THE STATS

Industry(ies): Art/Museum

Location(s): Dolores, CO

Number of interns: *Annual*: 4

Pay: $100/week. Free housing at a communal, 3-bedroom house located on 6 acres adjacent to the Anasazi Heritage Center; academic credit

Length of internship: 8-12 weeks

THE SCOOP

The Anasazi Heritage Center works to preserve and display archaeological evidence from the ancestral Puebloan culture. The organization also works to bring information and cultural resources to the American public. Located in the Four Corners area of Colorado, The Center is on rich ground for archaeological finds. It's also close to the descendant populations of the ancestral Pueblos, the Pueblo Indians of New Mexico and Arizona.

ON THE JOB

AHC interns work in collections management, exhibit design and museum education and interpretation. Collections management interns assist the museum curator, working with the museum's cataloging system and helping to reorganize and inventory existing collections at the AHC. Exhibit design interns brainstorm and mount a display at the AHC themselves, with the help of the curator and the exhibit specialist. Education interns put together programs that focus on topics such as the history of Puebloans, culture of the Four Corners area and archaeological scientific methods. These interns also work at the museum's front desk.

GETTING HIRED

Apply by: Rolling. Go to www.co.blm.gov/ahc/intern.htm to apply or send resume and letter of intent via mail or e-mail.

Qualifications:
Open to college freshmen, sophomores, juniors and seniors and recent grads, as well as grad students. Archaeology, anthropology and education majors preferred.

Contact:
Susan Thomas, Curator and Internship Coordinator
Bureau of Land Management
Anasazi Heritage Center
27501 Highway 184
Dolores, CO 81323
Phone: (970) 882-5600
Fax: (970) 882-7035
E-mail: susan_thomas@co.blm.gov
www.co.blm.gov/ahc/intern.htm

Anchorage Daily News

 THE BUZZ
- "See some grizzly bears and moose"
- "Hot job, hot climate (at least when the interns are there)"

THE STATS

Industry(ies): Journalism

Location(s): Anchorage, AK

Number of interns: *Summer*: 2-4

Pay: Unpaid; On-the-job mileage reimbursement

Length of internship: *Summer*: 12 weeks

THE SCOOP

The Anchorage Daily News started as a weekly in 1946, but just two years later it published six days a week. By 1965, the paper was the only one of the two in Alaska to publish on Sundays. It has also been the proud recipient of two Pulitzer Prizes, one in 1976 and the other in 1989. The now-daily newspaper has continued to grow with the editorial and photo teams winning several notable awards, including a first-place standing the Society of Environmental Journalists, two McClatchy President's Awards and inclusion in the Associated Press Top 10.

ON THE JOB

The Anchorage Daily News hires interns as reporters and photographers each summer. Reporting interns are treated like general assignment journalists and cover a variety of topics. While some stories are assigned, reporters at the paper usually develop their own ideas. Photography interns work in the office and out in the field. They do some clerical and darkroom work, and act as general assignment photographers. Interns are treated as full members of the photography staff.

GETTING HIRED

Apply by: *Summer/reporting*: December 1; *summer/photography*: February 1. Send a resume and cover letter, along with six published clips, or photos (20 samples as tearsheets, prints, slides, CD, zip, or disc/for Macs), to the address below.

Qualifications:
Open to college sophomores, juniors and seniors, as well as grad students and college graduates who have studied journalism for at least two years.

Contact:
Kathleen Macknicki, Reporter Internship Coordinator
or Richard Murphy, Photo Editor
Anchorage Daily News
P.O. Box 149001
Anchorage, AK 99514
Phone: (907) 257-4200
www.adn.com

The Andy Warhol Museum

THE BUZZ

- "For lovers of Campbell soup, Marilyn Monroe and Technicolor"
- "Believe it: high art in Pittsburgh"

THE STATS

Industry(ies): Art/Museum

Location(s): Pittsburgh, PA

Number of interns: *Annual:* 20

Pay: None. Free entry to museums; 20 percent off at the Warhol Museum Store; free entry to gallery openings and lectures

Length of internship: Varies; flexible

THE SCOOP

With support from the Carnegie Institute and Dia Center for the Arts, the Andy Warhol Museum has a vast collection and archive of one of the most influential artists of the late 20th century. The museum's motto, "more than a museum," is evident with celebrations like 2003's "Summer of Andy." In honor of what would have been the late artist's 75th birthday, the Warhol filled the summer with a celebratory exhibition from its permanent collection, unique online projects, a 13-country tour of Warhol's work, a special exhibition of work by former Charlie's Angel Farrah Fawcett and, of course, lots of parties. The man himself would have loved it!

ON THE JOB

Internships at the Warhol are extremely flexible and positions are available in just about every department – archives, marketing, exhibitions, education, and more. Intern tasks are wide ranging and depend on abilities, interests and department. Interns can do anything from entering archive data to mounting exhibitions.

GETTING HIRED

Apply by: Rolling. Due to a high volume of applications, however, the museum recommends that interested parties have applications for summer internships submitted by January. Apply by mail only; send cover letter and resume.

Qualifications:
Open to high school students, college freshmen, sophomores, juniors and seniors, as well as recent grads and grad students.

Contact:
Rachel Baron-Horn
Financial Officer
The Andy Warhol Museum
117 Sandusky Street
Pittsburgh, PA 15212
www.warhol.org/get_involved/index.html

Visit Vault at **www.vault.com** for insider company profiles, expert advice, career message boards, expert resume reviews, the Vault Job Board and more.

VAULT CAREER LIBRARY   41

Anheuser-Busch Adventure Parks

 ## THE BUZZ

- "The blissful crossroads of beer and fun"

 ## THE STATS

Industry(ies): Broadcast & Entertainment; Tourism/Recreation

Location(s): Langhorne, PA; Orlando, FL; San Antonio, TX; San Diego, CA; Tampa, FL; Williamsburg, VA

Number of interns: *Annual*: 30-40

Pay: Paid; *undergraduates*: $375-$700/week; *grad students*: $700-$1,100/week. Free uniforms; free admission; complimentary tickets

Length of internship: *Intern*: 10-14 weeks; *summer/co-op*: at least 1 semester

 ## THE SCOOP

Anheuser-Busch, the company that brews, imports and distributes the vast majority of beer in America, including its own Budweiser brand, also boasts an entertainment arm and runs several popular theme parks. It's one of the largest adventure park companies in the world. Its parks include three SeaWorlds, two Busch Gardens, Discovery Cove, Adventure Island, Water Country USA and Sesame Place.

 ## ON THE JOB

Depending on age, experience and educational background, interns can work in a variety of roles. Opportunities are usually available in ticket selling, guest relations, ride operations, food services, entertainment and merchandising. For college students, especially, there are some positions open on the administrative/business side of running the parks. All interns are thoroughly trained.

GETTING HIRED

Apply by: Rolling. Apply online: www.becjobs.com/student.asp. Interview required.

Qualifications:

Most programs open to college freshmen, sophomores, juniors and seniors, grad students and recent grads. Certain programs are also open to high school students. (See www.becjobs.com/student.asp for specifics.)

Contact:

Busch Gardens Tampa and Adventure Island
3605 Bougainvillea
Tampa, FL 33612
Phone: (813) 987-5400

Busch Gardens Williamsburg and Water Country USA
One Busch Gardens Blvd.
Williamsburg, VA 23187
Phone: (757) 253-3020

Sesame Place
100 Sesame Road
Box L579
Langhorne, PA
Phone: (215) 752-7070, ext. 231

SeaWorld of Florida and Discovery Cove
7007 SeaWorld Drive
Orlando, FL 32821
Phone: (407) 370-1562

SeaWorld of California
500 SeaWorld Drive
San Diego, CA 92109
Phone: (619) 226-3842

SeaWorld of Texas
10500 SeaWorld Drive
San Antonio, TX 78251
Phone: (210) 523-3198
www.anheuser-busch.com
www.becjobs.com/student.asp

The Antarctic and Southern Ocean Coalition (ASOC)

THE BUZZ
- "Help preserve Earth's polar regions"
- "A unique opportunity for those who care about the environment"

THE STATS

Industry(ies): Environmental; Nonprofit; Science/Research

Location(s): Washington, DC

Number of interns: *Annual*: 2-3

Pay: None

Length of internship: *Summer/fall/spring*: 12-16 weeks each

THE SCOOP

The Antarctic and Southern Ocean Coalition is a nonprofit conservation organization, representing the global environment community at Antarctica Treaty System meetings. It's the only one of its kind in the world, focusing on the environmental protection of Antarctica and the surrounding Southern Ocean, about 10 percent of the Earth. Current efforts are aimed at implementing the Environmental Protocol to the Antarctic Treaty, gaining agreement on large marine protected areas such as the Ross Sea and to protect the Southern Ocean's marine ecosystem – which includes the Southern Ocean Whale Sanctuary – by regulating commercial tourism and bio-prospecting, and stopping illegal fishing and 'scientific whaling.'

ON THE JOB

Interns work closely with the ASOC small global staff. However, they should be able to work independently, since most interns are given one major project pertaining to the organization's current priorities, to develop throughout their term. Interns also complete a variety of administrative tasks.

GETTING HIRED

Apply by: Rolling. Send resume, cover letter, a writing sample long enough to evaluate, and at least one recommendation. Please review web site first and use only e-mail to apply.

Qualifications:
Open to all juniors and seniors with a 3.0 GPA or greater. Those studying international relations, environmental studies or law are especially encouraged to apply.

Contact:
ASOC
1630 Connecticut Avenue, NW, 3rd Floor
Washington, DC 20009
Phone: (202) 234-2480
Fax: (202) 387-4823
E-mail: info@asoc.org
www.asoc.org

Aperture Foundation

THE BUZZ
- "Publishing for serious shutterbugs"

THE STATS

Industry(ies): Art/Museum; Publishing

Location(s): New York, NY

Number of interns: 11 every 6 months

Pay: $250/month. Free *Aperture* magazines; academic credit available

Length of internship: 6 months (January-June or July-December); no summer internships

THE SCOOP

Aperture started as a quarterly photography magazine back in 1952. From that seed, the Aperture Foundation has grown. The magazine is still alive and thriving, and The Foundation now also publishes books, portfolios and limited edition prints, while also running a program of traveling exhibitions and overseeing the Paul Strand archive. The Foundation also organized a 50th-anniversary retrospective show, which opened at Sotheby's in New York in January 2003 and moved on to other venues worldwide.

ON THE JOB

The Foundation accepts interns (or "work-scholars") across the board. Interns may contribute to the writing, editing, design, production and marketing of the magazine, or they can work on traveling exhibitions and the publicity involved, on both the domestic and international fronts. Interns can also learn the business side of running a nonprofit, working in the executive director's office and gaining experience in foreign rights sales.

GETTING HIRED

Apply by: Rolling. Early applications are recommended. Include a short writing sample with a resume and a cover letter describing your background, skills and reasons for wanting to intern at the Aperture Foundation. Review the web site and clearly state which department you want to work in.

Qualifications:
Open to college freshmen, sophomores, juniors and seniors, recent college grads and graduate students.

Contact:
Melanie Levy
Aperture Foundation
547 West 27th Street, 4th Floor
New York, NY 10010
Phone: (212) 505 5555
Fax: (212) 475-8790
E-mail: MLevy@Aperture.org
www.aperture.org/about-Scholar.html

Visit Vault at **www.vault.com** for insider company profiles, expert advice, career message boards, expert resume reviews, the Vault Job Board and more.

VAULT CAREER LIBRARY   **43**

Appalachian Mountain Club

 THE BUZZ
- "Combine work and play protecting the mountains, rivers and trails of the Appalachian Region"

 THE STATS

Industry(ies): Environmental

Location(s): Blairstown, NJ; Boston, MA; Bretton Woods, NH; Gorham, NH

Number of interns: *Annual*: 40

Pay: Unpaid; academic credit. Free membership to AMC and opportunity to use AMC facilities

Length of internship: 2-12 weeks; available year-round

 **THE SCOOP**

Founded in 1877, the Appalachian Mountain Club maintains 350 miles of trails and creates new ones to conduct tours. AMC also runs recreation centers and manages more than 50 recreational facilities in the northeastern United States. AMC's various chapters offer hiking, paddling, skiing, mountaineering, biking, trail work projects, the annual AMC White Mountain Guide, *AMC Outdoors* magazine and a literary journal called *Appalachia*.

 ON THE JOB

Most years, internship positions are available in publishing, advertising, research, curriculum development, education or research in an office, or working out on the trails at one of three facilities – the Boston office, the Pinkham Notch facility in New Hampshire and the Mohican Outdoor Center in New Jersey. Interns can also choose to work in conservation or web site services.

 GETTING HIRED

Apply by: Rolling. Visit www.outdoors.org to find specific application information for the different locations.

Qualifications:
Open to college freshmen, sophomores, juniors and seniors, as well as grad students interested in research. Interns must receive academic credit through their educational institution.

Contact:
Human Resources
Appalachian Mountain Club
5 Joy Street
Boston, MA 02108
Phone: (617) 523-0636
Fax: (617) 367-8878
www.outdoors.org

Apple Computer

 THE BUZZ
- "One word: iPod"
- "This company is hot!"

THE STATS

Industry(ies): Hardware; Music/Records; New/Interactive Media; Software; Technology

Location(s): Cupertino, CA

Number of interns: *Annual*: 100-200

Pay: Paid; competitive compensation and benefits

Length of internship: Usually 3 months

 THE SCOOP

Steve Jobs and Stephen Wozniak created Apple Computers in 1976 to make affordable, innovative computers for home and office use. Apple ignited the personal computer revolution in the 1970s with the Apple II, and "reinvented" the PC itself in the 1980s with Macintosh. Today, Apple remains committed to creating superior PCs with G4 processor-powered computers, iPod music devices, iMac and Power books, as well as a collection of products now used in schools and offices all over the world.

ON THE JOB

Apple offers full-time and part-time paid internships in technical operating functions, hardware engineering, software engineering, applications, finance, operations and marketing. The company sponsors speaking events and holds contests for interns – with Apple products as prizes.

GETTING HIRED

Apply by: Rolling. Submit a resume and cover letter to the address, fax or e-mail below.

Qualifications:
Open to college freshmen, sophomores, juniors and seniors, as well as graduate students. Students must be working toward a BS, BA, MA, MS, MBA or PhD.

Contact:
Attention: University Relations
Apple Computer, Inc.
1 Infinite Loop MS-38-3CE
Cupertino, CA 95014
Fax: (408) 974-5957
E-mail: applejobs@apple.com
www.apple.com/jobs/internship.html

Arab American Institute

 THE BUZZ
- "Embrace Arab culture and promote the Arab voice"

 THE STATS

Industry(ies): Government; Law

Location(s): Washington, DC

Number of interns: *Spring/summer/fall*: 4-6 each

Pay: Paid; $280/week

Length of internship: *Summer/spring/fall*: 10-12 weeks each

 THE SCOOP

The Arab American Institute was created in 1985 to foster Arab American participation and interest in politics, government and research, as well as to serve as an organized forum for domestic and foreign issues. AAI maintains a direct liaison to the Arab American congressional delegation and functions as a resource for U.S. policy makers on a range of Arab American concerns, including post-September 11 discrimination, the Israeli-Palestinian conflict, civil liberties, immigration and global terrorism.

ON THE JOB

Interns work on various projects and assignments in the government relations, communications and community relations departments, as well as in the executive offices. They may also be placed in outside agencies, including the White House, human rights organizations and in the offices of the major political parties. Through their assignments, interns may also have an opportunity to meet with the AAI president and director, attend meetings, briefings, interviews and parties hosted by visiting dignitaries.

GETTING HIRED

Apply by: *Spring*: December 5; *summer*: April 7; *fall*: August 8. Submit a resume and cover letter, including dates of availability, references, letters of recommendation and a three- to four-page writing sample.

Qualifications:
Open to college freshmen, sophomores, juniors and seniors, recent college graduates, graduate students and international applicants.

Contact:
Arab American Institute
Attention: Dianne Davidson
1600 K Street, NW, Suite 601
Washington, DC 20006
Phone: (202) 429-9210
Fax: (202) 429-9214
E-mail: ddavidson@aaiusa.org
www.aaiusa.org/for_students.htm#internships

ARAMARK

 **THE BUZZ**
- "Where opportunity is as limitless as your ability"

THE STATS

Industry(ies): Food & Beverage

Location(s): Norwell, MA (*marketing internships*); Philadelphia, PA (*accounting internships*)

Number of interns: *Annual*: over 100

Pay: Paid. Some programs provide housing during the internship

Length of internship: *Summer*: 10-12 weeks

 THE SCOOP

ARAMARK is a leader in professional services, providing award-winning food services, facilities management, and uniform and career apparel to health care institutions, universities and school districts, stadiums and arenas, international and domestic corporations, as well as providing uniform and career apparel. ARAMARK was ranked No. 1 in its industry in the 2004 and 2006 Fortune 500 surveys and was also named one of America's Most Admired Companies by *Fortune* magazine in 2006. Since 1998, ARAMARK has consistently ranked as one of the top three most admired companies in its industry as evaluated by peers. Headquartered in Philadelphia, ARAMARK has approximately 240,000 employees serving clients in 20 countries.

 ON THE JOB

As an ARAMARK intern, you will spend your summer learning from the best in the industry. All programs are "hands-on" and your drive will determine your success. Internships are offered for candidates interested in sales, engineering, food and beverage, lodging, accounting, human resources, IT, and facilities management.

GETTING HIRED

Apply by: It is recommended to apply before March 1. Apply online at www.ARAMARK.com.

Qualifications:

Open to undergraduate students working towards a Bachelor's degree Strong organizational, time management and leadership skills are required. Candidates must possess the ability and desire to communicate effectively with clients, client's customers, and support staff as well as the flexibility to work in an environment with changing demands. Positions may require flexibility for event-based hours, which may include nights and weekends.

Contact:
ARAMARK
College Relations
1101 Market Street
Philadelphia, PA 19107
Phone: (800) 999-8989 x3184
Email: collegerelations@aramark.com
www.aramark.com

Visit Vault at **www.vault.com** for insider company profiles, expert advice, career message boards, expert resume reviews, the Vault Job Board and more.

VAULT CAREER LIBRARY **45**

Arden Theatre Company

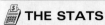 **THE BUZZ**
- "Seeking ambitious future theater leaders"
- "Intense hands-on experience in running a nonprofit theater"
- "Network with the Philly theater community"

THE STATS

Industry(ies): Nonprofit; Theater/Performing Arts

Location(s): Philadelphia, PA

Number of interns: *Annual*: 10-20 interns; 6 apprentices

Pay: Paid. *Interns*: Stipends may be available for some internships; free tickets to performances *Apprentices*: $310/week. Health benefits; paid time off; complimentary tickets to Arden productions, as well as opportunities to meet, network and attain understudy oppotunities with members of the Philadelphia theater community. Equity Membership Candidate credit is available. Housing and transportation are the apprentice's responsibility

Length of internship: *Interns*: varies; *Apprentices*: full-time, plus commitment from late August to mid-June.

THE SCOOP

Arden Theatre Company is a full-service, nonprofit professional regional theater, offering high quality theatrical and educational productions and programs to the artists, audiences and students of the greater Philadelphia region. Founded in 1988 by Terrence J. Nolen, Amy Murphy and Aaron Posner, the Arden is dedicated to bringing to its audiences great stories by the most prolific storytellers. The company draws from inherently dramatic and theatrical sources – fiction, nonfiction, poetry, music and drama.

ON THE JOB

Arden offers both intern and apprentice positions. Interns get hands-on experience and learn from a staff of theater professionals. Internships are available in production (stage management, lighting, sound, props, costuming and scenic construction – helping in the build, rehearsal, technical rehearsal, and performance of productions) and all administrative departments.

The Arden Professional Apprentice (APA) philosophy is to provide a comprehensive knowledge of the inner workings of a nonprofit regional theater through intense hands-on experience. Apprentices work in every area of the theater's operations including artistic, marketing, box office, development, production (strike, run crew, prop/set/costume building, etc.), stage management, finance, front of house and general management.

GETTING HIRED

Apply by: Contact the appropriate coordinator at the address below. *Internships*: Rolling. Send a current resume that includes two references, preferably from an educator, mentor or employer and a cover letter that highlights specific areas of interest and time commitment. If interested in more than one internship position, indicate order of preference.

Apprenticeships: May 15. Send a cover letter, a current resume, a one-page essay of a five-year plan, two letters of recommendation, and contact information for two to three professional, academic and/or employment refernces. Check

www.arden theatre.org/education/apa.html for more information.

Qualifications:

Internships: Open to all college freshmen, sophomores, juniors and seniors, as well as some high school students.
Apprenticeships: Open to college graduates and graduate students. Bachelor's degree or equivalent required.

Contact:
Intern or APA Coordinator
Arden Theatre Company
40 North 2nd Street
Philadelphia, PA 19106
Fax: (215) 922-7011
Internship e-nmail: jobs@ardentheatre.org
Apprentice e-mail: apa@ardentheatre.org

www.ardentheatre.org/education/apa.html

Arena Stage

 THE BUZZ
- "One of the premier regional theaters"

 THE STATS

Industry(ies): Nonprofit; Theater/Performing Arts

Location(s): Washington, DC

Number of interns: *Annual*: 18-20

Pay: Modest stipend. Academic credit; free tickets to all performances; free tickets to local theaters

Length of internship: Flexible; full-time

THE SCOOP

Producing performances since the 1950s, Arena Stage has many "firsts" to its name. It was one of the first not-for-profit theaters in the United States, the first regional theater to transfer a play to Broadway and the first theater to win a Tony award. Arena Stage premieres new plays every season and actively supports works-in-progress. Arena boasts an annual audience of 250,000.

ON THE JOB

Arena offers internships in a number of areas, including arts administration, artistic and technical production and community engagement. Interns focus on one specialty within an area, such as graphic design, ticket operations, directing, casting, costumes, sound, or communities and schools, and work with experienced professionals on the productions during the internship period. Arena Stage also brings in guest speakers for monthly intern seminars, and sponsors regular field trips and luncheons for its interns.

GETTING HIRED

Apply by: *Summer*: March 1; *fall*: May 1; *winter/spring*: October 1. To apply, send a resume, cover letter, two letters of recommendation, a transcript, a writing sample (for some positions), and responses to questions listed on the web site.

Qualifications:
Open to college freshmen, sophomores, juniors and seniors, recent grads and graduate students, as well as career-changers.

Contact:
Jacqueline E. Lawton
Fellows, Intern and Volunteer Coordinator
Arena Stage
1101 Sixth Street, SW
Washington, DC 20024
Phone: (202) 234-5782
Fax: (202) 797-1043
E-mail: jlawton@arenastage.org
www.arenastage.org/about/employment/internships/index.shtml

Argonne National Laboratory

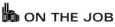 **THE BUZZ**
- "Pioneering science and technology"
- "Work at the epicenter of scientific innovation"

 THE STATS

Industry(ies): Energy/Utilities; Government; Science/Research

Location(s): Argonne, IL

Number of interns: *Annual*: 220

Pay: Paid; $400/week. Round-trip transportation; housing allowance

Length of internship: *Summer*: 10-12 weeks; *fall*: 15 weeks; *spring*: 15 weeks

THE SCOOP

The Argonne labs are operated by the University of Chicago for the United States Department of Energy. Steps to forming the lab began in 1942, when a team at the University of Chicago (lead by Enrico Fermi) produced the world's first sustained nuclear chain reaction. Just five years later, Argonne was a firm partner of the U.S. government, developing nuclear submarine power plants and working with the Atomic Energy Commission. Today, Argonne's efforts power much of the United States, and the labs continue to push scientific and technological innovation to the next level.

ON THE JOB

Undergrad interns work on Argonne's continuing research projects, usually relating to physical and life sciences, mathematics, computer science and engineering. Topics have included coal, conservation, environmental impact and technology, fission and fusion technology.

GETTING HIRED

Apply by: *Summer*: February 1; *fall*: rolling; *spring*: rolling. Online application available at www.dep.anl.gov.

Qualifications:
Argonne's research positions are open to undergraduate sophomores, juniors or seniors with a 2.5 GPA or higher.

Contact:
Division of Educational Programs
Argonne National Laboratory
Argonne, IL 60439
Phone: (630) 252-4495
Fax: (630) 252-3193
E-mail: Lreed@dep.anl.gov

For information about the internship
www.dep.anl.gov

For information about the organization
www.anl.gov

Visit Vault at **www.vault.com** for insider company profiles, expert advice, career message boards, expert resume reviews, the Vault Job Board and more.

VAULT CAREER LIBRARY **47**

Arms Control Association

 THE BUZZ
- "Work for the nation's No. 1 authority on arms control"

 THE STATS

Industry(ies): Education; Government; Nonprofit; Publishing

Location(s): Washington, DC

Number of interns: *Annual*: 7-10

Pay: Small daily stipend for lunch and travel

Length of internship: *Spring*: January-May; *summer*: June-September; *fall*: September-December; 4- to 5-month commitment

 THE SCOOP

Since 1971, the nonpartisan Arms Control Association has been making arms control a public issue. The Association hosts a variety of education programs and publishes *Arms Control Today (ACT)*, a magazine covering the gamut of arms control policy and opinion.

 ON THE JOB

Two internships are available: the ACA Research Internship and the *ACT* Journalism Internship. Research interns research arms control and security issues, keep track of legislative activity on Capitol Hill and provide crucial support for analysts. The journalism internship is a relatively new and very flexible program. These interns work with *ACT* staff to produce the magazine.

 GETTING HIRED

Apply by: *Summer*: April 4; *fall*: August 15; *spring*: December 19. Send cover letter, resume, and a relevant three- to five-page writing sample.

Qualifications:

Open to college freshmen, sophomores, juniors and seniors, as well as recent grads and grad students. Undergraduates are preferred, however.

Contact:

The Arms Control Association
Attention: Internship Director
1150 Connecticut Avenue, NW, Suite 620
Washington, DC 20036
Fax: (202) 463-8273
E-mail: aca@armscontrol.org
www.armscontrol.org/internships.asp

The Arnold Arboretum of Harvard University

 THE BUZZ
- "Take time to smell the roses – and grow them, too"
- "Especially for green thumbs"

 THE STATS

Industry(ies): Environmental; Horticulture; Forestry

Location(s): Jamaica Plain, MA

Number of interns: *Summer*: 14

Pay: Paid; $9.00/hour

Length of internship: *Spring/Summer*: 12-24 weeks

 **THE SCOOP**

The Arnold Arboretum dates back to 1872 and has served as a model for outdoor horticulture since its inception. James Arnold, its creator, envisioned the grounds to be both scientific and picturesque, and it lives up to this goal. Today, the Arboretum is a verdant escape for visitors (open every day of the year from sunrise to sunset) and is a serious place of scientific research, with continuing studies on everything from molecular systematics to pest management.

 ON THE JOB

The majority of interns at the Arboretum are placed in the grounds maintenance department, with a couple of them working in the Dana Greenhouses and another few working in the plant records department. Tasks vary with department, but may include clerical responsibilities. The Arboretum designs classes to enhance the interns' time there – in summer 2006, for example, the courses included Cultural Maintenance of Woody Plants and Plant Propagation. The Arboretum also takes interns on field trips to other gardens and to additional outside lectures.

 GETTING HIRED

Apply by: February 9. Fill out and send an online application (available at www.arboretum.harvard.edu/intern). Letters of reference are recommended and can be sent in separately. Current resumes or CV's are required.

Qualifications:

Open to sophomores, juniors and seniors. Must have a minimum of one year of college-level biology, life science, horticulture or forestry.

Contact:

Steve Schneider, Internship Coordinator
The Arnold Arboretum of Harvard University
125 Arborway
Jamaica Plain, MA 02130
Phone: (617) 524-1718, ext. 112
Fax: (617) 524-1418
E-mail: Stephen_Schneider@harvard.edu
www.arboretum.harvard.edu/intern

Arthritis Foundation

 THE BUZZ
- "Work with the largest private arthritis researcher in the world"

 THE STATS

Industry(ies): Health Care; Nonprofit

Location(s): Palo Alto, CA (Stanford); San Francisco, CA (UCSF)

Number of interns: *Summer*: 7-9

Pay: Paid; *high school student*: $1,500/summer; *undergraduate*: $2,000/summer

Length of internship: *Summer*: 8 weeks, full-time

 THE SCOOP

With offices in all 50 states and DC, the Arthritis Foundation is the largest private, nonprofit arthritis research organization in the world. This allows the Foundation to focus on training new investigators – including interns through its George Hagan Memorial Summer Science Fellowship Program – and on following radical and exciting research paths to a cure for arthritis. The Foundation also maintains a web site with a wealth of information on the disease, its treatments and ongoing research.

 ON THE JOB

Internships at the Foundation emphasize hands-on work in arthritis research labs either at the University of California at San Francisco or at Stanford University. There, interns assist a select few principal investigators with their work on projects related to finding a cure for the disease. Research covers a wide range of fields, from the most basic chemistry to molecular biology and genomics.

GETTING HIRED

Apply by: *Summer*: early March. Call for an application (available in January).

Qualifications:
Open to high school juniors and seniors, as well as college freshmen and sophomores.

Contact:
Jennifer Thompson, MS
Arthritis Foundation, North California Chapter
657 Mission Street, Suite 603
San Francisco, CA 94105
Phone: (800) 464-6240
www.arthritisfoundation.org

Artists Space

  THE BUZZ
- "Intern in SoHo on the cutting edge of contemporary art"

THE STATS

Industry(ies): Art/Museum; Nonprofit

Location(s): New York, NY

Number of interns: *Spring/summer/fall*: 10 each

Pay: None. Academic credit; invitations to openings

Length of internship: Flexible; average 2-6 months, 2 days/week

 **THE SCOOP**

Artists Space has been a haven for cutting-edge contemporary visual artists since 1972. In the summer of 2003, for example, the organization mounted a show of Zaha Hadid's work, who most recently designed the news-making Rosenthal Center for Contemporary Arts in Cincinnati. In addition to its curatorial work, Artists Space also maintains a large computerized slide library of contemporary art, the Irving Sandler Artists File.

ON THE JOB

Internships at Artists Space are largely left to the intern to design. They work on various projects with the regular staff, acquiring knowledge of everyday tasks for arts organizations. In the past, interns have also completed long-term projects such as digitized Artists File slide exhibitions, reviews of past and current exhibitions at the Artists Space and slide presentations of their own work.

GETTING HIRED

Apply by: Rolling. Download the online version at: www.artists space.org/intern_app.pdf or call Hillary Wiedemann.

Qualifications:
Open to college sophomores, juniors and seniors, graduate students and recent grads.

Contact:
Hillary Wiedemann
Artists Space
38 Greene Street, 3rd Floor
New York, NY 10013
Phone: (212) 226-3970, ext. 302
E-mail: hwiedemann@artistsspace.org
www.artissspace.org/intern.html

Visit Vault at **www.vault.com** for insider company profiles, expert advice, career message boards, expert resume reviews, the Vault Job Board and more.

V∧ULT CAREER LIBRARY   **49**

Arup

Boston, Detroit and New York offices
Keri Brady
HR Generalist
155 Avenue of the Americas
New York, NY 10013
Phone: (212) 229-2669
Fax: (212) 229-1056

THE BUZZ
- "Build on your interest in architecture"
- "Help design the cities of tomorrow"

THE STATS

Industry(ies): Engineering

Location(s): Boston, MA; Detroit, MI; Houston, TX ; Los Angeles, CA; New York, NY; San Francisco, CA; Seattle, WA; Toronto

Number of interns: Varies

Pay: Usually paid (amount varies with position and experience)

Length of internship: Varies with student availability

THE SCOOP

Arup is a leading global firm in the provision of design and business services and is the creative force behind many of the world's most innovative and sustainable buildings, transport and civil engineering projects. The firm's work includes the Sydney Opera House, the Oresund Bridge between Denmark and Sweden and, in the U.S., the Seattle Central Library, San Francisco's de Young Museum and New York's Second Avenue Subway. Founded in 1946, Arup now has 7,000 employees in more than 70 offices in 32 countries, with core businesses focusing on buildings, infrastructure and consulting.

ON THE JOB

Interns work closely with the professional staff on specific projects, though duties and qualifications vary depending on office location and position availability. Most jobs demand engineering, science and math skills.

GETTING HIRED

Apply by: Rolling. Visit the company web site, www.arup.com/americas, and go to the Careers Section to see available intern positions.

Qualifications:
Open to undergraduate juniors and seniors. Qualifications may vary from office to office. Contact desired location for specifics.

Contact:
Chicago, Houston and Los Angeles offices
Paula Balfoort
Senior HR Generalist
2440 South Sepulveda Blvd., Suite 180
Los Angeles, CA 90064
Phone: (310) 312-5040
Fax: (310) 312-5788

San Francisco and Seattle offices
Julie Jeffery
HR Generalist
901 Market Street, Suite 260
San Francisco, CA 94103
Phone: (415) 957-9445
Fax: (415) 957-9096

Ashburn Institute

THE BUZZ
- "A global internship with freedom and democracy at stake"

 THE STATS
Industry(ies): Government; Nonprofit

Location(s): Washington, DC

Number of interns: *Annual*: 2-3

Pay: $250/month

Length of internship: *Spring/summer/fall*: 12 weeks; minimum of 2 months and a maximum of 6 months. Full-time and part-time internships are available

 THE SCOOP
The Ashburn Institute is a nonprofit dedicated to uniting democratic governments. In particular, AI promotes Euro-Atlantic cooperation and the enlargement of the Euro-Atlantic community where newly democratic nations can find support. Through conferences and video conferences, publications and distant learning programs, the Ashburn Institute is focusing on educational and cultural exchange among representatives of the global community.

ON THE JOB
The internship program is designed to teach students the inner workings of a nonprofit in an international environment, and about AI's specific mission of promoting democracy and freedom. Duties include program development, database maintenance, event planning, newsletter writing and editing, specific research, marketing and administrative tasks.

GETTING HIRED
Apply by: *Spring*: December 15; *summer*: April 15; *fall*: August 15. Fill out the online application form and send it with a resume and cover letter by fax, e-mail or mail.

Qualifications:
Open to college juniors and seniors, preferably in their third or fourth year of study, as well as grad students. Interest in international relations or a closely related field strongly preferred. Must be in excellent academic standing and have good command of English. Computer skills are also necessary. Foreign language skills are a plus.

Contact:
Internship Coordinator
The Ashburn Institute
P.O. Box 77164
Washington, DC 20013-7164
Phone: (202) 220-1388
Fax: (202) 220-1389
E-mail: info@ashburninstitute.org
www.ashburninstitute.org

Ashoka

THE BUZZ
- "Do-gooders unite!"
- "Help solve some of society's toughest problems"

 THE STATS
Industry(ies): Nonprofit

Location(s): Arlington, VA

Number of interns: *Annual*: 35-40

Pay: Paid

Length of internship: 3-6 months

THE SCOOP
Ashoka – a global citizen organization – works to develop "social entrepreneurs," individuals committed to solving problems within society. These Ashoka Fellows, of which there have been more than 1,600 since the organization was established in 1980, work on specific issues in societies around the world. The organization is named after Ashoka, the Indian emperor in the third century B.C., who renounced violence by uniting the Indian subcontinent and dedicating his life to establishing social welfare programs and supporting the tolerance of all religions.

ON THE JOB
Interns should be dedicated to "advancing and supporting an influential civil society sector worldwide." Internships vary each year according to the needs of the organization. Usually interns can work in the following departments: Global Venture; Global Academy; Fellowship Support Services; US/Canada Program; CBI Best Practices; or Recruiting.

GETTING HIRED
Apply by: Rolling. Interested parties should see the web site for additional information: www.ashoka.org/involved/internships.cfm.

Qualifications:
Some Ashoka programs are open to undergrads, while other positions are reserved for graduate students only. (See web site for specifics.) Internship candidates are evaluated regarding the criteria that represent Ashoka's culture, as well as the specific qualifications for each internship.

Contact:
Ashoka Internship Program
1700 North Moore Street, Suite 2000 (20th Floor)
Arlington, VA 22209
Phone: (703) 527-8300
Fax: (703) 527-8383
E-mail: interns@ashoka.org
www.ashoka.org

Visit Vault at **www.vault.com** for insider company profiles, expert advice, career message boards, expert resume reviews, the Vault Job Board and more.

VAULT CAREER LIBRARY   **51**

Asian American Arts Centre

 THE BUZZ
- "Art history major nirvana"
- "Study a fusion of Asian cultures in the melting pot of New York City"

 THE STATS

Industry(ies): Art/Museum

Location(s): New York, NY

Number of interns: *Annual*: 12

Pay: None; academic credit

Length of internship: Varies

 **THE SCOOP**

Founded in 1974, the Asian American Arts Centre (AAAC) encourages and preserves the Asian American culture through artistic creativity. The Centre promotes its mission by mounting exhibitions that showcase a union of contemporary American and Asian art. AAAC also maintains slide and research archives, (one of the largest in the country on Asian Americans artists from 1945-present) organizes community outreach programs, and produces catalogs and Artspiral, a webzine e-publication on the arts.

 ON THE JOB

Internships at the Asian American Arts Centre teach the basics of running a nonprofit arts organization. Interns work on everything from answering phones to organizing exhibitions to writing up grant proposals, and also have the opportunity to work in the AAAC's extensive archives, assist in ongoing art history research and help produce the Artspiral webzine. Other duties include preparing materials to be posted on the web site and working with young children and middle school students on Saturdays to create ceramic tile mosaics for the program Stories of Chinatown.

 GETTING HIRED

Apply by: Rolling. To apply, e-mail a cover letter, resume and examples of visual/written material to aaac@artspiral.org.

Qualifications:
Open to high school students and college freshmen, sophomores, juniors and seniors, as well as graduates.

Contact:
Robert Lee, Executive Director
Asian American Arts Centre
26 Bowery Street
New York, NY 10013
E-mail: aaac@artspiral.org
www.artspiral.org/internship.html

Asian American Journalists Association

 THE BUZZ
- "Increasing fair and accurate portrayals of Asians in the media"
- "Work to diversify the news"

 THE STATS

Industry(ies): Event and Meeting Planning

Location(s): San Francisco, CA

Number of interns: *Annually*: 1

Pay: Stipend

Length of internship: Mid-March to early August

 **THE SCOOP**

The Asian American Journalists Association (AAJA) was established in 1981 by a group of journalists in Los Angeles (KCBS-TV anchor Tritia Toyota, the *Los Angeles Times*' business editor Bill Sing, and *Times* fashion editor Nancy Yoshihara). They felt there were too few Asian Americans represented in the American media, and the organization works to change that. Since it was founded, AAJA has grown to 19 national and international chapters and over 2,000 active members.

 ON THE JOB

The AAJA intern works with staff to coordinate logistical details for the national convention (to be held in Miami in 2007) and other national programs for students. The intern has opportunities for developing professional skills in event planning and management, advertisement sales and coordination, and program tracking.

 GETTING HIRED

Apply by: January 2007. Send or e-mail a resume and cover letter to the address below.

Qualifications:
Open to college seniors and grad students. Only for those seriously considering a career in event and meeting planning.

Contact:

Internship Coordinator
Asian American Journalists Association
1182 Market Street, Suite 320
San Francisco, CA 94102
Phone: (415) 346-2051
Fax: (415) 346-6343
E-mail: national@aaja.org
www.aaja.org

Asian American Justice Center

THE BUZZ

- "A relatively new voice in advancing Asian-American legal rights"

THE STATS

Industry(ies): Law; Civil Rights; Nonprofit

Location(s): Washington, DC

Number of interns: *Spring*: 1-4; *summer*: 4 undergraduate, 4 law; *fall*: 1-4; *winter*: 1-4

Pay: Unpaid. Assistance finding funding and housing

Length of internship: 10 weeks

THE SCOOP

The Asian American Justice Center (AAJC) opened its doors in 1993 as the National Asian Pacific American Legal Consortium (NAPALC). A nonprofit, nonpartisan organization, the AAJC is committed to advancing the civil and legal rights of Asian Pacific Americans in the areas of affirmative action, immigration, language rights, naturalization, violence prevention and voting rights. The organization's channels of change include litigation, public education and public policy.

ON THE JOB

The AAJC hosts year-round internships and the summer legal clerkship program. Intern tasks vary, but include research, writing, fieldwork, program development and advocacy. Year-round, undergraduate interns contribute to the AAJC in many differnt capacities on several projects. Among other duties, they conduct research, both legal and in the news, and sometimes write Op-ed pieces. Summer clerkship interns are paired (one undergraduate and one law student) for work on a project in a specific area. All interns get opportunities to see Congressional hearings and participate in office events. For more details, visit the web site.

GETTING HIRED

Apply by: *Year-round:* Rolling. The AAJC prefers to receive applications three months prior to the internship. *Summer clerkship:* Rolling (recommended by January 15). See the opportunities section of the AAJC web site, http://www.advancinge quality.org/?id=33, for specific requirements for each internship.

Qualifications:
Open to undergraduates and law students.

Contact:
Aimee Baldillo, Staff Attorney
AAJC
1140 Connecticut Avenue, NW, Suite 1200
Washington, DC 20036
Phone: (202) 296-2300
Fax: (202) 296-2318
E-mail: abaldillo@advancingequality.org
www.advancingequallty.org

Aspen Center for Environmental Studies

THE BUZZ

- "Take in the natural beauty of the Rockies and Aspen"
- "Get to know birds of prey up close"

THE STATS

Industry(ies): Education; Environmental; Nonprofit

Location(s): Aspen, CO

Number of interns: *Annual*: 14

Pay: $125/week stipend. Housing provided; tuition-free participation in one or more of ACES' Naturalist Field School courses

Length of internship: June 2-September 1 (10-day mandatory staff training included)

THE SCOOP

The Aspen Center for Environmental Studies (ACES) means "to inspire a life-long commitment to the earth by educating for environmental responsibility, conserving and restoring the balance of natural communities, and advancing the ethic that the earth must be respected and nurtured." Breathtaking in its array of flora and fauna, the lands and animals serviced by ACES are in close proximity to the cultural well source of Aspen.

ON THE JOB

Interns are responsible for a variety of duties, including assisting with the management of the visitor center and nature preserve, environmental education programs for children, interpretive nature walks, birds of prey programs and special projects such as caring for the resident birds of prey, indoor plants and live animals.

GETTING HIRED

Apply by: March 1. An application is available online.

Qualifications:
Experience in the natural sciences, environmental education or related field; interest in environmental education; first aid and CPR certification; and experience working with the public.

Contact:
ACES Summer Naturalist Internship Coordinator
100 Puppy Smith Street
Aspen, CO 81611
Phone: (970) 925-5756
Fax: (970) 925-4819
E-mail: aces@aspennature.org

Summer naturalist internship
www.aspennature.org/template.cfm?s1=7&s2=29

Summer environmental internship
www.aspennature.org/template.cfm?s1=7&s2=30

Visit Vault at **www.vault.com** for insider company profiles, expert advice, career message boards, expert resume reviews, the Vault Job Board and more.

V\ULT CAREER LIBRARY **53**

Assistant Directors Training Program

 THE BUZZ
- "The sunny side of Sunset Boulevard"
- "A direct route to a career as an assistant director"

 THE STATS

Industry(ies): Broadcast & Entertainment; Film

Location(s): Sherman Oaks, CA

Number of interns: *Annual*: 10-20

Pay: Paid; trainees start at $610/week and increase to a final wage of $749/week

Length of internship: 400 days of on-the-job training and classroom-based seminars

 THE SCOOP

The mission of the Directors Guild-Producer Training Plan is to provide motion picture and television industry training as directed by the Alliance of Motion Picture & Television Producers and the Directors Guild of America. The Assistant Directors Training Program recruits a diverse group of applicants from across the country and provides selected candidates with education, training and paid experience in professional settings, facilitating their development into successful assistant directors. The Training Program's ultimate goal is to provide the Directors Guild of America and the alliance of Motion Picture & Television Producers with assistant directors of the highest quality and professionalism.

ON THE JOB

Under the supervision of the unit production manager and assistant directors, the assistant director trainee helps provide support to all of the actors, crew and production personnel working on a production. Possible productions include episodic television, television movies, pilots, miniseries and feature films. Duties may include errands and administrative tasks.

GETTING HIRED

Apply by: Rolling. Application is available online. See web site for more information.

Qualifications:
The program requires applicants to be at least 21 years of age, have a legal right to work in the U.S., a bachelor's degree from an accredited four-year college or university, or an associate of arts or science degree from an accredited two-year college and/or two years of paid employment may be treated as equivalent to a bachelor's. Academic credit and work experience may be combined to meet the program's eligibility requirements. Applicants must have a demonstrated interest and/or experience in the motion picture, television, entertainment or related industries.

Contact:
Directors Guild – Producer Training Plan
14724 Ventura Blvd., Suite 775
Sherman Oaks, CA 91403
Phone: (818) 386-2545
E-mail: mail@trainingplan.org
www.trainingplan.org

Association of Trial Lawyers in America

THE BUZZ
- "A great chance to see justice done"

THE STATS

Industry(ies): Law

Location(s): Atlanta, GA

Number of interns: *Spring/summer/fall*: 6 each

Pay: None

Length of internship: *Spring/summer/fall*: 8-12 weeks each session

THE SCOOP

The Association of Trial Lawyers (ATLA) was founded in 1946 by a group of plaintiffs' attorneys representing workers' compensation claims. Originally dubbed the National Association of Claimants' Compensation Attorneys, the group renamed itself in 1972 to acknowledge its growth and expansion into all facets of law. Today, the association is one of the biggest bars in the United States and counts over 56,000 members worldwide.

ON THE JOB

Interns are placed in several departments, including public affairs, state affairs, legal affairs, media relations, meetings and conventions, continuing legal education, publications, production and foundations. Responsibilities vary with department, but may include answering phones and handling administrative tasks.

GETTING HIRED

Apply by: March 1. Send in a resume and cover letter to the address below.

Qualifications:
Open to high school seniors, college freshmen, sophomores, juniors and seniors, recent college graduates and grad students.

Contact:
Internship Coordinator
Association of Trial Lawyers of America
The Leonard M. Ring Law Center
1050 31st Street, NW
Washington, DC 20007
Phone: (202) 965-3500
www.atlanet.org/index.aspx

AT&T Finance

 THE BUZZ
- "Finance-oriented internships at the leading communications company"

 THE STATS

Industry(ies): Communications Services; Directory Publishing; Advertising Services

Location(s): San Antonio, TX (HQ); Dallas, TX; San Ramon, CA; Pleasanton, CA; Hoffman Estates, IL; Bedminster, NJ; Morristown, NJ; locations across the US

Number of interns: *Annual*: 15 MBA candidates

Pay: Varies.

Length of internship: 12-14 weeks

 THE SCOOP

AT&T traces its history back to Alexander Graham Bell and his most famous invention, the telephone, in 1895. He started the Bell Telephone Company, an ancestor to today's telecommunications conglomerate, in 1877, and a giant was born. Today, AT&T specializes in local, long-distance, Internet and transaction-based voice and data services and employs about 189,500 people worldwide.

 ON THE JOB

AT&T's summer finance interns work with staff implementing what they've learned in school. They're assigned to one of AT&T's finance areas such as auditing; corporate planning, financial analysis, investor relations, tax, treasury, business case development and regulatory compliance. Interns receive feedback from their management team while working toward established objectives and their performance is reviewed at the end of the term by their supervisors. Those deemed "high performers" are asked to interview for full-time employment in the company's Financial Leadership Program.

GETTING HIRED

Apply by: Rolling. Apply online at: www.att.com/flp.

Qualifications:
Open to first year MBA students in finance, accounting, economics or business administration. Applicants should have prior internship or coporate work experience, a minimum 3.5 GPA and display leadership and communication skills. Applicants must also have U.S citizenship or hold a permanent work authorization Qualifications may vary with position (see the web site, www.att.com/flp/fsip, for more information).

Contact:
www.att.com/flp/fsip

AT&T Labs

 THE BUZZ
- "The best internship for aspiring telecom engineers"

 **THE STATS**

Industry(ies): Communications Equipment; Science/Research; Technology; Telecom & Wireless

Location(s): Florham Park, NJ; Menlo Park, CA; Middletown, NJ; Piscataway, NJ

Number of interns: *Annual*: 60

Pay: Varies. Transportation provided

Length of internship: *Summer*: 10 weeks beginning in early June

 THE SCOOP

AT&T, perhaps the leading communications company in the world, specializes in local, long-distance, Internet and transaction-based voice and data services. The folks at AT&T Labs handle the research end of things and work on IP networks, artificial intelligence, broadband, human-computer interfaces, mobile wireless networks and much more.

ON THE JOB

Most AT&T Labs-Research interns work one-on-one with a supervisor and on specific projects that may deal with IP networks, artificial intelligence, broadband, human-computer interfaces, and other interesting projects. Duties vary with department placement, but will likely include technical research and laboratory work. Interns give a half-hour talk on their work at the end of the term.

GETTING HIRED

Apply by: December 1. Submit a resume, cover letter and a list of references (with e-mail addresses whenever possible) online at: www.research.att.com/~kbl/cgi-bin/resume.pl?URP. After you have successfully submitted this application, instructions for sending a personal statement will be e-mailed to you.

Qualifications:
Open to college juniors and seniors, as well as recent college graduates and graduate students. PhDs can apply at: www.research.att.com/academic/alfp.html.

Contact:
AT&T Labs
Undergraduate Research Program Administrator
Room D32-B03
200 Laurel Avenue
Middletown, NJ 07748
Phone: (732) 420-5092
www.research.att.com/academic

Visit Vault at **www.vault.com** for insider company profiles, expert advice, career message boards, expert resume reviews, the Vault Job Board and more.

VAULT CAREER LIBRARY **55**

AT&T Summer Management

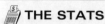 **THE BUZZ**
- "Management-oriented internships at the leading communications company"

THE STATS

Industry(ies): IP-based communications services (high speed DSL Internet, local and long distance voice, wireless); directory publishing; advertising services

Location(s): San Antonio, TX (HQ); Dallas, TX; San Ramon, CA; Chicago, IL; Bedmisnter, NJ; Multiple locations across the US

Number of interns: *Annual*: Varies. Approximately 25 per session

Pay: *Undergraduates:* $3,500-3,850/month; Graduate students: $5,000-5,500/month

Length of internship: 10-12 weeks

THE SCOOP

AT&T traces its history back to Alexander Graham Bell and his most famous invention, the telephone, in 1895. He started the Bell Telephone Company, an ancestor to today's

telecommunications conglomerate, in 1877, and a giant was born. Today, AT&T specializes in local, long-distance, Internet and transaction-based voice and data services and employs about 189,500 people worldwide.

ON THE JOB

The AT&T Summer Management Program (SMP) is designed for high-caliber undergraduate and graduate students who are within one year of graduation. The program gives students a jump start into a career with a telecommunications industry leader, providing challenging work assignments and an opportunity for students to evaluate their compatibility for full-time employment at AT&T. Interns receive orientation and work in network operations, sales, customer service, and marketing. Each student is paired with a supervisor who they work with in addition to peers. Interns attend executive lunches and regular meetings with the Leadership Development Program staff, and participate in SMP committees. Interns also have the opportunity to make site visits, attend social events and network. Another benefit of the Summer Management Program: consideration for AT&T's Leadership Development Program upon graduation.

GETTING HIRED

Apply by: Students are recruited from career fairs at schools across the United States - individuals may submit their resumes directly to recruiters; applications are not accepted online.

Qualifications: Open to students in the last year of a bachelors or masters program.

Applicants should demonstrate strong academic performance, significant leadership experience (work, campus or community efforts), and teamwork experience (supervising, delegating, or achieving results through others). Applicants should also be US citizens or permanent residents.

Contact:
www.att.jobs/
www.sbc.com/gen/careers?pid=28

Atlanta Ballet

THE BUZZ
- "Learn marketing and ballet simultaneously"

THE STATS

Industry(ies): Theater/Performing Arts

Location(s): Atlanta, GA

Number of interns: *Annual*: 8-10

Pay: None. Free tickets; dance classes; gym membership; parking

Length of internship: 4 week minimum, but very flexible

THE SCOOP

As the oldest professional dance company in America, the Atlanta Ballet not only serves as an ambassador for Georgia, but for the United States, having regularly toured internationally. Dorothy Alexander started the company as a dance concert group and renamed it the Atlanta Ballet in 1967, when it earned professional status. In 1996, the company opened the Centre for Dance Education and in 2002 it created the Teacher Training Institute.

ON THE JOB

A variety of positions are available – marketing, administrative, production – and interns can mix and match different interests, so duties vary. In fact, the Atlanta Ballet virtually offers prospective interns a design-your-own-internship in terms of hours, departments and length of commitment. It's also a great way to rub elbows and toe shoes with professionals in the performing arts.

GETTING HIRED

Apply by: Rolling. Send a resume and cover letter to the address below.

Qualifications:
Open to college sophomores, juniors and seniors.

Contact:
Heather Kelly
Atlanta Ballet
1400 Peachtree Street, NW
Atlanta, GA 30309
Phone: (404) 873-5811, ext. 203
Fax: (404) 874-7905
E-mail: hkelly@atlantaballet.com
www.atlantaballet.com

Atlanta Braves

 THE BUZZ

- "Batter up your professional skills"
- "Take your career goals out to the ballgame"
- "Live out a Bull Durham summer"

 THE STATS

Industry(ies): Sports

Location(s): Atlanta, GA

Number of interns: Varies

Pay: Paid; $9.00/hour. Free tickets

Length of internship: 12 weeks; at least 37.5 hours/week

 THE SCOOP

The Braves, Atlanta's professional baseball team, moved to the city from Boston via Milwaukee in the 1960s. Under the ownership of CNN-mogul Ted Turner, the team hit its stride in the 1990s, winning multiple World Series. In 1991, the Braves became the first baseball team in history to win the ultimate prize (the Series) just one season after having the worst record in the league.

ON THE JOB

The Atlanta Braves Career Initiative Program is designed for students interested in a behind-the-scenes professional sports career. Each summer, interns work closely with full-time employees in a variety of departments including baseball operations, player personnel, marketing, promotions and public relations. Depending on position, some interns will also have game-day responsibilities.

GETTING HIRED

Apply by: *Summer:* March 10. Send resume between January 9, 2006 and March 10, 2006 for 2006 season. Submit materials to www.braves.jobs@turner.com. No resumes will be received after the deadline, and no calls or e-mails will be accepted regarding status.

Qualifications:
Open to college juniors and seniors, as well as grad students, with a GPA of 2.8 or higher.

Contact:
Atlanta Braves Career Initiative Program
Attention: Human Resources
P.O. Box 4064
Atlanta, GA 30302
atlanta.braves.mlb.com/NASApp/mlb/mlb/help/jobs.jsp?c_id=atl

Atlanta Spirit, LLC (Atlanta Hawks, Atlanta Thrashers and Philips Arena)

 THE BUZZ

- "A top sports franchise in the 'Dirty South'"

 THE STATS

Industry(ies): Sports; Entertainment

Location(s): Atlanta, GA

Number of interns: Varies according to departmental need

Pay: Varies. *Course credit internship (Fall/spring/summer):* none; *paid internship (season):* approximately $10/hour, not entitled to benefits (i.e. insurance, vacation). All interns are responsible for travel and housing arrangements.

Length of internship: Varies with availability. *Course credit:* an average 12 weeks; *paid:* the season, typically from September through May

THE SCOOP

The Atlanta Spirit, LLC is the parent company of the NBA's Atlanta Hawks and the NHL's Atlanta Thrashers and has operating rights to Philips Arena.

ON THE JOB

Atlanta Spirit Student Programs are designed to give top students as well as recent four year college and Masters graduates hands-on experience in the sports and entertainment industry. Interns with Atlanta Spirit work for the two teams and the arena in various departments including sales, marketing, operations, customer service, media relations, business development, information technology, human resources, community development and game operations. Some intern positions include game and event day duties.

GETTING HIRED

Apply by: Rolling. Visit www.atlantaspirit.com and look under "Student Programs" for openings. Send a resume and cover letter stating area(s) of interest.

Qualifications:
Course credit: open to college students only (junior, senior or graduate level). Course credit interns must prove that they can receive academic credit toward graduation; *paid positions:* open to college graduates whose graduation date is within one year of the position start day. All interns must have a GPA of at least 3.0.

Contact:
Student Programs Coordinator
Atlanta Spirit, LLC
101 Marietta Street
Atlanta, GA 30303
Fax: (404) 878-3710
Email: atlantaspiritstudentprograms@atlantaspirit.com
www.atlantaspirit.com

Visit Vault at **www.vault.com** for insider company profiles, expert advice, career message boards, expert resume reviews, the Vault Job Board and more.

V**A**ULT CAREER LIBRARY   **57**

Atlantic Council of the United States

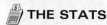 **THE BUZZ**
- "A constructive nonpartisan approach to foreign policy"

 THE STATS

Industry(ies): Government; Nonprofit

Location(s): Washington, DC

Number of interns: *Annual:* 10-15 per session

Pay: None

Length of internship(s): 12 weeks

THE SCOOP

Founded in 1961, the Atlantic Council of the United States (ACUS) is a nonprofit public policy center advancing U.S. global interests within the Atlantic and Pacific communities. ACUS is also a nonpartisan organization working with various entities, including the executive and legislative branches of the government, the international business community, academia and foreign leaders.

ON THE JOB

The John A. Baker Internship Program offers 10 to 15 positions during the fall, spring and summer academic terms. ACUS projects involve new relationships within Europe and between Europe and North America; the transformation of the newly independent Slavic and Eurasian states; new relationships among the Asian and Pacific nations, as well as their ties to North America and Europe; new opportunities for strengthening global and regional security; international education; government and corporate relations; international business; and global interdependence in energy, the environment, trade, economic growth and development.

GETTING HIRED

Apply by: *Summer*: March 30; *fall*: June 30; *spring*: November 24. Send resume, academic transcript, a brief writing sample, two letters of recommendation and a cover letter by mail, fax or e-mail.

Qualifications:
Open to college freshmen, sophomores, juniors and seniors, as well as recent grads and grad students. Strong interest in international affairs and U.S. foreign policy is required. Applicants should have some scholarly research and administrative or office experience.

Contact:
Internship Coordinator
The Atlantic Council of the United States
910 17th Street, NW, Suite 1000
Washington, DC 20006
Phone: (202) 778-4954
Fax: (202) 463-7241
E-mail: internships@acus.org
www.acus.org/education/intern.htm

The Atlantic Monthly

THE BUZZ
- "Join one of America's oldest magazines"

THE STATS

Industry(ies): Journalism

Location(s): Washington, DC

Number of interns: *Summer:* 4; *fall:* 4; *Spring:* 4

Pay: Unpaid. Metrochecks provided for transportation; one-year subscription to the magazine. The Monthly will also grant academic credit

Length of internship(s): Varies. *Summer:* June through August; *Fall:* September through December; *Spring:* January through May

THE SCOOP

Founded in Boston in 1877 and currently celebrating its 150th anniversary, The Atlantic Monthly is a general-interest magazine known for its contributions to the American dialogue on literature, politics and international affairs. Historically, its content has run the gamut from short stories to world news to commentary on civil rights. Its contributors have included Ralph Waldo Emerson, Mark Twain, Martin Luther King, Jr., Vladimir Nabokov and Ernest Hemingway, and the Atlantic has received 19 National Magazine Awards since 1971. Today the Atlantic boasts an editorial staff of approximately 40 people with headquarters in Washington, D.C., and writers all over the world.

ON THE JOB

Atlantic interns assist the magazine's editorial staff. They research and fact-check projects, act as first readers on thousands of unsolicited submissions, and perform numerous administrative tasks such as opening and sorting mail. Interns meet with members of the editorial staff in informal seminars to discuss the functions of the different departments of the magazine. Although the program does not usually offer opportunities for writing, interns gain a thorough understanding of the Atlantic's behind-the-scenes editorial operations.

In addition to the editorial internship, the Atlantic also offers human resources and marketing internships. Applicants should consult the Atlantic's career and internship web site, www.theatlantic.com/a/intern.mhtml, to see positions and descriptions.

GETTING HIRED

Apply by: *Summer:* March 1; fall: July 1; *Spring:* November 1. Applicants should submit a cover letter and resume electronically. Refer to "Atlantic Internship" in the heading. For more information visit the website at www.theatlantic.com/a/intern.mhtml

Qualifications: Open to college juniors, seniors, graduate students and recent graduates of all ages.

Contact:
Josephine Vu, Intern Coordinator
600 New Hampshire Ave., NW
Washington, D.C. 20037
Fax: (202) 266-7227
E-mail: jvu@theatlantic.com
www.atlanticmediacompany.com

Australian Embassy

 THE BUZZ

- "Shrimps on the barbie and valuable government work experience"

 THE STATS

Industry(ies): Government

Location(s): Washington, DC

Number of interns: *Summer/fall/spring*: 3 each

Pay: None

Length of internship: Varies

 **THE SCOOP**

The Australian Embassy is the official diplomatic site for relations between the land down under and the United States. The Embassy also assists Australians traveling to America (and vice versa) by providing a wealth of useful material on passports, current news and information for businesses thinking of expanding into Australia.

 ON THE JOB

Internships are available in three areas: the Congressional Liaison Office, the Public Affairs Office and cultural relations. Cultural relations interns help the staff with basic event management, database tasks, administrative assistance and research. Public affairs interns write embassy news briefs, compose press releases and scan U.S. newspapers for Australia-related clippings, among other duties. Congressional liaison interns assist with research on U.S. domestic and foreign trade policy, report on hearings and legislative developments, and perform general administrative duties.

 GETTING HIRED

Apply by: *Summer*: March 31; *fall*: July 2; *spring*: December 10. Fill out an application form at www.austemb.org/PDFS/InterApply.dot. Check web site (www.austemb.org) for exact dates and for more information on how to apply.

Qualifications:
Open to freshman, sophomore, junior and senior undergrads with strong writing, research and organizational skills.

Contact:
Internship Coordinator
Congressional Liaison Office or
Public Affairs Branch or
Cultural Relations Branch
Embassy of Australia
1601 Massachusetts Avenue, NW
Washington, DC 20036
Phone: (202) 797-3071
Fax: (202) 797-3414
E-mail (cultural affairs): cultural.affairs@austemb.org
E-mail (public affairs): media@austemb.org
www.austemb.org/internships.html

Avaya Inc.

 THE BUZZ

- "Lots of networking opportunities – and not just in the telecom sense of the word!"

 THE STATS

Industry(ies): Communications Equipment; Operations & IT Consulting; Technology

Location(s): Basking Ridge, NJ

Number of interns: *Annual*: 20-30

Pay: Varies depending upon department placement and experience

Length of internship: *Summer*: 10-12 weeks

 THE SCOOP

Love telecom? Then cheer the birth of Avaya. Avaya Inc. was born in October 2000, when Lucent Technologies spun off some of its communication solutions holdings, including Octel Communications, though elements of the company had existed for over 100 years as parts of AT&T and Lucent. The resulting company helps large corporations and other organizations integrate voice and data services into communications networks. Avaya also offers consulting and outsourcing services to its clients, many of which are Fortune 500 companies.

 ON THE JOB

Interns have the option to choose their placements from Avaya's multifarious business units (financial, sales, marketing and manufacturing, to name a few). They are assigned to work projects geared toward their academic and future career goals. The company uses its intern program to target and track potential future employees.

 GETTING HIRED

Apply by: May 15. Send resume and cover letter to the address below.

Qualificati.ons:
Open to college freshmen, sophomores, juniors and seniors, as well as grad students. International student applications are welcome. Applicants must be majoring in a technical field or in business/economics.

Contact:
Internship Coordinator
Avaya Inc.
211 Mt. Airy Road
Basking Ridge, NJ 07920
Phone: (908) 953-6000
jobs.brassring.com/en/asp/tg/cim_home.asp?partnerid=261&sit eid=5069

Visit Vault at **www.vault.com** for insider company profiles, expert advice, career message boards, expert resume reviews, the Vault Job Board and more.

VAULT CAREER LIBRARY **59**

VAULT CAREER LIBRARY

INTERNSHIP PROFILES:
B

BAE Systems

THE BUZZ
- "Perform work of national importance"

THE STATS

Industry(ies): Aerospace

Location(s): Rockville, MD (U.S. HQ); Global

Number of interns: *Annual*: 200-300

Pay: Determined by the business unit, function, hiring department and level of experience

Length of internship: *Summer*: 2-3 months

 THE SCOOP

BAE Systems North America has grown to become one of the top 10 suppliers to the U.S. Department of Defense – solving customers' needs with both highly innovative and leading edge solutions across the defense electronics, systems, information technology and services arenas. Employing approximately 30,000 people, BAE Systems North America has operations across 30 states, the District of Columbia and the UK, generating annual sales of more than $5 billion. BAE Systems designs, develops, integrates, manufactures and supports a wide range of advanced aerospace products and intelligent electronic systems for government and commercial customers. BAE Systems North America is a U.S. corporation and a wholly-owned subsidiary of BAE Systems plc.

ON THE JOB

Internships are offered for students in both engineering- and business-related disciplines in support of programs in electronic systems, information systems, technology services and business operations. Opportunities vary based on the type of project, however all students have a unique opportunity to apply their classroom learning to a real-world setting, working closely with a mentor in a team-based environment. Interns have the opportunity to develop their skills in an environment that encourages innovation, collaboration and creativity.

GETTING HIRED

Apply by: Rolling. Search jobs and apply at: http://careers.na.bae systems.com/cgi-bin/prjps/req_Postings.cfm?searchtype=G. Check with your college recruiting office to see if and when BAE will be visiting your school.

Qualifications:

Open to college sophomores and juniors generally with a GPA of 3.0 or greater, leadership experience, extra-curricular activities and related coursework, and/or project experience in the following: engineering (aerospace engineering, computer engineering, computer science, information technology/MIS, mechanical engineering, industrial/manufacturing engineering, optical engineering, math, physics) and business (accounting, finance, economics, business administration, human resources).

Contact:
BAE Systems, North America Corporate Office
1601 Research Blvd.
Rockville, MD 20850
Phone: (301) 838-6000
Fax: (301) 838-6925
www.na.baesystems.com

Bain & Company

THE BUZZ
- "Management and strategy consulting gone global"

THE STATS

Industry(ies): Management & Strategy Consulting

Location(s): Boston, MA (HQ); Atlanta, GA; Chicago, IL; Dallas, TX; Los Angeles, CA; New York, NY; Palo Alto, CA; San Francisco, CA; international offices in Asia, Australia, Canada, Europe, Johannesburg, Mexico City and Sao Paulo

Number of Interns: Varies according to location

Pay: Paid; competitive salary

Length of Internship: *Summer*: 10 weeks

 THE SCOOP

Since its founding in 1973, Bain & Company has grown to be one of the world's leading business consulting firms. Bain's business is to help make companies more valuable. Consultants work with senior executive teams to convert opportunity into action, and action into economic performance. Bain is comprised of 3,000 employees from varied backgrounds working in 31 offices throughout the world. Collectively, they have served more than 2,700 clients – that historically have outperformed the stock market by 4 to 1 – from every sector in every region of the world.

ON THE JOB

Most of Bain's global offices offer summer internship opportunities for first-year MBA students and undergraduates between their junior and senior years. The summer experience mirrors the work performed by full-time team members. Interns are contributing members of their teams, working on real business problems, collaborating with clients and delivering lasting results. As is also the case with full-time hires, interns attend formal training with their global colleagues. Many former interns return to Bain for full-time positions following graduation.

GETTING HIRED

Apply by: Internship recruiting varies across schools and Bain offices. Contact your career management center and/or visit www.bain.com for a description of the application process. If Bain does not actively recruit on your campus, complete an online application at www.bain.com.

Qualifications:

Summer associate: open to first-year MBA students; *associate consultant intern*: open to rising seniors. Bain looks for eager, driven and committed individuals who are continually motivated to seek new challenges. Applicants should have strong analytical skills, the ability to "think outside of the box" and solid communication skills. Being friendly and down to earth are also important qualities.

Contact:
E-mail: recruiting@bain.com

BalletMet Columbus

 THE BUZZ
- "Grace and business smarts alike"
- "Enhance your passion for the arts"

 THE STATS

Industry(ies): Theater/Performing Arts

Location(s): Columbus, OH

Number of interns: *Spring/summer/fall/winter:* 2 each

Pay: Varies. Complimentary tickets to performances

Length of internship: *Summer/spring/fall/winter:* 8-10 weeks each

 THE SCOOP

BalletMet Columbus has provided high caliber dance performances in Central Ohio since 1978. With an annual budget of $5.3 million, it ranks among the 15 largest dance companies in the U.S. BalletMet's Dance Academy, housed in the 35,000-square-foot Dance Centre, is also one of the five largest professional dance-training centers in the country. BalletMet celebrates dance by exposing the community to quality performances, instruction, education programs and new work. The company has developed extensive educational and outreach programs serving nearly 50,000 people a year, as well as a Community Outreach Scholarship program providing full tuition for talented minority and underserved youth.

 ON THE JOB

Interns work in marketing, communications, development or education departments dealing with ongoing projects such as organizing photos and press clippings or writing a commercial or press release.

GETTING HIRED

Apply by: Rolling. Submit a resume and cover letter at least three months prior to intended start date.

Qualifications:
Open to college juniors and seniors, graduate students, recent graduates and international applicants.

Contact
Patty Donahey
BalletMet, Columbus
322 Mount Vernon Avenue
Columbus, OH 43215
Phone: (614) 229-4860, ext. 160
Fax: (614) 229-4858 or (614) 224-3697
E-mail: pdonahey@balletmet.org
www.balletmet.org

Baltimore Zoo

 THE BUZZ
- "An important name in zoo internships"

 THE STATS

Industry(ies): Education; Science/Research; Tourism/Recreation

Location(s): Baltimore, MD

Number of interns: *Annual:* 20

Pay: None

Length of internship: *Spring/summer/fall:* 10 weeks

 **THE SCOOP**

The Baltimore Zoo was established over 125 years ago – it's the third-oldest zoo in the United States. Because of this, it is currently raising funds for a huge renovation project. The zoo offers an impressive selection of education (which it wittily calls "edzoocation") programs.

 ON THE JOB

Interns at the Baltimore Zoo work in a variety of departments. Generally, the zoo matches interns with a position based on their educational background, experience and career goals. Possible departments are animal care, aviculture, education, graphic design, group sales, herpetology, horticulture, mammals, management and administration, marketing, public relations, special events, veterinary care and volunteer management.

GETTING HIRED

Apply by: Rolling. Contact the volunteer office to request an internship application.

Qualifications:
Open to college freshmen, sophomores, juniors and seniors, grad students and recent college graduates.

Contact:
The Baltimore Zoo
c/o Volunteer Department
Druid Hill Park
Baltimore, MD 21217
Phone: (410) 396-7623
www.baltimorezoo.org

Visit Vault at **www.vault.com** for insider company profiles, expert advice, career message boards, expert resume reviews, the Vault Job Board and more.

VAULT CAREER LIBRARY   **63**

Bank of America

 THE BUZZ

- "Work for one of America's largest banks"

 THE STATS

Industry(ies): Financial Services

Location(s): Charlotte, NC; New York, NY; San Francisco, CA (principal offices); additional locations in California; Colorado; Florida; Georgia; Illinois; Maryland; Massachusetts; Missouri; New York; North Carolina; Oregon; Tennessee; Texas; Washington; Washington, DC; London; Hong Kong; Mexico City; Santiago; São Paolo; Singapore; Tokyo

Number of interns: Varies

Pay: Paid; competitive salary

Length of Internship: *Summer*: 10-12 weeks

THE SCOOP

Bank of America (NYSE: BAC) is one of the world's leading financial services companies. The company's Global Corporate and Investment Banking group (GCIB) provides investment banking, equity and debt capital raising, research, trading, risk management, treasury management and financial advisory services. Through offices in 32 countries, GCIB serves domestic and international corporations, institutional investors, financial institutions and government entities. Many of the bank's services to corporate and institutional clients are provided through its U.S. and UK subsidiaries, Banc of America Securities LLC and Banc of America Securities Limited.

ON THE JOB

Bank of America offers a variety of summer associate (open to students entering their second year of MBA candidacy) and summer analyst (open to rising college seniors) positions. Outstanding performers may be considered for full-time positions upon graduation. Students may seek positions in the following internship programs: Corporate & Investment Banking; Capital Markets; Global Markets — Sales & Trading Research — Debt & Equity; Global Markets Technology; or Global Portfolio Management. See the company web site for descriptions of each program and day-to-day responsibilities.

GETTING HIRED:

Apply by: January 15. Check with your school's career services office for information on how to apply. If your career office directs you to apply online, or if Bank of America does not recruit on your campus, check the company's web site (corp.bank ofamerica.com/public/career/howtoapply.jsp) for application details.

Qualifications:

Summer associate and analyst candidates must demonstrate a combination of academic aptitude, quantitative skills, strategic and creative thinking, and distinguished written and oral communications skills.

Contact:

corp.bankofamerica.com/public/career/opportunitieslanding.jsp

Barrington Stage Company

 THE BUZZ

- "Bringing award winning theater to the masses in the heart of the Berkshires"

 THE STATS

Industry(ies): Theater/Performing Arts

Location(s): Pittsfield, MA

Number of interns: *Summer*: 15-20

Pay: Stipend; housing provided

Length of internship: *Summer*: 3-5 months (Memorial Day-Labor Day)

THE SCOOP

Barrington Stage, originally Berkshire Music Hall, reopened in August 2006 after seven months of renovations. BSC was founded in 1995 and, until 2006, rented performing spaces in southern Berkshire County. Now that renovations are complete, the theater is back in business in Pittsfield. The 2007 season will include three main stage productions, four stage ii productions and youth theater shows, and at least two special events.

ON THE JOB

Barrington Stage Company will continue its tradition of hiring interns during the summer months to help with all aspects of the company. Opportunities range from production internships (in areas such as carpentry and electrics) to administrative and stage management internships. Interns work alongside Broadway designers and talented staff, expanding their contacts and skills to new levels.

GETTING HIRED

Apply by: Rolling. BSC will begin accepting resumes in January. Send a resume and cover letter to the address below.

Qualifications:

Open to undergraduate and graduate students. Knowledge of a specific field is a plus, as is theater experience.

Contact:

Intern Coordinator
Barrington Stage Company
30 Union Street
Pittsfield, MA 01201
E-mail: lbayne@barringtonstageco.org

Baxter Healthcare Corporation

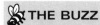 **THE BUZZ**
- "A serious internship that's a lot of fun"
- "Get the feedback you deserve"

 THE STATS

Industry(ies): Health Care; Pharmaceuticals

Location(s): Deerfield, IL

Number of interns: *Summer*: 50-60

Pay: Varies

Length of internship: *Summer:* 12 weeks

THE SCOOP

Baxter, a health care and pharmaceutical company, creates and delivers treatments for conditions such as cancer, kidney disease, immune disorders and other chronic and life-threatening ailments. Baxter was chosen as one of *Fortune* magazine's 100 Best Companies to Work For in 2003.

ON THE JOB

Summer internships are available in finance, engineering, biochemistry, accounting, chemistry, information technology, human resources and marketing.

GETTING HIRED

Apply by: Resumes accepted between September 1 and February 1. Apply by sending a resume to the address below or through the company's web site. Decisions are generally made before the end of April.

Qualifications:
Open to college freshmen, sophomores, juniors and seniors, recent college graduates and grad students who exhibit ambition, enthusiasm and interest in innovation. Applicants must be enrolled in or recently graduated from an accredited university with either a bachelor's degree or PhD and must have less than one year of post-graduation full-time work experience.

Contact:
Baxter Healthcare Corporation
College Relations
1 Baxter Parkway
Deerfield, IL 60015
www.baxter.com/job_seekers/index.html

Beach Associates

 THE BUZZ
- "New media, Virginia-style"
- "Gain experience in creating visual media presentations"

 THE STATS

Industry(ies): Government; New/Interactive Media; Public Relations

Location(s): Arlington, VA

Number of interns: *Summer/fall/winter/spring*: 2 each

Pay: None

Length of internship: Flexible, but not exceeding 3 months

THE SCOOP

Founded in 1979, Beach Associates handles the communication needs of government agencies, associations and business organizations. Using a wide array of media, BA focuses on two main objectives: "to communicate information clearly in order to motivate the desired response from the audience, and to create a package that makes the medium transparent to the audience, allowing them to focus and act on the information without distraction by the vehicle."

ON THE JOB

Interns are accepted into either the marketing or video production/new media departments. Video production intern duties include research, dubbing, preparing copy for the teleprompter, operating the teleprompter, archiving and assisting on location.

GETTING HIRED

Apply by: Rolling. Send cover letter and resume by e-mail or fax.

Qualifications:
Open to college students; juniors and seniors preferred.

Contact:
Deb Ellis
Beach Associates
200 North Glebe Road, Suite 720
Arlington, VA 22203-3728
Phone: (800) 598-6567
Fax: (703) 812-9710
E-mail: dellis@beachassociates.com
www.beachassociates.com

Visit Vault at **www.vault.com** for insider company profiles, expert advice, career message boards, expert resume reviews, the Vault Job Board and more.

VAULT CAREER LIBRARY **65**

Beacon Press

 THE BUZZ
- "Publishing careers for deep thinkers"
- "Small size enables interns to get real hands-on experience"

 THE STATS

Industry(ies): Nonprofit; Publishing

Location(s): Boston, MA

Number of interns: Varies

Pay: None

Length of internship: Varies; available year-round

 THE SCOOP

As an independent, nonprofit publisher of "serious" fiction and nonfiction, Beacon Press works with authors such as Octavia Butler, Cornel West and James Baldwin. The company has a 150-year history and its titles have received National Book Awards, American Book Awards, Christopher Awards and PEN New England Friend to Writers Awards, among others. The company focuses on issue-based works (such as freedom of speech, diversity and religious pluralism, for example), challenging readers to assess the ways in which they think.

 ON THE JOB

Interns work primarily in two departments: editorial and publicity/marketing. Editorial interns help with permissions and unsolicited manuscripts, while publicity interns' responsibilities include pasting up reviews and sending out galley mailings. Since the company is relatively small, there can be spillover work, allowing interns to experience many aspects of an independent publishing environment.

 GETTING HIRED

Apply by: The company posts for interns on it's web site, www.beacon.org. Send resume and cover letter, expressing areas of interest to the specific departments for which you would like to work. Direct application materials to the individual posting for intern assistance.

Qualifications:
Open to college freshmen, sophomores, juniors and seniors, recent grads and grad students.

Contact:
Internship Coordinator
Beacon Press
25 Beacon Street
Boston, MA 02108
Phone: (617) 742-2110
Fax: (617) 723-3097
www.beacon.org/contentjo.html

The Bear Stearns Companies, Inc.

 THE BUZZ
- "It's no bear market at America's most admired securities firm"

 THE STATS

Industry(ies): Financial Services

Location(s): New York, NY (HQ); Atlanta, GA; Boston, MA; Chicago, IL; Dallas, TX; Denver, CO; Los Angeles, CA; San Francisco, CA; San Juan, PR; Beijing; Dublin; Hong Kong; London; Lugano; Milan; São Paulo; Shanghai; Singapore; Tokyo

Number of Interns: *Summer analyst*: 62; *summer associate*: 66

Pay: Paid; competitive salary

Length of Internship: *Summer*: 10-12 weeks

 **THE SCOOP**

The Bear Stearns Companies, Inc., founded in 1923, is a leading global investment banking, securities trading and brokerage firm. Bear Stearns works with corporations, institutions, governments and individuals offering a variety of financial services. The firm focuses its business in three core areas: capital markets, wealth management and global clearing services. Headquartered in New York City, Bear Stearns currently employs 11,500 people in its eight American offices and nine international outposts. In 2005, Bear Stearns was recognized as the Most Admired securities firm in a *Fortune* magazine survey.

 ON THE JOB

Bear Stearns offers a variety of departmental summer internships. Summer associate positions are available in financial management, investment banking, equity research, asset management, institutional equity and fixed income. Summer analyst positions are available in the asset management, controllers groups, global credit, fixed income, institutional equity, investment banking, and public finance.

 GETTING HIRED

Apply by: Bear Stearns participates in on-campus recruiting at a limited number of college campuses for its summer analyst positions. On-campus and on-site interviews take place from January to March, or until all positions are filled. Qualified and interested candidates are encouraged to apply online (go to www.bearstearns.com/careers) and submit a resume and cover letter. *Investment banking summer associates*: applications accepted in November; interviews take place in January and February. Check for on-campus resume drops; if none, apply online. *Equity research and sales & trading summer associates*: applications accepted in November; interviews begin in December and continue until all positions are filled.

Qualifications:
Summer analysts must have completed their junior year of undergraduate work or be expecting to graduate in December of 2006. Summer associates must be first- or second-year MBA students.

Contact:
www.bearstearns.com/careers

Bechtel

 THE BUZZ
- "Construct a top engineering career"

 **THE STATS**

Industry(ies): Architecture; Construction/Building Materials; Engineering

Location(s): San Francisco, CA (HQ); Federick, MD; Glendale, AZ; Houston, TX; Richland, WA; Montreal; Singapore; Toronto

Number of interns: *Annual*: 25-50

Pay: Paid; varies based on experience and schooling

Length of internship: Varies with availability

 **THE SCOOP**

As one of the world's largest engineering/construction firms, Bechtel provides technical, management and related services to develop, manage, engineer, build and operate facilities for its worldwide customers. The firm employs 47,000 employees in nearly 60 countries.

ON THE JOB

Internships and co-op positions are available in a number of fields, including engineering, business, accounting and computer science. Duties vary with position but may include number-crunching, programming or administrative tasks.

GETTING HIRED

Apply by: Rolling. Send a letter to the College Relations Department requesting more information about the program and how to apply – contact information can be found on the company's web site. (If you e-mail your letter, be sure it is in ASCII text format and left justified.)

Qualifications:

Open to college juniors and seniors, recent grads and grad students. Formal college or university cooperative education program students may apply if they have satisfactorily completed at least one year of study in engineering or in a professional academic discipline such as business, accounting/finance or computer science. Interns and co-ops are only hired from local colleges and universities closest in proximity to Bechtel's appropriate hiring office. Priority is given to students within one year of graduation, to recipients of Bechtel scholarships, and to students who have previously worked for Bechtel and have been identified as high performing and/or having high potential.

Contact:
Bechtel College Relations Department
P.O. Box 193965
San Francisco, CA 94119-3965
Phone: (415) 768-1234
Fax: (415) 768-2675
E-mail: collegsf@bechtel.com
www.bechtel.com/careers/coop.asp

Benetton

THE BUZZ
- "Work in fashion, Italian-style"
- "If you speak Italian and want a retail gig, read on"

THE STATS

Industry(ies): Consumer Products; Fashion; Manufacturing

Location(s): Ponzano-Treviso, Italy

Number of interns: *Annual*: 4

Pay: None

Length of internship: 6-12 weeks; available year-round

THE SCOOP

United Colors of Benetton is Europe's Gap; they're on every other corner in most cities. The Benetton Group's five brands – United Colors of Benetton, Sisley, The Hip State (for teens), Playlife and Killer Loop (both sportswear lines) – are sold in 120 countries. The hugely successful clothing company was founded in 1965 by four Italian siblings. Benetton's advertising campaigns have often stirred much discussion and controversy for their political and social angles.

ON THE JOB

The global fashion company, Benetton Group, offers internships at its gorgeous headquarters, the Villa Minelli, near Venice, Italy. Open positions depend on the company's need, so you should check the web site for current opportunities (www. benetton.com, click on "Career"). Past positions include an assistant accessories designer and a graphic designer for the Sisley and Playlife lines.

GETTING HIRED

Apply by: Rolling. Submit your resume online at www.benetton. com, click on "Career."

Qualifications:

Open to college freshmen, sophomores, juniors and seniors, grad students and recent college graduates who have at least a working knowledge of Italian.

Contact:
Benetton
Internship Coordinator, Human Resources
Villa Minelli
Via Villa Minelli, 1
Ponzano – Treviso
Italy
Phone: +39 0422 519111
Fax: +39 0422 519227
E-mail: selezione@benetton.it
www.benetton.com

Visit Vault at **www.vault.com** for insider company profiles, expert advice, career message boards, expert resume reviews, the Vault Job Board and more.

VAULT CAREER LIBRARY **67**

Berkeley Repertory Theatre

 THE BUZZ

- "The next step toward a career in professional theater"

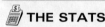 **THE STATS**

Industry(ies): Education; Theater/Performing Arts

Location(s): Berkeley, CA

Number of interns: *Annual*: 5-15

Pay: $4,000 stipend

Length of internship: August/September-June/July

 **THE SCOOP**

The Berkeley Repertory Theatre won the 1997 Tony award for outstanding regional theater. There are seven productions in its season, running the gamut from classic to contemporary. In addition, the Berkeley Rep School of Theatre tours annually with a fully staged professional production to elementary and/or secondary schools throughout the greater Bay Area.

ON THE JOB

Interns are placed in arts and administration or production and they work closely with the company's artists, administrators, guest directors and designers to help them reach as many career objectives as possible and give them networking opportunities. Berkeley Rep also offers its interns regularly scheduled informal seminars and evaluations.

GETTING HIRED

Apply by: No earlier than January 1. All materials must be received by April 1. Submissions include an application form, personal statement, resume and three letters of recommendation. Apply by U.S. mail only.

Qualifications:
Open to college freshmen, sophomores, juniors and seniors who are serious about their career goals and highly motivated individuals, already having basic training and experience in theater. Not open to high school students.

Contact:
Rachel Fink
Berkeley Repertory Theatre
2025 Addison Street
Berkeley, CA 94704
Phone: (510) 647-2900
Fax: (510) 647-2976
E-mail: internship@berkeleyrep.org
www.berkeleyrep.org/HTML/AboutTheRep/internships.html

Bermuda Institute of Ocean Sciences

 THE BUZZ

- "Explore ocean science in Bermuda"

 THE STATS

Industry(ies): Environmental; Nonprofit; Science/Research

Location(s): St. George's, Bermuda

Number of interns: *Spring/summer/fall*: 3-4 VIP (volunteers), 3-4 GIP per season (graduate students)

Pay: Varies; *VIP*: room and board; *GIP*: none

Length of internship: *VIP*: 3-6 months; *GIP*: flexible

THE SCOOP

The Bermuda Institute of Ocean Sciences (BIOS), formerly known as the Bermuda Biological Station for Research (BBSR), studies ocean science from an island in the North Atlantic. Established by Harvard and NYU over a century ago, BIOS is now a nonprofit with endowments allowing it to support world-class labs, a 115-foot research vessel called the Atlantic Explorer, and a specialized resident research faculty.

ON THE JOB

BIOS has two internships: the Graduate Internship Program (GIP), for graduate students researching their thesis or dissertation topic, and the Volunteer Internship Program (VIP), aimed at undergraduates studying ocean sciences. During their three to six months at BIOS, VIP interns may go on research cruises to Antarctica, scuba dive around St. George's, work with the BIOS education program or publish research. Interns in the GIP program work one-on-one with a member of BIOS's resident faculty, researching the biology or oceanography of subtropical, shallow-water environments.

GETTING HIRED

Apply by: Rolling. *VIP*: send application, cover letter, resume and one letter of recommendation. Apply directly to faculty member whose work interests you (see web site for participating faculty). *GIP*: send cover letter, research proposal, graduate transcripts and two letters of recommendation. Apply directly to faculty member whose work matches your research interest.

Qualifications:
VIP: open to college juniors and seniors, as well as recent college graduates. *GIP*: open to enrolled PhD or MS students.

Contact:
J.P. Skinner, Education Officer
Bermuda Institute for Ocean Sciences
17 Biological Lane
Ferry Road, St. George's GE 01
Bermuda
Phone: (441) 297-1880, ext. 241
Fax: (441) 297-8143
E-mail: skinner@bbsr.edu
www.bbsr.edu

Bernstein-Rein

THE BUZZ
- "Get a great background in advertising in the Gateway to the West"

THE STATS
Industry(ies): Advertising

Location(s): Kansas City, MO

Number of interns: *Summer*: 8

Pay: Paid; $8/hour

Length of internship: *Summer*: 9 weeks

 THE SCOOP
A full-service advertising firm, Bernstein-Rein is the 33rd-largest ad agency in the U.S. Founded in 1964, the company offers database, direct, interactive media, research, business-to-business, creative, account management and strategic planning. Some of its clients include Wal-Mart, McDonald's, Bayer Animal Health, USAA, United Online, Commerce Bank and The Kansas City Zoo.

ON THE JOB
Interns are placed in a number of different departments where they work on real advertising-related projects. Interns also work together on group projects. At the end of the summer, each intern presents his or her project to Bob Bernstein, Skip Rein and the company's executive committee.

GETTING HIRED
Apply by: *Summer*: February 1. Send cover letter, resume and a completed application (e-mail the human resource contact below to get a link to it), three reference names and a one-page writing sample. Creative applicants must complete a separate assignment (e-mail the human resource contact for details).

Qualifications:
Open to college juniors and seniors who have at least one semester remaining.

Contact:
Human Resources Department
Bernstein-Rein
4600 Madison, Suite 1500
Kansas City, MO 64112
Phone: (816) 756-0640
Fax: (816) 531-5708
E-mail: human_res@bradv.com
www.bernstein-rein.com

Bertelsmann AG

THE BUZZ
- "Learn the inner workings of a media giant"
- "Known as a great place to network"

THE STATS
Industry(ies): Broadcast & Entertainment; Journalism; Music/Records; Publishing

Location(s): California; Indiana; Maine; Maryland; New Jersey; New York; North Carolina; Pennsylvania; South Carolina; Virginia; additional facilities across the United States

Number of interns: Varies

Pay: Paid or for academic credit only positions available

Length of internship: Varies; available year-round

 THE SCOOP
Bertelsmann AG is an international media and entertainment company with approximately 73,221 employees in 50 countries. In fiscal year 2003, the company generated global revenues of 16.3 billion Euros. Bertelsmann employs some 15,000 people in the United States, which is its second-largest market after Germany, contributing approximately 25.1 percent of global revenues in 2003. The Bertelsmann media family includes Bertelsmann Music Group (BMG), Random House, Gruner + Jahr and many more divisions.

ON THE JOB
During an internship at Bertelsmann, college students will expand their professional experience while learning about the media industry first hand. Interns will be involved in one or more projects, ranging from organizing a large event to developing and implementing a marketing study. They will also get an insider's perspective on what makes an international media corporation tick. Positions are available in departments including sales, marketing, operations, art/design, HR, IT, photography, editorial, research, direct mail, Web design, finance, adminsitration and music.

GETTING HIRED
Apply by: Rolling (some divisions may have hard deadlines). Check site (myfuture.bertelsmann.com) for details. Applications must be completed online.

Qualifications:
Open to college sophomores, juniors, seniors and graduate students. Interns must be enrolled in a college or university in the U.S. that allows them to receive credit for their internship. Must be enthusiatic, have a passion for media and strong communication and analytical skills. Prior experience a plus.

Contact:
For inquiries
E-mail: myfuture@bertelsmann.com (note division of interest)
www.myfuture.bertelsmann.com

Visit Vault at **www.vault.com** for insider company profiles, expert advice, career message boards, expert resume reviews, the Vault Job Board and more.

 **69**

Best Buddies

 THE BUZZ
- "Help enrich the lives of children and adults with intellectual disabilities"

 THE STATS

Industry(ies): Education; Nonprofit

Location(s): Baltimore, MD; Baton Rouge, LA; Boston, MA; Chicago, IL; Des Moines, IA; Houston, TX; Indianapolis, IN; Los Angeles, CA; Miami, FL; New Haven, CT; New York, NY; Orlando, FL; Phoenix, AZ; Pittsburgh, PA; Providence, RI; Washington, DC

Number of interns: Varies

Pay: Stipend (varies)

Length of internship: 6 weeks

 **THE SCOOP**

Anthony K. Shriver founded Best Buddies in 1989 to assist people with intellectual disabilities worldwide (today numbering over 7.5 million). It's now an international nonprofit organization that has grown to include over 1,000 chapters based in middle schools, high schools and colleges. Best Buddies provides contact relationships and integrated employment opportunities for its clients.

ON THE JOB

Best Buddies interns work as part of the e-Buddies Training Corps on the e-buddies program. They attend a training session in Washington, DC, where they learn how to teach e-mail skills to persons with intellectual disabilities, then return to their "home" cities and work with local agencies to provide one-on-one e-mail training to members of the intellectually disabled community.

GETTING HIRED

Apply by: Rolling. Applicants must send in a completed online application (www.ebuddies.org/downloads/internapp.pdf), a resume and two letters of recommendation.

Qualifications:
Open to college freshmen, sophomores, juniors and seniors, and recent grads. Must have reliable transportation and computer skills.

Contact:
Lisa Derx
Best Buddies
401 Ninth Street, NW, Suite 750
Washington, DC 20004
Phone: (202) 266-2293
Fax: (202) 266-2260
E-mail: e-buddies@bestbuddies.org
www.ebuddies.org/etcfacts.html
www.bestbuddies.org

BET

 THE BUZZ
- "No bigger name in black television"

THE STATS

Industry(ies): Broadcast & Entertainment; Music/Records; New/Interactive Media

Location(s): Chicago, IL; New York, NY; Southfield, MI; Studio City, CA; Washington, DC

Number of interns: *Annual*: 75-100

Pay: *Undergraduate intern*: unpaid; *legal intern*: hourly wage

Length of internship: 12 weeks

THE SCOOP

A subsidiary of Viacom, BET has been the biggest name in African-American entertainment for over 20 years. It was the first African-American owned cable television network. The station offers a wide variety of programming, ranging from talk shows to music videos, as well as a reality TV show.

ON THE JOB

BET offers internships in every department: BET Pictures, BET on Jazz, sports, creative services, marketing, advertising, art, public relations, human resources, legal, finance, news and programming, information services, computer, music programming and many more. Intern duties, naturally, vary from department to department.

GETTING HIRED

Apply by: *Summer*: March 30; *fall*: July 1; *spring*: November 15. Submissions should include transcripts, three recommendations, a resume and a letter from your current school. Application forms are available by mail.

Qualifications:
Open to high school seniors, college freshmen, sophomores, juniors and seniors, and grad students. Legal interns must be enrolled in law school.

Contact:
Patrice Huckleberry
BET
1235 W Street
Washington, DC 20018
Phone: (202) 608-2020
E-mail: human.resources@bet.net
www.bet.com

Bet Tzedek

 THE BUZZ

- "Help bring justice to those who can't afford legal aid"

 THE STATS

Industry(ies): Law; Nonprofit

Location(s): Los Angeles, CA; North Hollywood, CA

Number of interns: Varies

Pay: None

Length of internship: 12 weeks minimum

THE SCOOP

Bet Tzedek, literally meaning "House of Justice" in Hebrew, is a nonprofit center providing free legal services to low-income individuals, the elderly and disabled people of any racial or religious background. The organization was founded in 1974, and currently serves over 5,000 people in need every year on cases such as Holocaust reparations, landlord/tenant, consumer protection, conservatorship, guardianship, supplemental security income disability and wills.

ON THE JOB

Interns begin working as "intake assistants." After training, they will pre-screen clients for financial eligibility and for case type, arrange subsequent appointments and make referrals, as needed. It is possible for interns to be promoted to legal assistants, which means that, after more training, they will conduct in-person client consultations and work with attorneys on specific cases.

GETTING HIRED

Apply by: *Academic year*: rolling; *summer*: April 1. Send a cover letter and resume.

Qualifications:

Open to college freshmen, sophomores, juniors, seniors and recent grads interested in law but who have not yet entered law school.

Contact:

Robin Summerstein
Human Resource Director/Volunteer Coordinator
Bet Tzedek Legal Services
145 South Fairfax Avenue
Los Angeles, CA 90036
Phone: (323) 939-0506
Fax: (323) 939-1040
E-mail: humanresources@bettzedek.org
www.bettzedek.org/html/pre-law_volunteers.html

Betsey Johnson

 THE BUZZ

- "Start your fashion career with an icon of the New York scene"

 THE STATS

Industry(ies): Fashion

Location(s): New York, NY

Number of interns: Varies

Pay: None

Length of internship: Varies

THE SCOOP

Betsey Johnson has been designing since the 1960s and is now an icon in New York fashion world. Known for funky, youthful, over-the-top fashion statements, Johnson's clothing is available in her own signature stores, upscale department stores and over 1,000 specialty boutiques in the U.S., Europe and Japan.

ON THE JOB

Interns are hired regularly and at various times during the year, (the company doesn't follow a specific internship program) and they work closely with regular full-time staff (not each other). Departments offering positions include design, production, public relations, sales and merchandising. Applicants choose the department for which they want to work.

GETTING HIRED

Apply by: *Academic year*: rolling; *summer*: February 1. Log on to the company's web site, www.betseyjohnson.com/html/all_about_betsey.asp?ask_betsey=Y, and click on the department for which you want to intern. Then send an e-mail to that department with a cover letter and resume.

Qualifications:

Open to college freshmen, sophomores, juniors and seniors, as well as recent grads, grad students and individuals changing careers.

Contact:

Internship Coordinator
Betsey Johnson
498 Fashion Avenue
New York, NY 10018
Phone: (212) 244-0843
Fax: (212) 244-0855
(Specify which department you would like to work in on the outside of the envelope.)
www.betseyjohnson.com/html/all_about_betsey.asp?ask_betsey=Y

Visit Vault at **www.vault.com** for insider company profiles, expert advice, career message boards, expert resume reviews, the Vault Job Board and more.

VAULT CAREER LIBRARY   71

Biltmore Estate

 THE BUZZ
- "Work where the Vanderbilts once played"

 THE STATS

Industry(ies): Art/Museum; Equestrian; Hospitality; Tourism/ Recreation; Marketing; Horticulture; Retail; Finance; Human Resources

Location(s): Asheville, NC

Number of interns: Varies

Pay: Varies

Length of internship: Varies

 THE SCOOP

The Biltmore Estate was designed to be George Vanderbilt's country retreat in North Carolina's Blue Ridge Mountains, built over a century ago. Visitors can now tour the 250-room chateau and landscaped gardens, as well as over 8,000 acres of forest, farmlands and rivers. They can also enjoy wine and food products from The Estate's farms, and stay overnight at the Biltmore Inn. Biltmore was named one of America's best travel destinations by *National Geographic Traveler*.

 ON THE JOB

Available positions include the "creative services intern" (print production and graphic design for client services), the "arboricultural intern" (forestry and tree maintenance projects) and the "special collections intern" (museum services cataloging collection books and managing the curatorial database).

GETTING HIRED

Apply by: Rolling, but vaguely follows a semester schedule. Interns can only apply for open positions, so see www.biltmore.com/special/employment/internships.shtml for an updated list. Complete and send in an online application at www.biltmore.com/special/pdfs/biltmore_employment_app.pdf, a cover letter, resume, an interest form (also available on the web site), transcripts, one letter of recommendation and three letters of reference.

Qualifications:
Open to college juniors, seniors and grad students who attend an accredited school and who will receive credit for the internship.

Contact:
Human Resources, Re: Internships
The Biltmore Company
One North Pack Square
Asheville, NC 28801
Phone: (828) 225-6776
Fax: (828) 225-6744
E-mail: employmentquestions@biltmore.com
www.biltmore.com/special/employment/internships.shtml

Black & Veatch

 THE BUZZ
- "Kansan engineering internships focusing on water and energy"

 THE STATS

Industry(ies): Architecture; Construction/Building Materials; Engineering; Investment Management; Management & Strategy Consulting

Location(s): Kansas City, MO; Overland Park, KS (sporadic openings in other U.S. cities)

Number of interns: Varies

Pay: None

Length of internship: Varies

 THE SCOOP

Black & Veatch, a global engineering, consulting and construction company founded in 1915, specializes in energy and water fields. Its client services include conceptual and preliminary engineering and design, construction, asset management and management consulting. One of *Forbes*' 500 largest private companies in the U.S., B&V is an employee-owned business, with offices in more than 90 cities worldwide.

 ON THE JOB

Internship positions vary depending on the company's needs. The program includes weekly "lunch n' learn" sessions, which introduce interns to different branches of the company. B&V also hosts social events (dinners, plays, etc.), offering interns a broader look at Kansas City and to facilitate networking and informal interaction between colleagues. College-level senior participants are expected to deliver a presentation on what they've learned to firm managers at the end of the summer.

GETTING HIRED

Apply by: Rolling. To browse open positions and apply online, go to: www2.bv.com/careers/college/internship.htm.

Qualifications:
Open to college freshmen, sophomores, juniors and seniors. Other qualifications depend on specific job openings. See site for details.

Contact:
Precious Dean, Internship Coordinator
Black & Veatch
11401 Lamar Avenue
Overland Park, KS 66211
Phone: (913) 458-8239
Fax: (913) 458-9018
E-mail: Collegerecruiter@bv.com
www2.bv.com/careers/college/internship.htm

Black Enterprise

 THE BUZZ
- "A venerable magazine for black Americans"

 **THE STATS**

Industry(ies): Journalism; New/Interactive Media; Publishing

Location(s): Chicago, IL; Los Angeles, CA; New York, NY (editorial internships in New York only)

Number of interns: *Summer*: 6-10

Pay: Paid; varies

Length of internship: *Summer*: 10 weeks

 THE SCOOP

Earl G. Graves founded Black Enterprise in 1968 as a corporate vehicle for African American professionals in the business world. The company is now divided into three sections: Earl G. Graves Publishing Company (print and electronic), Black Enterprise Unlimited (ancillary products and services), and the Black Enterprise/Greenwich Street Corporate Growth Fund (investment funding). Graves is also the founder and publisher of *Black Enterprise* magazine.

 ON THE JOB

Though every department at Black Enterprise uses interns as program assistants, hiring is done on a case-by-case basis. Departments include human resources, advertising, online, marketing and corporate. The only established and planned summer internship program at the company is at its magazine. *Black Enterprise* interns work in the editorial department on all facets of publishing the magazine.

$ GETTING HIRED

Apply by: *Summer*: January 31. Send a resume, cover letter and published writing samples (for magazine internship only) to the address below.

Qualifications:
Open to college juniors and seniors as well as recent grads and graduate students. Minimum 3.0 GPA required. For the editorial internship program (at the magazine), applicants must demonstrate an interest in publishing.

Contact:
Natalie M. Hibbert, Employment & Benefits Manager
Black Enterprise Magazine
130 Fifth Avenue, 10th floor
New York, NY 10011
Phone: (212) 242-8000
E-mail: careers@blackenterprise.com
www.blackenterprise.com/AboutUsOpen.asp?Source=AboutBe/hr.html

The Blackstone Group

 THE BUZZ
- "A prestigious alternative"

THE STATS

Industry(ies): Financial Services

Location(s): New York, NY (HQ); Atlanta, GA; Boston, MA; Los Angeles, CA; Hamburg; London; Mumbai; Paris; Hong Kong

Number of interns: Varies depending on market performance and firm's expected growth

Pay: Paid; competitive salary

Length of Internship: *Summer*: 10 weeks

 THE SCOOP

The Blackstone Group opened its doors to business in 1985 with a staff of four, striving to create an alternative for clients looking outside the enormous corporate giants in the investment banking world. Since then the firm has raised approximately $46 billion for alternative asset investing across its Private Equity, Real Estate, Corporate Debt, Distressed Securities and Marketable Alternative Investments groups. The Corporate Advisory Services and Restructuring & Reorganization Advisory Services businesses have handled assignments valued at over $450 billion. Headquartered in New York City, TBG maintains offices in New York, Atlanta, Boston, Los Angeles, London, Paris, Mumbai, Hamburg and Hong Kong, and employs nearly 700 people.

ON THE JOB

Blackstone offers summer internships for analyst and associate positions in many of the business groups. Interns at TBG have the opportunity to participate in all aspects of projects and can expect to be staffed on a number of assignments at a time. The small size of each group affords the opportunity for interns to assume important and integral roles and to work closely with senior members of the firm.

$ GETTING HIRED

Apply by: *Summer analyst*: late December of junior year in college. Submit a cover letter and resume through The Blackstone Group's online application process at www.blackstone.com/careers/analyst.html (click on the link for "Analyst Recruiting" to access the application). *Summer associate*: late December of first year in business school. Submit a cover letter and resume through The Blackstone Group's online application process at www.blackstone.com/careers/associate.html (click on the link for "Associate Recruiting" to access the application).

Qualifications:
Summer analyst: applicants must be rising college seniors; *summer associate*: applicants must be first year MBA students. Candidates are selected based on academic record and class ranking, degree of interest, work experience and level of ambition. Entrepreneurial spirit and ability to work on a team are also critical. Prior experience in financial services preferred, but not required.

Contact:
Summer analyst
www.blackstone.com/careers/analyst.html

Summer associate
www.blackstone.com/careers/associate.html

Visit Vault at **www.vault.com** for insider company profiles, expert advice, career message boards, expert resume reviews, the Vault Job Board and more.

 **73**

BMW Group

THE BUZZ

- "The 'Rolls Royce' of auto internships – literally"

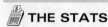 THE STATS

Industry(ies): Consumer Products; Manufacturing; Technology

Locations: Atlanta, GA; Chicago, IL; Los Angeles, CA; Spartanburg, SC; Woodcliff Lake, NJ; Austria; Germany

Number of interns: *Annual:* 15

Pay: Paid; $3,000/month. Subsidized housing

Length of internship: 3 month minimum; available year-round

THE SCOOP

Founded mainly as an aircraft engine manufacturer in Munich in 1916, BMW switched its focus to motorcycles in 1923 and then to automobiles in 1928. Today, BMW has become as much a status symbol (who doesn't want a spiffy "Beemer"?) as a transportation option. The global company, which has offices in Germany and Austria as well as in the United States, produces over 1 million vehicles per year.

ON THE JOB

Interns work in the business services, engineering, manufacturing or data services departments at plants around the globe. Experience will vary depending on where the intern is placed. Some positions require clerical duties. Longer internships are encouraged, and the company prefers that applicants work in a BMW office in their home countries first.

GETTING HIRED

Apply by: Varies by internship. Check the web site for specific upcoming deadlines and information. Apply online or send a resume and cover letter to the address below.

Qualifications:
Open to college sophomores, juniors and seniors "willing to show enthusiasm" for BMWs. Applicants are advised to intern in their home country first. U.S. intern opportunities are available at www.bmwusa.com and www.bmwusfactory.com.

Contact
BMW Group
PM-1
80788 Munich
Germany
E-mail: bewerber.hotline@bmw.de
www.bmwusa.com/About/internships.htm?dNav_loc=_root.internships

BMW of Manhattan, Inc./Mini of Manhattan

THE BUZZ

- "Learn to promote one of the world's highest-end luxury goods"

THE STATS

Industry(ies): Consumer Products; Retail

Location(s): New York, NY

Number of interns: *Summer:* 1

Pay: Varies

Length of internship: *Summer:* 10-12 weeks

THE SCOOP

The only official BMW/Mini Cooper dealer in Manhattan is located in a gleaming showroom on 11th Avenue and West 57th Street where cars and motorcycles are sold and leased and Manhattanites' luxury autos are fixed, polished and preened. The company sponsors several marketing events in the city, such as the Annual Ultimate Drive Event, Taste of the Nation, and Lenox Hill Hospital's Fantasy Express Fundraiser.

ON THE JOB

BMW's marketing interns work with the marketing team on all initiatives, including special events. They also maintain the print advertising portfolio, along with the press and event books. Interns help create advertisements for BMW of Manhattan Motorcycles, too. They handle all brochure requests and work with customer databases. Finally, they have unlimited opportunities to salivate over the attractive vehicles sold at the dealership.

GETTING HIRED

Apply by: *Summer:* March 5. Send cover letter and resume (as MS Word attachment) to the e-mail address below.

Qualifications:
Open to college juniors only. Minimum 3.5 GPA required. Must have experience with HTML, Excel and MS Word, as well as knowledge of the New York City marketplace.

Contact:
Laura Hauptman
BMW of Manhattan
555 West 57th Street
New York, NY 10019
Phone: (212) 586-2269
Fax: (212) 626-1890
E-mail: lhauptman@bmwnyc.com
www.bmwnyc.com

Boeing

 **THE BUZZ**
- "Good experience for the mechanically inclined"
- "The top aerospace engineering internship"

THE STATS

Industry(ies): Aerospace; Technology

Location(s): Chicago, IL; Philadelphia, PA; St. Louis, MO; Washington, DC; Wichita, KS; multiple cities in AL, AZ, CA, FL, OK, TX, WA

Number of interns: *Annual*: 150-400

Pay: Paid; varies depending on position. Health benefits, if needed; housing, if needed

Length of internship: *Summer*: 8-12 weeks; available year-round; *co-op*: 6 months

 **THE SCOOP**

Boeing is the world leader in aerospace technology, manufacturing more satellites, commercial jetliners and military aircraft than any other company. William Boeing and Conrad Westervelt founded the firm in 1916 in Puget Sound, Wash., 13 years after the Wright Brothers' first flight. Boeing has helped create aircraft history since that time. Boeing has expanded into a multibillion-dollar company, selling to customers in 145 countries with employees in 70.

ON THE JOB

Boeing interns work in a variety of roles. Available positions include electrical, industrial, mechanical and computer engineers, as well as technical and network designers. The company also looks for interns to work as information systems, procurement, market, budget, budget systems and systems analysts; database administrators; and systems programmers. All interns work with professional employees and managers on specific projects.

GETTING HIRED

Apply by: *Summer*: January 31; *co-op*: rolling.

Qualifications:

Open to all college juniors and seniors, recent college graduates, and grad students majoring in a relevant topic. Generally, applicants need to have a minimum GPA of 2.8 and strong communication skills. For further details, see www.boeing.com/employment/college.

Contact:
Internship Program
Boeing World Headquarters
100 North Riverside
Chicago, IL 60606
Phone: (312) 544-2000
www.boeing.com/employment/college

Bonhams & Butterfields

THE BUZZ
- "Learn the business of art and the art of auction"

THE STATS

Industry(ies): Art/Museum

Location(s): Los Angeles, CA; San Francisco, CA

Number of interns: Varies

Pay: *Students:* None; stipend of $10/7.5 hour workday, academic credit available. *Graduates:* minimum wage/hour.

Length of internship: *Summer*: June-August 15; *fall*: September-December 15; *spring*: February-May 15

THE SCOOP

Specializing in appraising and selling fine arts and antiques, Bonhams & Butterfields is the largest U.S. auction house on the West Coast and the third-largest auction establishment in the world. B&B provides a variety of services including appraisals and consignment management. Its experts hail from a variety of backgrounds and bring clients a wealth of extensive experience.

ON THE JOB

B&B interns work with the property and specialists and learn about the auction business. Internships offered by the San Francisco and Los Angeles offices vary, however they include fine arts, Asian arts, furniture and decorative arts, rugs, jewelry, arms and armor, Native American, pre-Columbian and tribal art, sunset sales, and books and manuscripts.

GETTING HIRED

Apply by: *Summer*: April 10; *fall*: August 25; *spring*: January 6. Request an internship application at hr.US@bonhams.com. Complete and send the application, along with a resume and cover letter, to the adress below. If the application is accepted, candidates will be interviewed by Bonhams. To view more detailed internship descriptions, opening and application procedures, go to the Bonhams web site. www.bonhams.com, and under "Services" click on "Recruitment." Follow the link "USA vacancies" to see the internship program.

Qualifications:

Open to college juniors and seniors and grad students majoring in art or art history, as well as all college graduates.

Contact:
Human Resources
Attention: Internship Coordinator
Bonhams & Butterfields
220 San Bruno Avenue
San Francisco, CA 94103
Fax: (415) 861-8486
E-mail: hr.US@bonhams.com
www.bonhams.com

Visit Vault at **www.vault.com** for insider company profiles, expert advice, career message boards, expert resume reviews, the Vault Job Board and more.

VAULT CAREER LIBRARY **75**

Booz Allen Hamilton

THE BUZZ

- "Boozing to improve business and government"

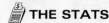

THE STATS

Industry(ies): Management & Strategy Consulting; Operations & IT Consulting

Location(s): McLean, VA (HQ); Baltimore, MD; Washington, DC. Undergraduate internships are offered all over the U.S., though mostly concentrated in McLean. Summer associate positions available worldwide.

Number of interns: *Government Markets and Technology*: varies (100+/year); *Emerging Leaders*: 12; *MBA/summer associate*: varies (100+/year)

Pay: Varies; competitive salary

Length of internship: Varies; *undergraduate programs*: flexible; available year-round; *MBA/summer associate*: 9 weeks in the summer

THE SCOOP

Founded in 1914, Booz Allen Hamilton, Inc., is a global strategy and technology consulting firm that employs over 16,000 people on six continents. Headquartered in McLean, Virginia, Booz Allen is one of the oldest firms of its type. The firm currently separates its consulting divisions into two business sectors: WCB (Worldwide Commercial Business) and WTB (Worldwide Technology Business). WCB provides services to the top-management of the world's leading corporations, while WTB serves government agencies, institutions and infrastructure organizations worldwide. In April 2006, however, the firm will be re-organizing, no longer operating through two separate business units, but rather presenting itself as one firm with three market focuses: Global Commercial Markets, Global Government Markets and Integrated Markets.

ON THE JOB

Booz Allen offers internships during the summer and the academic year. The majority (50 to 60 percent) of undergraduate internships are located in McLean, Va., while MBA opportunities are available around the world. Undergraduate interns join a small, dynamic project team and have the opportunity to apply coursework concepts to real-world situations. All interns will get hands-on experience, use cutting-edge technology, receive mentoring from Booz Allen staff, and be eligible for full-time employment opportunities upon graduation.

Booz Allen is also the founder of the Emerging Leaders internship program for students with disabilities, a program founded in 2001 that offers internships to applicants who have proven records of scholastic achievement and leadership excellence. Emerging Leaders interns are hired by various companies and gain valuable work experience, exposure to senior leadership, networking opportunities and an invitation to attend the annual Leadership Development Conference in Washington, DC. Booz Allen plans, sponsors and hosts the annual conference, which gives Emerging Leaders interns the chance to meet with government, nonprofit and business leaders in the disability field and receive career and leadership training.

Booz Allen's summer associate program is for MBA students who have completed their first year of business school. They work on teams serving commercial clients. Associates work with clients through all stages of strategy-based transformation projects, conducting analysis, developing conclusions and recommendations, writing reports and implementing strategies.

GETTING HIRED

Apply by: Rolling. *Government Markets and Technology*: submit resumes online. Once an online profile is created it is visible to all Booz Allen recruiters and hiring managers. Applicants are then evaluated for all current and upcoming internship opportunities as they become available. If qualified, Booz Allen will contact the applicant through a letter, e-mail or phone call.

Emerging Leaders: apply online at www.emerging-leaders.com /beAnEmergingLeaderApplyNow.htm. The application packet must include a current resume, an information sheet and a 500-word statement of interest.

MBA/summer associate: apply on the company web site.

Qualifications:

Government Markets and Technology: open to college students with more than 30 hours of coursework with a declared major in any field who have a GPA of 3.0 or above. Applicants must be either U.S. citizens or aliens legally authorized to work in the U.S.

Emerging Leaders: applicants must self-identify as a person with a qualified disability under the Americans with Disabilities Act; have completed a minimum of 45 university-level credits; maintain at least a 3.0 GPA; sustain full-time student status for the semester following the internship (graduating seniors immediately continuing on to graduate level study may apply); and be either a U.S. citizen or an alien legally authorized to work in the U.S.

MBA/summer associate: open to MBA students between their first and second years of study. Applicants must be legally authorized to work in the country where they apply for an internship.

Contact:
www.boozallen.com

Emerging Leaders program
www.emerging-leaders.com/aboutUs.htm

Boston Consulting Group

 THE BUZZ
- "Begin your consulting career with the top dogs"

 THE STATS

Industry(ies): Management & Strategy Consulting

Location(s): Boston, MA (HQ); Atlanta, GA; Chicago, IL; Dallas, TX; Detroit, MI, TX; Los Angeles, CA; Miami, FL; New York, NY; San Francisco, CA; Short Hills, NJ; Washington, DC; 27 offices in Europe; 15 offices in Asia and Oceania

Number of interns: Varies according to location

Pay: Paid; varies

Length of internship: *Summer*: 12 weeks

 THE SCOOP

Boston Consulting Group, founded in 1963, is an international strategy and general management firm that works with individuals and organizations. BCG is a global firm comprised of 2,900 consultants working in 61 offices in 36 countries, with 2004 revenues of $1.3 billion. BCG counsels clients in numerous industries, and conducts research and analysis in fields of expertise including branding, corporate development, diversity, financial services, health care, industrial goods, intellectual property, national security initiatives, organization, operations, technology, and communication, tourism, strategy, innovation, consumer behavior and media.

 ON THE JOB

During the summer program, BCG summer associates become part of a BCG consulting team under the direction of a consultant sponsor. The program includes experiences with client cases, other summer interns, full-time associates and any BCG events. The summer program exposes summer associates to the daily requirements and expectations of the associate position in hopes that interested and capable interns will return to BCG following graduation.

⑤ GETTING HIRED

Apply by: Applicants are encouraged to contact specific BCG offices for more information about the summer program. BCG suggests potential candidates ask their placement offices about specific application deadlines and interview scheduling.

Qualifications:
Open to college juniors. Applicants should have an intellectual curiosity about consulting in specific and business in general. Potential applicants are advised to undergo practice case studies located on the BCG web site as interview preparation. Go to www.bcg.com/careers/interview_prep/interview_prep_splash.jsp for more information.

Contact:
Local BCG offices
www.bcg.com/offices/office_list.jsp

BCG campus events
www.bcg.com/careers/bcg_on_campus/AreaSelection/area1.jsp

The Boston Globe

 THE BUZZ
- "Bean-town beat"
- "Serious newspaper gig"
- "Get your own writing coach"

 **THE STATS**

Industry(ies): Journalism

Location(s): Boston, MA

Number of interns: *Summer*: around 16

Pay: Paid; weekly wage

Length of internship: *Summer*: 12 weeks

 THE SCOOP

Founded in 1872 by six businessmen, *The Boston Globe* has become one of the best-respected daily newspapers in the U.S. and is the leading paper for the New England area. The *Globe* merged with the New York Times Company in 1993, which caused the largest newspaper merger and acquisition in American history.

 ON THE JOB

The Boston Globe's summer newsroom internship program has been giving college students interested in journalism a peek into the industry for over 45 years. Most interns work as "general assignment reporters," in the metropolitan section, or may be assigned to work in sports, arts, business or the Washington bureau. Each intern works with a writing coach/intern supervisor, and the program includes weekly seminars on journalism issues.

⑤ GETTING HIRED

Apply by: *Summer*: November 1. Application form can be obtained after August 31 at www.bostonglobe/newsintern, or by sending a request to the address below. Interview required.

Qualifications:
Open to all undergraduate students, as well as journalism graduate school students who have not had professional experience as a newspaper reporter. Applicants must have had at least one prior daily newspaper internship. Must have a driver's license and be able to type at least 30 words per minute.

Contact:
Donna Bains
Newsroom Summer Internship
The Boston Globe
P.O. Box 55819
Boston, MA 02205-05819
Phone: (617) 929-3212
www.bostonglobe.com/newsintern

Visit Vault at **www.vault.com** for insider company profiles, expert advice, career message boards, expert resume reviews, the Vault Job Board and more.

VAULT CAREER LIBRARY   **77**

Boston Magazine

 THE BUZZ
- "Get the buzz on Beantown"
- "One of the few editorial internships outside New York"

 THE STATS

Industry(ies): Journalism; Publishing

Location(s): Boston, MA

Number of interns: Varies by department

Pay: None

Length of internship: *Spring*: 12 weeks; *summer*: 8-10 weeks; *fall*: 12 weeks

 THE SCOOP

Boston Magazine provides in-depth stories and local features to offer its readers a complete view of Boston and its rich culture. This lifestyle magazine has a readership of 471,000, much of which is affluent and influential – and its content reflects its audience. Monthly sections include "Party Pics," "Food & Dining," and "City Journal." The company also publishes *Elegant Wedding*, *Social Datebook*, *New England Travel*, and *Home & Garden*.

 ON THE JOB

Interns can work in one of five departments: editorial, marketing, advertising and sales, art or special projects. The editorial internship is the most demanding, as interns write, edit and research pieces for the magazine. Interns in the marketing department work on client relations and magazine promotions. Advertising and sales interns see some overlap with the marketing interns, but concentrate more heavily on database work and research. Art interns are able to participate in all aspects of the magazine's art department, though the internship is mostly photography based. Special projects interns are responsible for taking ownership of promotional materials and distributing those materials, updating information in multiple databases, distributing information to department clients and prospects and becoming familiar with Special Projects publications.

$ GETTING HIRED

Apply by: *Spring*: November 1; *summer*: March 15; *fall:* July 15. Send resume and cover letter to the address below. Editorial applicants should also send two to three writing samples.

Qualifications:
Open to college juniors and seniors as well as recent college graduates and grad students.

Contact:
Boston Magazine, Attn: Internship Coordinator
300 Massachusetts Avenue
Boston, MA 02115
Phone: (617) 262-9700
Fax: (617) 262-5670
www.bostonmagazine.com

Boston University International Programs

 THE BUZZ
- "Combine travel, study, and work experience"

 THE STATS

Industry(ies): Education

Location(s): Los Angeles, CA; Washington, DC; Auckland; Beijing; Dresden; Haifa; London; Madrid; Moscow; Paris; Sydney

Number of interns: Varies

Pay: Interns pay tuition program fees and receive academic credit for the program (some financial aid is available)

Length of internship: *Summer*: 8 weeks; *fall/spring*: 12-16 weeks each

 THE SCOOP

As the study abroad division of Boston University, the International Programs office has sent more than 18,000 students from over 400 universities to study away from their own schools and countries for over 25 years. BU was one of the first U.S. universities to feature a study abroad program. All programs are also open to non-BU students, who get a BU transcript and transferable credits upon completion.

 ON THE JOB

The programs combine classes (taught by adjunct BU professors) and practical work experience in a wide variety of fields. In most, students concentrate on core classes. At the end of their time, they work in their host-country or city, applying what they've learned in the core classes. Some programs continue classes in the evenings.

$ GETTING HIRED

Apply by: *Summer*: March 1; *fall*: March 15; *spring*: October 15. Online applications available at https://app.applyyourself.com/?id=BU-I. Log on to www.bu.edu/abroad/internships/index.html to peruse each program's work specialties and fields.

Qualifications:
Open to college sophomores, juniors and seniors, and grad students.

Contact:
Joe Finkhouse
Boston University International Programs
232 Bay State Road, 5th Floor
Boston, MA 02215
Phone: (617) 353-9888
Fax: (617) 353-5402
E-mail: abroad@bu.edu
www.bu.edu/abroad/internships/index.html

Boys Hope Girls Hope

 THE BUZZ
* "Change a child's life"

 **THE STATS**

Industry(ies): Education; Nonprofit

Location(s): Baltimore, MD; Baton Rouge, LA; Chicago, IL; Cincinnati, OH; Denver, CO; Detroit, MI; Kansas City, KS; Las Vegas, NV; New Orleans, LA; New York, NY; Northeast, OH; Orange County, CA; Phoenix, AZ; Pittsburgh, PA; San Francisco, CA; St. Louis, MO; Brazil; Guatemala; Ireland

Number of interns: *Annual:* 40

Pay: $200/month. Room and board; loan deferment; health insurance; transportation assistance; chance to receive the AmeriCorps Education Assistance Award

Length of internship: 1 year minimum

 **THE SCOOP**

Founded by Father Paul Sheridan in 1977, Boys Hope Girls Hope is a nonprofit providing homes and support for at-risk youth in 16 U.S. cities, Brazil, Guatemala and Ireland. The organization is privately funded and multidenominational. The homes are noninstitutional and staffed with live-in counselors and support volunteers. Families voluntarily place their children in the organization's care. The emphasis is placed on education.

ON THE JOB

The organization's "residential volunteers" live with, and work as role models for, at-risk youth. All are trained and work with professional staff to provide surrogate parenting for groups of children (usually six to eight children, ages 10-18) in homes across the country. Volunteers help transform these youth into competent young adults. After completing the year, volunteers can apply for full-time employment with the organization.

GETTING HIRED

Apply by: July 1. Request an application on the web site (www.boyshopegirlshope.org/m-contactus3.html).

Qualifications:
Open to recent college graduates and graduate-level students.

Contact:
Boys Hope Girls Hope, National Office
Attention: Recruitment & Volunteer Coordinator
12120 Bridgeton Square Drive
Bridgeton, MO 63044-2607
Phone: (877) 878-HOPE
Fax: (314) 298-1251
E-mail: rvs@bhgh.org
www.boyshopegirlshope.org/jobtypes/m-residential/
volunteer.html

BP

 THE BUZZ
* "Fuel a career in the energy industry"

THE STATS

Industry(ies): Energy/Utilities

Location(s): Various locations, including: Anchorage, AK; Blaine, WA; Carson, CA; Houston, TX; La Palma, CA; Naperville, IL; Texas City, TX; Toledo, OH; Warrenville, IL; Whiting, IN; Calgary

Number of interns: *Average, U.S.*: 200 annually; *average, Canada*: 50 annually

Pay: Paid; competitive salary (varies)

Length of internship: Generally mid-May to mid-August

 THE SCOOP

BP is the second-largest energy company in the world, with employees working in more than 100 countries and annual revenues of around $285 billion. BP is divided into segments: exploration and production; manufacturing and marketing; and gas, power and "renewables."

ON THE JOB

BP hires interns on an as-needed basis so check its web site for open positions: https://www.bp.com/careers/us. Past positions have included business internships in land administration and negotiation, engineering, geosciences, industrial safety internships and environmental specialist positions. Interns/co-ops are thoroughly trained to work independently at the company.

GETTING HIRED

Apply by: Rolling. Apply for specific positions online: www.bp.com/careers/us.

Qualifications:

Open to college freshmen, sophomores, juniors and seniors, recent grads (three years or less) and graduate students. Requirements necessary for placement vary greatly depending on the positions available; log on to the company's web site for more details.

Contact:

www.bp.com/careers/us

Visit Vault at **www.vault.com** for insider company profiles, expert advice, career message boards, expert resume reviews, the Vault Job Board and more.

 **79**

Breakthrough Collaborative

THE BUZZ

- "Be a teacher while you're still a student"

THE STATS

Industry(ies): Education

Location(s): Atlanta, GA; Austin, TX; Boca Raton, FL; Cambridge, MA; Cincinnati, OH; Denver, CO; Fort Lauderdale, FL; Fort Worth, TX; Houston, TX; Long Island, NY; Manchester, NH; Miami, FL; Minneapolis, MN; New Haven, CT; New Orleans, LA; New York, NY; Norfolk, VA; Philadelphia, PA; Providence, RI; Sacramento, CA; Saint Paul, MN; San Francisco, CA (2 locations); San Jose, CA; San Juan Capistrano, CA; Santa Fe, NM; Hong Kong

Number of interns: *Summer:* 700

Pay: *College students:* $1000/summer; *high school students:* $750/summer. "Home stays" for out-of-town staff at some sites; financial aid is available based on financial need

Length of internship: *Summer:* 8 weeks

THE SCOOP

Breakthrough offers tuition-free tutoring and academic programs for motivated elementary and middle school students with limited educational opportunities. Most students attend programs for two to four years. Their teachers are high school and college students, trained and supported by professional educators.

ON THE JOB

Interns work as teachers and lead up to three academic courses and one elective per summer session. They are responsible for designing and evaluating the entire curriculum after a one-week training program. There are also other leadership opportunities, such as department and committee head positions.

GETTING HIRED

Apply by: *Summer:* March 5, 2007. Complete and send in an application (see breakthroughcollaborative.org/apply/index.html). After passing first review, applicants will be notified of their interview by phone or e-mail.

Qualifications:
Open to high school sophomores, juniors and seniors, as well as college freshmen, sophomores, juniors and seniors (ages 15-23). All majors are welcome.

Contact:
Breakthrough Collaborative
Attention: Jen Moon
Teacher Recruitment and Training Manager
40 First Street, Fifth Floor
San Francisco, CA 94105
Phone: (415) 442-0600, ext. 105
Fax: (415) 442-0609
E-mail: jmoon@breakthroughcollaborative.org
breakthroughcollaborative.org/apply/index.html

Breckenridge Outdoor Education Center

 THE BUZZ
- "Life-changing experiences in the open air"

 **THE STATS**

Industry(ies): Education; Nonprofit

Location(s): Breckenridge, CO

Number of interns: *Summer* (May-September): 12; *winter* (November-April): 12

Pay: Room and some board; $50/month; free pass to Breckenridge Recreation Center

Winter intern: 3-mountain season ski pass; ski lessons; adaptive instructor training; certification opportunities; deals on outdoor gear

Summer intern: wall-climbing training; off site rock climbing; high ropes course/top rope/elements experience set-up; paddling experience; hiking/mountaineering training; deals on outdoor gear

Length of internship: *Winter*: November 1-April 30; *summer*: May 15-September 30

 THE SCOOP

Founded in 1976, the Breckenridge Outdoor Education Center (BOEC) is for "experiential education," providing outdoor activities for all people, including those with disabilities and special needs. BOEC focuses on adaptive skiing and snowboarding, and on wilderness courses offered on its 39 acres and in the surrounding area filled with ropes courses, rivers and lakes for rafting and canoeing, a climbing wall, and miles of trails and slopes.

ON THE JOB

Interns at the BOEC are given "an unlimited amount of responsibility," according to administrators. While the summer and winter programs are markedly different, both allow people of all abilities to participate in outdoor activities. Summer interns, become staff on wilderness programs after a month of intense training, and plan, implement and evaluate outdoor therapeutic courses for unique groups (made up of children or adults with epilepsy, traumatic brain injuries, cancer, sensory integration disorder, developmental disabilities, learning disabilities, multiple sclerosis, at-risk youth, corporate groups, etc.). Responsibilities range from food and gear logistics, to safely guiding activities, to having client's determine their goals and discuss their experiences.

Winter interns undergo a similar introductory month of hard training before becoming assistants and primary instructors at the ski office, specifically for students with special needs. Off the slopes, interns are responsible for maintaining the BOEC wilderness site where they live, driving participants, fulfilling administrative duties at the ski office and leading winter wilderness courses.

GETTING HIRED

Apply by: *Summer*: March 1; *winter*: September 1. Online application at www.boec.org/ver2/internship_app.cfm.

Qualifications:

Open to high school graduates, college juniors and seniors, college graduates and grad students. Minimum age is 21. First aid and CPR certification are required.

Contact:
Brook Yates, CTRS
Breckenridge Outdoor Education Center
P.O. Box 697
Breckenridge, CO 80424
Phone: (970) 453-6422
Fax: (970) 453-4676
E-mail: internship@boec.org
www.boec.org/ver2/internships.cfm

Visit Vault at **www.vault.com** for insider company profiles, expert advice, career message boards, expert resume reviews, the Vault Job Board and more.

VAULT CAREER LIBRARY   **81**

Brethren Volunteer Service

 THE BUZZ
- "Advocate justice and meet basic human needs"

 THE STATS

Industry(ies): Nonprofit; Religious

Location(s): Locations throughout the U.S. and world

Number of interns: *Annual*: 120

Pay: $60-80/month stipend. Room and board; medical insurance; transportation to projects

Length of internship: *National*: 1-year minimum; *international*: 2-year minimum

 THE SCOOP

Fifty-six years ago, the Church of the Brethren decided that it was time to establish a formal group for "sharing God's love through acts of service." The Brethren Volunteer Service took this original goal as its motto and still lives by it today, with over 100 volunteers serving in 18 countries worldwide and 25 states across the nation. Projects range from lobbying for the environment in Brno, Czech Republic, to driving clinic patients around in Walker, Kentucky.

ON THE JOB

Once accepted, interns attend one of five annual orientation sessions held nationwide. Along with fellow BVS volunteers, they discuss social problems, explore their own faith and settle on project placement with the help of the permanent BVS staff. After three weeks of orientation, volunteers ship out across the country and around the world to complete their time of service. See web site for a complete listing of current BVS projects.

GETTING HIRED

Apply by: Application process must be completed six weeks or earlier prior to orientation. Complete and send in an application packet (e-mail bvs_gb@brethren.org to request one or call the number below), an essay, a transcript, a current photo and a resume.

Qualifications:
Open to high school graduates, college freshmen, sophomores, juniors and seniors, recent grads and grad students. Applicants must be at least 18 years old for domestic projects. International interns must be at least 21 years old and have a college degree or similar life experience.

Contact:
Brethren Volunteer Service Recruitment
1451 Dundee Avenue
Elgin, IL 60120
Phone: (800) 323-8039, ext. 454
Fax: (847) 742-0278
E-mail: bvs_gb@brethren.org
www.brethrenvolunteerservice.org

Brick Wall Management

 THE BUZZ
- "Entertainment and nonprofit work, a unique combo"

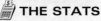 **THE STATS**

Industry(ies): Broadcast & Entertainment; Health Care; Nonprofit

Location(s): New York, NY

Number of interns: *Annual*: 1-3

Pay: None; academic credit available

Length of internship: *Spring/summer/fall*: 12-16 weeks each

 **THE SCOOP**

Brick Wall manages the careers of some big name artists. The firm also runs the Kristen Ann Carr Fund, which doles out grant money for cancer research and works to improve the lives of young cancer patients. The fund has enjoyed support from artists such as Bruce Springsteen and Shania Twain. Brick Wall also provides consulting services to other entertainment organizations (such as Star Polish and Musicians on Call). Current management clients include The Clarks, the Duhks, Slow Runner, Marc Broussard and Citizen Cope.

ON THE JOB

Since the company is small, interns do everything and anything in Brick Wall's world of artist management and entertainment consulting, gaining invaluable work experience. They often review submitted demos, work on the database, and perform general office tasks. Interns also have the option of attending live shows and other music events where they can network with industry bigwigs.

GETTING HIRED

Apply by: Rolling. Send resume by fax, e-mail or regular mail.

Qualifications:
Open to all college juniors and seniors, grad students and recent college graduates. International applicants eligible with documentation.

Contact:
Coordinator/Internship Director
Brick Wall Management
648 Amsterdam Avenue, Suite 4A
New York, NY 10025-7456
Phone: (212) 501-0748
Fax: (212) 724-0849
E-mail: internships@brickwallmgmt.com
www.brickwallmgmt.com

Brookfield Zoo

THE BUZZ
- "200 acres of wild animals in the Windy City"

 THE STATS
Industry(ies): Science/Research; Tourism/Recreation

Location(s): Brookfield, IL

Number of interns: *Summer*: 20; *fall*, *winter*: 15 each

Pay: None

Length of internship: 12 weeks

 THE SCOOP
Brookfield Zoo, just outside of Chicago, is open every day of the year. Big hits at the zoo include its dolphin shows, the Australia House, the Tropic World rainforest and the Hamill Family Play Zoo. Sponsored by the Chicago Zoological Society, the zoo has a well-established internship program boasting over 800 past participants.

ON THE JOB
Zookeeper internships are available in many different animal areas. Interns become familiar with animal management, exhibit maintenance, diet preparation and distribution, animal observation and documentation, animal handling and informal education programs. A small number of non-zookeeping internships are also available in various departments including marketing, education, design, water quality lab and conservation biology.

GETTING HIRED
Apply by: *Summer*: February 1; *fall*: August 1; *spring*: December 1. Download the information packet, including an application, at www.brookfieldzoo.org.

Qualifications:
Open to all college juniors and seniors, grad students and recent college graduates. Must have 2.5 GPA or higher.

Contact:
Zookeeper Internships
Brookfield Zoo
3300 Golf Road
Brookfield, IL 60513
Phone: (708) 485-0263, ext. 449
Fax: (708) 485-3140
E-mail: zookeeper_internships@brookfieldzoo.org
www.brookfieldzoo.org

Brookhaven National Laboratory

 THE BUZZ
- "Like summer camp, with beakers"

THE STATS
Industry(ies): Engineering; Science/Research

Location(s): Upton, NY

Number of interns: *Annual*: 250-300

Pay: Paid; $325-$400/week. Housing

Length of internship: *Spring*: 10 weeks; *summer*: 8-10 weeks; *fall*: 10 weeks

 THE SCOOP
Located on New York State's Long Island, Brookhaven was established in 1947 as a multi-program science lab, operated by Brookhaven Science Associates for the U.S. Department of Energy. Around 3,000 scientists, engineers and support staff work at the lab, with specialist guest researchers (usually around 4,000 each year). Discoveries made at Brookhaven have resulted in six Nobel Prizes. Focuses include nonproliferation, nuclear physics, environmental research and medical imaging.

ON THE JOB
Brookhaven, which has had its own undergrad summer intern program since 1952, is now one of the sites for the U.S. Department of Energy's Science Undergraduate Laboratory Internships (SULI). However, SULI at Brookhaven has many of the same features of the former Brookhaven summer program. Interns work with science professionals on research projects concerning chemistry, physics, biology, nuclear medicine, applied mathematics, high and low energy particle accelerators, and science writing.

GETTING HIRED
Apply by: *Spring*: November 30; *summer*: April 1; *fall*: July 15. See the online application at www.bnl.gov/scied/programs/suli/index.html.

Qualifications:
Open to college freshmen, sophomores, juniors and seniors studying a science-related field, with a GPA of 3.0 or higher.

Contact:
Internship Coordinator
Brookhaven National Laboratory
Building 438-Science Education Center
Upton, NY 11973
Phone: (631) 344-4503
E-mail: oep@bnl.gov
www.bnl.gov

Visit Vault at **www.vault.com** for insider company profiles, expert advice, career message boards, expert resume reviews, the Vault Job Board and more.

VAULT CAREER LIBRARY   83

The Brookings Institution

 THE BUZZ
- "For the nonpartisan at heart"

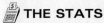 **THE STATS**

Industry(ies): Nonprofit

Location(s): Washington, DC

Number of volunteers: *Spring/summer/fall/winter*: 8-10 each

Pay: None

Length of internship: *Spring/summer/fall/winter*: 1 semester each; part-time

 THE SCOOP

The Brookings Institution was founded from the Institute for Government Research (IGR), established in 1916. One of IGR's principals, Robert Somers Brookings, created the Institute for Economics (1922) and an eponymous graduate school (1924), both of which merged in 1927 with IGR to become the Brookings Institution, which works to improve U.S. public policy through research and education. Current projects for 2004 include "The Future of Children," "Korea," and "Homeland Security."

ON THE JOB

Several formal and informal internship opportunities are available, including the Economic Studies Program, Governance Studies, Information Technology Services, Communications and the Brookings Press. The 11 programs offering internships have specific requirements and responsibilities. Log on to www.brookings.edu/admin/internships.htm for a list of available student positions with descriptions.

 **GETTING HIRED**

Apply by: Rolling. Deadlines vary according to program. Requirements differ but a resume and cover letter are standard.

Qualifications:
Open to college freshmen, sophomores, juniors and seniors and grad students.

Contact:
General Questions
Administration
The Brookings Institution
1775 Massachusetts Avenue, NW
Washington, DC 20036
Fax: (202) 797-2479
E-mail: hrjobs@brookings.edu
www.brookings.edu/admin/internships.htm

Governance Studies Program
Internship Coordinator
The Brookings Institution
1775 Massachusetts Avenue, NW
Washington, DC 20036
E-mail: GSCOMMENTS@brookings.edu

Foreign Policy Studies
Internship Coordinator
The Brookings Institution
1775 Massachusetts Avenue, NW
Washington, DC 20036

Metropolitan Policy Program
Elena Sheridan
The Brookings Institution
1775 Massachusetts Avenue, NW
Washington, DC 20036
Phone: (202) 797-6139
Fax: (202) 797-2965

Brookings Center for Executive Education
Adina Lord
Program Associate
The Brookings Institution
1775 Massachusetts Avenue, NW
Washington, DC 20036
Phone: (202) 797-6276
Fax: (202) 797-6133

Office of Communications
Adrianna Pita
Phone: (202) 797-6302
Fax: (202) 797-2495

Information Technology Services
Ms. Stuart Allen
Assistant to the CIO
Phone: (202) 797-6183
Fax: (202) 797-6264

Brookings Institution Press
Uwi Basaninyenzi
Publicity Coordinator
1775 Massachusetts Avenue, NW
Washington, DC 20036

Jaime Fearer
Sales and Marketing Coordinator
1775 Massachusetts Avenue, NW
Washington, DC 20036

Brooklyn Botanic Garden

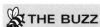 THE BUZZ
- "Go green in the Big Apple"
- "A horticultural oasis in urbania ..."

 THE STATS

Industry(ies): Education; Environmental

Location(s): Brooklyn, NY

Number of interns: *Annual*: 26 paid, post-high school positions

Pay: Paid; $7.00/hour for all except Horticulture Therapy, in which a stipend is paid. Access to garden collections, Gardener's Resource Center, Science Library and Rare Book Room; field trips

Length of internship: 3 months-1 year

 THE SCOOP

What began as an ash dump at the turn of the century has grown into the beautiful Brooklyn Botanic Garden, an international landmark in urban gardening. Not only an oasis of flora, BBG is also an active research site and educational center, playing host to a plethora of exhibits, workshops, celebrations and programs, including the annual Cherry Blossom Festival.

ON THE JOB

Horticulture internships are available in BBG's Discovery Garden and in its Children's Garden, as well as other educational programs. These interns work directly with The Garden's acclaimed horticulture staff. BBG also offers one horticulture internship with The Garden's plant propagator and one with The Garden's rosarian in the Rose Garden. Discovery Garden and Children's Garden interns should have some experience working with children. Discovery Garden interns work with the Discovery programs coordinator in an outdoor adventure garden, educating visitors and maintaining the gardens themselves. Children's Garden interns work with groups of young students, planning lessons and activities as well as gardening.

Other summer education internships include the plant investigator/junior botanist and summer science adventurers, which also involve working with children and providing garden and science-based activities. The Horticulture Therapy and Community Horticulture position is for one year and requires horticulture experience as well as experience in children's education. This intern works with different local community groups.

GETTING HIRED

Apply by: *Horticulture Therapy*: December 1; *Community Horticulture*: January 15; *Discovery Garden*: March 1; all others: April 1. See web site for specific program information.

Qualifications:
Open to high school graduates, college freshmen, sophomores, juniors and seniors, college grads and graduate students. Some positions require horticulture or education experience.

Contact:
Inquiries
Romi Ige
Coordinator of Interpretation and Internships
Phone: (718) 623-7298
E-mail: romiige@bbg.org

Applications
Director of Human Resources
Brooklyn Botanic Garden
1000 Washington Avenue
Brooklyn, NY 11225-1099
Fax: (718) 622-7826
E-mail: personnel@bbg.org
www.bbg.org/edu/internships

Visit Vault at **www.vault.com** for insider company profiles, expert advice, career message boards, expert resume reviews, the Vault Job Board and more.

VAULT CAREER LIBRARY **85**

Brooklyn Museum

THE BUZZ
- "Something for every art history buff"

 THE STATS

Industry(ies): Art/Museum; Education

Location(s): Brooklyn, NY

Number of interns: *Annual:* 5-10

Pay: $14,800 stipend. Monthly transit card. Health insurance

Length of internship: 10 months (September-June)

THE SCOOP

The Brooklyn Museum is the second-largest art museum in New York City, located just 30 minutes from Manhattan and next door to the verdant Brooklyn Botanic Garden. The museum has a permanent collection of more than 1.5 million objects of extraordinary range, from ancient Egyptian pots to contemporary canvases.

ON THE JOB

Each year, the museum's education division offers several full-time, 10-month internship positions. Intern educators spend the first month in intensive training where they are introduced to the various museum collections and museum education from the intern coordinator, as well as other museum staff members who monitor, observe and guide their professional development. Regularly scheduled seminars introduce interns to other Brooklyn Museum departments and to education programs at other New York museums.

GETTING HIRED

Apply by: March 31. Send a resume, a statement of interest and two letters of recommendation to the address below. The Museum prefers that all application materials arrive in the same envelope. Do not send academic transcripts.

Qualifications:
Open to recent grads and grad students. Applicants should have an interest in working with diverse museum audiences and/or teaching from art objects. International applicants must be eligible to work in the U.S. and are responsible for securing their own immigration documents. The museum will not sponsor immigrant visa applications for intern educators, though in the past, interns have worked with international student organizations to secure non-immigrant visas (ie, J-1 or F-1). Proof of applicant's ability to work in the United States must be submitted to the museum before work starts.

Contact:
Education Intern Coordinator
Brooklyn Museum
200 Eastern Parkway
Brooklyn, NY 11238
Phone: (718) 501-6589
Fax: (718) 501-6129
E-mail: education.internships@brooklynmuseum.org
www.brooklynmuseum.org/info/internships

Bucks County Courier Times

THE BUZZ
- "Small paper, big Philly experience"

THE STATS

Industry(ies): Journalism

Location(s): Bucks County, PA

Number of interns: *Summer:* approximately 5

Pay: Paid; $365/week. Daily transportation reimbursement

Length of internship: *Summer:* 12 weeks

THE SCOOP

The Bucks County Courier Times is a daily newspaper with a circulation of over 70,000. It was founded in 1910, and has all the traditional newspaper sections, including local features and national headlines. *The Bucks County Courier Times* (in its online form) is available at www.phillyburbs.com.

ON THE JOB

After an orientation, interns are treated like regular employees. Some are reporters covering news and bureau beats, others work as desk assistants, and some even write for features sections, like sports and lifestyles. Interns can also work as photographers. All work with professional mentors.

GETTING HIRED

Apply by: *Summer:* February 1. Send cover letter, resume and writing samples.

Qualifications:
Open to freshman, sophomore, junior and senior undergrads and graduate students. Applicants should have a car along with a valid driver's license.

Contact:
Patricia Walker
Bucks County Courier Times
8400 Route 13
Levittown, PA 19057
Phone: (215) 949-4160
Fax: (215) 949-4177
E-mail: pwalker@phillyburbs.com
www.phillyburbs.com/onlineedition

Buffalo Bill Historical Center

 **THE BUZZ**
- "Definitely for the American history buff"
- "Where 'New West' meets 'Old West'"

 THE STATS

Industry(ies): Art History; Museum; Tourism/Recreation; Natural History; Western Studies, Native American Studies; Oral History

Location(s): Cody, WY

Number of interns: *Summer*: 5

Pay: Paid; $7.60/hour

Length of internship: *Summer*: 12-14 weeks

 THE SCOOP

The Buffalo Bill Historical Center examines the history and culture of the American West. The Center's exhibits focus on Western art, the culture and natural history of the Mountain Plains West, Native American cultute and life, firearms and the life and times of W.F. "Buffalo Bill" Cody and his impact on the Wild West. Cody became the public face of the Army in the West and one of the most famous Americans of his time. The Center runs five museums (including one that focuses on the Plains Indians) and a research library.

ON THE JOB

Interns work 40-hour weeks in different museum departments after a required orientation session, where they receive reading lists and formal job descriptions. Each intern works with a supervisor who assigns general department duties. Interns also learn the overall operations of running a museum. There are multiple training and evaluation programs throughout the summer.

GETTING HIRED

Apply by: *Summer*: February 1. Send a resume, three reference letters, a current transcript and a cover letter to the address listed below with an application found at www.bbhc.org/edu/internship.cfm.

Qualifications:
Open to college juniors and seniors, as well as graduate students.

Contact:
Intern Coordinator
Buffalo Bill Historical Center
720 Sheridan Avenue
Cody, WY 82414
Phone: (307) 587-4771
Fax: (307) 578-4090
www.bbhc.org/edu/internship.cfm

Bunim/Murray Productions

 THE BUZZ
- "Get the background on reality TV"

THE STATS

Industry(ies): Broadcast & Entertainment; New/Interactive Media

Location(s): Los Angeles, CA

Number of interns: 5-12 depending on season

Pay: None; academic credit

Length of internship: *Summer*: 8 weeks; *fall/spring*: 14-15 weeks each; must work a minimum of two full days per week

 THE SCOOP

For well over a decade, television networks and viewers around the globe have looked to Bunim/Murray Productions for ground-breaking reality entertainment. Known for the hit series, *The Real World* (MTV), *Road Rules* (MTV), *The Simple Life* (FOX) and *Starting Over* (NBC), Bunim/Murray Productions turns the tales of ordinary real people into extraordinary television programming and filmed entertainment. Whether they are documenting the lives and loves of the MTV generation, or writing scripted dramas grounded in relatable life experiences, the team at Bunim/Murray Productions, led by Jonathan Murray, is continually expanding an innovative body of work that is, as the company says, "as real as it gets™."

ON THE JOB

Interns learn television pre-production, post-production and business processes, gaining valuable industry experience. During the first half of the program interns can rotate throughout various departments (unless they're working in a business area, where they will remain in that specific department). In the second half, interns choose where they want to be assigned for the remainder of the program. Available departments include casting, story, editing, pre-production/research, post-production, new show development, business development, accounting/finance, human resources, legal affairs and web site design.

GETTING HIRED

Apply by: *Summer/fall*: April 1; *spring*: November 1. Those interested in the internship program after the deadline has passed can e-mail the coordinator at the address below for further consideration with "Internship" in the subject line. Complete an application, writing test and submit one letter of reference. (Application and writing test can be found at www.bunim-murray.com.)

Qualifications:
Open to college juniors and seniors, as well as graduate and law students. Applicants must have their own health insurance and be able to receive academic credit at a four-year college or university.

Contact:
Bunim/Murray Productions
Internship Coordinator
P.O. Box 10421
Van Nuys, CA 91410-0421
Phone: (818) 756-5100
Fax: (818) 756-5140
E-mail: humanresources@bunim-murray.com
www.bunim-murray.com/aboutus/working_interns.html

Visit Vault at **www.vault.com** for insider company profiles, expert advice, career message boards, expert resume reviews, the Vault Job Board and more.

VAULT CAREER LIBRARY **87**

Burson-Marsteller

 THE BUZZ
- "Get on the short list for a long career in public relations"

 THE STATS

Industry(ies): Public Relations

Location(s): New York, NY (HQ); Chicago, IL; Los Angeles, CA; Miami, FL; San Francisco, CA; Washington, DC

Number of interns: *Annual*: 40

Pay: Varies

Length of internship: 8 weeks minimum

 THE SCOOP

Established in 1953, Burson-Marsteller is a leading global public relations firm with a network of 47 wholly owned offices and 45 affiliate offices operating in 54 countries. Burson-Marsteller is a part of Young & Rubicam Brands, a subsidiary of WPP Group plc (Nasdaq: WPPGY), one of the world's leading communications services networks.

 ON THE JOB

Summer interns are placed in advertising/creative, brand marketing, corporate/financial, health care, media, public affairs or technology departments. Interns do real work, attend seminars and complete a special project, which they must present to a senior management panel.

GETTING HIRED

Apply by: February 3. Send a resume, cover letter, an official college transcript, writing sample and two essays, one to three pages in length (topics found on the web site: www.bm.com).

Qualifications:

Open to college juniors and seniors with a minimum 3.0 GPA. Journalism, political science, communications, computer science, economics, English, psychology, mathematics and history majors preferred.

Contact:

Internship Coordinator
Burson-Marsteller
2425 Olympic Blvd., Suite 200-E
Santa Monica, CA 90404

Business Executives for National Security

 THE BUZZ
- "Use business know-how to improve our nation's security"

 THE STATS

Industry(ies): Government; Nonprofit

Location(s): Washington, DC

Number of interns: *Annual*: 2-3 per term

Pay: Varies; academic credit possible

Length of internship: *Spring*: January-May; *summer*: June-August; *fall*: September-December. Interns work 4-5 days/week

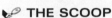 **THE SCOOP**

Business Executives for National Security (BENS) is a nationwide, nonpartisan group of senior business execs working to improve U.S. national security. BENS finds resources to reshape U.S. military forces for the 21st century, and partners businesses with government entities to strengthen homeland security.

 ON THE JOB

Interns work on substantive research and writing assignments in one or more of BENS's major policy areas. These include the "New Threats" activities in homeland, cyber and port security, terrorist finance, and ways of building the militatry (for a complete list see www.bens.org/what.html). Interns also have ample opportunity to meet with governmental figures and make contacts. All interns must create and present an original proposal for new BENS action. Several past projects have been implemented. Some interns may also work with the BENS Business Force, which raises money and facilitates public-private homeland security collaboration.

 GETTING HIRED

Apply by: *Spring*: November 30; *summer*: April 1; *fall*: July 31. Send a cover letter, a one-page resume and a two- to three-page writing sample to the address below.

Qualifications:

Open to college sophomores, juniors and seniors, as well as recent college graduates and grad students. BENS accepts interns from all backgrounds and degree programs. Strong writing and research skills are a must, as is an interest in national security issues. Applicants must be computer-literate in MS Office and Internet-savvy.

Contact:

Internship Coordinator
Business Executives for National Security
1717 Pennsylvania Avenue, NW, Suite 350
Washington, DC 20006-4603
Phone: (202) 296-2125
Fax: (202) 296-2490
E-mail: internships@bens.org
www.bens.org/contact_internships.html
www.bensbusinessforce.org/

INTERNSHIP PROFILES: C

Cabrillo National Monument

 THE BUZZ
- "San Diego: average temperature 72 degrees"

THE STATS

Industry(ies): Environmental; Tourism/Recreation

Location(s): San Diego, CA

Number of interns: Varies

Pay: None; academic credit available. Free entry to Cabrillo National Monument

Length of internship: Flexible

 **THE SCOOP**

President Woodrow Wilson established the Cabrillo National Monument in 1913 to commemorate Juan Rodríguez Cabrillo, the first European on the West Coast, who claimed land for Spain in 1542. Today, the National Park Service manages the monument and its 160 acres. People come from around the world to watch Pacific gray whales migrate south, visit the tidepool area, learn about military history and more. The park also offers volunteer programs and exhibits on various subjects.

ON THE JOB

Internships at the Cabrillo National Monument are really introductions to park management and environmental preservation. Interns study the science of natural resource by doing fieldwork in the park. They learn about the geography of the area by putting data in Cabrillo's Geographic Information System. They help with the Resource Management & Visitor Protection division by restoring the native plants of the coastal sage scrub ecosystem around the park. Interns also help staff the visitor center's front desk and work on special projects.

GETTING HIRED

Apply by: Rolling. Volunteer application is available on the web site (www.nps.gov/volunteer/volunteerapp1.htm). Send completed form with cover letter indicating the jobs that interest you.

Qualifications:
Open to college freshmen, sophomores, juniors and seniors, as well as recent grads and grad students.

Contact:
Marcy Marquez
National Park Service
Cabrillo National Monument
1800 Cabrillo Memorial Drive
San Diego, CA 92106
Phone: (619) 523-4573
Fax: (619) 557-5469
E-mail: marcy_marquez@nps.gov
www.nps.gov/cabr

California Governor's Office

THE BUZZ
- "Brush up on your government and surfing skills"

THE STATS

Industry(ies): Government; Law

Location(s): Los Angeles, CA; Riverside, CA; Sacramento, CA (summer only); San Diego, CA; San Francisco, CA

Number of interns: *Annual*: 100

Pay: None; academic credit available

Length of internship: *Summer*: June-August; *fall*: varies; *spring*: varies

THE SCOOP

There's a new California governor in town, and it's not Gray Davis. Arnold Schwarzenegger is the governor of one of America's most celebrated states, and he needs some sharp interns to help him govern from San Diego to San Francisco (whether the San Franciscans like it or not). Are you up to the task?

ON THE JOB

Interns work with the governor's staff on everything from public policy issues to state politics. They can work in Sacramento (the state capital) or in the field offices during the summer or during the year. Interns may work in the cabinet, press, constituent affairs, communications, special projects and speechwriting units. Intern responsibilities range from administrative work to unit-specific duties, including attending cabinet hearings, organizing press conferences and working with the public. Communications interns work on special events and must be available on Fridays for at least four hours.

GETTING HIRED

Apply by: *Summer*: May 1, field offices vary; *fall/spring*: rolling. Interns must send an application, cover letter, resume, a copy of their driver's license or state ID, and a letter of recommendation.

Qualifications:
Open to high school seniors and college freshmen, sophomores, juniors and seniors. High school students must have at least a 2.5 GPA. College students must have at least a 3.0 GPA.

Contact:
Community Relations and Internship Coordinator
Office of Governor
State Capital
Sacramento, CA 95814
Phone: (213) 897-0322
Fax: (213) 897-0319
www.governor.ca.gov

California Museum of Photography

 THE BUZZ
- "A West Coast boost to a visual arts career"

 **THE STATS**

Industry(ies): Art/Museum; New/Interactive Media

Location(s): Riverside, CA

Number of interns: *Annual*: 20

Pay: None; academic credit

Length of internship: 9 weeks minimum

 **THE SCOOP**

With over 350,000 historical prints and negatives including works by photo icons such as Ansel Adams and Walker Evans, the California Museum of Photography is home to one of the country's premier photography collections. The museum was founded in 1973 by the University of California at Riverside and has kept pace with new technology with its cutting-edge digital studio.

ON THE JOB

Interns can work in collections management, curatorial, digital studio, education or public relations. Collections interns catalogue historical images and rare books, do research and help prepare exhibitions in the museum and online. Digital studio interns create web sites, download collections and teach visitors about new media. Education and public relations interns work with professionals on specific projects.

GETTING HIRED

Apply by: Rolling. E-mail resume and cover letter, or send by U.S. mail.

Qualifications:
Open to college freshmen, sophomores, juniors and seniors, as well as recent grads and grad students. Digital studio internships are also open to qualified high school students. These interns must have experience with Macintosh and digital imaging software. Graphic design training preferred.

Contact:
Jennifer Stratton
UCR/California Museum of Photography
University of California
3824 Main Street
Riverside, CA 92501
Phone: (909) 787-4787
Fax: (909) 787-4797
E-mail: jenstrat@pop.ucr.edu
www.cmp.ucr.edu

California Senate Fellows

 THE BUZZ
- "Catapult yourself into California politics"

 **THE STATS**

Industry(ies): Government; Law

Location(s): Sacramento, CA

Number of interns: *Annual*: 18

Pay: Paid; $1,882/month. 12 units of graduate credit; health, dental and vision coverage

Length of internship: 11 months (October-September)

THE SCOOP

The California Senate Fellows program was created in 1973 to give college graduates from diverse backgrounds experience in the legislative process. Sponsored by the California Senate and California State University, Sacramento, the program has launched hundreds of interns into the world of politics.

ON THE JOB

Fellows work as full-time staffers in one of the California Senators' Capitol offices or in Senate policy committees. Fellows assigned to senators' personal offices develop and staff legislative proposals, handle constituent issues and write press releases and speeches. Fellows assigned to policy committees analyze legislation before it is heard in committee. All fellows attend a free weekly graduate seminar conducted by the university faculty advisor.

GETTING HIRED

Apply by: February 23. Those interested must submit an application, college transcript, two letters of recommendation and a personal statement. Applications are available online (www.csus.edu/calst/Programs/senate/04-05_application.pdf) or through the mail.

Qualifications:
Open to college graduates and grad students (anyone who has completed at minimum a four-year college or university program, from recent grads to mid-career professionals). High GPA, community activism and interest in politics and public policy preferred.

Contact:
David Pacheco
California Senate Fellows
Center for California Studies
California State University, Sacramento
6000 J Street
Sacramento, CA 95819-6081
Phone: (916) 278-5408
Fax: (916) 278-5199
E-mail: david.pacheco@sen.ca.gov
www.csus.edu/calst/programs/senate_fellows.html

Visit Vault at **www.vault.com** for insider company profiles, expert advice, career message boards, expert resume reviews, the Vault Job Board and more.

VAULT CAREER LIBRARY   91

California State Assembly

 THE BUZZ

- "Jumpstart a political career in sunny California"

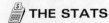 **THE STATS**

Industry(ies): Government; Law

Location(s): Sacramento, CA

Number of interns: *Annual:* 18

Pay: Paid; $1,972/month. Health, dental and vision coverage; graduate credit

Length of internship: 11 months (October-September)

THE SCOOP

The California State Assembly is the legislative arm of the sunny west coast state. Founded in 1957, the Jesse M. Unruh Assembly Fellowship Program is one of the nation's oldest and most prominent legislative fellowships. A year-long submersion into Golden State politics puts interns of all ages behind the scenes of the legislative process. The program was created by the State Assembly and renamed in 1987 to honor California's former Assembly Speaker and State Treasurer.

ON THE JOB

Interns work as full-time staffers in one of the California Assembly members' capitol offices. They may draft legislation, write speeches, track bills and research policy issues, and may also work at schools. The program includes two grad-level government seminars.

GETTING HIRED

Apply by: February 22. Candidates must submit a completed application, college transcript, three evaluations, a policy statement on a topic in the application and a personal statement. An application is available online at www.csus.edu/calst/Programs/about_programs.html. Interview required.

Qualifications:

Open to college graduates (anyone with a BA or higher, from recent grads to mid-career professionals). High GPA, community activism and interest in politics and public policy preferred.

Contact:
Robbin Lewis-Coaxum
Program Director
The Jesse M. Unruh Assembly Fellowship Program
The Center for California Studies
California State University, Sacramento
6000 J Street
Sacramento, CA 95819-6081
Phone: (916) 278-6906
Fax: (916) 278-5199
E-mail: calstudies@csus.edu
www.csus.edu/calst/Programs/jesse_unruh.html

Callaway Engineering

 THE BUZZ

- "This internship is too fast, too furious"

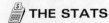 **THE STATS**

Industry(ies): Engineering; Manufacturing; Technology

Location(s): Old Lyme, CT

Number of interns: Varies

Pay: None

Length of internship: *Summer/fall/spring:* 12 weeks each

THE SCOOP

Founded in 1987, Callaway Engineering delivers a range of contract engineering and manufacturing services, with special focus developing high-performance vehicles, systems, and components. The Callaway staff uses PTC Pro/ENGINEER® design software solutions, prototype fabrication techniques and component production processes, and also offers complete testing and validation services. Engineers are able to specify, source and manage complex OEM supply chains while also performing craftsman-quality assembly of small- to medium-sized production runs.

ON THE JOB

Specific duties vary, but normally include basic engineering tasks. Interns work closely with seasoned staff.

GETTING HIRED

Apply by: Rolling.

Qualifications:

Open to college freshmen, sophomores, juniors and seniors, as well as recent grads.

Contact:
Scott Rawling
Internship Coordinator
Callaway Engineering
3 High Street
Old Lyme, CT 06371
Phone: (860) 434-9002
Fax: (860) 434-1704
E-mail: srawling@callawaycars.com
www.callawaycars.com

Campbell Soup Company

 THE BUZZ
- "Get in with the largest soup maker in the world"
- "An M-m-m good way to spend the summer"

 **THE STATS**

Industry(ies): Food & Beverage

Location(s): Camden, NJ (HQ); Norwalk, CT

Number of interns: *MBA*: Marketing: 12-15, Finance: 4-6; *undergraduate*: approximately 40

Pay: Varies for each department and education level

Length of internship: *Summer*: 3 months, 40 hours/week; *spring/fall co-op*: 3-6 months, 20-40 hours/week

 **THE SCOOP**

The Campbell Soup Company is the largest soup maker in the world – leading the industry in 120 countries globally. The bulk of the company's sales are brought in with their classic recipes like chicken noodle, cream of mushroom and tomato soups. Other Campbell products and brands include V8, Godiva, Franco American, Swanson, Pace and Pepperidge Farm. Combined national and international sales reflect $7.5 billion. Headquartered in Camden, N.J., the company employs approximately 24,000 people.

ON THE JOB

Campbell offers internships in several divisions: Brand Marketing (MBA candidates only), Corporate and Brand Finance (MBA candidates strongly preferred), Research & Development, Tax, Advertising, IT, Global Design, Creative Services and more. Most of the positions are based in Camden, NJ. The company also offers internships in its Pepperidge Farm offices in Norwalk, CT and Godiva, NY. At the Camden location, Campbell offers a health and fitness center, a child care facility, full-scale cafeteria serving breakfast and lunch, company store, sports leagues, dry cleaning and several other perks. Several of the mentioned services can also be found at the Pepperidge Farm location.

GETTING HIRED

Apply by: *Academic year/co-op*: rolling. *MBA summer*: February. If Campbell does not recruit on your campus, visit: careers.campbell soupcompany.com; internships are posted as-needed. You can also set up an online profile on Campbell's job board (http://careers. campbellsoup company.com/careers_ campus.asp) to be notified when Campbell posts new positions.

Qualifications:

Open to rising undergraduate juniors and seniors majoring in a field related to the internship. Candidates should have at least a 3.0 GPA and be U.S. citizens. For several of the internships, relocation is not covered, so local candidates are preferred (this information is available online). MBA candidates should be in a competitive MBA program with a minimum of two years of progressing work experience. Teamwork, leadership, analytic skills and consumer insights are highly valued.

Contact:
Campbell Soup Company
Campus Relations Program
1 Campbell Place
Box 35D
Camden, NJ 08103-1701
Phone: (856) 342-4800
Fax: (856) 342-3765
careers.campbellsoupcompany.com

Visit Vault at **www.vault.com** for insider company profiles, expert advice, career message boards, expert resume reviews, the Vault Job Board and more.

VAULT CAREER LIBRARY   93

Camphill Soltane

 THE BUZZ
- "An internship of 'heart work' as well as hard work"

THE STATS

Industry(ies): Education; Nonprofit

Location(s): Glenmoore, PA

Number of interns: *Annual*: 12-15

Pay: $170/month. Room and board; health care after 3 months; $700 vacation stipend after one year. AmeriCorps Education Award of $4,725 after 1 year of service for eligible American applicants

Length of internship: 11 months (August-July)

THE SCOOP

Located on a 50-acre stretch of Pennsylvania countryside, Camphill Soltane caters to handicapped young adults aged 18-35, relying on interns or co-workers to create a community with the people they serve. The Camphill Movement was founded in Scotland in 1940 around the philosophy of anthroposophy, which highlights spirituality in humanity. However, interns of all religious or spiritual affiliations are accepted.

ON THE JOB

Interns live and work with other interns, as well as the young adults with disabilities they help. They handle many types of tasks including household work, gardening, crafts, tutoring and direct care for the disabled. The work is challenging but rewarding. Interns get one day off each week, plus longer breaks at Christmas and Easter.

GETTING HIRED

Apply by: May 1. An interview is required (may be conducted over the telephone). Fill out an application online at http://www.camphillsoltane.org/coworkers.htm.

Qualifications:
Open to college juniors and seniors, and all individuals at least 20 years old. Applicants must be in good health and able to speak English well.

Contact:
Camphill Soltane
Anne-Marie McMahon, Co-Worker Admissions
224 Nantmeal Road
Glenmoore, PA 19343
Phone: (610) 469-0933
Fax: (610) 469-1054
E-mail: amcmahon@camphillsoltane.org
www.camphillsoltane.org/coworkers.htm

Canadian Embassy

 THE BUZZ
- "Get some Northern resume exposure"

THE STATS

Industry(ies): Government

Location(s): Washington, DC

Number of interns: *Annual*: 39-45; *spring*: 11-13; *summer*: 17-19; *fall*: 11-13

Pay: None. Tours of the Capitol, Pentagon, FBI, etc.; briefings by the Ambassador and other Embassy officers; pot luck dinners; gym; cafeteria

Length of internship: As per the academic calendar (September-December, January-April/May, May-August)

THE SCOOP

Designed to foster better relations with our northern neighbors, the Canadian Embassy internship program gives interns a "behind the scenes" look into international political policy by working in Canada's embassy located in Washington, DC. The Embassy oversees maple leaf natives living in areas from eastern Pennsylvania to Virginia, and is one of 13 consulate offices throughout the US.

 ON THE JOB

Interns work four-and-a-half days a week and are screened for the department that best suits their skills and interests. Placements include public affairs, academic relations, culture, press/media, information services, trade, environment, energy and congressional relations.

GETTING HIRED

Apply by: *Summer:* March 1; *fall*: July 1; *spring*: November 1. Fax or e-mail an application form, autobiography, resume, transcript and three letters of recommendation.

Qualifications:
Open to college juniors, seniors and graduate students.

Contact:
Ingrid Summa
Intern Coordinator
Canadian Embassy
501 Pennsylvania Avenue, NW
Washington, DC 20001
Phone: (202) 448-6595
Fax: (202) 682-7791
E-mail: ingrid.summa@international.gc.ca
www.canadianembassy.org/embassy/internships-en.asp

Canoe & Kayak Magazine

THE BUZZ
- "Hone your kayaking skills, as well as your writing skills"

THE STATS

Industry(ies): Journalism; Publishing; Sports

Location(s): Kirkland, WA

Number of interns: 1 editorial and 1 graphic design position per semester

Pay: None; academic credit available. Editorial intern can sometimes write for trade journals at 15 cents per word

Length of internship: Varies

THE SCOOP

Canoe & Kayak (C&K) Magazine is devoted to those boating sports and has found the perfect location in the coastal town of Kirkland, a suburb of Seattle. Many staff bios list not only the aforementioned sports, but also a love for hiking – and what better place to do it than the state that boasts the only rainforest in the continental United States?

ON THE JOB

Immerse yourself in the journalism trade. *C&K*'s small staff and flexible deadlines (remember, this is a bi-monthly publication). Interns may also indulge in canoeing and kayaking, in addition to photography, reporting and editing.

GETTING HIRED

Apply by: Rolling. Submit your resume via e-mail.

Qualifications:

Open to college freshmen, sophomores, juniors and seniors. Some experience with MS Word, Photoshop and Quark necessary.

Contact:

Ross Prather
Editor, Canoe & Kayak Magazine
10526 NE 68th Street, Suite #3
Kirkland, WA 98033
Phone: (425) 827-6363
E-mail: ross@canoekayak.com
www.canoekayak.com

CARE USA

 THE BUZZ
- "For those voted most likely to save the world"

THE STATS

Industry(ies): Construction/Building Materials; Education; Environmental; Health Care; Nonprofit

Location(s): Atlanta, GA; Boston, MA; Chicago, IL; Minneapolis, MN; New York, NY; Philadelphia, PA; San Francisco, CA; Seattle, WA; Washington, DC; dozens of overseas locations

Number of interns: Varies

Pay: Varies

Length of internship: 6 weeks-9 months

THE SCOOP

With nearly 13,000 staff fighting international poverty and salvaging communities in crisis, CARE is one of the world's foremost international charitable organizations. CARE sponsors volunteers in more than 60 of the world's poorest countries, from Ethiopia to Afghanistan. The group's mission is to work with local communities to find long-term solutions to poverty.

ON THE JOB

Interns work in agriculture and natural resources, education, emergency relief, health, nutrition, finance, external relations (fundraising, marketing), human resources, sanitation or small economic activity development. Positions vary by project, but can range from training local medical workers to constructing sewage systems to advising fledgling businesses. International interns work full time. U.S.-based interns work full- or part-time.

GETTING HIRED

Apply by: Rolling. Send resume and cover letter, reason for interest and dates of availability directly to the domestic office or international location where you are interested in working. For a complete list of all domestic offices and contact information, go to www.careusa.org.

Qualifications:
Open to college freshmen, sophomores, juniors, seniors, graduate students and recent grads.

Contact:
Internship Coordinator
CARE USA
Atlanta Headquarters
151 Ellis Street
Atlanta, GA 30303
Phone: (404) 681-2552
Fax: (404) 589-2651
E-mail: internships@care.org
www.careusa.org/careers/internship.asp

Visit Vault at **www.vault.com** for insider company profiles, expert advice, career message boards, expert resume reviews, the Vault Job Board and more.

VAULT CAREER LIBRARY   95

Carnegie Endowment for International Peace

 THE BUZZ
- "A great place to hone diplomatic skills"
- "Ambitious political researchers will be in heaven here"

 THE STATS

Industry(ies): Government; Nonprofit

Location(s): Washington, DC

Number of interns: *Annual*: 8-10

Pay: Paid; $2,500/month. Health care and benefits package

Length of internship: 1 year

 THE SCOOP

Founded in 1910, the Carnegie Endowment for International Peace is a private, nonprofit and nonpartisan organization advancing international cooperation and promoting America's international involvement. The Carnegie Junior Fellows program is a highly competitive position that draws applicants from more than 300 colleges across the country for a chance to work hand-in-hand with the Endowment's senior researchers.

ON THE JOB

Junior Fellows research topics like nonproliferation, democracy-building, trade, U.S. leadership, China-related issues and Russian/Eurasian studies. Fellows also research for books, contribute to journal articles and policy papers, sit in on meetings with high-level officials, contribute to congressional testimony and organize briefings attended by scholars, activists, journalists and government officials.

GETTING HIRED

Apply by: January 15. Individual colleges may have earlier deadlines. Two references are required.

Qualifications:
Open to college seniors and recent grads up to a year after graduation. Candidates must come from a university in the fellowship network and be nominated by their university.

Contact:
Your school career office. Carnegie does not accept applications directly from students.
www.ceip.org/files/about/about_Junior.asp

Carolyn Ray

 THE BUZZ
- "A stitch away from a design career"

 THE STATS

Industry(ies): Architecture; Manufacturing

Location(s): Yonkers, NY

Number of interns: Varies

Pay: Academic credit; pay possible upon inquiry

Length of internship: 4-12 weeks; flexible hours within Monday-Friday, 9-5:30 schedule

 THE SCOOP

Founded in 1977, Carolyn Ray is an international interior design powerhouse specializing in fabric production. Run by a small team of artists in a loft, the New York-based company has built its reputation on creating unique, top-of-the-line fabrics and wall coverings.

ON THE JOB

Interns pitch in wherever needed, working in the production studio, office, sample department or the warehouse. There are two specific intern positions. The business intern works with IT and computers and in the office, in sales, marketing and business management. The studio intern assists with handpainted production; studio maintenance, sample making and clerical work. Qualified interns can go on to paid, part-time work and potentially a full-time position.

GETTING HIRED

Apply by: Rolling. Send or fax resume, cover letter, transcript and recommendations. Slides of artwork are a plus for studio intern applicants.

Qualifications:
Open to college freshmen, sophomores, juniors and seniors, as well as recent grads up to one year after graduation. *Business intern:* Computer skills are required, good writing skills are preferred. *Studio intern:* mat cutting, sewing, printmaking and other design course work is recommended.

Contact:
Janice Cervera
Carolyn Ray
578 Nepperhan Avenue
Yonkers, NY 10701
Phone: (914) 476-0619
Fax: (914) 476-0677

E-mail: janice@carolynray.com

www.carolynray.com

The Carter Center

THE BUZZ

- "Help Jimmy Carter bring peace to the world"

 THE STATS

Industry(ies): Environmental; Government; Health Care; Nonprofit

Location(s): Atlanta, GA

Number of interns: *Summer*: 40-45; *fall*: 35- 40; *spring*: 35-40

Pay: None; academic credit available. Need-based financial aid available

Length of internship: *Summer* (May-June): 10 weeks; *fall* (September-December): 15 weeks; *spring* (January-April): 15 weeks

THE SCOOP

The Carter Center is the nexus of Jimmy Carter's post-presidential activities and is dedicated to improving human rights and living conditions across the globe. Activities include resolving conflicts, monitoring elections, advocating for transparency in government and reducing poverty.

ON THE JOB

The Carter Center internship program began in 1984. Over 110 students intern each year and most work in the Peace Programs area, monitoring activities and writing reports on assigned countries, and assisting with planning international conference/meetings. Interns work a minimum of 20 hours a week (preferably 40 hours a week) in one of The Center's three program divisions: peace programs, health programs and operations.

GETTING HIRED

Apply by: *Summer*: March 1; *fall*: June 15; *spring*: October 15. All application materials must be postmarked by these dates. An application is required. See site for details.

Qualifications:

Open to college juniors and seniors (with a minimum of 60 credit hours), recent graduates (less than two years after graduation), graduate students and international applicants.

Contact:

The Carter Center
Educational Program
Christina Jordan or Lauren Kent-Delaney
One Copenhill Avenue
Atlanta, GA 30307
Phone: (404) 420-5179
Fax: (404) 420-5196
E-mail: carterweb@emory.edu
www.cartercenter.org

Catholic University of America

THE BUZZ

- "It's Parliamentary, my dear Watson"

THE STATS

Industry(ies): Education; Government

Location(s): London; Dublin; Levven, Belgium

Number of interns: Varies

Pay: None; academic credit available

Length of internship: *Summer*: 12-16 weeks (London only); *fall*: 12-16 weeks (all locations); *spring*: 12-16 weeks (Dublin and Belgium)

THE SCOOP

Established as a graduate and research college in 1887, the Catholic University of America has expanded to include 12 schools. As part of its curriculum, the Washington, DC-based CUA offers undergraduate and graduate students the chance to study abroad for a semester in programs that incorporate class work with internships in foreign government. Possible locations include the British House of Commons, British Parliament, Irish Parliament and Belgium Parliament.

ON THE JOB

Interns divide their time between class and performing legislative work for the government bodies. Interns in Belgium study post-WWII history while working in the European Commission or Parliament. Interns in London study comparative politics and British drama while working in the British Parliament. Interns in Ireland live with a family, study local history and economy, and work in the Irish Parliament. Interns typically work as aides, answering letters and helping to research and draft speeches.

GETTING HIRED

Apply by: *Summer*: February 1; *fall*: April 15; *spring*: October 15.

Qualifications:

Open to college juniors and seniors, as well as graduate students. Minimum 3.0 GPA required. Must be enrolled at the Catholic University of America. Applicants must have completed foreign language and English composition requirements and be accepted into field of study.

Contact:

John Kromkowski
Assistant Dean for International Programs and Internships
The Catholic University of America
107 McMahon Hall
620 Michigan Avenue, NE
Washington, DC 20064
Phone: (202) 319-6188
E-mail: kromkowski@cua.edu
financialaid.cua.edu/study_abroad.htm

Visit Vault at **www.vault.com** for insider company profiles, expert advice, career message boards, expert resume reviews, the Vault Job Board and more.

V/\ULT CAREER LIBRARY **97**

Caux Scholars Program

 THE BUZZ

- "Learn about peace by living and working in a neutral country"
- "Develop skills in conflict resolution"

 THE STATS

Industry(ies): Education; Government; Nonprofit

Location(s): Washington, DC; Caux, Switzerland

Number of interns: *Summer*: 20

Pay: None. $2,300 fee (includes tuition, meals and board)

Length of internship: *Summer*: July 12-August 12. Participants work 10 hours/week

 THE SCOOP

The Caux Scholars Program strives for world peace through education. Participants learn about ethics and what leads individuals and nations to conflicts that hinder peaceful relations. Students take the month-long course at the Mountain House, a former Swiss palace, where the Franco-German peace talks were held in 1946. Participants work with delegations from the Balkans, Russia, the Middle East, Somalia, South Africa and other nations.

ON THE JOB

Program participants study with experts on conflict resolution, learning why conflicts occur and how they affect the peace process. They take a trip to Geneva to see nongovernmental organizations in action. Students also work a minimum of 10 hours a week assisting Caux Center's peace conference organizers. At the end of the program, students give mini-workshops based on what they've learned.

GETTING HIRED

Apply by: March 15. Download the application online (at www.cauxscholars.org/downloads/application.doc) and send the completed form to the address below. A 500-word essay on why you would like to participate in the program is required, as is a transcript.

Qualifications:
Open to college juniors and seniors, recent college graduates and graduate students. Applicants must have a high GPA, exhibit leadership ability and have studied a foreign language. Community service and an interest in the ethics of international affairs preferred.

Contact:
The Caux Scholars Program
Krista Rigalo, Program Director
1156 15th Street, NW, Suite 910
Washington, DC 20005
Phone: (202) 872-9077
Fax: (202) 872-9137
E-mail: CauxSP@aol.com
www.cauxscholars.org/about.html

Cavaliers/Gund Arena Company

 THE BUZZ

- "Britney, basketball and the Barons"
- "Work for one of the busiest arenas in the country and learn about event management"

 THE STATS

Industry(ies): Broadcast & Entertainment; Sports

Location(s): Cleveland, OH

Number of interns: *Summer/fall/spring*: 5 each

Pay: None; academic credit

Length of internship: *Summer*: 6-8 weeks; *fall/spring*: 12-16 weeks

 THE SCOOP

Located in Cleveland, the Gund Arena is home to the NBA's Cleveland Cavaliers, as well as the AHL's Cleveland Barons. Most big-name music acts appearing in Cleveland (like Britney Spears and Kid Rock) play at Gund. The stadium holds 20,500 spectators and hosts over 200 events every year.

ON THE JOB

The sports marketing department hires three interns. One intern works in facility operations, and the others work in basketball public relations. Interns work directly with professional staff in each department on general office duties and specific hands-on projects. For most positions, game-time work is necessary. The facility operations intern may also work during other arena activities (concerts, shows, and so on).

 GETTING HIRED

Apply by: Three to six months before internship begins. Download the application at: www.gundarena.com/internships/Application.pdf, or submit online: www.gundarena.com/internships/application.php. Send the completed application form (unless submitted online), a resume and a cover letter to the address below. Prospective interns will be called for an interview.

Qualifications:
Open to college sophomores, juniors and seniors and graduate students (must receive academic credit for program).

Contact:
Cavaliers/Gund Arena Company
Kevin Lednik
Human Resources Department
1 Center Court
Cleveland, OH 44115-4001
Phone: (216) 420-2000
Fax: (216) 420-2235
E-mail: internship@gundarena.com
www.gundarena.com/internships/internships.html

CBS News

 THE BUZZ

- "Nirvana for communications majors"

 **THE STATS**

Industry(ies): Broadcast; Communications; Journalism

Location(s): New York, NY (HQ); Los Angeles, CA; Washington, DC; London; Tokyo

Number of interns: *Annual*: 150-200

Pay: None; academic credit only

Length of internship: *Summer*: full time; *spring/fall*: 2 full days/week

 **THE SCOOP**

CBS, home to popular shows such as *CSI* (a 2003 Best Drama nominee), the *Late Show with David Letterman* and *60 Minutes*, is owned by media giant Viacom. A division of the CBS television network, CBS News produces a mix of radio and television news programs, including *CBS Evening News*, *60 Minutes* and *48 Hours*.

ON THE JOB

Duties vary depending upon departmental assignments. They include, but are not limited to, logging tapes, coordinating scripts, research, reading viewer mail and clerical duties. Possible placements include *The Early Show*, *CBS Evening News*, *48 Hours*, *60 Minutes*, *Face the Nation*, Public Relations, CBS Promotions, CBS Production, *Sunday Morning*, *Weekend News*, *Up to the Minute*, New Media and NewsPath, a satellite news-gathering system providing news feeds, as well as editorial and technical support, to CBS affiliates. Interns have the opportunity to attend most staff meetings and may occasionally accompany correspondents on shoots. Summer interns also attend workshops with CBS executives.

GETTING HIRED

Apply by: *Summer*: February 28; *spring/fall*: rolling. Applicants must forward the application (available for download at www.cbs news.com). Send a resume, two letters of recommendation, a letter of credit from your university/college, school transcript and a one-page essay on why you want to work in broadcast journalism to the mailing address listed below. (Only those eligible to receive academic credit will be considered.)

Qualifications:

Open to undergrad juniors and seniors currently enrolled in an undergraduate institution. Eligible majors: Journalism, Broadcasting, Communications, Public Relations, Marketing, Advertising, English, History, International Studies, and Political Science. Participants should have basic computer skills, as well as excellent written and oral communication skills, and have at least a 3.0 GPA.

Contact:

Katie Curcio, Internship Coordinator, CBS News
524 West 57th Street
New York, NY 10019
Phone: (212) 975-2114
Fax: (212) 975-6699
E-mail: internships@cbsnews.com

CCUSA

 THE BUZZ

- "Sunscreen not included"
- "Be more than a tourist "

THE STATS

Industry(ies): Education; Camp; Tourism/Recreation

Location(s): Australia; New Zealand; Russia, United Kingdom; China

Number of interns: *Annual*: Australia: 240; New Zealand: 250; Russia: varies

Pay: Varies. *WADU (Australia/New Zealand)*: salary depending on job; CCUSA will sponsor visas, can help with job placement; *CRussia/UK/Teach in China*: room, board, small stipend; in the Russia program, airline flight is included. All participants can purchase travel insurance from CCUSA

Length of internship: *Australia*: 4 months maximum; *New Zealand*: 4-12 months; *Russia*: 4-8 weeks; *UK:* 8 weeks; *China:* 6 weeks, 6 months or 12 months. Programs are year-round, but all may take place over the summer

THE SCOOP

CCUSA's Work Adventures Outbound places American students in its Work Abroad Down Under (WADU) program in Australia and New Zealand for work and travel. The company helps students apply for a work/travel visa and prepares them for life abroad, and while U.S. students go down under, Australians and New Zealanders head to America for work. The Camp Counselors Russia program has also placed Americans in Russian youth summer camps as counselors, for four to eight weeks during the summer, for 15 years. The most recent addition to CCUSA's programs is the Teach China Program, which places Americans in private schools in China to teach English.

ON THE JOB

Independence is a must, as participants on the Australian and New Zealand programs are responsible for finding their own jobs and living arrangements. Australian visas last for only three months, after which interns can travel for a month before heading home or on to New Zealand, where interns can work for up to 12 months. Experience with children is a must for the UK and Russia camps, and an interest in the Russian culture is essential for the Camp Counselor Russia program. Applicants to the China program should be equally adventurous and eager to teach English to non-native speakers.

GETTING HIRED

Apply By: *WADU:* Rolling; *CRussia and UK:* April 15. *Teach in China:* Rolling, but depends on program. Download applications at www.ccusa.com.

Qualifications:

All programs: Open to high school graduates, college students, college grads and graduate students (U.S. citizens 18-30 years old).

Contact:

Work Experience, Outbound Program
2330 Marinship Way, Suite 250
Sausalito, CA 94965
Phone: (800) 999-2267
E-mail: danaf@ccusa.com
www.ccusa.com

Visit Vault at **www.vault.com** for insider company profiles, expert advice, career message boards, expert resume reviews, the Vault Job Board and more.

VAULT CAREER LIBRARY   99

CDS International, Inc., Internship Program in Argentina

 THE BUZZ

• "Work and live in Argentina"

 THE STATS

Industry(ies): Engineering; Financial Services; Technology; Tourism/Recreation; and others

Location(s): Buenos Aires; Córdoba

Number of interns: Unlimited

Pay: None. Participants may apply for financial support or stipends through the CDS International Scholarship Fund

Length of internship: 2 program options are available: 1-month intensive Spanish language course followed by a 2-month unpaid internship placement (combination language/internship option); or a 3-month unpaid internship placement (internship option)

 **THE SCOOP**

CDS, now in its 37th year, is a nonprofit organization committed to the advancement of international career training opportunities customized to provide individuals with in-depth practical knowledge of other nations' business practices, cultures and political traditions. These experiences help strengthen global cooperation and understanding among individuals, businesses, organizations and communities. Each year, CDS serves approximately 1,700 individuals from almost 60 nations around the globe. For U.S. college/university students and recent graduates, CDS offers a variety of programs in Germany, Argentina, Spain, Switzerland and Russia.

ON THE JOB

CDS works in cooperation with its partner organization, COINED (Comisión de Intercambio Educativo), to provide internship opportunities for U.S. students and young professionals in either Córdoba or Buenos Aires, Argentina. Unpaid placements are available in business/finance, hotel management/tourism, computer science and engineering fields. Two program options are available: a four-week Spanish language course followed by an eight-week internship with an Argentinian company (Combination Language/Internship Option), or a 12-week internship at a host company (Internship Option). The program will start at the beginning of each month and applications are accepted on a rolling basis throughout the year.

GETTING HIRED

Apply by: Rolling (candidates should submit a completed application at least three months before desired start date). Download the application online from www.cdsintl.org/fromusa/iparg.htm. Only completed applications
(with application fee) will be considered.

Qualifications:

Candidates must be U.S. or Canadian citizens, between the ages of 18-30. At least two years at a university or college in a field related to one of the following is required: business (general administration, marketing, PR, sales, advertising, finance, hotel management); technical fields (chemical, electrical, industrial, mechanical engineering, information technology, logistics, Internet, multimedia, graphic design, architecture); liberal arts (international relations, Spanish majors with requisite business or technical experience and exceptional Spanish skills may also apply. Please note that placement for other liberal arts majors is almost impossible). Candidates must have at least two years post-secondary study of Spanish (fluency required for Internship Option). For complete eligibility requirements, please visit the web site.

Contact:
CDS International
Internship Program in Argentina
871 United Nations Plaza, 15th Floor
New York, NY 10017-1814
Phone: (212) 497-3500
Fax: (212) 497-3535
E-mail: usabroad@cdsintl.org
www.cdsintl.org

CDS International, Inc., Internship Program in Germany

 THE BUZZ
- "Cultural immersion in Germany"

 THE STATS

Industry(ies): Engineering; Financial Services; Technology; Tourism/Recreation; and others

Location(s): Various cities; Germany

Number of interns: Unlimited

Pay: Paid and unpaid. Financial support may be available through the CDS International Scholarship Fund. Interns pay program fee ($700 – includes work authorization, internship placement, orientation materials or seminar, and program support)

Length of internship: Up to 18 months for year-round programs; 3 months for summer program

 THE SCOOP

CDS International, now in its 37th year, is a nonprofit organization committed to the advancement of international career training opportunities customized to provide individuals with in-depth practical knowledge of other nations' business practices, cultures and political traditions. These experiences help strengthen global cooperation and understanding among individuals, businesses, organizations and communities. Each year, CDS serves approximately 1,700 individuals from almost 60 nations around the globe. For U.S. college/university students and recent graduates, CDS offers a variety of programs to Germany, Argentina, Spain, Switzerland and Russia.

 ON THE JOB

This program provides practical training opportunities in Germany for American students and recent graduates and non-U.S. citizens enrolled in an accredited U.S. college or university. Paid and unpaid placements are available in business, finance, technical and engineering fields for usually six (enrolled students) to 12 months (extension possible up to a total of 18 months for graduates). An optional one-month intensive language course is available prior to the start of the internship phase. Programs start individually at the beginning of each month (June for summer programs). Apply approximately five months prior to your desired start date, or by December 15 for summer program.

GETTING HIRED

Apply by: Rolling. Candidates should submit a complete application at least five months prior to desired start date. Candidates for the Summer Internship Program must submit application materials by December 15 for consideration. Download the application online at: www.cdsintl.org/fromusa/ipgerm.htm (year-round program) or www.cdsintl.org/fromusa/sip.htm (summer program). Only complete applications (with application fee) will be considered.

Qualifications

Candidates must be U.S. or Canadian citizens, between the ages of 18-30. Non-U.S. citizens enrolled full-time at a U.S. college/university may be eligible. Please contact the program officer for more information. At least one two years at a university/college in a field related to one of the following is required: business (general administration, marketing, PR, sales, advertising, finance, hotel management); technical fields (chemical, electrical, industrial, mechanical engineering, information technology, logistics, Internet, multimedia, graphic design, architecture); liberal arts (international relations, German majors with requisite business or technical experience and exceptional German skills may also apply. Please note that placement for other liberal arts majors is almost impossible). Candidates must have at least two years post-secondary study of German. For complete eligibility requirements, please visit the web site.

Contact:
CDS International
Internship Program in Germany
871 United Nations Plaza, 15th Floor
New York, NY 10017-1814
Phone: (212) 497-3500
Fax: (212) 497-3535
E-mail: usabroad@cdsintl.org
www.cdsintl.org

Visit Vault at **www.vault.com** for insider company profiles, expert advice, career message boards, expert resume reviews, the Vault Job Board and more.

VAULT CAREER LIBRARY 101

CDS International, Inc., Summer Internship Program in Spain

 THE BUZZ

- "Live and work in Spain next summer!"

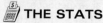 **THE STATS**

Industry(ies): Engineering; Financial Services; Technology; Tourism/Recreation; and others

Location(s): Various cities; Spain

Number of interns: Unlimited

Pay: None. Host companies are asked to provide non-monetary compensation such as free housing, meal stipends, through the CDS International Scholarship Fund. Interns pay program fee ($700 – includes work authorization, internship placement, orientation materials or seminar, and program support)

Length of internship: *Summer*: June-August

THE SCOOP

CDS, now in its 37th year, is a nonprofit organization committed to the advancement of international career training opportunities customized to provide individuals with in-depth practical knowledge of other nations' business practices, cultures and political traditions. These experiences help strengthen global cooperation and understanding among individuals, businesses, organizations and communities. Each year, CDS serves approximately 1,700 individuals from almost 60 nations around the globe. For U.S. college/university students and recent graduates CDS offers a variety of programs to Germany, Argentina, Spain, Switzerland and Russia.

ON THE JOB

This program (June to August) provides an opportunity to American and Canadian students to complete professional internships in Spain in a variety of fields. Internships start in early June for three months in Spain. The program ends mid-August for all participants. All internships are unpaid. However, host companies will be asked to provide some form of nonmonetary compensation, such as free housing, meals, and/or public transportation to and from work.

GETTING HIRED

Apply by: January 15. Candidates should submit a complete application for consideration. Download the application online at www.cdsintl.org/fromusa/sipsp.htm. Only complete applications (with application fee) will be considered.

Qualifications:

Candidates must be U.S. or Canadian citizens. U.S. citizens must be full-time enrolled students at an accredited U.S. college or university before, during and after the program. Applicants must be between the ages of 19-30. The equivalent of two years of post-secondary study of Spanish is required. Participants must be able to function in a Spanish-speaking work environment. It is in the participants' best interest to practice and take additional Spanish classes before the program starts. At least two years of study in business, marketing, sales, advertising, public relations, finance, engineering, information technology, logistics, multimedia, graphic design, mass communication, biosciences, computer science, hotel management/tourism or liberal arts such as international relations, Spanish, social sciences or economics. For complete eligibility requirements, visit the web site.

Contact:
CDS International, Inc.
Summer Internship Program in Spain
871 United Nations Plaza, 15th Floor
New York, NY 10017-1814
Phone: (212) 497-3500
Fax: (212) 497-3535
E-mail: usabroad@cdsintl.org
www.cdsintl.org

Center for an Urban Future

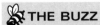 **THE BUZZ**
- "A think-on-your-feet think tank"
- "Report-and shape-NYC policy"

 **THE STATS**

Industry(ies): Public Policy; Research; Journalism

Location(s): New York, NY

Number of interns: *Per session:* 1

Pay: Unpaid; can receive academic credit

Length of internship: *Winter session:* February-May; *Summer session:* June-September; *Fall session:* September-January; minimum 20 hours/week

 **THE SCOOP**

Founded nearly 10 years ago, the Center for an Urban Future is a New York-based think and policy organization known for credible, fact-based research and solutions-oriented studies. Its aim is to produce policy solutions for urban problems, especially in New York City. The Center accomplishes this by conducting journalistic research, producing policy reports, providing extensive links to policy and news resources on its web site, and by hosting forums, often in partnership with other New York City organizations. The sister organization of City Limits magazine, the Center's policy analysis focuses on economic development, higher education and workforce development.

ON THE JOB

The policy research intern will assist staff in researching a variety of issues impacting New York City, primarily on studies related to economic and workforce development. The intern's responsibilities include conducting phone interviews, doing Web research, attending policy meetings and writing. Other duties include coordinating meetings with government officials, maintaining the Center's database and assisting on all reports.

GETTING HIRED

Apply by: *Winter:* January 1; *Summer:* May 1; *Fall:* August 15. To apply, send resume and cover letter by fax, e-mail or traditional mail to the address below.

Qualifications:
No age requirement. Experience in journalism or public policy research preferred.

Contact:
Center for an Urban Future
120 Wall Street, 20th Floor
New York, NY 10005
Fax: (212) 344-6457
E-mail: Intern@nycfuture.org
www.nycfuture.org

Center for Investigative Reporting

 THE BUZZ
- "For the future Woodwards and Bernsteins out there"

THE STATS

Industry(ies): Journalism

Location(s): San Francisco, CA; Washington, DC

Number of interns: *Annual:* 4-6

Pay: $500 monthly stipend

Length of internship: About 5 months (15-20 hours/week minimum); shorter internships in the summer are sometimes considered

THE SCOOP

Since the founding of the Center for Investigative Reporting in 1977, hundreds of investigations and stories have exposed social injustice and abuse of power. CIR launches hard-hitting investigations and intensive research to cover stories that local media often miss.

ON THE JOB

CIR internships allow future investigative reporters to develop necessary skills by working part-time for five months with investigative journalists. Once assigned a project, they provide research assistance and perform administrative duties from the project's beginning stages to publication or broadcast.

GETTING HIRED

Apply by: *Winter/spring:* December 1; *summer/fall:* May 1. Regular starting dates are approximately February 1 (*winter/sring*) and July 1 (*summer/fall*). Applicants for *winter/spring* will be notified of a decision by December 21. To apply submit a resume, a cover letter stating your interest and summarizing your background, and a few writing samples with your name on each sheet. Samples should demonstrate a clear and concise writing style. Published work is not a prerequisite for consideration. Include a transcript for review if you would like to receive academic credit.

Qualifications:
Open to college juniors and seniors.

Contact:
Center for Investigative Reporting
Attention: Erica Baker, Operations Manager
131 Steuart Street, Suite 600
San Francisco, CA 94105
Phone: (415) 543-1200, ext. 301
Fax: (415) 543-8311
E-mail: center@cironline.org
www.muckraker.org/jobs_internships.php

Visit Vault at **www.vault.com** for insider company profiles, expert advice, career message boards, expert resume reviews, the Vault Job Board and more.

V∆ULT CAREER LIBRARY **103**

Center for Strategic and International Studies

 THE BUZZ
- "Analyze global strategy at this top DC think tank"

 THE STATS

Industry(ies): Government

Location(s): Washington, DC

Number of interns: *Annual*: 150

Pay: None

Length of internship: *Summer*: 3 months; *fall*: 4 months; *spring*: 5 months

 THE SCOOP

The Center for Strategic and International Studies (CSIS) works to provide leaders of the world with an analytical look at existing and emerging global issues, along with strategic solutions. Founded over 40 years ago, The Center is now run by former Deputy Secretary of Defense John Hamre. CSIS has a staff of 190 researchers and assistants who work in three subject areas: addressing challenges to international and national security; maintaining resident experts on all of the world's regions; and developing new methods of governance. CSIS is private and nonpartisan.

 ON THE JOB

Interns' duties include research, writing and clerical tasks. They also attend seminars and meetings with leaders in the public policy field. Interns work on a variety of programs, depending on the organization's needs. Programs include those focusing on technology and public policy, international trade and finance, and energy.

$ GETTING HIRED

Apply by: *Summer*: March 1; *fall*: July 1; *spring*: November 1. Send resume, cover letter, writing sample (1,150 words or less), official transcript(s) and three letters of reference to the address below.

Qualifications:
Open to college juniors and seniors, recent college graduates and graduate students. Applicants must have 3.0 GPA or higher and be eligible to work in the U.S.

Contact:
Shavshigeh Howard
Internship Coordinator
Center for Strategic and International Studies
1800 K Street, NW, Suite 400
Washington, DC 20006
Phone: (202) 887-0200
Fax: (202) 775-3199
E-mail: internships@csis.org
www.csis.org
.

Center for Talented Youth

 THE BUZZ
- "Work with kids smarter than you"

 **THE STATS**

Industry(ies): Education

Location(s): Alexandria, VA; Baltimore, MD; Bethlehem, PA; Bristol, RI; Carlisle, PA; Chestertown, MD; Easton, PA; Kaneohe, HI; Lancaster, PA; Los Angeles, CA; Loudonville, NY; Owings Mills, MD; Palo Alto, CA; Sandy Spring, MD; Santa Cruz, CA; Saratoga Springs, NY; South Hadley, MA; St. Mary's City, MD; Tempe, AZ; Thousand Oaks, CA

Number of interns: *Annual*: About 1,500 in total of all locations

Pay: Paid; *instructional assistants*: $950/session; *resident assistants*: $1,050/session; *instructors*: $1,800-$2,800/session, depending upon experience. Room and board are provided at residential sites

Length of internship: 3 weeks, offered in 2 separate summer sessions

Contact:
CTY Summer Programs Employment
Johns Hopkins University
2701 North Charles Street
Baltimore, MD 21218
Phone: (410) 516-0053
Fax: (410) 516-0093
E-mail: ctysummer@jhu.edu
www.cty.jhu.edu/summer/employment.html

THE SCOOP

The Center for Talented Youth at Johns Hopkins University has been offering academic summer enrichment programs for high-achieving young students since 1979. Students range from second- to 11th-graders and all have scored in the top two percent nationally on standardized tests. The classes are designed to challenge and develop the students' academic skills by providing them with an opportunity to learn at a pace and depth that matches their abilities. CTY offers both residential and day programs.

ON THE JOB

CTY instructors are responsible for planning and conducting class sessions, as well as monitoring and assessing the students' progress. Instructional assistants work in both classroom and laboratory settings preparing materials for class, supervising study sessions, tutoring and assisting instructors during class sessions. Resident assistants are responsible for students at all times when they are out of class and are involved in preparing and conducting student activities. Other administrative positions may also be available. A complete list can be found on the web site.

GETTING HIRED

Apply by: Rolling. Applications are accepted beginning January 31 and recruiting continues until all positions are filled. An application form (available on the web site), transcript and a letter of recommendation are required. Applications may be submitted by fax, but original materials must follow in the mail.

Qualifications:
Open to college freshmen, sophomores, juniors and seniors, recent grads and graduate students. Teaching assistants and resident assistants are usually college students or recent graduates. They should have a GPA of 3.2 or above and some experience working with children. Graduate students who have teaching experience with children or adolescents may be considered for instructor positions.

Visit Vault at **www.vault.com** for insider company profiles, expert advice, career message boards, expert resume reviews, the Vault Job Board and more.

VAULT CAREER LIBRARY 105

Center for the Study of Conflict

 THE BUZZ
- "All we are saying is give peace a chance"
- "Look for a nonviolent conflict resolution"

 THE STATS

Industry(ies): Government; Nonprofit

Location(s): Baltimore, MD

Number of interns: *Annual*: 3

Pay: None; academic credit; assistance finding an apartment if from outside the Baltimore area

Length of internship: 2-5 months or more; available year-round

 THE SCOOP

Established in 1982, the Center for the Study of Conflict works to understand how conflicts can be resolved through nonviolent methods. The group studies interindividual, intergroup and international conflict. Examples include domestic issues (like Baltimore's ongoing criminal activity) and international unrest (like Swiss social policies and its political structure). The Center is currently researching nonmilitary solutions to nuclear threats and attacks.

 ON THE JOB

Interns get a variety of hands-on experience while working for The Center. Responsibilities may include administrative tasks, researching history and social science, and writing and editing Center reports and publications. Interns also help in The Center's fundraising events.

$ GETTING HIRED

Apply by: Send a resume and cover letter and names and phone numbers of at least one work reference and one academic reference to address below.

Qualifications:
Open to college freshmen, sophomores, juniors and seniors, recent college graduates and grad students.

Contact:
Center for the Study of Conflict
Dr. Richard Wendell Fogg, Director
5846 Bellona Avenue
Baltimore, MD 21212
Phone: (410) 323-7656

Central Intelligence Agency

 THE BUZZ
- "The ultimate patriot game"
- "Potheads need not apply"

 **THE STATS**

Industry(ies): Government

Location(s): Washington, DC

Number of interns: Varies

Pay: None. Scholarships available for housing

Length of internship: *Spring* (January-July) and *fall* (July-December): 6 months; *summer*: 3 months

 THE SCOOP

The Central Intelligence Agency was created in 1947 as part of President Truman's National Security Act. The agency collects, analyzes and coordinates foreign intelligence and counter-intelligence. The CIA is an independent agency that reports to the President and is accountable to the American people.

ON THE JOB

Undergrads can apply for the general three-month summer program (which they must combine with a semester internship or another summer at the CIA). Or they can apply to the six-month internships, which focus on a specific regional or transnational issue division, supporting intelligence reporting operations and overseas outposts. The agency also offers a six-month graduate program, which provides similar job experience as the undergrad program at a slightly higher level. Or they can do a more basic internship in the summer. Students who complete the six-month program can apply for the Professional Trainee program or the Clandestine Service Trainee program.

 GETTING HIRED

Apply by: *Spring*: July; *fall*: January; *summer*: November. To download the application, go to: www.cia.gov/employment/student.html#dousp, or submit a resume online at www.cia.gov/employment/resume.html.

Qualifications:
The undergraduate programs are open to college freshmen, sophomores, juniors and seniors. The graduate programs are open to all graduate courses. A minimum 3.0 GPA is required. Previous international and military residency, the ability to speak at least one foreign language, good communication skills and a strong interest in foreign affairs are all recommended. Minority students are encouraged to apply. Applicants must be American citizens.

Contact:
Internship Coordinator
Phone: (800) 368-3886
www.cia.gov/employment/student.html#req

Centro para los Adolescentes de San Miguel de Allende

 THE BUZZ
- "Not just for Spanish-speaking MD wanabees"
- "Give your time and energy where it's needed most"

 **THE STATS**

Industry(ies): Education; Health Care (especially adolescent and reproductive); Nonprofit

Location(s): San Miguel de Allende, Mexico

Number of interns: *Annual*: around 10

Pay: None

Length of internship: 10 weeks minimum

 THE SCOOP

Centro Para Los Adolescentes De San Miguel, or C.A.S.A. is a non-profit organization that has been serving the poor, particularly adolescents and rural women, through health, social service and educational outreach programs since 1981. It offers reproductive and general health information, as well as family health care, prenatal and childbirth services, day care, and health training/education. Located in the lovely colonial town of San Miguel de Allende, C.A.S.A. employs over 80 doctors, nurses and support staff, and reaches over 50,000 clients each year.

 ON THE JOB

C.A.S.A. interns must be self-motivated and willing to take the initiative in working with staff to identify unmet needs and projects. Depending on availability, interns may work in any C.A.S.A program that interests them, including the educational outreach program, maternity hospital/family health clinic, library, child development center, and the counseling and anti-violence program. Past intern projects have included the development of health education materials, program evaluation and volunteer management. Since the center sees so many cases in a day (it's located in the state of Guanajuato, which has over 4 million residents and one of the bleakest health records in Mexico), while working together toward their individual learning goals, interns also assist with fundraising, writing newsletters, grant-writing and other administrative tasks.

GETTING HIRED

Apply by: Rolling; apply three months from the desired start date. Send resume, cover letter, two letters of recommendation and the answers to two short essay questions in Spanish.

Qualifications:
Open to college freshmen, sophomores, juniors and seniors, recent college graduates and grad students. Applicants must speak and understand Spanish fluently.

Contact:
Centro Para Los Adolescentes De San Miguel
Internship Program
Santa Julia 15, San Miguel de Allende
Guanajuato
Mexico 37734
E-mail: internos@sanmiguel-casa.org
www.sanmiguel-casa.org

CH2M Hill

 THE BUZZ
- "Budding civil engineers wanted"
- "Build stuff that works with the environment"

 THE STATS

Industry(ies): Engineering

Location(s): Denver, CO

Number of interns: Varies

Pay: Paid; varies according to position

Length of internship: Varies; available year-round

THE SCOOP

An employee-owned, multinational engineering firm, CH2M Hill works on infrastructure projects from start to finish. The company's strange name is a combination of the four founders' initials (two of whom had names beginning with H), who joined forces in 1946. Hill came later, when CH2M merged with Clair A. Hill & Associates in 1971.

ON THE JOB

Interns work closely with professional staff in a variety of departments. Open positions depend on the company's need. Interns may work on projects surrounding agricultural development, erosion control, roads and highways, ports and harbors, telecommunications, fossil fuels and water treatment, for example. Many of the internship positions have an environmental component.

GETTING HIRED

Apply by: Rolling. Apply for specific positions online: www.ch2m.com/flash/careers/careers_frame.htm.

Qualifications:
Open to college freshmen, sophomores, juniors and seniors, recent college graduates and graduate students. Some positions are open to high school students, as well. Some positions have more specific criteria; see www.ch2m.com/flash/careers/careers_frame.htm for more details. An educational background in the sciences, environmental studies or architecture is helpful.

Contact:
Internship Coordinator
CH2M Hill
9191 South Jamaica Street
Englewood, CO 80112
Phone: (303) 774-0900
Fax: (720) 286-9250
E-mail: feedback@ch2m.com
www.ch2m.com

Visit Vault at **www.vault.com** for insider company profiles, expert advice, career message boards, expert resume reviews, the Vault Job Board and more.

V\ULT CAREER LIBRARY **107**

Chamber Music America

 THE BUZZ
- "Future Bach heads should apply"
- "Music to your resume"

 THE STATS

Industry(ies): Music/Records; Publishing; Theater/Performing Arts

Location(s): New York, NY

Number of interns: Varies

Pay: Stipend of $250-$500/month

Length of Internship: Varies

 THE SCOOP

Chamber Music America was established in 1977 by a group of musicians to further artistic quality and adequate funding for chamber music professionals. It also produces *Chamber Music*, a full-color magazine featuring news, interviews and reviews all about chamber music. With a membership totaling nearly 10,000, CMA offers residencies for musicians, professional and educational activities, and various chamber music services across the country.

ON THE JOB

CMA interns' duties include proofreading the magazine and membership directory, Internet research and clerical tasks. Interns work in the membership department, on the magazine, coordinating conferences and CMA events, in administration, or in the program or development departments.

GETTING HIRED

Apply by: Rolling. See the web site for details.

Qualifications:
Open to college sophomores, juniors, seniors and grad students. Send a cover letter and resume via e-mail or fax. General office skills and a passion for music are a plus.

Contact:
Chamber Music America
Kevin Russell
Director of Administration
305 Seventh Avenue, 5th Floor
New York, NY 10001
Phone: (212) 242-2022
Fax: (212) 242-7955
E-mail: krussell@chamber-music.org
www.chamber-music.org/about_cma/opportunities.htm

Charlesbridge Publishing

 THE BUZZ
- "Learn about inner-workings of a major publishing firm"
- "The write stuff"

THE STATS

Industry(ies): Publishing

Location(s): Watertown, MA

Number of interns: *Summer/fall/winter/spring*: 1 editorial intern and 1 design intern per term

Pay: None

Length of internship: *Summer/fall/winter/spring*: 12 weeks each

 THE SCOOP

Founded in 1980, Charlesbridge Publishing produces books for children, including picture books, transitional "bridge books" and books that range in age and audience from early readers to middle-grade chapter books. The company works with leading authors in the science, education, reading and writing fields to develop classroom materials that teach thinking strategies, the writing process and scientific methods. Charlesbridge's nonfiction addresses nature, science, social studies and multicultural topics, and their fiction titles are plot-driven stories with strong, engaging protagonists. Titles range from *Ace Lacewing: Bug Detective* and *Alice In Pastaland* to *Sir Cumference and the First Round Table* and *Wood-Hoopoe Willie*.

ON THE JOB

Charlesbridge relies on its interns to do substantive work, and interns learn the process of picture book publishing, from submission and production to publication. The editorial intern acts as an editorial assistant, reading and evaluating unsolicited manuscripts, writing rejection letters, fact-checking, and providing clerical support for the department, including copyright and catalog-in-publication submissions to the Library of Congress. The design intern aids and assists the art director and designers in the trade book department. In the process, the intern learns about art direction, the organization of original art work, its preparation for in-house review, and the printing process.

GETTING HIRED

Apply by: *Fall*: July; *winter*: October; *spring*: January; *summer*: March/mid-April. Submit a resume and cover letter.

Qualifications:
Open to college juniors and seniors, recent college graduates and graduate students.

Contact:
Alyssa Pusey
Managing Editor
Charlesbridge Publishing
85 Main Street
Watertown, MA 02472
Phone: (617) 926-0329
www.charlesbridge.com

The Charlie Rose Show

 THE BUZZ

- "For ardent PBS watchers and aspiring TV pros"

 **THE STATS**

Industry(ies): Broadcast & Entertainment

Location(s): New York, NY

Number of interns: *Fall/spring/summer*: 8 each

Pay: None; academic credit

Length of internship: 4 months; *fall*: September-December; *spring*: January-May; *summer*: May-August

 **THE SCOOP**

An award-winning former anchor of *Nightwatch*, Charlie Rose now has his own weeknight television series interviewing the best thinkers, writers, politicians, athletes, entertainers, business leaders, scientists and other newsmakers. Rose and his guests discuss a wide range of current events in both one-on-one interviews and roundtable discussions.

ON THE JOB

Interns handle administrative needs (filing, faxing, running errands), but their main responsibility is researching the show's guests. Recent guests have ranged from rapper Jay-Z to actor Leonardo DiCaprio. Interns are also responsible for meeting and greeting guests, setting up the greenroom and facilitating taping segments. For more information, please visit www.charlierose.com.

GETTING HIRED

Apply by: Rolling. Apply with resume and letter of interest. Candidates require an on-site interview.

Qualifications:

Open to college freshmen, sophomores, juniors and seniors, as well as recent grads and graduate students. Preferred majors include communications, journalism, English, history, drama/arts and economics.

Contact:
Noelle Balnicki
The Charlie Rose Show
731 Lexington Avenue, 7E
New York, NY 10022
Phone: (212) 617-1600
E-mail: crinterns@bloomberg.com
www.charlierose.com

Chevron

THE BUZZ

- "A major name in oil; no gas pump time required"

THE STATS

Industry(ies): Energy/Utilities; Science/Research

Location(s): Anchorage, AK; Coral Gables, FL; Houston, TX; Lafayette, LA; Los Angeles, CA; Midland, TX; New Orleans, LA; San Ramon, CA; select international locations

Number of interns: *Summer*: 450

Pay: Paid; *undergraduate*: $750-$1200/week; *grad student*: $1,000-$2,000/week. Round-trip travel; temporary lodging allowance

Length of internship: Varies

THE SCOOP

An integrated energy company, Chevron Corporation also sells products internationally under the brand names Caltex, Havoline and Delo, with a main focus on developing additives, aviation products, chemicals, lubricants, marine products, fuels, power services, specialty products and energy services. Based in Northern California and Houston, Texas, the company's roots stem from an 1876 oil discovery at Pico Canyon, near Los Angeles, Calif. and an 1879 discovery in Texas. It employs over 53,000 people worldwide.

ON THE JOB

Interns hold a variety of roles in several Chevron offices around the world and are placed in departments such as accounting, engineering, earth science, finance development, human resources and information technology. The firm also offers an extensive MBA Development Program internship for grad students. As the company often hires for entry-level positions from its intern pool, the programs are set up to help Chevron learn about the intern, as well as teaching the intern about the company.

GETTING HIRED

Apply by: Rolling. The company prefers that those interested apply through their college's career center (the company recruits at specific schools). You can also apply for open positions online: http://www.chevron.com/about/careers/.

Qualifications:

Most programs are open to junior and senior undergraduates, but several seek graduate students or those pursuing doctoral degrees. Check the Chevron careers web site for specific program requirements.

Contact:
Chevron Corporation
6001 Bollinger Canyon Road
San Ramon, CA 94583
Phone: (925) 842-1000
www.chevron.com/about/careers/internship_index.asp
www.chevron.com/about/careers/

Visit Vault at **www.vault.com** for insider company profiles, expert advice, career message boards, expert resume reviews, the Vault Job Board and more.

VAULT CAREER LIBRARY **109**

Chicago Botanic Garden

 THE BUZZ
- "An internship by any other name would be as sweet"

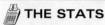 **THE STATS**

Industry(ies): Education; Environmental; Public Relations; Sciencec

Location(s): Glencoe, IL

Number of interns: *Annual*: 18-25

Pay: Paid; $8.65/hour

Length of internship: Depends on program; generally from 3-12 months, working 37.5-40 hours/week

 THE SCOOP

The Chicago Botanic Garden is 385 acres in total, consisting of 23 gardens, three natural habitat facilities, 81 waterway acres, nine islands, six miles of shoreline, 15 prairie acres and 100 acres of woodlands. The Garden was built in 1965 by the Chicago Horticultural Society, which has been putting on flower shows and gardening events in Chicago since 1890.

ON THE JOB

Interns gain skills in education, horticulture, public relations or research as they pertain to horticultural studies and related fields. They can work in conservation science, community garden, horticulture, plant breeding, plant information and living plant documentation.

GETTING HIRED

Apply by: Most positions fill up by March 15, although applicants are encouraged to apply as late as May 31. Applications can be submitted through the web site (at www.chicagobotanic.org/internship/InternApplication.html). Send applications along with a cover letter, resume, an essay (minimum of 1,000 words, answering the following questions: What kind of work-study do you envision yourself performing at the Chicago Botanic Garden? What skills would you like to attain and/or improve upon? How will this work experience help you to achieve future work-related goals?), and current transcripts. Three letters of recommendation are also required, all mailed directly to the internship coordinator. Applications will not be considered until all five components are received. Applications are considered "active" for up to six months from date of receipt.

Qualifications:
Open to college freshmen, sophomores, juniors and seniors, graduate students and recent grads. Most divisions require a horticulture major, botany or related experience.

Contact:
Human Resources
Attention: Internships
Chicago Botanic Garden
1000 Lake Cook Road
Glencoe, IL 60022
Fax: (847) 835-4263
E-mail: humanresources@chicagobotanic.org
www.chicagobotanic.org/internship/index.html

Chicago Bulls

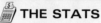 **THE BUZZ**
- "Start a sports career of Micheal Jordan-like prominence"
- "Heaven for basketball fanatics"

THE STATS

Industry(ies): Sports

Location(s): Chicago, IL

Number of interns: 10-14 full-time ticket sales representatives

Pay: Paid; $6.50/hour (minimum wage). Flat-fee tiered commission structure for all sales that exceed the minimum wage draw; potential weekly/monthly bonus; parking and lunch at United Center provided daily; 2 complimentary tickets to each Bulls home game

Length of internship: Approximateley 9 months (July-February)

THE SCOOP

The Bulls, Chicago's professional basketball team, debuted in 1966. The team was made famous, however, by Michael Jordan and his 1990s NBA dynasty. Since Jordan's departure from the sport, the team has been "re-organizing."

ON THE JOB

The team hires interns as ticket sales representatives, and their job is to drum up new season and group ticket sales through phone leads provided by the company. Each is expected to make 50 calls per workday. Interns also follow up the phone leads with mailings, and field incoming requests for season ticket and group ticket sales information, as well as provide back up assistance to other departments, such as marketing, when needed. For current openings, see www.nba.com/bulls/news/employment_010328.html.

GETTING HIRED

Apply by: Rolling. Send a cover letter and resume to the address below.

Qualifications:
Open to recent graduates and grad students (the company prefers that applicants have a four-year college degree in sports administration, business, advertising, marketing, communications or liberal arts). Sales experience is a plus.

Contact:
Internship Coordinator
Chicago Bulls
1901 West Madison Street
Chicago, IL 60612-2459
www.nba.com/bulls/news/employment_010328.html

Chicago Children's Museum

 THE BUZZ

- "Work on Navy Pier"
- "Reach the whole of Chicago"
- "Great community connections"

 THE STATS

Industry(ies): Art/Museum; Education

Location(s): Chicago, IL

Number of interns: Varies

Pay: $100 stipend

Length of internship: 200 hours; available year-round

THE SCOOP

The Chicago Children's Museum aims "to create a community where play and learning connect." CCM receives more than 500,000 visitors annually, with its primary audience consisting of children up through the fifth grade and their families.

ON THE JOB

CCM's interns work in various departments, including human resources, volunteer and intern services, public relations, special events, exhibits and education. Mentoring opportunities are available with a supervisor in the intern's chosen field. Interns usually work 10-25 hours a week, depending on the season.

GETTING HIRED

Apply by: Rolling. Send cover letter, resume and three outside references. Applications are available on the web site.

Qualifications:
Open to college juniors, seniors and graduates.

Contact:
LaWanda M. May
Director of Volunteer & Intern Resources
Chicago Children's Museum
700 East Grand Avenue, Suite 127
Chicago, IL 60611
Phone: (312) 464-7652
Fax: (312) 527-9082
E-mail: LaWandaM@Chichildrensmuseum.org
www.ChiChildrensMuseum.org/voluntr.cfm

Children's Defense Fund

THE BUZZ

- "Now's your chance to work on behalf of children"

THE STATS

Industry(ies): Education; Health Care; Law; Nonprofit

Location(s): Washington, DC

Number of interns: *Annual*: 60-70

Pay: None; academic credit

Length of internship: *Summer*: 8-10 weeks; *fall/spring*: 10-16 weeks each

THE SCOOP

The Children's Defense Fund was founded in 1973 by its current president, Marian Wright Edelman. Headquartered in Washington, DC, the main office staffs about 100 workers who speak for the children of America who cannot vote, lobby or speak for themselves. CDF strives to ensure that all American children who need it gain access to immunizations, health care, child care, Head Start programs, education, adoption, mental health attention, protection in the juvenile justice systems and welfare programs, as well as a chance to escape poverty. The organization is nonprofit and supported by foundations, corporation grants and individual donations.

ON THE JOB

CDF interns are split into four working groups: programs and policy, movement-building and outreach programs, nonprofit management and legal internships. Interns support professional staff by drafting memoranda, issue analyses, research, planning rallies and conferences, attending meetings, and tracking relevant legislation. They work as part of a children's advocacy education program exploring CDF's mission and goals, and attend eight to 10 seminar lunches.

GETTING HIRED

Apply by: *Summer*: March 1; *fall*: July 15; *spring*: November 1. Online application form available at: www.childrensdefense.org/internships/application.asp. Send the completed form, a cover letter, resume, three references or two letters of recommendation and a writing sample (no longer than 2,500 words) – required for all legal intern applicants – to the address below. Phone interview required.

Qualifications:
Open to college freshmen, sophomores, juniors, seniors and recent grads, as well as graduate and law students.

Contact:
Warren Buford, Internship Coordinator
Children's Defense Fund
25 E Street, NW
Washington, DC 20001
Phone: (202) 662-3502
Fax: (202) 662-3570
E-mail: wbuford@childrensdefense.org
www.childrensdefense.org/internships

Visit Vault at **www.vault.com** for insider company profiles, expert advice, career message boards, expert resume reviews, the Vault Job Board and more.

 VAULT CAREER LIBRARY 111

Children's Museum of Indianapolis

 THE BUZZ
- "Passionate Midwestern educators wanted"
- "Intern at the world's largest museum built for children"

 THE STATS

Industry(ies): Art/Museum; Education; Nonprofit; Tourism/Recreation

Location(s): Indianapolis, IN

Number of interns: *Annual:* 60

Pay: None; limited number of museum scholarships available. Academic credit given; access to museum; professional development series with field trips; discount at food court and museum store

Length of internship: *Summer/winter/fall:* 10-16 weeks each

 THE SCOOP

The Children's Museum of Indianapolis has been enriching and educating children through exhibitions, galleries and theater since 1925. The 433,000 square foot museum houses 10 major art galleries, and 13 galleries overall, which take an interactive approach to nature, science, history and the arts. The Children's Museum offers over 4,000 programs and activities every year and maintains a collection of over 110,000 artifacts.

 ON THE JOB

Interns learn the day-to-day operations of a major museum in fields related to education, collections, graphic arts, exhibit design, theater, gallery interpretation, marketing, public relations, and development from hands-on experience and assigned staff mentors.

GETTING HIRED

Apply by: *Summer:* April 4 29; *fall:* August 4; *spring:* December 4. Applications should be in by these dates, or approximately 6 weeks before the start of each semester. Download the online application form, available under the general information tab, at www.childrensmuseum.org/generalinfo/interns.htm. Mail, e-mail or fax a cover letter, resume, transcript and completed application.

Qualifications:

Open to two- or four-year college students, recent graduates and graduate students. A passion to work with or for children, good interpersonal skills and the ability to articulate goals are required. Students from all majors and interests are encouraged to apply, and international students are accepted.

Contact:
Intern Program Manager
The Children's Museum of Indianapolis
P.O. Box 3000
Indianapolis, IN 46206
Phone: (317) 334-3830
Fax: (317) 920-2028
E-mail: interncentral@childrensmuseum.org
www.childrensmuseum.org

Child's Play Touring Theatre

 THE BUZZ
- "Play dress up with the kids"
- "Open kids up to a world of endless possibilities"

 THE STATS

Industry(ies): Theater/Performing Arts

Location(s): Chicago, IL

Number of interns: *Annual:* 8-12

Pay: Stipend available for lunch and transportation

Length of internship: Varies; available year-round. Minimum commitment of 8 weeks; 15 hours/week. Interns can also work full time

 THE SCOOP

Child's Play Touring Theatre, a nonprofit performance arts theater, focuses on producing and presenting stage works written by children. Based in Chicago for the past 21 years, Child's Play strives to ignite a child's imagination using theater professionals and educators. Its unique mission gives children an outlet for their writing and for their creative voices to be heard and appreciated.

 ON THE JOB

Interns' duties vary depending on department, but may include organizing touring material, clerical work, tracking financial income, gathering audit material, updating and maintaining mailing lists, organizing photo galleries, reading submissions, designing costumes and building sets.

GETTING HIRED

Apply by: Rolling.

Qualifications:

Open to high school students and college freshmen, sophomores, juniors and seniors, career changers and those returning to employment.

Contact:
Child's Play Touring Theater
2518 West Armitage Avenue
Chicago, IL 60647
Phone: (773) 235-8911 or (800) 353-3402
Fax: (773) 235-5478
E-mail: cptt@cptt.org
www.cptt.org/g-intern.htm

Chincoteague National Wildlife Refuge

THE BUZZ
- "Get a bird's eye view of an environmental career"

THE STATS

Industry(ies): Education; Environmental; Nonprofit; Science/ Research

Location(s): Chincoteague, VA

Number of interns: *Annual*: 1-5 within each department

Pay: Paid; $125/week. Housing provided

Length of internship: *Summer*: mid-May thru mid-August; *fall*: early-September thru late-November

THE SCOOP

Founded in 1943 to protect migratory birds, Chincoteague National Wildlife Refuge is made up of over 14,000 acres of beach, dunes, maritime forest and marsh, and is home to waterfowl, and various other animals and plants, including the famous wild horses. The Refuge helps restore threatened and endangered species, and provides environmental education to the public.

ON THE JOB

Placement is based on skills and interest. Participants can choose interpretative internships (communicating the refuge's mission to the public), environmental internships (designing environmental educational programs), or field research assistant/wildlife management positions (researching and conducting scientific activities). Interns may be able to participate in other refuge management programs.

GETTING HIRED

Apply by: Interpretive Internship/Field Research Assistant/ Wildlife Management Internship: *summer*: March 15; *fall*: August 1. Environmental Education Internship: *spring*: January 15. Submit a resume and cover letter, indicating area of interest.

Qualifications:

Open to college juniors and seniors, recent college graduates and graduate students with a background in wildlife biology, general biology, natural resource management, ecology or a related field. Good communication and writing skills, keen observational and recording skills, a willingness to work with people and a valid driver's license are required. Experience working with birds or a background in ornithology/general biology and computer skills are a plus.

Contact:
Chincoteague National Wildlife Refuge
Attention: Volunteer Coordinator
P.O. Box 62
Chincoteague, VA 23336
Phone: (757) 336-6122
Fax: (757) 336-5273

Choate Rosemary Hall

THE BUZZ
- "Choate students are blessed with an accomplished faculty and accomplished teaching interns"
- "Ideal for *Dead Poet's Society* fans"

THE STATS

Industry(ies): Education

Location(s): Wallingford, CT

Number of interns: *Summer*: 30-35

Pay: Paid; $2,800-$2,900/summer. Free room and board

Length of internship: *Summer*: 5-6 weeks

THE SCOOP

Dating back to 1890, Choate Rosemary Hall (often referred to simply as Choate) is a highly selective boarding and day secondary school in Connecticut. Choate students are fortunate to study with a very established faculty, and graduates typically go on to elite universities and colleges. Choate also runs a number of academic programs throughout the summer.

ON THE JOB

Teaching interns at the Choate summer program are very much part of the faculty. Interns assist two different senior teachers with classes of middle and/or high school students from around the world. The Choate Teaching Intern program is an especially good experience for those who are considering teaching in either public or private education. Interns live in the dormitory, serve as resident advisers, coach athletics and chaperone day trips.

GETTING HIRED

Apply by: January 13. Send an application plus a transcript, resume and two recommendations from college professors. Only completed applications are reviewed, and applications received after January 20 will not be reviewed. An on-campus interview may follow; interviews are scheduled for January 13 and January 27, 2007.

Qualifications:

Open to those completing at least their third year of college by summer 2007.

Contact:
James Irzyk
Director of Summer Programs
Teaching Internships
Choate Rosemary Hall
333 Christian Street
Wallingford, CT 06492-3800
Phone: (203) 697-2365
Fax: (203) 697-2519
E-mail: summer@choate.edu
www.choate.edu/summerprograms

Visit Vault at **www.vault.com** for insider company profiles, expert advice, career message boards, expert resume reviews, the Vault Job Board and more.

VAULT CAREER LIBRARY **113**

Christian Dior Couture

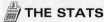 **THE BUZZ**

- "This fashion internship is très chic!"
- "Fashionable Francophiles wanted"

THE STATS

Industry(ies): Fashion; Retail

Location(s): New York, NY; Paris

Number of interns: Varies

Pay: Paid; varies depending on position

Length of internship: Varies with availability

THE SCOOP

Christian Dior studied political science before becoming the world's premier 1950s fashion designer. But in 1938, he had a change of heart. In 1953, he hired then-unknown Yves Saint-Laurent as his assistant. When Dior died in 1957, Saint-Laurent took the reigns as the company's head designer. With its goal to hit 1 billion euros in sales by 2007, Christian Dior is obviously optimistic about its future – and with good reason. The growth of this leading fashion company has been tremendous in the last years. Sales almost doubled between 1998 and 2002.

ON THE JOB

Christian Dior Couture offers a variety of internships through its parent company, LVMH. Most positions deal with sales in some capacity. Students interested in working for Dior should check out its ever-changing list of internship opportunities at www.lvmh.com under the "Internships" category. However, only students fluent in French and English need apply. (Other fashionable Francophile internships are available on the site as well, from fashion name Celine to bubbly purveyor Moet et Chandon.)

GETTING HIRED

Apply by: Deadlines vary depending on the position. E-mail resume to the address below.

Qualifications:
Open to college freshmen, sophomores, juniors and seniors fluent in both French and English. Fluency in a third language preferred.

Contact:
Christian Dior
19 East 57th Street
New York, NY
Phone: (212) 931-2200
Fax: (212) 751-7478
Paris headquarters
E-mail: mdrh@christiandior.fr
www.lvmh.com/lvmhetvous/pg_stages.asp?rub=13&srub=5

Christie's

THE BUZZ

- "Get closer to art than those pesky museum guards allow you to"
- "The internship for arts and antiques lovers"

THE STATS

Industry(ies): Art/Museum

Location(s): New York, NY

Number of interns: Varies

Pay: *Academic credit option*: weekly hours and the duration of the internship are in keeping with university requirements. *Paid option*: minimum wage (for those unable to receive academic credit)

Length of internship: *Spring* (January-May) and *fall* (September-December): 12-16 weeks each

THE SCOOP

English businessman James Christie held his first sale in 1766. Soon enough, members of the Royal Family were consigning works of art to him and Christie was negotiating with Catherine the Great. Today, Christie's, his legacy, holds auctions in major cities around the globe.

ON THE JOB

Christie's interns work on a variety of administrative projects meant to provide them with a basic understanding of the auction business. However, each intern also specializes in a department, depending on his or her own interests and educational background. Departments include publications and public relations, sales and appraisals, corporate collections, museum collections and education, among others.

GETTING HIRED

Apply by: *Spring*: November 30; *summer*: February 15; *fall*: July 15. E-mail or mail (see below) a resume and cover letter, listing all art history coursework.

Qualifications:
Open to college freshmen, sophomores, juniors and seniors, as well as recent graduates and grad students. Applicants must have taken some art history courses and it is preferred that they speak at least one language other than English.

Contact:
Christie's Human Resources
Internship Program
20 Rockefeller Plaza
New York, NY 10020
Fax: (212) 636-4945
E-mail: careers@christies.com
www.christies.com/careers/internship.asp

Chronicle of the Horse

 THE BUZZ
- "Giddy-up to a great editorial internship"
- "Spend your semester photographing man's other best friend"

 **THE STATS**

Industry(ies): Journalism; Publishing; Sports

Location(s): Middleburg, VA

Number of interns: *Annual*: 3 (1 per semester)

Pay: Paid; $6.50/hour

Length of internship: *Spring*: January-May; *summer*: June-August; *fall*: September-December

THE SCOOP

Since 1937, *Chronicle of the Horse* has operated as a weekly news magazine covering English riding and horse sports competitions. The magazine serves over 22,000 subscribers, featuring news, rider profiles and how-to articles related to English horse sports.

ON THE JOB

Internships give students an interactive experience in magazine publishing where the editorial department offers personal staff attention. Interns develop skills through a variety of activities including proofreading, researching, the chance to interview professionals for profiles and covering equestrian events. Interns may have the opportunity to serve as reporters on cover stories and learn about photography through events.

GETTING HIRED

Apply by: Rolling. Interviews must take place three to four months before intended start date. Send a resume and cover letter, including equestrian background, and writing sample.

Qualifications:

Open to college sophomores, juniors and seniors, and recent graduates with an interest in journalism. Background knowledge of competitive English horse sports is strongly suggested and photography talent is helpful.

Contact:
Attention: Molly Sorge, Assistant Editor
The Chronicle of the Horse
P.O. Box 46
Middleburg, VA 20118
Phone: (540) 687-6341
E-mail: staff@chronofhorse.com
www.chronofhorse.com/intern_info.html

CIGNA

 THE BUZZ
- "200 years of American health care"

THE STATS

Industry(ies): Financial Services; Health Care; Insurance

Location(s): Bloomfield, CT; Hartford, CT; Philadelphia, PA

Number of interns: *Summer*: varies

Pay: Paid; varies with position and experience. Summer housing provided.

Length of internship: *Summer*: 10-16 weeks

THE SCOOP

CIGNA was formed from two early American insurance companies. The first, founded as the Insurance Company of North America (INA) in 1792, was out of Philadelphia's Independence Hall. As the first insurance company in America (then offering mostly marine insurance), INA is the oldest in operation today. INA paid out life insurance policies for the Great Chicago Fire. In 1865, the governor of Connecticut signed an agreement to incorporate the Connecticut General Life Insurance Company (CG). Both companies became early insurers of flight. They merged in 1981, becoming the insurance firm now known as CIGNA. Today CIGNA is notable as a health benefits company with a portfolio of health, pharmacy, behavioral, dental, disability, life, accident and international businesses.

ON THE JOB

CIGNA's Summer Associates Program was established to teach interns about the company's products and services. The program also allows CIGNA to identify potential candidates for full-time hire. Interns receive training before working with a team on specific projects. Interns are placed into actuarial, health care or technology, among others. The finance and health care programs are open to graduate students only.

GETTING HIRED

Apply by: Rolling. Download an online application: www.cigna.com/general/careers/current_programs.html.

Qualifications:

Positions vary, but most are open to college sophomores, juniors and seniors, as well as grad students (the finance program is open only to MBA students; the health care program is only open to grad students). Applicants must have at least a 3.2 GPA.

Contact:
Summer Associates Coordinator
CIGNA
1650 Market Street, Floor 52
Philadelphia, PA 19103
Phone: (215) 716-1000
www.cigna.com/general/careers/summer.html

Visit Vault at **www.vault.com** for insider company profiles, expert advice, career message boards, expert resume reviews, the Vault Job Board and more.

VAULT CAREER LIBRARY **115**

CIIT Centers for Health Research

THE BUZZ

- "Stop another Love Canal"

THE STATS

Industry(ies): Health Care; Science/Research

Location(s): Research Triangle Park, NC

Number of interns: *Summer*: 10

Pay: Paid; $480/week

Length of internship: *Summer*: 10-12 weeks

 THE SCOOP

A private, nonprofit institute that researches the potential impact of chemicals on human health, CIIT Centers for Health Research is one of the preeminent environmental and health research institutes in the U.S. Its president and CEO is Dr. William F. Greenlee, a well known researcher in molecular toxicology. Eleven major chemical companies started CIIT in 1974, when concerns over the effects of chemicals on the environment and humans first arose.

ON THE JOB

CIIT's internship program began in 1989 to give those studying science a peek into different careers in the field. Interns work with CIIT staff on research projects and may include literature review, experiments, data analysis and interpretation of results. Many past interns have gone on to study toxicology in advanced degree programs. At the end of the summer, all interns present their research results.

GETTING HIRED

Apply by: March 1. Download an application at www.ciit.org/careers/applications/education_app.doc and send the completed form to the address below.

Qualifications:
Open to college freshmen, sophomores, juniors and seniors in science-related majors.

Contact:
Rusty Bramlage, Human Resources Director
CIIT Centers for Health Research
P.O. Box 12137
Research Triangle Park, NC 27709-2137
Phone: (919) 558-1331
E-mail: bramlage@ciit.org
www.ciit.org/training_edu/undergrade.asp

Citigroup Corporate and Investment Banking

THE BUZZ

- "Learn the banking biz with the crème de la crème"

THE STATS

Industry(ies): Financial Services

Location(s): Chicago, IL; Dallas, TX; Houston, TX; New York, NY; Palo Alto, CA; San Francisco, CA; Toronto, ON (Canada)

Number of interns: *Summer*: 200 across all business and in all offices

Pay: Paid; competitive salary. Some businesses will provide a housing stipend and arrange housing, and also offer free use of corporate gym

Length of internship: *Summer*: 10 weeks

THE SCOOP

The largest bank in the U.S. and the No. 5 company on the Fortune 500, Citigroup seemingly offers every financial service under the sun to consumer and corporate customers, catering to some 200 million customer accounts and doing business in more than 100 countries. The company is organized into a few main divisions: the Global Consumer Group, Corporate and Investment Banking, Global Wealth Management, Alternative Investments and Corporate Center.

 ON THE JOB

Citigroup hires interns into the following businesses: investment banking, corporate banking, investment research, sales and trading, capital markets, finance, global transaction services, and technology and operations. Internship experiences vary by business, but typically, Citigroup summer programs tend to be small and very focused. Therefore, students are given more opportunity to function as real first-year analysts versus just a summer intern. Each program has a training component as well as a distinguished speaker series and social activities to introduce interns to the firm, the city and their colleagues.

GETTING HIRED

Apply by: Potential applicants at target schools should consult their career services office. Applicants at non-target schools should apply by January 1.

Qualifications:
Internships are reserved for students between their junior and senior year of college. Citigroup has a minimum GPA requirement of 3.5 in most businesses. The internship is open to students of all majors.

Contact:
www.oncampus.citigroup.com

Citizens for Global Solutions

 THE BUZZ

- "Help put an end to conflict"
- "Young activists, unite!"

THE STATS

Industry(ies): Education; Environmental; Government; Nonprofit

Location(s): Washington, DC

Number of interns: *Spring/summer/fall*: 10 each

Pay: $10/day stipend

Length of internship: *Spring/summer/fall*: 13-16 weeks

THE SCOOP

Citizens for Global Solutions, formerly the World Federalist Association, is a membership organization working to build political will in the United States. The mission of the organization is to create "a future in which nations work together to abolish war, protect our rights and freedoms, and solve the problems facing humanity that no nation can solve alone." To accomplish this goal, CGS educates Americans and public officials on global concerns and drafts proposals on how to strengthen international institutions.

ON THE JOB

Citizens for Global Solutions staff, interns and member activists carry out advocacy on issues within five program areas: U.S. Global Engagement; Peace and Security; International Law and Justice; International Institutions; and Health and Environment. There are also specific projects on the International Criminal Court, Peace Operations, UN Reform, Community of Democracies, the Earth Legacy project and Global Democracy. Interns will have a wide variety of responsibilities, including attending coalition meetings and meetings with Congressional staffers on the Hill; writing press releases; analyzing voting patterns; and updating the organization's web site. Staff and interns also regularly lobby members of the U.S. Congress and the Administration to support various issues.

GETTING HIRED

Apply by: Rolling. Submit a cover letter (should include your days-per-week availability, as well as preferred start and end dates), resume, and a three- to five-page writing sample (this can be a portion of a larger paper and can be on any issue). E-mail applications to internships@globalsolutions.org, or mail them to the address listed below.

Qualifications:

Open to undergraduates, grad students and recent graduates. Applicants must have knowledge of U.S. politics, international affairs, or journalism or an interest in electronic advocacy and information technology; excellent written and oral communication skills; and general computer skills (some knowledge of HTML or FrontPage is a plus but not required).

Contact:
Sara Bodenberg, Internship Coordinator
Citizens for Global Solutions
418 7th Street, SE
Washington, DC 20003
Phone: (202) 546-3950, ext. 118
E-mail: sbodenberg@globalsolutions.org
http://globalsolutions.org/internship

Citizens Network for Foreign Affairs

THE BUZZ

- "Know more about foreign affairs than Bush? Prove it!"

THE STATS

Industry(ies): Government; Nonprofit

Location(s): Washington, DC

Number of interns: *Annual*: 12

Pay: Paid; $1,000/month

Length of internship: *Spring*: 5 months (January-May); *summer*: 3 months (June-August); *fall*: 4 months (September-December)

THE SCOOP

Citizens Network for Foreign Affairs (CNFA), a nonprofit, was formed in 1986 to deal with issues of public policy, economic development and education in the global arena. Working with private-sector leaders in the U.S., CNFA increases the domestic dialogue on foreign affairs and the importance of America's stake in the global economy. CNFA also works to improve collaboration between public and private sectors on foreign affairs issues.

ON THE JOB

The CNFA internship program, touted as a springboard for careers in international relations, places interns with professionals. Some of the main policy areas in which interns work are in central and eastern Europe, the Middle East and Africa, new business development, and operations and compliance. Current and past interns have worked in the Agribusiness Partnership department (implementing and monitoring a USAID-funded project), the new business development department and special events planning (working on plans for CNFA's international conference).

GETTING HIRED

Apply by: *Spring*: November 1; *summer*: April 1; *fall*: July 1. Apply for one or more internship positions and submit documents (a resume, cover letter, and writing sample) online at http://www.cnfa.org/page.cfm?pageID=89. Additonal documents, namely three required recommentdation letters, should be e-mailed or mailed to the address below.

Qualifications:

Open to college juniors or seniors, as well as recent college graduates. A minimum 3.0 GPA is required. Interns may not be enrolled in classes during the internship. Certain positions have more specific requirements; see www.cnfa.com for current guidelines.

Contact:
Internship Coordinator
CNFA Internship Program
1828 L Street, NW, Suite 710
Washington, DC 20036
Phone: (202) 296-3920
Fax: (202) 296-3948
E-mail: intern@cnfa.org
www.cnfa.com

Visit Vault at **www.vault.com** for insider company profiles, expert advice, career message boards, expert resume reviews, the Vault Job Board and more.

  VAULT CAREER LIBRARY 117

Citizens Union

THE BUZZ

- "Watchdog that bites big"
- "Loves NYC more than ever"

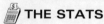

THE STATS

Industry(ies): Government; New/Interactive Media; Nonprofit

Location(s): New York, NY

Number of interns: *Annual*: 8

Pay: None; academic credit available

Length of internship: Varies according to position and student availability

THE SCOOP

The Citizens Union was established in 1897, and has been working for a municipal democracy ever since, encouraging New York City residents to take an active part in the election process through efforts including publishing *Voter's Guide*. This nonpartisan group works to better public policy and monitors the actions of the city council. GothamGazette.com, an award-winning news web site about New York City policy and politics, is published each weekday by the Citizens Union Foundation of the City of New York, the nonprofit research and education affiliate of Citizens Union. It functions as four publications in one – a daily digest of news about New York City, a news operation in itself, a policy magazine and a reference tool for students and serious researchers alike.

ON THE JOB

Interns work in the voting, public policy and city council departments assisting staff with writing position papers and educating the voting public about the process and the issues. Some interns may work in The Foundation assisting with research projects or publishing materials on voting and New York City politics. The company is also looking for Web-savvy researchers, reporters, writers, illustrators photographers and editors who will work for GothamGazette.com.

GETTING HIRED

Apply by: Rolling. Please include cover letter with resume.

Qualifications:
Open to all college freshmen, sophomores, juniors and seniors, as well as college graduates. Writing, editing, research, interviewing and phone skills are relevant. Interest in New York City and state politics, policy and civic life is necessary.

Contact:
Internship Coordinator
Citizens Union
299 Broadway, Suite 700
New York, NY 10007
Phone: (212) 227-0342
Fax: (212) 227-0345
E-mail: Internship@citizensunionfoundation.org

City Limits

THE BUZZ

- "Get to the core of the Big Apple with this political journalism internship"
- "A small full-time staff means big opportunities for interns"

THE STATS

Industry(ies): Government; Journalism; Nonprofit; Publishing

Location(s): New York, NY

Number of interns: *Annual*: 2-3

Pay: None; pay is given for for published work (freelance fee)

Length of internship: *Fall:* September-December; *winter:* January-April; *summer:* May-August

THE SCOOP

City Limits has covered the issues relevant to New York City's neighborhoods for 30 years. The paper provides information and analysis on city policies and players, strategies and programs. They cover everything-from the front lines of advocacy and politics to affordable housing, from federal spending to local political races, and from community gardens to inclusionary zoning. City Limits Weekly is the sister organization to the Center for an Urban Future, which produces in-depth policy reports on New York City.

ON THE JOB

Since the publication has a small staff (10), interns are treated like professional staff members. They are encouraged to report and write (pieces ranging from 300 to 3,000 words) for the magazine as much as possible, including some time-sensitive reporting. Areas of interest include government, housing, criminal justice, education and economic development. Interns also write for the weekly news bulletin. In addition, they work with staff to manage and produce the publications.

GETTING HIRED

Apply by: Rolling. Send resume and cover letter (detailing availability), along with three clips, to the address below.

Qualifications:
Open to college freshmen, sophomores, juniors and seniors, recent college graduates and grad students with some writing experience.

Contact:
City Limits Intern Program
120 Wall Street, 20th floor
New York, NY 10005
Phone: (212) 479-3345
www.citylimits.org

City of New York Parks & Recreation

 THE BUZZ
- "One of the nation's largest parks and rec departments"
- "Not just for the horticulturally inclined"

THE STATS

Industry(ies): Environmental; Government

Location(s): New York, NY

Number of interns: *Annual*: 80-100

Pay: None

Length of internship: 12-20 hours per week; length varies based on student availability

THE SCOOP

The New York City Department of Parks & Recreation does much more than just oversee the upkeep of its 28,000 acres of parkland (as if that weren't a big enough job). "Parks," as those in the department refer to it, also sponsors free events to get the community involved in its local parks, runs a workfare program, organizes nature walks and sports clinics, and maintains a substantial photo archive and a comprehensive web site, among other programs. Parks covers so much ground that it takes 2,200 employees to keep the agency running.

ON THE JOB

An internship at Parks can mean anything from acting as the park commissioner's aide to designing the agency's web site. Interns can choose to work in the marketing division, promoting current ad campaigns for the park. Or, they can perform social work in its work experience program, or study the parks' wetlands from an ecological viewpoint. In fact, Parks offers 24 different kinds of internships in all. See www.nycgovparks.org for complete descriptions.

GETTING HIRED

Apply by: Rolling. Send resume and cover letter, preferably by e-mail.

Qualifications:
Most internships are open to high school juniors and seniors, college freshmen, sophomores, juniors and seniors, recent college graduates and grad students. See the web site for details on requirements.

Contact:
City of New York Parks & Recreation
Attention: Leslie Nusblatt
830 Fifth Avenue
New York, NY 10021
Phone: (212) 360-8257
Fax: (212) 360-8263
E-mail: Leslie.Nusblatt@parks.nyc.gov
www.nycgovparks.org/sub_opportunities/internships.html

CITYarts, Inc.

 THE BUZZ
- "Making a difference through the arts"

 **THE STATS**

Industry(ies): Art/Museum; Education; Nonprofit

Location(s): New York, NY

Number of interns: *Annual*: 15-25

Pay: Stipend

Length of internship: 3-month minimum; available year-round

THE SCOOP

CITYarts was founded in 1968 as the first organization that makes and installs public art in communities where arts involvement is limited. Through this commitment, it maintains an innovative and productive New York City public arts program by partnering with youth, families, local businesses, schools and city administrators.

ON THE JOB

Interns conduct research projects in various divisions, including the development fundraising, public relations/communication, exhibition, marketing/promotions, clerical, program development, annual benefit, video or studio departments. Interns typically work as assistants with duties such as researching the logistics and locations for touring exhibitions, helping with publicity, developing marketing strategies, organizing and updating mailing lists, preparing press releases, creating promotional materials and working one-on-one with professional artists.

GETTING HIRED

Apply by: Rolling. E-mail resume to apply.

Qualifications:
Open to all students 18 years of age or older with an interest and/or background in the arts. Applicants should be able to work in all of NYC's five boroughs. Those interested in office opportunities should have some computer experience, especially with Microsoft Word and Excel.

Contact:
CITYarts, Inc.
525 Broadway, Suite 700
New York, NY 10012
Phone: (212) 966-0377
Fax: (212) 966-0551
E-mail: tsipi@cityarts.org
www.cityarts.org

Visit Vault at **www.vault.com** for insider company profiles, expert advice, career message boards, expert resume reviews, the Vault Job Board and more.

 **V/\ULT** CAREER LIBRARY **119**

Classic Stage Company

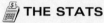 **THE BUZZ**
- "Stage fright? Work behind the curtain"
- "Don't worry about breaking your legs"

THE STATS

Industry(ies): Theater/Performing Arts

Location(s): New York, NY

Number of interns: *Fall/spring/summer*: 2 each

Pay: None. Complimentary ticket offers for other productions around the city

Length of internship: Flexible; minimum of 4 months

THE SCOOP

Founded in 1967, Classic Stage Company is the award-winning Off-Broadway theater that re-imagines classic plays for contemporary audiences. Each season the company produces a selection of classical plays and adaptations, a variety of education and outreach programs, and training opportunities for students and artists. CSC is where young and established actors, writers, directors and designers are nurtured and supported, and where audiences, young and old, can delight in discovering classical plays and new talent in the same evening.

ON THE JOB

CSC's internship program offers students the opportunity to learn more about theater management. The interns assist the producing director, development director and general manager with correspondence, budgets, contracts, schedules, grant writing, fundraising research and managing the company. Interns work in the areas of fundraising, marketing, education and outreach, and company management.

GETTING HIRED

Apply by: Rolling. Send resume with references and cover letter indicating primary area(s) of interest and season (summer, fall or spring) desired.

Qualifications:
Open to college freshmen, sophomores, juniors, and seniors, recent college graduates and grad students.

Contact:
Internship Coordinator
Classic Stage Company
136 East 13th Street
New York, NY 10003
Fax: (212) 477-7504
E-mail: info@classicstage.org
www.classicstage.org

The Cloisters

THE BUZZ
- "The best internship for both museum professionals – and wannabe monks"

THE STATS

Industry(ies): Art/Museum; Education

Location(s): New York, NY

Number of interns: *Summer*: 8

Pay: Paid; $2,750 paid in 3 installments over the course of the summer. Field trips

Length of internship: *Summer*: mid-June–mid-August

THE SCOOP

The Cloisters, a division of the Metropolitan Museum of Art devoted to medieval Europe dating from the 12th through the 15th centuries, can be found in northern Manhattan's Fort Tryon Park situated on four acres overlooking the Hudson River. The museum's structure incorporates medieval French cloisters with quadrangles enclosed by a vaulted passageway. It features gardens planted according to horticultural information found in medieval treatises, poetry, garden documents, herbals and medieval works of art, such as tapestries, stained-glass windows and column capitals.

ON THE JOB

During the nine-week program, interns run gallery workshops with New York City day campers and develop gallery tours, delivered during their last week. The internship provides intensive training sessions in The Cloisters' collection and in museum teaching techniques.

GETTING HIRED

Apply by: *Summer*: January 19. Potential candidates will be invited for a required interview at The Cloisters in March; all applicants will be notified by April 15. Applications (*not* submitted via e-mail or fax) must include academic transcripts; a 500-word essay describing why you would like to participate in the program; two academic recommendations; a resume highlighting all work and volunteer experience; and a cover letter detailing field of interest or specialization, special honors, major, class year and contact information, including an e-mail address. Go to the web site to download a cover sheet for the application.

Qualifications:
Open to college freshmen, sophomores and juniors.

Contact:
College Internship Program
The Cloisters
Fort Tryon Park
New York, NY 10040
Phone: (212) 650-2280
www.metmuseum.org/education/er_internship.asp#sum

The Coca-Cola Company

 THE BUZZ
- "Even people in Burkina Faso will know where you worked"

 THE STATS

Industry(ies): Consumer Products; Food & Beverage

Location(s): Atlanta, GA (HQ); many field locations

Number of interns: *Annual*: 50-100

Pay: Paid; *undergraduate*: $1,800-$2,500/month; *MBAs*: $4,000-$5,300/month

Length of internship: *Summer*: 8-12 weeks

 THE SCOOP

The Coca-Cola Company boasts the most recognized beverage in the world. Along with Coca-Cola, invented in 1886, the company also markets four of the world's top five soft drink brands, including Diet Coke, Fanta and Sprite, as well as a range of other diet and light soft beverages, waters, juices and juice drinks, teas, coffees and sports drinks. Consumers in more than 200 countries use the company's products at a rate exceeding 1 billion servings each day.

 **ON THE JOB**

As part of Coca-Cola's Functional Internship Program, undergraduate and graduate level interns work in various departments, including marketing and supply chain. Coca-Cola also offers a separate internship program through INROADS, which enhances educational opportunities for undergraduate students of African American, Hispanic American, Asian American and Native American descent. The Coca-Cola Company has partnered with INROADS for over 20 years.

 GETTING HIRED

Apply by: Deadline was not available at the time of publication. See www2.coca-cola.com/careers/internships.html for more information. A completed application (available at: www2.coca-cola.com/careers/submit_profile.html) must be sent for the Functional Internship Program. Go to www.inroads.org to apply for the INROADS program (for students of color and minority ethnicities).

Qualifications:
Open to all college freshmen, sophomores, juniors and seniors, recent college graduates and grad students. The INROADS program is open only to undergrad minorities with a GPA of 3.0 or higher.

Contact:
Human Resources Recruiter
The Coca-Cola Company
P.O. Box 1734
Atlanta, GA 30301
www2.coca-cola.com/careers/functional_intern_program.html
www2.coca-cola.com/careers/internships.html

College Light Opera Company

 THE BUZZ
- "What summer stock should be"
- "Whistle while you work"
- "Digs in Cape Cod"

THE STATS

Industry(ies): Nonprofit; Theater/Performing Arts

Location(s): Falmouth, MA

Number of interns: *Summer*: 65

Pay: Stipend; varies. Actors receive free room and board; orchestra members receive $1,000 plus room and board

Length of internship: *Summer*: 10 weeks

THE SCOOP

The College Light Opera Company was founded in 1969 as a nonprofit, educational, independent theater company, specializing in light opera and musicals. Based in Cape Cod, the company puts on Broadway shows for the summer vacationers, while giving young people experience in the different elements of musical theater. All members of the company (acting, music and support staff/interns) are students guided by professional staff. It's the largest resident theater company in the United States.

ON THE JOB

Each summer, interns are hired to work as stage managers, piano accompanists, costume designers, choreographers, associate conductors, actors, orchestra musicians, marketing directors, assistant business managers, box office treasurers and set designers/technical directors. In addition, the company hires interns with previous experience in cooperative residence and dining halls to work as cooks and directors of the cooperative work program. The company stresses that it never makes interns do work that they were not hired to do. Some positions require more independence and initiative than others.

 GETTING HIRED

Apply by: *Summer*: March 15. Download the application at www.collegelightopera.com/jobs and mail it to the address below.

Qualifications:
Open to freshman, sophomore, junior and senior undergrads and grad students. Qualifications vary depending on position; see www.collegelightopera.com/company.htm for details.

Contact:
Robert and Ursula Haslun, Producers
College Light Opera Company
162 South Cedar Street
Oberlin, OH 44074
Phone: (440) 774-8485
www.collegelightopera.com

Visit Vault at **www.vault.com** for insider company profiles, expert advice, career message boards, expert resume reviews, the Vault Job Board and more.

V/\ULT CAREER LIBRARY **121**

Columbia Journalism Review

THE BUZZ
- "Uncover media bias"
- "Learn journalism from the best"

THE STATS

Industry(ies): Broadcast & Entertainment; Journalism; New/Interactive Media; Publishing

Location(s): New York, NY

Number of interns: *Annual*: 6

Pay: Paid; $8/hour

Length of internship: *Summer*: 10 weeks; *fall*: September-December; *spring*: January-May

THE SCOOP

Founded under the auspices of Columbia University's renowned Graduate School of Journalism, the *Columbia Journalism Review (CJR)* is a bimonthly watchdog of all types of media – newspapers, magazines, radio, television, cable and Internet. It covers current events and analyzes the way they are reported. It covers media issues more generally as well, publishing articles that explore corporate ownership, international media, the effects of new legislation, and trends in journalism culture.

ON THE JOB

Interns work in the editorial department fulfilling administrative needs as they arise. They also get to report, research and fact-check articles, thus entering the thick of this "forum for journalists to examine and question their own practices and principles." They may even get a voice in that forum – past interns have had articles published in *CJR* during their internship.

GETTING HIRED

Apply by: *Summer*: March 1; *fall*: July 1; *spring*: November 1. Send resume, cover letter, names and phone numbers of two references, and three writing samples (clips preferred) to the address below.

Qualifications:
Open to college freshmen, sophomores, juniors, and seniors, recent college grads and grad students.

Contact:
Tom O'Neill
Columbia Journalism Review
2950 Broadway
Columbia University
207 Journalism Building
New York, NY 10027
Phone: (212) 854-9768
www.cjr.org

Comedy Central

THE BUZZ
- "Kiss Jon Stewart's ring"

THE STATS

Industry(ies): Broadcast & Entertainment

Location(s): New York, NY

Number of interns: 30-40 students per semester

Pay: None; academic credit may be available (check with your school). Meetings with executives; field trips

Length of internships: Length of 1 semester

THE SCOOP

From classic *Saturday Night Live* reruns to *The Daily Show with Jon Stewart*, the cable network Comedy Central brings its viewers comic-driven productions, sometimes with a political slant. Other Comedy Central programming includes *South Park* and *The Graham Norton Effect*. The channel also puts out an interactive web site, some publishing projects and radio syndication.

ON THE JOB

Interns are placed in marketing, corporate communications, finance, human resources, sales research, on-air promotions, production and many other company departments. Duties can vary, but may include clerical support and events coordination.

GETTING HIRED

Apply by: *Winter*: mid-late October; *spring*: mid-late December; *summer*: mid-late April; *fall*: mid-late July.

Qualifications:
Students in Comedy Central's unpaid internship program must be eligible to receive academic credit. Indicate the semester of interest (spring, summer or fall), department(s) of interest and if eligible to receive credit in a cover letter with a resume.

Contact:
Comedy Central
Attention: Human Resources
1775 Broadway
New York, NY 10019
For questions, contact the internship coordinator at:
Fax: (212) 767-4257
E-mail: interns@comedycentral.com
Post resume at jobs.comedycentral.com/postresume.htm
jobs.comedycentral.com/cgi-bin/wc.dll?EnterSearchJobs

Common Cause

THE BUZZ
- "Political heavyweight"
- "Grassroots experience"

THE STATS

Industry(ies): Government; Law

Location(s): Washington, DC; offices in 37 states

Number of interns: *Spring/fall*: approximately 4 each; *summer:* approximately 10

Pay: None. Daily travel reimbursement for public transportation

Length of internship: 3 months (flexible)

THE SCOOP

Founded in 1970 by John Garner, former Secretary of Health, Education and Welfare, the nonpartisan lobbying group Common Cause has become one of the nation's most influential lobbying organizations. Using grassroots campaigns, Common Cause watches the government and helps get citizens involved in shaping national public policies.

ON THE JOB

Interns work in program operations, media communications, research, membership and fundraising, state issues or Web design. In all areas, interns work closely with staff on grassroots campaigns and gain experience in political lobbying and activism.

GETTING HIRED

Apply by: Rolling. Application form is available at www.common cause.org/intern. Early applicants are welcome. Law intern positions are offered as needed; interested applicants should inquire about availability. State and legal interns should apply through the national office; they will be redirected as appropriate.

Qualifications:
Open to all undergraduates and postgraduates. Experience is not necessary; enthusiasm and interest are essential.

Contact:
Ian Storrar
Internship Coordinator
Common Cause
1133 19th Street NW, Suite 900
Washington, DC 20036
Phone: (202) 833-1200
Fax: (202) 659-3716
E-mail: internship@commoncause.org
www.commoncause.org/intern

Visit Vault at **www.vault.com** for insider company profiles, expert advice, career message boards, expert resume reviews, the Vault Job Board and more.

VAULT CAREER LIBRARY **123**

Congress-Bundestag Youth Exchange for Young Professionals

 THE BUZZ

"One-year work/study scholarship program to Germany"

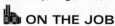 **THE STATS**

Industry(ies): All industries

Location(s): Various; Germany

Number of interns: *Annual*: 75

Pay: 1-year scholarship program to Germany funds most basic expenses, including round-trip transportation; transportation stipend (in Germany); language training; housing; health and accident benefits; orientation program

Length of internship: 1 year (July-July)

THE SCOOP

The Congress-Bundestag Youth Exchange for Young Professionals is a scholarship program with a strong focus on cultural exchange. It is designed to give participants an understanding of everyday life, education and professional training in Germany and the United States. In the U.S., the Bureau of Educational and Cultural Affairs of the Department of State under the authority of the Fulbright-Hays Act of 1961 funds the program. In Germany the program is funded through the administration of the Bundestag. The program is administered by CDS International, a nonprofit founded in 1968 to increase international exchange programs for young professionals. CDS offers international internship programs to Germany, Argentina, Spain, Switzerland and Russia.

ON THE JOB

The program is designed to give young Americans an idea of everyday life in Germany, as well as cultural understanding, education and professional training. The 12-month program includes two months of intensive German training, four months of classroom instruction at a German university and a five-month internship at a German company or organization. There are several orientations and training sessions throughout the year, both in the U.S. (before and after the program) and in Germany. Participants work at various host companies in Germany, not directly at CDS.

GETTING HIRED

Apply by: December 1 for the next program year. Applications are available online at www.cdsintl.org/cbyx/cbyxfromusa.htm, or contact cbyx@cdsintl.org to have one sent via post or e-mail. Send two recommendations, high school diploma and transcripts from your four most recent semesters.

Qualifications:

U.S. citizens and permanent residents aged 18-24 (at the start of the program) with a high school diploma and a sincere interest in Germany are invited to apply. No prior german knowledge is required. All fields of study are encouraged to apply.

Contact:

CDS International, Inc.
Congress-Bundestag Youth Exchange
871 United Nations Plaza, 15th Floor
New York, NY 10017-1814
Phone: (212) 497-3500
Fax: (212) 497-3535
E-mail: cbyx@cdsintl.org
www.cdsintl.org

Congressional Hispanic Caucus Institute

 THE BUZZ

- "Move forward and give back!"
- "Impressive networking opportunities"
- "Learn while you work"

 THE STATS

Industry(ies): Education; Government; Nonprofit

Location(s): Washington, DC

Number of interns: *Summer*: 30

Pay: $2,000/summer. Free housing; round-trip airfare

Length of internship: *Summer*: 8 weeks

 THE SCOOP

Since the 1978 establishment of the Congressional Hispanic Caucus Institute (CHCI) as a nonprofit, nonpartisan educational organization, its leadership development programs have provided resources that students can use in their educational pursuits and beyond. CHCI offers internship, scholarship and fellowship programs in hopes of producing more Latino leaders. This organization expresses pride in its emphasis on community.

 ON THE JOB

Interns for CHCI work in the offices of U.S. Representatives. In addition to practical work experience, interns also gain knowledge through weekly leadership development sessions. While networking and learning, interns have the chance to "give back" through CHCI's community service projects.

GETTING HIRED

Apply by: *Summer*: January 31. Download application from www.chci.org/chciyouth/internship/internshipprogram.htm and send it to the address below.

Qualifications:

Open to Latino undergraduates who are U.S. citizens or legal permanent residents. Strong analytical skills, writing skills and a history of community service required. 3.0 GPA preferred.

Contact:
Program Coordinator
CHCI Summer Internship Program
911 2nd Street, NE
Washington, DC 20002
Phone: (202) 543-1771 or toll free: (800) EXCEL-DC
www.chciyouth.org

Congressional Management Foundation

 THE BUZZ

- "Help Congress look like it knows what it's doing"
- "Pitch in to help the country run more smoothly"

 THE STATS

Industry(ies): Government; Law; Nonprofit

Location(s): Washington, DC

Number of interns: *Annual*: 6

Pay: None; academic credit available

Length of internship: *Summer/fall/spring*: 30-40 hours/week. Internships generally last at 2-4 months

 THE SCOOP

The Congressional Management Foundation began in 1977 as a nonprofit organization to help Congress improve its performance and become a more productive and effectively managed institution. CMF provides four primary management services to House and Senate offices: management training, consulting, reports and technological guidance.

 ON THE JOB

Interns support CMF's work through tasks ranging from writing evaluations and conducting research for current projects to preparing for training sessions and providing general office support (answering phones, overseeing reception and customer service, and maintaining office cleanliness and organization).

GETTING HIRED

Apply by: *Summer*: March 15; *fall/spring*: rolling. Send a resume, a cover letter and a brief writing sample (three to five pages on any subject).

Qualifications:

Open to college freshmen, sophomores, juniors and seniors, as well as recent college graduates and graduate students.Students on semester and quarter systems welcome to apply.

Contact:

Congressional Management Foundation
Attention: Internship Coordinator
513 Capitol Court, NE, Suite 300
Washington, DC 20002
Phone: (202) 546-0100
Fax: (202) 547-0936
E-mail: cmf@cmfweb.org
www.cmfweb.org/default.asp

Visit Vault at **www.vault.com** for insider company profiles, expert advice, career message boards, expert resume reviews, the Vault Job Board and more.

VAULT CAREER LIBRARY 125

Connecticut Judicial Branch

 THE BUZZ
- "In an internship program this vast, you're sure to find one that fits"
- "A less scary version of *Law & Order*"

 THE STATS

Industry(ies): Government; Law

Location(s): Cities across Connecticut

Number of interns: *Spring/summer/fall*: 150-175 each

Pay: None; academic credit available. Travel expenses

Length of internship: *Spring/fall*: 12-16 weeks; *summer*: 10 weeks

 THE SCOOP

The Connecticut Judicial Branch consists of 22 courts across 15 judicial districts. Every year, Connecticut's Superior Courts hear a total of 750,000 cases on criminal, civil, juvenile, family, housing and administrative matters. It takes 2,500 employees to run Connecticut's courts and an accordingly large central administrative staff to tend to external affairs, court support services and court operations.

ON THE JOB

With over 200 interns in cities across Connecticut, duties for Connecticut Judicial Branch interns vary quite a bit. The Judicial Internship Program, for example, often takes current law school students to clerk, swear in documents, file and track case-flow information. A typical intern in the probation department, on the other hand, might go on field visits with a probation officer, assist officers with intakes and complete daily reporting on probation clients. See the Connecticut Judicial Branch web site (www.jud.state.ct.us/external/news/jobs/Intern.htm) for testimonies from past interns on specific departments.

 GETTING HIRED

Apply by: *Summer*: May 16; *fall*: August 26. Check web site for application deadline updates. Download application at www.jud.state.ct.us/external/news/jobs/Intern.htm.

Qualifications:
Open to college sophomores, juniors and seniors, recent college graduates, and graduate and law students.

Contact:
Robyn N. Oliver, Program Manager
Administrator of Volunteer/Intern Program
Connecticut Judicial Branch
99 East River Drive
Two Riverview Square, Room 701
East Hartford, CT 06108
Phone: (860) 282-6581
E-mail: Robyn.Oliver@jud.state.ct.us
www.jud.state.ct.us

Connecticut Magazine

 THE BUZZ
- "Nutmeg State-loving literary types wanted"
- "Get hands-on editorial experience"

 THE STATS

Industry(ies): Journalism; Publishing

Location(s): Trumbull, CT

Number of interns: 1-3 per semester

Pay: None. Interaction with editor; free copies of magazine, mentoring and advice from staff

Length of internship: *Summer/fall/winter/spring*: One full term each; 12-15 hours/week

 THE SCOOP

Founded in 1972, *Connecticut Magazine* is about all things Connecticut, featuring shopping, arts, politics and dining. There is a section detailing things to do, a dining out guide (which can be accessed online) and county maps to help visitors to the state get around. The magazine has a readership of over 86,000 subscribers.

ON THE JOB

Interns work as assistants in the editorial department. Duties include reading manuscripts, answering phones, fact checking, copy editing and proofreading. They also handle editorial correspondence, return manuscripts and queries from freelance writers, cross-index articles from back issues on a database and occasionally contribute short pieces for the magazine.

 GETTING HIRED

Apply by: Rolling. Submit a cover letter detailing why you're interested in interning at *Connecticut Magazine*, as well as a resume and writing sample.

Qualifications:
Open to college freshmen, sophomores, juniors and seniors, recent graduates and graduate students.

Contact:
Cathy Ross, Calendar Editor
Connecticut Magazine
35 Nutmeg Drive
Trumbull, CT 06611
Phone: (203) 380-6600, ext. 326
E-mail: cross@connecticutmag.com
www.connecticutmag.com

Coors Brewing Company

 THE BUZZ
- "Be the envy of every frat boy in the world"

 THE STATS

Industry(ies): Food & Beverage

Location(s): Golden, CO

Number of interns: *Annual*: 20

Pay: Competitive stipend. Volleyball tournament; luncheons and picnics; influential speakers

Length of internship: *Summer*: 10-16 weeks

 THE SCOOP

Founded in 1873, Coors Brewing Co. is a family-owned and -operated business that has grown into the nation's third-largest beer brewer. The Coors Brewing Co. uses about 2.6 million gallons of water per day in order to brew over two dozen varieties of alcoholic beverages, including Coors Light, which is the fourth best-selling beer in the country. The company recently reported consolidated net sales of $1.1 billion with more than 30 international offices.

ON THE JOB

Coors insists that each workday should be fun. Interns work with designated supervisors who assign tasks and projects related to personal and professional development. The interns are then placed in their specialty and given focal and collaborative goals. Departments with intern positions include corporate relations, engineering, environmental health and safety, finance, human resources, information technology, manufacturing, public affairs, quality control, and research and development. Interns are also encouraged to share their ideas in meetings, discussions and forums.

GETTING HIRED

Apply by: Rolling. Apply online at www.coorsjobs.com.

Qualifications:

Open to all college freshmen, sophomores, juniors, seniors and graduate students.

Contact:
Internship Coordinator
Coors Brewing Company
P.O. Box 4030
Golden, CO 80401-0030
www.coorsjobs.com

Coro

 THE BUZZ
- "Boot camp for community leaders"
- "Learn about city management and gain a sense of civic pride"

 THE STATS

Industry(ies): Education; Government; Nonprofit

Location(s): Kansas City, MO; Los Angeles, CA; New York, NY; Pittsburgh, PA; San Francisco, CA; St. Louis, MO

Number of interns: *Annual*: 64

Pay: None; fellows must pay tuition for the program

Length of internship: *Youth and Summer Programs*: 10 weeks; *Fellows Program*: 9 months

 THE SCOOP

Coro offers real-world training for future community leaders. Attorney W. Donald Foster founded Coro in 1942 in San Francisco with investment counselor Van Duyn Dodge when they realized there was no professional school for such leaders. The nonprofit soon expanded to several U.S. cities.

ON THE JOB

Coro offers three types of internship programs. Youth Programs (in New York and San Francisco) help junior and senior high school students understand how a city works. The Fellows Program in Public Affairs (in all Coro cities) allows college graduates to analyze resources and needs of different community organizations, design and evaluate projects relating to civic affairs, and complete field work assignments. Coro's Summer Internship in Public Affairs exposes Midwestern college students to city government, using Kansas City as a microcosm; and the Pittsburgh-based Community Problem-Solving Internship allows African-American college students to assess issues of diversity.

GETTING HIRED

Apply by: Rolling. Deadlines vary depending on program. See web site for more information. Apply online at www.coro.org/how_to_apply/how_to_apply.html.

Qualifications:

Youth Programs are open to junior and senior high school students. *Summer Internship in Public Affairs*: open to college juniors and seniors, primarily from the Midwest; *Community Problem-Solving Internship*: open to African-American college sophomores, juniors and seniors; *Fellows Program*: open to all college graduates.

Contact:
Coro National Office
1010 West 39th Street
Kansas City, MO 64111
Phone: (816) 931-0751
Fax: (816) 756-0924
E-mail: national@coro.org
www.coro.org

Visit Vault at **www.vault.com** for insider company profiles, expert advice, career message boards, expert resume reviews, the Vault Job Board and more.

VAULT CAREER LIBRARY 127

Corporation for National and Community Service

THE BUZZ
- "Like the Peace Corps, but without the jet lag"
- "Joining the military isn't the only way to serve your country"

THE STATS
Industry(ies): Education; Environmental; Government; Nonprofit

Location(s): Washington, DC (HQ); Albany, NY; Atlanta, GA; Austin, TX; Baltimore, MD; Baton Rouge, LA; Birmingham, AL; Boise, ID; Boston, MA; Charleston, WV; Cheyenne, WY; Chicago, IL; Columbia, SC; Columbus, OH; Concord, NH; Denver, CO; Des Moines, IA; Detroit, MI; Hartford, CT; Helena, MT; Honolulu, HI; Indianapolis, IN; Jackson, MS; Kansas City, MO; Lincoln, NE; Little Rock, AR; Los Angeles, CA; Milwaukee, WI; Minneapolis, MN; Nashville, TN; Orlando, FL; Philadelphia, PA; Phoenix, AZ; Pierre, SD; Portland, OR; Providence, RI; Raleigh, NC; Reno, NV; Richmond, VA; Salt Lake City, UT; Seattle, WA; Topeka, KS; Trenton, NJ; San Juan

Number of interns: *Annual*: 35

Pay: None

Length of internship: *Fall/spring*: 12-16 weeks each; *summer*: 10 weeks

THE SCOOP
Managed by the federal government, the CNS works to engage Americans in addressing national issues, such as education, public safety and the environment, and thereby fosters civic responsibility. The national CNS office is in DC, but most states have a branch, as well. CNS administers AmeriCorps, Learn and Serve America, and the National Senior Service Corps.

ON THE JOB
Interns in the national office conduct research and coordinate special events. They may work in AmeriCorps Recruitment, AmeriCorps, Chief Financial Office, Chief Operating Office, Learn and Serve America, Planning and Program Integration, Congressional Relations, Public Affairs, Public Liaison, Senior Corps, General Counsel and the Chief Executive Office. State offices also offer internships, but each program is different.

GETTING HIRED
Apply by: *Spring*: December 1; *summer*: April 1; *fall*: July 1. For the DC internship, send a cover letter and resume to the address below. For state offices, find contact information at www.cns.gov/about/family/state_offices.html.

Qualifications:
Open to college freshmen, sophomores, juniors and seniors, recent college graduates and grad students. Requirements vary by position; see www.cns.gov/jobs/internships/index.html for detailed information.

Contact:
Intern Coordinator
Corporation for National Service
1201 New York Avenue, NW
Washington, DC 20525
Fax: (202) 565-2784
www.cns.gov

Council of Energy Resource Tribes

THE BUZZ
- "Play a role in the future of Indian tribes"
- "Put your energy into energy resource"

THE STATS
Industry(ies): Energy/Utilities; Environmental; Science/Research

Location(s): Denver, CO; local tribal locations in CO

Number of interns: *Annual*: approximately 10-14

Pay: Paid; hourly. Dorm rooms and round-trip travel provided

Length of internship: *Summer*: 10 weeks; *fall*: 1 year

THE SCOOP
The Council of Energy Resource Tribes (CERT) works to develop programs that improve the environment and save energy throughout the country. Recently, CERT partnered with the Southern States Power Company, Inc., to develop energy projects that would benefit citizens as a whole. The organization's goal is to have Indian tribes gain control of their own resources by protecting, managing and developing their land while keeping their Native American traditions and priorities intact.

ON THE JOB
Interns work with experienced Council of Energy Resource Tribe members and alongside employees of sponsoring companies. Interns are trained in scientific, technical and policy areas, including resource management, environmental protection and energy business operations with a focus on the connection between science and technology and tribal governance.

GETTING HIRED
Apply by: *Summer*: March 15; *fall*: rolling.

Qualifications:
Open to Native American freshmen, sophomores, juniors and seniors, and graduate students enrolled in tribal or nontribal colleges and universities. Send a resume, writing sample, transcripts and two letters of recommendation (one from instructor or counselor).

Contact:
Internship Program
CERT
695 South Colorado Blvd., Suite 10
Denver, CO 80246
Phone: (303) 282-7576
Fax: (303) 282-7584
www.certredearth.com/Education/internship.html

Council on Foreign Relations

 THE BUZZ
- "Use your education to help educate the country"
- "Work locally, but think globally"

 THE STATS

Industry(ies): Government; Nonprofit

Location(s): New York, NY; Washington, DC

Number of interns: *New York*: 15-20 per semester; *Washington, DC*: 5 per semester

Pay: None; stipend offered upon completion

Length of internship: *Fall*: September-December; *spring*: January-May; *summer*: May-August

 THE SCOOP

The Council on Foreign Relations, a nonprofit organization founded in 1921, works to get America thinking and talking about world issues focusing on U.S. foreign policy. Members include almost every U.S. president and various other former senior cabinet members. The Council's journal on global issues, *Foreign Affairs*, promotes its goals of educating the public and sparking interest in international issues.

ON THE JOB

Interns at the Council of Foreign Relations are involved in various projects related to the work of The Council. Most internships have an administrative component. Internships are available in New York and Washington, DC, and include working in various departments including foreign affairs, www.cfr.org and publications.

GETTING HIRED

Apply by: Rolling. E-mail or fax resume and cover letter stating days and hours of availability.

Qualifications:
Open to undergrads, graduate students and recent graduates. Individual internships require specific qualifications. See list of internships at www.cfr.org/about/jobs.php.

Contact:
Council on Foreign Relations
Nicolle Szewczyk
Human Resources Office
58 East 68th Street
New York, NY 10021
Fax: (212) 434-9893
E-mail: humanresources@cfr.org or nszewczyk@cfr.org
www.cfr.org/about/jobs.php

Council on Hemispheric Affairs

 THE BUZZ
- "Help promote healthy relations across the hemisphere"

THE STATS

Industry(ies): Nonprofit

Location(s): Washington, DC

Number of interns: *Summer*: 25 interns; varies with need the rest of the year

Pay: None

Length of internship: *Summer*: 14 weeks; *fall*: 18 weeks; *winter*: 18 weeks

 THE SCOOP

The Council on Hemispheric Affairs (COHA) is a hard-hitting, highly respected, nonprofit organization founded in 1975 to raise awareness of regional issues, research and influence U.S. policies toward Latin America. COHA also monitors Canadian/Latin American relations. COHA is run by a small group of professionals with a large intern staff and is supported by professors on sabbatical leave, volunteers and retired government employees.

ON THE JOB

Internships are offered on a rolling basis in U.S., Latin American and Canadian relations. Interns may assist in issuing statements and providing commentary to the media, writing articles, keeping an eye on human rights violations and attending briefings and Congressional hearings. Much of an intern's time is spent writing and researching.

GETTING HIRED

Apply by: Rolling. Print out the application posted online and send it along with a resume, brief writing sample, transcript and two recommendations to the address below. COHA's internships are highly competitive; usually there are 10 applications for every vacancy.

Qualifications:
Open to college freshmen, sophomores, juniors, seniors, and graduate students. Candidates should have an interest in or knowledge of U.S./Latin American affairs or international affairs, as well as strong research and writing skills. Some Portuguese or Spanish language skills are a plus. Candidates with journalism or English backgrounds will be considered.

Contact:
Council on Hemispheric Affairs
Attention: Internship Coordinator
1250 Connecticut Avenue, NW, Suite 1C
Washington, DC 20036
Phone: (202) 223-4975
Fax: (202) 223-4979
E-mail: coha@coha.org
www.coha.org

Visit Vault at **www.vault.com** for insider company profiles, expert advice, career message boards, expert resume reviews, the Vault Job Board and more.

VAULT CAREER LIBRARY **129**

Council on International Education Exchange

 THE BUZZ
- "Learn what it's like to travel and work in Spain"

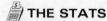 **THE STATS**

Industry(ies): Education; Nonprofit; Tourism/Recreation

Location(s): Seville; additional locations worldwide

Number of interns: *Summer*: varies

Pay: Paid; varies. Academic credit available; $4,900 program fee

Length of internship: *Summer*: 7 weeks

 **THE SCOOP**

Founded in 1947, the Council on International Education Exchange (CIEE) was created to help develop international relations and understanding after World War II. Student and teacher travel was seen as one of the most effective ways to meet the goals and the educational needs of the participants.

ON THE JOB

This program, run through the organization's Portland office, is geared toward students looking to gain practical experience working in a foreign company and to improve their Spanish language skills. The internship program incorporates an intensive Spanish for Students of Business course, which increases the students' business vocabulary and conversational skills, and an internship in a local Spanish company. For the internship, students complete a minimum of 120 hours of on-site work, conduct a research project, and participate in weekly seminars, which involve company visits and training in public speaking and leadership. Students will also engage in learning outside of the classroom through cultural visits, company site visits, and practical trips. CIEE helps arrange the visas and work permits, and gives students advice on how to secure employment and accommodations in the host country. The organization also offers internships in the U.S. to international students. Contact the CIEE Boston office (800-448-9944) for more information on U.S. placements.

GETTING HIRED

Apply by: March 15. Application forms and procedures can be accessed at www.ciee.org/study/apply.aspx. CIEE offers various programs, so see web site for further details.

Qualifications:

Open to college, sophomores, juniors and seniors. Applicants must have completed five semesters of college-level Spanish, or the equivalent, and must have a GPA of 2.75 or higher.

Contact:

Seville internship program
CIEE
7 Custom House Street, 3rd Floor
Portland, ME 04101
Phone: (207) 553-7600
Fax: (207) 553-7699
E-mail: studyinfo@ciee.org
www.ciee.org/study
www.ciee.org/program_search/program_detail.aspx?program_id
=126&type=part

For more programs
www.ciee.org/participant.aspx

Creative Time

 THE BUZZ
- "Work on some of New York City's most creative projects"
- "Add nonprofit and art to your resume"
- "Hear interesting stories about interesting people"

 THE STATS

Industry(ies): Art/Museum; Nonprofit

Location(s): New York, NY

Number of interns: About 8-15 each session

Pay: None; possible academic credit

Length of internship: Approximately 12-16 weeks, depending on intern availability; must work a minimum of 15 hours/week

 THE SCOOP

Creative Time, a nonprofit organization that employs less than 10 people, supports artists in new and innovative projects, and encourages them to create alternative pieces around the environment and real objects. Recent events the group has sponsored include a pyrotechnic display at Central Park, a street performance engaging chance pedestrians, and a film that takes the viewer on an unusual tour of a gothic mansion. Creative Time has been serving artists for 30 years.

 ON THE JOB

Interns are given a variety of tasks throughout the internship. From writing press releases and doing research to working in technology, Creative Time offers interns a real look into the world of nonprofit art organizations.

(S) GETTING HIRED

Apply by: Rolling. Mail, fax or e-mail resume, cover letter and application form. To download the application form and read descriptions of each internship, go to www.creativetime.org/oin/interns.html.

Qualifications:
Open to college freshmen, sophomores, juniors, seniors and graduate students, as well as recent graduates. (Note: interns are not required to be students.) An interest in art is preferred.

Contact:
Lauren Friedman
Creative Time
307 Seventh Avenue, Suite 1904
New York, NY 10001
Phone: (212) 206-6674
Fax: (212) 255-8467
E-mail: internships@creativetime.org
www.creativetime.org
www.creativetime.org/join/interns.html

Credit Suisse Group

 THE BUZZ
- "Better than chocolate"

 THE STATS

Industry(ies): Financial Services

Location(s): Zurich (Credit Suisse HQ); New York, NY; London; Tokyo; Hong Kong; numerous other branches throughout North America and across the world

Number of interns: Varies

Pay: Paid; competitive salary

Length of internship: *Summer*: 10-14 weeks

 THE SCOOP

Founded in Zurich in 1856, the Credit Suisse Group contains the three divisions of Credit Suisse: Investment Banking, Private Banking and Asset Management, as well as the Winterthur business which specializes in life and non-life insurance and pensions. The Credit Suisse Private Banking division provides private banking services to high-net-worth individuals through wealth management products and services. It also offers banking products and services, mortgages, secured and unsecured corporate loans, trade finance, consumer loans, and leasing and credit cards, as well as investment products and services, payment transactions and foreign exchange. The Credit Suisse Investment Banking division, formerly known as CSFB, is a leading global investment bank serving institutional, corporate and government clients. Its businesses include securities underwriting, sales and trading, investment banking, private equity, alternative assets and investment research. The Credit Suisse Asset Management division is a leading global asset manager focusing on institutional, mutual fund and private client investors, providing investment products and portfolio advice in the Americas, Asia Pacific and Europe. The company operates in over 50 countries and employs 60,000 people.

 ON THE JOB

Credit Suisse Investment Banking offers a variety of summer associate positions for MBA and PhD students and summer analyst positions for undergraduates. The summer programs are intended to attract top talent and ultimately for participants to join the firm full-time. There is a wide variety of specialties available to summer analysts and associates. See the company web site for details about individual programs.

(S) GETTING HIRED

Apply by: Undergraduate and graduate students should check with their on-campus career services center for information about Credit Suisse campus visits and the application process.

Qualifications:
Summer analyst: open to undergraduate juniors; *summer associate*: open to MBA and PhD students. Applicants should be highly motivated and creative individuals who have demonstrated academic achievement, specifically in finance and accounting. See the web site for specific requirements based on department.

Contact:
Internship
www.csfbcampusrecruiting.com
U.S. campus recruitment
uscampus.recruiting@csfb.com

Visit Vault at **www.vault.com** for insider company profiles, expert advice, career message boards, expert resume reviews, the Vault Job Board and more.

VAULT CAREER LIBRARY 131

Creede Repertory Theatre

 THE BUZZ
- "Spend the summer in a creative atmosphere"
- "Fulfill your dreams of working in theater"

 THE STATS

Industry(ies): Theater/Performing Arts

Location(s): Creede, CO

Number of interns: *Summer*: 5-10

Pay: Paid; $200/week. Housing

Length of internship: *Summer*: 10-18 weeks

 THE SCOOP

Creede Repertory Theatre, located near the picturesque Rio Grande, keeps Creede, Colo., residents and visitors entertained all summer with children's shows, a one-act play and four main-stage productions. As Creede's largest summer employer, the theater brings in more than 35,000 people to watch performances each year. A gallery in the lobby hosts musical and visual arts that make attending theater more enjoyable.

 ON THE JOB

Interns at Creede Repertory Theatre are given a variety of tasks to perform. Interns working with the set designer may help build sets or work on costumes and props and those working with the development director may assist with writing grant proposals, mailings or planning special events. There are also acting internships available.

💲 **GETTING HIRED**

Apply by: *Summer*: March 1.

Qualifications:

Open to students 18 or older. Mail, fax or e-mail resume and a list of three references with names and telephone numbers.

Contact:
Tristan Wilson
Creede Repertory Theater
P.O. Box 269
Creede, CO 81130
Phone: (719) 658-2541
Fax: (719) 658-2343
E-mail: crt@creederep.org
www.creederep.org

Cromarty & Co.

 THE BUZZ
- "Help promote Broadway theater to the masses"

 THE STATS

Industry(ies): Public Relations; Theater/Performing Arts

Location(s): New York, NY

Number of interns: Varies

Pay: $6/day for lunch; $4/day for transportation

Length of internship: Approximately 12-16 weeks; hours can be full-time or part-time

 THE SCOOP

Cromarty & Co. was founded in 1988 and focuses its business on providing public relations services for the theater industry, including Broadway and Off-Broadway theater, as well as dance, music, cabaret, benefits, special events and various festivals. Services that Cromarty & Co. provides include public relations plans, conceptual marketing designs, promotional plans, story placement, column item placement, photography consultation and advertising consultation.

ON THE JOB

Cromarty internships will suit those students who are interested in theater, show business, public relations, journalism, and the entertainment industry in New York City. Interns are given a variety of tasks, including creating press kits, communicating with the press, coordinating schedules, attending photo shoots, and writing program materials. Interns work directly with a publicist and internships are structured toward each intern's level. Some other responsibilities include coordinating performer's schedules, writing program materials and arranging interviews. Interns are also encouraged to attend the performances put on by Cromarty & Co.'s clients.

💲 **GETTING HIRED**

Apply by: Rolling. Send a resume, cover letter, and a short note on how your previous theatre or performing arts experiences would make you a qualified candidate for this opportunity.

Qualifications:

Open to all interested parties. General office skills are required (typing, computers, etc.). A strong interest in the theater or public relations and theater background (can be school experience) preferred. (Note: interns are not required to be students.)

Contact:
Internship Supervisor
Cromarty & Co.
Ansonia Station P.O. Box 237154
New York, NY 10023
Phone/Fax: (212) 580-4222
E-mail: mailbox@cromarty.com
www.cromarty.com/internship.htm

Crow Canyon Archaeological Center

THE BUZZ

- "Dig into the history of the Pueblo Indians"

THE STATS

Industry(ies): Education; Environmental

Location(s): Cortez, CO

Number of interns: Varies

Pay: Small stipend. Free meals in dining hall; housing; travel allowance up to $350

Length of internship: *Spring/summer/winter*: varies

THE SCOOP

Crow Canyon Archaeological Center, founded in 1983, studies and teaches the history of the ancient Pueblo Indians. Researchers at The Center use findings from the archaeology of the Mesa Verde region to educate the public.

ON THE JOB

Lab interns process specimens, maintain records, analyze artifacts, manage collections and supervise visitors. Cataloging and analyzing pottery and stone tools are major parts of the internship. Interns may also analyze and interpret artifact collections. Interns assist Crow Canyon's research staff of nine archaeologists and interact with visitors. Interns also work on The Center's current research project, "Communities Through Time: Migration, Cooperation and Conflict."

GETTING HIRED

Apply by: Refer to the web site for the deadline. Download an application from Crow Canyon web site at www.crowcanyon.org /Jobs/intern_research.html.

Qualifications:
Open to graduate and undergraduate students. Advanced undergraduate or graduate work in archaeology, anthropology, museum studies or related fields; minimum of four weeks laboratory or archaeology field experience for the lab internship; desire to work in a team; ability to instruct lay persons; and ability to perform technical work required.

Contact:
Moria Robinson
Crow Canyon Archaeological Center
Internship Program
23390 Road K
Cortez, CO 81321
Phone: (970) 565-8975
Fax: (970) 565-4859
E-mail: mrobinson@crowcanyon.org
www.crowcanyon.org/Jobs/jobs_opportunities.html

Crown Capital

THE BUZZ

- "Make useful connections as you work with top executives"
- "Learn commercial mortgage banking and real estate from top to bottom"

THE STATS

Industry(ies): Financial Services; Real Estate

Location(s): San Francisco, CA

Number of interns: *Summer*: 1-2

Pay: Paid; $1,500/month

Length of internship: *Summer*: 12 weeks

THE SCOOP

Crown Capital offers commercial real estate services including acquisitions, financing, development and management. Crown owns and manages in excess of $250 million in real estate and has originated over $750 million in real estate loans. Product types include multifamily, office, retail, industrial, hotels and others.

ON THE JOB

Interns at Crown Capital are given the chance to work with the company's executives. Interns may assist on various levels and deals including acquisitions management, commercial mortgage loans and more.

GETTING HIRED

Apply by: April 1. Send resume, cover letter, SAT scores and GPA. Also include any other information you feel qualifies you for the position.

Qualifications:
Open to sophomores, juniors and seniors in undergrad programs in the U.S. Strong SATs and a high GPA required.

Contact:
David W. Yancey
Crown Capital
540 Pacific Avenue
San Francisco, CA 94133
Phone: (415) 398-6330
Fax: (415) 398-6057
E-mail: dyancey@crowncapital.com
www.crowncapital.com

Visit Vault at **www.vault.com** for insider company profiles, expert advice, career message boards, expert resume reviews, the Vault Job Board and more.

VAULT CAREER LIBRARY **133**

C-SPAN

🐝 THE BUZZ

- "Be in the know!"
- "Hands-on experience"
- "Fast-paced environment for fast-paced learning"

📟 THE STATS

Industry(ies): Broadcast & Entertainment; Government; Journalism; New/Interactive Media; Nonprofit

Location(s): Washington, DC

Number of interns: *Spring*: 15; *summer*: 20; *fall*: 15

Pay: None

Length of internship: *Spring/summer/fall*: 12 weeks each

✒ THE SCOOP

C-SPAN (Cable-Satellite Public Affairs Network) began in 1979 as a public service cable television network broadcasting the live proceedings of the House of Representatives. In addition to the original C-SPAN, the company now includes C-SPAN2, C-SPAN3, C-SPAN Radio and C-SPAN.org. This corporation takes pride in its unbiased broadcasts. It receives no government funding and is a nonprofit educational organization.

🏢 ON THE JOB

The broad goal of the C-SPAN internship program is to introduce the best and the brightest interested in communications and politics to (what else?) the running of a cable television network and contemporary politics. Six departments accept interns: marketing, programming, programming operations, new media, C-SPAN Radio 90 and engineering. Intern duties include researching, learning video production and assisting public relations. C-SPAN interns may also be involved in community outreach programs. Expect at least 16 hours of work per week and interaction with interns from other departments.

💲 GETTING HIRED

Apply by: Rolling. Apply online at www.c-span.org; click on the "jobs" link and select the appropriate internship. Include a cover letter – indicating desired department and term (spring, summer or fall) – and resume via online application.

Qualifications:

Open to college juniors and seniors.

Contact:

C-SPAN
Human Resources
400 North Capitol Street, NW, Suite 650
Washington, DC 20001
www.c-span.org

Cummins, Inc.

🐝 THE BUZZ

- "Study engine design with a global leader"
- "Get actual hands-on experience"

📟 THE STATS

Industry(ies): Manufacturing

Location(s): Columbus, IN (HQ)

Number of interns: *Annual*: over 100

Pay: Paid; competitive salary

Length of internship: *Summer*: May-August; *fall*: August-December; *spring*: January-May

✒ THE SCOOP

Cummins, Inc., is a network of companies that designs, manufactures, distributes and services (diesel) engines and related technologies, including electrical power generation systems, emissions solutions, air handling, filtration, fuel systems and controls. The company also makes and manufactures construction equipment and generators. Cummins is present in 160 countries and distributes engines from 550 distribution facilities worldwide. Headquartered in Columbus, Ind., Cummins employs 24,000 people and has reported sales of $8.4 billion.

🏢 ON THE JOB

Co-ops and interns work in various capacities. Research and development students get hands-on experience applying their education to real and complex problems. Information technology co-ops and interns directly participate in the development of new, leading technology. Electronics technology interns and co-ops develop cutting-edge communications systems and engine design while getting comprehensive experience in hardware and software design. The manufacturing engineering department offers students first-hand experience in metrology, controls, industrial and manufacturing engineering. Service engineer students learn how to predict problems, conduct field tests and develop solutions for client support. Finance and accounting students participate in financial planning, including accounting, pricing and long-term planning.

💲 GETTING HIRED

Apply by: Rolling. Complete online application and submit resume to: http://64.89.40.26/servlet/resp/rf?jobid=1446626&boardid=1692&Template=ResponseFormCampus.html. Check with your campus career placement center to see if and when Cummins representatives will be visiting your school.

Qualifications:

Open to undergraduate, graduate and MBA candidates enrolled in a full-time technical, finance, human resources, business, marketing or related program. Students must possess at least a "B" average.

Contact:

Cummins Corporate Headquarters
Box 3005
Columbus, IN 47202
Phone: (812) 377-5000
Fax: (812) 377-3334
www.cummins.com

The Cushman School

 THE BUZZ
- "Help shape the lives of Miami's youth"
- "A unique teaching experience"

 THE STATS

Industry(ies): Education

Location(s): Miami, FL

Number of interns: *Annual*: 2-4

Pay: Paid; $118/week for U.S. citizens; $175/week for non-U.S. citizens

Length of internship: 17 weeks with the option to extend

 THE SCOOP

The Cushman School is Miami's oldest independent day school. It focuses on character development and educational excellence. Since 1924, the school has maintained the same philosophy of founder Dr. Laura Cushman, who felt that good citizens resulted from instilling a love of learning in students and teaching good character. The United States Department of Education has recognized Cushman as a National School of Excellence.

 ON THE JOB

Interns handle a variety of classroom duties, including organizing thematic units, working with small reading groups or math groups, assisting teachers in drama, art and music, and helping to plan drama assemblies. In addition, interns are encouraged to teach students about their own backgrounds, bringing cultural education to Cushman students. Interns work with three-year-olds through eighth graders.

$ GETTING HIRED

Apply by: Rolling. Mail resume, cover letter and photo.

Qualifications:
Open to undergraduate juniors and seniors, and recent college graduates. An interest in education is preferred.

Contact:
Ann Gorman
The Cushman School
592 North East 60th Street
Miami, FL 33137
Phone: (305) 757-1966
Fax: (305) 757-1632
E-mail: agorman@cushmanschool.org
www.cushmanschool.org

Visit Vault at **www.vault.com** for insider company profiles, expert advice, career message boards, expert resume reviews, the Vault Job Board and more.

VAULT CAREER LIBRARY **135**

INTERNSHIP PROFILES:
D

D.C. Booth Historic National Fish Hatchery

 THE BUZZ

- "Intern in the aptly named Spearfish, South Dakota"

 THE STATS

Industry(ies): Art/Museum

Location(s): Spearfish, SD

Number of interns: *Annual*: 1-2

Pay: Housing or stipend; varies according to funding

Length of internship: *Summer*: 3-5 months

 **THE SCOOP**

Formed in 1896, the D.C. Booth Historic National Fish Hatchery is run by the U.S. Fish and Wildlife Service and is one of the oldest fish hatcheries in the West, located in tiny Spearfish, South Dakota (population 9,000). The museum's collection focuses on the history of fish hatcheries and includes tools, photographs, personal papers and archeological items. An historic house is also connected to the museum.

ON THE JOB

Interns work with the curator on inventory, cataloging, preservation maintenance and storage. They also research topics relating to fish hatcheries and work on archival, processing, photography and exhibit work. Internship procedures follow those set by the Department of the Interior, so the program closely resembles those at National Parks.

GETTING HIRED

Apply by: Rolling. Send detailed resume (career goals, experience, academic requirements) with three references to the address below.

Qualifications:
Priority given to college juniors and seniors and graduate students in museum studies or historic preservation.

Contact:
Curator, D.C. Booth HNFH
423 Hatchery Circle
Spearfish, SD 57783-2643
Phone: (605) 642-7730
E-mail: randi_smith@fws.gov
dcbooth.fws.gov/internship.htm

The Daily Press

 THE BUZZ

- "Be inside the newsroom and watch the news unfold"
- "For Virginian newspapermen and newspaperwomen"

 THE STATS

Industry(ies): Journalism

Location(s): Newport News, VA

Number of interns: *Summer*: 1-10

Pay: Paid; 80 percent of a full time reporter's salary

Length of internship: *Summer*: 10 weeks

 THE SCOOP

The Daily Press covers breaking news, sports, entertainment, business and more for Virginia, from Newport News to Williamsburg. *The Daily Press*, which has been published since 1896, has about 550 employees, 150 of which work in the newsroom.

ON THE JOB

Interns at *The Daily Press* do real work, from reporting and writing stories to taking photos or copy editing and designing graphics. Interns also attend team meetings and brown bag lunch programs on current topics. This is a true reporting position, in which interns drive to local story locations to cover events or news and return to the office to write their stories, making a car necessary for the job. Interns in graphic design will work with graphic designers and those taking photos will work directly with the photography staff.

GETTING HIRED

Apply by: *Summer*: December 1. Mail resume, cover letter, five to 10 clips or classroom writing samples, a list of three professional references, and a 450- to 700-word essay on "the one that got away."

Qualifications:
Open to rising college juniors and seniors.

Contact:
Ursula E. Nofal
Administrative Coordinator
Daily Press Internships
7505 Warwick Blvd.
Newport News, VA 23607
Phone: (757) 247-4745
E-mail: unofal@dailypress.com
www.dailypress.com/dp-careers-intern.htmlstory

DaimlerChrysler

 **THE BUZZ**
- "Design vehicles of the future"
- "Work for one of the largest automobile companies in the world"

THE STATS

Industry(ies): Manufacturing; Technology

Location(s): Auburn Hills, MI (U.S. HQ)

Number of interns: Varies

Pay: Paid; *undergraduates*: $340-$740/week; *graduate students*: $595-$1,000/week. $700 stipend and round-trip travel for out-of-towners

Length of internship: 17 weeks maximum

 **THE SCOOP**

Now called DaimlerChrysler, the company oversees automotive makers Maybach, Mercedes-Benz, Chrysler, Jeep and Dodge, along with several commercial vehicle brands. Daimler (a German company) merged with the American carmaker Chrysler at the turn of the current century. The company's official language is English, and it employs over 350,000 people worldwide. Its headquarters are now located in Stuttgart, Germany, and Auburn Hills, Michigan.

ON THE JOB

The internship is designed to foster personal growth and allow interns to decide whether a career with the DaimlerChrysler Group specifically, or in automotive business, more generally, is right for them. Offices accepting interns include global sales and marketing, finance, human relations, information technology management, manufacturing, procurement and supply, product design and vehicle engineering. For more information, see www.careers.chrysler-group.com.

GETTING HIRED

Apply by: Rolling. Chrysler recruits at specific schools each fall. Check with your career office (where interested students must apply).

Qualifications:
Open to college students who have finished their sophomore year (junior year for human relations) and have above-average grades (3.0 GPA or above). The finance program accepts MBA students only. The information technology management internship requires advanced computing skills.

Contact:
If DaimlerChrysler doesn't recruit at your school, contact www.careers.chrysler-group.com.

Dallas Cowboys

THE BUZZ
- "Did somebody say cheerleaders?"
- "Work for one of the most successful NFL franchises"

THE STATS

Industry(ies): Sports

Location(s): Irving, TX

Number of interns: *Summer*: 40-50

Pay: Varies depending on department

Length of internship: *Summer*: 5-6 weeks

THE SCOOP

The Dallas Cowboys is one of the NFL's most famous football teams. Darren Woodson, the Cowboy's oldest player at 34, is currently the talk of the team. Other players bringing team notoriety include wide receiver Antonio Bryant, linebacker Dexter Coakley and offensive lineman Larry Allen. The five-time world championship team, founded in 1960, plays at Texas Stadium in Irving, Texas.

ON THE JOB

Interns for the Dallas Cowboys may work in various departments, including public relations, marketing, training, equipment, coaching, merchandising, operations and the Internet. Interns are given a wide range of jobs, from researching and filing to interacting with the media, and may work with coaches, players or any other Dallas Cowboys employee.

GETTING HIRED

Apply by: Applications are accepted between January and April. Mail a resume including related experience. No e-mail or telephone calls.

Qualifications:
Open to college juniors and seniors studying in fields related to the department for which they will intern.

Contact:
Dallas Cowboys
Human Resources Department
7 Cowboy Parkway
Irving, TX 75063
Phone: (972) 556-9900
Fax: (972) 556-9984

Visit Vault at **www.vault.com** for insider company profiles, expert advice, career message boards, expert resume reviews, the Vault Job Board and more.

V/\ULT CAREER LIBRARY **139**

Decatur House Museum

THE BUZZ
- "Spend a summer just up the street from the White House"

THE STATS
Industry(ies): Art/Museum; Education; Tourism/Recreation

Location(s): Washington, DC

Number of interns: *Summer/fall/spring*: 1-4 each

Pay: None. Free entry to other museums throughout DC area

Length of internship: *Summer*: 8-10 weeks; *fall/spring*: 10-12 weeks each; dates are flexible

THE SCOOP
Benjamin Henry Latrobe, the "Father of American Architecture," designed the Decatur House in 1818 for naval hero Stephen Decatur. Situated one block away from the White House, the Decatur House has seen many great residents since its original owner (Henry Clay and Martin Van Buren among them) and is a landmark of Washington's earliest days. Presently, the Decatur House serves as a museum and educational site.

ON THE JOB
Internships at the Decatur House are largely up to the interns' designs and will be modeled according to each intern's talents, interests and educational requirements. Past interns have focused on a wide range of museum work, including education programs, curatorial work, archive research, and managing the museum's shop. Interns very much become part of the staff during their time at Decatur House. Summer internships are conducted in tandem with those at the National Trust, and Decatur House interns are able to go on field trips and attend lunch seminars with National Trust interns.

GETTING HIRED
Apply by: Rolling. Apply with a cover letter, transcript and resume listing two to three references.

Qualifications:
Open to undergraduates, recent grads, as well as grad students.

Contact:
Katherine Malone-France
Director of Collections and Programs
Decatur House
1610 H Street, NW
Washington, DC 20006
Phone: (202) 842-0920
Fax: (202) 842-0030
E-mail: katherine_malone-france@nthp.org
www.decaturhouse.org

Dell

 THE BUZZ
- "Live the TV commercial"

 **THE STATS**

Industry(ies): Hardware; Technology

Location(s): Austin, TX; Nashville, TN

Number of interns: *Summer*: 75

Pay: Paid; varies. Travel reimbursement for travel to and from internship location; fully furnished corporate apartment; discount on Dell products; discounted health club membership

Length of internship: *Summer*: 10-12 weeks

 **THE SCOOP**

Founded in 1984 by Michael Dell, this namesake corporation was once a small company that was based on the simple concept of selling computers directly to customers. Today, Dell is one of the largest computer manufacturers and the biggest direct-sale computer company worldwide.

ON THE JOB

Interns at Dell share the same job responsibilities as full-time employees; they are given real work with business-related problems to solve. Interns commit to working with one group during the summer and work with full-time employees to accomplish the goals outlined in their performance plan. Undergraduate and master's interns can choose finance, human resources, IT, engineering, supply chain, logistics or operations. MBA students have opportunities in marketing, finance, human resources, corporate strategy, supply chain, logistics and operations. All interns will participate in an extensive orientation program and various intern events, as well as in the Intern Executive Speaker Series, which includes sessions with Michael Dell and Kevin Rollins.

GETTING HIRED

Apply by: Rolling. Attend one of Dell's scheduled campus visits or submit a resume and cover letter online. See the company web site for a listing of upcoming campus events.

Qualifications:
Open to undergraduate sophomores and juniors, first-year MBA students, and first-year master's students. Applicants must be in good academic standing and must be pursuing a field consistent with Dell's intern assignments.

Contact:
Internship Coordinator
University Relations
Dell Computer Corporation
2214 West Braker Lane
Austin, TX 78758
E-mail: Dell_College_Relations@Dell.com
www1.us.dell.com/content/topics/topic.aspx/global/hybrid/career
s/content/139d3ad4-3216-49bd-919f-ed933865e6bf?c =
us&l = en&s = corp

Deloitte & Touche

 **THE BUZZ**
- "You choose the location and get your own laptop"

THE STATS

Industry(ies): Financial Services; Manufacturing; Aviation and Transport Services; Life Sciences and Healthcare; Energy and Resources; Consumer Business; Public Sector; Real Estate; Media, Technology; Telecom

Location(s): New York, NY (HQ); offices in more than 80 American cities and 140 countries

Number of interns: Varies according to location

Pay: Paid; competitive salary

Length of internship: *Summer*: 8-10 weeks; *winter/spring*: approximately 10 weeks. In certain offices, part-time internships are available.

THE SCOOP

In the United States, Deloitte & Touche USA LLP (DT) is the member firm of Deloitte Touche Tohmatsu (DTT), an organization of member firms across the globe providing professional services and advice in four principal areas – audit, tax, consulting and financial advisory services. DTT serves over half of the world's largest companies, as well as public institutions, locally significant clients and rapid-growth global companies. The subsidiaries of DT employ nearly 33,000 people in more than 80 U.S. cities.

ON THE JOB

During a Deloitte internship, college students will join a client service team in one of four service functions: audit and enterprise risk services from DT; consulting from Deloitte Consulting LLP; financial advisory services from Deloitte Financial Advisory Services LLP; or tax from Deloitte Tax LLP. Interns will work first-hand with clients, gaining an understanding of what a full time position with Deloitte entails. Interns will be issued a laptop computer for access to the Internet and the firm's technology via intranet. Interns will undergo an orientation program and several weeks of technical and functional training specific to their department. Interns should expect to receive the same assignments and face the same expectations as first-year hires.

GETTING HIRED

Apply by: Rolling. Apply online through Deloitte's web site. Resume, transcripts and location preferences are required. Applicants are also encouraged to attach a resume to their job-specific profiles.

Qualifications:
Open to college sophomores, juniors and seniors. Leadership is essential, in the classroom, at work and on campus. Applicants should display an ability to balance a strong academic record with extracurricular activities.

Contact:
careers.deloitte.com/students_internships.aspx

Internship recruiting
careers.deloitte.com/students_internships.aspx?Country

Visit Vault at **www.vault.com** for insider company profiles, expert advice, career message boards, expert resume reviews, the Vault Job Board and more.

 **141**

DesignTech International

 THE BUZZ
- "Help design smart products for the future"

 THE STATS

Industry(ies): Consumer Products; Technology

Location(s): Springfield, VA

Number of interns: *Annual*: 10-12

Pay: Stipend of $375-$500 paid every 2 weeks based on expertise. Travel to trade shows; possible bonus at end of internship; free housing

Length of internship: *Summer/fall/winter/spring*: minimum 6-month commitment

 THE SCOOP

DesignTech International is a small consumer company that has developed and marketed innovative consumer products in the "automotive, smart home and smart phone" areas since 1984. Over 90 percent of the company's product assembly is done at the headquarters in Springfield, Va. DesignTech's best known pioneering products include remote car starter systems, wireless home automation products, and other home and automotive electronics.

 ON THE JOB

Interns work in all facets of DesignTech International, from clerical duties to product quality control. They also experience an intense degree of interaction with the president and vice president, depending on their fields of concentration. Interns work as assistants in accounting, graphic design, production, marketing, engineering and database development.

$ GETTING HIRED

Apply by: Rolling. Submit resume and cover letter stating availability and intended start dates.

Qualifications:

Open to all college juniors and seniors, as well as recent grads and grad students. (Applicants should be 18-24 years of age.) International applications are welcome. The company prefers that students have completed at least two years of college prior to application.

Contact:

Arturas Rainys – Director of Sales
DesignTech International
7955 Cameron Brown Court
Springfield, VA 22153
Phone: (703) 866-2000
Fax: (703) 866-2001
E-mail: arturas@designtech-intl.com
www.designtech-intl.com/Content/jobs/interns

Deutsche Bank

 THE BUZZ
- "A global bank with classic German engineering"

 **THE STATS:**

Industry(ies): Financial Services

Location(s): Frankfurt (HQ); additional HQ offices in London and New York, NY; Singapore; various locations worldwide

Number of interns: Varies

Pay: Paid; competitive salary

Length of internship: *Summer*: 10 weeks

 THE SCOOP

Founded in Germany in 1870, Deutsche Bank is a multinational bank headquartered in Frankfurt with additional head offices in London, New York City and Hong Kong. Through its three divisions – the Corporate and Investment Bank, Private Clients and Asset Management, and Corporate Investments – Deutsche Bank provides financial services to global corporations, financial institutions, sovereign and multinational organizations, and retail and high-net-worth individuals. The bank employs over 65,000 people across the globe.

 ON THE JOB

Deutsche Bank offers summer analyst and summer associate positions in a variety of groups or divisions. Groups accepting summer associates include Asset Management, Global Banking, Corporate Finance and Global Markets. Summer analysts can work in Controlling and Finance, Global Banking, Global Markets, Human Resources, Operations, Risk Management, Credit Risk and Technology. Visit the company web site for details on each group and the programs associated with them.

 GETTING HIRED

Apply by: Unless you have a particular campus process that Deutsche Bank is working with, applications are generally accepted November through February until the programs are filled. Interviews take place from January to March. All applications are available online and candidates are asked to review the various opportunities online prior to applying, as each candidate is allowed to submit only one application. The online application is available at http://career.deutsche-bank.com/wms/dbhr/index.php?language=2&ci=1514.

Qualifications:

Summer analyst: open to rising college seniors; *summer associate*: open to MBA students who have completed their first year. See the web site for more details on each of the various groups.

Contact:

Undergraduate internship
career.deutsche-bank.com/wms/dbhr/index.php?language=2&ci=2655

MBA internship
career.deutsche-bank.com/wms/dbhr/index.php?language=2&ci=2617

Deutsche Post World Net/DHL

 THE BUZZ
- "Get your career moving in a global network"

 **THE STATS**

Industry(ies): Transportation

Location(s): Various locations in at least 12 countries including Singapore and other Southeast Asian countries, the United States, Germany and Belgium

Number of interns: *Annual*: 90

Pay: Varies

Length of internship: 9-12 months

 THE SCOOP

Deutsche Post World Net/DHL began in 1969 as an express document shipping company. The firm is now a leading express and logistics company offering a variety of customized express solutions from a single source to its clients. DPWN/DHL combines worldwide coverage with an in-depth knowledge of its customers' local markets. The company's international network links more than 220 countries and territories worldwide. At the forefront of technology and with over 150,000 employees, DPWN/DHL guarantees fast and reliable service. DPWN/DHL is based in Bonn, Germany, and is wholly owned by Deutsche Post World Net.

 ON THE JOB

DPWN/DHL has a number of intern positions available. Audit interns perform internal control system revision; human resource trainees work on organization design policy and HR information systems; training and development executives; corporate affairs trainees work on brand relaunching and organize press conferences; macro economic analysts learn market analysis and forecasting; and industry knowledge support analysts coordinate customer satisfaction surveys and work on analyzing customer supply chains and strategies.

GETTING HIRED

Apply by: Rolling. DPWN/DHL hires its interns through AIESEC (www.aiesec.org).

Qualifications:
Open to college graduates and grad students selected through AIESEC to be part of their international traineeship exchange program.

Contact:
www.aiesec.org
www.dpwn.com/career

Discovery Communications

 THE BUZZ
- "The leading brand in televised lions"

 THE STATS

Industry(ies): Broadcast & Entertainment; Education; New/Interactive Media; Publishing

Location(s): Silver Spring, MD (corporate HQ); Berkeley, CA; Bethesda, MD; Charlotte, NC; Chicago, IL; Detroit, MI; Florence, KY; Los Angeles, CA; Miami, FL; New York, NY; Argentina; Australia; Brazil; Canada; Denmark; England; Germany; Hong Kong; India; Japan; The Netherlands; Poland; Singapore; Taiwan

Number of interns: *Summer*: 90

Pay: Paid; $8-13/hour. Weekly "lunch and learn" seminars with executives; mentoring program; field trips and tours

Length of internship: *Summer*: 10 weeks

 THE SCOOP

Launched in 1985 by founder and chairman John Hendricks, Discovery Communications Inc. is a private multimedia company for home entertainment, interactive multimedia, publishing, merchandising, and international sales and distribution. Discovery Communications' U.S networks include the Discovery Channel, Animal Planet, TLC, Travel Channel, Discovery Kids, Discovery Health, Fit TV, The Science Channel, Discovery Home Channel, Discovery Wings, Discovery en Espanol, Discovery HD Theater and BBC America. Through popular programs such as *The New Detectives* and *Unsolved History*, Discovery Communications is explores insightful topics related to science, technology, culture, history, human adventure and health with programs that reach over 1 billion households in 155 countries.

 ON THE JOB

Internships are available in every facet of the company, including sales, advertising, product development, technical support, marketing, manufacturing, finance and human resources. Interns' duties vary between departments.

GETTING HIRED

Apply by: *Summer*: application review begins in late January. Apply online at secured.kenexa.com/discoveryv4/newhr/jobsearch.asp.

Qualifications:
Open to college juniors and seniors (minimum 3.0 GPA), grad students, MBA students and international applicants.

Contact:
Internship Coordinator
Discovery Communications, Inc.
Human Resources
One Discovery Place
Silver Spring, MD 20910
Phone: (240) 662-0000
www.discovery.com

Visit Vault at **www.vault.com** for insider company profiles, expert advice, career message boards, expert resume reviews, the Vault Job Board and more.

VAULT CAREER LIBRARY **143**

Disney Theme Parks and Resorts College Program

 THE BUZZ
- "Magical resume builder"
- "Ride Space Mountain for free!"

 THE STATS

Industry(ies): Broadcast & Entertainment; Hospitality; Tourism/Recreation

Location(s): Orlando, FL

Number of interns: *Spring/fall*: Varies

Pay: Paid; $6.40/hour; additional premiums for some positions. Housing and free park admission

Length of internship: *Spring/fall*: 5-7 months, beginning in either January, May, or August; 30-45 hours/week

 THE SCOOP

Through his drawing talent, Walt Disney literally conjured up an empire. One of his most well-known creations, the Florida-based theme park Walt Disney World opened in 1971 and became home to some of Disney's most beloved characters, including Mickey Mouse, Donald Duck and Goofy. The giant resort has grown over the years, now encompassing 47 square miles of land. It includes the Magic Kingdom Park, Epcot, Disney-MGM Studios, Disney's Animal Kingdom Theme Park, the Downtown Disney area, two water parks and over 20 themed resorts for its visiting guests.

 ON THE JOB

Disney College Program interns work in the food and beverage, entertainment, operations, retail or culinary departments (as sous-chefs in culinary), or in the front offices or housekeeping sections of Walt Disney World resorts. Responsibilities vary by department, but may include customer service, operations, sales, food service or administrative duties. Operational interns may handle janitorial tasks or man the ticket windows. Interns learn time management, decision making, communication, planning and organizational skills.

$ GETTING HIRED

Apply by: *Spring:* interviews during prior fall semester; *fall:* interviews in prior spring semester. Online application (go to disneycollegeprogram.com and click on "Walt Disney World Resort" for details) Viewing an on-campus presentation or E-Presentation online is required prior to interview. An audition is also required for entertaiment interns.

Qualifications:

Open to college freshmen, sophomores, juniors and seniors who have completed at least one semester. Must be enrolled in college, at least 18 years of age at time of arrival, and a U.S. citizen or have unrestricted U.S. work authorization. A minimum GPA of 2.0 required. Not limited to specific majors.

Contact:
E-mail: wdw.college.recruiting@disney.com
www.wdwcollegeprogram.com

Donna Karan

 THE BUZZ
- "A *Sex and the City*-caliber internship"

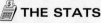 **THE STATS**

Industry(ies): Fashion; Retail

Location(s): New York, NY

Number of interns: Varies

Pay: None

Length of internship: *Spring/summer/fall/winter*: 3 months each

 THE SCOOP

In 1985, Donna Karan launched her own clothing line, the Donna Karan New York Collection. Four years later, Donna Karan International Inc. expanded with the introduction of DKNY, a more affordable line. Now Donna Karan International Inc., purchased by LMVH in 2001, also offers accessories, home furnishings and eyewear among its many products. Donna Karan remains the chief designer and chairman, and the company has become one of the world's fashion powerhouses.

ON THE JOB

Donna Karan International Inc. offers internships year-round in a variety of departments. Although specific intern duties will vary depending on placement – advertising, design, finances, etc. – tasks may include assisting the design teams, answering phones and handling administrative duties. Students can expect an in-depth introduction to the fashion business.

GETTING HIRED

Apply by: Rolling. Send a cover letter indicating area of interest and resume to the address below. Log on to www.pcrecruiter.com/clients/dkny/welcome.html for a list of openings.

Qualifications:

Open to college freshmen, sophomores, juniors and seniors enrolled in an accredited university; various departments within Donna Karan may have additional requirements.

Contact:
Donna Karan International
240 West 40th Street
New York, NY 10018
Phone: (212) 789-1643 (internship hotline)
Fax: (212) 768-5937
E-mail: dkinterns@dkintl.com
www.pcrecruiter.com/clients/dkny/welcome.html

Dow Chemical Company

THE BUZZ

- "Mix together the formula to your future"
- "One word: plastics"

 THE STATS

Industry(ies): Chemicals; Science/Research

Location(s): Midland, MI (HQ); California; Freeport, TX; Georgia; Louisiana; New Jersey; West Virginia; Africa; Asia-Pacific; Europe; Latin America; Middle East

Number of interns: *Annual*: 100-115

Pay: *Undergraduate*: $2,100-$3,400; *graduate*: $3,300-$5,500 stipend. Round-trip travel; furnished housing for $12/day; gym access

Length of internship: *Summer/fall/spring*: 12 weeks

THE SCOOP

Established in 1897, Dow has since grown into a leading science and technology company with approximately 50,000 employees. Dow services more than 170 countries and provides innovative chemical, plastic and agricultural products and services to many essential consumer markets. The firm's recent revenues of $28 billion were achieved through the sale of such popular consumer products as "adhesives, sealants, coatings, Styrofoam brand insulation fibers and films, as well as performance chemicals such as acrylic acid," among others.

ON THE JOB

Opportunities for both alternating term co-ops and interns include manufacturing, research, information systems, accounting, sales and human resources (MS degrees only). For students pursuing an MBA, opportunities are available in finance, treasury and marketing.

GETTING HIRED

Apply by: *Spring/summer/fall*: October 31. Submit resume and cover letter.

Qualifications:
Open to sophomore, junior and senior undergraduates with a minimum GPA of 3.0, as well as graduate students and international applicants.

Contact:
National Student Program
Dow Chemical Company
P.O. Box 1655
Midland, MI 48641-1655
www.dow.com/careers/students/intern.htm

Dow Jones & Company

THE BUZZ

- "In the journalism field, it doesn't get much more prestigious than this"
- "A good step toward that Pulitzer"

THE STATS

Industry(ies): Journalism

Location(s): New York, NY; South Brunswick, NJ

Number of interns: Varies

Pay: Paid; *publishing*: $700/week minimum; *technology*: $525/week

Length of internship: *Summer*: 8-10 weeks

THE SCOOP

Dow Jones & Company, publisher of *The Wall Street Journal*, produces the world's most vital business and financial news and information. Company operations are divided into three segments: print publishing, electronic publishing and community newspapers.

ON THE JOB

Internships are offered primarily during May through August. Students will be introduced to careers in the exciting world of business news and information reporting. Publishing interns will spend the summer working in one of the *Journal*'s news bureaus. Technology interns will be involved with technical support of desktop systems and networks affecting real-time news delivery, programming in C++, JAVA, GUI, HTML, related databases, systems and database administration, or networking and information security.

GETTING HIRED

Apply by: *Publishing*: November 1; *technology*: May 1.

Qualifications:
Open to college freshmen, sophomores, juniors and seniors, as well as grad students.

Contact:
Dow Jones & Company
Attn: IT Internship Dept – HR
P.O. Box 300
Princeton, NJ 08543-0300
www.dowjones.com/careers/internships/internships.htm

Visit Vault at **www.vault.com** for insider company profiles, expert advice, career message boards, expert resume reviews, the Vault Job Board and more.

VAULT CAREER LIBRARY 145

The Dow Jones Newspaper Fund

 THE BUZZ
- "Deadlines and headlines"
- "Stop the presses!"

 THE STATS

Industry(ies): Journalism

Location(s): Various U.S. newspapers and news services in cities including Denver, CO; Erie, PA; Houston, TX; Los Angeles, CA; Miami, FL; New York, NY; San Francisco, CA; Washington, DC

Number of interns: *Summer*: 100 or more nationwide

Pay: Paid; $350/week minimum. $1,000 scholarship for the following school year

Length of internship: *Summer*: 10 weeks

 **THE SCOOP**

The Dow Jones Newspaper Fund is a nonprofit on a mission to improve journalism education and the quality of candidates for newspaper jobs. In this spirit, DJNF offers journalism-related internships, scholarships, fellowships, training and literature. The Dow Jones Newspaper Fund was founded in 1958 and is supported by Dow Jones & Company, Inc., in addition to other newspaper corporations.

 ON THE JOB

There are four internship programs available: the Business Reporting Program, the Newspaper Copy Editing Program, the Online Copy Editing Program and the Sports Copy Editing Program. All offer hands-on journalism experience and pre-internship training sessions on college campuses. The Business Reporting Program is specifically designed for minority students on the sophomore- or junior college-level. Participating newspapers include *The New York Times*, *The Tennessean* and *The Wall Street Journal*.

 GETTING HIRED

Apply by: November 1 – postmark deadline. An application, resume, 500-word essay, transcript, and Dow Jones Newspaper Fund test are required. Business Reporting candidates must also submit three to five published clips.

Qualifications:
Business Reporting: open to minority college sophomores and juniors. *Online/Sports/Newspaper Copy Editing*: open to all college juniors, seniors and graduate students.

Contact:
Dow Jones Newspaper Fund, Inc.
P.O. Box 300
Princeton, NJ 08543-0300
Phone: (609) 452-2820
E-mail: newsfund@wsj.dowjones.com
djnewspaperfund.dowjones.com/fund/cs_internships.asp

The Drawing Center

 THE BUZZ
- "Oil gets all the press – start promoting drawings"

 **THE STATS**

Industry(ies): Art/Museum; Nonprofit; Public Relations; Publishing

Location(s): New York, NY

Number of interns: 4-5 per semester

Pay: None; academic credit available

Length of internship: Internships run for approximately 2-4 months, with the potential to continue for subsequent sessions. *Summer*: May-July; *fall*: September-December; *winter/spring*: January-April; minimum 15 hours/week

 THE SCOOP

The Drawing Center is the only fine arts institution in the the U.S. that focuses solely on the exhibition of drawings, both historical and contemporary. The Center was established in 1977 to provide opportunities for emerging and under-recognized artists; to demonstrate the significance and diversity of drawings throughout history; and to stimulate public dialogue on issues of art and culture. The Center is located in SoHo, known for its large number of galleries, museums and artists' studios.

 ON THE JOB

Rotational internships provide opportunities to acquire practical experience in a small art museum. Interns rotate through one of two groupings of several departments: the departments of contemporary curation and the Viewing Program for emerging artists, education and operations; or historical curation, registration, publications and development/marketing. Interns work with museum staff to become familiar with each department. Interns will have the opportunity to assist in exhibition installations and de-installations. Interns must attend opening receptions for all exhibitions, and assist with at least one special event each month during the duration of the internship.

GETTING HIRED

Apply by: *Fall*: July 1; *spring*: November 10; *summer*: April 1. Submit an application form and resume indicating dates of availability and areas of interest or expertise via mail or fax. Online application available at www.drawingcenter.org.

Qualifications:
Open to undergraduates (with at least one year of study completed), graduate students and recent grads.

Contact:
Education Coordinator
The Drawing Center, Education Program
35 Wooster Street
New York, NY 10013
Phone: (212) 219-2166, ext. 119
Fax: (212) 966-2976
E-mail: agood@drawingcenter.org

Dublin City Internships

 THE BUZZ
- "Get real-life business experience in the roaring Celtic Tiger economy"
- "Forget London; Dublin is calling"

 THE STATS

Industry(ies): All industries

Location(s): Dublin

Number of interns: Varies

Pay: None; academic credit available

Length of internship: *Spring/fall*: 15 weeks; *summer*: 10 weeks

 **THE SCOOP**

The Dublin City program offers professional-level internships across the spectrum of majors. The program offers full-time international work experience for interns in a progressive city more than 1,000 years old — a city rich in traditions, history, music, literature, theater and heritage.

 ON THE JOB

Dublin City Internships links college students with companies in their chosen fields that are located in and around Dublin.

 GETTING HIRED

Apply by: *Fall*: May 15; *spring*: October 15; *summer*: March 15. Send a letter of interest via e-mail to the address below. Include your name and address, your educational level (i.e., junior, senior), the type of internship you're seeking and an e-mail address for a quick response.

Qualifications:

Open to college juniors and seniors, as well as college graduates and grad students. Match your college courses and career interests with a professional level placement.

Contact:

E-mail: mhrieke@eircom.net

http://homepage.eircom.net/~dublininternships

Visit Vault at **www.vault.com** for insider company profiles, expert advice, career message boards, expert resume reviews, the Vault Job Board and more.

VAULT CAREER LIBRARY 147

Duke University Talent Identification

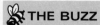

THE BUZZ
- "Work with junior Einsteins"

THE STATS

Industry(ies): Education; Nonprofit

Location(s): Summer Studies Programs in multiple locations including Durham, NC, and Lawrence, KS; Domestic Field Studies Programs in multiple locations including Orange, CA, and Ghost Ranch, NM; International Programs in multiple locations such as England and Costa Rica

Number of interns: *Summer*: 1 teacher's assistant and 1 instructor per class; 1 on-site coordinator; 1 academic coordinator; 2 office staff members; 1 counselor per campus; number of residential staff varies according to campus size

Pay: Paid; $1,100-$6,400/3-6 weeks

Length of internship: *Summer*: 2 months

THE SCOOP

The Duke University Talent Identification Program (Duke TIP) provides resources and guidance to students in grades seven through 11 with exceptional academic promise. The first Summer Residential Program was held in 1981 with 151 students; enrollment for the same program was more than 2,300 in 2001. Current Duke TIP programs offering advanced academic courses include Summer Studies Programs, the PreCollege Program, Domestic and International Field Studies Programs, the Global Dialogues Institute and the Leadership Institute. This leading nonprofit educational organization was founded in 1980 through a grant from The Duke Endowment.

ON THE JOB

Interns may apply for a variety of different positions in academic, residential and administrative departments. Available positions include instructor, teaching assistant, residential counselor and office assistant. Responsibilities vary according to position and department; however, all interns may expect a lot of hands-on experience.

GETTING HIRED

Apply by: Rolling, but applications received by February 28 receive priority. Application (available for downloading at www.tip.duke.edu/Employment/Summer-Employment-Application.pdf), court record release, equal opportunity form, cover letter, resume, college transcript(s) and letters of reference required.

Qualifications:
Residential counselor and office assistant positions open to college students who have completed one year of study. Teaching assistant, residence hall leaders, operations coordinator, and all pre-college positions open to college students who have completed two years of study. Instructor positions open to applicants who have completed college and one year of graduate study or teaching. On-site coordinator positions open to applicants who have completed college (and are usually filled by returning staff).

Contact:
Duke TIP 2006 Summer Employment
1121 West Main Street
Durham, NC 27701
Phone: (919) 684-3847
Fax: (919) 681-7921
E-mail: jobs@tip.duke.edu
www.tip.duke.edu

DuPont

THE BUZZ
- "Techies"

THE STATS

Industry(ies): Chemicals; Construction/Building Materials; Manufacturing; Science/Research; Techology

Location(s): Waltham, MA; Wilmington, DE; U.S. region plants and research laboratories are predominately in mid-Atlantic, mid-South, Southeast and Gulf Coast

Number of interns: *Annual*: 100

Pay: Varies based on education and experience. Orientation; workshops; mentors; round-trip travel expenses

Length of internship: *Summer*: 10-16 weeks

THE SCOOP

DuPont is one of the world's most well-known names in science, providing quality solutions for nutrition, security, apparel, electronics and construction. With operations in more than 70 countries around the world, nearly 79,000 employees and revenues of nearly $24 billion for 2002, the company strives to improve people's lives through scientific innovation.

ON THE JOB

Interns work on assignments that pertain to their related field of study under the direct supervision of an experienced DuPont employee. At the end of the internship, supervisors personally discuss performance and professional interests with interns and assist with goals and career development.

GETTING HIRED

Apply by: *Summer*: December 31. Submit a resume and cover letter online, indicating dates of availability and areas of interest or expertise.

Qualifications:
Open to full-time undergraduates with a GPA of 3.0 or higher and a major in engineering (ChE, ME, EE) or science (chemistry, biology).

Contact:
Corporate Headquarters
DuPont Building
1007 Market Street
Wilmington, DE 19898
Phone: (800) 774-2271
Fax: (800) 978-9774
E-mail: gsb-staffservices@usa.dupont.com
www1.dupont.com/dupontglobal/corp/careers/univ_internships.html

Dykeman Associates

THE BUZZ
- "Learn all about PR, Texas style"

THE STATS

Industrie(s): Advertising; Public Relations

Location(s): Dallas, TX

Number of interns: 2-3 per semester

Pay: Interns are paid in barter dollars that may be used for many necessities, gifts and entertainment

Length of internship: 3 months-1 year

THE SCOOP

Since 1974, Dykeman Associates, Inc., has been a full-service advertising, public relations and marketing firm that assists clients with the creation, implementation and maintenance needed to reach audiences through media-related sources such as video production, advertising, public relations and marketing services. Dykeman creates results for clients ranging from Fortune 500 companies to small firms.

ON THE JOB

In an internship with Dykeman, you never really know what duties you're going to be assigned, as they differ for each client. Interns should be adept at handling a multitude of tasks that may include web site and commercial production, creating brochures and compiling media lists. Interns join staff for client meetings and attend special events, seminars and workshops.

GETTING HIRED

Apply by: Rolling. Apply two to three months prior to your intended start date as an intern. Send a resume, cover letter and your availability.

Qualifications:
Open to college juniors and seniors and graduate students. A basic knowledge and/or related course work in advertising, public relations or journalism is helpful.

Contact:
Alice Dykeman, President
Public Relations
Dykeman Associates
4115 Rawlins Street
Dallas, TX 75219
Phone: (214) 528-2991
Fax: (214) 528-0241
E-mail: adykeman@airmail.net
www.dykemanassociates.com

Visit Vault at **www.vault.com** for insider company profiles, expert advice, career message boards, expert resume reviews, the Vault Job Board and more.

VAULT CAREER LIBRARY **149**

INTERNSHIP PROFILES:
E

E/The Environmental Magazine

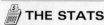 **THE BUZZ**
- "For the serious environmentalist"
- "Saving the earth, one issue at a time"

THE STATS

Industry(ies): Environmental; Journalism

Location(s): Norwalk, CT

Number of interns: *Summer*: 4; *fall/winter/spring*: 3 each

Pay: None

Length of internship: 3 months

THE SCOOP

With a circulation of 50,000, *E Magazine* is the world's leading independent environmental magazine. Founded in 1990 and sponsored by the Earth Action Network, *E Magazine* is devoted to expanding environmental awareness in all areas. The people at *E* practice what they preach, printing the magazine on recycled paper.

ON THE JOB

Editorial interns are responsible for writing, researching and fact-checking the magazine's editorial content; proofreading layouts; generating ideas for articles; participating in editorial meetings; and assisting staff with special projects. Advertising interns prospect for new advertisers, research markets/industries with advertising potential, assemble media kits and work closely with the art department on ad production, placement and layout of ads.

GETTING HIRED

Apply by: Rolling. Send resume and cover letter to the appropriate address below. Writing samples are required for editorial candidates.

Qualifications:
Open to college freshmen, sophomores, juniors and seniors, recent college graduates and grad students.

Contact:
E Magazine
28 Knight Street
Norwalk, CT 06851
Editorial
Jim Motavalli, Editor
Phone: (203) 854-5559, ext. 107
Fax: (203) 866-0602
E-mail: jimm@emagazine.com

Advertising
Karen Soucy
Phone: (203) 854-5559, ext. 104
Fax: (203) 866-0602
E-mail: karen@emagazine.com

E! Entertainment Television

THE BUZZ
- "E! Networks invest time in their interns"
- "An internship can improve your chances of working at E! later on!"

THE STATS

Industry(ies): Broadcast & Entertainment; Internet; Journalism; New/Interactive Media

Location(s): Los Angeles, CA; New York, NY; London

Number of interns: *Annual*: 200

Pay: None; academic credit only

Length of internship: Requires at least 15 hours/week for a 2-month minimum

THE SCOOP

E! Entertainment Television, Inc., is the world's largest producer and distributor of entertainment news and lifestyle-related programming. The company operates E! Entertainment Television, the 24-hour network with programming dedicated to the entertainment world; The Style Network, the 24-hour network where life gets a new look; and E! Online, located at www.eonline.com.

ON THE JOB

Internships are available in E! original programming, The Style Network, E! Online, marketing, public relations, promotions, information technology, human resources, talent/casting, international operations, business development, on air design, affiliate relations, music, set design, production, development, short form production and new media content.

GETTING HIRED

Apply by: Rolling. Interested students can apply online (at www.eentertainment.com/careers).

Qualifications:
Open to college juniors and seniors. Underclassmen are considered. Opportunities are also available for grad students.

Contact:
Internship Coordinator
Human Resources
E-mail: interns@eentertainment.com
www.eentertainment.com/careers

Eastman Kodak Company

 THE BUZZ
- "Work with the cutting edge of imaging technology"

 THE STATS

Industry(ies): Consumer Products; Technology

Location(s): Rochester, NY

Number of interns: *Annual*: 100

Pay: Paid; competitive salary based on work experience and education level. Round-trip travel expenses; paid holiday; vacation; health benefits

Length of internship: Varies

 THE SCOOP

Kodak is not just disposable cameras and color film; it's also the world leader in "infoimaging," a $385-billion industry. Constantly pushing the envelope with new image technology, Kodak claims responsibility for the technology behind 75 percent of the images you see on the Web. Kodak employs almost 40,000 people in the U.S. and nearly 70,000 worldwide.

ON THE JOB

Internships are available in computer technology, engineering, manufacturing, optics, sciences, business, mathematics and statistics, and more. Duties vary according to department. The Cooperative Internship Program (CIP) boasts of learning opportunities with top professionals and a dedication to interaction with peers.

GETTING HIRED

Apply by: Rolling. Submit resume in print to the address below or apply online. Include GPA and anticipated graduation date.

Qualifications:
You must be enrolled full-time in a bachelor's, master's or PhD program and have completed your freshman year. You must be able to work a minimum 10-week work block during the year and maintain a minimum GPA of 2.8. You must also complete and pass a drug screen.

Contact:
Jen Camelio
Internship Coordinator
Eastman Kodak Company
343 State Street
Rochester, NY 14650-00915
E-mail: jen.camelio@kodak.com
www.kodak.com/US/en/corp/careers/students/internships.jhtml

Ecco Press

 THE BUZZ
- "Spend a summer reading great literature"
- "Learn all about the publishing biz"

 THE STATS

Industry(ies): Publishing

Location(s): New York, NY

Number of interns: *Summer*: 8

Pay: None

Length of internship: *Summer*: 10 weeks

THE SCOOP

An imprint of HarperCollins, Ecco Press began by printing classic literature and grew from there. Ecco Press publishes authors such as Louise Glück (appointed U.S. poet laureate in August of 2003), Joyce Carol Oates and Cormac McCarthy. The company is also responsible for The Essential Poet Series, a collection of portable works by influential poets introduced by contemporary writers.

ON THE JOB

During their 10-week stint with Ecco Press, interns will assist in several different departments. While being exposed to the various aspects of publishing, the interns will develop and pitch a book idea. Interns should also expect networking opportunities. The internship is ideal for students interested in publishing careers.

GETTING HIRED

Apply by: April 10. Send resume with cover letter to the e-mail address below, with "Internship" in the subject line.

Qualifications:
Open to college juniors and seniors. Organized students with related experience, strong written and verbal communication and computer skills preferred.

Contact:
E-mail: collrec@HarperCollins.com
www.harpercollins.com/hc/aboutus/careers.asp#internship

Visit Vault at **www.vault.com** for insider company profiles, expert advice, career message boards, expert resume reviews, the Vault Job Board and more.

V∧ULT CAREER LIBRARY **153**

EchoStar Communications Corporation

THE BUZZ
- "Seniors and MBAs approaching graduation wanted"
- "Learn about the business of satellite entertainment"

THE STATS

Industries: Broadcast & Entertainment

Location(s): Englewood, CO (corporate HQ); over 150 additional locations throughout the U.S.

Number of interns: *Annual*: 60-100

Pay: Paid; $8-$25/hour depending on degree, year in school, prior experience and other related factors

Length of internship: *Summer*: 11 weeks; *recent college/MBA grad*: full-time

THE SCOOP

Founded in 1980, EchoStar Communications is a direct broadcast satellite television service provider, serving more than 12 million U.S. customers with its DISH Network. Through its fleet of in-orbit satellites, EchoStar offers DISH Network customers hundreds of video and audio channels, Interactive TV, HDTV, sports and international programming, together with professional installation and 24-hour customer service.

ON THE JOB

Interns complete a specific project (related to their major) over the summer under the guidance of a VP sponsor, manager and mentor. Interns also participate in field trips, specialized training and other company events and activities. In addition to interns, EchoStar recruits recent college and MBA graduates for full-time positions.

GETTING HIRED

Apply by: During January-March. Check the company web site for university recruitment information (www.dishnetwork.com/college).

Qualifications:
Open to students majoring in accounting; communications; computer engineering; computer science; economics; electrical engineering; finance; human resources; information systems; journalism; leadership; liberal arts; management; marketing; MBA and psychology. Candidates should have a GPA of 3.2 or higher, as well as demonstrated energy and achievements.

Contact:
EchoStar Corporate Headquarters
Attn: Angela Heyroth
9601 South Meridian Blvd.
Englewood, CO 80112
Phone: (303) 723-1000
Fax: (720) 514-8439
www.dishnetwork.com

Economic Research Service

THE BUZZ
- "Just the thing for eco-minded, political agriculturalists"

THE STATS

Industry(ies): Food & Beverage; Government; Science/Research

Location(s): Washington, DC

Number of interns: Varies

Pay: Varies, depending on education and experience. Subsidized passes for public transportation

Length of internship: Varies

THE SCOOP

The Economic Research Service is a division of the United States Department of Agriculture (USDA). Utilizing roughly 450 employees, ERS provides economic research and information to the USDA and the public through various studies and publications. Employees work within four divisions: Food and Rural Economics; Information Services; Market and Trade Economics; and Resource Economics.

ON THE JOB

Interns for ERS are hired as either economics assistants/ economists or computer clerks/assistants/IT specialists. Duties include research, data compilation, and Web design. In addition to salary, perks include a convenient downtown DC location and subsidized travel via bus or subway.

GETTING HIRED

Apply by: March 5. E-mail, fax or send resume, most recent transcript, and cover sheet (available at www.ers.usda.gov/AboutERS/Employment/summerinternship.htm).

Qualifications:

Economics assistant/economist: open to students who have completed one economics course and plan to continue study the following year. Undergraduate junior or senior economics majors or graduate students studying economics preferred.

Computer clerk/assistant/IT specialist: open to college freshmen, sophomores, juniors and seniors and grad students who plan to continue study the following year. Undergraduate IT/computer science majors or graduate students with experience in areas such as data visualization or multimedia technologies preferred.

Contact:
Gwen Donovan
USDA/Agricultural Research Service
HRD/Metropolitan Services Branch
Mail Stop 0308
1400 Independence Avenue, SW
Washington, DC, 20250-0308
Fax: (202) 690-2239
E-mail: erssummerinterns@ers.usda.gov

The Economist

 THE BUZZ
- "Its writers may not be well known, but the magazine is"
- "Test the limits of your international erudition"

 THE STATS

Industry(ies): Journalism

Location(s): London

Number of interns: *Summer*: 2-3

Pay: Paid; approximately £200-£300/week (roughly $325-$500/week)

Length of internship: *Summer*: 3 months

 THE SCOOP

Although *The Economist* has called London its home for more than 160 years, nearly 80 percent of its circulation is outside the UK. A champion of free trade, internationalism and minimum government interference, *The Economist* also prides itself on anonymity, refusing to list the bylines of its writers.

 ON THE JOB

Internships are regularly available in the foreign and business departments, and occasionally in the Britain department. Interns are treated like staff members and invited to participate in meetings and activities. Special internships are open during the year and are listed in the magazine.

 GETTING HIRED

Apply by: January/February. Send cover letter, resume and writing samples to the appropriate contact at the address below. See the web site for details.

Qualifications:
Open to recent college graduates and grad students.

Contact:
Foreign: Peter David
Business Affairs: John Peet
Britain: Emma Duncan
The Economist
25 St. James's Street
London SW1A 1HG
United Kingdom
Phone: 011-44-207-830-7000
Fax: 011-44-207-839-2338
E-mail: recruitment@economist.com
www.economistgroup.com/employment/internships.html

Edelman Public Relations

 THE BUZZ
- "Become the latest entrepreneur at a firm of entrepreneurs"
- "PR pros start at the biggest shops"

 THE STATS

Industry(ies): Public Relations

Location(s): Chicago, IL (HQ); New York, NY (HQ); Atlanta, GA; Austin, TX; Dallas, TX; Los Angeles, CA; Portland, OR; San Francisco, CA; Seattle, WA; Silicon Valley, CA; Washington, DC

Number of interns: *Annual*: 50 each in Chicago and New York; other locations vary

Pay: Varies

Length of internship: 3-6 months

 **THE SCOOP**

With over 50 years of public relations experience, Edelman employs almost 2,000 professionals and is the world's largest independently-owned public relations firm. Edelman's mission is "to provide public relations counsel and strategic communications services that enable our clients to build strong relationships and to influence attitudes and behaviors in a complex world."

 ON THE JOB

Internships are available in a number of departments and locations. Some responsibilities include media relations, web site and press material development, video production, special event and press conference planning, internal strategy sessions and new business research. Although the program varies according to location, interns can be assured of daily account involvement and an introduction to broader PR strategies.

 GETTING HIRED

Apply by: Rolling. Refer to the web site for current availabilities, as well as methods of application. Online application available at www.edelman.com/careers/want_to_join_us/internships/secure/index.asp.

Qualifications:
Open to college juniors and seniors, as well as recent graduates. Candidates must be Microsoft Word proficient. Interns must be able to work effectively with a variety of account service staff within a specific set of accounts. They must have good organizational skills and the ability to adapt to new conditions, assignments and deadlines. Familiarity with the public relations discipline through past coursework or other trainee/internships is desirable.

Contact:
Internship Specialist
E-mail: chicagointerns@edelman.com
www.edelman.com

Visit Vault at **www.vault.com** for insider company profiles, expert advice, career message boards, expert resume reviews, the Vault Job Board and more.

V∧ULT CAREER LIBRARY **155**

Educational Programmes Abroad

 THE BUZZ

- "The one-stop study abroad shop"
- "Bring your suit and your backpack"

THE STATS

Industry(ies): Education; Nonprofit

Location(s): Berlin; Bonn; Brussels; Cologne; Edinburgh; London; Madrid

Number of interns: 80-120 per semester in all locations combined

Pay: None; monthly housing allowance

Length of internship: Varies; available year-round

 THE SCOOP

Educational Programmes Abroad was incorporated in 1972 as a central, nonprofit body to assist students in finding employment internships overseas. EPA is committed to equipping future workers with the global experience they will need in the 21st century.

ON THE JOB

EPA's internship program is designed "to provide work experience in a realistic environment. You trade your intelligence and willingness to work for the opportunity to become intimately involved on the inside of an organization or system which is related to your field of academic study or career interest." Initial work assignments may seem mundane, but successful completion promises more interesting opportunities. In the fall and spring semester internships, students take two classes along with their internships.

GETTING HIRED

Apply by: Rolling. If you are from an institution affiliated with EPA, your home institution will decide if you are accepted into the program. If you want academic credit but cannot obtain it from your home institution, you can apply to the University of Rochester with the exceptions of social science, urban studies and town planning, and education. For these fields you can apply to Northern Illinois University. Positions are offered in a variety of departments, including finance, sales, marketing, IT, human resources, editorial, PR, education/outreach and psychology.

Qualifications:

Open to college juniors and seniors, as well as college graduates and grad students with a GPA of 3.0 or above.

Contact:

Educational Programmes Abroad
UR/Lattimore 206
P.O. Box 270375
Rochester, NY 14627-0375
Phone: (585) 275-8850
Fax: (585) 276-2167
E-mail: usoffice@epa-internships.org
www.epa-internships.org/home.html

University of Rochester
Internships in Europe
Lattimore 206
P.O. Box 270376
Rochester, NY 14627-0376
Phone: (585) 275-7532
Fax: (585) 461-5131
E-mail: abroad@mail.rochester.edu

Northern Illinois University
Study Abroad Office
Williston Hall 417
DeKalb, IL 60115-2854
Phone: (815) 753-0304
Fax: (815) 753-0825
E-mail: niuabroad@niu.edu

EdVenture Partners/General Motors Marketing Internship

 THE BUZZ
- "A secret road into a top General Motors opportunity"

 THE STATS

Industry(ies): Advertising; Public Relations

Location(s): Various college campuses throughout the U.S. and Canada. See a complete list on the firm's web site, www.edventure partners.com/educators/rosterOfSchools.asp

Number of interns: Varies

Pay: None

Length of internship: *Fall/spring*: around 4 months each

 THE SCOOP

General Motor's and EdVenture Partners have brought over 40,000 students and companies together since 1990. Programs include the Student Area Manager Program, the Research Program and the Marketing Internship Program. The EdVenture Partners/General Motors Marketing Internship is offered as a class at various colleges and universities across the U.S. and Canada.

ON THE JOB

Students taking the EdVenture Partners/General Motors Marketing Internship class at their university develop and execute a promotional event for an assigned vehicle or truck brand of General Motors. The team budget must cover all aspects of the project including research, advertising, public relations and actual event and promotion implementation.

GETTING HIRED

Apply by: Enroll in class.

Qualifications:
Open to students enrolled at a university offering this class.

Contact:
E-mail: info@edventurepartners.com
Phone: (800) 739-7476
www.edventurepartners.com

Electronic Arts

 THE BUZZ
- "All that time in front of the PlayStation is about to pay off!"

 THE STATS

Industry(ies): Consumer Products; Software

Location(s): Los Angeles, CA; Orlando, FL; Chicago, IL; Redwood City, CA; London; Montreal; Tokyo; Vancouver; Shanghai; Singapore

Number of interns: *Annual*: 150

Pay: Paid; varies based on skills and experience. Relocation assistance; housing and transportation stipend; free and discounted games

Length of internship: 12-16 weeks (most internships are filled during the summer)

 THE SCOOP

Electronic Arts is the world's leading independent developer and publisher of interactive entertainment software for advanced entertainment systems such as the PlayStation®2 computer entertainment system, PlayStation®, Xbox™ video game console from Microsoft, the Nintendo GameCube™ and the Game Boy® Advance, as well as PCs. The company employs over 6,000 staff members.

ON THE JOB

Electronic Arts' internship program is known as the "EA Academy." Students gain hands-on experience, whether they are working in one of the company's development studios, marketing or in a corporate department. The weekly speaker series gives interns a chance to network with some of the brightest minds in the industry. There are also social and teambuilding events throughout the summer, often including an exhibition of interns' work for company leaders.

GETTING HIRED

Apply by: January 1-March 1. Students are asked to apply online at jobs.ea.com/eaacademy/how.html. Applicants must submit a resume; those applying for art-related positions must also submit a demo reel and/or portfolio.

Qualifications:
Open to college juniors and seniors, as well as graduates. Interns assigned to one of the company's studios generally are pursuing a degree in computer science, computer engineering or electrical engineering, and have strong mathematical and programming backgrounds. For art positions, applicants must have some experience with 2-D and/or 3-D graphic software packages. Students will also need to submit a demo reel and/or portfolio. Interns in the company's production or marketing/public relations departments should have strong verbal and written communications.

Contact:
eaacademy.ea.com

Visit Vault at **www.vault.com** for insider company profiles, expert advice, career message boards, expert resume reviews, the Vault Job Board and more.

V\ULT CAREER LIBRARY **157**

Elite Model Management Corporation

 THE BUZZ
- "Work with the beautiful people"

 **THE STATS**

Industry(ies): Broadcast & Entertainment; Fashion; Public Relations

Location(s): New York, NY (HQ); Atlanta, GA; Chicago, IL; Los Angeles, CA; Miami, FL; multiple international locations

Number of interns: *Annual*: 1-5

Pay: None; academic credit only

Length of internship: 10 weeks

 THE SCOOP

Alain Kittler and John Casablancas started Elite Model Management Corporation in 1972 in the world's fashion Mecca: Paris, France. The agency quickly merged as a high-level firm. In 1977, Elite opened its first international office in the new fashion capital, New York City. Not content with just two locations, Elite built a network of firms around the world. Today, Elite Model Management is one of the most recognized names in the industry, with over 30 locations worldwide.

 ON THE JOB

Interns work alongside staff learning the ropes of managing a modeling agency. Duties vary with department and location but may include assisting marketing and sales staff with leads, answering the phones and handling administrative functions. Participants have many networking opportunities and may attend some gala events.

$ GETTING HIRED

Apply by: Rolling. Send a resume and cover letter to the desired location (see web site for locations).

Qualifications:
Open to college sophomores, juniors and seniors, recent college graduates and grad students.

Contact:
Elite Model Management Chicago
58 West Huron
Chicago, IL 60610
Phone: (312) 943-3226
Fax: (312) 943-2590

Elite Atlanta
Victoria Duruh, Internship Coordinator
1708 Peachtree Street, NW, Suite 210
Atlanta, GA 30309
Phone: (404) 872-7444
Fax: (404) 874-1526
E-mail: vduruh@eliteatlanta.com
www.elitemodel.com

Elite New York
404 Park Ave South 10th Floor
New York, NY 10010
Phone: (212) 529-9700
Elite Miami

119 Washington Ave
Suite 501
Miami Beach, FL 33139
Phone: (305) 674-9500

Elizabeth Dow

 THE BUZZ
- "Make wallpaper out of your previous resume"
- "Work for an artist in a working artist's internship"

 **THE STATS**

Industry(ies): Consumer Products; Manufacturing

Location(s): Amagansett, NY

Number of interns: *Annual*: 40-50

Pay: Unpaid and paid (starting at $7.00/hour). Limited housing available.

Length of internship: Varies; available year-round

 **THE SCOOP**

As a manufacturer of hand painted wall coverings and interior decorative painting, Elizabeth Dow is considered by many to be the most influential wallpaper designer of the decade. The Cooper Hewitt Museum recently acknowledged her achievements by including her wallpapers in their permanent collection. The new location in Amagansett houses a state of the art applied arts center, complete with digital, photography, printmaking, and painting studios.

 ON THE JOB

Art and design internship responsibilities include sampling, painting and studio work. Marketing/managerial internship responsibilities include Macintosh skills and data entry. Summer interns have the opportunity to work with the children's camp as teacher's assistants.

 GETTING HIRED

Apply by: Rolling. Students should apply as early as possible for summer.

Qualifications:
Open to high school students, college freshmen, sophomores, juniors and seniors, as well as recent grads, grad students, career changers and individuals re-entering the workforce.

Contact:
Daniel Waldron, Internship Coordinator
11 Indian Wells Highway
P.O. Box 2310
Amagansett, NY 11930
Phone: (631) 267-3401
Fax: (631) 267-3408
danielwaldron@mac.com
www.elizabethdow.com/internships.html

Elizabeth Gillett, Ltd.

 THE BUZZ
- "For future fashion entrepreneurs"
- "Accessorize your internship by trying on a little of everything"

 THE STATS

Industry(ies): Fashion; Manufacturing

Location(s): New York, NY

Number of interns: *Summer/fall/winter*: 2-4 each

Pay: Stipend based on hours/week given upon completion

Length of internship: 8-week minimum

 THE SCOOP

Recently featured in the pages of *Lucky*, *InStyle* and *The New York Times Magazine*, the fashions of Elizabeth Gillett are the height of chic. Based in New York's Garment District, Elizabeth Gillett has been creating accessories – including scarves, shrugs, and shawls – since 1990.

 ON THE JOB

Internships are available in merchandising (which includes sales and marketing), design, business and graphic design/photography. Many interns overlap their focuses, dabbling in two or three of the internship categories. It's a great opportunity for those interested in entrepreneurship and a small business environment.

GETTING HIRED

Apply by: Rolling.

Qualifications:
Open to high school students, college freshmen, sophomores, juniors and seniors, as well as recent grads and grad students.

Contact:
Tara Marek, Internship Coordinator
Elizabeth Gillett NYC
242 West 38th Street, 9th Floor
New York, NY 10018
Phone: (212) 629-7993 or toll free: (800) 273-4773
Fax: (212) 629-7454
E-mail: design@elizabethgillett.com
www.elizabethgillett.com

Visit Vault at **www.vault.com** for insider company profiles, expert advice, career message boards, expert resume reviews, the Vault Job Board and more.

V∧ULT CAREER LIBRARY 159

Elizabeth Glaser Pediatric AIDS Foundation

 THE BUZZ
- "Gain satisfaction from helping those who can't help themselves"

 THE STATS

Industry(ies): Health Care; Nonprofit

Location(s): New York, NY; Santa Monica, CA; Washington, DC; and various international locations

Number of interns: Over 1,000 (volunteers)

Pay: None

Length of internship: Flexible

 THE SCOOP

The Elizabeth Glaser Pediatric AIDS Foundation began in 1988 with a mission to rapidly raise money for pediatric AIDS research. Now, the nonprofit raises money, as well as provides treatment and care to those infected with HIV/AIDS.

 ON THE JOB

More than 1,000 volunteers fill positions such as office assistant, software applications specialist, development assistant and executive staff assistant. Research/program volunteers are professionals such as doctors that provide training or grant writing assistance. Even more opportunities exist in the company's 17 Call to Action Program international sites.

 GETTING HIRED

Apply by: Rolling. Required application available for download at www.pedaids.org/fs_volunteer.html.

Qualifications:
Open to people of legal working age.

Contact:
Jeff Gaffney
2950 31st Street, #125
Santa Monica, CA 90405
Phone: (310) 314-1459
Fax: (310) 314-1469
E-mail: jeffg@pedaids.org
www.pedaids.org/fs_volunteer.html

Paige Alona Sass
420 Lexington Avenue, Suite 2216
New York, NY 10170
Phone: (212) 682-8152
Fax: (212) 682-8643
E-mail: paige@pedaids.org

or

1140 Connecticut Avenue, NW, Suite 200
Washington, DC, 20036
Phone: (202) 296-9165
Fax: (202) 296-9185

Emerson Electric

 THE BUZZ
- "Seeking MBA students for internships and corporate sponsorship positions"

 THE STATS

Industries: Energy/Utilities

Location(s): St. Louis, MO (HQ); Global

Number of Interns: *Annual*: 25-30 MBA students; 20 corporate sponsorship positions

Pay: Paid; competitive salary and benefits

Length of internship: 24-36 month rotations

 THE SCOOP

Since 1980, Emerson Electric has been manufacturing process control systems, climate control technologies, reliable power technologies, electric motors and other products such as ceiling fans and hand tools. The company's eight brands are Emerson Process Management, Emerson Network Power, Emerson Climate Technologies, Emerson Industrial Automation, Appliances Solutions, Storage Solutions, Professional Tools and Motor Techniques. The company operates 60 divisions in 245 global locations, marketing products in over 150 countries. Emerson employs over 107,000 people.

 ON THE JOB

Internships take place in a global work environment where students are exposed to top management. Emerson offers promotion and management opportunities based on performance. Positions are available in auditing, business systems, finance, human resources, international planning, manufacturing and operations, materials analysis, marketing, technology and strategic planning.

 GETTING HIRED

Apply by: Check with your college recruitment office to see if/when Emerson will be at your school. Potential candidates may apply online at www.gotoemerson.com/careers/ca_epp.html by utilizing the company's affiliation with CareerBuilder.com. For opportunities at Emerson's St. Louis headquarters, write to: Director, Corporate Personnel, Emerson, 8000 W. Florissant Avenue, P.O. Box 4100, St. Louis, MO 63136.

Qualifications:
Open to motivated, strong leaders preferably with technical undergraduate degrees and three to five years in manufacturing. Multilingual grads preferred.

Contact:
Emerson Electric Corporate Office
8000 West Florissant Avenue
St. Louis, MO 63136
Phone: (314) 553-2000
Fax: (314) 553-3527
www.gotoemerson.com

EMI Records Group North America

THE BUZZ
- "Work your way up in the music industry"
- "Great for music enthusiasts who lack professional experience"

 THE STATS
Industry(ies): Music/Records

Location(s): New York, NY

Number of interns: *Spring/summer/fall*: 30

Pay: *Legal/finance/IT internships*: $15/hour; all other internships are unpaid

Length of internship: *Spring/summer/fall*: 4 months each

THE SCOOP
The artists represented by EMI are a veritable who's who of the music industry, including Garth Brooks, Coldplay, The Beatles, AC/DC, Tina Turner and many more. With over 10,000 employees in more than 70 countries, EMI Records Group is one of the world's largest recording and publishing companies, and consists of EMI Records, Hut, Innocent, Parlophone and Virgin, in addition to a catalogue division, imprints and related labels.

ON THE JOB
Many different departments of EMI accept interns, including legal, finance, IT, publicity, marketing and sales. Although responsibilities vary depending on the department, all interns do office work in addition to participating in projects. The same internship coordinator handles internships for Virgin Records, Angel Records and Blue Note Records. These companies are committed to giving students without prior experience (but with relevant education) a chance.

GETTING HIRED
Apply by: Rolling. Send resume and cover letter to the address below. Interview required.

Qualifications:
Open to college freshmen, sophomores, juniors and seniors and law students (for legal internships). The student must be enrolled in courses relevant to the internship.

Contact:
Internship Coordinator
EMI Records
150 Fifth Avenue
New York, NY 10011
E-mail: ushrdept@emicap.com
www.emirecordedmusic.com

EMILY's List

THE BUZZ
- "The pro-choice, Democratic, support-your-local-congresswoman internship"
- "Help women candidates get the dough they deserve"

THE STATS
Industry(ies): Government; Nonprofit

Location(s): Washington, DC

Number of interns: *Fall/spring/summer*: 15-20 each

Pay: Monthly stipend; varies from $100-$500. $30/month Metro card

Length of internship: Varies; generally 1 semester

THE SCOOP
EMILY is an acronym for "Early Money Is Like Yeast," and adds, "it makes the dough rise." EMILY's List is a grassroots political network that assists in fund-raising for pro-choice, Democratic women candidates. EMILY's List strives to create a positive snowball effect in the election of woman into office, helping to organize a network of viable candidates and fervent supporters.

ON THE JOB
Internships are available in four departments: political, development, research and communications. EMILY's List considers its interns to be a crucial part of the organization and relies greatly on their energy and achievements.

GETTING HIRED
Apply by: *Summer*: March 1; *fall*: July 1; *spring*: November 1.

Qualifications
Open to college students, recent graduates and grad students. Good judgment and an ability to maintain confidentiality are a must. Knowledge of Microsoft Word is required. Experience with the Internet, Excel and PowerPoint preferred.

Contact:
Courtney Fry, Intern Coordinator
EMILY's List
1120 Connecticut Avenue, NW, Suite 1100
Washington, DC 20036
Phone: (202) 326-1400
Fax: (202) 326-1415
www.emilyslist.org/internships

Visit Vault at **www.vault.com** for insider company profiles, expert advice, career message boards, expert resume reviews, the Vault Job Board and more.

VAULT CAREER LIBRARY   161

The Emma L. Bowen Foundation

 THE BUZZ
- "Giving the underrespresented an edge"

THE STATS

Industry(ies): Broadcast & Entertainment

Location(s): New York, NY; Studio City, CA; Washington, DC

Number of interns: *Annual*: Varies

Pay: Varies; hourly salary and matching scholarship dollars to pay for college expenses

Length of internship: *Summer*: 4-5

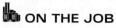 **THE SCOOP**

Co-founded in 1989 by the community activist it's named after, the Emma L. Bowen Foundation places minority students in summer internships with major media companies. Partners include NBC, CBS, ABC, Turner, Time Warner Cable, Comcast Communications and Tribune/WB, among others.

ON THE JOB

Students work in various departments (production, human resources, finance, sales, marketing, etc.) within their sponsoring company. EBF interns also attend yearly conferences to learn about the latest trends in the media industry and network with prominent media professionals and fellow EBF interns.

GETTING HIRED

Apply by: *Summer*: January 31. See www.emmabowen foundation.com for more information and to download an application.

Qualifications:

Open to minority high school juniors and seniors, and college freshman of African, Asian/Pacific Islander, Hispanic or Native American/Alaskan descent with at least a 3.0 GPA; an interest in media/communications; and who plan to attend a four-year accredited university.

Contact:

West Coast

Robbin Turner, M.Ed., Program Manager, Western Region
Emma L. Bowen Foundation for Minority Interests in Media
CBS Studio Center, Administrative Building, Suite 300
4024 Radford Avenue
Studio City, CA 91042
Phone: (818) 655-5708
Fax: (818) 655-8358

East Coast

Sandra D. Rice, Vice President, Eastern Region
Emma L. Bowen Foundation for Minority Interests in Media
524 West 57th Street
New York, NY 10019
Phone: (212) 975-2545
Fax: (212) 975-5884
www.emmabowenfoundation.com

Emory University

 THE BUZZ
- "Enjoy a challenging summer in the sunny South"

THE STATS

Industry(ies): Education

Location(s): Atlanta, GA

Number of interns: *Summer*: 25 non-Emory students

Pay: $3,000/10 weeks. Paid housing

Length of internship: *Summer*: 10 weeks (May 30-August 4)

THE SCOOP

Emory University was established in 1836 and includes undergraduate and graduate schools of arts and sciences, the Roberto C. Goizueta Business School, a medical school and the School of Law. Their last school, the Rollins School of Public Health, was added in 1990. Approximately 11,600 students received education from 2,700 faculty members at this well-respected Atlanta institution.

ON THE JOB

During their 10-week stay, students in the Summer Undergraduate Research Program at Emory (SURE) will conduct scientific research under the supervision of a faculty mentor. The culmination of their research is participation in a formal academic symposium. Intern responsibilities include working 40 hours per week, attending workshops and seminars on science careers and research ethics, and presenting their research at the symposium. The Howard Hughes Medical Institute sponsors the program.

GETTING HIRED

Apply by: *External applications*: January 27; *Emory applications*: February 20. Send to the address below an application form, online application form, letter of recommendation, transcript, a two-page essay for visiting students, and a three-page research proposal for Emory students. Applications are available at cse.emory.edu/sciencenet/undergrad/SURE/SURE.html.

Qualifications:

Open to undergraduate juniors and seniors. The program is designed for students who plan to enter PhD programs upon graduation.

Contact:

SURE Program
c/o Center for Science Education
Emory University
1399 Oxford Road
Atlanta, GA 30322

Dr. Cathy Quiñones
SURE Program Director
Phone: (404) 727-3439
E-mail: SRP@learnlink.emory.edu
cse.emory.edu/sciencenet/undergrad/SURE/SURE.html

Entertainment Weekly

THE BUZZ
- "Get paid to research entertainment's biggest stars"

THE STATS

Industry(ies): Broadcast & Entertainment; Journalism; Publishing

Location(s): New York, NY

Number of interns: *Summer/fall/spring*: 2 each

Pay: Paid; $10/hour. Occasional movie passes and invitations to events and screenings

Length of internship: *Fall/spring*: 4 months; *summer*: 2.5 months. Interns work full time, 35 hours/week.

THE SCOOP

Established in 1990, *Entertainment Weekly* provides an inside scoop into the world of movies, television, music and, of course, celebrities. Every week, the magazine gives its readers interviews, exclusive photos, reviews and current news on the latest movies, TV shows and music hits, and the stars that make them.

ON THE JOB

Interns are assigned to the editorial, photo and design departments. They assist with the day-to-day upkeep of the magazine through general administrative duties that can involve making phone calls, filing, organizing databases and opening mail. Interns also assist writers with research for upcoming pieces, which may sometimes lead to interns publishing articles.

GETTING HIRED

Apply by: *Summer*: February 15; *fall*: June 15; *spring*: October 15. Submit resume, cover letter and a writing sample of four to five published clips.

Qualifications:
Open to senior undergraduates, graduate students and recent college graduates.

Contact:
Internship Coordinator
Entertainment Weekly
1675 Broadway
New York, NY 10019
Phone: (212) 522-5600
www.ew.com

Environmental Careers Organization

THE BUZZ
- "Saving the planet never looked so rewarding"

THE STATS

Industry(ies): Environmental; Government; Nonprofit

Location(s): Locations in almost every state in the country, including Alaska and some U.S. territories and possessions

Number of interns: *Annual*: 800+

Pay: Paid; $10-20/hour wage, with $12-15 most typical, but varies depending on the program, education, experience and skill set of the individual. Worker's compensation provided; some programs offer employee-paid health insurance coverage

Length of internship: 3 months-2 years, depending on program

THE SCOOP

Founded in 1972, the Environmental Careers Organization is a Boston-based, national, nonprofit organization that develops future professionals for the environmental field, through paid environmental internship programs that provide experiential learning and training opportunities.

ON THE JOB

Each year, ECO places approximately 800 interns with government agencies, corporations and nonprofit organizations. ECO Associates work in offices, in the field and in the lab. Past projects have included monitoring coral reefs in the Virgin Islands, surveying desert plants in Southern California, planning environmental education programs for Maryland school children and evaluating tire recycling technologies in Texas. Others included measuring the effects of salvage logging on songbirds and mammals in South Dakota, photographing and mapping archaeological artifacts in Alaska, assessing recovery trends of sensitive river fish species in Oregon and identifying abandoned properties for redevelopment on Long Island, NY. Among current intern opportunities are projects such as surveying trail conditions, monitoring beach water quality, doing a wildlife census, assessing vehicle emissions, GIS, creating web site content, sea floor mapping, migrant farm worker health and safety, smart growth, tribal affairs, youth gardening projects, air and water quality, chemical exposure, legal research, and international policy.

GETTING HIRED

Apply by: Rolling. See web site postings at www.eco.org/internships for specific requirements.

Qualifications:
Open to all college and graduate students, as well as recent graduates at all degree levels. Other requirements vary depending on position; see web site for details.

Contact:
The Environmental Careers Organization
30 Winter Street, 6th Floor
Boston, MA 02100
Phone: (617) 426-4375
Fax: (617) 423-0998
Staff contacts: www.eco.org/contact
www.eco.org

Visit Vault at **www.vault.com** for insider company profiles, expert advice, career message boards, expert resume reviews, the Vault Job Board and more.

V/\ULT CAREER LIBRARY **163**

Ernst & Young

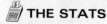 THE BUZZ

- "State-of-the-art learning and technology"
- "A great name on your resume"
- "An ideal place for budding bean counters"

THE STATS

Industry(ies): Accounting; Financial Services

Location(s): 95 offices nationwide

Number of interns: Varies

Pay: Varies

Length of internship: Flexible

 THE SCOOP

With 2004/2005 fiscal year revenues of $16.9 billion and offices in 140 countries, Ernst & Young is a global powerhouse in professional services. Its 106,000 people provide a range of industry-focused services centered on the firm's core competencies of auditing, accounting, tax and transactions.

ON THE JOB

Ernst & Young interns are exposed to a variety of responsibilities. Assignments typically include research, assisting with mergers, capital-sourcing efforts, tax-planning engagements, or learning the firm's audit process and getting practical experience with audit concepts. Recognized as a top employer and top 10 learning organization, the firm boasts resources and programs to help interns put their academic learning to work in the business world. These include a hands-on orientation, practice-oriented functional and technical instruction, and the opportunity to gain professional skills, such as writing and presentation techniques. Interns get the chance to attend an international conference held especially for interns each August.

GETTING HIRED

Apply by: Contact your college placement or career services office for a campus interview schedule. An updated resume and interview are required.

Qualifications:
Open to college freshmen, sophomores, juniors and seniors.

Contact:
www.ey.com/us/careers

ESPN

THE BUZZ

- "Sports 24/7! Need we say more?"
- "Work at one of the country's fastest-growing cable networks"

THE STATS

Industry(ies): Sports Media, Broadcast & Entertainment

Location(s): Bristol, CT; Charlotte, NC; Los Angeles, CA; New York, NY; Orlando, FL; Miami, FL; Denver, CO

Number of interns: *Summer*: 120; *fall*: 40; *spring*: 40

Pay: Paid; *undergraduate*: $9/hour; *graduate*: $13/hour; *law clerk*: $18/hour. Discounts on ESPN merchandise; subsidized housing for summer interns

Length of internship: *Summer/fall/spring*: 12 weeks each

THE SCOOP

ESPN, Inc., The Worldwide Leader in Sports, is the leading multinational, multimedia sports entertainment company, featuring the broadest portfolio of multimedia sports assets with over 40 business entities. The company is comprised of seven domestic television networks (ESPN, ESPN2, ESPN Classic, ESPNEWS, ESPN Deportes, ESPN Now ,ESPN Today), ESPN HD, (a high-definition simulcast service of ESPN), ESPN Regional Television, ESPN International (25 international networks and syndication), ESPN Radio, ESPN.com, *ESPN The Magazine*, SportsTicker, ESPN Enterprises, ESPN Zones (sports-themed restaurants) and other growing new businesses including ESPN Broadband, ESPN Wireless, ESPN Video-on-Demand, ESPN Interactive, and ESPN PPV. ESPN has 25 networks reaching over 147 countries and territories, including Latin America, Brazil, Mexico, Canada, Asia, India, Taiwan, South East Asia, Korea, Japan, Australia, New Zealand; Africa, Israel, France and Italy.

ON THE JOB

Interns work in the Bristol., New York, Los Angeles, Orlando, Miami, Charlotte and Denver offices in production, programming, communications, broadcast, promotions, sales, marketing, finance, MIS or engineering.

GETTING HIRED

Apply by: *Summer*: April 1; *fall*: August 1; *spring*: December 1. Visit www.espn.com/joinourteam to apply.

Qualifications:
To qualify as an intern, students must be in good academic standing; be a full-time junior or senior enrolled in a relevant degree program; meet minimum qualifications and requirements of the position; and be authorized to work in the U.S. for any company.

Contact:
www.espn.com/joinourteam

Essence

 THE BUZZ
- "A venerable name in ethnic publishing"
- "Spend the summer at one of today's most popular fashion and beauty magazines"

 THE STATS

Industry(ies): Fashion; Journalism; Publishing

Location(s): New York, NY

Number of interns: *Annual*: 8

Pay: Paid; $325/week

Length of internship: *Summer*: 6 weeks

 **THE SCOOP**

Essence magazine was created to serve the African-American female population. The magazine currently boasts 1 million subscribers and reaches 7.6 million readers. Published by Essence Communications Partners Publishing, the magazine is based in New York City.

ON THE JOB

Essence offers two summer internship programs: Essence Communications Summer Internship Program and Essence Summer of Beauty Program. The Essence Communications Summer Internship Program offers positions in editorial, art and sales/marketing.

GETTING HIRED

Apply by: *Communications Summer*: December 26; *Summer of Beauty*: April 14. E-mail resume and writing sample to internships@essence.com. See the web site (www.essence.com /essence/jobs/intern/internapply) for details.

Qualifications:
Open to college seniors.

Contact:
Communications Summer
Elaine P. Williams
Human Resources Department
Essence Communications Partners
1500 Broadway, 6th Floor
New York, NY 10036
E-mail: internships@essence.com
www.essence.com/essence/jobs/intern

Summer of Beauty Internship
1500 Broadway, 6th floor
New York, NY 10036

ExxonMobil

THE BUZZ
- "Taking on the world's toughest energy challenges"

THE STATS

Industry(ies): Energy/Utilities; Science/Research; Technology

Location(s): Operations exist in nearly 200 countries and territories

Number of interns: 250-300 in the U.S. and 450-600 outside the U.S.

Pay: Paid

Length of internship: Varies depending on position

THE SCOOP

In 1998 the companies Exxon and Mobil merged to create ExxonMobil. Exxon and Mobil were once the Standard Oil Company of New Jersey and the Standard Oil Company of New York, respectively, both founded in 1882. Although these companies once thrived on kerosene production, they made the switch to gasoline in 1911. Today, ExxonMobil is decidedly a powerhouse in energy and petrochemicals.

ON THE JOB

Students who wish to intern with ExxonMobil must apply using the appropriate country recruiting process, which can be found at www.exxonmobil.com/careers. ExxonMobil actively recruits intern candidates in engineering, geoscience, mathematics, accounting, finance, business, human resources, and MBAs, as well as other disciplines. While responsibilities vary depending on discipline and assignment, all ExxonMobil internship positions offer candidates significant responsibilities, the ability to work both independently and in teams, and the opportunity to make a contribution.

GETTING HIRED

Apply by: Rolling, but most U.S. and Northern Hemisphere recruiting takes place in the fall of each year. Candidates can find the country-specific application process online at www.exxon mobil.com/careers.

Qualifications:
Open to college freshmen, sophomores, juniors and seniors and grad students. Other requirements may exist for specific positions.

Contact:
www.exxonmobil.com/careers

Visit Vault at **www.vault.com** for insider company profiles, expert advice, career message boards, expert resume reviews, the Vault Job Board and more.

VAULT CAREER LIBRARY **165**

Get the BUZZ on Top Schools

Read what STUDENTS and ALUMNI have to say about:

- Admissions
- Academics
- Career Opportunities
- Quality of Life
- Social Life

Surveys on thousands of top programs
College • MBA • Law School • Grad School

INTERNSHIP PROFILES: F

Fairness and Accuracy in Reporting

 THE BUZZ
- "Who watches the watchmen? You"

 THE STATS

Industry(ies): Journalism; Nonprofit

Location(s): New York, NY

Number of interns: *Annual*: 2-3 per semester

Pay: None

Length of internship: 1 semester; available year-round

 **THE SCOOP**

Fairness and Accuracy in Reporting (FAIR) is a media watchdog that strives to expose biased journalism and fight all forms of censorship. FAIR works to create publicity for underreported news stories and defends the rights of journalists to have their voices heard. As part of its mission to defend dissenting opinions, FAIR opposes the consolidation of media ownership. The group publishes *Extra!* magazine, and produces the radio show *CounterSpin*. Both focus on media criticism and commentary.

 ON THE JOB

The internship program at FAIR is largely tailored to the individual interests of each student. In the past, internships focusing on research and media monitoring have been developed. Interns may also choose to assist at *Extra!*, *CounterSpin*, or work on the FAIR web site. A staff member will be assigned to supervise each intern and will act as a mentor during the internship.

 GETTING HIRED

Apply by: Rolling. The required application form is available on the web site.

Qualifications:
Open to all students.

Contact:
Peter Hart
FAIR
112 West 27th Street
New York, NY 10001
Phone: (212) 633-6700, ext. 304
Fax: (212) 727-7668
E-mail: PHart@fair.org
www.fair.org/internships.html

Families USA

 THE BUZZ
- "Help ensure access to affordable high quality health care for all Americans"

 THE STATS

Industry(ies): Health Care; Nonprofit

Location(s): Washington, DC

Number of interns: 6 per semester

Pay: Paid; $7.00/hour

Length of internship: *Fall/spring/summer*: 1 per semester

 THE SCOOP

Families USA is a national, nonpartisan, nonprofit, advocacy organization that strives to make health care available and affordable to all Americans. They publish reports on a variety of health policy issues and conduct public information and media outreach campaigns.

 ON THE JOB

The specific responsibilities of each intern will vary depending upon which department they work in. Families USA offers internships in its health policy, health assistance partnership, communications and field departments. Sometimes a government affairs internship is also offered. For more information about specific internships, log on to www.familiesusa.org.

 GETTING HIRED

Apply by: Rolling, but candidates should apply as early as possible.

Qualifications:
Some positions open to college sophomores, juniors, seniors and grad students. Varies according to position. Go to www.familiesusa.org for more information.

Contact:
Melissa Rosenblatt, Director, Internship and Fellowship Program
Families USA
1201 New York Avenue, Suite 1100
Washington, DC 20005
Phone: (202) 628-3030
Fax: (202) 347-2417
E-mail: internship@familiesusa.org
www.familiesusa.org

Fantagraphics

THE BUZZ
- "Not your parents' comic books – cartoons as high art"
- "The underground is up-and-coming"

THE STATS

Industry(ies): Publishing

Location(s): Seattle, WA

Number of interns: *Annual*: 7-8 (2 per semester)

Pay: None, unless the internship is arranged as part of a college work-study program

Length of internship: Internships begin each semester (4 times/year) and usually last 3 months; range from 6 weeks-6 months, depending upon availability and interns' interest

THE SCOOP

Fantagraphics is a Seattle-based alternative comic book publisher. Blending traditional comics with a more literary and fine art style, Fantagraphics was one of the pioneers of the new breed of underground comics. Recently, the company has published work by notable artists such as Daniel Clowes (*Ghost World*), Joe Sacco (*Safe Area Gorazde*) and Chris Ware (*Jimmy Corrigan*). Fantagraphics also publishes *The Comics Journal*, a magazine that examines the world of comics from an "arts-first perspective."

ON THE JOB

Interns work in the marketing, art and editorial departments. Marketing interns assist the Fantagraphics publicsit by updating databases, proofreading copy and maintaining press files. Art interns scan and clean up artwork using Photoshop and other graphic design tools. Editorial interns conduct research, proofread, fact check and practice writing. All Fantagraphics interns spend some time filing, sending out mass mailings, photocopying and helping out in the library.

GETTING HIRED

Apply by: *Fall* (October-December): July 7; *winter* (January-March): October 6; *spring* (April-June): January 7; *summer* (July-September): April 7. Applicants should include in their cover letter a brief statement outlining what they hope to learn from an internship with Fantagraphics. Applications should either be mailed or faxed.

Qualifications:
Open to all college freshmen, sophomores, juniors and seniors, recent grads and graduate students.

Contact:
Kristy Valenti
Assistant Editor, The Comics Journal
Fantagraphics
7563 Lake City Way NE
Seattle, WA 98115
Phone: (800) 657-1100 or (206) 524-1967
Fax: (206) 524-2104
E-mail: kvalenti@fantagraphics.com
www.tcj.com
www.fantagraphics.com

FAO Schwarz

THE BUZZ
- "More than stomping on keyboards"

THE STATS

Industry(ies): Retail

Location(s): Boston, MA; Chicago, IL; New York, NY; San Francisco, CA

Number of interns: *Annual*: 18

Pay: None

Length of internship: *Summer/fall*: 10-13 weeks; *winter*: 4-6 weeks

THE SCOOP

From its humble beginnings in 1870 as an ordinary shop, FAO Schwarz has expanded to become a national toy empire. Today the chain operates 16 stores coast to coast. Not just ordinary retail outlets, the stores also serve as showrooms for the latest toys, making them magnets for enthusiastic kids. The store has been featured in several motion pictures including Big, starring Tom Hanks.

ON THE JOB

Internships can be arranged in both the sales and management departments. Sales interns work on the floor of the "ultimate toy store" – FAO Schwarz's flagship Fifth Avenue location. Individuals with an interest in retail management can also be placed as an assistant to an FAO manager.

GETTING HIRED

Apply by: Rolling.

Qualifications:
Open to anyone interested in learning the business of toy retailing.

Contact:
Nancy Tarascio, Senior Human Resource Manager
FAO Schwarz
767 Fifth Avenue
New York, NY 10153
Phone: (212) 644-9400
Fax: (212) 644-9410
E-mail: ntarascio@faoinc.com
www.fao.com

Visit Vault at **www.vault.com** for insider company profiles, expert advice, career message boards, expert resume reviews, the Vault Job Board and more.

VAULT CAREER LIBRARY 169

Farm Sanctuary

THE BUZZ

- "Save the cows"
- "Promote responsible agriculture"

THE STATS

Industry(ies): Nonprofit; Animal Welfare/Animal Rights

Location(s): Orland, CA; Watkins Glen, NY

Number of interns: Usually 12 interns each month (6 at each location)

Pay: None. Housing is provided for all interns who work at the California and New York Shelters. Occasionally, off-site internship opportunities may be available; in these special cases, housing is not provided.

Length of internship: 1-3 months; 2-3 month commitment preferred. Internships run year-round and begin on the first of each month

THE SCOOP

Farm Sanctuary, a nonprofit organization dedicated to stopping farm animal abuse, is a leading farm animal protection organization with 150,000 supporters. Since incorporating in 1986, Farm Sanctuary has worked to expose and stop cruel practices of the "food animal" industry through research and investigations, legal and institutional reforms, public awareness projects, youth education, and direct rescue and refuge efforts. The group operates farm animal shelters in New York and California, where rescued livestock recuperate and are given long-term care.

ON THE JOB

Interns advocate for and connect with farm animals, establish communities with like-minded people, and acquire valuable knowledge of the various facets of animal protection. Since Farm Sanctuary was founded in 1986, interns help operate shelters, conduct educational programs, and initiate campaigns to end the suffering of farm animals. Farm Sanctuary internships are available at both shelters, as well as in various departments within the organization. For a full list of available positions, as well as qualifications and responsibilities for each position, visit the web site.

GETTING HIRED

Apply by: Apply early, at least 1 month prior to desired start date and by February for summer positions. Apply online at http://www.farmsanctuary.org/join/intern_main.htm. Letters of recommendation are welcome but not required; send to PO BOX 150 Watkins Glen, NY 14891 Attn: Internship Program.

Qualifications:

Qualified applicants will be 18 years or older with a strong personal commitment to Farm Sanctuary's goals and veganism. Interns live a vegan lifestyle for the duration of their internship.

Contact:

Internship Coordinator
Farm Sanctuary
P.O. Box 150
Watkins Glen, NY 14891
Phone: (607) 583-2225
E-mail: Intern@farmsanctuary.org
www.farmsanctuary.org/join/jobs.htm#internship

Farrar, Straus & Giroux

THE BUZZ

- "Intern for one of the most distinguished publishing houses in New York City"

THE STATS

Industry(ies): Publishing

Location(s): New York, NY

Number of interns: 12-16 per semester

Pay: None

Length of internship: 1-4 months

THE SCOOP

Farrar, Straus, & Giroux is a distinguished trade publishing house based in New York. Founded in 1946 by Roger Straus, the company's authors have won multiple National Book Awards, Pulitzer Prizes and Nobel Prizes for literature. FSG publishes fiction, poetry and nonfiction, including recent work by Jonathan Franzen, Michael Cunningham and Philip Gourevitch. Imprints published by FSG include Faber & Faber, Hill & Wang and North Point Press.

ON THE JOB

Interns will assist in various departments depending on the intern's interests and the needs of the company. Departments may include editorial, marketing and publicity. Some office administrative work may also be required.

GETTING HIRED

Apply by: Rolling. Prospective interns should e-mail Linda Rosenberg for details on the application process.

Qualifications:

Open to all undergraduates, recent graduates and graduate students.

Contact:

Linda Rosenberg, Associate Publisher
Farrar, Straus and Giroux
19 Union Square West
New York, NY 10003
Phone: (212) 741-6900
E-mail: linda.rosenberg@fsgbooks.com
www.fsgbooks.com

Federal Bureau of Investigation

 THE BUZZ
"Pierce the inner G-man sanctum"

 THE STATS

Industry(ies): Government; Law

Location(s): Quantico, VA; Washington, DC; San Diego, CA

Number of interns: *Annually: NCAVC:* 10 interns per year; Honors Program: highly selective; *FBI Academy:* varies, current openings are posted on the web site; *FBI Office of International Operations/INTERPOL: 3; Visiting Scientist:* varies (selective); *Performance, Recognition And Awards Unit:* varies (selective); *Community Relations Unit:* varies; *Personnel Relations:* 1-2; *San Diego Division Administrative Squad:* varies

Pay: *NCAVC:* unpaid; *FBI Academy:* none; *Honors Internship Program:* paid; $470/week for undergrads; $522/week for graduate students; *FBI Office of International Operations/INTERPOL:* unpaid volunteer; *Visiting Scientist:* monthly stipend based on level of education; *Performance, Recognition And Awards Unit:* unpaid volunteer; *Community Relations Unit:* unpaid volunteer; *Personnel Relations:* unpaid volunteer; *San Diego Division Administrative Squad:* unpaid volunteer

Length of internship: *NCAVC:* 14 weeks, beginning in September and January; *FBI Academy:* 12 weeks, minimum; offered in the spring, summer, and fall; *Honors internship program:* 10 weeks, beginning in June; *FBI Office of International Operations/INTERPOL:* 10 weeks; *Visiting Scientist:* Student and faculty appointments are 3 months in the summer, sometimes during the year, and postgraduate appointments can be 1-2 years; *Performance, Recognition And Awards Unit:* 10 weeks, 40 hours/week; *Community Relations Unit:* 10 weeks, 40 hours/week; *Personnel Relations:* 10 weeks, 40 hours/week; *San Diego Division Administrative Squad:* minimum 10 weeks, 8-40 hours/week, 8:15 A.M. to 5:00 P. M., Monday through Friday, with a few optional Saturdays; preference given to those who will commit over 6 months

 THE SCOOP

One of the most well-known U.S. government agencies, the FBI investigates crimes on behalf of the Department of Justice. The Bureau is charged with examining all violations of federal law not specifically assigned to another organization. Most visibly, the FBI is responsible for fighting organized crime, foreign espionage, major violent crimes and terrorism.

ON THE JOB

The FBI offers nine different internship programs. Interns at the National Center for the Analysis of Violent Crime (NCAVC) are assigned a research project that will be the main focus of their program. The FBI Academy alone offers thirteen different internships in several different areas such as behavioral science, investigative training and law enforcement communications. Specific activities will vary according to the particular division to which the intern is assigned. These programs are based at the FBI Academy in Quantico, Va. In Washington, students selected for the prestigious Honors internship program are assigned to Quantico (including the NCAVC), to Clarksburg, W.V., or to a

department at FBI Headquarters according to their academic specialty. They work closely with agents and support personnel and gain a thorough understanding of FBI practices and procedures. The FBI Office of International Operations/INTERPOL offers interns the opportunity to work in either the Terrorism and Violent Crime Division or the Alien/Fugitive Division of the United States National Central Bureau of INTERPOL (USNCB).

The Visiting Scientist Program, a joint program between the FBI Laboratory's Counterterrorism and Forensic Science Research Unit (CFSRU) and Oak Ridge Associated Universities (ORAU), is designed for university students and faculty studying forensic sciences, toxicology, chemistry, and biology. Visiting scientists do lab and computer research at the FBI Lab in Quantico and work in the areas of analytical chemistry, molecular biology, and computation of datasets. All visiting scientists are supervised by FBI mentors.

The FBI also offers opportunities in human relations, personnel, and administrative divisions. Interns in the Performance, Recognition And Awards Unit work with analysts and human resources personnel on performance management and awards programs. Community Relations Unit interns work with public relations executives and program analysts in the FBI's Office of Public Affairs. They help facilitate relationships between the FBI and minority, ethnic, community-based and industry organizations. Personnel Relations interns help formulate FBI advertising, marketing and recruiting campaigns, influencing FBI hiring and recruiting decisions. Finally, interns at the San Diego Division Administrative Squad provide the division with administrative support.

GETTING HIRED

Apply by: *NCAVC:* November 1 for fall internships, March 1 for spring internships; *FBI Academy:* March 1 of previous year for spring; May 1 of previous year for summer; November 1 of previous year for fall. Specify 1 of the 13 divisions in application; *Honors Program:* October 10 of preceding year for summer; *FBI Office of International Operations/INTERPOL:* October 10 of preceding year for summer; *Visitng Scientist:* rolling; *Performance, Recognition And Awards Unit:* October 10 of preceding year for summer; *Community Relations Unit:* October 10 of preceding year for summer; *Personnel Relations:* October 10 of preceding year for summer; *San Diego Division Administrative Squad:* rolling.

Application forms, requirements, and procedures vary by program; see the FBI careers web site, www.fbijobs.gov, to view specific program descriptions and download forms.

Qualifications:

Open to college juniors and seniors and graduate students (exception: the San Diego Squad requires that volunteers be 16 years of age or older). Required GPA varies depending on program, usually 2.5-3.0 minimum. All applicants must be U.S. citizens and pass a background check.

Visit Vault at **www.vault.com** for insider company profiles, expert advice, career message boards, expert resume reviews, the Vault Job Board and more.

VAULT CAREER LIBRARY **171**

Federal Bureau of Investigation, cont.

 GETTING HIRED, CONTINUED

Contact:

NCAVC Internship Program
Cynthia Lent
FBI Academy - NCAVC
Quantico, VA 22135
Phone: (703) 632-4358
E-mail: clent@fbiacademy.edu

FBI Academy Internship Program
See individual unit postings on web page:
www.fbijobs.gov/234.asp

Honors Internship Program
Submit application materials to your nearest FBI field office. A list of field offices can be found at: www.fbijobs.gov/FBIOffice.asp

FBI Office of International Operations/INTERPOL Internship Progam
Makeda Manasseh, Volunteer Internship Coordinator
Federal Bureau of Investigation
935 Pennsylvania Avenue, N.W.
PA 1301-200
Washington, DC 20535
Phone: (202) 278-2424
www.fbijobs.gov/233.asp#6
www.usdoj.gov/usncb
www.interpol.int

Visiting Scientist Program
Go to ORAU/ORISE site for application, procedures and contacts, see.orau.org/ProgramDescription.aspx?Program = 10063

Performance, Recognition And Awards Unit Volunteer Internship Program
Makeda Manasseh, Volunteer Internship Coordinator
(see FBI/Interpol contact directly above)
www.fbijobs.gov/235.asp

Community Relations Unit Volunteer Internship Program
Makeda Manasseh, Volunteer Internship Coordinator (see above)
www.fbijobs.gov/236.asp

Personnel Relations Unit Volunteer Internship Program
Makeda Manasseh, Volunteer Internship Coordinator
(see above)
www.fbijobs.gov/237.asp

San Diego Division Administrative Squad Volunteer Internship Program
SSA Roxanne West
Administrative, Applicant and Training Squad
San Diego FBI
9797 Aero Drive
San Diego, CA 92123
Phone: (858) 499-7612
www.fbijobs.gov/238.asp

Federal Bureau of Prisons

 THE BUZZ
- "Lock down a unique summer experience"
- "See the legal system from the 'inside'"

THE STATS

Industry(ies): Government; Law

Location(s): Washington, DC, and over 100 locations throughout the U.S. Addresses and phone numbers available at www.bop.gov

Number of interns: *Annual:* 71

Pay: Paid; varies according to number of hours worked and experience level

Length of internship: Varies; available year-round. 1 semester minimum

 THE SCOOP

Established in 1930, the Federal Bureau of Prisons is a part of the U.S. Department of Justice. It operates all of the nation's 106 federal correctional institutions and is responsible for approximately 180,000 federal inmates. The FBP confines offenders in facilities that are safe, humane, cost-efficient and appropriately secure, and that provide work and other self-improvement opportunities to assist offenders in becoming law-abiding citizens.

ON THE JOB

The Bureau of Prisons offers internship programs in its Washington, DC, headquarters, as well as facilities in the field. Interns will learn from FBP professionals in the legal and psychology departments, among others. At the conclusion of the program, interns may be considered for permanent placement at the Bureau.

GETTING HIRED

Apply by: Rolling. Application materials and instructions are available by contacting the local institution or office where the applicant is interested in working. Addresses and phone numbers available at www.bop.gov.

Qualifications:
Open to undergraduates and graduate students. Applicants must be 18 years of age or older and U.S. citizens.

Contact:
Staffing, Examining, and Employee Relations Section
Federal Bureau of Prisons
320 First Street, NW, Room 700
Washington, DC 20534
Phone: (202) 307-3177
E-mail: Recruitment@bop.gov
www.bop.gov

Federal Emergency Management Agency

THE BUZZ
- "Strengthen American cities against natural disasters"

 THE STATS

Industry(ies): Government

Location(s): Washington, DC (HQ); field locations

Number of interns: *Annual*: 1-3

Pay: Stipend and free housing during summer. Travel reimbursement for field work; tuition reimbursement for credits earned in independent study portion of the fellowship

Length of internship: 1 academic year

 THE SCOOP

The Federal Emergency Management Agency (FEMA) aids victims of natural disasters and promotes mitigation. As part of its effort to reduce the amount of damage caused by catastrophes, FEMA, along with the Multihazard Mitigation Council of the National Institute of Building Sciences, sponsors one-year Mitigation Planning Fellowships, that promote the integration of hazard mitigation techniques into the practice of urban and regional planning.

 ON THE JOB

Students in the Community Planning Fellowship develop an independent study project on hazard mitigation in a specific target community. Fellow(s) attend an eight-week orientation program in Washington, visiting the FEMA headquarters and other federal agencies. At the end of the summer, fellows travel to a chosen community for field work after which they return to their universities to continue their projects, consulting with faculty sponsors. At the conclusion of the program, fellows submit a paper detailing their experiences.

GETTING HIRED

Apply by: January 21. Submit an application form, available on the MMC web site, along with a three-page statement of educational and career goals, original copies of academic transcripts and letter of nomination by a faculty member.

Qualifications:

Open to master's students who have completed one year of study in regional, environmental or urban planning. U.S. citizens only. Doctoral students not eligible.

Contact:
Claret M. Heider
National Institute of Building Sciences
Multihazard Mitigation Council
1090 Vermont Avenue, NW, Suite 700
Washington, DC 20005-4905
Phone: (202) 289-7800, ext. 131
Fax: (202) 289-1092
E-mail: cheider@nibs.org
www.nibs.org/MMC/mmcactiv4.html

Federal Reserve Bank of New York

THE BUZZ
- "Keeping the economy running smoothly"
- "A prized position for aspiring economists"

THE STATS

Industry(ies): Financial Services; Government

Location(s): New York, NY

Number of interns: *Summer*: 30 (15 undergraduate and 15 graduate students)

Pay: Varies; up to $1,300/week for graduate students

Length of internship: *Summer*: 12-14 weeks

THE SCOOP

The Federal Reserve Bank of New York is one of the 12 regional reserve banks that make up the U.S. Federal Reserve System. Serving New York State, Puerto Rico, the Virgin Islands, and parts of New Jersey and Connecticut, the New York Fed serves a comparatively small area, yet is the largest reserve bank in terms of assets and volume of activity. Reserve banks engage in a number of different activities such as regulating financial institutions, executing monetary policy through the purchase and sale of treasury securities, and providing various financial services to the federal government and U.S. commercial banks. Approximately one-third of the world's monetary gold reserves are housed in the New York Fed's vault.

ON THE JOB

Some of the projects in which interns may be involved include assessing banking applications, writing research papers and conducting bank examinations. The program also provides interns with the opportunity to participate in weekly seminars and luncheons with senior management.

GETTING HIRED

Apply by: *Summer*: January 31. A transcript is required. Applications must be submitted online.

Qualifications:

Undergraduate positions are open to college juniors majoring in a business discipline such as economics, finance, business administration or accounting. Graduate positions are available for students who have completed their first year in an MBA or public policy program. All applicants should have strong computer, writing and analytical skills and demonstrate academic excellence.

Contact:
Internship Coordinator
Federal Reserve Bank of New York
33 Liberty Street
New York, NY 10045
Phone: (212) 720-5000
www.newyorkfed.org/careers/summerintern.html

Visit Vault at **www.vault.com** for insider company profiles, expert advice, career message boards, expert resume reviews, the Vault Job Board and more.

VAULT CAREER LIBRARY **173**

Federal Reserve Board

THE BUZZ
- "Bank on Bernanke"
- "Participate in a finance internship at the highest level"

THE STATS

Industry(ies): Financial Services; Government

Location(s): Washington, DC

Number of interns: *Annual*: 9 (6 undergraduates and 3 doctoral students)

Pay: Most undergraduate internships are unpaid, however a limited number of paid positions are available in the Division of Research and Statistics. Doctoral level internships are paid

Length of internship: *Summer*: 10-12 weeks

THE SCOOP

The Federal Reserve is the central banking system of the United States. Founded in 1913, the Fed polices U.S. financial institutions and safeguards the stability of the economy by setting monetary policy.

ON THE JOB

The Federal Reserve currently offers internship programs in its information technology (IT), research and statistics, and banking supervision departments. IT interns will develop software for mainframe and workstation systems and assist staff in the installation of hardware and software. Research interns will assist Board economists on an assigned project. Interns in the banking supervision section will have the chance to serve in a support role to analysts reviewing banking applications and monitoring bank holdings.

GETTING HIRED

Apply by: Banking Supervising Program
Summer (June 1-September 1): March 31

Research and Statistics Program; Dissertation Internship
Summer (June 1-September 1): April 1; *fall* (September-December): April 1; *spring* (March-May): November 15

Project Internship
Summer (June 1-September 1): April 1

Unpaid Internship
Summer (June 1-September 1): April 1; *fall*: July 31; *spring*: November 15

Division of Information Technology: first week of March

Qualifications:
Open to doctoral candidates in economics, as well as undergraduate students majoring in economics, finance, mathematics, statistics, computer science or other relevant disciplines. Requirements vary by program; see web site for more details.

Contact:
Banking Supervision Program
Board of Governors of the Federal Reserve System
Management Division, Recruiting Section, MS 129
20th Street and Constitution Avenue, NW
Washington, DC 20551

Information Technology Program
Nakia Lucas
Mail Stop 163
Board of Governors of the Federal Reserve System
20th Street and Constitution Avenue, NW
Washington, DC 20551

Research and Statistics Program
Rebecca Young
Mail Stop 65
Board of Governors of the Federal Reserve System
20th Street and Constitution Avenue, NW
Washington, DC 20551
Phone: (800) 448-4894
www.federalreserve.gov/careers/info.cfm?WhichCategory=8

Fellowship of Reconciliation

THE BUZZ
- "Achieve peace through religious dialogue"
- "Work toward resolution of the most intractable conflicts"

THE STATS

Industry(ies): Education; Nonprofit; Religious

Location(s): Nyack, NY; San Francisco, CA; St. Paul, MN; Washington, DC

Number of interns: *Annual:* 4

Pay: $650/month. Housing provided

Length of internship: 11-12 months beginning in September

THE SCOOP

The Fellowship of Reconciliation is a nonprofit using interfaith dialogue to resolve conflict. FOR opposes violence in all its forms, and seeks to attain a just, free and peaceful world. The organization engages in educational and community-building programs to train the next generation of nonviolent leaders and organizers.

ON THE JOB

The Fellowship offers several different internship program tracks, all dealing with various aspects of nonviolent conflict resolution. Currently, programs are being offered in both adult and youth nonviolence training. Interns in these courses will learn how to facilitate workshops and build grassroots education campaigns. There are also internships in the Israel/Palestine peace-building program and the Latin American task force. These interns will have the opportunity to help organize demonstrations and training events and produce written materials. For more details on the individual programs, see the FOR web site.

GETTING HIRED

Apply by: March 15. Print out an application from FOR's web site. Some positions require a resume. Send one copy of the application to the general internship coordinator and one copy to the specific internship department you are interested in (see full instructions on the web site).

Qualifications:
Open to all applicants.

Contact:
Maryrose Dolezal, Internship Coordinator
Fellowship of Reconciliation
1050 Selby Avenue
St. Paul, MN 55104
Phone: (651) 647-4465
Fax: (651) 647-4271
E-mail: internships@forusa.org
www.forusa.org/programs/internships/internships.html

Feminist Majority Foundation

 THE BUZZ
- "Fight for your (equal) rights"

THE STATS

Industry(ies): Education; Nonprofit; Publishing

Location(s): Washington, DC; Los Angeles, CA

Number of interns: *Summer:* 9-10; *fall/spring:* 6 each

Pay: None; some students may qualify for grants or financial aid.

Length of internship: 2-month minimum; available year-round

THE SCOOP

Founded in 1987, the Feminist Majority Foundation (FMF) one of the nation's leading research and advocacy organizations working for women's rights, develops creative long-term strategies and permanent solutions for the pervasive social, political, and economic obstacles facing women. In addition to publishing *Ms.* magazine, FMF conducts a variety of education, research, and outreach projects, and mobilizes grassroots political support for issues of women's equality, reproductive rights, and non-violence.

ON THE JOB

Interns work on a range of activities, from monitoring hearings and press conferences to research projects and organizing events. Interns also work closely with FMF's Campus Program to conduct outreach and launch pro-choice feminist student groups on college campuses nationwide. Current Campus Campaigns include the Women's Leadership Program, Get Out Her Vote, the Emergency Contraception Campaign, and the Global Reproductive Rights Campaign.

GETTING HIRED

Apply by: Rolling. E-mail a resume, cover letter detailing interest in working with FMF, and contact information for two references, at least one preferably academic.

Qualifications:

Open to all undergraduate men and women of any major, as well as recent graduates and graduate students. Applicants with experience working in women's issues are preferred.

Contact
Los Angeles, CA internship
Jessie Raeder
Feminist Majority Foundation
433 South Beverly Drive
Beverly Hills, CA 90212
Phone: (310) 556-2500
Fax: (310) 556-2509
E-mail: jraeder@feminist.org

Washington, DC internship
Crystal Lander
Feminist Majority Foundation
1600 Wilson Boulevard, Suite 801
Arlington, VA 22209
Phone: (703) 522-2214
Fax: (703) 522-2219
E-mail: internship@feminist.org
www.feminist.org/intern

Visit Vault at **www.vault.com** for insider company profiles, expert advice, career message boards, expert resume reviews, the Vault Job Board and more.

VAULT CAREER LIBRARY 175

Fenton Communications

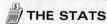 **THE BUZZ**
- "PR that's not for huge corporations"
- "Spin for a cause"

THE STATS

Industry(ies): Public Relations

Location(s): New York, NY; San Francisco, CA; Washington, DC

Number of interns: *Summer*: 1-2 per office

Pay: None

Length of internship: 15-20 hours/week

THE SCOOP

Fenton Communications is a public relations company specializing in nonprofit clients. It has a diverse client list comprising some of the most influential environmental, health and civil rights organizations such as the Sierra Club and Greenpeace. Fenton operates offices in New York, Washington, DC, and San Francisco.

ON THE JOB

Students in the internship program work closely with account executives on media and advocacy campaigns. Interns will manage mailings, monitor press reports for clips, create digests of media coverage and maintain databases. Campaigns focus on public interest issues and can typically range from such topics as global warming to cancer prevention.

GETTING HIRED

Apply by: Rolling. Submit a cover letter and resume via e-mail, fax or mail.

Qualifications:
Open to college juniors, seniors and recent graduates.

Contact:
San Francisco office
Intern Hiring Committee
Fenton Communications
182 Second Street, 4th Floor
San Francisco, CA 94105
Phone: (415) 901-0111
Fax: (415) 901-0110
E-mail: sfintern@fentonwest.com
www.fenton.com/contact/intern_sf.asp

Florida Grand Opera

THE BUZZ
- "Training for serious opera devotees"
- "High culture in Scarface country"

THE STATS

Industry(ies): Art/Museum; Theater/Performing Arts

Location(s): Miami, FL

Number of interns: *Annual*: 8

Pay: Paid; $200/week. Round-trip travel, housing, and health insurance provided

Length of internship: 9 months, beginning each September

THE SCOOP

The Florida Grand Opera is a southern cultural mainstay. Recent FGO productions have included *Don Giovanni*, *Romeo et Juliette* and *La Traviata*.

ON THE JOB

The Young Artist Studio at the Florida Grand Opera is a program designed to impart the necessary skills to aspiring opera singers. Young artists attend voice, acting and language classes, as well as receive individual coaching. Members of the program will also have the chance to perform recitals, sing in the FGO chorus and cover mainstage roles.

GETTING HIRED

Apply by: October 15. A CD or tape of two arias, a photograph, application form and fee are required. See web site for details. Those selected will be invited to a live audition.

Qualifications:
Open to all college grads.

Contact:
Audition Coordinator
Florida Grand Opera Ensemble
1200 Coral Way
Miami, FL 33145
Phone: (305) 854-1643
Fax: (305) 856-1042
E-mail: info@fgo.org
www.fgo.org/fgo-ensemble

Food for the Hungry

THE BUZZ
- "Relieve hunger around the world"
- "Poverty reduction as a vocation"

THE STATS

Industry(ies): Nonprofit; Religious

Location(s): Phoenix, AZ; Washington, DC; select international fields

Number of interns: *Annual:* 50

Pay: Unpaid

Length of internship: *Fall*: 10-15 weeks; *spring*: 10-15 weeks; *summer*: 8-10 weeks; *Micah*: 9 months

THE SCOOP

A Christian nonprofit, Food for the Hungry is devoted to international development and to providing both physical and spiritual aid to poor communities around the world, lending those individuals the skills and materials necessary to escape poverty. Founded in 1971 by Dr. Larry Ward, Food for the Hungry is based in Phoenix and works in 38 countries around the world.

ON THE JOB

Interns can expect a supervised work experience. Phoenix interns work in several areas, including research, administrative support, filmmaking and urban development. Washington, DC, interns work in public policy, health care, political science, and relief. Some summer interns do field work abroad in Africa, Asia, and Latin America, on projects such as child development, agriculture, water and sanitation, and community health (including HIV/AIDS). Finally, interns in the highly selective Micah program work with the Phoenix office. They provide support for FH progrects, sit in on strategic meetings, and may have contact with FH's President, CEO and field staff. Some may also have the opportunity to travel, both domestically and abroad. All interns work in small groups, participate in seminars and retreats, and are provided with one-on-one mentoring. See the web site, http://www.fh.org/internship_opps, for individual program details and opportunities.

GETTING HIRED

Apply by: *Fall*: May 1; *spring*: October 1; *summer*: March 1. Download the application at http://www.fh.org/application-process-internship. Mail the application, a current resume, two faculty references, a student affairs or student life recommendation, and signed agreement with FH's corporate identity statement to the address below. Also have your school mail an official transcrip directly to FH.

Qualifications:
Open to college juniors and seniors, recent graduates. Applicatns should have a minimum cumulative GPA of 3.3 for the Micah internship and 2.75 for all other internships.

Contact:
Julie Short
Food for the Hungry
1224 East Washington Street
Phoenix, AZ 85034
Phone: (480) 609-7762
Fax: (480) 99809448
E-mail: julies@fh.org
www.fh.org/internships

Visit Vault at **www.vault.com** for insider company profiles, expert advice, career message boards, expert resume reviews, the Vault Job Board and more.

VAULT CAREER LIBRARY 177

Food Network

 THE BUZZ
- "Hungry for TV success?"
- "Bam! The top name in food TV"

THE STATS

Industry(ies): Broadcast & Entertainment; Food & Beverage; New/Interactive Media

Location(s): New York, NY

Number of interns: Varies

Pay: None; academic credit

Length of internship: Varies; available year-round

 THE SCOOP

The Food Network is a cable television station devoted to all things food related. Though primarily considered an instructional cooking channel, the Food Network also airs programs examining the culture of food appreciation. Along with its companion web site, www.foodnetwork.com, the network's content reaches over 80 million people worldwide. Food Network is home to hit shows like *Emeril Live* and *Iron Chef*.

ON THE JOB

Internships at the Food Network offer hands-on experience. Students will learn how television programs are produced and how the network operates. Internships are offered in the production, research, programming and creative services departments. Interns may be involved in creating on-air promos, screening tapes for programming research and acting as production assistants for various Food Network programs.

GETTING HIRED

Apply by: Rolling. Intern positions are posted and filled on an individual basis. The Scripps employment web site lists open positions for the Food Network, as well as other Scripps companies such as HGTV, Fine Living and the DIY networks. Resumes accepted by e-mail only.

Qualifications:
Open to all students. Interns must receive academic credit for their internship. Candidates pursuing a degree in television and/or communications preferred.

Contact:
E-mail: hresources@scrippsnetworks.com
www.foodnetwork.com
cfapps.scripps.com/jobposting/jobopp.asp

Forbes

 THE BUZZ
- "The inside scoop on the most powerful business leaders"
- "One of the 'big three' business magazines"

THE STATS

Industry(ies): Journalism; New/Interactive Media; Publishing

Location(s): New York, NY

Number of interns: *Summer*: 12-15

Pay: Paid; $10/hour

Length of internship: *Summer*: 10 weeks

THE SCOOP

Forbes is a privately held publishing and new media company. Its flagship publication, *Forbes*, the oldest major business magazine in the U.S., celebrated its 85th anniversary in 2002. In an industry increasingly dominated by public conglomerates, Forbes remains one of the largest and most successful family businesses of its kind. In recent years, the company has expanded to include several new divisions, including Forbes.com, Forbes Management Conference Group, and Forbes Custom Media, which also encompasses *American Heritage*, *American Legacy*, and *American Heritage of Invention & Technology* magazines.

ON THE JOB

Interns at Forbes will rotate through the editorial and business departments, working on special projects and assisting staff members as needed. This rotation is designed to give interns an idea of the different aspects of magazine publishing. Some of the duties typically assigned are fact checking, conducting research for the Forbes Lists, working on marketing campaigns and assisting in the human resources and information technology departments.

GETTING HIRED

Apply by: *Summer*: March 15. To apply, submit a resume and cover letter by e-mail or mail.

Qualifications:
Open to undergraduate freshmen, sophomores, juniors and seniors, as well as recent college grads.

Contact:
Internship Coordinator
Forbes
Human Resources Department
60 Fifth Avenue
New York, NY 10011
Fax: (212) 206-5105
E-mail: careers@forbesinc.com
forbesinc.com/careers/internship.shtml

The Ford Foundation

THE STATS

Industry(ies): Education; Nonprofit

Location: New York, NY

Number of interns: *Summer*: typically 10-15

Pay: Paid; $13-$14/hour

Length of internship: Summer

THE SCOOP

The Ford Foundation – which is unaffiliated with a certain Michigan car company, although created by the gent we all know and love as Henry Ford – was founded in 1936 with the mission of promoting democracy, reducing poverty and funding projects that aim to solve social and economic problems.

ON THE JOB

Interns at The Ford Foundation perform administrative tasks and become involved in the process of selecting grant proposals to be funded. They also handle grant applications.

GETTING HIRED

Apply by: *Summer*: May. Apply by submitting a cover letter and resume by fax or mail.

Qualifications:
Restricted to "economically disadvantaged" 18- to 23-year-old undergraduates residing in the New York City area. Must have a minimum 2.5 GPA and receive financial aid for education.

Contact:
Human Resources
The Ford Foundation
320 East 43rd Street
New York, NY 10017
Phone: (212) 573-5000
Fax: (212) 351-3644
www.fordfound.org

Ford Models

THE STATS

Industry(ies): Broadcast & Entertainment; Fashion; Public Relations

Location(s): Chicago, IL; Los Angeles, CA; Miami, FL; New York, NY; Scottsdale, AZ; Paris; São Paulo; Toronto; Vancouver

Number of interns: *Annual*: 15-20 for the New York location; 8-10 for other offices

Pay: None; academic credit. Lunches; subway fare

Length of internship: *Spring/summer/fall*: 3-week minimum; available year-round

THE SCOOP

Established in 1946 by Eileen and Jerry Ford, Ford Models is now one of the world's most recognized modeling agencies. Known as an innovator in business and marketing, Ford Models represents the industry's top models. The agency is known for being especially protective of its gorgeous, often very young, models.

ON THE JOB

Interns work in the marketing and public relations departments. Some intern duties include using Word Perfect, Microsoft Excel, PowerPoint and Internet applications, as well as calling clients, answering phones, assisting in model calls, opening mail and organizing files.

GETTING HIRED

Apply by: Rolling. Submit a resume and cover letter via fax or e-mail.

Qualifications:
Open to college juniors and seniors, as well as grad students. International applicants welcome.

Contact:
Refer to the web site for contact information for each office.

Ford Models
142 Greene Street
New York, NY 10012
Phone: (212) 219-6500
Fax: (212) 966-1531
E-mail: mschwartz@fordmanagment.com

Ford Models
8826 Burton Way
Beverly Hills, CA 90211
Phone: (310) 276-8100
Fax: (310) 276-9299
www.fordmodels.com

Visit Vault at **www.vault.com** for insider company profiles, expert advice, career message boards, expert resume reviews, the Vault Job Board and more.

VAULT CAREER LIBRARY 179

Ford Motor Company

 THE BUZZ
- "One of the bluest of the automotive bluechips"

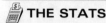 **THE STATS**

Industry(ies): Consumer Products; Engineering; Manufacturing; Technology

Location(s): Detroit, MI

Number of interns: *Summer*: 1,000-1,200

Pay: Paid; *undergraduates*: $1,935-$3,170/month; *graduate students*: $3,525-$5,800/month. Return travel; free housing and transportation if qualified (Dearborn) or housing allowance (non-Dearborn)

Length of internship: *Summer*: 3 months

 **THE SCOOP**

The storied history of the Ford Motor Company dates back to 1903, when Henry Ford produced his first Model-T. Today, the company is one of the "Big Three" U.S. automakers and sells nearly 7 million vehicles annually. In addition to the Ford make of automobiles, the company also produces vehicles under the Mercury, Lincoln, Volvo, Land Rover, Jaguar and Aston Martin brands.

ON THE JOB

Ford's internships are structured around its various career development programs. Each department offers both a summer internship and a two-year program for college graduates. Departments accepting interns include product development, manufacturing, finance, marketing, information technology, purchasing and human resources. The internships aim is to provide practical experience in an area related to each student's academic study.

GETTING HIRED

Apply by: Rolling. There is no deadline for the program. Intern positions are filled on an individual basis. See the web site for current openings and to apply. Ford does not accept paper resumes. Submit application online.

Qualifications:
Open to college sophomores, juniors and seniors and grad students. A minimum GPA of 3.0 and an academic background relevant to the internship is required. Most interns are from the business or technical fields. Specific qualifications vary by department.

Contact:
Phone: (313) 322-7500
E-mail: career@ford.com
www.mycareer.ford.com

Foreign Affairs

THE BUZZ
- "Gain perspective on international relations"
- "Shaping opinions on the world's big issues"

THE STATS

Industry(ies): Government; Journalism; Publishing

Location(s): New York, NY

Number of interns: *Full-year editorial internship*: 1 per year

Pay: Paid, full-time position

Length of internship: 1 year, starting in August

THE SCOOP

Foreign Affairs is the prestigious international issues journal published by the Council on Foreign Relations. The journal is committed to be a nonpartisan forum for debate and analysis. Since 1922, *FA* has published lively discussions by well-respected scholars of the most pressing issues in contemporary international politics.

ON THE JOB

The academic year internship is a full-time, paid position offering training in serious journalism. The intern works as an assistant editor with substantial responsibility and is involved in all aspects of the editorial process — editing, proofreading, evaluating manuscripts, research, fact-checking, and production work. Other internship opportunities are available through the Council of Foreign Relations. Those positions amy be found on the CFR web site at http://www.cfr.org/about/career_opportunities/internships.html.

GETTING HIRED

Apply by: March 10, 2007, for the 2007-2008 academic year position. Please consult the web site for specific dates (www.foreignaffairs.org/about/employment). Submit three writing samples of five pages or less and three letters of recommendation, either professional or academic, cover letter and resume. *Foreign Affairs* does not accept applications by e-mail, and only finalists will be interviewed.

Qualifications:
The full-year editorial internship is open to recent graduates of either undergrad or graduate level programs. Candidates should have a serious interest in international relations, a flair for writing, and a facility with the English language.

Contact:
Editorial Internships
Foreign Affairs
58 East 68th Street
New York, NY 10021
Phone: (212) 434-9507
Fax: (212) 434-9849
www.foreignaffairs.org/about/employment (links to information on all internship programs)

Foreign Policy Research Institute

THE BUZZ
- "A global view from Philadelphia"

 THE STATS
Industry(ies): Education; Government; Nonprofit; Publishing

Location(s): Philadelphia, PA

Number of interns: 6-10

Pay: None; work-study positions (Pennsylvania residents only)

Length of internship: *Spring/summer/fall:* 3 months, or shorter by arrangement

THE SCOOP
The Foreign Policy Research Institute is a nonprofit organization that performs research and runs educational programs on international issues. American foreign policy, China's role in Asia, terrorism and the Israel/Palestine conflict are focal points for the FPRI's recent work. The Institute also publishes the foreign policy journal *Orbis* and runs the Marvin Wachman Fund for International Education.

ON THE JOB
Internships are available in three different support roles. Research assistants maintain databases, search for literature and create indices. Editorial assistants work mainly on *Orbis*, proofreading, fact checking, copyediting and performing other administrative duties. Administrative assistants are involved with public relations, event planning and development.

GETTING HIRED
Apply by: *Summer:* Close of business on first Friday of April; *fall:* September 15; *spring:* January 15. Send a writing sample (preferably a 3-10 page paper) along with your resume and cover letter by e-mail. Accepted applicants will usually be contacted within two weeks of the application deadline.

Qualifications:
Open to all college freshmen, sophomores, juniors and seniors and graduate students. Knowledge of a foreign language (particularly Russian, Arabic, French, German or Spanish) is helpful. Interns must be able to commit at least 10 hours per week.

Contact:
Internship Coordinator
Foreign Policy Research Institute
1528 Walnut Street, Suite 610
Philadelphia, PA 19102-3684
Phone: (215) 732-3774
Fax: (215) 732-4401
E-mail: intern@fpri.org
www.fpri.org/about/internships.html

Forty Acres and a Mule

THE BUZZ
- "Still one of the most vibrant film internships"
- "Do the film thing"

THE STATS
Industry: Broadcast & Entertainment; Film

Location: Brooklyn, NY

Number of interns: *Annual:* around 15 (varies). Interns accepted only when a movie is in production

Pay: None; academic credit available. Stipend provided for local transportation and meals

Length of internship: 8-11 weeks; coincides with production dates

THE SCOOP
Forty Acres and a Mule was founded in 1986 by Spike Lee as a career vehicle for black writers, actors and directors seeking a chance to work with peers and develop skills in a supportive environment. Internships are offered at the mercy of production schedules – there are no internships when there is nothing to do. Forty Acres produces all of Spike Lee's movies, such as *Jungle Fever* and *X*.

ON THE JOB
Interns work in wardrobe, props, casting and accounting; as extras or director's assistants; and in production and editing. Some are even cast as extras.

GETTING HIRED
Apply by: Rolling.

Qualifications:
Open to college freshmen, sophomores, juniors and seniors, as well as grad students. Submit a resume and cover letter in order to be invited for an admissions test and interview.

Contact:
Forty Acres and a Mule
Internship Program
75 South Elliot Place
Brooklyn, NY 11217

Visit Vault at **www.vault.com** for insider company profiles, expert advice, career message boards, expert resume reviews, the Vault Job Board and more.

VAULT CAREER LIBRARY **181**

Fourth World Movement

THE BUZZ

- "Demonstrating solidarity with the world's poor"
- "Improve your karma"

THE STATS

Industry(ies): Education; Nonprofit

Location(s): Appalachia, VA; New Orleans, LA; New York, NY; Washington, DC

Number of interns: *Spring/summer/fall*: up to 4 each

Pay: None. Housing, local work-related transportation provided

Length of internship: *Spring/summer/fall*: 12 weeks each

THE SCOOP

The Fourth World Movement is dedicated to fostering partnerships with families in persistent poverty and other members of society in a way that recognizes each person's efforts and the role they have to play in overcoming social exclusion due to extreme poverty. This commitment to the cause of those living in persistent poverty takes various forms, including cultural and educational programs in disadvantaged neighborhoods; long-term research into poverty and efforts made to combat it; public information campaigns; and working to ensure that the voice of the poorest and most excluded is heard through forums for representation and dialogue.

ON THE JOB

The internship introduces the philosophy and work of the Fourth World Movement through a flexible program of reading, research, videos and discussion, as well as some manual work (maintenance and renovation), regular writing projects, and ongoing evaluation and feedback. Interns then participate in Fourth World Movement/USA activities with families and children living in poverty in New York City, New Orleans, Appalachia or Washington, DC.

GETTING HIRED

Apply by: Rolling. Request an application form on the Fourth World Movement web site. An application fee, three reference letters, an interview and/or a visit to the national center are also required.

Qualifications:
Interns must be at least 19 years old, have a high school diploma or GED, and have at least one year of college or work experience.

Contact:
Internship Coordinator
7600 Willow Hill Drive
Landover, MD 20785
Phone: (202) 393-2822
Fax: (202) 393-2443
E-mail: nationalcenter@4thworldmovement.org
www.4thworldmovement.org

Fox Networks Group

THE BUZZ

- "Doh! Even Homer could start a TV career with this internship"

THE STATS

Industry(ies): Broadcast & Entertainment

Location(s): Atlanta, GA; Bellevue, WA; Charlotte, NC; Denver, CO; Houston, TX; Irving, TX; Los Angeles, CA; Minneapolis, MN; New York, NY; Orlando, FL; Phoenix, AZ; Pittsburgh, PA; St. Louis, MO; Tampa, FL

Number of interns: *Fall*: 150

Pay: Most positions are unpaid (limited number of paid available on occasion); academic credit required

Length of internship: Varies; usually about 3 months; available year-round

THE SCOOP

Fox Networks Group supports a wide range of television programming, including Fox Sports Net, FX, Fox Movie Channel, Fox Sports en Español, Fox Reality Channel, Fox Soccer Channel, SPPED, Fuel TV and National Geographic Channel. FNG is part of Fox Entertainment Group, one of the most recognized producers and distributors of films and television programs, with a collection of diverse program networks extending to almost every popular genre.

ON THE JOB

Internships are available in the legal, sales, marketing, production, music, network development and other departments. Typical duties may include preparing sales materials and presentations, assisting with the post-production of programs and researching information for press releases. Fox Networks Group also offer business development and strategy positions for MBA candidates.

GETTING HIRED

Apply by: Rolling. See the web site for current internship openings and e-mail resumes to fng.jobs@fox.com. Applications are accepted online. Visit www.foxcareers.com.

Qualifications:
Open to college juniors and seniors enrolled in an accredited college or university and in good academic standing. Interns must receive academic credit from their institutions and/or may be paid a weekly salary. Interns are eligible to participate in the program for a maximum of two consecutive semesters.

Contact:
Fox Cable Networks
Human Resources
P.O. Box 900
Beverly Hills, CA 90213
www.foxcareers.com

Franconia Sculpture Park

THE BUZZ

- "Get a head start on your first exhibition"

 THE STATS

Industry(ies): Art; Museum

Location(s): Franconia, MN

Number of interns: *Winter:* 4; *spring:* 6; *summer:* 6; *fall:* 6

Pay: Unpaid. Free room and board. Some free materials, machinery, and engineering.

Length of internship: 8 weeks-4 months

THE SCOOP

Founded in 1996, Franconia Sculpture Park is a professional artists' organization dedicated to providing opportunities to artists and audiences through a diverse program of creation, education, and experimentation. An outdoor sculpture park open to the public 365 days a year, from dawn until dusk, Franconia allows visitors to tour its rotating collection of over 75 pieces. FSP is committed to nurturing artistic excellence and giving emerging artists the experience of working and exhibiting with more established artists.

ON THE JOB

FSP actively recruits student artists, post-grad artists and students of museum studies to participate in its intern/mentor program. Half of an intern's time is spent on their own sculptural work with the other half spent on park duties. Interns create work to be included in exhibitions. In addition, they assist visiting artists with fabrication, site preparation, and installation of all types and sizes of 3-D work, landscaping, and maintenance.

GETTING HIRED

Apply by: March 10, 2007. Send a letter of application, resume, 12 Slides or a CD, a slide script, and the names, e-mail addresses, phone numbers and addresses of two references. Check the web site for up to date information.

Qualifications: Open to college students, post-graduates and adults. Applicants should be career-bound emerging artists. Interns range from juniors in college to 45 years of age.

Contact:
John Hock
Artist Interns/Franconia Sculpture Park
29815 Unity Ave
Franconia, MN 55074
Phone: (651) 465-3701
Fax: (651) 465-3701
E-mail: info@franconia.org
www.franconia.org

Franklin D. Roosevelt Library

THE BUZZ

- "A New Deal for summer internships"
- "Preserving the legacy of FDR"

THE STATS

Industry(ies): Education; Nonprofit

Location(s): Hyde Park, NY

Number of interns: *Summer:* Usually 5; varies based on funding

Pay: Varies; $300/week for paid summer internships (limited number); unpaid internships available year-round for academic credit

Length of internship: *Summer:* 6-8 weeks

THE SCOOP

The Franklin D. Roosevelt Library was the first presidential library in the U.S. Built under the guidance of Roosevelt himself, the library opened in 1941 and is today operated by the National Archives. The Library complex consists of a museum, as well as an archive of the former President's personal papers and historical documents.

ON THE JOB

Interns with an interest in the history of the New Deal era will have the unique opportunity to work with primary source materials from the Roosevelt presidency. They will work with Library staff, helping to catalogue museum and archival materials, create databases, and scan documents and photographs for digital retrieval.

GETTING HIRED

Apply by: *Summer:* April 15. Send application form, available on the web site, and a current college transcript to the address below.

Qualifications:
Open to college freshmen, sophomores, juniors and seniors, recent college graduates and grad students.

Contact:
Clifford Laube
Franklin D. Roosevelt Presidential Library
4079 Albany Post Road
Hyde Park, NY 12538
Phone: (845) 486-7745
Fax: (845) 486-1981
E-mail: clifford.laube@nara.gov
www.fdrlibrary.marist.edu/intern.html

Visit Vault at **www.vault.com** for insider company profiles, expert advice, career message boards, expert resume reviews, the Vault Job Board and more.

V/\ULT CAREER LIBRARY **183**

Freedom Theatre

 THE BUZZ
- "An African American cultural treasure"
- "Uncover your dramatic talents"

 THE STATS

Industry(ies): Art/Museum; Theater/Performing Arts

Location(s): Philadelphia, PA

Number of interns: *Annual*: 4-5

Pay: None; academic credit

Length of internship: Flexible

 THE SCOOP

Founded in 1966, the Freedom Theatre is the oldest African-American theater in Pennsylvania. The renowned Freedom Repertory Theatre Company stages four productions each year and recently moved into a brand-new state-of-the-art facility. The theater performs a variety of works including dramas, comedies and musicals that showcase the African American experience. Freedom Theatre also offers the Performing Arts Training Program, which provides education in acting, dance and vocal arts to children and adults.

ON THE JOB

The Freedom Theatre offers an individualized internship program that is tailored to the interests and abilities of each person. Opportunities exist for internships on both the creative and business sides. Placements are available in production, directing, acting, marketing or development. All interns will receive support and guidance from a designated mentor.

GETTING HIRED

Apply by: Rolling. Send cover letter and resume to the address below.

Qualifications:

Open to all individuals 18 years of age or older. College freshmen, sophomores, juniors and seniors, recent college graduates, grad students and anyone interested in exploring a career change are all encouraged to apply.

Contact:
Thom Page
Freedom Theatre
1346 North Broad Street
Philadelphia, PA 19121
Phone: (215) 765-2793
www.freedomtheatre.org

French Embassy Press Office

 THE BUZZ
- "Put those high school French classes to good use"
- "Promote U.S./French relations in the realm of public diplomacy"

 THE STATS

Industry(ies): Government; Public Relations

Location: Washington, DC

Number of interns: *Annual*: 5-7/semester

Pay: None; academic credit available. Free tickets (or reduced prices) for Embassy cultural events; access to Embassy boutique and cafeteria

Length of internship: Varies; usually 4-6 months (1 semester); 3 days/week, 24 hours/week

 THE SCOOP

The main task of the French Embassy's Press and Information Office is to research and answer questions, mostly from the American public (journalists, businessmen, researchers, students, etc).

 ON THE JOB

Interns serve as liaisons between the French government and the public, with duties ranging from fielding questions to writing articles and looking for photos for the *News from France* newsletter. Some also write reports on certain issues of media interest, or background press releases for the Embassy's web site. Interns having some experience in Web design programs may help keep the Embassy's site updated. Most French Embassy interns come from the U.S. or France with a background in political science, foreign affairs and/or communications.

 GETTING HIRED

Apply by: Rolling. Internships are available year-round. Send resume (in English), cover letter (in French), a one-to two-page academic writing sample (in English) and one page journalistic writing sample on a French current event (also in English) to the address below.

Qualifications:

Open to college sophomores, juniors and seniors. Must be enrolled in a university at the time of the internship. Interns must be fluent in French. Applicants should familiarize themselves with *News From France (NFF)* before applying at http://www.ambafrance-us.org/publi/.

Contact:
Mr. Thomas Rottcher
Press and Communication Office
French Embassy
4101 Reservoir Road, NW
Washington, DC 20007
Phone: (202) 944-6060
Fax: (202) 944-6040
E-mail: info@ambafrance-us.org
www.ambafrance-us.org

Friends Committee on National Legislation

 THE BUZZ
- "Quaker morals meet Beltway power brokers"

 **THE STATS**

Industry(ies): Government; Nonprofit

Location(s): Washington, DC

Number of interns: Varies; usually between 2-5 annually

Pay: Paid; salary is subsistence level for the Washington, DC, area

Length of internship: 11 months (early September-late July)

 **THE SCOOP**

The Friends Committee on National Legislation (FCNL) functions as a nonprofit, Quaker-affiliated advocacy and lobbying organization. The FCNL is committed to social and economic justice, conflict resolution and civil rights. In recent years, The Committee has worked to ban nuclear weapons and landmines, stop the war in Iraq, promote civil liberties in the United States, and advocate for Native People in the United States.

ON THE JOB

Interns will work as full-time members of the FCNL staff during the course of the internship, gaining a thorough understanding of the relevant issues, as well as the governmental process. They will attend committee hearings, examine government reports, write background briefs, and correspond with FCNL members and other grassroots activists. Interns will have the opportunity to work closely with experienced FCNL lobbyists and communications and field program staff.

GETTING HIRED

Apply by: March 1. An application form and recommendations from the web site are required. Send in complete application via U.S. mail.

Qualifications:
Open to all college graduates and graduate students. Applicants without a college degree but with equivalent experience will also be considered.

Contact:
Kathie Guthrie
Field Program Secretary
Friends Committee on National Legislation
245 Second Street, NE
Washington, DC 20002-5795
Phone: (800) 630-1330 (inside U.S. only)
Phone: (202) 547-6000, x2506
Toll-free: (800) 630-1330
Fax: (202) 547-6019
E-mail: fcnl@fcnl.org
www.fcnl.org/intern.htm

Frito Lay

 THE BUZZ
- "Munch your way through this resume builder"

 THE STATS

Industry(ies): Consumer Products; Food & Beverage

Location(s): Dallas, TX; Orlando, FL; many other locations

Number of interns: *Summer*: 25

Pay: Paid; *undergraduate*: $375-$649/week; *graduates*: $649-$953/week. Maximum $500 relocation allowance

Length of internship: *Summer*: 10-12 weeks

 THE SCOOP

Frito Lay began its illustrious history in 1932 with two young entrepreneurs. Elmer Doolin of San Antonio, Texas, took his new, then-unknown, food snack, Fritos corn chips to the market and named the company after the product. The Frito Company went on to hold the biggest chip market in the Southwest. At the same time, Herman W. Lay was delivering potato chips in his Model A truck in Nashville, Tenn. He later bought the potato chip company in 1938 and named it H.W. Lay & Company. It went on to hold the biggest chip market in the Southeast. Frito granted Lay one of the first exclusive deals to manufacture Frito chips in the Southeast. The rest is delicious history.

 ON THE JOB

Interns can work in sales, marketing, operations, finance, purchasing, service and distribution. Duties vary with department and placement but may include assisting the sales and marketing staff with promotional literature, crunching numbers in finance or handling administrative tasks. Interns work closely with mentors on the staff and attend a three-day intern conference.

GETTING HIRED

Apply by: May 1. Apply online at www.fritolayjobs.com or send a cover letter and resume, indicating GPA, position preference and location desired, to the address below.

Qualifications:
Open to college juniors and seniors, as well as grad students; minimum 3.0 GPA required. International students accepted.

Contact:
Frito Lay, Inc.
Staffing Department
Dept: Intern
P.O. Box 225458
Dallas, TX 75222-5458
www.fritolayjobs.com

Visit Vault at **www.vault.com** for insider company profiles, expert advice, career message boards, expert resume reviews, the Vault Job Board and more.

VAULT CAREER LIBRARY 185

Frontier Nursing Service

 THE BUZZ

- "Improving access to health care in rural and underserved areas"
- "Health care with a pioneering spirit"

 THE STATS

Industry(ies): Education; Health Care; Nonprofit

Location(s): Wendover, KY

Number of interns: 20

Pay: None

Length of internship: 12 weeks

 **THE SCOOP**

The Frontier Nursing Service is a nonprofit organization devoted to providing comprehensive, primary health care to families in rural and underserved areas. Founded by Mary Breckinridge in 1925, FNS continues to provide service through the Mary Breckinridge Hospital, a licensed Critical Access Hospital, six rural health care clinics, a home health agency, and through the Frontier School of Midwifery and Family Nursing.

 ON THE JOB

The Courier Program seeks volunteers with an interest in health care and education. Interns provide a variety of vital support services to FNS workers and the local community. These tasks can include host/hostess duties and performing community outreach in a variety of fields, as well as supporting the work of the midwifery school, the local hospital and FNS clinics.

 **GETTING HIRED**

Apply by: Rolling. Send in three letters of recommendation and completed application forms, available on the web site, www.frontiernursing.org.

Qualifications:

All applicants must be over 18 and have graduated from high school. Couriers must hold a valid driver's license and are required to provide their own vehicles for personal use. A $250 housing fee is required prior to arrival.

Contact:

Courier Program
Frontier Nursing Service
132 FNS Drive
Wendover, KY 41775
Phone: (606) 672-2317
Fax: (606) 672-3022
E-mail: fnstours@yahoo.com
www.frontiernursing.org

INTERNSHIP PROFILES: G

Gap

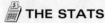 **THE BUZZ**
- "Stake your claim to the khaki empire"
- "Learn the retail business – and look good doing it"

 THE STATS

Industry(ies): Consumer Products; Fashion; Retail

Location(s): San Francisco, CA; New York, NY; Field

Number of interns: *Summer*: 15-50

Pay: Paid; $15/hour

Length of internship: *Summer*: 10 weeks

 THE SCOOP

The San Francisco-based clothing retailer Gap has grown rapidly since its start as a single store in 1969. What began as one brand has grown to encompass several under the Gap Inc. umbrella, uncluding Gap, Banana Republic, Old Navy, and Forth & Towne, with worldwide revenues in excess of $16 billion. In addition to its near-ubiquitous presence in the United States, Gap operates stores in Canada, the United Kingdom, France, Japan and Germany and has further expansion plans into several overseas markets.

ON THE JOB

The Gap summer internship program is designed to help students gain an understanding of the retail industry and see if they wish to pursue a career at Gap Inc. after graduatuonm. Placements are available in several different concentrations. Interns in the logistics and import compliance department will learn the finer points of international trade and customs regulations. Distribution analysts will develop a supply plan that supports the marketing goals of one of Gap's departments. Students in the information technology department provide tech support and may work as members of a project team. Gap also offers graduate-level internships for MBA candidates in finance, merchandising, strategy and business development.

All interns attend weekly presentations by senior executives, which provide an overview of Gap's brands. Each intern is assigned to a group project that will be presented to senior management at the end of the summer. Outside of the office, interns participate in volunteer projects and attend events such as baseball games and dinners in San Francisco.

GETTING HIRED

Apply by: *Summer*: March 1. Choose an open position on the web site and apply via e-mail with a cover letter, resume and a job reference number.

Qualifications:
Open to college juniors and MBA candidates with a GPA of 3.0 or higher.

Contact:
College Internship Coordinator
Gap Inc. College Recruiting
2 Folsom Street, 6th Floor
San Francisco, CA 94105
Fax: (415) 427-6804
E-mail: college_recruiting@@gap.com
http://gapinc.com/public/Careers/car_col_intern.shtml

Gazette Communications

 THE BUZZ
- "Real responsibility for cub journalists"
- "A multimedia internship opportunity in Iowa"

 THE STATS

Industry(ies): Broadcast & Entertainment; Journalism

Location(s): Cedar Rapids, IA

Number of interns: *Gazette newsroom*: 2-3/semester; *Gazette photography*: 1-2/semester; *KCRG newsroom*: 5/semester; *public relations*: 1; *ad sales*: 1-2

Pay: Paid; $8-9.50/hour

Length of internship: *Summer/fall/winter*: 3 months each. Newsroom and photography internships are offered in the winter, summer, and fall; advertising and marketing internships are offered in the summer only

 THE SCOOP

Gazette Communications is a Cedar Rapids, Iowa-based media company which owns the local ABC affiliate, KCRG-TV and the KCRG-AM sports radio station, and it publishes *The Gazette* newspaper. Gazette employs approximately 700 people and reaches an audience of over 325,000 in eastern Iowa.

ON THE JOB

Gazette offers both editorial and business-oriented internships. On the editorial side, interns may serve as reporters or photographers. Positions are also available in advertising, sales, marketing and public relations.

GETTING HIRED

Apply by: *Newsroom/photography*: *summer*: January 1; *fall*: May 1; *winter*: September 1. Send cover letter and resume, including clips or slides, with application. *Advertising/marketing*: March 1. To apply, send cover letter and resume.

Qualifications:
News and photo internships are open to college sophomores, juniors and seniors. Advertising and marketing internships are open to college sophomores and juniors.

Contact:
Patricia Thoms, Employment Manager
Gazette Communications
P.O. Box 511
Cedar Rapids, IA 52406
Phone: (319) 398-5845
Fax: (319) 399-5915
E-mail: gazcohr@gazettecommunications.com
gazettecommunications.com/internships.htm

GE

 THE BUZZ

- "Work for a company that will light up your resume"

 **THE STATS**

Industry(ies): Broadcasting & Entertainment; Energy/Utilities; Financial Services; Health Care; Transportation

Location(s): Fairfield, CT (HQ); operations in over 100 countries around the globe

Number of interns: *Annual*: approximately 2,200 in the U.S.

Pay: Paid; competitive pay rate based on year in school, major and work experience. Relocation assistance or housing stipend; informational sessions; career fairs; social events and recreational activities

Length of internship: *Summer*: 10-12 weeks; *co-op*: 3-9 months, usually January-June or June-December

THE SCOOP

GE traces its beginnings to Thomas A. Edison, who established Edison Electric Light Company in 1878. GE is the only company listed in the Dow Jones Industrial Index today that was also included in the original index in 1896. It has been ranked number 1 by Universum for the best rotational leadership programs, and number 3 for the quality of its internships. The company has also been rated by Fortune as the "Most Admired," both in America and globally. With a wide range of products and services,from aircraft engines, locomotives and plastics to medical equipment, financial services and media, GE offers candidates the ability to grow professionally while working in different industries. Last year, GE posted revenues of $150 billion and earnings of $18.3 billion.

ON THE JOB

Interns may work in various businesses, including Advanced Materials, Commercial Finance, Consumer Finance, Equipment Services, Energy, Global Research, Health Care, Infrastructure, Insurance, NBC/Universal and Transportation. Interns work side-by-side with industry experts on projects. Duties vary by department and location, and cover a wide array of disciplines, including human resources, finance, information technology, engineering, operations, and sales and marketing.

GETTING HIRED

Apply by: GE focuses the core of its recruiting efforts at 39 select "Executive Schools" each year, and prefers that students interview with them by applying through their university career offices. Check your university career office or GE's corporate web site for dates: www.gecareers.com/GE CAREERS/jsp/us/studentOpportunities/studentOpportunities.jsp. If your university isn't listed, you may apply online for any of GE's Corporate Leadership Programs or direct-hire positions. GE conducts second-round interviews at its various offices.

Qualifications

Open to full-time university students enrolled at any level in a related concentration. Minimum 3.0/4.0 GPA required for undergraduates and 3.2/4.0 GPA for master's students. All applicants must have U.S. work authorization.

Contact:
GE
3135 Easton Turnpike
Fairfield, CT 06828
Phone: (203) 373-2211
Fax: (203) 373-3131
www.ge.com
www.gecareers.com

Visit Vault at **www.vault.com** for insider company profiles, expert advice, career message boards, expert resume reviews, the Vault Job Board and more.

V/\ULT CAREER LIBRARY **189**

GEICO

THE BUZZ
- "Meet the Gekko"
- "Take the GEICO road to success"

THE STATS

Industry(ies): Insurance

Location(s): Chevy Chase, MD (HQ); Buffalo, NY; Coralville, IA; Dallas, TX; Fredericksburg, VA; Honolulu, HI; Lakeland, FL; Macon, GA; San Diego, CA; Tucson, AZ; Virginia Beach, VA; Woodbury, NY

Number of interns: *Summer:* 12

Pay: $12.75-$13.00 per hour (varies by location)

Length of internship: *Summer:* 8-10 weeks

THE SCOOP

GEICO's full name, Government Employees Insurance Company, goes back to its first customers in 1936: government employees and military personnel. Founder Leo Goodwin went into business determined that he could deliver automobile insurance at reduced prices by selecting to prime customer groups and marketing directly to them. By doing so, Goodwin succeeded in driving down operating costs and passing the savings to GEICO's customers. The company offers insurance products for motorcycles, all-terrain vehicles (ATV's), boats, homes, apartments and mobile homes. Personal umbrella protection and life insurance are also available. GEICO is also the largest direct writer of private passenger auto insurance in the country.

In 1996, GEICO became a subsidiary of Berkshire Hathaway, headed by Warren Buffett, one of the country's most successful investors. For the past two years, Fortune magazine has named Berkshire Hathaway's property-casualty insurance operation the most admired in the country. Today GEICO is the fourth-largest private-passenger auto insurer in the United States, a ranking established each year by A. M. Best based on direct written premiums. The company has $21.2 billion in assets and over 20,000 employees.

ON THE JOB

GEICO offers internships at its Fredericksburg and Virginia Beach offices, where interns get a good look at how the company operates as they progress through various operating units. Each intern is assigned a senior management mentor, and interns interact with senior management to present analysis and research on consulting projects. During their internship, students complete both individual and group projects on topics relevant to GEICO and the insurance industry. In addition, interns participate in a two-day summit at GEICO's corporate headquarters in Washington, D.C., where they meet with senior management and GEICO CEO Tony Nicely. The biggest perk: interns are considered for future employment with the company.

GETTING HIRED

Apply by: Summer: May 1.. Submit a resume, online application and transcript to one of the two internship locations below.

Qualifications: Applicants should be currently enrolled sophomores or juniors at an accredited college or university, have a minimum GPA of 3.2, and be majoring in or studying risk management, business, economics, finance and accounting, management and statistics (research methods).

Contact:

Fredericksburg internship:
Kristie Woodside
One GEICO Boulevard,
Fredericksburg, VA 22412
Phone: (540) 286-4821
Fax: (305) 503-7343
E-mail: kwoodside@geico.com

Virginia Beach internship:
Jill Stover
One GEICO Landing,
Virginia Beach, VA 23454
Phone: (757) 222-6393
Fax: (206) 508-9021
E-mail: jistover@geico.com

www.geico.com/careers

Genentech

THE BUZZ

- "Learn from the granddaddy of gene splicers"
- "On the cutting edge of biotechnology"

THE STATS

Industry(ies): Biotech; Pharmaceuticals; Science/Research

Location(s): San Francisco, CA

Number of interns: *Summer*: 165

Pay: Paid; *undergraduates*: $475/week; *grad students*: $575/week

Length of internship: *Summer*: 3 months

THE SCOOP

Genentech, founded by Herbert Boyer and Robert Swanson in 1976, was one of the first biotechnology companies in existence. Boyer, in fact, was one of the co-inventors of recombinant DNA technology, a method of altering the genetic content of cells. Genentech works to develop novel treatments and diagnostics for a number of diseases including asthma, diabetes, arthritis and cancers of all kinds.

ON THE JOB

Genentech has placed interns in nearly all of its departments, including immunology, bioinformatics, protein engineering and many others. The internships allow students to conduct high-level scientific research and observe how scientific findings are translated into real-world products. At the end of the summer, all interns make a presentation of their findings to the Genentech scientists.

GETTING HIRED

Apply by: *Summer*: February 13.

Qualifications:

Open to college sophomores, juniors and seniors, as well as MBA students. Most intern positions are reserved for students with a background in biology, chemistry, engineering and other relevant fields. However, there are some internships available for nonscience students. (See the company's web site for more details.)

Contact:
Internship Coordinator
Genentech
Attention: Summer Internship Program
1 DNA Way MS 39A
South San Francisco, CA 94080
Phone: (650) 225-1000
Fax: (650) 225-6000
www.genentech.com/gene/careers/college/internships

General Mills

THE BUZZ

- "Better eat your Wheaties"
- "Great experience for anyone interested in working in consumer products"

THE STATS

Industry(ies): Consumer Products; Food & Beverage

Location(s): Minneapolis, MN (HQ); Albuquerque, NM; Allentown, PA; Avon, IA; Bakersfield, CA; Belvidere, IL; Boston, MA; Buffalo, NY; Buffalo Mill, NY; Carson, CA; Cedar Rapids, IA; Chanhassen, MN; Cincinnati, OH; Covington, GA; Federalsburg, MD; Great Falls, MT; Hannibal, MO; Hazelton, PA; Joplin, MO; Kansas City, MO; Lloyds, MN; Lodi, CA; Los Angeles, CA; Martel, OH; Methuen, MA; Milwaukee, WI; Mufreesboro, TN; New Albany, IN; Poplar, WI; Reed City, MI; Swedesboro, NJ; Tempe, AZ; Vernon, CA; Vineland, NJ; Vinita, OK; Wellston, OH; West Chicago, IL

Number of interns: *Annual*: approximately 75

Pay: Paid; *undergraduates*: about $700/week; *grad students*: about $900/week

Length of internship: Usually 3 months

THE SCOOP

Yoplait. Wheaties. Cheerios. All of these and more are produced by food conglomerate General Mills, which started out as a single flour mill perched on the banks of the upper Mississippi River in 1866. Charles Pillsbury, the man behind the omnipresent doughboy, purchased the mill in 1869. The company introduced Wheaties (1921), Bisquick (1931), and Cheerios (1945) and purchased Chex in 1997.

ON THE JOB

Interns are treated like employees. Departments accepting interns include promotions, sales, human resources, research and development (at the company headquarters). At food processing plants, interns work in manufacturing, engineering and logistics.

GETTING HIRED

Apply by: February 1.

Qualifications:

Open to college students majoring in an area related to the position sought (i.e., accounting for the finance department). Market research and brand management groups are only open to graduate students.

Contact:
Internship Recruiting Program
General Mills
P.O. Box 1113
Minneapolis, MN 55440
Phone: (763) 764-3393
E-mail: marilyn.callaway@genmills.com
www.generalmills.com

Visit Vault at **www.vault.com** for insider company profiles, expert advice, career message boards, expert resume reviews, the Vault Job Board and more.

VAULT CAREER LIBRARY 191

Gensler

 THE BUZZ
- "Better living through architecture"
- "Beautifying the built environment"

 THE STATS

Industry(ies): Architecture

Location(s): Arlington, VA; Atlanta, GA; Baltimore, MD; Boston, MA; Charlotte, NC; Chicago, IL; Dallas, TX; Denver, CO; Detroit, MI; Houston, TX; LaCrosse, WI; Los Angeles, CA; New Jersey; Newport Beach, CA; New York, NY; San Francisco, CA; San Ramon, CA; Seattle, WA; London; Tokyo

Number of interns: *Annual*: 50

Pay: Paid; determined by individual office

Length of internship: 2 months-1 year

 THE SCOOP

Gensler is a leading global architecture, design planning and strategic consulting firm with offices in 25 different cities. The company offers a full range of services including architecture, interior, urban and graphic design to both corporate and government clients. Recent Gensler design projects have included Toys "R" Us in Times Square; North Harris Community College, Cypress Fairbanks Campus in Houston; Moscone West in San Francisco; and the Allsteel Headquarters in Muscatine, IA. *Fast Company* magazine has called Gensler "one of America's most influential design firms." For two years in a row, Gensler was named "most admired firm" in a *Contract Magazine* survey of 4,500 professional architects and interior designers.

 ON THE JOB

The availability of internship placements depends upon the company's needs at each particular office. Though internships can be arranged in any Gensler department, most students work in interior design, architecture or graphics. Interns are assigned to a market sector and join the staff on regular projects. Specific duties vary will vary according to the abilities and interests of the intern.

💰 **GETTING HIRED**

Apply by: Please visit www.gensler.com/careers/internships.htm to learn how to apply.

Qualifications:
Open to students at accredited design schools who have completed their third year of undergraduate education or the first year of a master's program.

Contact:
www.gensler.com/careers/internships.htm

Georgetown University Law Center Criminal Justice Clinic

 THE BUZZ
- "Help defend the poor and fight crime in our nation's capital"
- "Great prep for DAs"

 THE STATS

Industry(ies): Government; Law

Location(s): Washington, DC

Number of interns: *Spring/summer/fall*: 10 each

Pay: None. Interns will be reimbursed for mileage and other work-related expenses

Length of internship: *Spring/fall*: 15 weeks minimum; *summer*: 12 weeks minimum

 THE SCOOP

The Criminal Justice Clinic at the Georgetown University Law Center was founded in 1960 with the mission of providing legal services to poor defendants. Pre-trial defense investigations play a crucial role in presenting a strong legal defense and determining the strengths and weaknesses of the state's case. The Criminal Justice Clinic's internship allows interns to work on actual cases.

🏢 **ON THE JOB**

Interns will take on significant responsibilities as members of the investigative staff at the Clinic. They will locate and interview witnesses, conduct criminal background checks, photograph crime scenes, and produce maps and diagrams. Interns must document all of their investigative work in a manner that is admissible in court. The Criminal Justice Clinic is a small program and, as such, participants will have the opportunity to work closely with the seasoned professionals on staff.

💰 **GETTING HIRED**

Apply by: *Fall*: March 15 for first round; July 1 for supplemental round; *spring*: December 1; *summer*: April 1. A required application form is available online.

Qualifications:
Open to all undergraduates, recent grads and graduate students with an interest in law or criminal justice.

Contact:
Rebecca O'Brien, Investigations Supervisor
Criminal Justice Clinic
Georgetown University Law Center
111 F Street NW
Washington, DC 20001
Phone: (202) 662-9589
Fax: (202) 662-9681
E-mail: obrienra@law.georgetown.edu
www.law.georgetown.edu/clinics/cjc/iip.html

Georgia Governor's Intern Program

THE BUZZ
- "An insider's view of state government"
- "A tradition of public service dating back to Jimmy Carter"

THE STATS

Industry(ies): Government

Location(s): Atlanta, GA, and multiple GA cities

Number of interns: Varies by semester and various agency involvement

Pay: Paid. *Fall/spring*: 40 hours/week: $5,400 (graduate), $4,680 (undergraduate); 30 hours/week: $4,050 (graduate), $3,510 (undergraduate); 20 hours/week: $2,700 (graduate), $2,340 (undergraduate)

Summer: 40 hours/week: $3,900 (graduate), $3,380 (undergraduate); 30 hours/week: $2,925 (graduate), $2,535 (undergraduate); 20 hours/week: $$1,950 (graduate), $1,690 (undergraduate)

Law interns: 40 hours/week: $4,420

Length of internship: *Fall/spring*: 18 weeks/each; *summer*: 13 weeks

THE SCOOP

Jimmy Carter started the Georgia Governor's Internship Program in 1971, which is intended to provide practical experience to promising young students with an interest in government or public policy.

ON THE JOB

The Governor's Internship Program attempts to place applicants in a state agency corresponding to their interests. Interns are encouraged to seek academic credit for the program.

GETTING HIRED

Apply by: *Spring*: October 2; *summer*: March 3; *fall*: pending; *Law* (summer only): March 3. An application form is available on the web site. An essay and two reference names with contact information are required.

Qualifications:
Open to college juniors and seniors, grad students and law students. Law students are eligilbe for legal internships, and grad students are considered for fellowships.Applicants must have a GPA of 2.8 or above, and they must either be a Georgia resident or be enrolled at a Georgia college.

Contact:
Sumner Holman, Intern Coordinator
Governor's Internship Program
111 State Capitol
Atlanta, GA 30334
Phone: (404) 656-3804
Fax: (404) 651-5110
E-mail: sholman@gov.state.ga.us
www.ganet.org/governor/intern

Glen Helen Outdoor Education Center

THE BUZZ
- "Eco-education"
- "Spread good eco-citizenship"

THE STATS

Industry(ies): Education; Environmental; Nonprofit

Location(s): Yellow Springs, OH

Number of interns: *Spring/fall*: 10 each (called naturalist interns)

Pay: $260/month. Full room and board provided; academic credit (10 graduate/12 undergraduate credits) at Antioch College; individual bedrooms (other facilities shared)

Length of internship: *Spring*: 5 months; *fall*: 4 months

THE SCOOP

The 1,000-acre Glen Helen Nature Preserve sits next to the campus of Antioch College in southwestern Ohio. The Outdoor Education Center, part of the Glen Helen Ecology Institute, provides overnight, camp-style environmental education programs for elementary and middle school students. Also on the grounds is the Raptor Center, a facility devoted to educating the public on birds of prey and providing them with rehabilitative care.

ON THE JOB

Naturalist interns educate visiting students with the organization's environmental education curriculum. Naturalists lead hikes in areas such as geology, forest community, birds, critters, living history and environmental problem solving. Interns also serve as educators at the Raptor Center. Additionally, naturalist interns can apply for a second term as a naturalist or one of the organization's three administrative internship roles: program coordination, extension naturalists or Raptor Center assistant.

GETTING HIRED

Apply by: Rolling. Contact The Center by phone or e-mail to obtain the required application form. The form is also available on the web site, along with the reference form.

Qualifications:
Open to all college juniors and seniors, recent college graduates and grad students. International applicants are welcome.

Contact:
Attention: Director
Glen Helen Outdoor Education Center
1075 SR 343
Yellow Springs, OH 45387
Phone: (937) 767-7648
Fax: (937) 767-6655
www.glenhelen.org/oec/nat/nat.htm

Visit Vault at **www.vault.com** for insider company profiles, expert advice, career message boards, expert resume reviews, the Vault Job Board and more.

VAULT CAREER LIBRARY **193**

Global Exchange

 THE BUZZ

- "Ride a bike, take a trip, eat fresh produce...all in the name of social justice"

 THE STATS

Industry(ies): Government; Law; Nonprofit

Location(s): San Francisco, CA

Number of interns: Varies

Pay: None

Length of internship: 8 weeks minimum; available year-round

 THE SCOOP

An international human rights organization dedicated to promoting environmental, political and social justice, Global Exchange works primarily on economic issues such as promoting fair pay for overseas factory workers and ending human rights violations (in Cuba, Palestine/Israel, Brazil, Iraq, U.S., etc.). The organization was founded in 1988 and is based in San Francisco. Programs include Reality Tours (socially responsible travel programs), Fair Trade Centers (physical and online stores that allow artisans from around the world to directly sell their goods), and Bike-Aid (bike rides in which participants raise money for GE causes).

 ON THE JOB

Global Exchange offers a structured summer internship program, and less structured positions during the school year. Interns work closely with the organization's staff on pressing country-specific campaigns supporting local nongovernmental organizations, as well as programming activities, such as the Fair Trade Coffee Speaking Tour, Bike-Aid and Reality Tours. Positions are available in development, communications, the speakers' bureau and public education.

GETTING HIRED

Apply by: *Summer*: March 15; *fall/winter/spring*: rolling. Mail the online application (available at: www.globalexchange.org/getInvolved/internapp.html) along with a resume, cover letter and two letters of recommendation or contact info for references.

Qualifications:

Open to college freshmen, sophomores, juniors and seniors. Qualifications differ depending on the department and position available (log on to www.globalexchange.org/getInvolved/interninfo2.html for more details).

Contact:
Global Exchange Internship Program Coordinator
2017 Mission Street, Room 303
San Francisco, CA 94110
Phone: (415) 255-7296
Fax: (415) 255-7498
E-mail: interns@globalexchange.org
www.globalexchange.org/getInvolved/volunteer.html

Global Volunteers

 THE BUZZ

- "Travel that feeds the soul"

 THE STATS

Industry(ies): Education; Environmental; Health Care; Nonprofit

Location(s): U.S. locations in MN, MS, MT, SD and WV; international locations in Australia, Brazil, China, Cook Islands, Costa Rica, Ecuador, Ghana, Greece, Hungary, India, Ireland, Italy, Jamaica, Mexico, Peru, Poland, Romania, Sri Lanka and Tanzania

Number of interns: *Annual*: 200 teams (more than 2,000 volunteers)

Pay: None. Tax-deductible program fees range from $750-$2,650 (airfare extra) and vary by program location and duration. Discounts available to students, Internet users and families. Fees include all food, accommodation and ground transportation costs. Check with your school's advisors to arrange for possible academic credit

Length of internship: 1-3 weeks; available year-round. Extended stay opportunities available in China and Poland

 THE SCOOP

Founded in 1984, Global Volunteers pioneered the concept of "volunteer vacations," focusing on waging "peace through people." The organization offers short-term placements in ongoing development projects in more than 100 host communities worldwide. Participants in the program receive a unique cultural experience while providing vital assistance to an underserved rural community. Financial assistance to the host community (as part of the effort to encourage each community's self-sufficiency) is included as part of each volunteer's service program fee. Today, Global Volunteers operates programs in 20 different countries around the world.

ON THE JOB

Project categories are teaching conversational English, child care, labor, health care and environmentalism. Many projects involve repairing homes, schools, clinics and other community buildings. Individuals with a particular interest in health care, education or the environment may also choose to participate in rainforest conservation projects, teach adult literacy or English as a second language, care for orphans and disabled children, or provide medical services at small rural clinics.

GETTING HIRED

Apply by: Rolling. Download application from web site and mail or fax it to the address below. Volunteers may also enroll by phone or online.

Qualifications:

Open to people of all ages and backgrounds. Minors may not travel unaccompanied.

Contact:
Global Volunteers
375 East Little Canada Road
St. Paul, MN 55117-1628
Phone: (800) 487-1074 or (651) 407-6100
Fax: (651) 482-0915
E-mail: info@globalvolunteers.org
www.globalvolunteers.org

Goldman Sachs

 **THE BUZZ**
- "The #1 bank on Wall Street"
- "Intern with the Masters of the Universe"

THE STATS

Industry(ies): Financial Services; Investment Banking

Location(s): New York, NY; Hong Kong; London; Tokyo; Limited opportunities in: Atlanta, GA; Boston, MA; Chicago, IL; Dallas, TX; Houston, TX; Los Angeles, CA; Miami, FL; Philadelphia, PA; Princeton, NJ; Salt Lake City, UT; San Francisco, CA; Seattle, WA; Washington, DC; Bangalore; Beijing; Frankfurt; Geneva; Milan; Paris; Seoul; Singapore; Taipei; Zurich

Number of interns: *Annual*: 1,000+ (many locations)

Pay: Paid; competitive salary (varies)

Length of internship: *Summer*: approximately 10 weeks; *additional programs*: 10-12 weeks; *Frankfurt/Zurich*: year-round

 **THE SCOOP**

Goldman Sachs, founded in 1869, is one of the top investment banking, securities and investment management firms in the world. GS offers a full range of financial services, such as accounting and investment strategies, to clients around the world, which includes top corporations, financial institutions, governments and (extremely) high-net-worth individuals. The firm is based in New York and maintains offices in London, Frankfurt, Tokyo, Hong Kong and other major financial centers around the world.

ON THE JOB

Goldman Sachs interns do much of the same work as entry level GS employees, from investment banking to investment management, sales and trading to research and financial analysis. Goldman Sachs hires both undergrads and MBA students for its highly coveted and competitive internships. GS also provides scholarships and MBA fellowships to students from traditionally under-represented groups in Europe and the Americas. The company also offers spring, fall and winter internship programs in its Frankfurt and Zurich offices. Most internships run from 10 to 12 weeks and are offered to students one to two years from graduation.

GETTING HIRED

Apply by: Goldman Sachs recruits on campus at some universities. Check with your school career center. If GS does not visit your campus, apply by January. The company interviews potential interns in the spring. There are varying application deadlines for each university and/or Goldman Sachs location. Visit the Goldman Sachs career web site (www.gs.com/careers) for more details on deadlines and various scholarship and fellowship programs. Aspiring interns can also apply directly on the web site.

Qualifications:

Open to college sophomores and juniors at the undergrad level, and first-year MBA students at the graduate level. All majors are encouraged to apply, but students should show a keen interest in financial services, as well as a strong GPA. MBA fellowships are also available.

Contact:
www.gs.com/careers

Good Morning America

 THE BUZZ
- "Be sure to bring your sunny personality to this TV internship"

 THE STATS

Industry(ies): Broadcast & Entertainment; Journalism

Location(s): New York, NY

Number of interns: *Annual*: 25

Pay: None; academic credit

Length of internship: 8-12 weeks, offered in 5 different sessions year-round

 THE SCOOP

Good Morning America is ABC News' long-running morning talk show, showcasing lifestyle features and current news. Based in New York, the program is broadcast every weekday from 7 to 9 a.m. Currently, *Good Morning America* is hosted by Diane Sawyer and Charles Gibson.

ON THE JOB

Internships at *Good Morning America* offer a broad introduction to broadcast journalism. Interns have the opportunity to sit in on editorial meetings and learn about the different aspects of television production. They also play a vital role in the day-to-day operation of *GMA* by managing the flow of information and handling administrative duties in the office. Interns are needed to work both day and evening shifts.

 GETTING HIRED

Apply by: *Spring I* (mid-January–mid-April): November 15; *spring II* (early April–early June): February 1; *summer* (early June– mid/late August): April 1; *fall* (early September–mid/late December): July 1; *winter* (early/mid December–mid-January): October 1. Apply by mail. Include a transcript, two recommendations and a notice of credit approval from your college with your application.

Qualifications:

Open to undergraduate juniors and seniors enrolled in an accredited college or university. Previous journalism experience is a plus. Students must receive academic credit for their internship.

Contact:
New York internship
ABC, Inc.
Attn: Internship Program
77 West 66th Street, 13th Floor
New York, NY 10023

Los Angeles internship
ABC, Inc.
Attn: Internship Program
500 South Buena Vista Street
Burbank, CA 91521-4391
abcnews.go.com/sections/GMA/GoodMorningAmerica/GMA030
602Internships.html

Visit Vault at **www.vault.com** for insider company profiles, expert advice, career message boards, expert resume reviews, the Vault Job Board and more.

VAULT CAREER LIBRARY **195**

Goodman Theatre

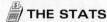 **THE BUZZ**
- "Prepare for a theater career in the Loop"
- "Experience the vibrant Chicago theater scene"

THE STATS

Industry(ies): Theater/Performing Arts

Location(s): Chicago, IL

Number of interns: *Annual*: 60

Pay: All interns receive a stipend. Amount varies between $350-$825 depending on the position and number of hours worked

Length of internship: *Summer*: 3 months; *fall*: 4 months; *winter/spring*: 5 months. Stage management internships are usually 6-8 weeks

THE SCOOP

The Goodman Theatre, Chicago's oldest and largest regional theater company, is home to the Goodman Artistic Collective. The collective includes members such as Robert Falls, Frank Galati and Mary Zimmerman (all Tony Award-winning directors) and Henry Godinez,. Chuck Smith and Regina Taylor. The nationally renowned theater stages both revivals and new works. Recent Goodman productions have included *The Light in the Piazza, Pericales, Electricidad, The Clean House, Romance,* and *Crumbs from the Table of Joy.* In addition to performances, the theater also provides educational theater appreciation and community outreach programs for local students.

ON THE JOB

Interns work in the artistic, casting, costume, development, dramaturgy, education and community programs, general management, literary management, marketing/PR/press, production management, sound, and stage management departments. Detailed descriptions of the program for each department are available on the Goodman web site. All interns work under the guidance of a mentor and will have the opportunity to interact with resident and guest artists.

GETTING HIRED

Apply by: *Fall*: April 1; *winter/spring*: September 1; *summer*: February 1. An application form (available on the web site), a resume, a 500-word personal statement, and two letters of recommendation are required.

Qualifications:
Open to college students and recent grads pursuing a career in theater.

Contact:
Julie Massey, Internship Coordinator
Goodman Theatre
170 North Dearborn Street
Chicago, IL 60601
Phone: (312) 443-3813
Fax: (312) 443-7448
E-mail: juliemassey@goodmantheatre.org
www.goodmantheatre.org

Gould Farm

THE BUZZ
- "The therapeutic power of nature"
- "A model program for treating mental illness"

THE STATS

Industry(ies): Health Care

Location(s): Boston and Monterey areas of Massachusetts

Number of interns: *Annual*: 1-2

Pay: $100-$250/month, depending on financial need. Some interns receive grants or other forms of funding to participate in the program; medical coverage for interns with a 12-month and longer commitment. Interns live on the premises; free room and board provided

Length of internship: 12-24 months; available year-round; 40 hours/week

THE SCOOP

Gould Farm is a therapeutic treatment program for people with mental illnesses. Located in the Berkshire Mountains of Western Massachusetts, the program is designed to create a supportive and communal environment where clients can develop practical skills and gain a sense of independence to aid their recovery. Staff and clients live and work together on the 650-acre working farm. Gould Farm also provides outpatient treatment in the Boston area for clients preparing for independent living.

ON THE JOB

Internships are available in the residential support, grounds maintenance, gardening, food service and administrative departments. Interns in residential support perform crisis management, teach living skills and assist with counseling and treatment planning. Other interns contribute to the operation of the farm in a range of areas including planting crops, caring for the farm animals, cooking and administrative work. Placements are also available in the Boston-area residential and nonresidential programs.

GETTING HIRED

Apply by: Rolling. Fax, email or send a letter of interest and resume to Cynthia Meyer.

Qualifications:
Open to college freshmen, sophomores, juniors and seniors and recent college graduates. All positions require a full-time, live-in commitment.

Contact:
Cynthia Meyer, Human Resources Director
Gould Farm
P.O. Box 157
Monterey, MA 01245
Phone: (413) 528-1804, ext. 17
Fax: (413) 528-5051
E-mail: humanresources@gouldfarm.org
www.gouldfarm.org/opportunity.htm

Government Affairs Institute

 THE BUZZ
- "Go behind the scenes on the Hill"
- "Become a 'fixer' in the government"

 **THE STATS**

Industry(ies): Education; Government

Location(s): Washington, DC

Number of interns: *Spring/summer/fall*: 1 each

Pay: Modest stipend

Length of internship: 1 semester

 **THE SCOOP**

The Government Affairs Institute is an educational nonprofit corporation in the Public Policy Institute at Georgetown University. The Institute offers courses and simulations to federal employees on the operations of Congress. The courses are conducted on Capitol Hill and feature members of Congress, congressional staff, journalists, lobbyists and academics.

ON THE JOB

Interns at the Government Affairs Institute research and write issue briefs and help conduct simulations. The briefs usually cover issues in Congress of relevance to particular agencies, departments or service branches of the military. Interns have the opportunity to spend time on Capitol Hill during some of the courses.

GETTING HIRED

Apply by: Rolling. Send cover letter, resume, college transcript and a writing sample to the address below.

Qualifications:
Open to all college students – sophomores, juniors and seniors preferred. Academic background in U.S. government is required.

Contact:
John Haskell
The Government Affairs Institute at Georgetown University
3333 K Street, NW, Suite 112
Washington, DC 20007
Phone: (202) 333-4838
Fax: (202) 333-8165
www.georgetown.edu/ssce/gai

Visit Vault at **www.vault.com** for insider company profiles, expert advice, career message boards, expert resume reviews, the Vault Job Board and more.

VAULT CAREER LIBRARY **197**

Graduate Public Service Internship (GPSI) at the University of Illinois at Springfield

THE BUZZ
- "One of Illinois' premier governmental internship programs"
- "Begin your professional career in Illinois government while simultaneously earning a master's degree"

THE STATS

Industry(ies): Education; Government

Location(s): Springfield, IL

Number of interns: *Annual:* Approximately 50 new interns

Pay: Paid; $850/month during academic terms while working 20 hours/week; $1700/month during the summer term while working 37.5 hours/week. Interns receive a 40 credit hour tuition waiver (9 hours for fall and spring semesters and 4 hours for the summer term), as well as a $300 professional development budget/year

Length of internship: 21 months – while earning a master's degree from the University of Illinois at Springfield

THE SCOOP

The Graduate Public Service Internship (GPSI) program is a competitive, 21-month internship with Illinois state government and municipal agencies. Interns work part-time during the academic year and full-time during the summer between their first and second year of graduate school. Interns earn a master's degree from the University of Illinois at Springfield and almost two years of professional work experience through their GPSI placement.

ON THE JOB

GPSI placements are geared toward interns from all academic programs. Responsibilities vary greatly, depending on the placement agency and the intern's academic program. Examples of job responsibilities include, but are not limited to: general accounting and auditing functions; policy development and implementation; preparation of statistical reports; design and development of computer programs; maintenance and design of database systems; staffing legislative hearings; development and dissemination of marketing/promotional resources; design, implementation and statistical reports for public health surveys; Web application design; conducting environmental laboratory and field studies; data collection and data analysis; development of digital outreach materials; design and implementation of epidemiology studies; management of prisoner review board crime victim's toll-free reporting line; administrative/executive office assistance for agency directors; and fiscal and procurement support.

GETTING HIRED

Apply by: March 15. Applicants can complete the UIS graduate admission application (Section I and Section II) online at www.uis.edu/admissions/apply.html. Required application materials are a UIS graduate admission application (Section I),

GPSI application (Section II), official transcripts from each college attended, current resume, three letters of recommendation and a personal goal statement. GPSI applicants must be admitted to a graduate studies program at the University of Illinois at Springfield. For first-round consideration, the applicant's file must be complete by March 15.

GPSI is a competitive internship program. Applying for the GPSI program does not guarantee placement as a GPSI intern.

Qualifications:
Open to college graduates from all academic backgrounds. The GPSI program requires a minimum cumulative undergraduate GPA of 2.5 or higher. UIS graduate programs may have higher minimum cumulative undergraduate GPA requirements.

Contact:
Shawn Craig Shures
Assistant Director/Graduate Intern Recruiter
Office of Graduate Intern Programs
One University Plaza, MS PAC 514
Springfield, IL 62703-5407
Phone: (217) 206-6153
Fax: (217) 206-7508
E-mail: shures.shawn@uis.edu
http://gpsi.uis.edu

Great Projects Film Company

 THE BUZZ
- "Be part of a great film project"

 **THE STATS**

Industry(ies): Broadcast & Entertainment; Film

Location(s): New York, NY

Number of interns: *Annual*: 1; depends upon current production schedule and needs

Pay: Paid; $225/week

Length of internship: 15-20 weeks; available year-round

 **THE SCOOP**

Great Projects is an independent film company based in New York whose documentaries have aired on PBS, A&E and Discovery Networks. Some of its most recent films have examined the clean-up effort at the World Trade Center site, Boston's Big Dig construction project and Jewish partisans during World War II. Great Projects has won an Emmy Award for Outstanding Historical Programming for *George Marshall and the American Century* (1993) and was nominated for an Academy Award for Best Short Documentary for *An Essay on Matisse* (1996).

ON THE JOB

Interns are involved in all areas of the company, performing administrative duties such as answering phones, logging tapes and bookkeeping. They also have the opportunity to write proposals and assist with film editing. About half of all Great Projects interns are invited to remain on the staff full time.

GETTING HIRED

Apply by: Rolling. Include a five- to 10-page writing sample with your resume and cover letter. The writing sample should ideally be an English, history or other research paper – not a paper about film.

Qualifications:
Open to recent college grads and graduate students.

Contact:
Internship Coordinator
Great Projects Film Company
594 Ninth Avenue
New York, NY 10036
Phone: (888) 326-6536 or (212) 581-1700
Fax: (212) 581-3157
E-mail: internship@greatprojects.com
www.greatprojects.com/internship.html

Guggenheim Museum

 THE BUZZ
- "Modern art fans need look no further"
- "Spend an aesthetically pleasing summer on Museum Mile"

THE STATS

Industry(ies): Art/Museum; Education; Tourism/Recreation

Location(s): New York, NY; Venice; Bilbao

Number of interns: *Annual*: 110

Pay: *Academic year:* Unpaid; academic credit arranged through school. *Summer:* Paid. $1,000 stipends awarded to some graduate candidates. Two $2,500 diversity stipends are also available

Length of internship: *Summer*: June through mid-August; requires a full-time commitment. *Academic year*: Both 3 and 6 month internships are offered to correspond with academic cycles. Fall: September 15-December 15; Spring: January 15-April 15

THE SCOOP

The Solomon R. Guggenheim Museum was named in honor of its founder, who insisted on a novel approach to art and all of its unique forms, and worked closely with designer Frank Lloyd Wright on the museum's creation. In 1992, the museum was restored by Thomas Krens. The museum is considered a top modern art facility and one of the most remarkable architectural works of the 20th century.

ON THE JOB

The museum offers numerous internships in art services and preparations, conservation, curatorial, exhibition and collection management and design, development, the director's office, education, finance, information technology, library and archives, membership, public affairs, photography, registrar, special events and visitor services.

GETTING HIRED

Apply by: *Summer*: January 10; *fall*: May 1; *spring*: November 1. Send applications to the address below. Applications must include a cover letter, resume, two letters of recommendation, current transcripts, a list of all relevant course work and an essay (not more than 500 words) clearly stating the cycle for which the candidate is applying and describing the applicant's interest in the internship program, museum work and his or her reasons for applying.

Qualifications:
Open to undergraduate and graduate students in all relevant disciplines.

Contact:
Internship Coordinator
Solomon R. Guggenheim Museum
1071 Fifth Avenue
New York, NY 10128
Phone: (212) 423-3500
E-mail: mjubin@guggenheim.org
www.guggenheim.org/education/get_involved.shtml

Visit Vault at **www.vault.com** for insider company profiles, expert advice, career message boards, expert resume reviews, the Vault Job Board and more.

VAULT CAREER LIBRARY **199**

INTERNSHIP PROFILES:
H

H.O.M.E.

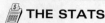 **THE BUZZ**
- "Help build homes and communities in rural Maine"
- "Empowering the rural poor"

THE STATS

Industry(ies): Nonprofit

Location(s): Orland, ME

Number of interns: *Annual:* 2-6

Pay: None. Housing and some meals provided

Length of internship: 1-12 months

THE SCOOP

Homeworkers Organized for More Employment (H.O.M.E.) was established in 1970 as a craft cooperative where local residents could sell their handmade goods. Over the years, it has grown into a full-fledged community development organization offering a variety of services including a homeless shelter, food bank, learning center and medical clinic. H.O.M.E. also runs the Covenant Community Land Trust and a home construction program in which low-income families and volunteers assist in building new homes.

ON THE JOB

Many volunteers assist in housing construction projects during their stay, but opportunities are available for helping out in other ways as well. Volunteers may teach, work in the pottery or weaving shops, tend to the organic garden, write grant proposals or help with fundraising. All participants in the program live together in the Saint Francis Community located about five miles from the H.O.M.E. headquarters.

GETTING HIRED

Apply by: Rolling. Call with or e-mail a letter of interest and you will be provided with an information package.

Qualifications:
Open to all college freshmen, sophomores, juniors and seniors, college graduates, grad students and volunteers of all backgrounds.

Contact:
Jackie Rogan
Volunteer Coordinator
H.O.M.E. Inc.
P.O. Box 10
Orland, ME 04472
Phone: (207) 469-7961
E-mail: home@homecoop.net
www.homecoop.net/volunteers/oneyear.html

Habitat for Humanity International

 **THE BUZZ**
- "Hands-on experience—literally!"
- "Help house the poor around the world"

THE STATS

Industry(ies): Construction/Building Materials; Nonprofit; Religious

Location(s): Americus, GA (HQ); possibiliy of placement in other HFHI locations

Number of volunteers/interns: Varies; typically accept 1 in 5 internship applicants

Pay: Varies based on position

Length of internship: 1 month-1year

THE SCOOP

Habitat for Humanity International is a nonprofit Christian organization that has been building houses for those in need since 1976 and is affiliated with former U.S. President Jimmy Carter. Habitat has built more than 200,000 houses around the world, providing some 1,000,000 people in more than 3,000 communities with safe, decent, affordable shelter. Today, Habitat employees, volunteers and beneficiaries build a house every 26 minutes. These are sold to low-income families at no profit and with a no-interest mortgage. Habitat affiliates are located in all 50 states and in 92 other countries.

ON THE JOB

Habitat volunteers work under supervision to help build a house. There are several ways for students to get involved – found or join a high school or college club, found or join a teen summer team (ages 16-18), found or join a school break team, or volunteer for Habitat's international program. Interns work in finance, communications, human resources, construction, information systems, legal services, graphic arts, photography and language translation. Interns may also get the opportunity to hear international figures speak.

GETTING HIRED

Apply by: Rolling. Send an e-mail to volunteer@habitat.org to request an application.

Qualifications:
Open to high school students at least 16 years of age; college freshmen, sophomores, juniors and seniors, college graduates and grad students.

Contact:
Habitat for Humanity International
Attn: Domestic Volunteer Program Manager
121 Habitat St
Americus, GA 31709
Phone: (229) 924-6935 ext. 2920
E-mail: volunteer@habitat.org
www.habitat.org

Hallmark

THE BUZZ
- "When you care enough to intern at the very best"
- "A passion to create, a mission to enrich lives"

THE STATS

Industry(ies): Consumer Products; Retail

Location(s): Kansas City, MO; Metamora, IL; Center, TX

Number of interns: *Summer*: 20-30

Pay: Competitive total rewards program

Length of internship: *Summer:* 9-12 weeks (May-August)

THE SCOOP

Hallmark is the global leader in personal expression and one of the world's most recognized brands, enriching lives, helping people communicate, connect and celebrate. The company boasts that behind its legacy, and key to its future, are Hallmark's people.

ON THE JOB

Hallmark looks for sharp, optimistic people to create, engineer, market and deliver products worldwide. Challenging full-time and summer internship opportunities are available for those pursuing or holding an undergraduate or graduate degree in marketing, finance, accounting, human resources, business administration, engineering or information technology.

GETTING HIRED

Apply by: *Summer*: October 15. Most corporate internships are filled by the late fall.

Qualifications:
Open to college juniors entering their final year of undergrad following the program, as well as graduate students. Permanent authorization to work in the U.S. without company sponsorship is required. See web site for further qualifications specific to your interests.

Contact:
College Relations CR/VAULT
Hallmark Cards, Inc.
P.O. Box 419580 #112
Kansas City, MO 64141
Fax: (816) 274-4299
E-mail: hcolle1@hallmark.com
www.hallmark.com

Career Opportunities
Scroll to bottom of homepage and click on "About Hallmark," then on "Hallmark Careers"

Press Room
Scroll to bottom of homepage and click on "Press Room," then on "Site Index"

Halstead Communications

THE BUZZ
- "Friendly work environment"
- "Very hands-on"

THE STATS

Industry(ies): Public Relations

Location(s): New York, NY

Number of interns: Varies

Pay: None

Length of internship: *Spring/summer/fall*: approximately 15 weeks each; 30-40 hours/week

THE SCOOP

Halstead Communications was founded in 1980 as College Connections by Carol P. Halstead. This public relations and marketing communications firm represents educational institutions and nonprofit organizations.

ON THE JOB

Intern responsibilities include writing press releases, pitching story ideas to media sources and building media lists. The small office environment provides plenty of hands-on PR experience. There is a high learning curve and Halstead Communications expects as much from interns as it does from full staff. The culture is relaxed and informal, but not lazy. If interns want to make copies and sit in a skyscraper all summer, this isn't the position for them. (Note: The firm says it has an office cat. Bear this in mind if you are allergic to, or are afraid of, animals.)

GETTING HIRED

Apply by: Rolling. Send resume, cover letter and writing sample to the address below. Call or e-mail for details.

Qualifications:
Open to college juniors, seniors, and recent graduates with excellent written and verbal communication skills. PR experience and a sense of humor strongly preferred.

Contact:
Ashley Deiser
Halstead Communications
329 East 82nd Street
New York, NY 10028
Phone: (212) 734-2190
Fax: (212) 517-7284
E-mail: deiser@halsteadpr.com
www.halsteadpr.com

Visit Vault at **www.vault.com** for insider company profiles, expert advice, career message boards, expert resume reviews, the Vault Job Board and more.

VAULT CAREER LIBRARY 203

HALT – An Organization of Americans for Legal Reform

 THE BUZZ

- "Demystifying the legal process"

 THE STATS

Industry(ies): Government; Law; Nonprofit

Location(s): Washington, DC

Number of interns: *Fall*: 2-3; *spring*: 2-3; *summer*: 4-5

Pay: *Full-time interns*: $300/week; *part-time interns*: $60/day

Length of internship: *Fall/spring/summer*: 10-12 weeks each

 THE SCOOP

HALT is a public interest nonprofit organization dedicated to improving access to and accountability within the civil legal system. Among its goals are expanding self-help resources and alternatives to traditional legal channels so that more Americans can handle their own legal affairs, as well as holding legal professionals accountable for their actions. Aside from its lobbying efforts, HALT also publishes books and pamphlets to help educate citizens on the legal process.

 **ON THE JOB**

The HALT internship program strives to expose students to the difficulties and rewards of engaging in public interest work. Each intern will be involved in research and writing on issues related to civil justice reform and improving legal access. Students will also have the opportunity to write one or more articles for the HALT newsletter and become involved in lobbying and public education campaigns.

GETTING HIRED

Apply by: Rolling. Send resume, cover letter and writing sample (three to 10 pages) to the address below.

Qualifications:
Open to undergraduates and graduate students with an interest in public service and legal reform.

Contact:
Suzanna Blonder, Associate Counsel
HALT
1612 K Street, NW, Suite 510
Washington, DC 20006
Phone: (202) 887-8255
Fax: (202) 887-9699
E-mail: internship@halt.org
www.halt.org/internship_program

Hansard Scholars Programme

 THE BUZZ
- "Access to London power brokers"
- "A primer on Parliament"

 THE STATS

Industry(ies): Communications; Education; Government; Public Policy; Law; Media; Human Rights; International Development

Location(s): London

Number of interns: *Hansard Scholars Programme (undergraduate)*: approximately 20/semester; *Research Scholars Programme (postgraduate)*: approximately 10/semester

Pay: None. The program charges a fee of £6,850/semester, which includes tuition at the London School of Economics, housing, a public transportation pass, social and cultural activities, and political study visits.

Length of internship: *Spring/fall*: 12 weeks; *summer*: 11 weeks

 **THE SCOOP**

The Hansard Society was formed in 1944 to promote the ideals of parliamentary government when it seemed threatened by fascist and communist dictatorship. Its first subscribers were Winston Churchill and Clement Richard Attlee, then prime minister and deputy prime minister of the UK. The society's activities, meetings and publications focus on educating people in how the UK parliament works. In addition, the Hansard Society has developed an international perspective, becoming active in teaching about the ideas of parliamentary government, following the break up of colonial empires and in the newly emerging democracies in Eastern Europe and the former Soviet Union.

 **ON THE JOB**

Participants in the Hansard Scholars Programme spend one day a week attending classes at the London School of Economics and three days per week in their internships. In addition to pursuing an individual research dissertation, undergraduate Hansard Scholars take two lecture courses, while Research Scholars take one more focused course. All Scholars have regular lectures with politicians and other senior figures from a variety of organizations at the cutting edge of the UK public policy agenda and take an intensive internship at one of the many influential political organizations in the UK. These include campaign organizations, lobbying companies, interest groups, research institutions and the UK Parliament itself. As part of the program, scholars will participate in political study visits to Edinburgh and Oxford, where they will attend lectures given by prominent figures from the British political establishment.

GETTING HIRED

Apply by: *Spring*: August 1; *summer*: February 1; *fall*: May 1. Download the application form from the web site. Mail it, along with transcript, resume, two letters of recommendation, a writing sample and a personal statement to the address below. Applicants from non-English-speaking countries should also submit TOEFL scores.

Qualifications:

The undergraduate Hansard Scholars Programme assumes no previous knowledge of British Politics or any experience of political internships. More important is that the applicants show a genuine interest in politics and public policy, and a commitment to working in a high level political environment. Scholars will often be involved in work of a sensitive nature, so personal integrity – in addition to comittment and enthusiasm – are crucial. Applicants should have a GPA of 3.0 or above (if from the U.S.).

The Research Scholars Programme is designed to be a challenging opportunity for graduates and professionals to pursue a specific area of political academic interest while participating in an internship placement within the world of British politics.

For both programs, applicants from non-English speaking countries require a TOEFL score of at least 220 (under the computerized testing) or 550 under the paper-based tests.

Contact:
Hansard Scholars Programme
Hansard Society
40-43 Chancery Lane
London WC2A 1JA
United Kingdom
Phone: +44 207 438 1222
Fax: +44 207 438 1221
E-mail: study@hansard.lse.ac.uk
www.hansardsociety.org.uk

Visit Vault at **www.vault.com** for insider company profiles, expert advice, career message boards, expert resume reviews, the Vault Job Board and more.

VAULT CAREER LIBRARY **205**

HarperCollins

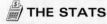 THE BUZZ

- "Become a player in the book biz"
- "All your reading needs, from highbrow literature to Emeril's latest cookbook"

THE STATS

Industry(ies): Publishing

Location(s): New York, NY

Number of interns: *Summer*: 8

Pay: None

Length of internship: *Summer*: 10 weeks

 THE SCOOP

HarperCollins, a division of the News Corp. media company, is one of the world's leading English-language publishers with over $1 billion in annual revenues. The Ecco, Avon, Fourth Estate, Perennial and Amistad presses are among the company's many imprints. Recent HarperCollins bestsellers include Eric Schlosser's stomach-churning *Fast Food Nation*, Michael Moore's broadside *White Men* and Ann Patchett's magical *Bel Canto*.

ON THE JOB

The HarperCollins internship program provides an ideal introduction to the book publishing business. Students participate in a rotational program that gives them experience in various departments such as publicity, production, advertising, sales and editorial. Interns will make valuable contacts in the industry and may even have the chance to pitch their book concept to HarperCollins executives.

GETTING HIRED

Apply by: *Summer*: April 10. E-mail a cover letter and resume with the subject line "Internship".

Qualifications:
Open to college juniors and seniors. Prior related experience with a school newspaper or another publishing internship is preferred.

Contact:
Internship Coordinator
HarperCollins Publishers
10 East 53rd Street
New York, NY 10022
Phone: (212) 207-7000
E-mail: collrec@harpercollins.com
www.harpercollins.com/hc/aboutus/careers.asp#rotassoc

Harper's Magazine

THE BUZZ

- "This is the cream of the literary crop"

THE STATS

Industry(ies): Journalism; Publishing

Location(s): New York, NY

Number of interns: *Spring/summer/fall*: 4 each

Pay: None

Length of internship: *Spring/summer/fall*: 4-5 months each

THE SCOOP

First published in 1850, *Harper's* is the oldest monthly magazine in the U.S. It's also one of the most prestigious, having received numerous honors including 12 National Magazine Awards. *Harper's* has featured journalism, essays and short fiction works by authors including Joyce Carol Oates, Richard Russo and Michael Chabon.

ON THE JOB

Internships are available in the magazine's art and editorial departments. Art interns perform page layout, color separation and photo research, as well as correspond with freelancers. On the editorial side, interns research items for the *Harper's* index section, perform fact-checking duties and screen unsolicited manuscripts. Interns work closely with an assigned editor and are encouraged to suggest ideas.

GETTING HIRED

Apply by: *Spring* (January-May): October 15; *summer* (June-August): February 15 for editorial department, March 15 for art department; *fall* (September-December): June 15. Download the application and accompanying assignment, or request materials by phone. Mail these, a personal statement (500 words or less) and the names and contact information of two references, to the appropriate address below.

Qualifications:
Open to all college freshmen, sophomores, juniors and seniors, recent college graduates and grad students.

Contact:
Editorial internship
Rachel Monahan
Harper's Magazine
666 Broadway, 11th floor
New York, NY 10012
Phone: (212) 420-5720
E-mail: rachel@harpers.org

Art department internship
Stacey Clarkson
Harper's Magazine
666 Broadway, 11th floor
New York, NY 10012
Phone: (212) 420-5749
Fax: (212) 228-5889
www.harpers.org/contact_us/internships.php3

Hastings Center

 THE BUZZ
- "Addressing the ethical dilemmas posed by technology"

 **THE STATS**

Industry(ies): Health Care; Nonprofit; Publishing; Science/Research

Location(s): Garrison, NY

Number of interns: *Annual*: 8-10

Pay: None. The Center can assist interns in finding low-cost housing

Length of internship: 2-8 weeks; available year-round but mostly in the summer

 THE SCOOP

Founded in 1969, the Hastings Center is a nonprofit institute conducting independent research in the field of bioethics. The work is carried out by Center staff and interdisciplinary teams that convene at The Center to frame and examine issues that inform professional practice, public conversation and social policy. The Center also publishes *Hastings Center Report* and *IRB: Ethics & Human Research*, two leading peer-reviewed bioethics journals. The Center's publications and research projects address ethical questions in a wide range of fields including genetics, biotechnology, health policy and environmental issues.

ON THE JOB

The internship program provides undergraduate and graduate students with the opportunity to work on a particular research project or in a particular Hastings Center program or department, such as library, editorial, or development. All interns will be paired with one or more Center staff, who will set out in advance the specific goals of the internship and oversee the intern's work.

 **GETTING HIRED**

Apply by: Rolling. For summer internships (May-August), apply by March 1. At all other times, prospective interns need to apply at least six weeks before they anticipate beginning the internship. Send or fax letter of application, along with a CV, writing sample and the names of two references to the address below.

Qualifications:
Open to all college freshmen, sophomores, juniors and seniors, and grad students.

Contact:
Intern Program
The Hastings Center
21 Malcolm Gordon Road
Garrison, NY 10524-5555
Phone: (845) 424-4040, ext. 208
Fax: (845) 424-4545
E-mail: visitors@thehastingscenter.org
www.thehastingscenter.org

Hawk Mountain Sanctuary

 THE BUZZ
- "Preserve birds of prey"

THE STATS

Industry(ies): Education; Environmental; Science/Research

Location(s): Kempton, PA

Number of interns: *Annual*: 12-14

Pay: $500/month. Free housing

Length of internship: Approximately 4 months (intensive); offered April-July and August-December

THE SCOOP

Raptors, a group that includes hawks, falcons and eagles, are migratory birds of prey. Raptors are at the top of the food chain and are considered important indicators of the overall health of an ecosystem. Since 1934, Hawk Mountain Sanctuary has promoted environmental awareness and raptor conservation through education programs and field research.

ON THE JOB

All Hawk Mountain interns develop and complete a research project and work closely with a member of senior staff in a mentor-student relationship. The internship is an intensive, four-month commitment and all interns, regardless of focus, help present public education programs, learn basic research and monitoring techniques, analyze data, and work on both group and individual projects. Interns have many opportunities to meet world-class visiting scientists and network with professionals in the business. Most Hawk Mountain interns go on to leadership roles in conservation.

GETTING HIRED

Apply by: Rolling. Download application (at www.hawk mountain.org) and send it, along with a personal statement and the names of three references, to the address below. See the web site for details.

Qualifications:
Open to college juniors and seniors, recent college graduates and grad students. Applicants must speak fluent English, should have a strong passion for birds of prey and a serious interest in a career in conservation. International applicants are welcome.

Contact:
Keith Bildstein
Acopian Center for Conservation Learning
Hawk Mountain Sanctuary
410 Summer Valley Road
Orwigsburg, PA 17961
Phone: (570) 943-3411, ext. 108
Fax: (610) 781-7358
E-mail: bildstein@hawkmtn.org
www.hawkmountain.org/default/internships.htm

Visit Vault at **www.vault.com** for insider company profiles, expert advice, career message boards, expert resume reviews, the Vault Job Board and more.

VAULT CAREER LIBRARY **207**

Hawthorne Valley Farm

 THE BUZZ

- "Spread the word about organic farming"

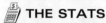 **THE STATS**

Industry(ies): Education; Environmental; Science/Research

Location(s): Ghent, NY

Number of interns: *Summer*: 20; *fall*: 2-3; *spring*: 3-4

Pay: *Academic-year interns*: $350/month; *summer counselors*: $1,500/summer; *Field Camp* (for ages 12-15): $1,700. Room and board (all vegetarian organic meals) provided for all interns and counselors

Length of internship: *Summer*: 8 weeks; *fall*: 3 months (end of August-end of November); *spring*: 4 months (end of January-beginning of June). Full academic year internships are also available

THE SCOOP

The Hawthorne Valley Farm is a 400-acre biodynamic farm in upstate New York. Biodynamic farms are almost completely self-sufficient. Composting, crop rotation and homeopathic treatments are used instead of fertilizers, pesticides and herbicides. As part of the farm's educational mission, the Hawthorne Valley Farm Visiting Students Program brings schoolchildren from throughout the region to visit the farm.

ON THE JOB

Interns/counselors will supervise and educate visiting students as they participate in the daily tasks of running a farm. During the school year, students spend one week on the farm; in the summer there are camps of one- and four-week sessions.

GETTING HIRED

Apply by: *Interns*: rolling; *summer camp*: begin interviewing in January. Visit the web site (www.vspcamp.com), call or e-mail vsp@taconic.net for an application.

Qualifications:
Open to college seniors, graduates, grad students and anyone 21 years of age or older. Individuals younger than 21 will be considered if the applicant has prior experience working with young children.

Contact:
Helen Enright
Hawthorne Valley Farm, Main House
Visiting Students Program
327 Route 21C
Ghent, NY 12075
Phone: (518) 672-4790
Fax: (518) 672-7608
E-mail: vsp@taconic.net
www.vspcamp.com

Herbert Scoville Peace Fellowship

THE BUZZ

- "Peace through disarmament"
- "Promote nonproliferation"

THE STATS

Industry(ies): Education; Nonprofit

Location(s): Washington, DC

Number of interns: *Fall/spring*: 2-4 each

Pay: Paid; $1,800/month. Health insurance and travel expenses covered

Length of internship: *Fall/spring*: 6-9 months

THE SCOOP

The Scoville Peace Fellowship program was established in 1987 to teach promising young scholars perspective on peace and security issues. Fellows are placed in one of 23 non-governmental organizations (NGOs) in Washington, DC, working on a range of issues related to international security. Participating groups include the Union of Concerned Scientists, the National Resource Defense Council, Physicians for Social Responsibility, the Nuclear Control Institute and many others.

ON THE JOB

Fellows will join the member NGO that best matches his/her interests. Typical activities include research, writing and political organizing. Fellows often write articles and fact sheets, attend congressional hearings and give interviews to members of the media. The sponsoring organization provides support, supervision and guidance for the fellow's project.

GETTING HIRED

Apply by: *Spring*: October 15; *fall*: February 1. Apply by mail only. See the web site for full application instructions. Applicants selected as finalists will attend an interview in Washington, DC.

Qualifications:
Open to all college graduates. Applicants with prior experience in public interest activism are preferred.

Contact:
Paul Revsine, Program Director
Herbert Scoville Jr. Peace Fellowship
322 4th Street, NE
Washington, DC 20002
Phone: (202) 543-4100, ext. 124
www.scoville.org

Heritage Foundation

 **THE BUZZ**
- "Promote personal liberties and traditional values"
- "Calling all deep-thinking young conservatives"

 **THE STATS**

Industry(ies): Nonprofit

Location(s): Washington, DC

Number of interns: *Spring/fall*: 20-25 each; *summer*: 50

Pay: *Fall/spring*: $10/day stipend; *summer*: $250/week

Length of internship: *Spring/summer/fall*: 3-4 months each

THE SCOOP

The Heritage Foundation is one of the preeminent conservative think tanks in the U.S. It is committed to the principles of free markets, reduced government, strong national defense, personal liberties and traditional values. Heritage conducts research, produces articles and position papers, and runs various information resources including the news web site townhall.com.

ON THE JOB

The Heritage Foundation seeks interns in its Asian studies, coalition relations, domestic policy, educational affairs, executive offices, foreign policy, government relations, lectures and seminars, and public relations departments. Specific duties vary by department, but all comprise a mix of research and administrative work. Some projects may involve working with congressional offices, federal agencies or other research institutions. Interns are encouraged to attend lectures, hearings and other events during their stay in DC.

GETTING HIRED

Apply by: *Summer*: February 1; *fall/spring*: rolling. Complete the online application and send two letters of recommendation, a one-page statement of interest and a writing sample (five pages maximum) to the address below.

Qualifications:
Open to college sophomores, juniors and seniors, recent college graduates and grad students. Applicants should have strong research and writing skills.

Contact:
Dan Szy, Internship Coordinator
The Heritage Foundation
214 Massachusetts Avenue, NE
Washington, DC 20002-4999
Phone: (202) 608-6032
Fax: (202) 546-8328
E-mail: internships@heritage.org
www.heritage.org/About/Internships/index.cfm

Hewitt Associates

 THE BUZZ
- "Don't apply to HR, be HR"
- "Get hands-on training from one of the biggies in the employee benefits industry"

THE STATS

Industry(ies): Human Resources & Recruiting; Management & Strategy Consulting

Location(s): Atlanta, GA; Bridgewater, NJ; Lincolnshire, IL; Newport Beach, CA; Norwalk, CT; Toronto; Vancouver

Number of interns: Varies

Pay: Paid; competitive salary. Furnished apartments in some locations

Length of internship: *Summer*: May-August

 THE SCOOP

Not only does Hewitt provide human capital management services to more than half of Fortune 500 companies, but it consults with more than a third of Fortune Global 500 companies. It handles more than 53 million HR-related customer interactions a year, spanning a worldwide network, which makes for ample opportunities for interns who might like to pursue a career at Hewitt upon graduation. Interns work on real projects as part of a Hewitt team.

ON THE JOB

Hewitt offers three types of internships: business analyst, programmer analyst and actuarial consultant. Business analyst interns work on teams that manage pension, 401(k), or health and welfare benefits issues; programmer analyst interns work with the technology that administers benefit plans; actuarial consultant interns help clients address various employee benefit issues such as mergers, pensions and financial analyses of health care benefits.

 GETTING HIRED

Apply by: The majority of recruiting starts the February prior to the internship summer. Hewitt accepts a resume anytime during an applicant's junior year, to review before visiting his/her campus.

Qualifications:
Open to college seniors; minimum 3.0 GPA is required. Traditional majors of Hewitt interns include accounting, actuarial science, computer science, economics, finance, information systems/science, math and statistics.

Contact:
Kathy Hancock
Hewitt Associates LLC
100 Half Day Road
Lincolnshire, IL 60069
Phone: (847) 295-5000
Fax: (847) 883-8001
www.hewitt.com/hewitt/careers/subcareers/campus/campus_internships.htm

Visit Vault at **www.vault.com** for insider company profiles, expert advice, career message boards, expert resume reviews, the Vault Job Board and more.

 **209**

Hewlett-Packard

THE BUZZ

- "Mother of all garages of innovation"

THE STATS

Industry(ies): Engineering; Hardware; Technology

Location(s): Multiple cities in CA, CO, DE, GA, ID, MA, NH, NJ, OR, TX and WA

Number of interns: *Annual*: 500-700

Pay: Paid; competetive salary. Health and welfare benefits; relocation assistance

Length of internship: 3 months

THE SCOOP

Hewlett-Packard is a technology solutions provider to consumers, businesses and institutions globally. The company's offerings span IT infrastructure, global services, business and home computing, imaging and printing.

ON THE JOB

HP offers internships in engineering, finance, marketing, information technology and operations. All interns benefit from the advice and support of HP staff members and have the opportunity to work on meaningful projects relevant to their field of study. While there are a number of different types of projects available to interns, the following is a sample. Engineering interns design and develop computer software and hardware; finance interns analyze and interpret financial results and forecasts (variance analysis, P&L impact) information technology interns conduct systems analysis and programming; operations interns coordinate physical and informational flows.

GETTING HIRED

Apply by: Rolling. Apply online at www.hp.com/go/jobs. Current intern openings are posted on the web site. Interested applicants should apply directly to positions of interest. Applications accepted online only.

Qualifications:
Open to full-time students actively pursuing a degree at an accredited university. Applicants should demonstrate high academic achievement in a technical or business field such as electrical engineering, computer science, computer engineering, mechanical engineering, industrial engineering, information technology, materials science, marketing, finance or business administration. Qualifications vary for individual positions. Consult the job postings on the company web site for details.

Contact:
www.hp.com/go/jobs

High Country News

THE BUZZ

- "Independent journalism for people who care about the West"
- "Covering environmental issues from the Plains to the Pacific"

THE STATS

Industry(ies): Environmental; Journalism

Location(s): Paonia, CO

Number of interns: *Spring/summer/fall*: 2 each

Pay: $500/month. Free housing provided

Length of internship: *Spring/summer/fall*: 4 months each

THE SCOOP

High Country News is a biweekly newsmagazine covering the American West's environment and communities. Topics of particular interest to the paper include Western politics and the environment, urban sprawl, wildlife, water and drought, logging, mining and citizen activism. *HCN* has a circulation of over 24,000.

ON THE JOB

Interns at *High Country News* are treated as full members of the editorial staff; aside from a few tasks such as sorting the mail and answering phones, interns research, interview and write intensively. Interns write the majority of HCN's news briefs; reporting for those stories is generally conducted over the phone and Internet. After gaining some experience, interns also wrote more in-depth 750- to 900-word stories. HCN also has the funds to send each intern into the field at least once in order to do on-the-ground reporting for these pieces.

GETTING HIRED

Apply by: Rolling. Check the web site for application deadlines and start dates.

Qualifications:
Open to all recent college graduates and grad students. Prior experience in journalism is not required; strong communication skills, initiative, background in the West and environmental issues, familiarity with HCN, and a sense of humor are. Native Americans and other minorities are especially encouraged to apply.

Contact:
Jodi Peterson, News Editor
High Country News
P.O. Box 1090
Paonia, CO 81428
Phone: (970) 527-4898
E-mail: jodi@hcn.org
www.hcn.org/about/interns.jsp

High Museum of Art

 THE BUZZ
- "High art and high culture at the High Museum"

THE STATS

Industry(ies): Art/Museum

Location(s): Atlanta, GA

Number of interns: *Annual*: 10 or more; varies depending on need

Pay: None

Length of internship: Varies; usually about 6 weeks; available year-round

 THE SCOOP

The High Museum houses its collection of over 11,000 works of art in two separate Atlanta locations. The main gallery is located in Atlanta's midtown arts area, the Woodruff Center – a facility that also includes the Alliance Theatre Company, the Atlanta College of Art, the 14th Street Playhouse and the Atlanta Symphony Orchestra. The High's photography and folk art collections are housed downtown at the Georgia Pacific Center. The Museum's collection also includes decorative arts and works of African, American, European and modern art. Over half a million people visit the High Museum each year, making it one of the premier cultural institutions in the South.

 ON THE JOB

Internships are available in the photography, membership, registrar, special events, exhibitions, publications, development, education, marketing, library and web site departments at the High Museum. Curatorial interns specialize in one of the High's collection areas: African art, decorative, modern, folk, European or media arts.

GETTING HIRED

Apply by: Rolling. Contact internship coordinator for the required application form.

Qualifications:
Open to high school seniors, college freshmen, sophomores, juniors and seniors, recent college graduates and grad students.

Contact:
Bobbi Edmond, Internship Coordinator
High Museum of Art
1280 Peachtree Street, NE
Atlanta, GA 30309
Phone: (404) 733-4400
E-mail: bobbi.edmond@woodruffcenter.org
www.high.org

Hill | Holliday

THE BUZZ
- "A top Boston communications firm"
- "Coffee and donuts for breakfast"

THE STATS

Industry(ies): Advertising; Communications; Public Relations

Location(s): Boston, MA

Number of interns: *Fall/spring*: 10-20 each; *summer*: 20-30

Pay: *Fall/spring*: unpaid; interns must receive academic credit; *summer*: paid; $7.50/hour

Length of internship: *Fall/spring*: 10 weeks, 10-15 hours/week (September-November, January-March, respectively); *summer*: 8 weeks, 40 hours/week (June-August)

 THE SCOOP

Hill | Holliday, is one of the top communications agencies in the U.S. Headquartered in Boston, with offices in New York, Miami Beach, San Francisco, and Greenville, S.C., Hill | Holliday has a roster of well-known clients including Anheuser-Busch, Cognos, CVS/pharmacy, Dell, Dunkin' Donuts, EMC, Harvard Pilgrim Healthcare, John Hancock, Putnam Investments and Tyco. In addition, Hill | Holliday, recognized by the American Association of Advertising agencies as one of the most "giving" agencies in the country, has a long-standing and extensive commitment to community service, each year undertaking more than 60 pro bono marketing assignments and donating over $1 million in cash to local nonprofits.

 ON THE JOB

Hill | Holliday's internship program is designed to offer college students a "real life" learning experience in advertising. Interns work closely with a mentor in one of the following departments: Accounting, Account Service, Art Buying, Brand Planning, Broadcast, Community Relations, Corporate Communications, Interactive, Relationship Marketing, Research, Media, New Business or Traffic. Interns attend a weekly seminar series that offers them exposure to areas outside of their assigned department. Summer interns also complete an intensive team project assignment on one of the firm's current clients.

GETTING HIRED

Apply by: Submit resume and cover letter to one of the following:

Fall: fallinterns@hhcc.com (deadline: July 1, decision by August 15)

Spring: springinterns@hhcc.com (deadline: November 1, decision by December 15)

Summer: summerinterns@hhcc.com (deadline: March 1, decision by May 15)

Qualifications:
All current college students are invited to apply. Graduate students are typically not eligible.

Contact:
Internship Coordinator
200 Clarendon Street
Boston, MA 02116
www.hhcc.com

Visit Vault at **www.vault.com** for insider company profiles, expert advice, career message boards, expert resume reviews, the Vault Job Board and more.

VAULT CAREER LIBRARY **211**

Hill & Knowlton

 THE BUZZ
- "Learn PR from the masters"

 THE STATS

Industry(ies): Public Relations

Location(s): Chicago, IL; Houston, TX; Los Angeles, CA; New York, NY; Portland, OR; San Francisco, CA; Seattle, WA; Spokane, WA; Tampa, FL; Washington, DC

Number of interns: *Annually*: usually around 10-20 across U.S. offices (varies depending upon labor market, economy and the business needs at each office)

Pay: Paid; $10-15/hour

Length of internship: *Summer:* 10 weeks; *Year-round:* 3-6 months

 THE SCOOP

Hill & Knowlton was founded in 1927 by John Hill in Cleveland, making it one of the oldest public relations consultancies in the world. In 1987, it became a part of the WPP Group, a set of marketing, advertising, communications and public relations companies that includes Burson-Marstellar, Cohn & Wolf, Ogilvy Public Relations Wordlwide, Cole and Weber United and GCI. Today, H&K is a global public relations firm with 71 offices in 40 countries. The firm's long list of clients includes Motorola, HP, Adidas, Yahoo!, Mazda, VeriSign, The Hershey Company, the Nuclear Energy Institute and Merck.

 ON THE JOB

H&K is divided into "core services" that include Marketing Communications, Public Affairs, Technology, Healthcare and Digital Communications. Interns are placed in the service or practice that offers the best fit with each individual's experience and interests. They participate in a structured orientation program that offers training in project management, news writing, media relations and news monitoring as well as basic writing, account management, time management, presentation skills and budget management. All interns are given a project that includes a formal presentation, which must be completed by the end of the internship.

Apply by: Rolling. Students are encouraged to apply early – summer interns are usually selected in the spring. Check the position description for exact application requirements. Applicants are usually asked to submit a writing sample with their resume, expected date of graduation, GPA and preferred office location(s). H&K posts open positions on www.CareerBuilder.com and their partner sites. Applicants are encouraged to check these sites for an updated list of openings. Students may also send inquiries to careers@hillandknowlton.com.

GETTING HIRED

Qualifications:

Open to rising college juniors and seniors, recent college graduates and grad students. A background in journalism, communications or another PR-related field is preferred.

Contact:
Denise Gordon
909 Third Avenue
New York, NY 10022
Phone: (212) 885-0547
E-mail: careers@hillandknowlton.com
www.hillandknowlton.com/index.php/careers/working_here.html

Hillel

 THE BUZZ
- "Enriching Jewish life on campus"

 **THE STATS**

Industry(ies): Education; Nonprofit; Religious

Location(s): Various college campuses

Number of interns: *Annual*: 75-85

Pay: *First-year fellows*: $22,000/11 months; *second-year fellows*: $24,000/year. Health and dental insurance; training and travel provided

Length of internship: 11 months; most fellows have the option to continue for an additional year. Some stay on the same campus, other fellows switch campuses

THE SCOOP

Hillel is the largest global Jewish campus organization, with over 500 chapters around the world. Hillel works to help students develop their Jewish identity through various educational, social, community service and arts/culture projects. Hillel's Steinhardt Jewish Campus Service Corps (JCSC) Fellowship program is part of the organization's ongoing effort to help students strengthen their Jewish identity and experience Judaism in meaningful ways with students who share their interests.

ON THE JOB

The JCSC Fellowship is an 11-month program providing recent college graduates crucial leadership roles on campuses in North America. Fellows develop and lead relationship and community-building efforts with Jewish students on campus, typically outside of the Hillel building and with students not connected to formal Jewish life on campus. Events organized by JCSC Fellows may include projects such as residence hall programs, service projects, arts/music festivals, alternative spring breaks and holiday celebrations. All Fellows gather for intensive training on community-building concepts, programming best practices and organizational skills in August and December of each year.

GETTING HIRED

Apply by: Applications are due at the beginning of March each year. Online application, four essays, two letters of recommendation and a $25 application fee are required. Applications must be submitted online at www.jcscfellowship.com. Please see the web site for detailed application instructions.

Qualifications:
Open to graduating college seniors and recent college graduates, not more than two years out of college. Applicants must be Jewish and should have campus leadership experience. No strong Jewish background or previous involvement in the Jewish community is required.

Contact:
Steinhardt Jewish Campus Service Corps
800 Eighth Street, NW
Washington, DC 20001
Phone: (202) 449-6500
E-mail: jcscapplication@hillel.org
www.hillel.org (Hillel website)
http://jcsc.hillel.org (JCSC website)

Hispanic Association of Colleges and Universities

 THE BUZZ
- "Opportunities in government and top corporations for Hispanic-Americans"

 **THE STATS**

Industry(ies): Education; Government

Location(s): Washington, DC; field sites throughout the country

Number of interns: *Annual*: Approximately 600

Pay: Paid; *sophomore/junior*: $440/week; *senior*: $470/week; *grads*: $540/week. Round-trip travel provided; academic credit available

Length of internship: *Spring*: January 12-April 29; *summer*: June 2-August 12; *fall*: August 24-December 9

THE SCOOP

The Hispanic Association of Colleges and Universities (HACU) is a consortium of over 300 institutions in the United States. The HACU National Internship Program (HNIP) recruits college students for paid summer- and semester-long internships at federal agencies and private corporations in Washington, DC, and throughout the country. Participating agencies and corporations hope to increase diversity in their workforce by providing these internships.

ON THE JOB

HACU staff matches academic backgrounds to internship descriptions provided by the host organizations. Representatives from the host organizations and HACU staff work to ensure that students' skills and goals are considered in placement. Past placements have included public affairs, accounting, human resources and information technology, as well as laboratories, airports and hospitals, among others.

GETTING HIRED

Apply by: *Spring*: November 4; *summer*: February 24 (early deadline: November 4); *fall*: June 16. Early deadlines are necessary for positions that require security clearance, extensive interviewing or drug screening. Apply online at www.hnip.net. Interns will need to submit online an application form, resume and a 250- to 500-word essay. Additionally, official college transcripts and certification of enrollment and class level must be mailed to the address below.

Qualifications:
Open to college sophomores, juniors and seniors and grad students enrolled in an undergraduate or graduate program with a GPA of 3.0 and above. Students graduating in May 2006 are still eligible for the summer 2006 session. Applicants must be authorized or eligible to work in the United States. Some internship assignments require U.S. citizenship.

Contact:
Internship Coordinator
HACU National Internship Program
One Dupont Circle, NW, Suite 605
Washington, DC 20036
Phone: (202) 467-0893; TTY users: (800) 855-2880
E-mail: HNIP@hacu.net www.hnip.net
www.hnip.net

Visit Vault at **www.vault.com** for insider company profiles, expert advice, career message boards, expert resume reviews, the Vault Job Board and more.

VAULT CAREER LIBRARY 213

Historic Deerfield Fellowship

THE BUZZ

- "Gain an appreciation for New England's heritage"
- "Curate a colonial village"

THE STATS

Industry(ies): Art/Museum; Education

Location(s): Deerfield, MA

Number of interns: *Summer:* 6-10

Pay: $7,500 fellowship award covers tuition, room, board and all expenses. In addition, a limited number of stipends ranging from $800-$1,500 are provided to outstanding candidates who demonstrate financial need. Academic credit (6 course hours) is available through the University of Massachusetts at Amherst

Length of internship: *Summer:* 9 weeks

THE SCOOP

Historic Deerfield is a preserved colonial-era village in rural Massachusetts. On the grounds are 14 historic buildings dating from the 18th and 19th centuries, as well as the Flynt Center of Early New England Life. The Center houses thousands of artifacts dating back as far as 1650.

ON THE JOB

Deerfield fellows study early New England history and material culture through a series of seminars and tours led by the Deerfield staff and lecturers from nearby colleges. Fellows then have the opportunity to put their knowledge to work by leading village tours for visitors. Each student also completes a short paper at the conclusion of the internship analyzing one of the objects in the Deerfield collection.

GETTING HIRED

Apply by: *Summer:* February 21. An application form, transcript, two letters of recommendation, an essay and a $15 application fee are required. See the web site for details.

Qualifications:
Open to college juniors and seniors. Applicants must have completed at least two years of studies, but still have undergraduate status as of January 1 of the year they wish to apply. Recent college graduates are also invited to apply.

Contact:
Office of Academic Programs
Historic Deerfield, Inc.
P.O. Box 321
Deerfield, MA 01342
Phone: (413) 775-7207
Fax: (413) 775-7224
E-mail: sfp@historic-deerfield.org
www.deerfield-fellowship.org

Historic Films

THE BUZZ

- "Get lost among the reels – a film buff's dream"
- "A slice of Hollywood history"

THE STATS

Industry(ies): Film

Location(s): Greenport, NY

Number of interns: *Annual:* 1-3

Pay: None

Length of internship: 6 weeks (full-time) or 13 weeks (part-time); available year-round

THE SCOOP

Historic Films maintains an extensive archive of vintage television shows, commercials, newsreels, feature films and more. The company owns or controls over 45,000 hours of footage spanning more than a century. Historic Films licenses its clips to film and television producers, advertising agencies and news organizations.

ON THE JOB

Interns generally work in the research department at Historic Films. They conduct searches for footage in the computer database, locate and compile clips for screening cassettes, and manage the delivery of tapes to Historic Films' clients.

GETTING HIRED

Apply by: Rolling. Send resume and cover letter to the address below.

Qualifications:
Open to college freshmen, sophomores, juniors and seniors, recent college graduates and grad students. Interns must have excellent English language skills. U.S. citizens are preferred.

Contact:
Kevin Rice, Internship Coordinator
Historic Films
211 Third Street
Greenport, NY 11944
Phone: (631) 477-9700
Fax: (631) 477-9800
E-mail: kevin@historicfilms.com
www.historicfilms.com

History Factory

 THE BUZZ
- "Understanding yesterday's history is good for tomorrow's business"
- "A blend of academia and consulting"

 THE STATS

Industry(ies): Art/Museum; Management & Strategy Consulting

Location(s): Chantilly, VA

Number of interns: *Summer*: 2-4

Pay: Stipend; amount varies

Length of internship: *Summer*: 8-12 weeks

 **THE SCOOP**

Essentially, the History Factory is a business consulting company that uses history to inform the present and hopefully improve the future. Since 1979, the company has hired historians, archivists, writers and researchers to explore companies' backgrounds and show them how to use their history to improve their businesses. They often help companies with special events, like anniversaries and mergers.

 ON THE JOB

The Archival Internship program allows graduate students the opportunity to conduct records surveys, identify historically important documents and artifacts, and appraise monetary values of historic pieces. Interns are responsible for establishing the archival guidelines, keeping records using a software database, storing records and providing research assistance. Undergrads can intern as part of the Interpretive Internship program, which invites "creative and intelligent" students to research the historical backgrounds of several American organizations and interpret those details for contemporary businesses.

 GETTING HIRED

Apply by: Rolling. Those interested can apply online at www.historyfactory.com/content/careers/careers.html.

Qualifications:
Archival Internship program: open to graduate students only; *Interpretive Internship program*: open to college freshmen, sophomores, juniors and seniors attending a liberal arts school.

Contact:
Internship Coordinator
The History Factory
14140 Parke Long Court
Chantilly, VA 20151-0500
Phone: (703) 631-0500
Fax: (703) 631-1124
E-mail: info@historyfactory.com
www.historyfactory.com

Home Box Office

 THE BUZZ
- "Tony Soprano would kill for this job. Really"
- "Learn all about the cable biz from one of the oldest and most successful companies in the industry"

 THE STATS

Industry(ies): Broadcast & Entertainment; Film

Location(s): Los Angeles, CA; New York, NY

Number of interns: *Annual*: 75

Pay: Stipend (equivalent to minimum wage) awarded upon completion of the internship; academic credit

Length of internship: 10 weeks minimum; available year-round

 **THE SCOOP**

Home Box Office (HBO), a division of Time Warner, is one of the leading providers of pay television services. Spread over multiple channels, the HBO and Cinemax networks reach subscribers in more than 35 countries. HBO broadcasts popular Hollywood films, exclusive boxing matches and original films and television series. Award-winning HBO productions include *The Sopranos* and *Six Feet Under*.

 ON THE JOB

The internship program gives students hands-on experience working at a major cable network and allows them to develop contacts in the industry. Interns are accepted in the sports, programming, casting, advertising, marketing, media relations, finance, accounting and human resources departments.

 GETTING HIRED

Apply by: Rolling. Applications may be submitted at the Time Warner careers web site. Indicate the department and semester for which you are applying. If applying by e-mail, cut and paste a cover letter and resume; do not send attachments.

Qualifications:
Open to college sophomores, juniors and seniors. Interns must receive academic credit from their college and be eligible to work in the U.S.

Contact:
Home Box Office
Human Resources
1100 Sixth Avenue
New York, NY 10036
Phone: (212) 512-1000
E-mail: hr.ny@hbo.com
www.aoltimewarner.com/careers

Visit Vault at **www.vault.com** for insider company profiles, expert advice, career message boards, expert resume reviews, the Vault Job Board and more.

VAULT CAREER LIBRARY **215**

Houghton Mifflin

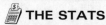 **THE BUZZ**
- "Textbook-perfect opportunity for aspiring educators"

THE STATS

Industry(ies): Education; Publishing

Location(s): Boston, MA

Number of interns: *Summer*: 12

Pay: Paid; $9/hour

Length of internship: *Summer*: 3 months

THE SCOOP

Houghton Mifflin is a Boston-based publishing house specializing in educational books. The company produces textbooks and reference materials for elementary, high school and college students. The HM Trade Division also publishes general interest titles, including the popular *Best American* series and the *Peterson Field Guides*. Founded in 1832, the company today has annual sales of over $1 billion.

ON THE JOB

Houghton Mifflin's college division offers internships in the editorial, marketing, art and design, production, rights and permissions, and custom publishing departments. Interns work a full-time schedule between June and August. Intern duties may include communicating with authors and reviewers, handling billing and budget/sales reviews, and administrative and clerical support.

GETTING HIRED

Apply by: *Summer*: March 30 (no earlier than January 1). Decisions on hiring are made in March and April. Send resume and cover letter to the address below. Selected applicants will be contacted for telephone interviews as positions become available.

Qualifications:

Open to college sophomores and juniors or those enrolled in a graduate program. Applicants must have excellent written and verbal communications and interpersonal skills, be able to multi-task, prioritize, be detail orientated and have a working knowledge of Microsoft Office, Lotus Notes and the Internet.

Contact:

Houghton Mifflin Company
College Division, Internship Coordinator
222 Berkeley Street
Boston, MA 02116
Phone: (617) 351-5000
E-mail: HRassist@hmco.com
www.hmco.com/company/careers/opp_for_students.html

Houston International Protocol Alliance

 THE BUZZ
- "Ride the Texas welcome wagon and learn about other cultures"

THE STATS

Industry(ies): Government; Hospitality; Nonprofit

Location(s): Houston, TX

Number of interns: *Annual*: 10 (2-4 per semester)

Pay: None. Parking and work-related expenses reimbursed

Length of internship: *Spring/summer/fall*: 3 months minimum each; 10 hour/week minimum

THE SCOOP

The Houston International Protocol Alliance serves as the official host to international dignitaries visiting the city, as well as the liaison to the 69 foreign consulates located in Houston and advisor to the Mayor and other city officials on international affairs and strategic communications. The organization, a department of the Greater Houston Convention and Visitors Bureau, acts as a resource for the city of Houston for information on protocol, etiquette and cross-cultural issues. The Alliance also promotes Houston's overseas reputation and strengthening its international ties.

ON THE JOB

The internship program at the Houston International Protocol Alliance provides an opportunity to observe both international diplomacy and city administration in action. All interns will choose a long-term project to work on independently during their internships. The choice of project will depend on both the interests of each student and the needs of the Alliance, often involving research, surveys, event planning or writing about countries dealing with the Alliance.

GETTING HIRED

Apply by: Rolling. Send resume, cover letter, and a writing sample (on any subject, any length) by e-mail or regular mail to the address below.

Qualifications:

Open to rising college juniors and seniors and grad students interested in international affairs and/or foreign languages. Knowledge of a foreign language and some experience living abroad are preferred, as are strong writing and computer skills.

Contact:

Tamara Hardikar, Internship Coordinator
Houston International Protocol Alliance
901 Bagby, Suite 100
Houston, TX 77002
Phone: (713) 227-3395
Fax: (713) 227-3399
E-mail: protocol@ghcvb.org
www.houston-guide.com/protocol

Howard Hughes Medical Institute

THE BUZZ
- "Discover the next biomedical breakthrough"
- "Curious med students discovering cures for disease"

THE STATS

Industry(ies): Health Care

Location(s): *HHMI Research Training Fellowships for Medical Students*: various universities and research institutions; *HHMI-NIH Research Scholars Program (Cloister Program)*: Bethesda, MD

Number of interns: *Research Training Fellowships*: 60; *Cloister Program*: 42

Pay: Paid; *Research Training Fellowships*: $23,000/year plus research and fellow's allowance; *Cloister Program*: $17,800/year; subsidized, furnished, on-campus housing provided; medical insurance and moving expenses covered

Length of internship: 1 year

 THE SCOOP

The Howard Hughes Medical Institute (HHMI) is a leading biomedical research organization. Its $11 billion endowment allows the Institute to employ over 350 scientists in labs across the country, as well as fund promising research at other facilities through its grants program. HHMI concentrates its research efforts on fields such as cell biology, computational biology, genetics, immunology, neuroscience and structural biology.

ON THE JOB

Scholars spend a year living and working on the National Institutes of Health (NIH) campus in Bethesda, Maryland. Each scholar selects a research project to join and works under the mentorship of a senior NIH scientist. All research scholars are housed together in the Cloister building on campus, creating a unique community and sense of camaraderie among the students. The HHMI Research Training Fellowships for Medical Students provides support for biomedical research for one year under the guidance of a mentor at an academic or nonprofit research institution in the United States or abroad, except at the NIH. Applicants for the fellowship choose their own mentor and research plan. Proposals for research should concentrate on basic biological processes or disease mechanisms.

GETTING HIRED

Apply by: *Research Training Fellowships*: January 6; *Cloister Program*: January 10. Students may apply to both programs in the same academic year. All application materials must be submitted online. The full list of application requirements for each program is available from the web sites.

Qualifications:
Open to students currently enrolled in a U.S. medical or dental school. Applicants who are enrolled in a joint MD/PhD or DDS/PhD program or have a PhD in a laboratory-based science are not eligible.

Contact:

HHMI Research Training Fellowships for Medical Students
Howard Hughes Medical Institute
Office of Grants and Special Programs/MedAp2005
4000 Jones Bridge Road
Chevy Chase, MD 20815
Phone: (301) 215-8883
Fax: (301) 215-8888
E-mail: fellows@hhmi.org
www.hhmi.org/medfellowships

HHMI-NIH Research Scholars Program (Cloister Program)
HHMI-NIH Research Scholars Program
1 Cloister Court, Building 60, Room 253
Bethesda, MD 20814-1460
Phone: (800) 424-9924
E-mail: research_scholars@hhmi.org
www.hhmi.org/cloister

Visit Vault at **www.vault.com** for insider company profiles, expert advice, career message boards, expert resume reviews, the Vault Job Board and more.

V\ULT CAREER LIBRARY **217**

The Howard Stern Show

 THE BUZZ
- "Add a little shock to your mornings"
- "Do more in radio production by 8 a.m. than most do all day"

 THE STATS

Industry(ies): Broadcast & Entertainment

Location(s): New York, NY

Number of interns: *Spring/summer/fall*: 15 each

Pay: None; interns must receive academic credit

Length of internship: *Spring/summer/fall*: usually 12 weeks (no minimum length)

 THE SCOOP

You know Howard Stern, don't you? You know Robin and Gary, right? Of course you do, that's why you're reading this. Howard Stern is the "shock jock" of Sirius Satellite radio. He's also branched out to On Demand Television, where he's making an honest living "from Playmates and farting contests to top celeb interviews."

ON THE JOB

Interns must put in the time, and if the web site is any guide, this is a pretty no-nonsense crew. Interns can participate in the show's production and be there every step of the way, from the writing to the editing to Howard's on-air performance. Must work at least 3 days a week, at least one shift from 6 a.m. to noon and two shifts from noon to 5:30 p.m.

GETTING HIRED

Apply by: Rolling. Fax resume, cover letter and letter from your school stating that you are receiving academic credit. Internships are available year-round as long as applicants are receiving academic credit.

Qualifications:

Open to college juniors and seniors. Must be at least 18 years old.

Contact:

Tracey Millman
Fax: (646) 313-2103
E-mail: tracey@howardstern.com

HSI Productions

 THE BUZZ
- "Make memorable commercials"
- "Work behind the scenes on a film or music video"

 THE STATS

Industry(ies): Advertising; Broadcast & Entertainment; Film; Music/Records

Location(s): Culver City, CA; New York, NY

Number of interns: *Annual*: 12-15 (4-5 per semester)

Pay: None

Length of internship: *Spring/summer/fall*: 2-3 months each

 THE SCOOP

HSI Productions is one of the largest music video and television commercial production companies in the U.S. The company has been recognized with numerous awards, including Grammys, MTV Music Video Awards, Clios and the Cannes Festival's Golden Lion. Lenny Kravitz, Eminem, Outkast and Christina Aguilera have all put out HSI-produced videos, and the firm's advertising clients include Mercedes-Benz, Coca-Cola, Adidas and Gap. HSI also produces full-length feature films.

ON THE JOB

HSI interns gain hands-on experience in a fast-paced film production company. Depending on shooting and production schedules, students may have the opportunity to work on the set of an HSI project in progress. The internship program is designed to prepare individuals for a career in production by providing a behind-the-scenes look at all of the ingredients that go into a successful commercial or music video.

GETTING HIRED

Apply by: Rolling. Apply as early as possible; interns for the upcoming semester are usually selected by the end of the first few weeks of the current semester. E-mail resume and cover letter to the address below.

Qualifications:

Open to college freshmen, sophomores, juniors and seniors; recent college graduates who have completed their studies within the past semester are also eligible.

Contact:

Apply by e-mail only to:
Todd Stringer, Internship Coordinator
E-mail: intern@hsiproductions.com
www.hsiproductions.com

Hudson Institute

 THE BUZZ
- "Help formulate ideas and solutions for prominent issues in public policy"
- "Welcome to the exciting world of talking heads"

 THE STATS

Industry(ies): Public Policy; Think Tanks

Location(s): Washington, DC

Number of interns: *Annual:* 35-50

Pay: Unpaid; will provide academic credit, job and graduate school recommendations

Length of internship: Flexible, usually 12 weeks minimum; minimum 15 hours/week; available summer, fall and spring

 THE SCOOP

The Hudson Institute is a nonpartisan policy think tank founded in 1961 by Herman Kahn. Conducting applied research on major issues in domestic and international affairs. One of the oldest think tanks, The Institute distinguishes itself from other public policy research organizations in its focus on hands-on research and the practical implementation of its ideas. In recent years, The Institute has been active in recommending a course of economic reform for the former Soviet states, proposing ideas for resolving ethnic conflict in the Balkans and conducting a UN-sponsored study of Kazakhstan and the Central Asian region.

 ON THE JOB

Interns work with Hudson research fellows on projects at The Institute's various policy centers. They analye policy issues, edit and write papers, and conduct research in areas such as campaign reform, economic and employment policy, Middle East studies, philanthropy and civic renewal, national and international security studies, and science in public policy. Past interns have created an index of global philanthropy, researched terrorism and homeland secuirity issues, and assisted with a Hudson-sponsored address by President Bush. Administrative interns assist with communications, marketing and other management tasks. All interns are encouraged to participate in office activities such as monthly staff luncheons, speed-debating, and movie nights.

GETTING HIRED

Apply by: Rolling. Submit a resume, cover letter and short writing samole to the director of the center of interest. See the internship section of the web site (under "Learn about Hudson") for a list of open internships and center contacts.

Qualifications:

Open to college sophomores, juniors and seniors, college graduates and grad students. See individual position descriptions on the web site for specific qualifications for each internship.

Contact:
Internship Coordinator
Hudson Institute
1015 15th St, 6th Floor
Washington, DC 20005
Phone: (202) 974-2400
www.hudson.org

Hunter House

 THE BUZZ
- "Books for healthy living and stronger communities"
- "Providing balanced information on underreported topics"

 THE STATS

Industry(ies): Health Care; Publishing

Location(s): Alameda, CA

Number of interns: *Annual:* 3-5

Pay: None

Length of internship: 3-month minimum; available year-round

 THE SCOOP

Hunter House is a small independent publisher specializing in books on physical, mental and emotional health. Several of the company's titles have been featured in *The New York Times* and have gone on to become bestsellers. Topics of particular interest to Hunter House include women's health, sexuality and relationships, domestic abuse and trauma recovery.

 ON THE JOB

Interns may work in the editorial, acquisitions, production, marketing or operations departments. Specific duties will depend upon which department the individual chooses but, typically, interns may be involved in laying out pages with Quark XPress, reading and evaluating manuscripts, creating press releases, reviewing page proofs, or developing the web site. The Hunter House staff is small, so interns can expect a substantive experience with real responsibilities.

GETTING HIRED

Apply by: Rolling. Mail, fax or e-mail resume and cover letter to the address below. Include writing samples if applying for an editorial internship.

Qualifications:

Open to college juniors and seniors, recent college graduates and grad students. A background in English, health, women's issues, psychology, graphic design, database programming or other relevant area is preferred.

Contact:
Alexandra Mummery
Hunter House Publishers
1515 1/2 Park Street
Alameda, CA 94501
Phone: (510) 865-5282
E-mail: editorial@hunterhouse.com
www.hunterhouse.com/ijobs.asp

Visit Vault at **www.vault.com** for insider company profiles, expert advice, career message boards, expert resume reviews, the Vault Job Board and more.

VAULT CAREER LIBRARY 219

INTERNSHIP PROFILES:

IAESTE

 THE BUZZ

- "Globetrotting technical students"
- "Technology – the international language"

 THE STATS

Industry(ies): Education

Location(s): Columbia, MD; 20 U.S. universities from coast to coast; over 80 countries worldwide

Number of interns: *Annual*: 100-200 from the U.S.; over 6,000 worldwide

Pay: Positions pay a wage sufficient to cover local living expenses; varies depending upon the company and country

Length of internship: *Summer*: 8-12 weeks; longer placements of up to 1 year are also available

 THE SCOOP

The International Association for the Exchange of Students for Technical Experience (IAESTE) was founded in England in 1948 to promote an appreciation and understanding of different cultures through technical exchanges. IAESTE United States dedicates itself to developing global skills in tomorrow's technical leaders. Local Committees, IAESTE chapters run by students, are found at over 20 of the nation's top technical universities. IAESTE-United States is a student and professional membership organization offering a reciprocal technical internship exchange program and an array of membership services and programs for international technical students and professionals.

 ON THE JOB

IAESTE-United States matches students in the U.S. with paid positions in industry, research institutes, universities, consulting firms and laboratories abroad. Applicants receive a list of international internships available and select the positions in which they are interested. The IAESTE selection panel then reviews the candidates and nominates one applicant for each available position. Over 95 percent of all nominated candidates are accepted by the international host organizations. IAESTE will also provide advice and assistance with work permits, visas and other required documents. IAESTE also arranges housing for over 98 percent of the interns in the host country.

GETTING HIRED

Apply by: January 1. Students should apply online at www.iaesteunitedstates.org between September 1 and January 1; a $35 (member) or $50 (nonmember) registration fee is required. See the web site for a list of universities with local committees, to become a member.

Qualifications:

Open to college sophomores, juniors and seniors and grad students pursuing a degree in science, engineering, mathematics, architecture, computer science or other technical fields. A full list of eligible fields of study is available on the web site. Applicants must be between 19 and 30 years of age.

Contact:

Info below is for students studying at a U.S. university or college. Students attending a university in other countries must contact IAESTE in their own country. Contact information for other countries is listed at the IAESTE International web site (www.iaeste.org).

IAESTE USA
10400 Little Patuxent Parkway, Suite 250
Columbia, MD 21044-3510
Phone: (410) 997-3069
Fax: (410) 997-5186
E-mail: iaeste@aipt.org
www.iaesteunitedstates.org

IBM

THE BUZZ

- "These three letters on your resume bring career success"

THE STATS

Industry(ies): Hardware; Management & Strategy Consulting; Operations & IT Consulting; Technology; Software

Location(s): Austin, TX; Raleigh, NC; San Jose, CA

Number of interns: *Spring*: 30; *summer*: 75 (18 MBA and 57 technical)

Pay: Paid; competitive salary, based on credit hours completed towards current degree. Relocation and housing program for summer interns

Length of internship: *Spring/summer*: 11-12 weeks each

THE SCOOP

The world's largest information technology, IBM was founded as the Computing-Tabulating-Recording Company in 1911. Measured by revenue, IBM is the biggest provider of IT services ($46 billion), hardware ($31 billion) and financing ($2.6 billion), and the company is second in software ($15 billion). The company's 2004 revenues were $96.2 billion. The IBM Extreme Blue™ internship program, one area within IBM's larger internship and co-op program, targets high-potential software development and business students.

ON THE JOB

During the Extreme Blue™ program, interns work in one of 3 labs in the US. Interns work in a team to conceive and deliver the technology, business plan and go-to-market strategy for an emerging business opportunity. Internships include executive presentations, mentoring, orientation, professional development, placement assistance, extracurricular activities and participation in the Extreme Blue Alumni Networking Group (EBANG). In 2004, 86 percent of alumni had received full time offers with IBM. In addition to creating solutions for clients and brining IBM prodcts to the market, Extreme Blue™ interns have filed over 270 patents, two for Alpha Works®.

GETTING HIRED

Apply by: *Technical applications*: Year-round. *Summer MBA applications*: February 28 (applications will be accepted as early as November). Online application required, which can be found at www-913.ibm.com/employment/us/extremeblue/apply2.html.

Qualifications:
Open to college juniors and seniors and graduate students enrolled full time at accredited American universities. Technical students should have a minimum of six months software development experience in industry, research or open source setting (equivalent to two semester-long internships), minimum GPA of 3.0 or 3.75 on a 5.0 scale, proficiency in Java, C and/or C++ programming languages and active contribution to professional communities. Examples include Open Source, IEEE, ACM, NSBE, UPE and HKN. MBA students should have experience in the industry, proven skills in business concept innovation, a history of personal initiatives for exploring technology and tech business trends, creativity and teamwork skills.

Contact:
IBM
E-mail: extremeblue@info.ibm.com
www.ibm.com/extremeblue
www-913.ibm.com/employment/us/extremeblue/apply2.html

Visit Vault at **www.vault.com** for insider company profiles, expert advice, career message boards, expert resume reviews, the Vault Job Board and more.

V∧ULT CAREER LIBRARY **223**

Illinois General Assembly

 THE BUZZ
- "Inside Springfield's corridors of power"
- "Legislation in the Land of Lincoln"

 THE STATS

Industry(ies): Government

Location(s): Springfield, IL

Number of interns: *Annual*: 24 (20 legislative analysts with partisan leadership staffs; 3 research positions with the Legislative Research Unit (LRU); and 1 science writing position with the LRU)

Pay: Paid; $2,026/month. Health insurance provided; interns also receive 8 hours of graduate course credit in political studies through the University of Illinois-Springfield. Tuition and all fees are covered by the ILSIP program

Length of internship: 10.5 months

 **THE SCOOP**

The Illinois Legislative Staff Intern Program (ILSIP) is a collaborative effort funded by the Illinois General Assembly and administered through the University of Illinois at Springfield. Interns are recruited for positions as legislative analysts with the four partisan leadership staffs (House and Senate Democrats, House and Senate Republicans), as well as research positions with the LRU.

 ON THE JOB

Legislative interns analyze bills and budget requests, conduct research on policy issues, and handle press and constituent relations. Research interns at the LRU respond to requests from members of the General Assembly for information on particular policy issues. The science writing internship offers an opportunity for individuals with a natural science background to gain experience writing on technical topics.

 GETTING HIRED

Apply by: February 1. Download the required application form at: http://cspl.uis.edu/InstituteForLegislativeStudies/IllinoisLegislativeStaffInternProgram/.

Qualifications:
Open to college graduates from all academic backgrounds.

Contact:
Barbara Van Dyke-Brown
Illinois Legislative Staff Intern Program
University of Illinois at Springfield
One University Plaza, MS PAC 466
Springfield, IL 62703-5407
Phone: (217) 206-6579
Fax: (217) 206-6461 or (217) 206-6542
E-mail: bvand1@uis.edu
http://cspl.uis.edu/InstituteForLegislativeStudies/IllinoisLegislativeStaffInternProgram/

The Indianapolis Star

 THE BUZZ
- "Get your foot in the journalism door"

 THE STATS

Industry(ies): Journalism

Location(s): Indianapolis, IN

Number of interns: *Summer*: 20

Pay: Paid; $650/week

Length of internship: *Summer*: 10 weeks

 **THE SCOOP**

The Indianapolis Star has been accepting interns into its editorial offices since 1974. Now owned by Gannett Co. Inc., the program still exists as the Pulliam Journalism Fellowship. The newspaper covers features and issues that affect those living in and around Indianapolis, Ind. The *Star* has recently tackled issues including the uproar over the U.S.-led war on Iraq and Indianapolis' local crime rate.

 ON THE JOB

The paper hires fellows to work in the editorial offices of both the *Star* and the *Arizona Republic* in Phoenix. Responsibilities vary according to company needs and student qualifications, but may involve writing short features and news items, as well as copyediting and proofreading. The *Star* sometimes dips into its intern pool when making full-time hires.

 GETTING HIRED

Apply by: November 15. Send a resume and cover letter to the address below.

Qualifications:
Open to college freshmen, sophomores, juniors and seniors, as well as recent college graduates.

Contact:
Editor
The Indianapolis Star
307 North Pennsylvania Street
Indianapolis, IN 46204
Phone: (317) 444-4000
www.gannett.com/job/jobs/internships.htm
www.indystar.com/pjf

Indianapolis Zoological Society

THE BUZZ

- "Go on safari in downtown Indy"

 THE STATS

Industry(ies): Education; Environmental; Science/Research; Human Resources; Marketing; Horticulture

Location(s): Indianapolis, IN

Number of interns: *Annual*: 30

Pay: None

Length of internship: *Summer/fall/spring*: 12-14 weeks

 THE SCOOP

The Indianapolis Zoo is home to over 320 species of animals, including 14 endangered and three threatened species. Conservation is an important part of the zoo's mission; it is in the top one percentile of all conservation organizations in the United States. The Indianapolis Zoo manages a successful captive breeding program with 19 species in the AZA Species Survival Plan (SSP).

ON THE JOB

Internships are available in animal care, animal nutrition, environmental education, horticulture, human resources, marketing and veterinary science.

GETTING HIRED

Apply by: *Summer*: March 10; *fall*: July 10; *spring*: November 10. Applications will not be accepted after the above dates. Applications are accepted two months prior to the deadline dates listed below. Download application (available at www.indyzoo.com/employment/internship_app_procedures. asp) and send it, along with resume, cover letter, two letters of recommendation and a current transcript, to the address below.

Qualifications:
Open to college juniors and seniors, recent college graduates and grad students. Some positions are reserved for students enrolled in veterinary science programs.

Contact:
Manager, Volunteer Services
Indianapolis Zoological Society
1200 West Washington Street
Indianapolis, IN 46222
Phone: (317) 630-2041
Fax: (317) 630-5119
E-mail: volunteer@indyzoo.com
www.indyzoo.com/content.aspx?cid=272

Infosys

THE BUZZ

- "A sunnier version of Redmond"

THE STATS

Industry(ies): Management & Strategy Consulting; Operations & IT Consulting; Software; Technology

Location(s): Bangalore; Japan; UK; U.S.

Number of interns: *Annual*: 125

Pay: Monthly stipend; varies according to base location, depending on the cost of living. Roundtrip airfare for India; all expenses paid including living accommodations in fully furnished apartments, as well as food and transportation (cab) for India office interns

Length of internship: 8-24 weeks; available year-round. InStep program is flexible to meet academic schedules for schools around the globe

THE SCOOP

Infosys, a leader in consulting and information technology services, partners with Global 2000 companies to provide business consulting, systems integration, application development and product engineering services. With a startup capital of a mere $250 in 1981, today the company has more than $1.6 billion in revenues and no debt. Infosys staffs more than 40,000 employees in over 30 offices worldwide.

ON THE JOB

InStep, Infosys's internship program, is a unique opportunity to gain international work experience. Interns can work on high-quality, live technical and business projects, ranging from application development to business consulting in Infosys' offices worldwide. Student mentors help interns settle into Infosys' international working environment, while project mentors guide them through the internship assignment.

GETTING HIRED

Apply by: March 15. Log on to: www.infosys.com/instepweb and apply online.

Qualifications:
Open to college freshmen, sophomores, juniors and seniors, as well as grad students and PhD students from top academic institutions around the world.

Contact:
Nidhi Alexander, Program Manager – InStep
Infosys Technologies Limited
44, Electronics City, Hosur Road
Bangalore – 560 100, India
Phone: + 91 80 2852 0261, ext. 67835
Mobile: + 91 98 4411 6217
Fax: + 91 80 2852 2394
E-mail: nidhi_alexander@infosys.com
www.infosys.com/instepweb

Visit Vault at **www.vault.com** for insider company profiles, expert advice, career message boards, expert resume reviews, the Vault Job Board and more.

VAULT CAREER LIBRARY 225

INROADS

 **THE BUZZ**
- "Get on the fast track to corporate America"
- "Planting the seeds of diversity at top companies"

THE STATS

Industry(ies): All industries

Location(s): Multiple cities throughout U.S.; Mexico City; Saskatchewan; Toronto

Number of interns: *Annual*: 5,000

Pay: Paid; $10-$25+/hour

Length of internship: Renewable 10-12 week career experience; year-round professional coaching, leadership training and academic support; ongoing for 2-4 years

 **THE SCOOP**

INROADS is a nonprofit organization that trains more than 5,000 college students each year to think, plan and execute strategically. They arrange multi-year internships with leading companies in various industries. Among the many Fortune 500s that regularly host INROADS interns are Target, United Technologies, Deloitte, MetLife, Pfizer, Lockheed Martin, Liberty Mutual, GE and others. Over 60 percent of graduating INROADS interns receive offers for full-time positions with sponsor companies each year.

ON THE JOB

Upon acceptance to the INROADS process, students have access to the organization's extensive career development resources. INROADS offers workshops and training sessions in leadership development, career guidance, and business and management skills. Internships are arranged in the summers and continue until graduation. On the job, interns receive coaching from corporate mentors and have access to unmatched networking opportunities.

GETTING HIRED

Apply by: Rolling, but most summer positions tend to be filled by late December. An application form, transcript and official copies of SAT/ACT scores are required. Application may be submitted online. Visit www.INROADS.org for details.

Qualifications:
Open to students of color enrolled in or planning to attend a four-year college or university. Applicants must have a minimum 2.8/3.0 GPA, a combined SAT score of 1,000 or ACT score of 20, and at least two summers remaining before college graduation.

Contact:
INROADS, Inc.
10 South Broadway, Suite 300
St. Louis, MO 63102
Phone: (314) 241-7488
Fax: (314) 241-9325
E-mail: info@INROADS.org
www.INROADS.org/interns/internApply.jsp

Inside Edition

 THE BUZZ
- "Start a tabloid TV career"

THE STATS

Industry(ies): Broadcast & Entertainment; Internet; Journalism; New/Interactive Media

Location(s): Los Angeles, CA (see web site for details); New York, NY

Number of interns: Varies each year, but normally 6-8

Pay: None. Travel stipend

Length of internship: Varies with number of interns hired, usually one semester (8-10 weeks)

THE SCOOP

Celebrating its 15th year in 2002, *Inside Edition* is television's longest-running syndicated newsmagazine program. Deborah Norville anchors *Inside Edition*, and a slew of dedicated news correspondents are actively involved in all areas of broadcast including "investigations, exclusive interviews and human-interest stories." Recent pieces have included reality TV scams, campus pornography, sanitary conditions on cruise ships and male anorexia.

ON THE JOB

Interns function as assistants in the newsroom, production, promotions, investigative unit and technical operations. They "assist news staff with research, production, tape dubbing/screening and related clerical tasks." In addition, interns can work in the investigative news, promotions or engineering departments to gain specific production experience related to their interests.

GETTING HIRED

Apply by: *Summer*: April 15. Submit a resume and cover letter to the e-mail address below.

Qualifications:
Open to college juniors or seniors who have completed at least 30 semester hours pursuing a career in broadcast media or other liberal arts fields.

Contact:
Jill Darowski, Internship Coordinator
Fax: (212) 586-1218
E-mail: jdarowski@kingworld.com
www.insideedition.com
No phone calls or regular mail accepted

Institute for International Cooperation and Development

 THE BUZZ
- "Alleviate third-world poverty"
- "Standing shoulder-to-shoulder with the world's poor"

 THE STATS

Industry(ies): Nonprofit

Location(s): Williamstown, MA (HQ); programs are offered in Angola, Brazil, Mozambique, Nicaragua and South Africa

Number of interns: Approximately 10 per program; several programs offered each year

Pay: None; program fees range from $3,300-$3,800. Partial scholarships may be available for students with financial need

Length of internship: 6-20 months; available year-round

 THE SCOOP

The Institute for International Cooperation and Development (IICD) trains volunteers for placement abroad with community development projects. IICD was founded in 1987 and sends its volunteers to programs in Africa, South America and Central America.

 ON THE JOB

All IICD programs consist of an intensive predeparture training program in Williamstown, an international period spent working on a development project and a follow-up session devoted to public education. Volunteers work on a variety of projects such as promoting AIDS prevention and awareness in Southern Africa, training teachers and tutoring students in Mozambique, and building homes and community facilities in Brazil.

 GETTING HIRED

Apply by: Rolling. Upcoming program trips are listed on the web site. Call or e-mail for application form.

Qualifications:
Open to everyone 18 years of age and older. Applicants should have an interest in international development and the desire to work closely with people from other cultures.

Contact:
Institute for International Cooperation and Development
1117 Hancock Road
Williamstown, MA 01267
Phone: (413) 441-5126
Fax: (413) 458-3323
E-mail: info@iicd-volunteer.org
www.iicd-volunteer.org

Institute for Local Self-Reliance

 THE BUZZ
- "Strategies for healthy communities and a sustainable future"
- "Work to encourage sustainable economic development"

 THE STATS

Industry(ies): Environmental; Nonprofit

Location(s): Washington, DC

Number of interns: *Annual:* 2-3

Pay: None

Length of internship: 3 months minimum

 THE SCOOP

The Institute for Local Self-Reliance (ILSR) is a nonprofit research and education organization working to promote sustainable economic development. the Institute publishes articles and reports and provides technical assistance on issues such as alternative energy sources, recycling, waste reduction and green building. ILSR's New Rules Project examines ways to strengthen local government and give citizens a stronger voice in how their community is developed. Founded in 1974, the Institute has offices in Washington, DC, and Minneapolis, Minnesota.

ON THE JOB

ILSR seeks interns to assist with various research and technical assistance projects and publications. Currently, interns can work on the Waste to Wealth program, which promotes recycling and community economic development. Interns are also involved with community projects such as compiling a local "DC green pages" directory, a listing of environmentally responsible companies and organizations.

GETTING HIRED

Apply by: Rolling. Mail, fax or e-mail a cover letter, resume, and a brief writing sample to the address below. See www.ilsr.org/interns.html for details.

Qualifications:
Open to college freshmen, sophomores, juniors and seniors, recent college graduates and grad students.

Contact:
Internship Coordinator
Institute for Local Self-Reliance
927 15th Street, NW, 4th Floor
Washington, DC 20005
Phone: (202) 898-1610
Fax: (202) 898-1612
E-mail: info@ilsr.org
www.ilsr.org

Visit Vault at **www.vault.com** for insider company profiles, expert advice, career message boards, expert resume reviews, the Vault Job Board and more.

VAULT CAREER LIBRARY 227

Institute for Policy Studies

 THE BUZZ
- "The people's think tank"
- "Upset the status quo"

 THE STATS

Industry(ies): Nonprofit

Location(s): Washington, DC

Number of interns: *Spring/summer/fall*: 5-10 each; *winter*: 5-7. Note that Everett internships are only available in the summer

Pay: None; a $230/week stipend is available for IPS interns who participate in the Everett Public Service Internship Program (see www.everettinternships.org for more information)

Length of internship: 1-3 months (extremely flexible)

 THE SCOOP

The Institute for Policy Studies is one of the oldest progressive think tanks in the United States. Founded in 1963, IPS has been active in the civil rights, environmentalist, women's rights, anti-apartheid and fair trade movements.

 ON THE JOB

Internships are available with IPS campaigns working on a diverse set of issues. A full list and detailed descriptions of each IPS program can be found on the web site. Administrative assistant and public relations internships are also available for students who wish to gain a broad overview of the Institute's work.

 GETTING HIRED

Apply by: Rolling. A required application form is available from the web site. Also include resume, cover letter, two letters of recommendation, and a brief writing sample (three pages or less). Transcripts are not required but recommended. Apply by mail or fax only.

Qualifications:

Open to college freshmen, sophomores, juniors and seniors, recent college graduates and grad students. Some positions require foreign language skills, overseas experience and/or organizing experience. Position descriptions can be found on the IPS web site.

Contact:

Dorian Lipscombe
Institute for Policy Studies
733 15th Street, NW, Suite 1020
Washington, DC 20005
Phone: (202) 234-9382
Fax: (202) 387-7915
E-mail: dorian@igc.org
www.ips-dc.org/projects/internship.htm

Institute for the International Education of Students

 THE BUZZ
- "Selling students on study abroad"

 THE STATS

Industry(ies): Education

Location(s): Chicago, IL

Number of interns: *Summer*: 4

Pay: $2,000 stipend

Length of internship: *Summer*: 10 weeks

 **THE SCOOP**

The Institute for the International Education of Students (IES) is a nonprofit educational organization that has been running study abroad programs for the past 53 years. IES is a consortium of over 130 top U.S. colleges and universities and offers programs in 22 cities throughout Europe, Asia, Australia and South America. The Institute's programs provide a high-quality academic experience while also encouraging cross-cultural interaction and understanding.

 ON THE JOB

The internship program changes annually, but past positions have included IES's marketing department. Recent summer intern projects have included designing and implementing a student mail survey, researching IES's competitors and exploring marketing opportunities with campus media outlets. See the organization's web site for current opportunities.

 GETTING HIRED

Apply by: *Summer*: March 15. Apply by mail or e-mail only. Send a resume and a cover letter detailing why you are interested in IES, study abroad and marketing to the address below.

Qualifications:

Open to college freshmen, sophomores, juniors and seniors with demonstrated interest or experience in international travel and/or study abroad. Previous marketing or marketing-related experience is also required.

Contact:

Tara Gibney
IES Summer Marketing Internship
33 North LaSalle Street, 15th Floor
Chicago, IL 60602
E-mail: intern@IESabroad.org
www.iesabroad.org/info/summerintern.htm

Institute for Unpopular Culture

THE BUZZ
- "Aid and abet artistic rule-breakers"

THE STATS
Industry(ies): Art/Museum; Music/Records; Nonprofit

Location(s): San Francisco, CA

Number of interns: *Annual*: 20

Pay: None

Length of internship: 10-15 weeks; available year-round

THE SCOOP

Since 1989, the Institute for Unpopular Culture has supported emerging artists and promoted artistic attempts to challenge the status quo. IFUC tries to lessen the financial disparity between subversive artists and those who cater to public taste and opinion to survive, and offers legal support to censored artists. Among its list of "unpopular" artists are Holly Hughes, Dan Das Mann and Julia "Butterfly" Hill, the environmental activist who famously lived in a tree to protest the desecration of Northern California forests. The Institute's latest project is the Punk Rock Orchestra, a 50-plus piece classical orchestra that reinterprets classic punk tunes on symphonic instruments.

ON THE JOB

Interns work closely with the small staff. Some participate in graphic arts and promotion/marketing work. Interns perform research to support casework, assist artists and participate in fundraising, promotion, graphic art, marketing and administration.

GETTING HIRED

Apply by: Rolling. Send resume and cover letter to the address below.

Qualifications:
Open to college freshmen, sophomores, juniors and seniors, college graduates of any age and grad students.

Contact:
Internship Coordinator
The Institute for Unpopular Culture
1592 Union Street, #226
San Francisco, CA 94123-4309
Phone: (415) 986-4382
Fax: (815) 717-7790
E-mail: ifuc2003@yahoo.com
www.ifuc.org

Visit Vault at **www.vault.com** for insider company profiles, expert advice, career message boards, expert resume reviews, the Vault Job Board and more.

VAULT CAREER LIBRARY **229**

Institute of Cultural Affairs

 THE BUZZ

- "Be part of an international effort to bolster communities everywhere"

 THE STATS

Industry(ies): Nonprofit

Location(s): Chicago, IL; Phoenix, AZ; Seattle, WA; Washington, DC

Number of interns: *Summer*: 100; *fall*: 20; *winter*: 10; *spring*: 10

Pay: $1,000/month stipend

Length of internship: 6-12 months

 **THE SCOOP**

The Institute of Cultural Affairs is a private nonprofit dedicated to achieving positive social change by helping community members find their own solutions to problems they face, along with the means necessary to implement those solutions. By encouraging participation and creativity, ICA fosters team building and consensus-based decision making in communities around the country. The U.S. branch is part of the international organization (in Brussels, Belgium), which has 35 independent member chapters.

 ON THE JOB

Depending on offices' needs, interns are hired to work with many of ICA's programs. For example, interns work with the Youth as Facilitative Leaders program, assisting with training projects, office support and community outreach. Other interns might work with the director of Hispanic community programs to support Neighborhood Activity programming in several cities, doing marketing, community outreach and office work, and documenting results.

 GETTING HIRED

Apply by: Rolling. Check the web site for open positions: www.ica-usa.org/org/orgwork.html, and apply from there.

Qualifications:

Open to college freshmen, sophomores, juniors and seniors, recent college graduates and grad students. Some programs have specific qualifications (like language skills), while others do not. Check www.ica-usa.org/org/orgwork.html for more details.

Contact:

Chicago
4750 North Sheridan Road
Chicago, IL 60640
Phone: (773) 769-6363
Fax: (773) 769-1144
E-mail: Chicago@ica-usa.org

Seattle
215 NE 40th Street, #C-2
Seattle, WA 98105
Phone: (206) 323-2100
Fax: (206) 547-4057
E-mail: Seattle@ica-usa.org

Phoenix
4220 North 25th Street
Phoenix, AZ 85016
Phone: (602) 955-4811
Fax: (602) 954-0563
E-mail: Phoenix@ica-usa.org

Washington, DC
2000 P Street, NW, Suite 408
Washington, DC 20036
Phone: (202) 828-1008
Fax: (202) 828-1008
E-mail: Washington@ica-usa.org
www.ica-usa.org

Institute of Government

 THE BUZZ
- "The academic fast track for civic-minded law students"

THE STATS

Industry(ies): Education; Government; Law

Location(s): Chapel Hill, NC

Number of interns: *Summer*: 3-5

Pay: $3,900/month

Length of internship: *Summer*: Varies, usually 10 weeks. Interns must be able to work at least 6 weeks

 THE SCOOP

The Institute of Government, part of the University of North Carolina-Chapel Hill's School of Government, is a research and training organization dedicated to studying and improving local government. The Institute organizes over 200 classes and provides training for more than 14,000 North Carolina public officials each year. In addition to publishing its own research, the Institute provides extensive coverage of North Carolina legislation through its legislative reporting service.

ON THE JOB

The Institute of Government sponsors a summer law clerk program for outstanding law students interested in public administration issues. Clerks engage mainly in research and writing projects on legal issues and governmental affairs. All summer clerks are evaluated as possible candidates for any future vacancies that may occur on the Institute's faculty.

GETTING HIRED

Apply by: Rolling. Second-year law students are recruited during the fall; first-year students in the spring. The Institute conducts on-campus recruiting at many law schools and at the Equal Justice Works Career Fair in Washington, DC. Applicants who attend one of the schools not visited by Institute recruiters should send a letter of interest, resume, transcript and writing sample to the address below.

Qualifications:

Open to law students. The positions are usually for students who have completed their second year of studies, though first-year students are occasionally accepted. Summer law clerks may be considered for appointment to the Institute's faculty, should any vacancies occur, and thus should demonstrate outstanding academic achievement.

Contact:
Thomas H. Thornburg, Associate Dean
Institute of Government, School of Government
CB# 3330
The University of North Carolina at Chapel Hill
Chapel Hill, NC 27599
Phone: (919) 966-4377
Fax: (919) 962-0654
E-mail: thornburg@iogmail.iog.unc.edu
www.iog.unc.edu/about/employment/summer_clerks.html

Insurance Services Office

 THE BUZZ
- "Ensure yourself a fast start in the insurance business"
- "A proving ground for aspiring actuaries"

THE STATS

Industry(ies): Insurance

Location(s): Jersey City, NJ

Number of interns: *Annual*: usually 3-4

Pay: Paid; $650-$750/week

Length of internship: *Summer*: 12 weeks

THE SCOOP

The Insurance Services Office is one of the first and most trusted provider of products and services that help measure, manage, and reduce risk. ISO provides data, analytics and decision-support solutions to professionals in many fields, including insurance, finance, real estate, health services, government and human resources. Professionals use ISO's databases and services to classify and evaluate a variety of risks and detect potential fraud. In the U.S. and around the world, ISO's services help customers protect people, property and financial assets.

ON THE JOB

ISO accepts interns in its New Jersey office. Participants learn the basics of insurance information and get to do some real, hands-on actuarial work. Interns can also take the CAS exam and, if they pass, get retroactive pay increases. They work in Commerical Lines Information Division, Actuarial and Personal Lines Information Division Services, or Financial Analysis.

GETTING HIRED

Apply by: *Summer*: February 1. Send resume and cover letter to the address below.

Qualifications:

The program is open to undergraduate sophomores or juniors enrolled in math, statistics, actuarial science or any other major, but must have 18 to 24 math credits. A minimum 3.2 GPA and a 1300 SAT, or corresponding ACT score, are required.

Contact:
Garvin Whitfield II, PHR
Human Resources Representative
Insurance Services Office, Inc
545 Washington Boulevard
Jersey City, NJ 07310
Fax: (201) 469-4010
Email: gwhitfield@iso.com
www.iso.com

Visit Vault at **www.vault.com** for insider company profiles, expert advice, career message boards, expert resume reviews, the Vault Job Board and more.

V**A**ULT CAREER LIBRARY **231**

Intel

 THE BUZZ
- "King of the chips"
- "Executive-level perks for tech-savvy interns"

THE STATS

Industry(ies): Hardware; Semiconductors; Technology

Location(s): Austin, TX; Chandler, AZ; Colorado Springs, CO; DuPont, WA; Folsom, CA; Hillsboro, OR; Hudson, MA; Rio Rancho, NM; Santa Clara, CA; R&D Labs: Berkeley, CA; Cambridge, MA; Pittsburgh, PA; Seattle, WA

Number of interns: *Annual*: 1,200; *spring*: 150, *summer*: 925, and *fall:* 125

Pay: All positions are paid competitive salaries; amount varies with experience. Vacation and holiday time; credit toward sabbatical; relocation assistance; access to professional development training classes at Intel University; networking opportunities with Intel managers and other interns at informational sessions and social events

Length of internship: *Summer*: 10-12 weeks; *co-op*: 3-9 months; available year-round

THE SCOOP

Tech-giant Intel was founded in 1968 by Robert Noyce, Gordon Moore and Andy Grove. The company introduced the world's first microprocessor in 1971, and over the years has consistently been at the forefront of semiconductor technology. Today, Intel is the world's leading chipmaker, with an 80 percent market share of all new PCs sold. In addition to its industry-leading Pentium and Celeron processors, the company is also a major manufacturer of flash memory and motherboard chipsets.

ON THE JOB

Intel offers both traditional summer internships and longer-term co-op positions during the academic year. Internship and co-op placements are available in each of Intel's departments including integrated circuit engineering, hardware engineering, materials, finance, human resources, e-business and others. Complete descriptions of Intel's departments and career paths are available on their web site. Doctoral candidates are eligible to apply for internships at one of Intel's four research and development laboratories. More than 60 percent of Intel's interns accept a full-time position with the company upon graduation.

GETTING HIRED

Apply by: *Summer*: most interns recruited between January and March, though applications accepted year-round; *co-op*: rolling. Applications must be submitted online.

Qualifications:

Open to college freshmen, sophomores, juniors and seniors, and grad students with a GPA of 3.0 and above. We are seeing more demand for advanced degree interns. All applicants must be eligible to work in the U.S. Students applying for technical positions should be pursuing degrees in computer science, computer engineering, materials science, electrical engineering, physics, chemical engineering, mechanical engineering, industrial engineering or a

related discipline. Research interns at Intel Labs are usually PhD students, though occasionally MS or undergraduate students are accepted.

Contact:

Online application
www.intel.com/jobs/usa/students/

R&D internship at Intel Labs
www.intel-research.net/internships.asp

Interlocken at Windsor Mountain

 THE BUZZ

- "A unique educational experience – for the campers and the counselors"

 THE STATS

Industry(ies): Education

Location(s): Windsor, NH; various other locations worldwide for travel programs

Number of interns: *Summer*: 80

Pay: Stipend of $1,400-$2,500/summer. Room and board provided

Length of internship: *Summer*: 1-3 months

 THE SCOOP

Since 1961, Interlocken at Windsor Mountain has been organizing summer camps and travel outings for students from all over the world. All Interlocken programs offer students the chance to "learn by doing" and strive to increase environmental awareness and cross-cultural understanding.

 ON THE JOB

Interlocken seeks camp counselors and travel leaders with a broad array of skills. Staff members are needed with skills in diverse areas such as rock climbing, theater, swimming instruction, photography, cycling, Spanish and ESL.

GETTING HIRED

Apply by: Rolling. Recruiting begins each fall for the following summer. Download the application form on the web site and send it, along with three letters of recommendation, to the address below.

Qualifications:

Open to college freshmen, sophomores, juniors and seniors, recent college graduates and grad students. Camp counselors must be 19 years of age or older and have completed one year of college. Travel leaders must be at least 24 years old. Applicants should have previous experience working with children in a residential education and/or camp setting. Travel staff are required to be certified in CPR and first aid. Wilderness first responder training is required for wilderness adventure program staff. Interlocken provides training and certification classes at reduced rates prior to orientation in June.

Contact:
Interlocken Center at Windsor Mountain
19 Interlocken Way
Windsor, NH 03244
Phone: (603) 478-3166
Fax: (603) 478-5260
E-mail: tom@windsormountain.org
www.windsormountain.org/general/jobs.html

Visit Vault at **www.vault.com** for insider company profiles, expert advice, career message boards, expert resume reviews, the Vault Job Board and more.

VAULT CAREER LIBRARY **233**

International Broadcasting Bureau

 THE BUZZ
- "Help bring America's voice to the world"
- "Engineers and journalists both welcome in this DC agency"

 THE STATS

Industry(ies): Broadcast & Entertainment; Government; Journalism; New/Interactive Media

Location(s): Washington, DC

Number of interns: Varies

Pay: None

Length of internship: Flexible

 THE SCOOP

The International Broadcasting Bureau operates a network that includes radio (Voice of America, or VOA), television (WORLDNET), and Internet (voanews.com) news and features delivered in 55 languages to a worldwide audience of around 94 million. VOA began broadcasting in 1942 as a propaganda tool during World War II. Today, it is no longer used for those purposes, but rather as a means of providing American news and culture to an international audience. IBB also runs the Radio Free network.

 ON THE JOB

IBB offers four types of internships. VOA offers journalism internships that give students the opportunity to help produce live and taped broadcasts and prepare stories with professional journalists. The Special English internship program teaches students how to write news and features pieces using the limited vocabulary needed to broadcast to parts of the world where English is not the listeners' native language. IBB also hires interns to work in its public affairs office, giving students interested in PR a chance to work on publicizing VOA's work to an American audience. Finally, the engineering internship concentrates on the technical aspects of radio, television and Internet broadcasting.

💰 **GETTING HIRED**

Apply by: Rolling. Contact the correct person below via e-mail for application information.

Qualifications:
Open to all enrolled college freshmen, sophomores, juniors and seniors, college graduates and grad students.

Contact:
Journalism internship
Janice Albritton-Pollock
E-mail: jalbritt@ibb.gov

Special English internship
R. Gollust
E-mail: rgollust@voanews.com

Public affairs internship
Joe O'Connell
E-mail: jdoconne@ibb.gov

Engineering internship
Terry Balazs
E-mail: tbalazs@ibb.gov

International Broadcasting Bureau
Office of Public Affairs
330 Independence Avenue, SW
Washington, DC 20237
Phone: (202) 401-7000
Fax: (202) 619-1241
E-mail: pubaff@voa.gov
www.voa.gov/vacancies/personnel.html

International Center

 THE BUZZ
- "Help foster international good will among former foes"

 **THE STATS**

Industry(ies): Nonprofit

Location(s): Washington, DC

Number of interns: *Spring/summer/fall*: 2-3 per term

Pay: None. Students are reimbursed for out-of-pocket expenses incurred for office work

Length of internship: *Spring/summer/fall*: 10 weeks or more

THE SCOOP

Founded in 1977, The International Center is a nonprofit organization divided into two programs, the US-Vietnam Trade Council and the New Forests Project. The US-Vietnam Trade Council (USVTC) is dedicated to informing the press, Congress, U.S. government officials, nongovernmental organizations and the public on the impact of American foreign policy through research programs, hosting of foreign delegations and the publishing of briefing books. The aim of the New Forests project is to conserve and enhance ecosystems, and this is accomplished by supporting grassroots campaigns in agroforestry, reforestation, watershed protection, sanitation, and water and renewable energy intiatives. The International Center has sponsored more than 50 delegations of prominent Americans - including members of Congress, journalists, foundation trustees and state officials - to over 20 countries. Center delegations to Haiti, South Korea, the Philippines, Paraguay, El Salvador, Nicaragua, Afghanistan, Vietnam, Myanmar and the former Soviet Union have attracted major media coverage.

ON THE JOB

Interns work with one of the two International Center divisions. Interns with the New Forests Project work in a people-to-people, direct action program established in an effort to initiate deforestation and provide clean water services in developing countries. Since its inception, the New Forests Project has worked with more than 4,400 communities in 120 countries. Its goals are to provide farmers, community organizations and environmental groups with the training and materials necessary to begin successful reforestation projects and to protect their watersheds and other natural resources.

Interns also work with the USVTC. The USVTC has played a leadership role in rebuilding a relationship between the U.S. and Vietnam, contributing to normalization of relations and improving the bilateral trade and investment environment. USVTC played a key role in the negotiation and implementation of the U.S.-Vietnam Bilateral Trade Agreement and has been working closely with Vietnam on its next major step in economic integration with the world, accession to the World Trade Organization.

GETTING HIRED

Apply by: *Spring*: January 15; *summer*: May 31; *fall*: August 30.

Qualifications:
Open to college juniors and seniors. Exceptional students entering

their sophomore year may be considered. The Center also welcomes applications from graduate students and students holding an undergraduate degree who wish to gain experience before pursuing a career.

Contact:
International Center
731 Eighth Street, SE
Washington, DC 20003

For the US-Vietnam Trade Council:
Neo Tran
Phone: (202)547-3800 ext. 115
Neo.tran@usvtc.org
www.usvtc.org

For the New Forests Project:
Michelle Gaudet
Phone (202) 537-3800 ext. 111
mgaudet@newforests.org
www.newforestsproject.com

Visit Vault at **www.vault.com** for insider company profiles, expert advice, career message boards, expert resume reviews, the Vault Job Board and more.

 CAREER LIBRARY **235**

International Creative Management

 THE BUZZ
- "Fetch coffee, run errands...and become an agent to A-list stars"
- "High-energy, people-persons wanted"

 **THE STATS**

Industry(ies): Broadcast & Entertainment; Film; Music/Records

Location(s): Los Angeles, CA; New York, NY

Number of interns: *Summer*: 200-250

Pay: None. Interns are first in line to become agent trainees

Length of internship: Minimum 4-week commitment

 THE SCOOP

So you want to be an agent to the stars? International Creative Management, formed in 1975 through a merger of The International Famous Agency and The Creative Management Association, can help get you there. The company has offices in Los Angeles and New York City. ICM represents professionals in show business, including producers, directors, actors, promoters and publishers. Its subsidiary, IMCA, represents talent in the classical music industry.

 ON THE JOB

Only the Los Angeles office accepts interns. Agent trainee positions are available on both coasts. The stars – Cameron Diaz, 98 Degrees, Denzel Washington, Julia Roberts, and so many more – are glamorous, even if the work isn't. Interns become assistants to assistants, handling clerical and administrative duties. But according to former participants, interns are first in line for agent training to eventually become full-fledged agents.

GETTING HIRED

Apply by: *Summer*: March 1. Send resume and cover letter to the appropriate address below.

Qualifications:
Open to college freshmen, sophomores, juniors and seniors, college graduates and grad students. No specific majors are preferred, but extroverted personalities are a plus.

Contact:
Internship Coordinator
8942 Wilshire Blvd.
Beverly Hills, CA 90211
www.icmtalent.com

Agent Trainee Coordinator
40 West 57th Street
New York, NY 10019
Phone: (212) 556-5600

International Foundation for Education & Self-Help

 THE BUZZ
 "Empowering African communities"

 **THE STATS**

Industry(ies): Nonprofit

Location(s): Various countries in sub-Saharan Africa

Number of interns: *Annual*: 1-10, depending on availability of funding

Pay: Paid; $800/month. Health insurance; travel expenses

Length of internship: 9 months

 THE SCOOP

The International Foundation for Education & Self-Help (IFESH) is a nonprofit, charitable organization that works to improve living conditions in sub-Saharan Africa. IFESH organizes programs aimed at reducing hunger and poverty, increasing literacy, providing health care and fostering increased cultural and economic relations between Africans and Americans. The International Fellows Program was established in 1987 to give college and graduate students the chance to work with an international development organization in sub-Saharan Africa.

 ON THE JOB

Fellows are placed with an international non-governmental organization (NGO) such as Save the Children, Africare, UNICEF or CARE and take part in community-based development activities. Each fellowship experience is unique, but students typically work on projects such as writing grant proposals, conducting community health surveys, implementing micro-lending programs or establishing local computer centers. All IFESH fellows participate in a one-week training and orientation session in Phoenix prior to departure.

GETTING HIRED

Apply by: February 28. An application form, letter of interest, transcript and three letters of recommendation are required. Write to address below for application.

Qualifications:
Open to college graduates and graduate students. Applicants must be U.S. citizens.

Contact:
Chair, Selection Committee
International Fellows Program
International Foundation for Education & Self-Help
5040 East Shea Blvd., Suite 260
Phoenix, AZ 85254
Phone: (480) 443-1800
Fax: (480) 443-1824
E-mail: ifesh@ifesh.org
www.ifesh.org

International Labour Organization

 THE BUZZ
- "Promote workers' rights and prevent exploitation"
- "Setting the social floor for globalization"

 THE STATS

Industry(ies): Government; Law; Nonprofit

Location(s): New York, NY; Washington, DC; Geneva

Number of interns: *Annual*: 130

Pay: None. Cost of local transportation reimbursed

Length of internship: *Spring/summer/fall*: 1 month minimum (usually 3-5 months)

 **THE SCOOP**

The International Labour Organization is the United Nations agency responsible for promoting social justice and protecting workers' rights. The organization was created by the Treaty of Versailles in 1919 and joined the UN system in 1946. The ILO Representation at the ILO's annual International Labour Conference includes delegates from governments, labor unions and employers.

 ON THE JOB

Internships are available in ILO departments such as international labor standards, job creation and enterprise development, social security, international migration and dozens of others. The ILO web site has details on the structure of the organization and the functions of each department. Applicants specify the ILO department in which they wish to work on their application. Interns are assigned a work plan related to their area of study. Typical duties may include analyzing data, writing reports, drafting legal documents and compiling statistics.

 GETTING HIRED

Apply by: *Spring*: October 1; *summer*: March 1; *fall*: June 1. For internships at the ILO headquarters in Geneva, apply online. For internships at one of the field locations, send resume directly to that office. Addresses for U.S. field offices in New York and Washington are listed below.

Qualifications:

Open to college sophomores, juniors and seniors, as well as grad students. Applicants must be between the ages of 20 and 35 and proficient in at least one of the ILO's official languages (English, Spanish, French). Interns should have an academic background in economic statistics, labor law, management development, occupational safety, human resources, finance or another field related to the ILO's work.

Contact:
Geneva internship (apply online)
www.ilo.org/public/english/bureau/pers/vacancy/intern.htm

New York internship
Internship Coordinator
ILO Liaison Office with the United Nations
220 East 42nd Street, Suite 3101
New York, NY 10017
Phone: (212) 697-0150

Washington internship
Internship Coordinator
ILO Branch Office in Washington
1828 L Street, NW, Suite 600
Washington, DC 20036
Phone: (202) 653-7652

Visit Vault at **www.vault.com** for insider company profiles, expert advice, career message boards, expert resume reviews, the Vault Job Board and more.

VAULT CAREER LIBRARY **237**

International Management Group

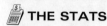 **THE BUZZ**

- "Work with top athletes and entertainers"
- "Learn how to manage a talent agency"

 THE STATS

Industry(ies): Broadcast & Entertainment; Fashion; Sports

Location(s): New York, NY; Cleveland, OH

Number of interns: *Annual*: 70

Pay: None

Length of internship: *Summer*: 8 weeks; *spring/fall*: 3 months

 THE SCOOP

The International Management Group is the world's largest sports marketing and management agency, representing athletes, broadcasters, models, writers and performing artists. IMG's client list includes Tiger Woods, Peyton Manning, Serena Williams and Heidi Klum. The company also owns and operates sports academies, arranges licensing deals, designs golf courses and promotes sporting events.

ON THE JOB

Internship placements are available in various IMG departments, including motorsports, racquet sports, golf, accounting, human resources, creative services, sales, marketing, investment advice, consulting and TWI productions. Most positions tend to be in the field of accounting or finance. Interns will assist with the daily operations of their assigned department and may also have the opportunity to help in organizing IMG events.

GETTING HIRED

Apply by: *Summer*: February 15; *spring/fall*: rolling. Send resume, and cover letter by mail or e-mail to the address below. Indicate your department placement preference in your cover letter. Prior to interviews, applicants must provide proof that their college will give academic credit for the internship.

Qualifications:

Open to college freshmen, sophomores, juniors and seniors, as well as grad students.

Contact:

Cleveland and branch locations other than New York
Sarah Thomas
IMG Center
1360 East 9th Street, Suite 100
Cleveland, OH 44114
E-mail: interns@imgworld.com

New York office
New York Internship Committee
IMG
825 7th Avenue, 8th floor
New York, NY 10019
E-mail: NY-Interns@imgworld.com
www.imgworld.com

The International Partnership for Service-Learning and Leadership

 THE BUZZ

- "Bring special ed around the globe"

 THE STATS

Industry(ies): Education

Location(s): International locations and Lakota Nation USA

Number of interns: *Annual*: around 160 (no limit)

Pay: None. Cost to interns varies depending on where they intern (typical semester is $9,000-$12,000); financial aid is available

Length of internship: 3 weeks-1 year

 THE SCOOP

The International Partnership for Service-Learning and Leadership (IPSL) is a unique study abroad/internship program allowing students to experience the host country through volunteer service and academic study. Over 4,000 students from 200 U.S. colleges/universities and 35 higher education institutions in 25 foreign countries have participated in the program since it began in 1982.

ON THE JOB

Students devote 15 to 20 hours per week to the community service internship while engaging in a rigorous academic program. Students serve individuals with special needs in clinics, residential settings, schools and workshops. In addition to regular programs, IPSL offers special education internships for autism, cerebral palsy, emotional disorders, fetal alcohol syndrome, learning disabilities, mental retardation, physical disabilities and visual impairments. Related coursework enhances the students' knowledge of the country, such as culture and civilization, ethnography, language, religion, and political and social issues.

GETTING HIRED

Apply by: *Summer*: March 15; *fall*: June 1, except for the Phillipines (March 15) and India (May 1); *spring*: November 1, except.for the Phillipins (September 1), India (October 1) and the Lakota Nation (December 15). Application available online at: www.ipsl.org/application/instructions.html.

Qualifications:

Open to college freshmen, sophomores, juniors and seniors, as well as college graduates from any nation. Qualified high school students are also accepted.

Contact:

The International Partnership for Service-Learning and Leadership
815 Second Avenue
New York, NY 10017
Phone: (212) 986-0989
Fax: (212) 986-5039
E-mail: info@ipsl.org
www.ipsl.org

International Planned Parenthood Association

 THE BUZZ
- "Help educate the public on some of today's most urgent health issues"
- "Promote safe sex worldwide"

 THE STATS

Industry(ies): Education; Health Care; Public Relations

Location(s): Chicago, IL; New York, NY; San Francisco, CA; Washington DC

Number of interns: *Annual*: Usually 10

Pay: None; academic credit available

Length of internship: 1 semester, usually only in the summer

 THE SCOOP

International Planned Parenthood is concerned with women's health and teaching safe sex. The organization also spends a good deal of time fighting for AIDS research. International Planned Parenthood was founded in 1952 in Bombay, India, as a joint effort between India, Germany, Hong Kong, The Netherlands, Singapore, Sweden, the United Kingdom and the United States.

 ON THE JOB

Interns work on all aspects of the organization's public relations, such as press releases and its web sites (plannedparenthood.org is the master site, and is constantly updated). Positions in international locations may be available, as IPP continues to extend its reach.

 GETTING HIRED

Apply by: Rolling. Send resume and cover letter to the address below.

Qualifications:
Open to college freshmen, sophomores, juniors and seniors, recent college graduates and grad students. Experience is a plus. Majors and strong backgrounds in politics and/or humanities (especially English literature, philosophy, political science and related fields) have an edge. Administrative or other office experience is helpful, but not required. Writing ability is essential.

Contact:
Internship Coordinator
International Planned Parenthood Federation
434 West 33rd Street
New York, NY 10001
Phone: (212) 541-7800
Fax: (212) 245-1845
E-mail: communications@ppfa.org
www.plannedparenthood.org

International Radio and Television Society Foundation

 THE BUZZ
- "Could be the foundation for great career in media"
- "Where the network moguls come to network"

 THE STATS

Industry(ies): Advertising; Broadcast & Entertainment; Internet; Journalism; Music/Records; New/Interactive Media

Location(s): New York, NY

Number of interns: *Summer*: 25-35

Pay: None. Living allowance; housing and travel covered

Length of internship: *Summer*: 9 weeks

 **THE SCOOP**

The International Radio and Television Society Foundation is a unique forum that unites voices from each of the sectors of today's electronic media. IRTS counts representatives from broadcast networks, radio stations, advertising agencies, local television stations, cable operators and Web publishers among its members. The Society offers educational luncheons, workshops and seminars to media professionals, academics, students and members of the public on contemporary issues in communications. The IRTS Summer Fellowship Program provides career advice and practical experience for students aspiring to a career in media.

 ON THE JOB

IRTS Summer Fellows are placed with a New York-based media company for a two-month summer internship. Internship opportunities are available in a variety of different roles, including: Television/Radio News, Productions, Commercial Production, Standards & Practices, Sales & Marketing, Entertainment PR, Research, Media Planning/Buying, Television/Radio Programming and others. All IRTS Fellows participate in a one-week orientation program prior to the start of their internships.

 GETTING HIRED

Apply by: *Summer*: December 1. The application form is available on the web site. Apply by e-mail only.

Qualifications:
Open to college juniors, seniors and grad students. Applicants do not have to be communications majors, but should have demonstrated interest in the field through extracurricular activities or prior experience.

Contact:
International Radio & Television Society Foundation, Inc.
420 Lexington Avenue, Suite 1601
New York, NY 10170
Phone: (212) 867-6650
Fax: (212) 867-6653
E-mail: apply@irts.org
www.irts.org

Visit Vault at **www.vault.com** for insider company profiles, expert advice, career message boards, expert resume reviews, the Vault Job Board and more.

V/\ULT CAREER LIBRARY **239**

International Relations Center

THE BUZZ
- "Cooperation, not confrontation"
- "A civics lesson for the global citizen"

THE STATS

Industry(ies): Nonprofit

Location(s): Silver City, NM

Number of interns: *Annual*: 1-4

Pay: None. Housing provided

Length of internship: 12 weeks minimum; available year-round

THE SCOOP

The International Relations Center, formerly the Interhemispheric Resource Center, is a nonprofit research organization dedicated to analyzing U.S. foreign policy and promoting a more responsible role for the United States in world affairs. The IRC's efforts are organized into three main projects: the Americas Program, which analyzes relations between the U.S. and Latin America; the Global Affairs Program, which looks at the role of the U.S. and international organizations in the wider realm of world politics (the Foreign Policy in Focus Project, part of the Global Affairs Program, is a joint effort between the IRC and the Washington-based Institute for Policy Studies); and Right Web, the mission of which is to "expose the architecture of power that's changing our world." Right Web explores the many ties that link the right-wing movement's main players, organizations and corporate supporters, hoping to add to the growing national movement of concerned citizens who are working to check the rightward drift of the country.

The IRC's books, briefs, reports and various other publications are used by dozens of progressive activist groups in their outreach and public education efforts.

ON THE JOB

Internships at the IRC provide the opportunity to contribute to one of the center's current books or other publications. Interns provide support to IRC analysts through Web-based research and database administration. Though some administrative duties are, at times, required, the IRC strives to create a meaningful and substantive experience for its interns.

GETTING HIRED

Apply by: Rolling. Include three references (two from professors, if possible) and three writing samples on topics relevant to the internship with the application. Send all application materials together as one package to the address below.

Qualification:

Open to college freshmen, sophomores, juniors and seniors, recent college graduates and grad students. A background in U.S. foreign policy, international affairs, U.S.-Latin American relations or a similar field is preferred. Being bilingual (English and Spanish) is a plus.

Contact:
Internship Coordinator
International Relations Center
P.O. Box 2178
Silver City, NM 88062
Phone: (505) 388-0208
Fax: (505) 388-0619
E-mail: siri@irc-online.org
www.irc-online.org

International Sculpture Center

THE BUZZ

- "Help bring sculpted beauty to the world"

THE STATS

Industry(ies): Art/Museum; Nonprofit

Location(s): Hamilton, NJ

Number of interns: *Annual*: Usually 6-10

Pay: Paid; $8/hour. Academic credit.

Length of internship: *New Jersey*: 1 semester (summer/spring/winter); *Minnesota*: 1 semester (summer)

 THE SCOOP

A nonprofit dedicated to sculpting (shocker), the International Sculpture Center was founded in 1960 and is made up of sculptors, collectors, patrons, developers, curators and others with an avid interest in the art form. ISC seeks to expand knowledge and appreciation of sculpture.

ON THE JOB

Interns work on press releases, client contact, donor contact and fundraising, and all integral parts of the organization. Interns also act as web and portfolio assitants, as administrative assistants, and as assistants to the Student Awards program, which gives awards annually. They also assist at conferences, events, and with development and research. In the process, interns get a chance to show their abilities and have a shot at the artist intern program, where they can hone their skills under the guidance of successful sculptors.

GETTING HIRED

Apply by: Rolling.

Qualifications:
Open to college freshmen, sophomores, juniors and seniors, college graduates and grad students. Applicants must submit 12 slides and a slide script, as well as two references. No electronic applications are accepted.

Contact:
Johannah Hutchison
Managing Director
International Sculpture Center
Publisher Sculpture Magazine
14 Fairgrounds Road, Suite B
Hamilton, NJ 08619
Phone: (609) 689-1051 ext. 304
Fax: (609) 689-1061
E-mail: isc@sculpture.org
www.sculpture.org

Internships in Francophone Europe

THE BUZZ

- "Experience France the way the French do"

THE STATS

Industry(ies): Advertising; Art/Museum; Broadcast & Entertainment; Chemicals; Commercial Banking; Consumer Products; Education; Energy/Utilities; Environmental; Fashion; Film; Financial Services; Food & Beverage; Government; Hospitality; Internet; Investment Banking; Journalism; Music/Records; New/Interactive Media; Nonprofit; Publishing; Retail; Telecom & Wireless; Tourism/Recreation

Location(s): Paris (HQ)

Number of interns: Varies

Pay: None. Interns are responsible for expenses (e.g., travel, accommodations). Program cost: 6,500 EUR; housing cost: an additional 2,200 EUR (approx.)

Length of internship: 18-weeks (5 weeks intensive preparation; 1 week vacation; 12 weeks full-time internship); Offered in the spring (late January) and fall (late August)

THE SCOOP

Founded in 1987 by a French-American couple wanting to improve cultural relations, Internships in Francophone Europe is a nonprofit organization that aims to enable American college students to experience France as a native would. The program's objective is to integrate the chosen students into French society so that they acquire an appreciation of it.

ON THE JOB

Those with French language competence (speaking, comprehension) can be placed in French-speaking regions throughout Paris. Most interns work in the public sector, though, "IFE is not allergic to the private sector." Interns work for various companies, and duties may include administrative work, travel, research or other assigned tasks.

GETTING HIRED

Apply by: Rolling. *Fall*: May 1; *spring*: November 1. Send the online application from http://ifeparis.org/apply.htm, and other required materials (see application for details), to the address below.

Qualifications:
Open to all undergraduates. Applicants must be at least 18 years of age and enrolled in college. They also must have French language competence (fluency is not a requirement).

Contact:
Internships in Francophone Europe
4 Boulevard Edgar Quinet
75014 Paris, France
Phone: (33-1) 43-21-78-07
Fax: (33-1) 42-79-94-13
E-mail: ife@ifeparis.org
http://ifeparis.org/apply.htm

Visit Vault at **www.vault.com** for insider company profiles, expert advice, career message boards, expert resume reviews, the Vault Job Board and more.

VAULT CAREER LIBRARY **241**

Internships International

 THE BUZZ
- "Pay somebody to find you your ideal international gig"

 THE STATS

Industry(ies): All industries

Location(s): Australia (multiple cities); China (Beijing, Shanghai); Budapest; Buenos Aires; Ecuador; Florence; Kenya; London; Paris; Spain (Bilbao, Madrid); Santiago; Scotland; Singapore; South Africa

Number of interns: *Summer*: 50; *fall*: 10; *winter*: 10; *spring*: 10

Pay: None. Applicants must pay a placement fee of $1,100

Length of internship: 8-12 weeks, possibly longer

 **THE SCOOP**

Internships International matches rising college seniors, those approaching graduation or graduates with professional international internships to help them reach their career needs and goals.

ON THE JOB

"You tell us what you want to do, where you want to do it, how long you want to do it, and when you want to do it. Then we find you a full-time, professional, nonpaying internship in any of the above locations."

GETTING HIRED

Apply by: Rolling. Download the application from www.internshipsinternational.org. Send a statement of purpose, two written recommendations, college transcript, resume, two photos and placement fee check. Phone interview required.

Qualifications:
Open to college seniors, recent college graduates and graduate students.

Contact:
January-May
Internships International, LLC
1612 Oberlin Road, #5
Raleigh, NC 27608
Phone: (919) 832-1575

June-December
Internships International, LLC
P.O. Box 480
23 Reed Road
Woolwich, ME 04579
Phone/Fax: (207) 442-7942
E-mail: internshipsinternational@gmail.com
www.internshipsinternational.org

INTERNSHIP PROFILES:

J

J. Paul Getty Trust

 THE BUZZ
- "Gorgeous views. Gorgeous art. Can you beat it?"

THE STATS

Industry(ies): Art/Museum; Education

Location(s): Los Angeles, CA

Number of interns: *Graduate program*: 20; *undergraduate program*: 20

Pay: Paid; *graduate*: $26,000/year plus health benefits; *undergraduate*: $3,500/summer

Length of internship: *Graduate*: 1 year, full-time; *undergraduate*: 10 weeks (summer)

THE SCOOP

The J. Paul Getty Trust studies all dimensions of visual arts through its museum, research institute, conservation institute, grant programs and leadership institute, and educates the public. Opened in 1997, the Getty Center is located in a stunning building overlooking Los Angeles. The museum – founded in 1953 – houses antiquities, drawings, manuscripts, paintings, photographs and sculptures. At his death in 1976, the Trust's founder, J. Paul Getty, was the richest man in the world, his fortune made in the oil industry.

ON THE JOB

The Getty Trust sponsors three different internship programs. Graduate students studying visual arts can intern at the museum, where they work in curatorial, education, conservation, research, public programs and information management. Through the Multicultural Undergraduate Summer Internships, college students of color can work in various administrative roles – conservation, collections, library, publications, education, etc. – at Getty Trust. Finally, the Trust sponsors the Multicultural Undergraduate Internship to Los Angeles Museums and Visual Arts Organizations program, which is similar to the other undergraduate program but allows interns to work at various arts institutions in Los Angeles.

GETTING HIRED

Apply by: *Graduate*: December 15; *Multicultural Undergraduate Summer Internship*: March 1; *Multicultural Undergraduate Internship to L.A. Museums and Visual Arts Organizations*: February 1. Online application for Graduate Program: www.getty.edu/grants/pdfs/Graduate_Internship_Application_2005.pdf. Online applications for undergraduate programs: www.getty.edu/grants/education/multicultural_getty.html, www.getty.edu/grants/education/multicultural_la.html.

Qualifications:

Graduate program: open to graduate students of all nationalities. Students must either be currently enrolled in a graduate program leading to an advanced degree in a field relevant to the internship(s) for which they are applying or have completed a relevant graduate degree in 2003 or later.

Undergraduate programs: open to undergraduate sophomores, juniors and seniors currently enrolled in a college or residing in Los Angeles County. Applicants must be members of groups currently underrepresented in museum professions and fields related to the visual arts and humanities (African American, Asian, Latino/Hispanic, Native American, and Pacific Islander). Candidates are sought from all areas of undergraduate study, including the sciences and technology, and are not required to have demonstrated a previous commitment to the visual arts.

Contact:
Attention: Graduate Internships or Multicultural Undergraduate Summer Internships or Multicultural Undergraduate Internships to Los Angeles Museums and Visual Arts Organizations
The Getty Grant Program
1200 Getty Center Drive, Suite 800
Los Angeles, CA 90049-1685
Phone: (310) 440-7320
Fax: (310) 440-7703
E-mail: gradinterns@getty.edu or summerinterns@getty.edu
www.getty.edu/about/opportunities/intern_opps.html

J. Walter Thompson

- "Anthropologists first, advertising people second"
- "Influence the world to think more creatively"

📟 THE STATS

Industry(ies): Advertising

Location(s): Atlanta, GA; Chicago, IL; Detroit, MI; Houston, TX; Los Angeles, CA; New York, NY; San Francisco, CA

Number of interns: Varies

Pay: Paid; amount varies with position

Length of internship: Varies

🖊 THE SCOOP

"Built Ford Tough," "The Few, the Proud, the Marines," "My bologna has a first name...," "That's Brisk, Baby." If these well-known taglines are a fabric of your culture, thank the folks at J. Walter Thompson who have been brand-building advertising specialists since 1864. The company is now an international communications firm, with more than 8,500 employees worldwide.

🏙 ON THE JOB

JWT's interns gain hands-on insight into the advertising industry and day-to-day business. They're mentored by and learn from seasoned professionals, and will have the opportunity to get involved in "real" work.

💰 GETTING HIRED

Apply by: Rolling. Each office recruits individually. Search for open positions and submit your resume online at www.jwt.com.

Qualifications:
Most internships are open to college seniors and graduate students. Go to the company's web site, https://recruitmax. jwt.com/ENG/candidates, for more details on open positions.

Contact:
Internship Coordinator
J. Walter Thompson U.S.A., Inc.
466 Lexington Avenue
New York, NY 10017
Phone: (212) 210-7000
Fax: (212) 210-7770
www.jwt.com

Jacob's Pillow Dance Festival

- "Dance and artistic expression in rural Massachusetts"
- "Many interns have graduated to full-time staff"

📟 THE STATS

Industry(ies): Theater/Performing Arts

Location(s): Becket, MA

Number of interns: *Summer*: 30; *fall/winter/spring*: varies

Pay: *Summer*: $500 stipend; free room and board; may qualify for academic credit. *Fall/winter/spring*: varies; academic credit available

Length of internship: *Summer*: 15 weeks; *fall/winter/spring*: flexible

🖊 THE SCOOP

Jacob's Pillow, the first American dance festival and one of the most acclaimed international dance festivals in the world, is now celebrating its 75th anniversary. It draws about 83,000 visitors annually to its performances, lectures, work-in-progress showings, exhibitions, dance classes and other events. Over 100 professional dancers and choreographers from all over the world perform in the festival.

🏙 ON THE JOB

Thirty summer positions are available in archives/preservation, business, development (institutional and individual support), education, general management, graphic design, editorial, press, operations, photojournalism, technical theater production, ticket services/accounting and analysis, ticket services (house management and development), and video documentation.

Full- and part-time internships for fall, winter and spring can be tailored to meet academic credit needs and individual interests. Dates and times are flexible.

💰 GETTING HIRED

Apply by: Please check www.jacobspillow.org for application details. Applications should be sent by February 9, 2007 for priority consideration, and will be accepted through March 2, 2007. Send a cover letter, resume, two letters of recommendation and contact information for two work-related references. Applicants for marketing, development, education, and general management must submit two writing samples. Applicants for graphic design and photojournalism must submit portfolios. If applying for more than one area, please list in order of preference.

Qualifications:
Open to high school graduates, college freshmen, sophomores, juniors and seniors, recent college graduates and grad students.

Contact:
The Intern Program at Jacob's Pillow
358 George Carter Road
Becket, MA 01223
Phone: (413) 243-9919
Fax: (413) 243-4744
E-mail: info@jacobspillow.org
www.jacobspillow.org

Visit Vault at **www.vault.com** for insider company profiles, expert advice, career message boards, expert resume reviews, the Vault Job Board and more.

VAULT CAREER LIBRARY 245

Japan-America Society of Washington, Inc.

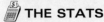 **THE BUZZ**

- "Bridge the gap between Japan and America"

 THE STATS

Industry(ies): Education; Nonprofit; Tourism/Recreation

Location(s): Washington, DC

Number of interns: *Annual*: 8; *spring/summer/fall*: 2-3 each

Pay: None. Attend Cherry Blossom festival, Japanese school, receptions with dignitaries; meet influential players in the DC area

Length of internship: *Fall/spring/summer*: 6-week minimum

 THE SCOOP

Founded in 1957, the Japan-America Society of Washington, Inc., is an educational and cultural organization that serves individuals and institutions with an interest in Japan and U.S.-Japan relations. It acts as the primary forum for the Mid-Atlantic region in promoting awareness of American and Japanese relations through cultural and public affairs, as well as through educational programs.

ON THE JOB

Interns learn about the inner workings of a small nonprofit office through projects designed to promote understanding of issues concerning U.S.-Japan relations. They perform basic clerical duties, compile data, aid research, proofread publications and assist with corporate and public affairs programs, annual fundraising events and educational outreach efforts. Administrative tasks include entering data of events attendees, answering questions about events via e-mail or telephone, assisting with permits needed for large events, developing and designing signage for events, and helping to organize and assisting participants during events.

GETTING HIRED

Apply by: *Spring*: November 15; *summer*: March 15; *fall*: July 15. Download application from www.us-japan.org/dc/. Send completed application, along with resume and cover letter, to the address below.

Qualifications:
Open to college freshmen, sophomores, juniors and seniors, and grad students.

Contact:
JASW Internship Program
Japan-America Society of Washington, DC
1819 L Street, NW, 1B Level
Washington, DC 20036
Phone: (202) 833-2210
Fax: (202) 833-2456
E-mail: jaswdc@us-japan.org
www.us-japan.org/dc

JCPenney Company Inc.

 THE BUZZ

- "'It's all inside' this internship"
- "Great business experience at an iconic American retailer"

 THE STATS

Industry(ies): Fashion; Retail

Location(s): Allentown, PA; Bronx, NY; Cedar Hill, TX; Columbus, OH; Dallas, TX; Kennewick, WA; Knoxville, TN; Langhorne, PA; Plano, TX; Warwick, RI; Wayne, NJ; 1,100 stores nationwide

Number of interns: *Summer*: 250

Pay: Paid; $11.50/hour

Length of internship: *Summer*: 10 weeks; 40 hours/week (some nights and weekends)

 THE SCOOP

James Cash Penney opened his first shop, Golden Rule Store, in 1902. Since then, JCPenney has become an American department store institution. The chain still follows its founder's philosophy, "Success will always be measured by the extent to which we serve the buying public." Today, his empire has grown to 1,100 stores across the U.S. and $349 million in profit at the end of last year's fourth fiscal quarter.

ON THE JOB

Interns can work in various departments, including information technology, merchandising, store management, marketing, accounting and many others, at one of the company's many locations. Responsibilities vary with position, but may include assisting store managers, crunching numbers, updating the web site and maintaining computer systems.

 GETTING HIRED

Apply by: March 1, but the company suggests early application is best. Apply online for each specific placement. See jcpenney.recruitmax.com/candidates/default.cfm for available positions and locations.

Qualifications:
Open to college juniors going into their senior year. Minimum 3.0 GPA required. Business, sales or marketing majors preferred. Retail experience is a plus.

Contact:
E-mail: jcpcr@jcpenney.com
jcpenney.recruitmax.com/candidates/default.cfm

Jim Henson Company

 THE BUZZ
- "Work with Kermie, Big Bird and Elmo"

 **THE STATS**

Industry(ies): Broadcast & Entertainment; Education

Location(s): Los Angeles, CA (HQ)

Number of interns: *Annual*: 25

Pay: None; academic credit

Length of internship: *Summer*: 10-16 weeks; *fall*: 12-16 weeks; *spring*: 12-16 weeks

 **THE SCOOP**

The Jim Henson Company redefines family entertainment, making it creatively educational and interesting to all members of the family. Henson, the late puppeteer most famous for creating the Muppets, founded the company 48 years ago. Today it's a multimedia production company headquartered in L.A.'s Charlie Chaplin Studios, with offices in New York and London.

ON THE JOB

Film/TV Development Interns support the creative team at the Jim Henson Company in its development of fantasy films and television programming. Interns read scripts and books, write materials and complete research for various projects. They also compile artwork and pitch materials. Interns do some office support work and assist executives.

GETTING HIRED

Apply by: Rolling. Fax or e-mail a resume and cover letter to the address below.

Qualifications:
Open to college freshmen, sophomores, juniors and seniors. Interns must receive academic credit for the internship.

Contact:
Intern Program
c/o Melissa Eaton
The Jim Henson Company
1416 North La Brea Avenue
Hollywood, CA 90028
Phone: (323) 802-1628
Fax: (323) 802-1835
E-mail: meaton@henson.com
www.henson.com

John Wiley & Sons

 THE BUZZ
- "Eureka! The source of CliffsNotes"

THE STATS

Industry(ies): Publishing

Location(s): Hoboken, NJ; Indianapolis, IN; San Francisco, CA; Somerset, NJ

Number of interns: *Annual*: 30

Pay: $350/week stipend (summer only)

Length of internship: *Summer*: 10 weeks

 THE SCOOP

Today, John Wiley & Sons is one of the powerhouses in American publishing, labeled one of the most respected companies in the U.S. Its holdings include *CliffsNotes*, the *Dummies* series, *Frommer's* travel guides, and Betty Crocker and WeightWatchers cookbooks.

ON THE JOB

Interns can work in marketing, editing, information technology, new media, customer service and publicity. There are four internship locations to choose from: the company's headquarters in Hoboken, NJ, the distribution center in Somerset, NJ, the imprint (Jossey-Bass) in San Francisco, CA., and Indianapolis, IN. All locations offer seminars and group luncheons so that interns can learn more about the publishing field.

GETTING HIRED

Apply by: *Summer*: February 15. Send a resume and cover letter that identifies the program in which you want to work.

Qualifications:
Open to college juniors going into their senior year.

Contact:
John Wiley & Sons, Inc.
Internship Program
Human Resources Department
111 River Street
Hoboken, NJ 07030-5774
Fax: (201) 748-6049, Attn: Internship Program
E-mail: opportunities@wiley.com, (subject: "Internship Program")

US Distribution Center-USDC
Attn: Internship Program
1 Wiley Drive
Somerset, NJ 08875-1272
Fax: (732)302-2386, Attn: Internship Program
E-mail: USDCopportunities@wiley.com, (subject: "Internship Program")

Jossey-Bass
989 Market Street
San Francisco, CA 94103
Fax: (415) 433-5015
E-mail: jobs@josseybass.com, (subject: "Internship Program")

Wiley Publishing Inc.
Attention: Internship Program
10475 Crosspoint Boulevard
Indianapolis, IN 46256
Fax: (317) 572-3000
E-mail: msaur@wiley.com (subject: Internship Program) wiley.com/WileyCDA/Section/id-163.html

Visit Vault at **www.vault.com** for insider company profiles, expert advice, career message boards, expert resume reviews, the Vault Job Board and more.

VAULT CAREER LIBRARY 247

Johnson & Johnson

 THE BUZZ
- "Get small-business attention with this global health product leader"

 THE STATS

Industry (ies): Consumer Products; Pharmaceuticals

Location (s): Internships and co-ops are available in Africa, Asia-Pacific, Europe, Latin America, the Middle East and North America (including CA, FL, NJ, NY and PA)

Number of interns: *Annual*: 75-80

Pay: Paid; compensation is based on local market factors for candidates with MBAs or master's degrees. International Internship Recruitment Program (IIRP) participants paid in local currency

Length of internship: *Summer*: 2-3 months (May-September); *co-op*: typically 6 months, full time (January-June/August, June-December); students generally take a full semester off from school. Depending on the college or university, students may receive academic credit for their co-op work experience

 THE SCOOP

Johnson & Johnson manufactures health care products for consumer, pharmaceutical, medical and diagnostic markets. The company specifically generates products for skin care, mental health, women's health, diagnostics, urology, cardiology, orthopedics, circulatory disease and anti-infectives, distributed throughout 175 countries. Johnson & Johnson employs over 100,000 people and generated global revenues of $47.3 billion in 2004.

 ON THE JOB

Internships are available in engineering, finance/accounting, information management, human resources, marketing operations, quality assurance, research and development, sales, logistics and information management. Interns adhere to a structured program that utilizes an individual internship work plan, developed during the first two weeks of the internship. The work plan includes monthly reports that highlight the key objectives and status of the intern's activities; performance reviews conducted by local managers at the conclusion of the assignment; an exit interview conducted before the intern departs; and a final presentation of the business results/findings of the internship position.

GETTING HIRED

Apply by: Visit www.jnj.com/careers/ucfair.html to view the university recruiting schedule. Prospective candidates may also submit a resume online and create a career profile at www.jnj.com.

Qualifications:

Open to prospective university candidates if they have received, or will receive within one year of hire, a bachelor's, master's, or doctoral degree (requirements vary by company and position). Interns must be authorized to work permanently in the geographic area that they select and must speak the language.

Contact:
Johnson & Johnson Corporate Office
1 Johnson & Johnson Plaza
New Brunswick, NJ 08933
Phone: (732) 524-0400
Fax: (732) 524-3300
www.jnj.com/careers

JPMorgan

THE BUZZ
- "Gordon Gekko would approve"

THE STATS
Industry(ies): Investment Banking

Location(s): New York, NY (corporate HQ)

Number of interns: *Summer*: 300 (undergraduate and MBA)

Pay: Paid; competitive entry-level salary and incentive bonus

Length of internship: *Summer*: 10 weeks

THE SCOOP

JMorgan is the Investment Banking branch of JP Morgan Chase & Co., a leading global financial services frims. Founded in 1799 JP Morgan Chase & Co. now has offices in more than 50 countries around the world and retains about $1.3 trillion in assets. JPMorgan is one of the world's leading investment banks, and it serves close to 8,000 issuers and 16,400 investor clients in more than 100 countries. Clients include corporations, governments, private firms, financial institutions, non-profit organizations and wealhty individuals. Extensive client relationships, global scale and reach are among the features that differentiate the firm from its investment banking peers. JPMorgan provides personal development and training opportunities throughout its summer internships and also recruits the majority of its full-time hires from summer classes.

ON THE JOB

Internship programs are offered in Corporate Finance, Sales & Trading and Research, summer analysts and associates and in the Honors Program. Summer analysts and associates go through three to four days of orientation and formal training before being assigned to their business group. They also receive on-the-job training and gain exposure to many of the same tasks and projects as their full-time counterparts. All interns have mentors to guide them through throughout their internships, and there are many opportunities to attend senior manager lunches, sports games, receptions, networking events, and senior speaker events.

GETTING HIRED

Apply by: *Summer*: Deadlines vary widely by school. Applicants should check with their campus career office and visit www.jpmorgan.com/careers for more specific application instructions. Interviews usually conclude in February.

Qualifications:

Summer associates: must be a first-year MBA student. *Summer analysts:* Open to undergraduate college juniors (rising seniors). *Honors Program:* Open to exceptional undergraduate freshmen and sophomores from diverse backgrounds, including, but not limited to, students of color, female students and students with disabilities.

Contact:
www.jpmorgan.com/careers

The Juilliard School

THE BUZZ
- "A peerless background for the musically inclined"
- "Dance lovers should take a close look at this school"

THE STATS
Industry(ies): Education; Theater/Performing Arts

Location(s): New York, NY

Number of interns: *Annual*: 24

Pay: Paid; $272/week

Length of internship: 9 months (September-May)

THE SCOOP

The Juilliard School is known as the preeminent performing arts school and institution in the U.S. Its campus located in New York City's scenic Lincoln Center. The school was founded in 1905 as a music academy that would rival the European conservatories.

ON THE JOB

For its Professional Intern Program, Juilliard offers positions in technical theater and arts administration. Twenty-one technical interns work in the costume shop, electrics, wigs/makeup, props, scene painting and as stage managers and production assistants. Three arts administration interns work in the Dance Division, Drama Division, and Concert Office. Detailed descriptions of every position are available online at www.juilliard.edu/about/profintern.html. Look under "About Juilliard."

GETTING HIRED

Apply by: June 1. Download the internship application at www.juilliard.edu/about/profintern.html. Send it with a resume, $15 application fee, photo, three letters of recommendation and a personal statement (250 words). The school interviews before hiring.

Qualifications:

Open to college freshmen, sophomores, juniors and seniors, college graduates and grad students.

Contact:
Helen Taynton
The Juilliard School
60 Lincoln Center Plaza
New York, NY 10023
Phone: (212) 799-5000, ext. 621
E-mail: htaynton@juilliard.edu
www.juilliard.edu/about/profintern.html

Visit Vault at **www.vault.com** for insider company profiles, expert advice, career message boards, expert resume reviews, the Vault Job Board and more.

VAULT CAREER LIBRARY **249**

INTERNSHIP PROFILES:
K

The Kennedy Center

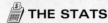 **THE BUZZ**
- "A center of arts in our nation's capital"
- "Learn how a top-notch arts organization works"

 THE STATS

Industry(ies): Education; Nonprofit; Theater/Performing Arts

Location(s): Washington, DC

Number of interns: *Spring/summer/fall*: 20 each

Pay: Paid; $250/week. Academic credit available; tickets to performances; weekly sessions led by Kennedy Center executives and other arts institutions in Washington, DC

Length of internship: *Spring/summer/fall*: 12-16 weeks

THE SCOOP

The Kennedy Center, founded in 1971, is America's living memorial to President John F. Kennedy. It is also the nation's busiest arts facility, producing over 3,000 performances annually in an effort to fulfill President Kennedy's vision. The Center offers hundreds of free performances each year through its Performing Arts for Everyone outreach program, featuring national and local artists.

ON THE JOB

Interns gain hands-on experience through assisting a Center staff member, who acts as mentor in various fields, including advertising, development, education, National Symphony Orchestra, press relations, production, technology, and volunteer management. Interns develop a working portfolio and participate in mid-semester and final evaluations.

GETTING HIRED

Apply by: *Summer*: March 1; *fall*: June 15; *winter/spring*: October 25. Send to the address below an application, resume, cover letter (detailing career goals, computer skills and three areas of interest), transcript, two letters of recommendation and a writing sample of no more than three pages. Applicants from non-English speaking countries must provide proof of English speaking and writing competence with a minimum TOEFL score of 600. International applications with a bachelor's degree may request an exemption from this requirement. All international applicants must provide proof of valid visa (the Center does not assist with visa applications). Download an application from: www.kennedy-center.org/education/vilarinstitute/internships/internapp.pdf.

Qualifications:

Open to college juniors, seniors, recent college graduates and grad students interested in arts careers.

Contact:
The Kennedy Center
Internship Program
PO Box 101510
Arlington, VA 22210
Phone: (202) 416-8821
www.kennedy-center.org/internships

KGO-TV

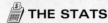 **THE BUZZ**
- "Enjoy a TV internship in a large local news market"
- "Wake up, San Francisco!"

THE STATS

Industry(ies): Broadcast & Entertainment; Journalism

Location(s): San Francisco, CA

Number of interns: *Annual*: 30-45

Pay: Paid; minimum wage

Length of internship: *Summer*: 8-12 weeks; *fall/spring*: 12-16 weeks each

THE SCOOP

KGO-TV is ABC-owed station serving San Francisco, San Jose, Oakland and Northern California. The station's signal reaches from Heyserville to Watsonville, a 75 mile radius, and it employs approximately 250 people. KGO-TV is known for its local news offerings, including an investigative team, a consumer research group (Seven On Your Side) and a local doctor delivering health news. The station has also made efforts to appeal to the area's Hispanic population, offering a mirror version of its web site in Spanish.

ON THE JOB

Specific internship opportunities and availabilities vary; however, interns usually work in the general newsroom, at the news assignment desk, on the sports segments and with the consumer unit. The public affairs, accounting, finance, promotions, sales, marketing, human resources, and engineering departments also hired interns in the past. Responsibilities vary with position, but the station strives to offer participants a genuine experience working in broadcasting.

GETTING HIRED

Apply by: Rolling. Download application from www.abc7news.com. On the "Jobs" tab, click on ABC 7 Jobs, ABC 7 Internships.

Qualifications:

Open to college juniors and seniors, as well as grad students.

Contact:
Human Resources Department
KGO Television
900 Front Street
San Francisco, CA 94111
Phone: (415) 954-7222
Fax: (415) 954-7514
E-mail: kgo-tv.hr@abc.com
http://abclocal.go.com/kgo/

Kimberly-Clark

 THE BUZZ
- "Peddle paper products"
- "Operations and engineers wanted"

THE STATS

Industry(ies): Consumer Products; Manufacturing; Science/Research

Location(s): Dallas, TX; Knoxville, TN; Neenah, WI; Roswell, GA

Number of interns: Varies

Pay: Paid; varies

Length of internship: *Summer*: 8-14 weeks

 **THE SCOOP**

In 2003, Kimberly-Clark netted $14.3 billion. This consumer products company specializes in tissues, personal care, and health care products, and employs 62,000 around the world. Its brands include Kleenex, Scott, Huggies and Kotex.

ON THE JOB

K-C has a well-established internship program. Interns may work in the following departments: research, development, engineering, logistics, operations and information services.

GETTING HIRED

Apply by: Rolling. Apply online: www.kimberly-clark.com/careers/ci_coopintern.asp.

Qualifications:

Open to college freshmen, sophomores, juniors and seniors, recent college graduates and graduate students. Some positions have specific requirements; see www.kimberly-clark.com/careers/ci_coopintern.asp for details.

Contact:
Internship Coordinator
Kimberly-Clark Corporation
P.O. Box 2020
Neenah, WI 54957
Phone: (888) 525-8388
www.kimberly-clark.com/careers/ci_coopintern.asp

The Kitchen

THE BUZZ
- "Starving artists come and get your fill in this kitchen"
- "Feed your appetite for theater"

THE STATS

Industry(ies): Art/Museum; Theater/Performing Arts

Location(s): New York, NY

Number of interns: *Annual*: 2-4 per semester

Pay: None. Free access to all performances

Length of internship: Varies; available year-round. Generally requires a 2- to 3-month commitment

THE SCOOP

The nonprofit multidisciplinary art center The Kitchen, believe it or not, really began in a kitchen back in 1971. The center outgrew its digs and moved twice; it's now ensconced at 512 West 19th Street. The space features one of the largest black box theaters in the United States as well as a gallery space for visual art and sound exhibitions. Developed through the years as a hub of artistic activity and performances that were "daring, nontraditional, and cutting edge," The Kitchen defines the American avant-garde and has achieved professional stature in its mission to "identify, support and present artists whose art influences its medium and contemporary culture."

ON THE JOB

Interns work with prominent arts professionals and focus on learning about all levels of the organization. Positions available include administration, marketing, development, technical and assistants for The Kitchen's Summer Institute. Interns generally perform the day-to-day activities of administrative production for a nonprofit theater, such as developing press kits, researching special projects, sending out mailings, coordinating special events or operating lights and sound as a member of the production crew.

GETTING HIRED

Apply by: Rolling. Submit resume and letter of interest that includes intended intern area of focus, what you would like to learn from the internship, your availability to start and how many hours per week you can commit to the program.

Qualifications:
Open to all college freshmen, sophomores, juniors and seniors who have related course work and experience in the arts.

Contact:
Rachael Dorsey
The Kitchen
512 West 19th Street
New York, NY 1003
Phone: (212) 255-5793, ext. 14
E-mail: rachael@thekitchen.org
www.thekitchen.org/intern.html

Visit Vault at **www.vault.com** for insider company profiles, expert advice, career message boards, expert resume reviews, the Vault Job Board and more.

VAULT CAREER LIBRARY **253**

KPIX TV

THE BUZZ
- "Keep an evening camera on San Francisco"

THE STATS
Industry(ies): Broadcast & Entertainment; Journalism

Location(s): San Francisco, CA

Number of interns: *Annual*: around 50; varies with station need

Pay: $5.50/day; academic credit

Length of internship: *Spring/fall*: 6 months each

THE SCOOP

KPIX-5 is San Francisco's local CBS affiliate. It's also the 49th station in the country that went on the air in 1949, the first in Northern California. With a wide variety of locally produced entertainment, KPIX is most proud of its *Missing Persons* program (in which the station shows photos of missing locals) that has been airing since the station's inception. Its *Evening Magazine*, detailing Bay Area life, is another old program that debuted in 1976. With brief periods of going off the air, it is back – and very popular – today.

ON THE JOB

Interns may work in TV news sports, community relations, TV news assignment desk, TV news production, marketing/creative service, evening magazine, reports/news special assignment unit, TV weather production, online services and political research/elections. They can also choose to work in the community relations office. All interns are evaluated at the end of their programs. Available positions and their responsibilities may vary slightly.

GETTING HIRED

Apply by: Rolling. Download application (available at beta.kpix.com/ about/jobs/application.html) and mail it, along with resume and cover letter, to the address below. Applicants will be interviewed.

Qualifications:
Open to local college sophomores, juniors and seniors with a GPA of 2.5 or higher. Must be able to receive academic credit.

Contact:
Internship Coordinator
KPIX Human Resources
855 Battery Street
San Francisco, CA 94111
Phone: (415) 765-8609
cbs5.com/about/jobs/overview.html

KQED-FM

THE BUZZ
- "Work for the people's network in San Francisco"

THE STATS
Industry(ies): Broadcast & Entertainment; Journalism; Nonprofit

Location(s): San Francisco, CA

Number of interns: *Spring/summer/fall*: 1-5 each

Pay: None; academic credit

Length of internship: *Spring/summer/fall*: 4 months each; 15-25 hours/week

THE SCOOP

KQED is San Francisco's public television, radio and online network. It all started with television in 1954. Becoming known as a controversial broadcaster, KQED ran the Teller-Pauling nuclear fallout debate in the 1970s. It was also the first to use membership drives and fundraisers to pay for its programming. Striving to meet the needs of the Bay Area, KQED now boasts a public TV station (Channel 9), a number of digital TV stations (KQED HD, KQED Encore, KQED World, KQED Life and KQED Kids), public radio stations (88.5 FM in San Francisco and 89.3 FM in Sacramento), an education network and a web site (kqed.org). Today, it is one of America's flagship public broadcasting networks.

ON THE JOB

KQED interns work in most offices of all three of the network's divisions (online, television and radio). TV interns participate in specific shows and with production teams. There are interactive Web journalism internships available, as well as positions in the education network. Departments such as information technology, marketing and communications also hire interns. Finally, KQED Radio offers practical training internships for those looking to break into the public radio field.

GETTING HIRED

Apply by: *Spring*: December 1; *summer*: April 1; *fall*: August 1. Apply online: www.kqed.org/about/internships.

Qualifications:
Radio internships are open to college graduates wanting to get into the field. All others are open to college juniors and seniors and grad students, with a GPA of 2.5 or higher and who are receiving academic credit for the internship.

Contact:
HR Manager, Employment
KQED-FM
2601 Mariposa Street
San Francisco, CA 94110
E-mail: hr@kqed.org
www.kqed.org/about/internships

Kraft Foods Inc.

THE BUZZ

- "The Cheesiest"
- "Good 'til the last drop"
- "Yum – you won't go hungry"

 THE STATS

Industry(ies): Consumer Products; Food & Beverage

Location(s): Northfield, IL

Number of interns: *Annual*: 50-100

Pay: Paid; *undergraduates*: $400-$600/week; *grad students*: $800-$1,200/week. Housing provided

Length of internship: Varies; available year-round

 THE SCOOP

J.L. Kraft started selling cheese slices from a wagon in 1903 – since then, Kraft Foods has come a long way. You can find its products in 99 percent of American households. The company owns several well-known brands that are ubiquitous in American kitchens – JELL-O, Oreo, DiGiorno, Tang, Maxwell House, Nabisco, Post, Oscar Mayer, Planters, Kool Aid, and Philadelphia Cream Cheese – in addition to its signatures, Kraft Singles and Kraft Macaroni and Cheese. Kraft has also acquired international brands such as Gevalia, Jacobs, Toblerone and Milka.

ON THE JOB

Interns work with assigned supervisors who guide them through the program. They attend management meetings, and work on significant projects with senior-level management. Though interns are usually placed in management, they can also explore the sales, manufacturing, and other business offices. All interns receive on-site training and attend an orientation. There is also a similar INROADS internship program, but it's only open to minority students (see the web site for more details).

GETTING HIRED

Apply by: Rolling. Kraft generally recruits interns through specific schools' career placement offices (check with yours); however, it is possible to contact the company if you're interested in applying and Kraft does not work with your school.

Qualifications:

Open to college juniors and seniors, grad students and recent college graduates.

Contact:

Internship Coordinator
Kraft Foods, Inc.
Three Lakes Drive
Northfield, IL 60093
Phone: (847) 646-2000
www.kraftfoods.com

Kupper Parker Communications

THE BUZZ

- "A rising star in the PR industry"

 THE STATS

Industry(ies): Public Relations

Location(s): St. Louis, MO

Number of interns: *Annual*: 4 (2 every 6 months)

Pay: Paid; *undergrad*: $7.50/hour; *graduate*: $9.50/hour

Length of internship: *Spring/summer/fall*: 6 months; possible extension for college graduates

THE SCOOP

Kupper Parker Communications is an integrated marketing firm providing advertising, public relations, direct marketing and interactive services. Based in Saint Louis, the company has 12 branch offices throughout the United States and Europe. Kupper Parker's clients include Anheuser-Busch, Coolsavings Inc., Anthem Blue Cross and Blue Shield, and First Bank.

ON THE JOB

Kupper Parker offers an excellent entry-level experience for recent graduates. Account coordinator level responsibilities include writing (press releases, pitches and articles), editing, media relations, event support, research and media list building. Motivated candidates with strong writing and interpersonal skills should apply.

GETTING HIRED

Apply by: Rolling. Send resume, cover letter and two to three writing samples to the address below. E-mail preferred.

Qualifications:

Open to college seniors, recent college graduates and grad students. Postgrads preferred.

Contact:

Tom Geiser, Internship Coordinator
Kupper Parker Communications
8301 Maryland Avenue
St. Louis, MO 63105
Phone: (314) 290-2156
Fax: (314) 290-2126
E-mail: tgeiser@kupperparker.com
www.kupperparker.com

Visit Vault at **www.vault.com** for insider company profiles, expert advice, career message boards, expert resume reviews, the Vault Job Board and more.

VAULT CAREER LIBRARY **255**

Use the Internet's
MOST TARGETED
job search tools.

Vault Job Board

Target your search by industry, function, and experience level,
and find the job openings that you want.

VaultMatch Resume Database

Vault takes match-making to the next level: post your resume
and customize your search by industry, function, experience
and more. We'll match job listings with your interests and
criteria and e-mail them directly to your in-box.

VAULT
> the most trusted name in career information™

INTERNSHIP PROFILES:
L

L.E.K. Consulting

 THE BUZZ
- "Get a jumpstart on your consulting career"
- "Work with the Fortune 500"

 THE STATS

Industry(ies): Management & Strategy Consulting

Location(s): London (HQ); Boston, MA; Chicago, IL; Los Angeles, CA; San Francisco, CA; Auckland; Bangkok; Beijing; Melbourne; Milan; Munich; Paris; Shanghai; Singapore; Sydney; Tokyo

Number of interns: Varies

Pay: Paid; varies

Length of internship: *Summer*: 8-10 weeks

 **THE SCOOP**

Based in the United Kingdom, L.E.K. is one of the top strategy consulting firms in the world and employs over 600 professional staff members in 16 offices. Consultants advise some of the world's most successful executives on how to conduct better business. Besides strategy consulting, the company works on merger and acquisition cases, advisory services and value management. L.E.K. has over 250,000 clients in all major industries.

 ON THE JOB

Many of L.E.K.'s regional offices hire interns as summer associates and summer consultants. The programs begin with an orientation program, which prepares interns to work on specific client cases as members of teams. Training and supervision, however, remain constant throughout the summer. To learn about strategy consulting, and the distinctions between associate and consultant responsibilities, interns work on real cases.

 GETTING HIRED

Apply by: *Summer*: Rolling. Contact the regional office for application details.

Qualifications:

Open to all college juniors and seniors, graduate students and recent college graduates. Requirements may vary slightly; check with the regional office contact.

Contact:

L.E.K. Consulting LLC
Karina Gutierrez
1100 Glendon Avenue
Los Angeles, CA 90024
Phone: (310) 209-9823
Fax: (310) 209-9125
E-mail: K.gutierrez@lek.com
www.lek.com

L.E.K. Consulting LLC
Tracy Amico
One North Wacker Drive
39th Floor
Chicago, IL 60606
Phone: (312) 913-6400
Fax: (312) 782-4583
E-mail: t.amico@lek.com

L.E.K. Consulting LLC
Tracy Amico
28 State Street
16th Floor
Boston, MA 02109
Phone: (617) 951-9500
Fax: (617) 951-9392
E-mail: t.amico@lek.com

Lamont-Doherty Earth Observatory

 THE BUZZ
- "If you loved Earth Sciences in eighth grade, this is the internship for you"

 THE STATS

Industry(ies): Environmental; Science/Research

Location(s): Palisades, NY

Number of interns: *Summer*: 33-35

Pay: $2,640 stipend. Free, air-conditioned housing at Columbia; free bus passes; may cover round-trip travel expenses to New York

Length of internship: *Summer*: 10 weeks

 THE SCOOP

Simply put, the Lamont-Doherty Earth Observatory (Lamont) is one of the leading scientific research centers in the world and leads the pack in climate research. Its studies cover the entire breadth of earth sciences, from global climate change to thermodynamics, from oceanography to toxic waste treatment.

 ON THE JOB

Lamont has over 100 PhDs on staff, and at least as many graduate students researching alongside them – a very rich learning environment for interns. Students work one-on-one with a researcher, assisting with his or her current project. In the summer of 2003, 33 Lamont researchers participated in the internship program, offering a wide range of work for interns, from "Determining How Ocean Circulation Responds to Climate Change Using the Trace Element Concentrations in Sediments from the South Atlantic" to "Detecting Holocene Climate Variations Using the Stable Isotope Composition of Fish Otoliths from Coastal U.S. Sediments." Other topics of research include planetary science and impact craters.

 GETTING HIRED

Apply by: *Summer*: March 10. Apply by mail with the application form available on the web site, a transcript, two letters of recommendation, a resume with a description of computer skills, and a statement of interest.

Qualifications:
Open to college sophomores and juniors; graduating seniors are not eligible. Geology, environmental science, chemistry, biology, physics, mathematics or engineering majors only. Minimum one year of calculus.

Contact:
Dr. Dallas Abbott
Summer Internship Program
Lamont-Doherty Earth Observatory
Palisades, NY 10964
Phone: (845) 359-2900
Fax: (845) 359-2931
E-mail: dallas@ldeo.columbia.edu
www.ldeo.columbia.edu/~dallas/abbott_sum.html

Land Between the Lakes

 THE BUZZ
- "Help manage a bison habitat in Kentucky"
- "Immerse yourself in a natural education"

 THE STATS

Industry(ies): Education; Engineering; Environmental; Science/Research; Tourism/Recreation

Location(s): Golden Pond, KY

Number of interns: *Annual*: 10

Pay: Paid; $150-$200/week. Housing provided

Length of internship: *Interns*: 12-16 weeks; *apprentices*: up to 1 year

 THE SCOOP

Applying the mantra "explore and learn," Land Between the Lakes is an environmental education center that hosts groups of all sizes and ages (mostly for overnight stays). The center, in rural Kentucky, features a 700-acre bison and elk prairie, numerous hiking trails and programs at woodlands stations. LBL also boasts a planetarium and a historical farm, as well as several outdoor activities.

 ON THE JOB

LBL interns and apprentices work in the following departments: recreation, environmental education, forestry, wildlife, history, graphic design, photography, public relations, environmental engineering, and health and safety. While most interns work in the organization's administrative offices, some work onsite at campgrounds, nature centers and resident group camps. Others work on a "living history" farm that dates back to 1850. All interns and apprentices work to make sure visitors enjoy their stays.

 **GETTING HIRED**

Apply by: Rolling. Send resume and cover letter to the address below.

Qualifications:
The internship program is open to all college juniors and seniors. The apprentice program is open to all recent college graduates who are not currently enrolled in school.

Contact:
Greg Barnes, Intern/Apprentice Coordinator
Land Between The Lakes
100 Van Morgan Drive
Golden Pond, KY 42211
Phone: (270) 924-2089
E-mail: rweakley@fs.fed.us
www.lbl.org/Internships.html

Visit Vault at **www.vault.com** for insider company profiles, expert advice, career message boards, expert resume reviews, the Vault Job Board and more.

VULT CAREER LIBRARY **259**

The Late Show with David Letterman

THE BUZZ

- "This intership is more than a stupid human trick"
- "Work with one of the heavies of late night TV"

THE STATS

Industry(ies): Broadcast & Entertainment

Location(s): New York, NY

Number of interns: *Summer/fall/spring*: 12 each

Pay: None; academic credit

Length of internship: *Spring*: December-May; *summer*: May-August; *fall*: August-December

THE SCOOP

David Letterman celebrated his 10th anniversary as host of *The Late Show* on CBS in 2003. During that time, the show has garnered eight Emmys and mass audience appreciation. David Letterman's show is known for its wry, topical humor and stupid pet tricks, among other things.

ON THE JOB

The Late Show takes full-time interns in research, talent, production, writing, writers' production and music. (There is one part-time production finance internship, too, open to finance or accounting majors only.) While all interns fulfill administrative duties, their tasks vary greatly between departments. Interns in "writers," for example, work directly with the writers of the show, while interns in "talent" work with the department that handles the show's guests. No day's tasks are the same in the fast-paced environment that surrounds a daily show. Occasionally, Dave himself seizes upon an intern to taunt on the show.

GETTING HIRED

Apply by: *Spring*: October 1; *summer*: March 1; *fall*: June. Apply by fax with cover letter and resume.

Qualifications:
Open to college freshmen, sophomores, juniors and seniors. All interns must receive academic credit.

Contact:
Janice Penino
VP, Human Resources
Late Show with David Letterman
Phone: (212) 975-5300
Fax: (212) 975-4734
www.cbs.com/latenight/lateshow

© 2006 Vault Inc.

Lazard

 THE BUZZ

• "Intellectual international finance"

THE STATS:

Industry(ies): Financial Services

Location(s): Chicago, IL; Houston, TX; Atlanta, GA; Los Angeles, CA; San Francisco, CA; New York, NY; Montreal; Toronto

Number of interns: *Summer analysts*: 16-18; *summer associates*: 8-10 in New York, 1 in San Francisco

Pay: Paid; competitive salary

Length of internship: *Summer*: 10-12 weeks

 **THE SCOOP**

Founded in New Orleans in 1848, Lazard now operates with headquarters in New York, Paris and London, with branches in 29 key business and financial centers spread across 16 countries in North America, Europe, Asia, Australia and South America. Lazard provides financial services to corporations, partnerships, institutions, governments and high-net-worth individuals around the world. The firm focuses principally on two business segments: financial advisory (which includes its mergers and acquisitions and financial restructuring practices) and asset management. Lazard differentiates itself from rivals by emphasizing its status as an independent financial advisory firm, unconflicted by balance sheet considerations.

 ON THE JOB

Summer analysts partake in an ongoing training program comprised of classes taught by Lazard bankers. These seminars stress the fundamentals of investment banking and emphasize modeling and relevant analytical techniques in particular. The training is intended to augment the experience gained by working with active transaction teams.

Day-to-day activities for the summer associate position vary according to the associate's prior experience and skills, but are equivalent to those of a full-time associate. In addition to client-related assignments, summer associates are encouraged to explore the workings of the firm and become acquainted with their colleagues via both formal and informal mentoring.

 GETTING HIRED

Apply by: Mid-December. Lazard visits leading universities and business schools on an annual basis. Hiring occurs at the regional level, leading to training and development opportunities that vary by geographical location. For schools included on Lazard's campus events schedule, refer to your school's career center for application procedures. Interested candidates from other schools should mail their cover letter and resume to the contact below.

Qualifications:

Summer analyst: open to rising college seniors; *summer associate*: open to MBA students between their first and second year of their program, though applicants entering their final year of a JD or JD/MBA degree are also considered. Strong quantitative experience and solid oral and written communications skills considered a must for application. Candidates should be highly driven, display a stellar academic record and exhibit comfort in a work atmosphere that prizes initiative, creativity, maturity and self-assurance. Though not required, previous investment banking experience is a benefit.

Contact:
Undergraduate applicants
Shannon Sullivan
Lazard Ltd
30 Rockefeller Plaza
New York, NY 10020

MBA applicants
Lisa Henkoff
Lazard Ltd
30 Rockefeller Plaza
New York, NY 10020

Visit Vault at **www.vault.com** for insider company profiles, expert advice, career message boards, expert resume reviews, the Vault Job Board and more.

V\ULT CAREER LIBRARY **261**

Legacy International

 THE BUZZ
- "It's a small world after all"
- "Make an African friend in Virginia"

THE STATS

Industry(ies): Education

Location(s): Bedford, VA

Number of interns: *Summer*: varies

Pay: $900-1,200/summer. Room and board

Length of internship: *Summer*: about 1 month

 **THE SCOOP**

Legacy International runs the Global Youth Village, an international summer training program for youth. GYV works to develop skills in leadership, dialogue and global thinking among youths aged 13-18 from all over the world. The camp tries to impart ideas on how to make a difference in the world and how to think and act responsibly at a local and global level. The model cooperative society at this "global village" follows a strict honor code developed by former campers and staffers.

ON THE JOB

Summer staff and interns work with the year-round staff in four capacities – program (workshops, events, etc.), counseling, support services (cooking, cleaning, health care, set-up, etc.) and administration. All applicants must choose one area in which to specialize. With a staff-to-camper ratio of almost 1:2, each staff member has a chance to make a real difference in the campers' lives. Staffers and interns must follow the same honor code as the campers.

GETTING HIRED

Apply by: Rolling. Download the application form available at http://www.globalyouthvillage.org/Staff/StaffCenter.htm.

Qualifications:

Open to all college seniors, grad students and recent college graduates. Those who do not feel qualified for a professional staff position can apply for an unpaid internship.

Contact:

Leila Baz, Staff Coordinator
Legacy International
1020 Legacy Drive
Bedford, VA 24523
Phone: (540) 297-5982
Fax: (540) 297-1860
E-mail: staff@legacyintl.org
www.legacyintl.org
www.globalyouthvillage.org

Legal Momentum

 THE BUZZ
- "Join the legal fight for equal rights for all"

 THE STATS

Industry(ies): Law; Nonprofit

Location(s): New York, NY; Washington, DC

Number of interns: 2 undergraduates in DC; 4 in NY; 6 legal interns in NY

Pay: Paid; *graduates*: $420/week; *undergraduates*: $230/week during the summer

Length of internship: *Summer*: 10-12 weeks (30 + hours/week); *fall/spring*: at least 10 hours/week

 THE SCOOP

Since its founding in 1970, Legal Momentum has been advancing the rights of women and girls by using the law and creating innovative public policy. Legal Momentum strives for equal rights for women in the home, schools and workplace, relying on education and litigation to achieve this aim. Considered an authority on gender equity issues, it is a resource for Congress and grassroots organizations. Legal Momentum was formerly known as NOW Legal Defense and Education Fund.

ON THE JOB

Legal Momentum has several internships for students interested in education, law, public policy or women's issues. Ongoing internship opportunities include: development (event planning, maintaining supporter relations, organizing), the National Judicial Education Program (providing communications support for programs), the Family Initiative (advocating for better child care, preschool and afterschool), outreach, public policy and public education. The communication department also hires one graduate student intern to help write/research the quarterly newsletter and the annual report. All interns are included in seminars and "brown bag lunches."

GETTING HIRED

Apply by: *Summer undergraduate*: March 15; *summer legal intern in NY*: January 1 for 2Ls, February 1 for 1Ls.

Qualifications:
Open to college freshmen, sophomores, juniors and seniors, graduate and law students.

Contact:
Undergraduate internship
E-mail: bwatson@legalmomentum.org

Accounting internship
Bob Geryk, Director of Finance & Administration
Legal Momentum
395 Hudson Street, 5th Floor
New York, NY 10014
Fax: (212) 226-1066

Child Care Policy internship
Nicole A. Brown, Policy Attorney
Legal Momentum
395 Hudson Street, 5th Floor
New York, NY 10014

Communications internship
Attention: Maureen McFadden
Legal Momentum
395 Hudson Street, 5th Floor
New York, NY 10014

Legal internship – Washington office
Internship Coordinator
Legal Momentum
1522 K Street, NW, Suite 550
Washington, DC 20005
E-mail: policy@legalmomentum.org
www.legalmomentum.org/about/jobop.shtml

Legal internship – New York office
E-mail: legalinternhiring@legalmomentum.org

Women Rebuild New York internship – New York office
Attention: Françoise Jacobsohn
Legal Momentum
395 Hudson Street, 5th Floor
New York, NY 10014

Visit Vault at **www.vault.com** for insider company profiles, expert advice, career message boards, expert resume reviews, the Vault Job Board and more.

 **263**

Lehman Brothers

 THE BUZZ
- "Options abound at this prestigious firm"

 THE STATS:

Industry(ies): Financial Services

Location(s): New York, NY (HQ); London (Europe HQ); Tokyo (Asia HQ); offices worldwide

Number of interns: Varies

Pay: Paid; competitive salary

Length of internship: *Summer*: 8-10 weeks

 **THE SCOOP**

Since its establishment in 1850, Lehman Brothers has become one of the most well-recognized financial services firms in the world. Lehman Brothers services include equity and fixed income sales, trading and research, investment banking, private investment management, asset management and private equity. The firm serves corporations, governments and municipalities, institutional clients and high-net-worth individuals across the globe. Along with global headquarters in New York City, European headquarters in London and Asian headquarters in Tokyo, Lehman Brothers operates a worldwide network of offices.

ON THE JOB

Lehman Brothers offers summer analyst and associate internships in a variety of divisions within the firm. Each program is seen as a primary source for hiring full-time analysts and associates. These programs include fixed income and equities, investment banking and private equity, asset management, operations, finance and information technology.

GETTING HIRED

Apply by: Varies; check with your school career center for application deadlines.

Qualifications:

Summer analyst: open to rising seniors. Recruiting begins during the junior year of college. The firm expects applicants to be currently pursuing an undergraduate degree or science-related MA degree, a record of distinctive academic performance, leadership and initiative taking, an interest in a career in finance and a strong professional presence marked by self-confidence and maturity. *Summer associate*: applicants are expected to be pursuing an MBA or PhD; a record of strong academic achievement; distinctive problem-solving skills; refined written and verbal skills; and, where necessary, technical knowledge of banking functions. *IT summer analyst*: applicants are expected to have computer science, computer/electrical engineering and information systems collegiate backgrounds.

Contact:

Please view contacts on www.lehman.com\careers

Library of Congress

 THE BUZZ
- "Become the ultimate primary source"
- "Work on your thesis during lunch"

 THE STATS

Industry(ies): Education; Government

Location(s): Washington, DC

Number of interns: *Summer*: 6-10

Pay: None

Length of internship: *Summer*: 8-12 weeks

 **THE SCOOP**

The oldest cultural institution in our country (mandated in 1800), the Library of Congress continues to serve the congressional arm of the U.S. government. As the largest library in the world, it houses and protects rare primary sources, ranging from Benjamin Franklin's papers to the Mongolian Buddhist Sutra. The enormous collection (128 million items on 530 miles of shelves) boasts items in 450 languages.

 ON THE JOB

LOC interns work in the conservation, acquisitions, geography and map, information services, Web design and information technology divisions. The conservation department offers the most positions, in book, paper, photograph and preventive conservation departments, all of which are open to grad students only. The LOC also acts as an umbrella organization, overseeing the following internship programs: American Folklife Center Internship Program, the Harvey Mudd Greater LA Internship Program, the John Carroll Internship Program, the Mary Washington College Internship Program, and the Paul Peck Humanities Institute Internship Program. All of these have very specific application requirements (see the web site for details).

 GETTING HIRED

Apply by: Deadlines and application procedures vary. Contact the correct person (information below), depending on the program you're interested in, for specifics.

Qualifications:
Qualifications vary greatly depending on the specific program. See www.loc.gov/hr/employment/umbrella/jobs-umbrella.html for more details.

Contact:
Acquisitions programs
Nancy Davenport
Director, Acquisitions Directorate
Library of Congress
101 Independence Avenue
Washington, DC 20540
Phone: (202) 707-5137
Fax: (202) 707-6269
E-mail: ndav@loc.gov
www.loc.gov

Conservation programs
Mark Roosa
Preservation Directorate

Library of Congress
101 Independence Avenue
Washington, DC 20540
Phone: (202) 707-5213
E-mail: mroo@loc.gov

Information services/Web design programs
Gerald Burguera
Senior MIS Analyst
Library of Congress
Operations Directorate
101 Independence Avenue
Washington, DC 20540
Phone: (202) 707-2067
Fax: (202) 707-5325
E-mail: gbur@loc.gov

Information technology programs
Dr. Carolyn T. Brown
Director, Area Studies Collections Directorate
Library of Congress
Area Studies Collections Directorate
101 Independence Avenue
Washington, DC 20540
Phone: (202) 707-1902
Fax: (202) 707-3566
E-mail: cbro@loc.gov
For all umbrella programs, see the web site for specific contact info

Visit Vault at **www.vault.com** for insider company profiles, expert advice, career message boards, expert resume reviews, the Vault Job Board and more.

VAULT CAREER LIBRARY **265**

Lincoln Center for the Performing Arts

 THE BUZZ

- "Want a career in arts administration? Learn how to bring music to New York City"

 THE STATS

Industry(ies): Art/Museum; Film; Music/Records; Nonprofit; Theater/Performing Arts

Location(s): New York, NY

Number of interns: *Summer*: approximately 30

Pay: Varies each summer

Length of internship: *Summer*: varies with need

 THE SCOOP

Lincoln Center is the largest performing arts complex in the world, weighing in at 16.3 acres. It houses 12 resident organizations – including the world-renowned Juilliard School, Metropolitan Opera and New York City Ballet – and has some 5 million visitors per year. Located in the heart of New York City, it attracts the world's finest artists.

ON THE JOB

Interns at Lincoln Center are hired to work in a variety of departments throughout the organization, including marketing, public relations and development. In addition, internship opportunities are offered to support summer programming events such as Lincoln Center Out-of-Doors, Midsummer Night Swing and Mostly Mozart. The Lincoln Center Festival also hires interns to assist in projects associated with presenting internationally acclaimed artists and productions. (Please note: applicants interested in working with Lincoln Center's resident organizations should apply directly to them.)

GETTING HIRED

Apply by: Rolling. Positions are posted on www.lincoln center.org. Follow the instructions written on each posting on how to apply.

Qualifications:

Open to college freshmen, sophomores, juniors and seniors, as well as recent college graduates and grad students.

Contact:
Human Resources
Lincoln Center for the Performing Arts, Inc.
70 Lincoln Center Plaza
New York, NY 10023
Phone: (212) 875-5300
Fax: (212) 875-5185
E-mail: humanresources@lincolncenter.org
www.lincolncenter.org

Liz Claiborne

 THE BUZZ

- "Work in a growing fashion company – it's more than just Liz"

 **THE STATS**

Industry(ies): Consumer Products; Fashion; Manufacturing; Retail

Location(s): New York, NY

Number of interns: *Summer*: 50

Pay: None

Length of internship: *Summer*: 8-10 weeks

 THE SCOOP

Four partners (including Liz herself) founded the design company Liz Claiborne in 1976. The apparel and accessories (men's and women's) corporation now represents several brands. Its holdings include Kenneth Cole, Ellen Tracy, Donna Karan New York, Lucky's and Juicy Couture, among many others. The company also sponsors the Liz Claiborne Foundation, a nonprofit that addresses needs (particularly women with HIV/AIDS) in communities where the company has its main distribution and manufacturing centers.

 ON THE JOB

Liz interns are hired to work in the design, merchandising/planning, production/manufacturing, sales, finance, information systems, human resources and legal departments. All interns, regardless of department, work on an individual project for six to eight weeks. The projects are designed to give interns hands-on experience in the various areas of the company. The program also sponsors weekly activities, such as lunch seminars and field trips to give interns exposure to other departments, as well as a chance to socialize and learn from each other.

GETTING HIRED

Apply by: *Summer*: March 1. Send resume and cover letter to the address below.

Qualifications:

Programs are open to college freshmen, sophomores, juniors and seniors, recent college graduates and grad students. Applicants to the design program must be design majors; finance interns must be finance/accounting majors; and IT interns must be computer science or MIS majors.

Contact:
Summer Internship Program
Liz Claiborne
1440 Broadway, 2nd floor
New York, NY 10018
E-mail: College_recruiting@liz.com

Longwood Gardens

 THE BUZZ
- "Cultivate a career in horticulture in Pennsylvania"

 THE STATS

Industry(ies): Horticulture; Education; Nonprofit; Science/ Research

Location(s): Kennett Square, PA

Number of interns: *Annual*: Up to 40

Pay: Paid; $7.50/hour. Free housing

Length of internship: 3-12 months, 35 hours/week; available year-round

 THE SCOOP

With 11,000 different plants in 40 outdoor and indoor gardens on 1,050 acres of land, Longwood is one of the premiere horticultural centers in the world. It attracts roughly 900,000 visitors annually. Though many generations worked to make the garden what it is today (beginning with Quakers who bought the land from William Penn and began planting trees on it), philanthropist Pierre S. DuPont (of the DuPont chemical company family) brought it to excellence.

ON THE JOB

Positions vary depending on the garden's needs and staffing demands, but they are offered in indoor and outdoor display gardening, continuing education, curatorial, library, performing arts, planning and design, public relations, research, greenhouse and nursery production, student programs and visitor education.

GETTING HIRED

Apply by: Rolling. Application available at: http://www.longwood gardens.org/StudentPrograms_1_3_4_3.html.

Qualifications:
Open to college freshmen, sophomores, juniors and seniors, grad students, and recent college grads of all ages.

Contact:
Mark Richardson, Student Programs Coordinator
Longwood Gardens
P.O. Box 501
Kennett Square, PA 19348
Phone: (610) 388-1000, ext. 508
Fax: (610) 388-2908
E-mail: MRichardson@longwoodgardens.org
www.longwoodgardens.org/StudentPrograms_1_3_4_3.html.

Los Angeles Lakers

THE BUZZ
- "Meet Shaq!"
- "Learn the ins and outs of sports PR in Los Angeles"

 THE STATS

Industry(ies): Sports

Location(s): Los Angeles, CA

Number of interns: Varies

Pay: None

Length of internship: *Summer*: 10 weeks; at least 1 day a week and game nights

THE SCOOP

The Los Angeles Lakers formed in Minneapolis in 1947 (in what was then the National Basketball League – or NBL), before the National Basketball Association (NBA) was even established. In their inaugural season, the Minneapolis Lakers only lost two games, winning the NBL crown. Plagued by falling attendance, the team moved to Los Angeles before the 1960-1961 season. Today, the Lakers are one of the NBA's most recognized franchises, with superstar players including the controversial Kobe Bryant.

ON THE JOB

Most interns for the Lakers work in public relations, assisting team staff with media inquiries and promotional activities. All interns work on home game nights. Some interns may also work on special activities such as the "Stay in School" project.

GETTING HIRED

Apply by: Rolling. Send a resume, cover letter and letters of recommendation to the address below.

Qualifications:
Open to college juniors and seniors and recent college graduates within two years of graduation. Must live in or around Los Angeles.

Contact:
Internship Coordinator
Los Angeles Lakers
Great Western Forum
P.O. Box 10
Inglewood, CA 90306
Phone: (310) 419-3100
www.nba.com/lakers/index.html

Visit Vault at **www.vault.com** for insider company profiles, expert advice, career message boards, expert resume reviews, the Vault Job Board and more.

V/\ULT CAREER LIBRARY **267**

Los Angeles Magazine

 THE BUZZ
- "Learn about reporting all that is Los Angeles"

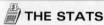 **THE STATS**

Industry(ies): Journalism; Publishing

Location(s): Los Angeles, CA

Number of interns: *Annual*: 20-25

Pay: None. Paid parking

Length of internship: *Summer/fall/winter/spring*: 13 weeks each

 **THE SCOOP**

Established in 1960, *Los Angeles Magazine* is a comprehensive lifestyle guide covering the contemporary life of all that is Los Angeles. Published by Emmis Communications Inc., the magazine circulates to over 150,000 readers and provides a combination of provocative articles, essays and columns, on a wide range of topics including politics, business, gossip, film, celebrities, sports, shopping, dining and the arts.

ON THE JOB

Interns assist in the editorial department and are generally assigned projects that change from day to day. Duties may include research, fact checking, submitting story ideas, transcribing and occasionally answering phones.

GETTING HIRED

Apply by: *Summer*: April 30; *fall*: July 30; *winter*: October 30; *spring*: December 30. Submit a resume, cover letter and any writing samples to the address below.

Qualifications:

Open to college juniors and seniors and graduate students majoring in English, communications or journalism.

Contact:
Eric Mercado
Research Editor
Los Angeles Magazine
5900 Wilshire Blvd., 10th Floor
Los Angeles, CA 90036
Phone: (323) 801-0062
E-mail: emercado@lamag.com
www.lamag.com

Los Angeles Municipal Art Gallery

THE BUZZ
- "Los Angeles' finest municipal art gallery"
- "See what artists in Los Angeles are doing"

THE STATS

Industry(ies): Art/Museum

Location(s): Los Angeles, CA

Number of interns: *Annual*: 3-6

Pay: None; academic credit

Length of internship: *Summer/fall/spring*: 15-20 weeks; 6 hours/week (3 in the morning and 3 in the afternoon). Academic credit requires 10 hours/week

THE SCOOP

Founded in 1971, the Los Angeles Municipal Art Gallery is operated by the City of Los Angeles Cultural Affairs Department. The Gallery focuses on contemporary art by both established and emerging artists, most from Southern California. The Gallery hosts the annual City of Los Angeles (COLA) Award Exhibition, which showcases the efforts of professional artists who have been awarded a grant by the Cultural Affairs Department of the City of Los Angeles.

ON THE JOB

Interns work as gallery educators in the Museum Education and Tours Program. They're trained to lead school tours, assist in developing curriculum materials and work on special education projects. Participation in the intern program teaches skills in art analysis, criticism and teaching, verbal communication, educational techniques and planning and writing art curriculum materials for elementary through high school grade levels. Interns may assist in daily operations. In addition, students interested in architecture can focus their internship on Hollyhock House, a house museum designed by Frank Lloyd Wright.

GETTING HIRED

Apply by: *Spring*: December 1; *Summer:* May 1; *Fall*: August 1. Submit resume, cover letter and the museum education intern application to the address below.

Qualifications:

Open to all college freshmen, sophomores, juniors and seniors, recent college graduates and grad students. International applicants are eligible. Prospective interns need to have an interest and/or background in contemporary art, enjoy teaching and working with the public, especially children, and possess a good to excellent grasp of the English language, both spoken and written.

Contact:
Sara L. Cannon, Director
The Los Angeles Municipal Art Gallery
Museum Education and Tours Program
Barnsdall Art Park, 4800 Hollywood Boulevard
Los Angeles, CA 90027
Phone: (323) 644-6269
Fax: (323) 644-6271
E-mail: met_scannon@sbcglobal.net

Los Angeles Times

 THE BUZZ
- "Work for one of the top California newspapers"

THE STATS

Industry(ies): Journalism

Location(s): Los Angeles, CA

Number of interns: *Summer*: 12-20

Pay: Paid; industry competitive

Length of internship: *Summer*: 10 weeks, full-time

 THE SCOOP

Founded in 1881, *The Los Angeles Times* has grown into one of the biggest urban dailies in the U.S. It consists of foreign, national, California, business, arts and features, and sports news, all of which contributed to 35 Pulitzer Prizes since 1942, including four gold medals for public service. The *Times* is published at three Southern California sites: the Los Angeles-based Olympic plant, an Orange County plant in Costa Mesa and a San Fernando Valley plant in Chatsworth. In 2000, the *Times* became part of the Tribune Co.

ON THE JOB

Interns work mostly in Southern California as business, news, sports and features reporters. There are positions available in visual journalism and copyediting. The paper is large and can be daunting to novices, which is why successful candidates usually have had two or three internships elsewhere before the *Times*. Interns should be self-starters ready to undertake complex tasks.

GETTING HIRED

Apply by: Official deadline is January 1, but early submission (October 15) is encouraged. Send a resume, cover letter, personal essay and clips to the address below.

Qualifications:
Open to all college freshmen, sophomores, juniors and seniors, as well as graduate students and recent graduates. Applicants must be within six months of graduation from an undergraduate or graduate program at the start of the internship to remain qualified.

Contact:
Los Angeles Times
Randy Hagihara
Editorial Internship Director
202 West 1st Street
Los Angeles, CA 90012
Phone: (213) 237-7992
E-mail: randy.hagihara@latimes.com
www.latimes.com

The Lowell Whiteman School

 THE BUZZ
- "Teach bright youngsters and ski all winter"
- "Academic schlussers wanted"

THE STATS

Industry(ies): Education; Sports

Location(s): Steamboat Springs, CO

Number of interns: *Annual*: 3-4

Pay: $11,500/year. Health benefits; season ski pass; room and board

Length of internship: 9 months

 THE SCOOP

Located in "Ski-Town U.S.A.," the Lowell Whiteman School – a co-ed, college prep boarding and day school – is nestled in the Rocky Mountains. Rigorous academics are paired with an experiential program, which focuses on outdoor activity, taking full advantage of all that Northwestern Colorado has to offer. Each student commits to a track of foreign travel or competitive skiing or riding. The school doesn't just educate minds; it educates "body and spirit." Lowell Whiteman, who died in 2001, launched the concept as a youth camp in 1946, expanding it to a school in 1957.

 ON THE JOB

Resident interns live and work in the high school students' dorms (one in each of the two boys' dorms and one or two in the girls' dorm). They assist the dorm parents in supervising the students in their residential lives, including kitchen work and weekend dorm duty. Interns also supervise afternoon activities such as backpacking, mountain biking, rock climbing, skiing, snowboarding, horseback riding, kayaking and canoeing. Interns teach one or two academic classes.

GETTING HIRED

Apply by: Rolling. Contact the head of school (see below) for application information.

Qualifications:
Open to all recent college graduates who have worked with high school students in the past.

Contact:
Walter H. Daub, Head of School
Lowell Whitman School
42605 Routt County Road #36
Steamboat Springs, CO 80487
E-mail: daubw@lws.edu
www.lws.edu

Visit Vault at **www.vault.com** for insider company profiles, expert advice, career message boards, expert resume reviews, the Vault Job Board and more.

 **269**

LucasFilm

 THE BUZZ

- "The film force must be with you if you nab this top slot"

THE STATS

Industry(ies): Broadcast & Entertainment; Film; New/Interactive Media; Technology

Location(s): Nicasio, CA (Skywalker Sound at the Skywalker Ranch); San Rafael, CA (Industrial Light & Magic)

Number of interns: *Annual*: 8-10, depending on project

Pay: Paid; $9/hour. Attend presentations and informal meetings conducted by award-winning artists and executives

Length of internship: *Summer*: June 9-August 15 (11 weeks); 40 hours/week, 9 a.m.-5 p.m.; *winter/spring*: October 14 -April 16; part-time, 16-24 hours/week

THE SCOOP

Founded in 1975 by *Star Wars* legend George Lucas, Industrial Light & Magic is one of the film industry's leading production and entertainment companies. ILM and Skywalker Sound have developed technical and creative innovations, which led to motion control cameras, optical composting and other advances in effects technology. ILM currently employs a core group of over 1,200 staff.

ON THE JOB

Internships at ILM or Skywalker Sound provide an opportunity to learn the business aspect of the entertainment industry. Assignments may be available in marketing, finance, human resources, information technology and services, ranch operations, Internet, archives, library and research, business affairs (legal), guest services, food services and corporate fitness.

GETTING HIRED

Apply by: *Summer*: April 30; *winter/spring*: August 30. Application available at: www.lucasfilm.com/lfl_internship_ programs.pdf. Submit transcripts, letters of recommendation and a one-page cover letter listing department preference and describing what duties you seek. See web site for details.

Qualifications:
Open to college juniors and seniors and college graduates with an overall GPA of at least 3.0 and a GPA of at least 3.5 in declared major.

Contact:
Lucasfilm Ltd.
Human Resources-Intern Department
P.O. Box 10228
San Rafael, CA 94912
Phone: (415) 258-2000
E-mail: resumes@lucasfilm.com
www.lucasfilm.com/employment/intern

Lunar and Planetary Institute

 **THE BUZZ**

- "Keep your eyes on the skies – research the solar system"

THE STATS

Industry(ies): Science/Research; Technology

Location(s): Houston, TX

Number of interns: *Summer*: 12

Pay: $500/week stipend. Assistance with travel expenses to a maximum of $1,000; shared low-cost housing near the LPI can be arranged

Length of internship: *Summer*: 10 weeks (June 5-August 11)

THE SCOOP

Founded in 1968, the Lunar and Planetary Institute researches the evolution, formation and current state of the solar system. The Institute is housed in the Universities Space Research Association's Center for Advanced Space Studies, which includes a computing center, extensive collections of lunar and planetary data, an image-processing facility and an extensive library. LPI also has educational and public outreach programs assisting local and national press on planetary issues.

ON THE JOB

LPI offers an opportunity for students to conduct real studies. Summer interns must complete a research project of current interest in planetary science on projects working one-on-one with a scientist at the Institute or at the Johnson Space Center, which may include the origins of meteorites, lunar resource utilization or any of a number of exciting topics.

GETTING HIRED

Apply by: January 20. Applicants must apply online at www.lpi. usra.edu/lpiintern/application/form.cfm. Paper applications are not accepted. Submit references online; college transcripts must be submitted by mail. Notification of selection will be made by February 22. Successful applicants should be prepared to make a decision regarding the offer to participate within two days of notification. Applicants should check the website for updates.

Qualifications:
Open to college freshmen, sophomores, juniors and seniors, with at least 50 semester hours of academic credit, interested in pursuing a career in the physical sciences. December 2006 graduates and 2007 spring semester graduates are also eligible.

Contact:
LPI Summer Intern Program
Attention: Jodi J. Jordan
3600 Bay Area Boulevard
Houston, TX 77058
Phone: (281) 486-2180
Fax: (281) 486-2127
E-mail: jordan@lpi.usra.edu
www.lpi.usra.edu/lpiintern

Lutheran Volunteer Corps

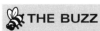 **THE BUZZ**

- "A year of service. A lifetime of commitment."

 **THE STATS**

Industry(ies): Nonprofit; Religious

Location(s): Baltimore, MD; Berkeley, CA; Chicago, IL; Milwaukee, WI; Minneapolis, MN; Oakland, CA; Seattle, WA; St. Paul, MN; Tacoma, WA; Washington, DC (national office); Wilmington, DE

Number of interns: *Annual*: 85-100

Pay: $100/month stipend. Housing, food, health insurance and transportation provided

Length of internship: 1-year commitment; commences in late August

THE SCOOP

The Lutheran Volunteer Corps operates on the belief that "living peacefully with one another is a life-long challenge." Volunteers provide direct service to the marginalized in society and work on the root causes of poverty and oppression. LVC is committed to dismantling racism and oppression within itself and its communities.

 **ON THE JOB**

Some programs involve coordination, development and management of projects. Volunteer placements may include schools, shelters, medical and legal clinics, public policy organizations and general social service agencies. A current list is available on the web site. LVC volunteers live in communities of four to seven, sharing meals and household responsibilities. LVC says this will "build and maintain a supportive community in a rewarding experience."

GETTING HIRED

Apply by: LVC has a rolling application process with four deadlines of February 1, March 1, April 1 and May 15. All volunteers (regardless of application date) have the same start date (late August). A downloadable application is available at www.lutheranvolunteercorps.org/volunteers.htm. Submit three references and a transcript with application.

Qualifications

Open to all individuals at least 21 years of age.

Contact:
Lutheran Volunteer Corps
1226 Vermont Avenue, NW
Washington, DC 20005
Phone: (202) 387-3222
Fax: (202) 667-0037
E-mail: lvcrecruitment@lutheranvolunteercorps.org
www.lutheranvolunteercorps.org

Visit Vault at **www.vault.com** for insider company profiles, expert advice, career message boards, expert resume reviews, the Vault Job Board and more.

VAULT CAREER LIBRARY **271**

INTERNSHIP PROFILES: M

MAD Magazine

THE BUZZ

- "What? You intern? Yes, if you like publishing and satire"

THE STATS

Industry(ies): Publishing

Location(s): New York, NY

Number of interns: *Summer*: 4 (2 editorial, 2 art)

Pay: None; academic credit

Length of internship: About 1 month

THE SCOOP

More than 400 issues of *MAD*, a comic entertainment magazine, have been published to date. the magazine uses humorous writing and comic illustrations to comment satirically on current events and the entertainment industry.

 ON THE JOB

Interns participate in all brainstorming sessions, and work on article conception and development. Previous editorial interns have been hired at *MAD* as full-time employees, and many have sold story ideas to the magazine. Art interns work on the layout of the magazine. Along with helping the art staff produce the publication, art interns should be prepared to fulfill some clerical roles.

GETTING HIRED

Apply by: *Summer*: April 19 (editorial), April 16 (art). Editorial applicants should send one original premise for an article that should be in *MAD* and three examples of how to develop it, along with personal information to the appropriate address below. Art applicants should send resumes and six samples of work to the appropriate address below.

Qualifications:

Editorial interns must be college juniors or seniors or grad students and must be able to receive academic credit. Art interns must be college freshmen, sophomores, juniors or seniors receiving academic credit for the program. They must have some experience in graphic design and typography, as well as Quark XPress experience, and Adobe Photoshop and Illustrator skills.

Contact:

MAD Magazine Internship Program
c/o Amy Vozeolas
1700 Broadway
New York, NY 10019
E-mail: amy.vozeolas@madmagazine.com

MAD Magazine Art Internship Program
c/o Patricia Dwyer
1700 Broadway
New York, NY 10019
E-mail: patty.dwyer@madmagazine.com
www2.warnerbros.com/madmagazine/files/interns/internsearch.html

Madison Square Garden

THE BUZZ

- "Shoot lay-ups during lunch break"
- "How cool is it to say you work at the Garden?"

THE STATS

Industry(ies): Broadcast & Entertainment; Sports

Location(s): New York, NY

Number of interns: *Annual*: 240

Pay: $25/day stipend; academic credit

Length of internship: *Spring*: 5 months; *summer*: 3 months; *fall*: 4 months

THE SCOOP

Madison Square Garden was built in 1879 in midtown Manhattan and is a major sports and events center. The Garden remains the Knicks' home court. Ringling Bros. performs its world-famous circus there when in town, and Ol' Blue Eyes himself (Frank Sinatra) made it a frequent venue, as well. Jimi Hendrix played The Garden in 1969, Tina Turner in 1987 and Jerry Garcia in 1994. Originally in Madison Square, the building's current version stands above the "new" Penn Station.

ON THE JOB

Though intern positions vary depending on management needs, most are related to The Garden's business activities. Applicants should express clearly their career interests, which will be accommodated, if possible. Some departments in which past interns have worked include public relations, advertising, sales and marketing, operations, information technology and new media. In all departments, interns work closely with full-time professionals.

GETTING HIRED

Apply by: *Spring*: December 1; *summer*: April 1; *fall*: August 1. Send resume and letter from an advisor approving academic credit.

Qualifications:

Open to all college sophomores, juniors and seniors, as well as grad students. Must be receiving academic credit for the internship.

Contact:

Internship Coordinator
Madison Square Garden
Human Resources
2 Penn Plaza, 16th Floor
New York, NY 10121
www.thegarden.com/inandaroundgarden_corporate_employment.html

Maine State Music Theatre

 THE BUZZ
- "Explore a top musical internship in gorgeous Maine"

 THE STATS

Industry(ies): Education; Nonprofit; Theater/Performing Arts

Location(s): Brunswick, ME

Number of interns: *Annual*: 22

Pay: $60/week stipend; $70/week stipend for meals. Interns live together for free in a rented fraternity house. Seminars on audition techniques; resume evaluation and preparation; valuable connections with some of the most successful directors, choreographers, designers and performers from New York and New England, whose credits include Broadway, national tours and regional theater

Length of internship: *Summer*: Early May-end of August (13 weeks)

 THE SCOOP

Maine State Music Theatre (MSMT) is a not-for-profit theater production company offering musical theater, live professional performances and outreach programs that entertain and educate. Maine State's productions, including set designs, costumes and musical arrangements, are original. MSMT seeks to preserve the American theatrical experience, holding high quality productions at affordable ticket prices.

 ON THE JOB

Interns work in carpentry, electrics, paints, properties, stage operations, costumes, wardrobe, stage management, company management, marketing and performance. MSMT requires all interns to work in areas other than their expertise so that they may develop an awareness of and appreciation for all areas of a production. Interns put together their own production at the end of the summer.

GETTING HIRED

Apply by: *Summer*: February 28. Send resume, cover letter and transcripts to the address below.

Qualifications:
Open to all students over 18 years of age, high school graduates, college freshmen, sophomores, juniors and seniors, grad students and recent college graduates.

Contact:
Kathi Kacinski
Company Manager
Maine State Music Theatre
22 Maine Street
Brunswick, ME 04011
Phone: (207) 725-8760, ext. 11
Fax: (207) 725-1199
E-mail: jobs@msmt.org
msmt.org/default.asp?contentID=666&rc=591&zm–666

Makovsky & Company

 THE BUZZ
- "Get a broad grounding in PR in the world's capital New York"

 **THE STATS**

Industry(ies): Public Relations

Location(s): New York, NY

Number of interns: *Spring/fall*: 1-2 each; *summer*: 2-3

Pay: Paid; $10/hour. Mentors and seminars in professional development; invitations to social functions

Length of internship: *Spring*: January-May; *summer*: June-August; *fall*: September–December

 THE SCOOP

Makovsky & Company is an independent, full-service public relations and investor relations firm with practice areas in health, technology, communications and financial and professional services. Voted one of the best agencies to work for by *Holmes Report* in 2006, Makovsky has business-to-business marketing expertise and an integrated branding and visual communications division.

 ON THE JOB

Interns generally work on a variety of PR projects and activities including media relations, research, updating media lists, compiling press kit materials and participating in internal account team and brainstorming meetings. Interns learn the PR business step by step as they are assigned their own projects to create and present to executives and staff. Interns are also encouraged to attend luncheons and professional development seminars sponsored by organizations such as the Public Relations Society of America (PRSA) or PR Newswire. The staff also organizes "field trips," most recently to the New York Stock Exchange, Bloomberg Business News and NBC studios, providing a broader perspective into the PR world.

GETTING HIRED

Apply by: *Spring*: December 15; *summer*: April 15; *fall*: August 15. Contact the internship coordinator by mail or email and include a cover letter, resume and writing samples. In-person interviews are required for finalists.

Qualifications:
Open to all college juniors and seniors with a career interest in public relations. Must be available a minimum 20 hours/week for the Fall/Spring and 40 hours/week for the Summer.

Contact:

Internship Coordinator
Makovsky + Company
575 Lexington Avenue, 15th Floor
New York, NY 10022
Phone (212) 508-9600
Fax (212) 751-9710
info@makovsky.com

Visit Vault at **www.vault.com** for insider company profiles, expert advice, career message boards, expert resume reviews, the Vault Job Board and more.

V∧ULT CAREER LIBRARY **275**

Manhattan Theatre Club

 THE BUZZ
- "An intense and involved New York theater internship"

 THE STATS

Industry(ies): Broadcast & Entertainment; Theater/Performing Arts

Location(s): New York, NY

Number of interns: *Annual*: 60; *spring/summer/fall*: 12-20 each

Pay: $235/week stipend. Free performances at MTC; free and discounted ticket offers to other companies Broadway and off-Broadway performances; invitations to readings of new plays and educational seminars.

Length of internship: *Spring*: January-May; *summer*: June-August; *fall*: September-December

 THE SCOOP

Manhattan Theatre Club is the center of some of America's most gifted theatrical artists, producing works by established and emerging playwrights for over three decades. Each year, MTC produces a season of works by established and emerging playwrights.

ON THE JOB

The Paul A. Kaplan Theatre Management Program at Manhattan Theatre Club is a full-time internship. Various positions are available in business, casting, development, education, general management, literary, marketing, production management, properties, theater management and as a production assistant. Interns will be assigned to work on specific projects within the office as well as general administrative duties.

GETTING HIRED

Apply by: *Spring*: second Friday in November; *summer*: second Friday in March; *fall*: last Friday in June. All applications must be received by 5 p.m. Eastern Standard Time. Submit an application, resume, cover letter and two reference letters to the address below. Application form available at: www.mtc-nyc.org/education/2005Intern_Application.htm.

Qualifications:
Open to all college freshmen, sophomores, juniors and seniors, recent college graduates, grad students and early-career professionals.

Contact:
The Paul A. Kaplan Theatre Management Program
Manhattan Theatre Club
Internship Coordinator
311 West 43rd Street, 8th Floor
New York, NY 10036
Fax: (212) 399-4329
E-mail: interns@mtc-nyc.org
www.mtc-nyc.org/education/internships.htm

Manice Education Center

 THE BUZZ
- "Help city kids learn about nature"

 THE STATS

Industries: Education; Environmental; Nonprofit

Location: Florida, MA; New York, NY

Number of interns: *Annual*: 10

Pay: $200/week. Room and board; insurance and equipment discounts

Length of internship: Varies; usually 3-6 months

 THE SCOOP

Manice Education Center is a nonprofit institution encouraging urban youth to take an interest in the environment and natural sciences. Manice coordinates field days and organizes courses in ecology, gardening, wilderness skills and geology.

ON THE JOB

Interns co-lead educational activities related to ecology, wilderness, leadership skills and group initiatives with Manice's field teachers. Summer wilderness education interns host and guide wilderness expeditions (canoeing and backpacking) in natural areas around the Northeast.

GETTING HIRED

Apply by: *Spring*: March 1; *summer*: May 1; *fall*: July 1; *winter*: September 1. Send an application, resume and cover letter to the address below. E-mail info@christodora.org to request an application form.

Qualifications:
Open to students with at least one year of college-level work in related subject, college graduates of any age and grad students. Lifeguard, first aid and CPR certifications are preferred.

Contact:
Christodora-Manice Education Center
One East 53rd Street
New York, NY 10022
Phone: (212) 371-5225
Fax: (212) 371-2111
E-mail: info@christodora.org
www.christodora.org
or

Mike Vecchiarelli
Manice Education Center
68 Savoy Road
Florida, MA 01247
Phone/Fax: (413) 663-8463
E-mail: mikev@christodora.org

Manus & Associates Literary Agency

 THE BUZZ
- "Book lovers, become a literary agent"
- "Bury your head in this spellbinding internship!"

THE STATS

Industry(ies): Publishing

Location(s): New York, NY; Palo Alto, CA

Number of interns: *Annual*: 8

Pay: None; free books

Length of internship: *Spring/summer/fall*: 12 weeks-1 year; at least 10 hours/week

 THE SCOOP

Manus & Associates Literary Agency, Inc., has represented independent authors in New York and the San Francisco Bay Area for the past 15 years. The firm has an office on each coast. Manus represents authors of commercial literary fiction, suspense and thrillers, multicultural fiction, biographies, parenting titles, travel and self-help books.

 ON THE JOB

Interns with Manus & Associates learn all facets of the literary agency market. Duties range from screening incoming queries to managing client and editorial correspondence. The firm helps its interns develop a "literary eye".

GETTING HIRED

Apply by: Rolling. Contact the internship coordinator in your area. Applicants pick up five 100-page manuscript excerpts, which they are asked to read and evaluate in writing (about one page each) in about a week's time. Their coverage is then read by the agency, and applicants are contacted by phone.

Qualifications:

Open to students who have completed at least one year of undergraduate work. Applicants who demonstrate critical reading or who have publishing, writing or editorial experience are preferred.

Contact:

Manus & Associates Literary Agency, Inc.
445 Park Avenue
New York, NY 10022
Phone: (212) 644-8020
Fax: (212) 644-3374

Manus & Associates Literary Agency, Inc.
425 Sherman Avenue, Suite 200
Palo Alto, CA 94306
Phone: (650) 470-5151
Fax: (650) 470-5159
E-mail: ManusLit@ManusLit.com
www.manuslit.com/old/Internship.htm

Marsh

 THE BUZZ
- "Can you handle a little risk?"
- "Innovative approach to risk solutions"

THE STATS

Industry(ies): Financial Services; Insurance; Management & Strategy Consulting

Location(s): Atlanta, GA; Boston, MA; Charlotte, NC; Chicago, IL; Cleveland, OH; Dallas, TX; Detroit; MI; Ft. Lauderdale, FL; Houston, TX; Los Angeles, CA; Minneapolis, MN; Morristown, NJ; Newport Beach, CA; New York, NY; Philadelphia, PA; Pittsburgh, PA; Richmond, VA; San Francisco, CA; Seattle, WA; St. Louis, MO; Washington, DC

Number of interns: *Summer*: 50

Pay: Paid; amount varies with placement

Length of internship: *Summer*: 10 weeks

 THE SCOOP

With over 400 of the Fortune 500 companies on its client roster and over 130 years of experience, Marsh Inc. is the No. 1 risk management specialist in the world. Marsh has over 400 offices in 100 countries, housing over 27,000 employees and over $5 billion in revenue. Organizations and individuals hire Marsh to protect their personal and financial assets through the broad range of industry and risk specialties it offers, including corporate governance, financial performance and global expansion. Marsh advises these companies and clients on their risk management needs, including international mergers and acquisitions, e-commerce, technology, cross-border trade and operations, and intellectual property.

 ON THE JOB

Marsh interns are offered a range of work experience and learning opportunities to develop and enhance skills and to acquire a career foundation. Interns work alongside a team of risk professionals, helping to analyze client accounts and assist with new client development. Responsibilities may include analyzing client data and compiling research results using company databases and other computer systems; maintaining billing control records and developing budgetary data; participating in the analyses of clients' existing insurance programs and requirements; helping to assess client needs by reviewing current policies and formulating recommendations for various policies; assisting team members in developing underwriting specifications; and preparing proposal presentations for existing and prospective clients.

GETTING HIRED

Apply by: *Summer:* February 1. Apply online at: www.marshcampuscareers.com.

Qualifications:

Intern opportunities open to college juniors with a 3.0 GPA or higher.

Contact:

Marsh, Campus Relations
1166 Avenue of the Americas
New York, NY 10036
Phone: (212) 345-6000
www.marshcampuscareers.com

Visit Vault at **www.vault.com** for insider company profiles, expert advice, career message boards, expert resume reviews, the Vault Job Board and more.

VAULT CAREER LIBRARY 277

The Martin Agency

 THE BUZZ
- "A crash course in advertising"
- "Get used to the fast-paced ad world"

THE STATS

Industry(ies): Advertising

Location(s): Richmond, VA

Number of interns: *Summer/winter*: about 15 each

Pay: None

Length of internship: *Summer/winter*: 10 days each

 THE SCOOP

The Martin Agency, a comprehensive advertising and marketing firm, started in Richmond, Va., and now has an additional office in New York City. It stresses a strategic and creative approach that has won over companies such as Coca-Cola, UPS, Hanes, TV Land, NASCAR and Olympus. Perhaps the most telling sign of the company's success, however, is the fact that it does advertising work for the Ad Council. Martin employs around 320 professionals between both offices.

ON THE JOB

In Martin's Student Workshop program, teams of five students work with one of the agency's professionals (usually an account manager) on a specific project. Each team creates an ad concept for its client and a strategy for implementing the concept, including an integrated marketing plan. At the end of the session, interns present their plan to agency execs and client representatives. The workshops are held twice a year at the company's Virginia offices during college breaks.

GETTING HIRED

Apply by: *Summer*: April 1; *winter*: November 1. Contact the company for an application.

Qualifications:
Open to all college freshmen, sophomores, juniors and seniors, and recent college graduates.

Contact:
Allison Mays, Internship Coordinator
Martin Agency
One Shockoe Plaza
Richmond, VA 23219
Phone: (804) 698-8219
Fax: (804) 698-8001
allison.mays@martinagency.com
www.martinagency.com

Marvel Comics

 THE BUZZ
- "If you loved comics as a kid, try this grown-up internship"

THE STATS

Industry(ies): Broadcast & Entertainment; New/Interactive Media; Publishing

Location(s): Los Angeles, CA; New York, NY

Number of interns: *Spring/summer/fall*: 15-20 each

Pay: None; must receive academic credit

Length of internship: *Spring/summer/fall*: 3-4 months each

THE SCOOP

Creators of the best-known comic book heroes, including Spider-Man, X-Men and the Incredible Hulk, it is no wonder Marvel boasts that 75 percent of American children have read its comic books. In addition to the above three superheroes, Marvel's entire collection of characters totals over 4,700. Encompassing comic book publishing, entertainment, licensing, toys and Internet/new media, Marvel stands at the forefront of the comic book industry.

ON THE JOB

Each intern is assigned to one department within the company. Departments include editorial, production, creative services, human resources, accounting, legal, scanning intern, manufacturing, sales and marketing, and marvel.com. Marvel's web site details intern functions in each of these categories. Nonetheless, much of the work is of the "run and fetch" variety.

GETTING HIRED

Apply by: Rolling. Send resume, cover letter and a letter from your college stating that you will receive academic credit to the address below.

Qualifications:
Open to college freshmen, sophomores, juniors and seniors. Must be able to receive academic credit. International applicants are eligible.

Contact:
Internship Coordinator
Marvel Enterprises, Inc.
10 East 40th Street
New York, NY 10016
E-mail: internship@marvel.com
www.marvel.com/company/careers.htm
(No phone calls, please!)

Mass Media Science & Engineering Fellows Program

THE BUZZ

- "Write for *Scientific American* or pitch stories at NPR"

THE STATS

Industry(ies): Engineering; Journalism; Science/Research

Location(s): Past sites have included: Albuquerque, NM; Atlanta, GA; Chicago, IL; Columbus, OH; Dallas, TX; Greeley, CO; Los Angeles, CA; Milwaukee, WI; New York, NY; Portland, OR; Raleigh, NC; Richmond, VA; Sacramento, CA; Seattle, WA; St. Louis, MO

Number of interns: *Summer:* 20-25

Pay: Paid; $450/week for 10 weeks; travel expenses

Length of internship: *Summer:* 10 weeks

 THE SCOOP

Sponsored by American Association for the Advancement of Science, as well as other nonprofit organizations, the Mass Media Science & Engineering Fellows Program was founded in 1975. The goal of the program is to engage scientists in the communications field and facilitate public understanding and appreciation of the sciences.

ON THE JOB

Fellows work with media professionals in mass media organizations nationwide, as reporters, researchers and production assistants. They participate in the news-making process, learning to communicate their scientific knowledge to the public.

GETTING HIRED

Apply by: January 15. Download an application at www.aaas.org/programs/education/MassMedia/. Send completed application, along with current resume, brief writing sample(s) as directed, transcripts of undergraduate and graduate work to date, and three letters of recommendation to the address below.

Qualifications:
Open to exemplary college seniors and graduate students in the fields of natural, health, physical, engineering or social sciences.

Contact:
AAAS Mass Media Science & Engineering Fellows Program
1200 New York Avenue, NW
Washington, DC 20005
Phone: (202) 326-6441
Fax: (202) 371-9849
www.aaas.org/programs/education/massmedia/

Mattel Toys

THE BUZZ

- "Get a great grounding in the world of toys"
- "Not just for Malibu Barbie fans"

THE STATS

Industry(ies): Consumer Products; Manufacturing

Location(s): El Segundo, CA; Mount Laurel, NJ

Number of interns: *Summer:* 24 (20 MBAs; 4 undergrads)

Pay: Paid; *undergraduates:* $450-$600/week; *grad students:* $900-$1,100/week. Fitness center; dry cleaning service; 25 percent company store discount

Length of internship: *Summer:* 10-12 weeks

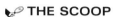 THE SCOOP

If you've ever played with toys, you're likely to be familiar with Mattel products. Makers of Barbie, American Girl, Hot Wheels and Fisher Price, Mattel trumps the toy competition; it's one of the largest toy sellers in the world. Founded in a garage in 1948 by Elliot and Ruth Handler and Harold Matson, Mattel now manufactures and sells its products around the globe.

ON THE JOB

Interns do project-based work. Mattel challenges them to use "teamwork, ingenuity, and creativity" while handling the responsibilities of a full-time employee. Mattel actively recruits for its coveted intern positions at select campuses, as well as the National Society of Hispanic MBA's and the National Black MBA Association, Inc.

GETTING HIRED

Apply by: February 28. See the web site (www.mattel.com/careers/ca_campusrec.asp) for details. E-mail resume to the appropriate address below.

Qualifications:
Open to first-year MBA students in marketing and finance.

Contact:
Mattel, Inc.
Corporate Staffing-Internships
333 Continental Blvd., MI-0210
El Segundo, CA 90245
Phone: (310) 252-2000
Fax: (310) 252-4423
E-mail: MBAIntern@Mattel.com (MBAs)
E-mail: UndergradInterns@Mattel.com (undergrads)
www.mattel.com

Visit Vault at **www.vault.com** for insider company profiles, expert advice, career message boards, expert resume reviews, the Vault Job Board and more.

V/\ULT CAREER LIBRARY 279

McLean Hospital

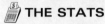 THE BUZZ
- "Hospital volunteers with a heart of gold"
- "McLean needs your help"

THE STATS

Industry(ies): Health Care

Location(s): Belmont, MA

Number of interns: *Psychiatry residents*: 73/annual; *psychology interns*: 15/annual

Pay: Varies with position and experience

Length of Internship: Varies with availability

THE SCOOP

McLean is the largest psychiatric clinical care, teaching and research facility of Harvard Medical School and also has the largest private psychiatric research program in neuroscience and psychiatry in the United States. With more than 1,000 employees, McLean offers the full spectrum of care for all psychiatric disorders for people of all ages.

ON THE JOB

Volunteers' main task, according to McLean, is to assist in a "variety of changing needs and help to create a friendly, caring climate." They perform a variety of specific duties throughout McLean's clinical services and programs, "including inpatient units, partial hospital and residential programs, rehabilitation programs, patient education programs and the Cole Mental Health Consumer Resource Center." Through volunteers' particular areas of concentration, they work under staff supervision and may also assist with basic clinical research, as well as support services for offices and the library.

GETTING HIRED

Apply by: Rolling. Download application at www.mclean hospital.org/HumanResources/volunteer_application.html. Send completed application, along with resume and cover letter, to the address below.

Qualifications:
Open to high school graduates, college freshmen, sophomores, juniors and seniors, colleges grads, graduate students, and all individuals who are at least 18 years of age.

Contact:
McLean Hospital
115 Mill Street
Belmont, MA 02478
Switchboard: (617) 855-2000
Phone: (800) 333-0338
E-mail: info@mclean.harvard.edu
www.mcleanhospital.org/HumanResources/volunteer.html

Mercer Oliver Wyman

THE BUZZ
- "A boutique international financial consulting firm"

THE STATS

Industry(ies): Financial Services; Management & Strategy Consulting

Location(s): New York, NY (HQ); various North American offices. Interns staffed out of offices in New York; London; Frankfurt; Madrid; Paris; Milan; Stockholm

Number of interns: *Summer*: approximately 30-50, globally

Pay: Paid; competitive salary

Length of Internship: *Summer*: 8-10 weeks

THE SCOOP

Mercer Oliver Wyman was formed in April 2003 following the merger of Oliver, Wyman and Company (founded in 1984) and the financial services sector of Mercer Management Consulting Inc., a subsidiary of Marsh & McLennan Companies, Inc. MOW is one of the leading international financial services strategy and risk management consulting firms. Headquartered in New York City, Mercer employs more than 950 staff members in 27 offices operating in 13 countries throughout North America, Europe and Asia Pacific.

ON THE JOB

MOW interns are treated like full-time entry-level consultants and have the opportunity to work on projects and complete a distinct piece of work. Feedback and formal review is presented upon completion of the project. The 8- to 10-week internship typically leads to an offer of permanent employment for strong performers.

In addition to real project work, the intern class is provided with training and events throughout the summer. These events (ranging from community service projects to sporting events) allow interns to get to know the majority of the directors and consultants in the office.

GETTING HIRED

Apply by: Varies between offices. Consult current consultant vacancies at www.merceroliverwyman.com/en/Careers/Vacancies/Consultants.xml for each office's application deadline. Online applications are available at www.mow.gtios.com/.

Qualifications:
Open to undergraduate juniors and seniors. Internship candidates should display extraordinary intellectual capacity, maturity and judgment as demonstrated by their academic achievements and extracurricular activities. Strong candidates will exhibit intellectual curiosity and be capable of learning quantitative techniques.

Contact:
Liz Herndon
NA Campus Recruiting
Mercer Oliver Wyman
99 Park Avenue, 5th Floor
New York, NY 10016
E-mail: recruitingna@mow.com
www.mow.gtios.com/

Merck

 THE BUZZ
- "Proscar and Propecia in your future"

THE STATS

Industry(ies): Health Care; Pharmaceuticals

Location(s): Multiple cities in AZ; CA; FL; GA; IL; IN; KS; MD; MA; MN; MO; NV; NJ; NC; OH; PA; TX; VA; WA; Puerto Rico; and multiple international locations

Number of interns: *Annual*: 300

Pay: Paid; *undergraduates*: $560-920/week; *graduates*: $950-1520/week. Daily transportation; housing; relocation assistance; sponsored activities

Length of internship: *Intern*: 12-14 weeks; *summer/co-op*: 1 or 2 6-month sessions; available year-round

THE SCOOP

Merck & Co., Inc, established in 1891, is one of the world's largest pharmaceutical companies. The company conducts research at 11 major centers in the U.S., Europe and Japan, publishes health information and distributes vaccines and drugs to 150 countries. Merck also donates some of its vaccines. Its product line includes vaccines for Hepatitis A and B, chicken pox and pneumonia, among others, as well as consumer drugs such as Zocor (modifies cholesterol), Singulair (for asthma) and Propecia (a hair loss remedy).

ON THE JOB

Interns/co-ops work in many sections including research, manufacturing, sales and marketing, public affairs, human resources, finance and computer resources. Interns are assigned to at least one project, including drug research using genomics, market research of cardiovascular drugs and helping to develop the company's computer infrastructure. The internship includes an ending presentation or report, with interns receiving evaluations from their managers.

GETTING HIRED

Apply by: February 15. Apply online at www.merck.com/careers/search_jobs/index.html.

Qualifications:

Open to college juniors and seniors and grad students.

Contact:
Merck & Company
1 Merck Drive
P.O. Box 100
Whitehouse Station, NJ 08889-0100
www.merck.com/careers/search_jobs/index.html

Merrill Lynch

THE BUZZ
- "The kind of bull you want on your resume"

THE STATS

Industry(ies): Investment Banking; Investment Management; Global Marketing; Global Private Client

Location(s): Global; internships available in Chicago, IL; Hopewell, NJ; Houston, TX; Jersey City, NJ; Los Angeles, CA; New York, NY; Palo Alto, CA; Princeton, NJ; Hong Kong; London; Tokyo; Toronto

Number of interns: *Summer*: 450 interns throughout the U.S., 550 globally

Pay: Paid; competitive salary

Length of internship: *Summer*: 10-12 weeks

 THE SCOOP

Founded in 1914, Merrill Lynch is one of the largest financial services firms in the world. Its businesses include investment banking, global markets, global private client, inverstment management (through Blackrock) and corporate and enterprose-wide businesses, such as technology and chief financial office. Its services are offered to clients in 36 countries. At the end of the second quarter of 2006 its impressive profile boasted $589 billion in client assets under mangement and record net revenues of $16.1 billion.

ON THE JOB

Merrill Lynch grooms interns to become future full-time employees and, in fact, 75 percent go on to do just that. Internships begin with a training session, followed by a placement in a specific group where interns learn on the job from experienced Merrill Lynch professionals and are given significant responsibilities.

GETTING HIRED

Apply by: December 15. Apply through the Merrill Lynch web site, which features a career match grid to help find the perfect fit for your skills and interests. Each position is clearly explained, along with application requirements.

Qualifications:

Open to rising college seniors. Qualifications vary by position and are detailed on the Merrill Lynch web site.

Contact:
Visit the Merrill Lynch web site for direct applications.
www.ml.com/careers

Visit Vault at **www.vault.com** for insider company profiles, expert advice, career message boards, expert resume reviews, the Vault Job Board and more.

 **VAULT** CAREER LIBRARY **281**

MetLife

 THE BUZZ
- "If it's good enough for Snoopy, it's good enough for you"

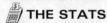 **THE STATS**

Industry(ies): Financial Services; Insurance

Location(s): Nationwide

Number of interns: *Annual*: 50

Pay: Commission; state licensing and NASD registration fees

Length of internship: *Spring/summer/fall*: 12-15 weeks; 15-20 hours/week

 THE SCOOP

MetLife (Met) is the leading insurance provider in the U.S. The company is ranked 36 in the Fortune 500, has $2.5 trillion of life insurance in force, over 49,000 employees, $36 billion in revenues and $2.22 billion in net income. In fact, it is the preferred financial advisor and insurance provider in over 10 million households, "including the Peanuts family." The company has made the list of *Working Mother* magazine's 100 Best Companies for Working Mothers for five consecutive years. MetLife provides private and business insurance, retirement planning and small business services.

 **ON THE JOB**

The internship program was founded in 1999. Interns work in sales. All are assigned mentors and then are put to work identifying and pursuing potential clients and accompanying the mentor on client calls. Interns are licensed, at Met's expense, and then trained in Met's services, as well as in prospecting, selling and underwriting.

$ GETTING HIRED

Apply by: Rolling. E-mail resume to salesinterns@metlife.com.

Qualifications:

Open to college juniors and seniors and grad students. Opportunities are also available for two-year community college graduates with work experience.

Contact:
MetLife
IB Recruiting Department
Sales Internship Program
E-mail: salesinterns@metlife.com
www.metlife.com

The Metropolitan Museum of Art

 THE BUZZ
- "Spend a summer surrounded by great works of art"

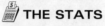 **THE STATS**

Industry(ies): Art/Museum

Location(s): New York, NY

Number of interns: *Summer*: 28 undergrads; 16 graduates

Pay: Paid; *Cloisters undergrads*: $2,750; *Met undergrads*: $3,250; *grad students*: $3,500

Length of internship: *Summer*: 10 weeks

THE SCOOP

The Metropolitan Museum of Art is one of the world's largest art museums, both in size and scope. Its impressive collection contains over 2 million works of art, ranging from Egyptian mummies and South American pottery, to American art and contemporary masterpieces. In particular, the Met prides itself on its 2,500 European paintings, which include several Rembrandts and Vermeers, as well as a cross section of Impressionists. The Met opened in 1870 with 174 paintings and has been at its current Central Park East location since 1880. It has 17 curatorial departments with 1,800 full-time staff and 900 volunteers.

ON THE JOB

Interns work in curatorial, administrative and educational departments, including conservation, communications, development, library, merchandising and registration. In addition, undergraduate interns take turns staffing the information desks and giving gallery talks.

$ GETTING HIRED

Apply by: January (inquire earlier). Send, via regular mail, a resume, official transcript(s), two academic references, a list of relevant courses and foreign languages, and a 500-word (maximum) essay describing your career goals, interest in museum work and reasons for applying. Cloisters applicants, send application to the Cloisters address. For more information on application procedures, visit the Met's internship web site at www.metmuseum.org/education/er_internship.asp.

Qualifications:

Open to college seniors and recent college graduates. Graduate internship is open to candidates who have completed one year of graduate work.

Contact:
Education Department Internship Program
The Metropolitan Museum of Art
1000 Fifth Avenue
New York, NY 10028-0198
Phone: (212) 570-3710
E-mail: mmainterns@metmuseum.org

College Internship Program
The Cloisters
Fort Tryon Park
New York, NY 10040
www.metmuseum.org/education/er_internship.asp

Microsoft

 THE BUZZ
- "It's Gates' world – this is your chance to live in it"

 **THE STATS**

Industry(ies): Software; Technology

Location(s): Silicon Valley, CA; Redmond, WA

Number of interns: *Summer*: 700

Pay: Paid; $450-$650/week. Round-trip transportation; subsidized housing (all amenities provided) and car rental/bike purchase; gym membership; software discounts; free t-shirts; training seminars

Length of internship: *Summer*: 12+ weeks

 THE SCOOP

Founded in 1975 by Harvard dropout Bill Gates, Microsoft is the largest computer software producer and provider in the world. The company led the personal computer revolution in the 1980s, then transformed the computing world when it launched its operating software Windows in 1990. Today, with 2003 net revenues of over $32 billion, Microsoft could well be the largest software company in the world.

 **ON THE JOB**

The first-week for interns is set aside for orientation. Interns are assigned to a full-time mentor and to one of four areas: program manager, software design engineer, software design engineer in test or software test engineer. They work on actual projects and in groups alongside full-time employees. The company uses its internship program to recruit full-time employees.

GETTING HIRED

Apply by: Rolling. Submit resume online (see www. microsoft.com/college/joinus/submit.asp for instructions) or send it to the address below.

Qualifications:
Open to college freshmen, sophomores, juniors and seniors with an interest in technology. While a technical major is not required, prospective interns must possess some technical aptitude. International applicants are welcome to apply.

Contact:
Attention: Recruiting
Microsoft Corporation
One Microsoft Way, Suite 303
Redmond, WA 98052-8303
Phone: (425) 882-8080
E-mail: resume@microsoft.com
www.microsoft.com/college/intern

Middle Earth Academy, Inc.

 THE BUZZ
- "A non-Tolkien-based internship to help at-risk youth"

THE STATS

Industry(ies): Education; Nonprofit

Location(s): Warminster, PA

Number of interns: *Annual*: 4

Pay: None. Free t-shirts; free lunch

Length of internship: 1 semester in the school year

THE SCOOP

Middle Earth is an alternative school and treatment center for at-risk youth. It was founded in 1974 to minimize the risk of institutionalization and incarceration. In addition to academic classes, Middle Earth offers rehabilitative treatment, job preparation and recreational activities.

ON THE JOB

Interns learn how to work with at-risk youth and attend training seminars in teaching, communication and conflict management. They assist in classrooms, counsel students, and supervise recreational activities including bowling, deep-sea fishing, horseback riding, skiing and softball.

GETTING HIRED

Apply by: Rolling. Write to the director at the address below for an application.

Qualifications:
Open to college freshmen, sophomores, juniors and seniors, all college graduates and grad students.

Contact:
Elizabeth Quigley, Ed. S.
Director
Middle Earth Academy
299 Jacksonville Road
Warminster, PA 18974
Phone: (215) 443-0280
Fax: (215) 443-0245

Visit Vault at **www.vault.com** for insider company profiles, expert advice, career message boards, expert resume reviews, the Vault Job Board and more.

VAULT CAREER LIBRARY **283**

Middle East Institute

 THE BUZZ
- "Educate Americans about the Middle East"
- "Great opportunity to brush up on your Arabic"

 THE STATS

Industry(ies): Nonprofit

Location(s): Washington, DC

Number of interns: 10-15

Pay: None; academic credit available. Local transportation stipend; free language course; 1-year membership to the Institute

Length of internship: *Spring/summer/fall*: 12-15 weeks; minimum 20 hours

 **THE SCOOP**

Founded in 1946, the nonprofit, nonpartisan Middle East Institute facilitates American understanding of the Middle East. It provides a forum for a free and unbiased exchange of ideas. MEI is concerned with both cultural and political understanding, which it promotes by offering performances, hosting conferences and presenting lecturers. MEI also publishes *The Middle East Journal*, offers language classes and houses a 25,000-volume library.

 ON THE JOB

Interns work in development (research prospective donors, handle correspondence), publications (write the chronology section of the *Journal*, annotations, compile bibliographies), programs (plan and administer lectures, exhibits, language courses, outreach materials), communications (edit press releases and opeds, monitor the Arab and European press, cover congressional hearings), in the Sultan Qaboos Cultural Center (plan and administer Omani and Gulf-related lectures, events, and outreach materials), and as research assistants for the scholars. All interns write policy briefs and assist with the annual conference held in the fall.

 GETTING HIRED

Apply by: *Spring*: November 15; *summer*: Mach 15; *fall*: july 15. Send cover letter, resume, official college transcript, five-page writing sample and letter of recommendation to the address below.

Qualifications:
Open to undergraduates, recent graduates and graduate students. Preferred skills include superior writing, organizing, word processing and Middle Eastern language skills.

Contact:
Internship Coordinator
Middle East Institute
1761 N Street, NW
Washington, DC 20036
Phone: (202) 785-1141 x206
www.mideasti.org

Middle East Research and Information Project

 THE BUZZ
- "Inform others about the Middle East and learn magazine journalism to boot"

 THE STATS

Industry(ies): Journalism; Nonprofit; Publishing

Location(s): Washington, DC

Number of interns: *Annual*: 9

Pay: None

Length of internship: *Spring*: 1 semester; *summer*: 2-3 months; *fall*: 1 semester

 THE SCOOP

Established in 1971, the Middle East Research and Information Project (MERIP) publishes a quarterly magazine and hosts a vibrant web site. As its name implies, MERIP is a cornerstone of English-language research and information on the Middle East. Respected and used by journalists and scholars in Europe and the United States, MERIP provides information that is not colored by political, religious or cultural bias. In addition to its 48-page journal, MERIP serves as an authority on Middle East issues, providing lectures and interviews.

 ON THE JOB

Interns gain exposure to and experience in magazine production, media relations and nonprofit services. Interns assist editors with a variety of projects, according to their interests and abilities, including research, proofreading, preparing web site content, producing the journal and finding photographs.

GETTING HIRED

Apply by: *Spring*: November 15; *summer*: April 15; *fall*: July 15. Paste a cover letter explaining your interest in MERIP and specifying your dates of availability in an email to ctoensing@merip.org and attach a resume. No writing samples, please. See www.merip.org/misc/internships.html for additional details.

Qualifications:
Open to college students, recent college graduates and grad students.

Contact:
MERIP Internship
1500 Massachusetts Avenue, NW, Suite 119
Washington, DC 20005
Phone: (202) 223-3604
E-mail: ctoensing@merip.org
www.merip.org/misc/internships.html

Miller Brewing Company

 THE BUZZ

- "Learn about the brewing business in beer heartland Milwaukee"

 THE STATS

Industry(ies): Food & Beverage

Location(s): Milwaukee, WI

Number of interns: *Summer*: 52

Pay: Varies depending on position

Length of internship: *Summer*: 10-12 weeks; 40 hours/week

 THE SCOOP

The Miller Brewing Company was founded in 1855 in Milwaukee, Wisconsin, by Frederick J. Miller. Now a subsidiary of SABMiller, plc, Miller has seven major breweries and a portfolio of award-winning beer brands and is a brewing presence in over 40 countries.

 ON THE JOB

Interns work in finance, I/S, sales, pricing, operations, engineering, supply chain, brewing research and quality assurance, breweries, and procurement. Interns are treated like full-time employees and are included in staff meetings, trained and have access to high-level management. Miller recruits at universities around the country and hires many past interns for full-time positions.

GETTING HIRED

Apply by: Rolling. Apply through the Careers page at www.millerbrewing.com.

Qualifications:
Open to college juniors. Minimum 3.0 GPA.

Contact:
www.millerbrewing.com/

Milwaukee Journal Sentinel

 THE BUZZ

- "Budding Wisconsin journalists start here"

 THE STATS

Industry(ies): Journalism

Location(s): Milwaukee, WI

Number of interns: *Annual*: 12 +

Pay: Paid; $450/week

Length of internship: *Summer*: 12 weeks

 THE SCOOP

The *Milwaukee Journal Sentinel* was formed in 1995 when the two largest Milwaukee newspapers merged. It has the second-largest metro market reach in the country – four out of every five people in metropolitan Milwaukee read the *Journal Sentinel*. Its circulation figures are 235,704 daily and 405,355 on Sunday. A publicly traded paper, it is self-described as "a community of creative people working together, telling stories, anticipating important issues."

 ON THE JOB

Mentorship and information sessions ensure that interns get on the fast track to working the newsroom. Interns are thrown into the pond with other reporters, vying for front-page stories. They work in specific departments including entertainment, local news, sports reporting, copyediting, graphic, layout and photography.

 GETTING HIRED

Apply by: November 1. Send resume, cover letter and clips/portfolio to the address below.

Qualifications:
Open to junior and senior journalism undergrads (though the paper has accepted younger students who have appropriate experience) and recent college graduates.

Contact:
Marilyn Krause, Senior Editor/Administration
Milwaukee Journal Sentinel
333 West State Street
P.O. Box 371
Milwaukee, WI 53201-0371
Phone: (414) 224-2185
Fax: (414) 224-2772
E-mail: mkrause@journalsentinel.com
www.jsonline.com/recruitment

Visit Vault at **www.vault.com** for insider company profiles, expert advice, career message boards, expert resume reviews, the Vault Job Board and more.

V\ULT CAREER LIBRARY **285**

Miniwanca Educational Center

 THE BUZZ
- "Youth education in Michigan"

THE STATS

Industry(ies): Education; Nonprofit

Location(s): Shelby, MI

Number of interns: *Fall/spring*: 3 each

Pay: $400/2 weeks. Room and board; full-year interns also receive health benefits

Length of internship: *Fall*: (mid-August–December); *spring*: (mid-January–early June); *full-year* (February 1-November)

 THE SCOOP

The Miniwanca Educational Center is one of two educational facilities run by the American Youth Foundation. Miniwanca is located on 360 acres of wooded sandy dunes that extend for a mile along Lake Michigan. The Center, with a self-stated mission "to develop leadership capacities of youth and the adults and institutions that serve youth," hosts youth leadership workshops and a summer camp.

ON THE JOB

Interns are initiated into the program through an intensive training, where they learn the Center's experiential education process that promotes cooperative community building, leadership development, service learning and personal growth. Once initiated, they join the community by coordinating and running the various educational, recreational and conference outreach programs. Interns will practice leadership skills and seek to live a balanced life. Visit Miniwana's internship web site, www.ayf.com/jobs_int_mw.asp, for details.

GETTING HIRED

Apply by: *Fall*: May 31; *spring*: November 30. Send cover letter, resume, application (available online), three references, police background check and copies of current certifications to the address below.

Qualifications:
Open to college freshmen, sophomores, juniors and seniors; college-age students; and recent graduates with experience working with youth. First Aid/CPR certification is required; lifeguard certification and an experimental/environmental education background are helpful.

Contact:
Miniwanca Education Center
Internship Program
8845 West Garfield Road
Shelby, MI 49455
Phone: (231) 861-2262
E-mail: adam.russell@ayf.com
www.ayf.com/jobs_int_mw.asp

Mixed Media

 THE BUZZ
- "An intimate entry into the world of PR"

THE STATS

Industry(ies): Music/Records; Public Relations

Location(s): Cranston, RI

Number of interns: *Annual*: 2

Pay: None

Length of internship: *Summer/fall/spring*: 15 weeks each

 **THE SCOOP**

Mixed Media, a small public relations firm, located in owner Ginny Shea's in-home office, specializes in music industry consulting – most of its artists are jazz and folk musicians. For these clients, Mixed Media makes press kits, marks music to radio stations, and develops and organizes publicity strategies.

ON THE JOB

Interns interface with the press, making follow-up calls to newspapers, radio and television stations; assemble press kits; and promote CDs.

GETTING HIRED

Apply by: *Summer*: May 31; *fall*: August 31; *spring*: December 31. Send resume and cover letter to the address below or e-mail Ginny Shea at ginny@mixedmediapromo.com.

Qualifications:
Open to college freshmen, sophomores, juniors and seniors.

Contact:
Internship Coordinator
Mixed Media
20 Lockmere Road
Mixed Media
Cranston, RI 02910
Phone: (401) 942-8025
www.mixedmediapromo.com

Mobility International

 THE BUZZ
- "Bring agency to the disabled"

 THE STATS

Industry(ies): Education; Nonprofit

Location(s): Eugene, OR

Number of interns: *Annual*: 2-5

Pay: $125/month for interns who commit to 6 months

Length of internship: 3-6 months

 THE SCOOP

Mobility International (MIUSA) is a nonprofit organization that empowers people with disabilities through international exchange and international development to achieve their human rights. It does this by coordinating leadership exchange programs and seminars. According to the organization's web site, "MIUSA exchange programs include training workshops and seminars, adaptive recreational activities, community service projects, home stays, language study and leadership development."

ON THE JOB

Interns help coordinate and facilitate the exchange programs. They are also involved with the activities, such as camping, horseback riding and whitewater rafting.

GETTING HIRED

Apply by: Rolling. Summer positions are often filled by March. Request an application by e-mailing info@miusa.org. Send application, along with your resume, letter of interest and two letters of recommendation to the address below.

Qualifications:
Open to high school graduates, college freshmen, sophomores, juniors and seniors, recent college graduates and grad students.

Contact:
Internship Coordinator
Mobility International
P.O. Box 10767
Eugene, OR 97440
Phone/TTY: (541) 343-1284
Fax: (541) 343-6812
E-mail: info@miusa.org
www.miusa.org

Visit Vault at **www.vault.com** for insider company profiles, expert advice, career message boards, expert resume reviews, the Vault Job Board and more.

VAULT CAREER LIBRARY **287**

Monitor Group

 THE STATS

Industry(ies): Management & Strategy Consulting

Location(s): Cambridge, MA; Chicago, IL; Los Angeles, CA; New York, NY; Palo Alto, CA; San Francisco, CA; Amsterdam; Beijing; Frankfurt; Hong Kong; Johannesburg; London; Madrid; Manila; Milan; Moscow; Mumbai; Munich; Paris; São Paulo; Seoul; Shanghai; Singapore; Stockholm; Tokyo; Toronto; Zurich

Number of interns: Varies year to year

Pay: Information not available

Length of internship: *Summer*: 10 weeks

 THE SCOOP

Monitor began at the Harvard Business School, where its founders taught and studied in the 1980s. Though focused primarily on strategy consulting, Monitor has developed client services in marketing strategy, operations analysis, systems dynamics and corporate finance. Monitor is organized into three over-arching business groups: the Action Group (enabling top management to resolve strategic problems and plan for and achieve long-term success); the Merchant Banking Group (providing advantaged capital markets investments and corporate finance advice by leveraging Monitor's networks); and the Intelligent Products Group (developing software products to support strategic decision making). Monitor advises clients across a variety of industries, including biotech; broadcast and entertainment; consumer products; energy/utilities; financial services; government; health care; nonprofit; pharmaceuticals; retail; and transportation.

 ON THE JOB

Monitor offers two summer programs: the summer intern program, open to rising undergraduate seniors; and the summer consultant program, offered to MBA students entering their second year. Both programs offer participants the opportunity to experience life as a full-time consultant on real client projects, as well as a comprehensive training and social program. In North America, summer intern positions are available in Cambridge, Chicago, Los Angeles, New York, San Francisco and Toronto, and summer consultant positions are available in Cambridge and Toronto. In Asia, summer intern positions are available in Hong Kong and Tokyo, and summer consultant positions are available in Beijing, Seoul, Hong Kong and Tokyo.

$ GETTING HIRED

Apply by: Monitor accepts applications from December 1 through January 20. For programs in U.S. offices, e-mail your cover letter and resume to recruiting_us@monitor.com. Refer to www.monitor.com/cgi-bin/iowa/work/common.html?text= toronto3 for summer positions in Toronto. To apply for summer intern and summer consultant positions in Asia, send application materials via e-mail to recruiting_asia@monitor.com.

Qualifications:

Summer intern: open to rising college seniors; *summer consultant*: open to MBA students entering their second year of business school.

Contact:

Application information
www.monitor.com/cgi-bin/iowa/careers/apply.html

Undergraduate opportunities
www.monitor.com/cgi-bin/iowa/about/positions.html?record = 17

MBA opportunities
www.monitor.com/cgi-bin/iowa/about/positions.html?record = 18

Montgomery County Pre-Release Center

 "THE BUZZ"

- "Help those down on their luck become functioning members of society"

 THE STATS

Industry(ies): Education; Government; Health Care

Location(s): Rockville, MD

Number of interns: *Spring/summer/fall*: 15 each

Pay: Paid; $120/week; academic credit available

Length of internship: 16 weeks-1 year

 THE SCOOP

The Montgomery County Pre-Release Center is a national model of community re-entry services. The Center offers both residential and home confinement services to sentenced offenders, services which address employment, substance abuse and recovery, education, family re-integration and mental health, all in a monitored and supervised environment.

 ON THE JOB

Interns work in the Pre-Release Center and in the community and can expect to supervise residents, direct the leisure and recreational programs, monitor alcohol and drug use, participate in group meetings and assist in inmate education. Most interns are also receiving academic credit.

GETTING HIRED

Apply by: Rolling. Apply online at www.montgomery countymd.gov; click on "Careers" and then "Internships". Once listed, please contact James Shannon, below.

Qualifications:

Open to college juniors and seniors, college graduates and grad students interested in a criminal justice and corrections career.

Contact:

James Shannon, Training Coordinator
Montgomery County Pre-Release Center
11651 Nebel Street
Rockville, MD 20852
Phone: (301) 468-4200
Fax: (301) 468-4420
E-mail: james.shannon@montgomerycountymd.gov
www.montgomerycountymd.gov

Visit Vault at **www.vault.com** for insider company profiles, expert advice, career message boards, expert resume reviews, the Vault Job Board and more.

VAULT CAREER LIBRARY **289**

Morgan Stanley

 THE BUZZ
- "Lots of options in an industry giant"

THE STATS

Industry(ies): Financial Services

Location(s): New York, NY (HQ); over 600 offices worldwide

Number of interns: Varies

Pay: Paid; competitive salary

Length of internship: *Summer*: 10 weeks; *co-op program (IT)*: 3-4 months

 **THE SCOOP**

Since a landmark merger in 1997, Morgan Stanley has combined the financial and knowledge capital of two influential American financial firms: Dean Witter, the San Francisco firm founded in 1924, and Morgan Stanley, established in New York in 1935. The company provides numerous investment portfolio opportunities to individual clients, including stocks, bonds, mutual funds, annuities, insurance, managed futures, UITs, and credit and lending services. MS also provides financial advice and implementation to institutional investors, corporations and investors around the world. Headquartered in New York City, Morgan Stanley's 53,718 employees represent over 120 nationalities and speak 90 languages in MS's 600 offices in 28 countries.

ON THE JOB

Morgan Stanley offers 10-week summer internships to both undergraduate and graduate students in a variety of fields, including equity research; financial controllers; fixed income; global operations; information technology; institutional equity; investment banking; investment management; private wealth management; public finance; and strategic planning. See the company web site for descriptions of various departments. The investment banking sector also offers the sophomore rotational program (SRP), which provides rising college juniors with a first-year analyst "buddy" to guide interns as they rotate every two or three weeks to a different aspect of the investment banking business; those SRP analysts who demonstrate the ability to succeed in IB will be offered returning positions as an IB analyst after their junior year.

GETTING HIRED

Apply by: *Summer*: February 1; apply online through contacts listed below. *Co-op program*: rolling.

Qualifications:
Summer analyst: open to rising college seniors; *SRP program*: open to rising college juniors; *summer associate*: open to MBA students. Morgan Stanley looks for applicants, in all majors, with a strong interest in business or finance. See the MS web site for various requirements for specific departments.

Contact:
Equity research
www.morganstanley.com/careers/recruiting/north_america/contact_us.html

Financial controllers group
www.morganstanley.com/careers/recruiting/north_america/financial_controllers_group_c.html

Fixed income
www.morganstanley.com/careers/recruiting/north_america/fixed_income_c.html

Global operations & services
www.morganstanley.com/careers/recruiting/north_america/finance_c.html

Information technology
www.morganstanley.com/careers/recruiting/north_america/information_tech_c.html

Institutional equity
www.morganstanley.com/careers/recruiting/north_america/inst_equity_c.html

Investment banking
www.morganstanley.com/careers/recruiting/north_america/invest_bank_c.html

Investment management
www.morganstanley.com/careers/recruiting/north_america/invest_manage_c.html

Private wealth management
www.morganstanley.com/careers/recruiting/north_america/private_wealth_manage_c.html

Public finance
www.morganstanley.com/careers/recruiting/north_america/public_finance_c.html

Strategic planning
www.morganstanley.com/careers/recruiting/north_america/strategic_planning_c.html

Morris Arboretum

 THE BUZZ
- "Rooted in tradition"
- "Grow an environmental career"

 THE STATS

Industry(ies): Environmental; Science/Research; Education; Horticulture; Landscape Design

Location(s): Philadelphia, PA

Number of interns: *Annual*: 8

Pay: Paid; $8.82/hour. Health and dental insurance; tuition and vacation benefits

Length of internship: 1 year, beginning mid-June; 40 hours/week

 **THE SCOOP**

The Morris Arboretum sits on 92 acres on the University of Pennsylvania Campus. It was originally the estate of Quaker brother and sister John and Lydia Morris, avid nature lovers who transformed their garden into a haven for diverse plant life. They sowed the seeds for a horticulture/botany school and laboratory, which became a part of U Penn in 1932.

ON THE JOB

The internship program was founded in 1979 and is renowned for its thorough mentorship experience, which prepares interns for administrative horticulture positions, as well as continued research, academia and service. One intern is chosen to work with a mentor in each of the following fields of interest: arboriculture, education, horticulture, Pennsylvania flora, plant propagation, plant protection, rose and flower garden, and urban forestry.

GETTING HIRED

Apply by: February 15. Send resume, letter of interest, specifying desired position, transcript and three letters of recommendation to the address below.

Qualifications:
Open to college juniors and seniors, all college graduates and grad students. Further requirements for specific fields are detailed on the web site.

Contact:
Jan McFarlan
Internship Coordinator
Morris Arboretum
9414 Meadowbrook Avenue
Philadelphia, PA 19118
Phone: (215) 247-5777, ext. 156
Fax: (215) 247-7862
E-mail: jim@pobox.upenn.edu
www.morrisarboretum.org

Mote Marine Laboratory

 THE BUZZ
- "Immerse yourself in a top Florida marine science program"

THE STATS

Industry(ies): Education; Nonprofit; Science/Research

Location(s): Sarasota, FL

Number of interns: *Annual*: 120

Pay: None; scholarships available

Length of internship: *Spring/summer/fall*: 8-16 weeks

THE SCOOP

Mote Marine Laboratory was founded in 1955 as an independent, nonprofit organization committed to advancement, education and research of the marine sciences. Its researchers focus on southern Florida, although their work is recognized in national and international journals. The laboratory is located on 10.5 acres on the Sarasota Bay. Other facilities include a public aquarium and several field stations.

ON THE JOB

College interns focus on a specific aspect of marine research in one of six centers: the Center for Fisheries Enhancement (aquaculture); the Center for Shark Research (biomedical and shark biology); the Center for Marine Mammal and Sea Turtle Research; the Center for Coastal and Tropical Ecology (invertebrate zoology); the Center for Eco-Toxicology (chemical fate and effects); or the Center for Coral Reef Research. There are also college interns in education/outreach, public relations and marketing. A separate internship is available for high school students. Check the web site for details.

GETTING HIRED

Apply by: *Spring*: November 1; *summer*: apply in fall; *fall*: July 1. See the scholarships web page (www.mote.org/ ~ccooper/ Intern/Scholarships.htm) for scholarship deadlines. Request an application package by e-mail.

Qualifications:
Open to high school students, college freshmen, sophomores, juniors and seniors, and recent college graduates.

Contact:
Dana O'Mara
College Intern Liaison
Mote Marine Laboratory
1600 Ken Thompson Parkway
Sarasota, FL 34236
Phone: (941) 388-4441
Fax: (941) 388-4312
E-mail: danaomara@mote.org
www.mote.org/code/8

Visit Vault at **www.vault.com** for insider company profiles, expert advice, career message boards, expert resume reviews, the Vault Job Board and more.

 V\ULT CAREER LIBRARY **291**

Mother Jones

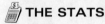 THE BUZZ

- "Raise hell, learn journalism"
- "Independent thinkers wanted"

 THE STATS

Industry(ies): Journalism; Nonprofit; Publishing

Location(s): San Francisco, CA

Number of interns: *Annual:* 15-20

Pay: $150/month stipend for internships (4 months); $1,381.25/month stipend for fellowships (4-8 months); scholarships available – see site for details

Length of internship: *Internships:* 4 months; *fellowships:* 4-8 months. Both 37.5 hours/week

THE SCOOP

Award-winning *Mother Jones* magazine was founded by the nonprofit Foundation for National Progress to educate the American public by investigating and reporting on important social and political issues. The FNP launched *Mother Jones* magazine in 1976 and MotherJones.com in 1993 to bring uncompromising reporting to a broad national audience. It takes its name from labor activist Mary Harris "Mother" Jones.

ON THE JOB

Interns perform various duties for the magazine. Editorial interns fact check articles and conduct research on upcoming issues. Online editorial interns develop skills as self-starting journalists. Art interns work with the creative director and photo editor to design and produce the magazine. Publishing interns learn how a nonprofit independent media organization operates through daily activities that include fundraising, marketing, promotion and outreach.

GETTING HIRED

Apply by: Rolling. Send application, cover letter, resume and writing samples to the address below. See site for information on obtaining an application.

Qualifications:

Open to college graduates and grad students with reporting, communications, activism and/or research experience.

Contact:

Editorial Internships: Research Editor

Online Editorial Internships: Assistant Web Editor

Art Internships: Photo Editor

Publishing Internships: Human Resources Manager

Mother Jones Magazine

222 Sutter Street, Suite 600

San Francisco, CA 94108

Phone: (415) 321-1700

Fax: (415) 321-1701

E-mail: internships@motherjones.com

www.motherjones.com/about/admin/internships.html

Ms.

THE BUZZ

- "Cover issues affecting women at the top feminist publication"

THE STATS

Industry(ies): Journalism; Nonprofit; Publishing

Location(s): *Publishing:* Washington, DC; *Editorial:* Los Angeles, CA

Number of interns: *Annual:* 18

Pay: None

Length of internship: *Spring/summer/fall:* at least 8 weeks. *Summer:* full-time; *fall/spring:* part- or full-time

THE SCOOP

Ms. magazine has been shaping American feminism since 1979. Launched by leaders of the women's movement, including Gloria Steinem, *Ms.* immediately blazed a path into the nation's consciousness. The magazine still presents thorough coverage of international women's issues. It has gone through several management changes in the past three decades and is currently owned by the Feminist Majority Foundation. Publishing internships are available at the Washington office, and editorial internships are available at the Los Angeles office.

ON THE JOB

Interns work in many areas of the magazine. Publishing interns may be involved in events organizing, press conferences and public hearings. Editorial interns do fact checking, research and writing.

GETTING HIRED

Apply by: Rolling. Submit resume, cover letter, writing sample (three to five pages on women's issues) and two or more reference phone numbers.

Qualifications:

Open to undergraduate women and men, recent graduates, and graduate students. Experience working with women's issues preferred. For the editorial internship in Los Angeles, experience with both journalism and women's issues is strongly preferred.

Contact:

Washinton D.C. – Ms. Magazine Publishing Office

Crystal Lander

Feminist Majority Foundation/Ms. Magazine

1600 Wilson Blvd., Suite 801

Arlington, VA 22209

Phone: (703) 522-2214

Fax: (703) 522-2219

Email: internship@feminist.org

www.feminist.org/intern

Los Angeles, CA – Ms. Magazine Editorial

Jessie Raeder

Feminist Majority Foundation/Ms. Magazine

433 South Beverly Drive

Beverly Hills, CA 90212

Phone: (310) 556-2500

Fax: (310) 556-2509

Email: jraeder@feminist.org

Fax: (310) 556-2509

E-mail: chahn@msmagazine.com

MTV Networks

 THE BUZZ
- "The pop culture generator for America"
- "A stepping-stone to a career in the entertainment industry"

 THE STATS

Industry(ies): Broadcast & Entertainment; Internet; Digital Media

Location(s): Burbank, CA; Miami, FL; Nashville, TN; New York, NY; Santa Monica, CA

Number of interns: *Annual*: 1,300 (NY)

Pay: None; academic credit required

Length of internship: *Spring/summer/fall*: 10-week minimum for each term; work at least 2 full days/week

 THE SCOOP

MTV Networks is a global company comprised of many different channels, including MTV: Music Television, MTV2, mtvU, VH1: Music First, Nickelodeon (including Nick at Nite, TV Land, Noggin and The N), Comedy Central, Spike TV, CMT, as well as Nickelodeon (GAS), Nick Too, Nicktoons, VH1 Soul, VH Uno, LOGO, Tempo, MTV World, MTV Espanol and VH1 Classic Rock. MTV Networks also operates a portfolio of leading Internet properties serving every interest of today's music fans and Internet-savvy kids.

 ON THE JOB

Interns are exposed to all levels of MTV Networks, an invaluable experience to individuals interested in pursuing a career in the entertainment industry. MTVN offers positions in almost every department, including advertising, editorial, programming, production, finance, talent and artist relations, special events and many more. There's no pay – and not many better ways to break into the entertainment business.

 GETTING HIRED

Apply by: Rolling for all except summer (April 1). Applicants should send a resume and cover letter stating the semester they are applying for and their area(s) of interest to the address below. For internships outside of New York, please consult the web site for addresses and contact information.

Qualifications:
Open to college juniors and seniors. Must be registered for academic credit with college or university, and must provide official documentation upon acceptance.

Contact:
MTV Networks
Internship Program
1515 Broadway – 35th Floor
New York, NY 10036
Fax: (212) 846-1320
E-mail: internships@mtvn.com
www.mtvncareers.com
jobhuntweb.viacom.com/jobhunt/main/internships.asp

The Museum of Contemporary Art, Chicago

 THE BUZZ
- "Sculpt a career path of your own"
- "Work in one of the city's finest art institutions"

 THE STATS

Industry(ies): Art/Museum; Nonprofit

Location(s): Chicago, IL

Number of interns: *Annual*: 80-90

Pay: None; possible academic credit

Length of internship: *Summer*: May-August; *fall*: September-December; *spring*: January-May

 THE SCOOP

The Museum of Contemporary Art opened in 1967 in a small building in Chicago. The new five-story building, designed by architect Josef Paul Kleihues, houses a sculpture garden, a 15,000-volume library and an education center. The permanent collection contains paintings, photography sculpture and video created since 1945, including works by Christo, Chuck Close, Max Ernst and Jeff Koons.

 ON THE JOB

MCA interns have the opportunity to participate in the development and expansion of the museum's cutting edge exhibitions and educational and outreach programs. Internships are available in all 20 departments, including administration, curatorial, graphic design, marketing, performance and education. Interns usually work on one or more main projects and help with daily departmental tasks.

 **GETTING HIRED**

Apply by: *Summer*: March 15; *fall*: July 15; *spring*: November 15. Applications should be submitted in triplicate, on or before the appropriate deadline, and include the application form, resume and two letters of recommendation.

Qualifications:
Open to college freshmen, sophomores, juniors and seniors, recent college graduates and grad students.

Contact:
Intern Coordinator
Museum of Contemporary Art
Office of Administration
220 East Chicago Avenue
Chicago, IL 60611
Phone: (312) 397-3822
Fax: (312) 397-4095
E-mail: SCleary@mcachicago.org
www.mcachicago.org

Visit Vault at **www.vault.com** for insider company profiles, expert advice, career message boards, expert resume reviews, the Vault Job Board and more.

VAULT CAREER LIBRARY **293**

Museum of Fine Arts, Boston

 THE BUZZ
- "Delve into the Boston art world"

 THE STATS

Industry(ies): Art/Museum

Location(s): Boston, MA

Number of interns: *Annual:* 100

Pay: None

Length of internship: *Spring/summer/fall:* 10 weeks; 12-30 hours/week

 THE SCOOP

The Museum of Fine Arts, Boston holds one of the top art collections in the United States. Founded in 1876, it features decorative arts, master works in painting and sculpture, and instruments and ceramics. The museum also hosts extensive supplemental education programs including classes, lectures, films and gallery talks.

ON THE JOB

Interns work in several departments, including Art of the Ancient World (Classical and Egyptian); Museum Learning and Public Programs, Public Relations and Registrar's Office. Interns gain insider privileges, including discounts on museum lectures, concerts and films, as well as contact with department heads and curators.

GETTING HIRED

Apply by: E-mail the internship coordinator for important dates, internship postings and application procedures, or visit www.mfa.org.

Qualifications:
Open to college students, recent college graduates and grad students.

Contact:
Jesse Tarantino
Volunteer and Intern Programs Coordinator
Museum of Fine Arts, Boston
465 Huntington Avenue
Boston, MA 02115
E-mail: jtarantino@mfa.org
www.mfa.org

Museum of Modern Art

 THE BUZZ
- "Wallow amidst Van Gogh and Miro during your New York arts internship"

 THE STATS

Industry(ies): Art/Museum

Location(s): New York, NY

Number of interns: *Summer:* 27; *academic year:* 50; *12-month:* 5-10

Pay: Varies; *12-month:* $21,000 plus health insurance; *summer:* $2,750; *academic year:* none

Length of internship: *Academic year:* 12 weeks (minimum 2 days/week); *summer:* 10 weeks (full-time)

 THE SCOOP

The Museum of Modern Art (MoMA) has hosted and housed dynamic exhibits of modern and contemporary art since 1929. Its permanent collection contains 100,000 works of art, including architectural plans, drawings, paintings, photographs, prints and sculpture.

 ON THE JOB

Internship content varies based on the project needs of the museum. Summer internships include orientation training and field trips to other museums, galleries and art spaces. The year-long program allows interns to work closely with a professional staff member, gain deeper knowledge of contemporary art through seminars and get help with job placement.

GETTING HIRED

Apply by: *Spring:* October 27; *summer:* January 19; *fall/12-month:* May 18. Applications should include the downloadable application form (available at www.moma.org/education/internships.html), two letters of recommendation, transcript or course list, and resume.

Qualifications:
Academic year internship is open to college juniors and seniors, grad students and recent college graduates. *Summer internship:* open to college juniors and seniors; *year-round internship:* open to recent college graduates only. Internships for high school students are also available; see web site for details.

Contact:
The Museum of Modern Art
Attention: Internship Coordinator
11 West 53 Street
New York, NY 10019
Fax: (212) 333-1118
E-mail: internships@moma.org
www.moma.org

My Sister's Place

 THE BUZZ
- "Help women in trouble get back on their feet"

 **THE STATS**

Industry(ies): Nonprofit; Women's Issues

Location(s): Washington, DC

Number of interns: *Annual*: 50

Pay: None

Length of internship: Minimum 4 month commitment; 10 hours/week

 THE SCOOP

My Sister's Place, Inc. (MSP) is a non-profit organization dedicated to the eradication of domestic violence via the provision of safe shelter, advocacy, counseling, and education for battered women and their children. Founded in 1979 by the Women's Legal Defense Fund, MSP has provided exemplary programs and services for families in crisis for more than 25 years.

 ON THE JOB

Volunteers and interns receive intensive training on issues of domestic violence and effective crisis intervention They support the 24-hour crisis hotline, community education,and the children's rehabilitation program. Volunteers and interns also support MSP by contributing to resource developent, fundraising, admistrative support and translation.

GETTING HIRED

Apply by: Rolling. Send resume and cover letter to the address below.

Qualifications:

Qualifications: Open to high school graduates, current undergraduate and graduate students, and recent graduates. Applicants should possess a willingness to become part of a team and work in a fast-paced environment, and a commitment to providing sanctuary for families in crisis.

Contact:
Volunteer Coordinator
My Sister's Place, Inc. (MSP)
P.O. Box 29596
Washington, DC 20017
Phone: (202) 529-5261
Fax: (202) 529-5984
www.mysistersplacedc.org

Visit Vault at **www.vault.com** for insider company profiles, expert advice, career message boards, expert resume reviews, the Vault Job Board and more.

VAULT CAREER LIBRARY **295**

INTERNSHIP PROFILES: N

Nabisco

THE BUZZ

- "Calling all 'tough cookies'"

THE STATS

Industry(ies): Consumer Products; Food & Beverage

Location(s): East Hanover, NJ

Number of interns: *Annual*: 70

Pay: Paid; *undergraduates*: $400-$600/week; *grad students*: $800-$1,000/week

Length of internship: *Summer/co-op*: 14 weeks

THE SCOOP

Animal Crackers, Oreos, Fig Newtons, Wheat Thins. Chances are, if you're an American you have eaten Nabisco's goods. Let's add Grey Poupon, LifeSavers and Planters peanuts to that and you'll see why Nabisco is one of the world's largest food companies. Nabisco employs 49,000 people, grosses $8.3 billion in annual sales and manufactures over 300 products.

ON THE JOB

Undergrad and graduate interns are hired to work in accounting/finance, information services, logistics and marketing. Interns participate in an orientation, "lunch and learn sessions," and bakery field trips. Interns' work is hands-on and current.

GETTING HIRED

Apply by: *Summer/co-op*: March 1. Send resume and cover letter to the address below.

Qualifications:
Open to college sophomores, juniors and seniors, and MBA students.

Contact:
Internship Coordinator
University Relations
Nabisco
100 De Forest Avenue
East Hanover, NJ 07936
Phone: (201) 503-2000

NAPSLO: National Association of Professional Surplus Lines Offices

THE BUZZ

- "Experience a summer working in the specialty insurance industry"
- "Networking with prospective employers"

THE STATS

Industry(ies): Insurance Claims

Location(s): Interns are placed with 2 NAPSLO member firms. NAPSLO membership consists of 800 member offices across the U.S.

Number of interns: *Annual*: 8-10

Pay: Paid; up to $500/week plus a stipend. Housing and travel expenses provided

Length of internship: *Summer*: 9 weeks (5 weeks with a member company and 4 weeks with a member broker)

THE SCOOP

Founded in 1975, the National Association of Professional Surplus Lines Offices (NAPSLO) acts as the voice and publicist of surplus lines. Surplus lines refer to specialty insurance that cannot be placed in traditional retail insurance markets.

ON THE JOB

NAPSLO places interns with member firms. The program is designed so that participants experience all aspects of the insurance business. They spend five weeks working for a member insurance company and four weeks with a NAPSLO member wholesale broker firm. Interns work in all departments of the member firm. Selected interns are asked to attend the NAPSLO Annual Convention the following fall, at which time one is chosen for a three-week London-based internship (expenses paid) for the following summer.

GETTING HIRED

Apply by: *Summer*: December 1. Applicants can apply online or submit a downloadable application, a resume, two letters of recommendation and a college transcript in to the address below.

Qualifications:
Open to college juniors and seniors, recent college graduates and grad students (insurance and risk management majors).

Contact:
Jessica Myers
Internship Coordinator
NAPSLO
200 NE 54th Street, Suite 200
Kansas City, MO 64118
Phone: (816) 741-3910
Toll-free: (888) 446-7414
Fax: (816) 741-5409
E-mail: internship@napslo.org
www.napslo.org/Content/Internships/Internships.htm

NASA

 THE BUZZ
- "Everything under the sun – and how"
- "An out-of-this-world resume booster for engineers and scientists"

 THE STATS

Industry(ies): Aerospace; Engineering; Government; Science/Research; Technology

Location(s): Washington, DC (HQ); Cleveland, OH; Edwards, CA; Hampton, VA; Houston, TX; Huntsville, AL; Greenbelt, MD; Kennedy Space Center, FL; Moffett Field, CA; Pasadena, CA; Stennis Space Center, MS

Number of interns: *Spring/summer/fall*: 1,000

Pay: Varies (civil service salary, stipend-supported or NASA contractor)

Length of internship: *Summer*: 8-12 weeks; *spring/fall*: 15-17 weeks each

 **THE SCOOP**

NASA has been a leader in scientific/technological research and space exploration since 1958. NASA is responsible for placing the first people on the moon, has launched scientific probes and conducts ongoing aerodynamics research.

 ON THE JOB

Hundreds of internships are available each year working directly with NASA scientists and engineers on research projects ranging from aerodynamics to biotechnology to satellite communications. Students can gain hands-on experience designing spaceflight hardware and software, and may even support real-time mission activities. Current students may participate in NASA's Cooperative Education Program, Student Temporary Experience Program or numerous education programs. Graduates seeking entry-level jobs may choose from the Federal Career Internship Program and the Presidential Management Internship.

 GETTING HIRED

Apply by: Varies by program; see the web sites listed below for specific program qualifications and application procedures/timelines.

Qualifications:
Internships are available for college freshmen, sophomores, juniors and seniors, recent college graduates and grad students. U.S. citizenship is required.

Contact:
www.nasajobs.nasa.gov
http://education.nasa.gov

NASCAR

 THE BUZZ
- "Help promote America's favorite car race"

 THE STATS

Industry(ies): Broadcast & Entertainment; Sports

Location(s): Brooklyn, MI; Charlotte, NC; Daytona Beach, FL; Dover, DE; Hoffman Estates, IL; Kansas City, KS; Long Pond, PA; Los Angeles, CA; Myrtle Beach, SC; Phoenix, AZ; Richmond, VA; Talladega, AL

Number of interns: *Summer*: 10-15

Pay: Paid; varies

Length of internship: *Summer*: 10 weeks

 THE SCOOP

NASCAR, which stands for the National Association for Stock Car Auto Racing, was founded by William H.G. France in 1948 to "organize and promote stock car racing," now the No. 1 live spectator sport in America (No. 2 in television ratings). Today, NASCAR sanctions almost 2,000 events annually, held at 110 tracks across the U.S. Some of its events include the Carolina Dodge Car 400, the Coca-Cola 600 and the Daytona 500.

 ON THE JOB

While NASCAR does offer some intern positions to people of "all cultural backgrounds," the company places most of its attention on its Diversity Internship Program, open only to minority students interested in a career in the motorsports industry. Interns work in the broadcasting department, design, competition and sales. Interns may also work with NASCAR's sanctioning body, NASCAR sponsors, NASCAR licensees, NASCAR teams and tracks, or other related organizations. Specific job offerings change annually, so check the company's web site for current offerings.

GETTING HIRED

Apply by: *Summer*: February 25. Applications are available online at www.diversityinternships.com/students_app.htm. Send the completed form with a resume, cover letter, references and a personal statement to the address below. NASCAR interviews candidates before hiring.

Qualifications:
Open to college sophomores, juniors and seniors, and graduate students of an underrepresented ethnicity.

Contact:
NASCAR Diversity Affairs Department
1801 West International Speedway Blvd.
Daytona Beach, FL 32114
E-mail: info@diversityinternships.com
www.diversityinternships.com

Visit Vault at **www.vault.com** for insider company profiles, expert advice, career message boards, expert resume reviews, the Vault Job Board and more.

VAULT CAREER LIBRARY **299**

The Nation

 THE BUZZ

- "A not-to-be-missed opportunity for fans of politics and good writing"
- "Rub shoulders with movers and shakers in the political field"

 THE STATS

Industry(ies): Journalism; Publishing

Location(s): Washington, DC; New York, NY

Number of interns: *Annual*: 27 (8 in New York, 1 in Washington, DC, per session)

Pay: Paid; $150/week. Academic credit possible; limited housing and transportation assistance available

Length of internship: *Spring/summer/fall*: 12 weeks, full-time (10 a.m.-6 p.m.)

 THE SCOOP

Founded in 1865, *The Nation* is America's oldest weekly magazine. It is a journal of politics and art that, since its founding, has aimed to maintain critical social and political discourse and shunned "exaggeration, violence, and misrepresentation" apparent in other political writing.

 ON THE JOB

The internship program is run through the nonprofit Nation Institute and participants get editorial experience with fact checking, reading and evaluating manuscripts, researching, and writing; and, on the publishing side, they assist with advertising, circulation and promotion. New York interns attend weekly seminars with authors, journalists and politicians on various topics, and with *Nation* staff members on editing and writing skills.

GETTING HIRED

Apply by: *Spring*: November 4; *summer*: March 24; *fall*: TBA. Mail resume, cover letter, two recommendations and two writing samples to the address below.

Qualifications:
Open to college sophomores, juniors and seniors, recent college graduates and grad students.

Contact:
Emily Biuso
Internship Program Director
The Nation Institute
33 Irving Place, 8th Floor
New York, NY 10003
Phone: (212) 209-5419
E-mail: emily@nationinstitute.org
www.thenation.com

The National Academies

 THE BUZZ

- "Engage in the analysis that informs the creation of science and technology policy"

 THE STATS

Industry(ies): Education; Engineering; Law; Science/Research

Location(s): Washington, DC

Number of fellows: Varies

Pay: *Summer/fall/spring*: $4,800. Travel stipend (up to $500)

Length of fellowship: *Spring/summer/fall*: 10 weeks each

 **THE SCOOP**

The National Academies brings together committees of experts in all areas of scientific and technological endeavor. These experts serve pro bono to address critical national issues and give advice to the federal government and the public. The fellowship program is named for former fellow Christine Mirzayan who, after completing her PhD in cell biology and neurobiology, died during the last week of her fellowship.

 ON THE JOB

Each fellow is assigned a mentor who is a senior staff member. The first week includes an orientation to introduce fellows to the National Academies and other organizations in DC who also influence, make or report on science and technology policy. Following this, the bulk of fellows' time is spent on a specific research project (such as wireless networks in developing countries, biotechnology and terrorism, demography of street children) and on fellowship program activities (briefings, field trips, seminar series).

 GETTING HIRED

Apply by: *Spring*: November 1; *summer*: March 1; *fall*: June 1. Complete the online application at www.nationalacademies.org/policyfellows and have a mentor/adviser complete the online reference form.

Qualifications:
Open to current graduate students and postdocs or scholars who have completed graduate studies or postdoctoral research within the past five years.

Contact:
The National Academies
Christine Mirzayan Science & Technology Policy Graduate Fellowship Program
500 5th Street, NW, Room 508
Washington, DC 20001
Phone: (202) 334-2455
Fax: (202) 334-1667
E-mail: policyfellows@nas.edu
www.nationalacademies.org
www.nationalacademies.org/policyfellows

National Aquarium in Baltimore

THE BUZZ
- "Learn about tourism, museum science, oceanography – and moray eels!"

THE STATS
Industry(ies): Science/Research; Tourism/Recreation

Location(s): Baltimore, MD

Number of interns: *Annual*: 60

Pay: None; academic credit available. 30 percent discount on Aquarium goods and services

Length of internship: *Summer/fall/winter/spring*: 120 hours

 THE SCOOP

With 1.6 million paying visitors a year, the National Aquarium in Baltimore is Maryland's leading tourist attraction and is dedicated to promoting local economic development. The 10,500 aquatic inhabitants are housed in the state-of-the-art, award-winning facility. It "strives to blend naturalistic exhibit elements with the most modern interpretive techniques."

ON THE JOB

Internships are available throughout the aquarium to match students' interests and fields of study. Departments include animal behavior, aquarist, aviculture, conservation, conservation education, membership/development, herpetology, horticulture, information systems, library science, the marine animal rescue program, marine mammal training, public relations, publications, and community and government affairs.

GETTING HIRED

Apply by: Download application at www.aqua.orgl and mail it with transcript to the address below.

Qualifications:
Open to college freshmen, sophomores, juniors, seniors and graduate students. Applicants must be enrolled in a two- or four-year college

Contact:
Internship Coordinator – Education Department
National Aquarium in Baltimore
Pier 3, 501 East Pratt Street
Baltimore, MD 21202-3194
Phone: (410) 576-3888
Fax: (410) 659-0116
E-mail: intern@aqua.org
www.aqua.org

National Association for Female Executives

THE BUZZ
- "A great place for young women to find thousands of role models"

THE STATS
Industry(ies): Marketing

Location(s): New York, NY

Number of interns: *Annual*: 6

Pay: None

Length of internship: *Spring/summer/fall*: 10-12 weeks each

THE SCOOP

The National Association for Female Executives (NAFE) is the largest women's professional and business owners' organization in the U.S. It is owned and operated by Working Mother Media, publishers of *Working Mother* magazine. The organization provides resources and services for its 125,000-plus members to help them achieve success. Offerings range from education and training to business and financial services, to name a few. NAFE also publishes *NAFE Magazine*.

 ON THE JOB

Interns for NAFE assist with association management, chapter management, customer service, marketing and events. Duties include administrative and clerical tasks. Interns benefit from networking opportunities and are able to attend industry meetings and seminars.

GETTING HIRED

Apply by: Rolling. Submit a resume and cover letter to the address below.

Qualifications:
Open to college freshmen, sophomores, juniors and seniors, college graduates and grad students.

Contact:
Internship Coordinator
National Association for Female Executives
60 East 42nd Street, Suite 2700
New York, NY 10165
Phone: (212) 445-6235
Fax: (212) 445-6228
E-mail: nafe@nafe.com, subject line: Internship Candidate
www.nafe.com

Visit Vault at **www.vault.com** for insider company profiles, expert advice, career message boards, expert resume reviews, the Vault Job Board and more.

VAULT CAREER LIBRARY **301**

National Association of College Broadcasters

 THE BUZZ
- "A great way to break into broadcasting"
- "Programming for students, by students"

 THE STATS

Industry(ies): Broadcast & Entertainment; Nonprofit

Location(s): Providence, RI

Number of interns: *Spring/summer/fall*: 5-7 each

Pay: None

Length of internship: *Spring/summer/fall*: 6-36 weeks

THE SCOOP

The National Association for College Broadcasters (NACB) was founded as a nonprofit in 1988 to encourage students interested and involved in electronic media to exchange ideas and information. NACB sponsors the National College Radio Awards, its own national conference and a network for college student television called U Network.

ON THE JOB

Interns work in production, publications or advertising/sales. Responsibilities vary with department but may include assisting the sales team with leads, copyediting and/or proofing content for the publications team, and various production work on U Network.

GETTING HIRED

Apply by: Rolling. Send a resume, cover letter and writing samples to the address below.

Qualifications:
Open to high school juniors and seniors; college freshmen, sophomores, juniors and seniors; and college graduates. International applicants welcome.

Contact:
Internship Coordinator
National Association of College Broadcasters
7 George Street
Providence, RI 02912-1824
Phone: (401) 863-2225
E-mail: NACB@aol.com

National Basketball Association

THE BUZZ
- "Slam dunk a resume grabber!"
- "Calling all sports nuts!"

THE STATS

Industry(ies): Sports

Location(s): New York, NY; Secaucus, NJ

Number of interns: Varies with need

Pay: Varies with position

Length of internship: *Summer*: 10 weeks

THE SCOOP

Chances are, if you want to intern with the NBA, you're already a huge basketball fan. The National Basketball Association was founded in 1946 as the Basketball Association of America, and it had 11 member teams. At present, 30 basketball teams belong to the NBA, which now grosses about 2 billion dollars a year in related sales. The organization also features the WNBA, Basketball U (where those who crave to learn more about the game on a higher level can go), and NBA City, a popular theme restaurant in Orlando, Florida.

ON THE JOB

NBA interns work in several different departments, including communications, human resources, interactive services, international television, and marketing and media. Placement depends on company need and the applicant's experience. Duties can vary depending on department, and there will probably be some clerical responsibilities.

GETTING HIRED

Apply by: Applications are accepted from September 15 through November 15. Visit the internship section of the NBA Careers web site, http://www.nba.com/careers/internship_program.html, to see the program description and complete the online application.

Qualifications:
Open to college juniors and seniors.

Contact:
Internship Coordinator
National Basketball Association
645 Fifth Avenue
New York, NY 10022
Phone: (212) 407-8087
Fax: (212) 407-7917
www.nba.com/careers/internship_program.html

National Collegiate Athletic Association

 THE BUZZ
- "Get a start in college sports management"

 **THE STATS**

Industry(ies): Sports

Location(s): Indianapolis, IN

Number of interns: *Annual*: 11

Pay: Varies

Length of internship: Varies

THE SCOOP

Over 1,200 college and universities belong to the National Collegiate Athletic Association (NCAA), which oversees college sports, establishing and enforcing consistent standards and policies across the board. Since 1906, the organization has dealt with all college sport-related issues, including recruiting, drug testing, sports playing rules and gender equity, among others. NCAA oversees a variety of popular sports, including college football, basketball and hockey.

ON THE JOB

NCAA interns in the past have worked in championships, education services, enforcement, membership services, finance, men's and women's basketball, governance or broadcasting/branding and promotions positions. The program is currently undergoing some changes, so check the web site (www.ncaa.org) for availability and requirements.

GETTING HIRED

Apply by: Check the organization's web site (www.ncaa.org) for deadlines and submission requirements.

Qualifications:
Open to college graduates. See site (www.ncaa.org) for details.

Contact:
Arthur Hightower
Assistant Director of Professional Development
National Collegiate Athletic Association
P.O. Box 6222
Indianapolis, IN 46206-6222
Phone: (317) 917-6263
www1.ncaa.org

National Committee for Responsive Philanthropy

 THE BUZZ
- "Get started on a philanthrophic career"
- "Find out where your donations really go"

 **THE STATS**

Industry(ies): Nonprofit

Location(s): Washington, DC

Number of interns: *Annual*: 2-3

Pay: Paid; $10/hour

Length of internship: 3 months-1 year

THE SCOOP

The National Committee for Responsive Philanthropy (NCRP) was founded in 1976 to make sure philanthropic funds go to those most in need. The organization functions as an advocate, overseer and researcher into philanthropic policies and practices most significant to the public. The NCRP also works with individual and corporate philanthropists to widen the breadth of their public impact.

ON THE JOB

The NCRP internship is research-intensive. Interns engage in the public interest and advocacy field directly through researching corporate and private philanthropy projects and working on related NCRP plans. The organization gives its interns a chance to develop capabilities and expand their knowledge of nonprofit institutions in a balanced work environment. Most interns have the chance to be published, either through an NCRP report or an NCRP journal.

GETTING HIRED

Apply by: Rolling. Send a resume and cover letter to the address below.

Qualifications:
Open to college freshmen, sophomores, juniors and seniors, as well as recent college grads and grad students.

Contact:
Jeff Krehely, Deputy Director
National Committee for Responsive Philanthropy
2001 S Street, NW, Suite 620
Phone: (202) 387-9177, ext. 26
Fax: (202) 332-5084
E-mail: jeff@ncrp.org
www.ncrp.org/about/employment.asp

Visit Vault at **www.vault.com** for insider company profiles, expert advice, career message boards, expert resume reviews, the Vault Job Board and more.

VAULT CAREER LIBRARY **303**

National Endowment for the Arts

 THE BUZZ
- "Work with the government to recognize the arts"
- "Still funded for the time being"

 THE STATS

Industry(ies): Art/Museum; Government; Nonprofit

Location(s): Washington, DC

Number of interns: *Annual*: 15-20

Pay: None

Length of internship: *Spring/summer/fall*: 15-20 weeks

 THE SCOOP

Created by Congress in 1965, the National Endowment for the Arts is an independent nonprofit agency of the federal government whose mission is to provide national recognition and support for artistic projects. Since its founding, it has given out more than 120,000 grants to organizations and artists all over the U.S. Some of The Endowment's grants have financed the Vietnam Veterans Memorial and provided support to legends like Dizzy Gillespie, Count Basie, Dr. Billy Taylor, Miles Davis and Sarah Vaughan.

ON THE JOB

Intern duties include clerical administrative functions, the arts library and Internet research, and independent projects assigned as needed. Interns also have access to resources such as "an extensive arts library, meetings with the advisory panels and the National Council on the Arts."

GETTING HIRED

Apply by: Rolling. Send materials at least four to six weeks prior to intended start date. Submit a resume, a cover letter detailing availability, interested areas of concentration, experience and typing ability. Letters of recommendation, references and college transcripts are suggested, but not required.

Qualifications:
Open to all college freshmen, sophomores, juniors and seniors, grad students and other volunteers.

Contact:
Office of Human Resources, Room 627
National Endowment for the Arts
The Nancy Hanks Center
Attention: Anita Green
1100 Pennsylvania Avenue, NW
Washington, DC 20506
Phone: (202) 682-5472
E-mail: webmgr@arts.endow.gov
arts.endow.gov/about/Jobs/Internships.html

National Football League

 THE BUZZ
- "Kick off your sports career"
- "A resume touchdown!"

 THE STATS

Industry(ies): Sports

Location(s): New York, NY

Number of interns: *Summer*: 20-25

Pay: Paid; $500/week

Length of internship: *Summer*: 9 weeks

 THE SCOOP

The American Professional Football Association, founded in 1920 out of the chaos that ensued from the birth of professional football some five decades earlier, was renamed the National Football League in 1922, now the governing body for over 30 professional football teams across the U.S. Its sole purpose is to coordinate teams, games and players. The League also oversees the many championship bowls, including the Super Bowl. The NFL has come under fire recently for the controversial halftime show MTV produced in 2004, which has sparked legislative debate over decency standards.

ON THE JOB

Interns work in various departments including legal, finance, marketing and football operations at the NFL headquarters in New York. Tasks include clerical duties, but interns learn about the business side of the sport and gain invaluable corporate experience. The NFL web site also posts internships with teams around the country.

GETTING HIRED

Apply by: *Summer*: fall. See web site for deadline details. Online applications available at www.nfl.com.

Qualifications:
Open to undergraduate juniors, as well as graduate and law students, but interns must be returning to school in the fall after the program.

Contact:
Internship Coordinator
National Football League
280 Park Avenue
New York, NY 10017
Phone: (212) 450-2000
footballjobs.teamworkonline.com/teamwork/jobs/jobs.cfm?supc at=321&supcat_name=Internships (for listings of available team internships)

The National GEM Consortium

 THE BUZZ
- "A sparkling internship for minority technical talent"

 THE STATS

Industry(ies): Education; Engineering; Nonprofit; Science/Research

Location(s): 90+ universities nationwide and in the Commonwealth of Puerto Rico

Number of interns: *Annual:* 100-200

Pay: Paid; $500-$750/week. Round-trip travel during summer internship; tuition, academic fees; $10,000-$14,000 annual stipend

Length of internship: *Master's fellows:* 2 summers; *PhD fellows:* 1 summer

 THE SCOOP

The National GEM Consortium was founded in 1976 as a vehicle for universities and employers around the nation partnering to provide fellowships for underrepresented minorities pursuing advanced degrees in science, technology, engineering, and mathematics. Since then, more than 3,000 GEM fellows have graduated from top colleges and research institutions, thanks to GEM's MS Engineering, PhD Engineering and PhD Science fellowship programs.

ON THE JOB

Chosen fellows attend one of 95 participating universities and spend the summer interning at one of 50 Fortune 500 companies and government labs. Tasks vary with position and placement, but may include science research or business training. An MS Science fellowship program is currently being developed.

GETTING HIRED

Apply by: November 1. Register and apply online at www.gemfellowship.org.

Qualifications:

Open to college juniors and seniors. Recent college graduates and degreed, experienced professionals are also eligible. Must be a U.S. citizen and from one of the following underrepresented groups: American Indians, African Americans, Mexican Americans, Puerto Ricans or other Hispanic Americans.

Contact:
The National GEM Consortium
P.O. Box 537
Notre Dame, IN 46556
Phone: (574) 631-7771
Fax: (574) 287-1486
E-mail: info@gemfellowship.org
www.gemfellowship.org

National Institutes of Health

 THE BUZZ
- "The world's largest biomedical research center, bar none"
- "Help discover cures and treatments"

 THE STATS

Industry(ies): Government; Health Care; Science/Research

Location(s): Baltimore, MD; Bethesda, MD; Detroit, MI; Frederick, MD; Hamilton, MT; Phoenix, AZ; Research Triangle Park, NC

Number of interns: Varies with department need; generally about 1,000

Pay: Paid; varies by position

Length of internship: 8-10 weeks (late May to mid-to-late August)

 THE SCOOP

The National Institutes of Health, an agency of the U.S. Department of Health and Human Services, is made up of 27 separate Institutes and Centers, each focusing on a different area of research. NIH is also the world's largest biomedical research institution. NIH employs 18,000 people, including 1,250 faculty and 3,800 postdoctoral fellows holding professional or graduate degrees. Some current research focuses on infectious diseases and bioterrorism defense.

ON THE JOB

In the Summer Internship Program in Biomedical Research, students work with researchers and scientists in laboratories, focusing on specific areas of research including cancer, child health, drug abuse, the human genome and mental health. Medical and dental students can apply to the Summer Research Fellowship Program. NIH recommends that students contact researchers directly if interested in particular labs.

GETTING HIRED

Apply by: March 1. Apply online at www.training.nih.gov/onlineApps/SIP/application/SIPApp.asp.

Qualifications:

Open to high school students over the age of 16, college freshmen, sophomores, juniors and seniors, and grad students who are U.S. citizens or permanent residents and are enrolled at least half-time in an accredited U.S. institution.

Contact:
NIH Office of Intramural Training and Research
2 Center Drive, Room 2W11A, MSC 0240
Bethesda, MD 20892
Phone: (800) 445-8283
E-mail: trainingwww@mail.nih.gov
www.training.nih.gov

Visit Vault at **www.vault.com** for insider company profiles, expert advice, career message boards, expert resume reviews, the Vault Job Board and more.

VAULT CAREER LIBRARY **305**

National Journal Group

 THE BUZZ
- "Political bloodhounds rejoice!"
- "Learn the fine art of political reporting"

 THE STATS

Industry(ies): Journalism; Publishing

Location(s): Washington, DC

Number of interns: *Spring/summer/fall:* 3 each

Pay: Paid; $10/hour, up to $400/week

Length of internship: 3-5 months

 THE SCOOP

Since 1969, the *National Journal* Group has produced non-partisan coverage of the federal policy-making process through monthly, weekly and daily publications and media outlets. The *National Journal*, a weekly political magazine covering national politics and federal policy, is the group's flagship publication. The magazine features articles on Washington's community of lobbyists, political consultants and journalists. It offers writing on politics, policy and government for readers with a professional interest in politics. It follows political trends, conducts public opinion polls and offers analysis of national developments.

 ON THE JOB

Interns work as journalists at *National Journal*, participating in research and political reporting. They are expected to assist other reporters in gathering information for stories, and to produce their own bylined articles for publication in the magazine. Internships are also offered with NationalJournal.com and The Hotline.

💰 **GETTING HIRED**

Apply by: *Summer:* March 15; *fall:* July 15; *spring:* October 15. Submit resume, cover letter and six writing samples to the address below.

Qualifications:
Open to college seniors, recent college graduates and grad students.

Contact:
Josephine Vu, Intern Coordinator
The Atlantic Media Company
600 New Hampshire Avenue, NW
Washington, DC 20037
Fax: (202) 266-7227
E-mail: jvu@nationaljournal.com

National Journalism Center

 THE BUZZ
- "A media junkie's dream"

 **THE STATS**

Industry(ies): Broadcast & Entertainment; Journalism

Location(s): Washington, DC

Number of interns: *Annual:* 60-70

Pay: None. Transportation and related expenses

Length of internship: *Spring/summer/fall:* 12 weeks; *winter:* 6 weeks

 THE SCOOP

Founded in 1977 by M. Stanton Evans, the National Journalism Center strives to teach balance and issue-comprehension to young reporters in an all-encompassing media/journalism program. Now directed by Kenneth Grubbs, the NJC educates budding journalists through extensive 12-week trainings and by arranging internships at various media locations. The organization has trained 1,400 students, some of whom have gone on to such prestigious media outlets as *The New York Times*, *The Washington Post*, *The Wall Street Journal*, CNN, NPR, Knight Ridder News Service and *Newsweek*, to name a few.

 ON THE JOB

Interns are placed with over 50 cooperating news organizations including ABC, BBC, CNN, National Geographic and many other local DC-, Virginia- and Maryland-based organizations. Interns work at one such organization and return once a week to The Center for a contextual lecture and a spot news writing assignment.

💰 **GETTING HIRED**

Apply by: *Spring 2007:* December 31, 2006; *summer 2007:* March 15; *fall 2007:* August 15. Download the online application from national journalismcenter.org/application.html.

Qualifications:
Open to college freshmen, sophomores, juniors and seniors, as well as college graduates and grad students.

Contact:
Krystle Weeks
Assistant to the Executive Director
National Journalism Center
A Program of the Young America's Foundation
529 14th Street NW
Suite 948
Washington, DC 20045
Phone: (703) 318-9608
Fax: (703) 318-9122
E-mail: kweeks@yaf.org
www.njc.yaf.org

National Organization for Women

 THE BUZZ
- "Work for equal rights"
- "Make your feminist voice heard!"

 THE STATS

Industry(ies): Nonprofit

Location(s): Washington, DC

Number of interns: *Annual:* 35-60

Pay: None

Length of internship: *Year-round:* full- and part-time, minimum 3 days/week; *fall/spring:* 16-16 weels; *summer:* 8-12 weeks

 THE SCOOP

The National Organization for Women is currently the largest and best-known feminist organization in the United States, with over 500,000 members. It was founded in 1966 to establish equality and further women's rights through grassroots organizing, lobbying and mass activism.

ON THE JOB

Interns learn grassroots organizing skills working with the Government Relations, Public Policy, Political Action Committees, Direct Marketing, Communications, Field Organizing or Racial Diversity Departments. NOW places a strong emphasis on building leadership skills by giving its interns responsibility and substantive work. Interns also attend workshops and discussion groups and are encouraged to represent NOW at various meetings and actions in the Washingto, DC, area.

GETTING HIRED

Apply by: *Spring:* November 20; *summer:* March 15; *fall:* July 30. Submit a cover letter, resume, application (online at www.now.org/organization/internap.html), two letters of recommendation, and a two-page writing sample.

Qualifications:
Open to all college, graduate or law student or recent graduate with a keen interest in women's issues.

Contact:
NOW Intern/Volunteer Coordinator
1100 H Street, NW, Third Floor
Washington, D.C. 20005
Phone: (202) 628-8669, ext. 103
Email: volunteer@now.org
www.now.org/organization/intern.html

National Park Service

 THE BUZZ
- "Work home on the range, where the buffalo, and now you, roam"
- "Get back in touch with nature"

THE STATS

Industry(ies): Environmental; Government; Tourism/Recreation

Location(s): Washington, DC; Nationwide

Number of interns: *Annual:* 5,000

Pay: Paid; $250-$350/week. Possibly free housing

Length of internship: *Summer/winter:* 12-16 weeks

THE SCOOP

Established in 1916 by the federal government, the National Park Service strives to preserve, protect and maintain the natural, historical and recreational resources of the United States. The idea for a national parks organization is credited to George Catlin who, in 1832, grew concerned with America's expansion into the West. Today, NPS includes over 370 parks in the United States and its territories, including Yellowstone, Yosemite, the Grand Canyon and Gettysburg.

ON THE JOB

NPS depends on seasonal employment to keep the sites functioning. Still, the positions are competitive, especially at better-known parks. NPS suggests that those interested in park internships contact the individual park directly to ask about available positions. In addition to park positions, cultural resource internships are offered, involving archaeology, curatorial and museums, history and historic architecture. The NPS Student Conservation Association also offers several volunteer programs.

GETTING HIRED

Apply by: *Summer:* January 15; *winter:* July 15.

Qualifications:
Open to college freshmen, sophomores, juniors and seniors (must be over age 18), college graduates and grad students.

Contact:
Seasonal Employment Unit, Room 2225
National Park Service
P.O. Box 37127
Washington, DC 20013-7127
Phone: (202) 208-5074
www.nps.gov/personnel/intern.htm

Visit Vault at **www.vault.com** for insider company profiles, expert advice, career message boards, expert resume reviews, the Vault Job Board and more.

VAULT CAREER LIBRARY **307**

National Partnership for Women and Families

 THE BUZZ
- "A great education/lobbyist organization"
- "Fight for equal rights and equal pay!"

 THE STATS

Industry(ies): Nonprofit

Location(s): Washington, DC

Number of interns: *Annual*: 24

Pay: None

Length of internship: *Spring/summer/fall*: 12-16 weeks; *summer*: full-time; *fall/spring*: 10-20 hours/week

 THE SCOOP

The National Partnership for Women and Families (NPWF) is a nonprofit, nonpartisan advocacy organization that uses public education and advocacy to promote fairness in the workplace, quality health care, and policies that help women and men meet the dual demands of work and family. Founded in 1971 as the Women's Legal Defense Fund, NPWF has been a powerful and effective advocate for women and families and was instrumental in bringing about reforms including the Family and Medical Leave Act of 1993, the Pregnancy Discrimination Act of 1978 and legal cases that ultimately prohibited sexual harassment in 1977.

 ON THE JOB

Internships are available in several departments including communications, the annual luncheon, fundraising and membership. There are also positions available in NPWF's program areas including health, work and family, and workplace fairness. In addition, the National Partnership offers law clerk internships in the health, work and family, and workplace fairness program areas.

$ GETTING HIRED

Apply by: *Spring*: November 15; *summer*: March 15; *fall*: July 15. Submit resume, cover letter, writing sample, a transcript and three references.

Qualifications:
Open to college freshmen, sophomores, juniors and seniors, grad students and law students.

Contact:
Volunteer Internship Coordinator
National Partnership for Women and Families
1875 Connecticut Avenue, NW, Suite 650
Washington, DC 20009
Phone: (202) 986-2600
Fax: (202) 986-2539
www.nationalpartnership.org

National Public Radio

 THE BUZZ
- "This just in: Media internships at NPR are as good as they get"
- "Interns get to produce their own show – try to beat that!"

 THE STATS

Industry(ies): Broadcast & Entertainment; Journalism

Location(s): Los Angeles, CA; Washington, DC

Number of interns: *Annual*: 60-80

Pay: *Summer*: $7/hour for 10 weeks (40 hour/week minimum), with the option to extend for an additonal 6 weeks unpaid; *spring/fall*: unpaid (flexible hours), but can receive academic credit

Length of internship: Minimum 10 weeks, with an option to extend to 16 weeks

 THE SCOOP

National Public Radio produces and broadcasts its award-winning journalistic, cultural, talk and music programs to nearly 30 million listeners over 600 public radio stations in the United States. Listeners can enjoy NPR on their radios or by streaming audio through a link on its web site.

 ON THE JOB

The work environment at NPR is creative but doesn't encourage flip flops, hip-huggers, low-riders or any kind of attire that doesn't represent a professional environment. But, if you wear a suit, be prepared to be teased about it. Specific programs include *All Things Considered, Talk of the Nation* and dozens more. Interns can also work in one of NPR's other departments, including audience and corporate research, audio engineering, business development, creative design, communications and public relations, finance, human resources, IT and legal.

 GETTING HIRED

Apply by: *Spring*: November 15; *summer*: February 15; *fall*: July 1. Download and send in a completed application form from the web site.

Qualifications:
It is very rare that a freshman gets in. Usually, NPR takes juniors, seniors and grad students, as well as those who are less than one year out of school

Contact:
Human Resources Department – Internship Program
National Public Radio
Human Resources Department
635 Massachusetts Avenue
Washington, DC 20001-3753
Phone: (202) 414-2909
Fax: (202) 513-3047
E-mail: internships@npr.org
www.npr.org/about/jobs/intern/index.html
www.npr.org/nextgen

National Review

THE BUZZ
- "The counter-liberal 'zine"

THE STATS

Industry(ies): Journalism; New/Interactive Media; Publishing

Location(s): New York, NY; Washington, DC

Number of interns: *Summer*: 1-2

Pay: Varies

Length of internship: *Summer*: 12 weeks

THE SCOOP

William F. Buckley Jr. established *National Review* in 1955 as a leading political journal for conservatives. The magazine covers both national and international issues, politics and American culture. With over 250,000 online readers, the *National Review* bills itself as "America's premier site for news, analysis and opinion."

ON THE JOB

Interns work as editorial assistants, fact checking and proofreading content for the *National Review*, as well as writing occasional paragraphs for the editorial section of the magazine. Some also handle readers' questions.

GETTING HIRED

Apply by: February 1. Send a resume and cover letter to intern@nationalreview.com or to the address below.

Qualifications:

Open to college juniors.

Contact:
Summer Editorial Internship
c/o Managing Editor
National Review
215 Lexington Avenue
New York, NY 10016
Phone: (212) 679-7330
E-mail: intern@nationalreview.com
www.nationalreview.com

National Rifle Association

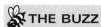

THE BUZZ
- "Working to protect out Second Amendment freedom"

THE STATS

Industry(ies): Nonprofit

Location(s): Fairfax, VA

Number of interns: *Annual*: 10

Pay: Paid; varies by department

Length of internship: 4-24 weeks; available year-round

THE SCOOP

The National Rifle Association was established in 1871 when Colonel William C. Church and General George Wingate, Union veterans of the Civil War, became frustrated with their troops' inability to shoot correctly. It has now grown into a national lobbying group, dedicated to preserving and upholding the Second Amendment, which gives U.S. citizens the right to bear arms. Thousands of volunteers and millions of members (think Charlton Heston and Tom Selleck) support NRA in its causes to promote education, safety, marksmanship training and the safeguarding of the Second Amendment.

ON THE JOB

Several departments hire interns, including administrative services, community services, development, field services, financial services, general counsel, legislative action, membership, purchasing, recreational shooting and security. Some tasks include clerical and administrative duties, and may require interaction with members and the public.

GETTING HIRED

Apply by: Rolling. Send resume and cover letter to the address below, indicating possible areas of interest.

Qualifications:
Open to college sophomores, juniors and seniors, as well as college graduates and grad students.

Contact:
Human Resources
National Rifle Association of America
11250 Waples Mill Road
Fairfax, VA 22030
Phone: (703) 267-1260
Fax: (703) 267-3938
Email: careers@nrahq.org
www.nra.org

Visit Vault at **www.vault.com** for insider company profiles, expert advice, career message boards, expert resume reviews, the Vault Job Board and more.

VAULT CAREER LIBRARY 309

National Security Agency

 THE BUZZ
- "Crack codes, get hired after graduation"
- "Puzzle out a real resume boost"

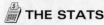 **THE STATS**

Industry(ies): Government; Science/Research

Location(s): Fort Meade, MD

Number of interns: *Summer:* 50

Pay: Paid; $500+/week

Length of internship: *Summer:* 12 weeks

THE SCOOP

The National Security Agency is the code-deciphering organization of the U.S. government, which protects security-sensitive information systems and gathers foreign signals intelligence information. As explained on its web site, NSA is composed of "the country's premier codemakers and codebreakers." Its mission is to stay on the cutting edge of communications and data processing while protecting government systems from hackers and others with malicious intent.

ON THE JOB

NSA is seriously committed to training potential employees through its internships and has developed a range of opportunities. In terms of summer employment, it offers six main programs: the College Summer Employment Program (for rising seniors majoring in math, computer science, electrical and computer engineering); the Math Summer Program (trains high-potential math students in cryptomathematical theory); Summer Network Evaluation Intern Program (network security program for engineering and computer science students); the Summer Program for Operations Research Technology; the Intelligence Analysis Summer Program (for graduating seniors and graduate students); and the Language Summer Program (for Arabic, Chinese and Farsi majors). Internships usually lead to employment offers.

GETTING HIRED

Apply by: Deadlines vary according to program, but most deadlines are mid-fall of the preceding year. Send resume, cover letter and transcripts to the appropriate address below. See the web site (www.nsa.gov/programs/employ/csp.cfm) for details.

Qualifications:

Most programs are open to college juniors or seniors and grad students. There are also programs open to high school students.

Contact:
Department of Defense
9800 Savage Road
Attn: S232 Co-op Education Program or Summer Intern Program
Fort George G. Meade, MD 20755-6779
Phone: (800) 962-9398
Fax: (800) 669-0703

Summer college program
National Security Agency
Attn: College Summer Employment Program
Office of Recruitment and Hiring, Suite 6779
P.O. Box 1661
9800 Savage Road
Fort George G. Meade, MD 20755-6779
www.nsa.gov/programs/employ/csp.cfm

Math summer program
National Security Agency
9800 Savage Road
Attn: R1 (DSP/MSEP/GMP)
Suite 6515
Fort George G. Meade, MD 20755-6515
Phone: (301) 688-0983

Operations research program
Summer Program for Operations Research Technology (SPORT)
National Security Agency
9800 Savage Road, Suite 6678
Fort George G. Meade, MD 20755-6678

STOKES educational scholarship program for high school students
National Security Agency, Attn: STOKES
Office of Recruitment and Staffing
9800 Savage Road, Suite 6779
Fort George G. Meade, MD 20755-6779
Phone: (866) 672-4473 (select Student Programs and then Stokes)

High school student program
www.nsa.gov/programs/employ/utp.cfm

National Space Society

 THE BUZZ

- "Help make *Star Trek* a reality"

 THE STATS

Industry(ies): Aerospace; Nonprofit; Science/Research

Location(s): Washington, DC

Number of interns: *Annual*: 2-3

Pay: None

Length of internship: *Summer/academic year*: 8 + weeks. *Summer*: 40 hours/week; *academic year*: 10 + hours/week

 THE SCOOP

The National Space Society is an independent nonprofit pushing for a future of human space exploration and colonization. It works to educate the public and promotes economic, political, social and technological change. NSS welceom recent efforts to restore moon research and initiate a mission to Mars. Currenty, NSS has over 20,000 members and 50 worldwide chapters.

 ON THE JOB

The breadth of activities at NSS allows interns to become involved in projects geared to their area of interest, including journalism, public outreach/education and public policy. Journalism interns work on *Ad Astra*, the bimonthly space publication. Public outreach interns interface with interested people, answering questions and assisting with event planning. Public policy interns attend Congressional briefings, track legislation, and help disseminate relevant information to the rest of NSS staff and to the public.

GETTING HIRED

Apply by: Rolling. To apply, applicants should e-mail or fax a resume and cover letter detailing their experience, qualifications, and area(s) of interest.

Qualifications:
Open to college sophomores, juniors and seniors with a minimum 3.0 GPA.

Contact:
Internship Coordinator
National Space Society
1620 I Street, NW, Suite 615
Washington, DC 20006
Phone: (202) 429-1600
Fax: (202) 463-8497
E-mail: nssinternships@gmail.com
www.nss.org

National Starch and Chemical Company

 THE BUZZ

- "Northeastern chemical engineers, take note of this non-starchy opportunity"

 THE STATS

Industry(ies): Chemicals; Manufacturing

Location(s): Bridgewater, NJ (HQ); multiple cities in CA, IL, IN, MA, MI, MO, NC, SC

Number of interns: Varies with need

Pay: Varies with position

Length of internship: Varies with student availability

 **THE SCOOP**

The National Starch and Chemical Company is a leading manufacturer of starches, adhesives, electronic and engineering materials, health care and industrial starches, specialty food, and synthetic polymers used in virtually every product category. It's staffed by almost 10,000 employees in 154 locations in 37 countries.

 ON THE JOB

Internships are available in the administrative, manufacturing, process development, product development, research and technical service areas. Interns work with professionals in the field: engineers, scientists and systems analysts. During the internship, students complete and present a special project assigned by their supervisors. Graduate students majoring in marketing or finance with an undergraduate degree in chemistry or engineering may be eligible for separate internships. Check the site for details.

 GETTING HIRED

Apply by: Rolling. Chemical engineering, chemistry, food science, paper science and materials/polymer science majors are eligible to apply. Go to resumebuilder.webhire.com/ resume_ add.asp?company = NSC and submit an online application.

Qualifications:
Open to college sophomore, junior and senior chemical engineering, chemistry, food science, paper science and materials/polymer science majors.

Contact:
National Starch and Chemical Company
10 Finderne Avenue
Bridgewater, NJ 08807-3300
Phone: (800) 797-4992
E-mail: nsc@rpc.webhire.com
www.nationalstarch.com/recruitment_pages.asp?lang_id = en&m kt = internships

Visit Vault at **www.vault.com** for insider company profiles, expert advice, career message boards, expert resume reviews, the Vault Job Board and more.

VAULT CAREER LIBRARY **311**

National Trust for Historic Preservation

 THE BUZZ
- "Preserve the past"
- "Ideal for hands-on historians"

 THE STATS

Industry(ies): Art/Museum; Nonprofit

Location(s): Washington, DC

Number of interns: *Summer*: 15-20

Pay: None

Length of internship: *Summer*: 10 weeks (full- or part-time)

 THE SCOOP

Since 1949, the National Trust for Historic Preservation has worked to preserve and protect historic buildings for future generations and operates 21 national trust sites around the country, supporting local historic preservation societies, creating programs and publications that foster awareness and education, and fighting to enact preservation laws. As stated in its motto, the organization "provides leadership, education and advocacy to save America's diverse historic places and revitalize our communities." The National Trust is sponsored by a quarter of a million members.

 ON THE JOB

Interns work on individual projects in the main office and in historic Washington, DC, sites, such as the Decatur House and the Woodrow Wilson House. Projects include compiling case studies, creating resources for local and national partners, developing databases and helping with communications and marketing, membership development and web site maintenance. Additionally, interns attend educational sessions on nonprofit management, preservation and Trust programs.

(\$) **GETTING HIRED**

Apply by: March 31. Submit a resume and cover letter to the address below.

Qualifications:
Open to college sophomores, juniors and seniors, college graduates and grad students.

Contact:
Internship Coordinator
National Trust for Historic Preservation
1785 Massachusetts Avenue, NW
Washington, DC 20036
Phone: (202) 673-4000
Fax: (202) 588-6059
E-mail: jobs@nthp.org
www.nationaltrust.org/volunteer/Search.asp

National Wildlife Federation

 THE BUZZ
- "Start an environmental career in conservation"
- "Environmentally conscious, supportive office"

 THE STATS

Industry(ies): Environmental; Nonprofit

Location(s): Offices in Anchorage, AK; Ann Arbor, MI; Atlanta, GA; Austin, TX; Boulder, CO; Missoula, MT; Montpelier, VT; Reston, VA; Seattle, WA; Washington, DC

Number of interns: *Annual*: 20

Pay: Paid; $320/week plus benefits

Length of internship: 24-48 weeks

 THE SCOOP

Founded in 1936, the National Wildlife Federation is the largest member-supported nonprofit conservation group in the United States, with more than 4 million members. Its goal is to raise public awareness for conservation and inspire people to work together to form a sustainable environment. The organization offers conservation education and leadership training, as well as networking contact opportunities.

ON THE JOB

Interns work in communications, conservation, education, grassroots organizing, policy issues, fundraising, and legal departments. They handle conservation projects on a community and national level, assisting and receiving support from professionals and the internship coordinator.

(\$) **GETTING HIRED**

Apply by: Rolling. Apply online at www.nwf.org/careergateway.

Qualifications:

Open to college juniors and seniors, as well as recent college graduates and grad students.

Contact:
National Wildlife Federation
Internship Coordinator
1100 Wildlife Center Drive
Reston, VA 20190-5362
E-mail: campus@nwf.org
www.nwf.org/careergateway

National Women's Health Network

 THE BUZZ
- "Get on the frontlines of promoting women's health"

 **THE STATS**

Industry(ies): Health Care; Nonprofit

Location(s): Washington, DC

Number of interns: *Spring/summer/fall/winter*: 4 each

Pay: Paid in fall/spring only; $160/week

Length of internship: *Spring/summer/fall*: 10-12 weeks (4 days/week); *winter*: 8-10 weeks (4 days/week)

 THE SCOOP

The National Women's Health Network (NWHN) is a nonprofit organization advocating for national policies that protect women's health. It supports, analyzes and disseminates health research information. It also connects activists and groups nationwide and monitors Congress and federal agencies. NWHN is fully supported by individuals and organizations, and acts independently of insurance agencies and pharmaceutical companies, enabling NWHN to provide women with unbiased health information and research.

ON THE JOB

NWHN values the contributions of its interns and uses the program to train new women's health activists. Interns conduct research on a variety of relevant women's health issues and develop skills and experience in the areas of education, feminist organizing and public policy. Past interns have produced and developed educational literature for women concerning new research, attended formal policy hearings on the latest health issues pertaining to women, and written articles for the organization's newsletter.

GETTING HIRED

Apply by: *Summer*: March 15; *fall/winter/spring*: rolling (three months prior is recommended). Send resume, cover letter and a two- to five-page writing sample to the address below.

Qualifications:
Open to college freshmen, sophomores, juniors and seniors, as well as college graduates and grad students.

Contact:
Electra Kaczorowski
National Women's Health Network
514 10th Street, NW, Suite 400
Washington, DC 20004
Phone: (202) 347-1140
Fax: (202) 347-1168
E-mail: ekaczorowski@womenshealthnetwork.org
www.nwhn.org

The Nature Conservancy

 THE BUZZ
- "'Saving the last great places on Earth'"

 **THE STATS**

Industry(ies): Environmental; Nonprofit

Location(s): Arlington, VA (HQ); regional offices in all 50 states

Number of interns: *Annual*: 130-150

Pay: Paid; $12/hour (depending on position and location). Free housing on preserves

Length of internship: *Summer/year-round*: 8 weeks-6 months

 **THE SCOOP**

The Nature Conservancy lives by its motto: "to preserve the plants, animals and natural communities that represent the diversity of life on Earth by protecting the lands and waters they need to survive." Since it was founded in 1951, the Nature Conservancy has preserved over 98 million acres of land through direct purchase and has also gained approximately 1 million members. Some of the lands it protects include Cumberland Marsh and the Virginia Coast Reserve in southeast Virginia.

ON THE JOB

Many of the Nature Conservancy's regional preserves and offices offer area-specific internships throughout the year. Interns working on the preserves help maintain them, monitor wildlife and handle related activities. Prospective interns can search for openings on the Nature Conservancy web page.

GETTING HIRED

Apply by: Rolling. For specific opportunities and application information, see the web site at nature.org/cgi-bin/zope.pcgi/careers/search_form (select "Internships").

Qualifications:
Open to college freshmen, sophomores, juniors and seniors, as well as college graduates and grad students.

Contact:
Internship Coordinator
The Nature Conservancy
Worldwide Office
4245 North Fairfax Drive, Suite 100
Arlington, VA 22203
nature.org/volunteer

Visit Vault at **www.vault.com** for insider company profiles, expert advice, career message boards, expert resume reviews, the Vault Job Board and more.

VAULT CAREER LIBRARY **313**

NBC Universal

 THE BUZZ
- "Must see TV internship program"

 THE STATS

Industry(ies): Broadcast & Entertainment; Film; Journalism; New/Interactive Media

Location(s): New York, NY (NBCU Corporate HQ); Burbank, CA (NBCU Entertainment Hub/Studios); Englewood Cliffs, NJ (CNBC); Hialeah, FL (Telemundo); Secaucus, NJ (MSNBC); Universal City, CA; 30 owned and operated stations across the U.S.

Number of interns: Varies at each location

Pay: None; academic credit only

Length of internship: *Spring*: 12-16 weeks; *summer*: 10-12 weeks; *fall*: 12-16 weeks

 THE SCOOP

NBC Universal, one of the world's leading media and entertainment companies in the development, production, and marketing of entertainment, news and information to a global audience, formed in May 2004 when NBCU combined with Vivendi Universal Entertainment. NBC Universal owns and operates the No. 1 television network, the fastest-growing Spanish-language network, a slew of noted news and entertainment networks, a motion picture company, significant television production operations, a leading television station group, and several world-renowned theme parks. NBC Universal is 80 percent owned by General Electric, with Vivendi Universal controlling the remaining 20 percent.

ON THE JOB

The bulk of NBCU's interns are in New York City and California, or at one of the 30 NBC-owned and operated stations across the country. There are also internships available at MSNBC, CNBC, Telemundo and mun2. Interns may also have the opportunity to work on the business-side, learning marketing, public relations, sales, advertising, operations, information technology and other duties. NBCU works to place interns in roles that suit their background and career interests.

GETTING HIRED

Apply by: Rolling. Visit www.nbcunicareers.com for more information.

Qualifications:
Open to all college sophomores, juniors and seniors and grad students in good academic standing with their university. Students must be able to receive academic credit for the internship.

Contact:
www.nbcunicareers.com

NETWORK

 THE BUZZ
- "Catholic (or any religious) women activists, this is your internship"

 THE STATS

Industry(ies): Nonprofit

Location(s): Washington, DC

Number of interns: *Annual*: 3

Pay: Paid; $1,056/month. Health benefits; travel stipend

Length of internship: 11 months (September-August). Inquire about the availability of shorter, unpaid internships

 THE SCOOP

NETWORK is a women-led nonprofit membership organization using Catholic social justice teachings about economic, racial and social equity to lobby the federal government for legislative changes. Its bimonthly magazine, *NETWORK Connection*, educates members on political issues and updates on legislation. NETWORK's issues have included a living wage, health care benefits for all, fair treatment for immigrants, fair trade, global peace and sustainable development.

ON THE JOB

NETWORK calls its internship the Associate Program. The organization hopes to offer its interns a faith-based advocacy experience and accepts two lobby associates and one field associate annually. Interns explore justice issues in depth and learn how to organize for legislative advocacy, attending press conferences, contacting Congressional members and staff, and working with other advocacy, civil rights and labor groups. Two internships focus on lobbying and one focuses on field organizing.

GETTING HIRED

Apply by: February 1. Download application from the web site and mail it, along with resume and two references, to the address below. See web site for the application.

Qualifications:
Open to college graduates from all faiths and backgrounds interested in political advocacy.

Contact:
Marjorie Bingham
Human Resources Coordinator
NETWORK
25 E Street, NW, 2nd Floor
Washington, DC 20001
Phone: (202) 547-5556
Fax: (202) 547-5510
E-mail: mbingham@networklobby.org
www.networklobby.org/about/associate/index.html

New Canaan Country School

 THE BUZZ
- "The ideal teaching experience in bucolic Connecticut"

 THE STATS

Industry(ies): Education

Location(s): New Canaan, CT

Number of interns: *Annual:* 22

Pay: Paid; $21,000/school year. Subsidized housing

Length of internship: 10 months (September-June)

 THE SCOOP

The New Canaan Country School, a private day school that was founded in 1916, works with families to help children attain their full academic potential. Seventy-three full-time teachers and 32 apprentices, assistants and part-time specialists work at NCCS, and 615 students attend the pre-K through ninth-grade school. Its resources include three art studios, three music classrooms, two gymnasiums, seven playing fields, a professional auditorium, a woodworking shop and a 40-acre nature preserve.

 ON THE JOB

The Apprentice Program, formerly known as the Teaching Fellowship Program, offers teaching experience to college graduates. Apprentices are assigned to a classroom in grades K through six and work alongside their mentor teachers. Apprentices' responsibilities increase as the year progresses and they learn to plan lessons, teach lessons, work with individual students and participate in parent-teacher conferences. Apprentices are also expected to supervise athletic and extracurricular activities.

GETTING HIRED

Apply by: April 1. Submit a resume, cover letter, transcript and recommendations to the address below.

Qualifications:
Open to college graduates and grad students.

Contact:
Dana Mallozzi
Coordinator of Apprentice Program
New Canaan Country School
P.O. Box 997
New Canaan, CT 06840
Phone: (203) 972-0771
Fax: (203) 966-5924
E-mail: dmallozzi@countryschool.net
www.countryschool.net

New Dramatists

 THE BUZZ
- "Rumor is, interns run the show – literally"
- "Go behind the scenes in the theater world"

 THE STATS

Industry(ies): Theater/Performing Arts

Location(s): New York, NY

Number of interns: *Annual:* 15-20

Pay: $50/week for full-time interns (40 hours/week) , $25/week for part-time interns (24 hours/week)

Length of internship: *Spring/summer/fall:* 12-20 weeks (generally starting January 1, June 1 and September 1)

 THE SCOOP

Founded in 1949, New Dramatists gives playwrights the time, space and tools to develop their craft so they may fulfill their potential and make lasting contributions to the theater. Fewer than 10 members are chosen to participate annually, and membership lasts for seven years. Notable alumni include Robert Anderson, Maria Irene Fornes, Donald Marguiles, John Patrick Shanley, Paula Vogel, Suzan-Lori Parks, Nilo Cruz and Doug Wright.

ON THE JOB

Interns are a valued part of the team and carry out much of the "real work", such as administration, literary services, fundraising/special events, casting and stage management. Duties also include clerical tasks and errands.

GETTING HIRED

Apply by: *Summer:* April 15; *fall/spring:* rolling. Submit an application, downloadable on the web site, www.new dramatists.org. Please include a cover letter and resume.

Qualifications:
Open to college students, college graduates, grad students and young theater professionals.

Contact:
Internship Coordinator
New Dramatists
424 West 44th Street
New York, NY 10036
Phone: (212) 757-6960
Fax: (212) 265-4738
www.newdramatists.org

Visit Vault at **www.vault.com** for insider company profiles, expert advice, career message boards, expert resume reviews, the Vault Job Board and more.

VAULT CAREER LIBRARY **315**

The New Republic

 THE BUZZ
- "One of the most prestigious American political magazines"
- "Intellectual rigor like nobody's business"

 THE STATS

Industry(ies): Journalism; Publishing

Location(s): Washington, DC

Number of interns: *Annual*: 5

Pay: Paid; $270/week plus healthcare and extensive overtime

Length of internship: Full year, beginning in mid-late summer

 THE SCOOP

The New Republic is the premier journal of liberal politics and cultural opinion. It was founded in 1914 and, since then, has been publishing sharp, cogent articles on the economy, the arts and politics. Staffers often make radio or television appearances to discuss their articles and political views.

ON THE JOB

Tasks include fact-checking, research, proofreading, writing and clerical duties. Applicants will have opportunities to write for both TNR online and the print edition. Five interns are hired yearly; three become reporter-researchers, one becomes an assistant to the editor, and one becomes an assistant Web editor.

GETTING HIRED

Apply by: February 10. All applications should be e-mailed to job@tnr.com. Submit a resume, cover letter, a 750-word critique of the Politics section of a recent issue and two clips (one news, one opinion). No phone calls and no snail mail.

Qualifications:
Open to college seniors, college graduates and grad students.

Contact:
E-mail: job@tnr.com
www.tnr.com

New Stage Theatre

 THE BUZZ
- "Perfect transition for aspiring theater buffs"
- "Fabulous theater experience in the Hospitality State"

 THE STATS

Industry(ies): Education; Theater/Performing Arts

Location(s): Jackson, MS

Number of interns: *Annual*: 4

Pay: Paid; $200/week. Health insurance

Length of internship: 9 months (August-May)

 THE SCOOP

New Stage Theatre is a nonprofit company producing quality performances in Mississippi and the Southeast. The organization produces five plays per year in its subscription series, which are performed for its 2,000 subscribers. New Stage has also developed a touring education program, bringing literary classics to life for students throughout Mississippi. It hosts summer camps and offers student and teacher workshops, as well.

 ON THE JOB

New Stage's intern program (Professional Acting Intern Company) is part of its educational area and provides aspiring theater professionals with the opportunity to gain necessary experience while performing and touring with New Stage Theatre.

 GETTING HIRED

Apply by: April 1. Submit a resume, cover letter, recommendations and a videotape of two monologues or arrange an in-person audition.

Qualifications:
Open to college graduates and grad students.

Contact:
Kate Roselle, Education Director
New Stage Theatre
1100 Carlisle Street
Jackson, MS 39202
Phone: (601) 948-3533 ext. 232
Fax: (601) 948-3538
E-mail: education@newstagetheatre.com
www.newstagetheatre.com

New York Arts Program

 THE BUZZ
- "New Yorkers with artistic souls – and interests – apply here"

 THE STATS

Industry(ies): Art/Museum; Broadcast & Entertainment; Film; Theater/Performing Arts

Location(s): New York, NY

Number of interns: Varies with artist/mentor availability

Pay: None. Tuition cost: $8,075/15-week semester (16 credits); $6,055/10-week semester (10 2/3 credits); additional fees

Length of internship: *Spring* (January-April), *fall* (September-December): 15 weeks; *winter* (January-March): 10 weeks

 THE SCOOP

The New York Arts Program arranges student apprenticeships with artists in all disciplines: communication arts, film, literary, publishing and visual arts. Over 3,000 participants have gone through the program since its inception in 1967. Resources offered to apprentices include a full-time support staff, facilities and housing.

 ON THE JOB

Interns gain exposure to the current thriving New York art scene (what it means to be an artist in an urban environment), which increases a student's specialized experience. Apprenticeships include acting and directing, advertising, arts administration, applied arts and design, creative writing, dance and choreography, design (theater), journalism, studio art and television. For details on participating universities, see www.newyorkartsprogram.org/info.html.

 GETTING HIRED

Apply by: *Fall*: March 31; *winter/spring*: October 31. Download application and recommendation form from www.newyorkarts program.org/application.html. Send completed application materials to the address below.

Qualifications:
Open to college sophomores, juniors and seniors.

Contact:
GLCA New York Arts Program
305 West 29th Street
New York, NY 10001
Phone: (212) 563-0255
Fax: (212) 563-0256
E-mail: office@newyorkartsprogram.org
www.newyorkartsprogram.org/apprenticeships.html

New York City Urban Fellows Program

 THE BUZZ
- "Learn about urban issues and government in a major metropolis"
- "The place to be both urban and scholarly"

 **THE STATS**

Industry(ies): Government

Location(s): New York, NY

Number of interns: 25 fellows

Pay: *Fellows*: $25,000 stipend/9 months. Health insurance; no housing

Length of internship: *Fellows*: 9 months

 THE SCOOP

The New York City Urban Fellows Program was founded in 1969 specifically to help those with a college education and an interest in policymaking learn about how urban issues meld with public policy. New York City politics and government are not for the faint-hearted. In a display of the program's prominence, every New York City mayor since 1969 has lent their support to it over the years.

 ON THE JOB

Fellows spend their time learning about the structure and functions of the New York City government, as well as the issues it faces, and work to find solutions. They sit in on meetings, look at budget requests and work side-by-side with senior city managers. Each fellow is assigned to a New York City agency.

 GETTING HIRED

Apply by: Application due in the Urban Fellows office by 5 p.m. on Friday, January 12, 2007.

Qualifications:
Urban Fellows must be graduates and not more than two years out of college. For 2007-2008 programs, applications will be accepted from those who graduate with a bachelor's degree in the Spring of 2006, 2007 or 2008.

Contact:
New York City Internship/Fellowship Programs
Department of Citywide Services
Division of Citywide Personnel Services
1 Centre Street, Room 2425
New York, NY 10007
Phone: (212) NEW-YORK
For further information, please visit:
www.nyc.gov/internships

Visit Vault at **www.vault.com** for insider company profiles, expert advice, career message boards, expert resume reviews, the Vault Job Board and more.

V∧ULT CAREER LIBRARY **317**

New York Presbyterian Hospital Westchester Division

 THE BUZZ
- "Get hands-on patient care experience"
- "Help treat the psychologically challenged"

 THE STATS

Industry(ies): Health Care

Location(s): White Plains, NY

Number of interns: *Summer*: 30-40

Pay: None

Length of internship: *Summer*: 8 weeks

 THE SCOOP

New York-Presbyterian, affiliated with both Columbia and Cornell universities, is one of the most comprehensive university hospitals in the United States. Its Westchester division specializes in psychiatry, providing a range of diagnosis and treatment services for patients suffering from behavioral, emotional and other psychiatric ailments. In fact, it was rated the second-best psychiatric clinic in America by *U.S. News & World Report*'s Best Hospitals 2002.

 ON THE JOB

The Pre-Career Practicum offered by New York-Presbyterian Hospital's Westchester Division allows students to learn in its prestigious hospital. Interns work in marketing, nursing, psychology, research, social services and therapeutic activities. Duties vary within the departments, but may include clerical tasks or assisting hospital staff members with patient care.

 GETTING HIRED

Apply by: March 15.

Qualifications:
Open to college sophomores, juniors and seniors, and grad students.

Contact:
Pre-Career Practicum
The New York Presbyterian Hospital
Westchester Division
21 Bloomingdale Road
White Plains, NY 10605
Phone: (914) 997-5780
Fax: (914) 682-6909
www.nyp.org

New York State Theatre Institute

 THE BUZZ
- "Solid, thorough work experience in theater"
- "Teach kids through performance art"

 THE STATS

Industry(ies): Education; Theater/Performing Arts

Location(s): Troy, NY

Number of interns: *Fall/spring*: 20 each

Pay: None

Length of internship: *Fall/spring*: 1 semester

 THE SCOOP

The New York State Theatre Institute was established through state legislation in 1974, to motivate disengaged students into finding interest in daily studies. The company uses its performances as a teaching tool and focuses on and its high quality family theater productions, which are also used to support arts in education programs. Its strong commitment to education is reflected in its solid internship participation: over 1,000 students have gone through the program.

 ON THE JOB

During the program, interns rotate through the different departments including the box office, costuming, education, lights, performance, properties, public relations, scenery and stage management. Interns can also audition for, and are sometimes cast in, Institute productions. In addition to the highly individualized and pragmatic training, interns benefit from a strong network of theater professionals.

 GETTING HIRED

Apply by: Rolling.

Qualifications:
Open to graduating high school seniors, college freshmen, sophomores, juniors and seniors, grad students and educators-in-residence. Prospective interns must be affiliated with an academic institution.

Contact:
Arlene Leff
Intern Program Director
New York State Theatre Institute
37 First Street
Troy, NY 12180
Phone: (518) 274-3573
Fax: (518) 274-3815
E-mail: aileff@nysti.org
www.nysti.org/education.shtm#internship

New York Times

 THE BUZZ
- "Vault to the top of the newspaper business by interning for the Gray Lady"

 THE STATS

Industry(ies): Journalism

Location(s): New York, NY

Number of interns: *Summer*: 12

Pay: Paid; $800 a week. Housing allowance for interns who reside in housing that the *Times* arranges

Length of internship: *Summer*: 10 weeks

 **THE SCOOP**

Since 1851, *The New York Times* has been publishing "all the news that's fit to print," with hard-hitting national and local articles. It is one of the best known and respected newspapers in the country and was awarded seven Pulitzer Prizes in 2002. *The New York Times* has a daily readership of 1.1 million and 1.7 million on Sundays.

 ON THE JOB

The internships offered include the James Reston Reporting Fellowships, which give interns regular reporting assignments and may be extended by six months, leading to full-time employment; the Thomas Morgan Internships in graphics, design and photography (each summer, the Thomas Morgan interns compete for a $1,500 award for excellent work); and the Dow Jones Newspaper Fund Editing Internship, which selects up to three interns to attend a two-week editing seminar and then work at the *Times*.

 GETTING HIRED

Apply by: November 15. Reporting fellow applicants must submit a resume and eight to 10 news-writing samples. Photography, graphics and design applicants should submit a resume and a portfolio of their creative work. Those applying for the Dow Jones editorial internship should call (609) 452-2820, log on to www.dowjones.com/newsfund or e-mail newsfund@wsj.dow jones.com.

Qualifications:
Reporting internships open to college seniors and grad students. Applicants for the other internship positions may be college sophomores, juniors and seniors, or grad students.

Contact:
Sheila Rule, Senior Editor
The New York Times
229 West 43rd Street
New York, NY 10036
Phone: (212) 556-4143
www.nytco.com/intern.html

Newsday

 THE BUZZ
- "Work for the top paper in Long Island, New York"

 **THE STATS**

Industry(ies): Journalism

Location(s): Melville, NY

Number of interns: *Summer*: 25

Pay: Paid; $523/week

Length of internship: *Summer*: 10 weeks; 35 hours/week

 THE SCOOP

Newsday is one of New York's largest daily papers, serving 400,000 daily and 480,000 Sunday Long Island and Queens residents. *Newsday* got its start in 1940, when Harry Frank Guggenheim bought the *Nassau Daily Journal*'s equipment for his wife, Alicia Patterson, to give her a project that would help her prepare for eventually taking the reins at her father's legacy newspaper, the *New York Daily News*. Due to an argument, she never did, but *Newsday* grew to become Long Island's most widely read paper. It has earned 18 Pulitzer Prizes in its history and employs almost 100 reporters and columnists.

 ON THE JOB

Newsday interns work as reporters, copyeditors, photographers or artists and are assigned to one of the paper's major sections including business, entertainment, features, news and sports. In addition to completing regular assignments, journalism interns attend seminars with staff members to discuss reporting and writing techniques.

GETTING HIRED

Apply by: November 15. Interns can obtain an application online by going to: www.newsday.com/internships.

Qualifications:

Open to college juniors and seniors, and grad students.

Contact:
Internship Coordinator
Newsday
235 Pinelawn Road
Melville, NY 11747
Phone: (631) 843-2637
E-mail: jobs@newsday.com
www.newsday.com/internships

Visit Vault at **www.vault.com** for insider company profiles, expert advice, career message boards, expert resume reviews, the Vault Job Board and more.

V/ULT CAREER LIBRARY **319**

The NewsHour with Jim Lehrer

 THE BUZZ
- "Somebody needs to replace MacNeil..."
- "News without commercial influence"

 THE STATS

Industry(ies): Broadcast & Entertainment; Journalism

Location(s): Arlington, VA

Number of interns: *Annual*: 7

Pay: Many unpaid positions; some paid (amount varies depending on position and experience)

Length of internship: *Summer* (starting early July), *winter* (starting mid-January): 6 months

 THE SCOOP

In 1972, Jim Lehrer and Robert MacNeil launched *The MacNeil/Lehrer NewsHour*, PBS's groundbreaking point-counterpoint news program, to cover the Watergate hearings. The duo earned an Emmy Award for it and continued winning awards for their show, which focused on a single current event or issue per episode. Many thought the show would fail when the episode length was changed to one hour, but it did just the opposite. Though MacNeil left in 1995, Lehrer continues in a similar style, working with several top-rated correspondents. Only the name has changed: *The NewsHour with Jim Lehrer*. One of PBS's mainstays, the show is one of the most highly respected news programs of its kind.

 ON THE JOB

NewsHour takes interns on an as-needed basis, so positions and duties vary greatly. Some past internships have included graphic design, where interns learned how to produce broadcast news graphics. Another position was an online internship that had interns working on the online version of *NewsHour*, gaining experience in online production, writing and audio editing. Interns can work in any department where a need exists.

 GETTING HIRED

Apply by: Rolling. Check the web site for current openings and application details: www.pbs.org/newshour/ww/openings.html.

Qualifications:
Open to college freshmen, sophomores, juniors and seniors, grad students and recent college graduates.

Contact:
3620 South 27th Street
Arlington, VA 22193
www.pbs.org/newshour/ww/openings.html

Newsweek

 THE BUZZ
- "One of the world's best-known news names"
- "Get your world news writing experience"

 THE STATS

Industry(ies): Journalism; Publishing

Location(s): New York, NY

Number of interns: *Summer*: 10-12

Pay: Paid; $595/week plus overtime

Length of internship: *Summer*: 13 weeks

 **THE SCOOP**

Newsweek, founded in 1922, now employs over 60 correspondents based throughout the world and enjoys a total circulation of over 4 million (with a readership numbering 21 million worldwide). *Newsweek* also has the distinction of holding more National Magazine Awards than any other weekly news publication. It's made up of six main sections: arts and entertainment, business, international affairs, national affairs, science and technology, and society.

 ON THE JOB

Interns meet and mingle with editors, writers and correspondents on a daily basis. Responsibilities for the editorial research interns include fact-checking, reporting and researching stories. The communications department also hires an intern to assist staff with clerical tasks.

 GETTING HIRED

Apply by: November 1. Submit a one-page cover letter describing qualifications and aspirations, resume, five published writing samples with the name and date of publication and the names and phone numbers of two references to the address below. *Newsweek* does not accept emailed application materials.

Qualifications:
Open to rising college seniors, grad students and recent college graduates with experience reporting and writing for their college newspapers or in previous internships at other publications. Must have proven eligibility to work in the United States (for foreign nationals and students, the appropriate INS paperwork).

Contact:
Internship Program
Newsweek
251 West 57th Street
New York, NY 10019
Phone: (212) 445-5416
www.msnbc.com/modules/newsweek/info/nwinfo_internships.asp

Nickelodeon Animation Studio

THE BUZZ
- "A television internship for those who are still kids at heart"

THE STATS

Industry(ies): Broadcast & Entertainment

Location(s): Burbank, CA

Number of interns: 3-10

Pay: None; academic credit available

Length of internship: 8-16 weeks; available year-round

THE SCOOP

Nickelodeon is the kid-branch of MTV Networks. It reaches more than 86 million U.S. households, which is more than all three major networks – CBS, NBC and ABC – combined. Related channels include Nick Jr. (for the toddler set), and Nick at Nite and TV Land, both of which air classic family comedies such as *I Love Lucy* and *The Cosby Show*. Nickelodeon Animation Studio creates, develops and produces various cartoons including the squishily popular *Spongebob Squarepants*, *The Fairly Odd Parents*, *Danny Phantom*, *Stripperella* and many more.

ON THE JOB

For the Nickelodeon Animation Studio Internship Program, students work in the Nicktoons division, which produces shows including *Dora the Explorer*, *The Fairly Odd Parents*, *Chalk Zone*, *Danny Phantom* and *Life as a Teenage Robot*. The internship involves a lot of hands-on work in animation and other departments. Interns also work in the production, post-production, finance, casting, development, administration, human resources and paralegal areas.

GETTING HIRED

Apply by: Rolling. Send a resume and cover letter, indicating the semester and departments in which you want to work. Must be able to receive academic credit.

Qualifications:
Open to all college freshmen, sophomores, juniors and seniors (internships are geared toward undergraduates).

Contact:
Internship Coordinator
Nickelodeon Animation Studio
Recruitment Office
231 West Olive Avenue
Burbank, CA 91502
Phone: (818) 736-3673
Fax: (818) 736-3539

Nightline

 THE BUZZ
- "Qualified gofers: run, watch and learn"
- "Help produce quality news"

THE STATS

Industry(ies): Broadcast & Entertainment; Journalism

Location(s): New York, NY

Number of interns: 4-5/semester; 1 fellow

Pay: None; academic credit

Length of internship: *Spring I* (January-April): 8-12 weeks (full- or part-time); *spring II* (April-June); *summer* (June-August); *fall* (September-December); *winter* (December-January); *fellowship*: 1 year (beginning July 15)

THE SCOOP

Nightline is ABC's late nightly news show hosted by Ted Koppel. The program is produced in its Washington, DC, office, where 35 staff members and interns bring together the extensive news coverage of current events and other investigative reports.

ON THE JOB

Nightline interns work in the Law & Justice Unit of the network's news division. These interns are generally responsible for garden-variety office work. However, they also fully participate in editorial conferences and television production. *Nightline* chooses interns who are sincerely interested in a career in broadcast journalism.

GETTING HIRED

Apply by: *Spring I*: November 15; *spring II*: February 1; *summer*: March 15; *fall*: July 1; *winter*: October 1. Send a resume, cover letter, two written recommendations, academic transcript, a completed application form and a notice of credit approval, if possible.

Qualifications:
Open to college juniors and seniors. Must receive academic credit.

Contact:
Nissa Walton Booker
ABC News Recruitment Coordinator
47 West 66th Street, 6th Floor
New York, NY 10023
E-mail: nissa.Walton-booker@abc.com
abcnews.go.com/service/DailyNews/internships.html

Visit Vault at **www.vault.com** for insider company profiles, expert advice, career message boards, expert resume reviews, the Vault Job Board and more.

VAULT CAREER LIBRARY 321

Nike

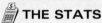 **THE BUZZ**
- "Spend the summer getting your career in shape with Nike"
- "Learn the apparel business from the bottom up"

 THE STATS

Industry(ies): Consumer Products; Fashion

Location(s): Beaverton, OR

Number of interns: *Summer*: 40+

Pay: Paid; competitive salary. $1,000 living stipend; travel compensation

Length of internship: *Summer*: 9 weeks (June-August)

 THE SCOOP

Nike is drenched in competition and personal potential with its mission "to bring inspiration and innovation to every athlete (and if you have a body, you are an athlete) in the world." The company hit the scene in 1964, started by former track coach Bill Bowerman and track runner/accounting student Phil Knight. Today, Nike is the largest sports equipment company in the world, with almost $10 billion in revenues. To keep it running smoothly, Nike employs 20,000 people worldwide. Its headquarters, dubbed the "Nike World Campus," sits on a 175-acre environmentally conscious haven for work and play.

ON THE JOB

Interns work in apparel, communications, contract manufacturing, customer service, design and development, equipment, finance, human resources, information technology, legal, logistics, marketing, marketing communications, public affairs, research, retail, sales and technology. Responsibilities vary with department placement.

GETTING HIRED

Apply by: November. Apply online at www.nike.com/nikebiz/nikebiz.jhtml?page=31&cat=internships.

Qualifications:
Open to college sophomores, juniors and seniors, as well as grad students.

Contact:
Nike
Internship Program
One Bowerman Drive
Beaverton, OR 97005
www.nike.com/nikebiz/nikebiz.jhtml?page=31&cat=internships

Norfolk Chamber Music Festival

 THE BUZZ
- "Work behind the scenes to make sure the show goes on"
- "Develop skills in event management as you help coordinate a huge arts festival"

 THE STATS

Industry(ies): Theater/Performing Arts

Location(s): Norfolk, CT

Number of interns: *Annual*: 1-2 unpaid; 5-6 paid

Pay: Varies. Unpaid interns receive housing and meals; paid interns receive housing, meals and $450/week

Length of internship: 12 weeks (mid-June–late August)

 THE SCOOP

Each summer the 70-acre Stoeckel Estate, willed to Yale University in 1939 by Ellen Batell Stoeckel and located in northwestern Connecticut, hosts 30-plus performances by world-famous chamber musicians, as well as 60 fellows from the Yale Summer School of Music. Featured artists include the Tokyo String Quartet, a group that has spent 20 summers in Norfolk.

ON THE JOB

Interns have access to all concerts and amenities, including an art gallery, dining hall, laundry room, library, seminars and theater. Internships fall into two categories: administrative and recording/production. Administrative interns assist with the daily operation of the Festival and the Yale Summer School of Music, handling clerical tasks, working at the box office, helping with marketing, publicity and special projects, and making arrangements for artists. Recording/production interns work in stage management, equipment management and preparations, assisting the concert hall manager, recording engineer and other staff members.

GETTING HIRED

Apply by: April 1. Submit a resume, cover letter and some contacts for recommendations.

Qualifications:
Unpaid internship: open to college juniors, seniors, graduate students and college graduates. *Paid internship*: open to applicants with a bachelor's degree. Previous experience required for Production Manager, Recording Engineer and Box Office Manager.

Contact:
Internship Manager
Norfolk Chamber Music Festival
Yale Summer School of Music
P.O. Box 208246
New Haven, CT 06520-8246
Phone: (203) 432-1966
Fax: (203) 432-2136
E-mail: Norfolk@yale.edu
www.yale.edu/norfolk

North Carolina Botanical Garden

THE BUZZ
- "A verdant place to start a career in plant conservation"
- "Keep America (or North Carolina) beautiful"

THE STATS

Industry(ies): Environmental; Science/Research

Location(s): Chapel Hill, NC

Number of interns: *Annual*: 4

Pay: Paid; $321/week

Length of internship: 3-12 months; available year-round

THE SCOOP

Emphasizing biological diversity and conservation of regional habitats, the North Carolina Botanical Garden is home to 4,700 species of North and South Carolina's native plants. The 600-acre public garden, part of the University of North Carolina at Chapel Hill, was opened in 1966. The Garden features two arboretums, a biological reserve, the herbarium and coastal plain, mountain and sandhills natural habitats.

ON THE JOB

Interns assist visitors, garden, keep records and work with volunteers. Tasks may include guiding tours, working with the garden staff and performing clerical duties in the records office. Interns work closely with staff members.

GETTING HIRED

Apply by: Rolling. Write to the address below for an application.

Qualifications:

Open to college freshmen, sophomores, juniors and seniors, college graduates and grad students.

Contact:
James L. Ward
North Carolina Botanical Garden
3375 Totten Center
University of North Carolina
Chapel Hill, NC 27599-3375
Phone: (919) 962-0522
Fax: (919) 962-3531
E-mail: wardjl@email.unc.edu
www.ncbg.edu

North Cascades Institute

THE BUZZ
- "Dust off your camping equipment"

THE STATS

Industry(ies): Education; Environmental; Nonprofit

Location(s): Skagit Valley, WA

Number of interns: *Spring/fall*: 3-10 interns each term

Pay: None. Training; food and housing; educational materials provided

Length of internship: *Spring/fall*: up to 9 weeks

THE SCOOP

Founded in 1986, North Cascades Institute is the Northwest's leader in field-based environmental education. Focusing on natural and cultural history, its mission is to conserve and restore Northwest environments through education. The organization teaches all ages and encourages hands-on discovery, believing that people need intimate, informed contact with the natural world. NCI teaches natural and cultural history, science, humanities and the arts, emphasizing wilderness, watersheds and biological diversity as unifying themes.

ON THE JOB

Interns provide the core of NCI's instructional staff and are involved in planning, camp set-up and breakdown, and logistics for the Northwest's premier environmental education organization. They participate in a comprehensive weeklong training in natural history, environmental education teaching methods and positive discipline. They also lead elementary and middle school children in daily field classes, including hike-based and evening activities, implement the Mountain School curriculum, and assist with other tasks that are involved in the operation and maintenance of an outdoor environmental education program.

GETTING HIRED

Apply by: *Fall*: mid-July; *spring*: mid-February. Send application, available at www.ncascades.org/about_us/employment/internships.ldmx and current resume to North Cascades Institute at the address below.

Qualifications:

Open to high school graduates, college freshmen, sophomores, juniors and seniors, college graduates and grad students. NCI seeks motivated interns interested in environmental education. Applicants should want to work with elementary and middle school students. Previous environmental education experience not required, but an asset. Good communication skills are important. Knowledge of, or an interest in, learning about the regional ecology is a must. Current first aid and CPR certification is required. Applicants should be at least 18 years of age.

Contact:
Internship Coordinator
North Cascades Institute
810 State Route 20
Sedro-Woolley, WA 98284
Phone: (360) 856-5700, ext. 209
Fax: (360) 856-1934
E-mail: nci@ncascades.org
www.ncascades.org/about_us/employment/internships.ldmx

Visit Vault at **www.vault.com** for insider company profiles, expert advice, career message boards, expert resume reviews, the Vault Job Board and more.

VAULT CAREER LIBRARY 323

Northfield Mount Hermon School

 THE BUZZ
- "Help prep kids for college"
- "Realize your dreams of becoming a teacher"

 THE STATS

Industry(ies): Education

Location(s): Northfield, MA

Number of interns: *Summer*: 30

Pay: Paid; $2,000/5 weeks. Free room and board; laundry service

Length of internship: *Summer*: 5 weeks (June 23-August 3)

 THE SCOOP

The Northfield Mount Hermon School is a college preparatory school for boys and girls located in western Massachusetts, close to the Vermont border. It provides a rigorous summer program, attended by 350-400 students from diverse ethnicities and nationalities. Northfield Mount Hermon School Summer Session offers three programs: College Prep (grades 7-9); Junior High Program (grades 10-13); and English as a Second Language (grades 7-13).

 ON THE JOB

The summer internship program introduces students to teaching in private schools through total immersion in one of the three student programs. Interns assist a professional teacher, conducting classroom observation, developing lesson plans, holding student conferences and teaching. Classes for major studies are held Monday through Saturday. Interns are also responsible for putting together and teaching a "minor course." Minor courses are held four afternoons a week and include drama, guitar and studio art. Interns also supervise recreational activities and dormitories.

 GETTING HIRED

Apply by: Rolling. Spaces filled by March 1. Submit an online application available at www.nmhschool.org/summer/interns/intern_forms.pdf PDF or www.nmhschool.org/summer/interns/intern_forms.doc, a personal statement, resume, transcript and two letters of recommendation.

Qualifications:
Open to college seniors, recent college graduates and grad students.

Contact:
Teaching Intern Program
Northfield Mount Hermon Summer Session
Drawer 5900
206 Main Street
Northfield, MA 01360
Phone: (413) 498-3290
Fax: (413) 498-3112
E-mail: summer_school@nmhschool.org
www.nmhschool.org/personnel/interns

Northwestern Mutual Financial Network

 THE BUZZ
- "Develop the skills to sell financial products"
- "Gain valuable financial services experience while continuing your studies"

 THE STATS

Industry(ies): Financial Services; Insurance

Location(s): Milwaukee, WI

Number of interns: *Annual*: 1,000-1,500

Pay: Commission; the top 50 interns' average commission in 2005 was $9,584 per semester, with additional bonuses and incentives available

Length of internship: 1 semester-2 years; 15-20 hours/week

 **THE SCOOP**

Northwestern Mutual Financial Network provides personalized financial services and offers inventive solutions for individuals' insurance and financial needs. Its success relies on the capacity of its sales force to build relationships with clients independently.

 ON THE JOB

The internship program began in 1967 to provide students with an opportunity to work as independent financial representatives while still in school. Interns' main objectives are to identify target markets, pursue and attain clients, and maintain client relationships. Interns receive substantive training, during which they become familiarized with Northwestern Mutual's products, sales methods, and policies and procedures. All interns must prepare for and pass a state licensing exam. Interns work with a mentor initially, until they are capable and confident enough to work independently.

 GETTING HIRED

Apply by: Rolling. Contact a recruiter for details.

Qualifications:
Open to college freshmen, sophomores, juniors and seniors.

Contact:
The Northwestern Mutual Life Insurance Company
720 East Wisconsin Avenue
Milwaukee, WI 53202-4797
Phone: (414) 271-1444
E-mail: resume@northwesternmutual.com
www.nminternship.com
www.nmfn.com

INTERNSHIP PROFILES:
O

Office of International Information Programs

 THE BUZZ

- "Educate the world about American foreign policy"
- "Get a fast-paced introduction to the world of DC policy and bureaucracy"

 THE STATS

Industry(ies): Government

Location(s): Washington, DC

Number of Interns: Varies

Pay: None

Length of internship: *Spring/fall*: length of academic semester or quarter; *summer*: 10 weeks

 **THE SCOOP**

The Office of International Information Programs (IIP), formerly the Information Bureau of the United States Information Agency until it merged with the Department of State, is responsible for educating international audiences on United States policies and foreign affairs. IIP creates electronic journals, printed material, CD-ROMs and web sites, and arranges speeches and training. Reliance on teamwork and technology are key elements of IIP success.

ON THE JOB

Interns should expect to hone their writing, researching, technological or business skills while working for IIP. Assignments may include researching government issues or writing reports. Interns might also assist in finding and engaging speakers for international programs. Although responsibilities vary for each intern, the bottom line is that they can expect real-world work experience.

GETTING HIRED

Apply by: *Spring*: July 1; *summer*: November 1; *fall*: March 1. Three copies required of each of the following: application form (available for download at www.careers.state.gov/student/interndownload.html), a one-page statement of interest and academic transcript(s).

Qualifications:

Open to college juniors and seniors, as well as graduate students who are pursuing areas relevant to their desired internship. Applicants must complete at least 60 semester hours or 90 quarter-hours before the internship begins. United States citizenship and good academic standing are also required.

Contact:

Intern Coordinator, Recruitment Division
United States Department of State
2401 E Street, NW, Room H518
Washington, DC 20522-0151
www.careers.state.gov/student/prog_intrn.html

Office of the Attorney General for the District of Columbia

 THE BUZZ

- "Immerse yourself in public law"
- "An A+ internship for wannabe JDs"

 THE STATS

Industry(ies): Government; Law

Location(s): Washington, DC

Number of interns: *Fall/spring*: 35-45; *summer*: 115-120

Pay: None

Length of internship: *Summer/fall/spring*: 8-12 weeks

 **THE SCOOP**

The Office of the Corporation Counsel (OCC) for the District of Columbia is one of the largest public law agencies in the U.S., with 250 attorneys, whose disciplines encompass appellate matters, affirmative litigation in consumer protection, tax fraud, welfare fraud, civil and criminal litigation in local and federal courts, and legal counsel for executive branch agencies. The internship program was developed in 1980 to assist lawyers and staff, and expose and orient students to the DC legal sphere.

ON THE JOB

The internship is highly educational, as interns participate in the inner workings of the OCC and its cases. Interns' work includes conducting research through Lexis/Nexis, drafting documents, interviewing witnesses and preparing cases. Weekly workshops and seminars are provided for additional enrichment.

GETTING HIRED

Apply by: See web site for deadlines. Send cover letter, resume, writing sample and two letters of recommendation to the address below.

Qualifications:

Open to college freshmen, sophomores, juniors and seniors and grad students concentrating in business, public management and pre-law.

Contact:

Internship Coordinator
Office of the Attorney General for the District of Columbia
441 4th Street, NW, Suite 1060 North
Washington, DC 20001
E-mail: keya.ross@dc.gov
www.oag.dc.gov

Office of the Speaker of the U.S. House of Representatives

 THE BUZZ
- "Enter the mix of politics on the Hill"
- "Snap up this ultra-prestigious DC internship"

 THE STATS

Industry(ies): Government

Location(s): Washington, DC

Number of interns: *Annual*: 4

Pay: None

Length of internship: *Spring/summer/fall*: 8 weeks or longer

 THE SCOOP

The Speaker of the House of Representatives holds a central role in Congress as the presiding officer. When each new Congress convenes, a Speaker is elected to supervise the House's proceedings. The Speaker recognizes members to speak and make motions, presides over most nonlegislative House business, and leads the majority party conference (including defending that party's agenda).

 ON THE JOB

Interns may be assigned to one of five areas: information technology, office administration, policy, press/communications and speaker's operations. Interns get hands-on experience in working for a major politico. Duties vary with position, but may include writing correspondence, clerical tasks and research.

(i) **GETTING HIRED**

Apply by: *Spring*: November 15; *summer*: March 15; *fall*: July 15. Send a cover letter, resume and four references (one personal, three professional/educational) to the address below.

Qualifications:
Open to college juniors and seniors with an interest in political science, as well as recent college graduates and grad students.

Contact:
Intern Coordinator
Office of the Speaker
H-419 C The Capitol
Washington, DC 20515
Phone: (202) 225-0600
www.speaker.gov

Oklahoma RedHawks

 THE BUZZ
- "Baseball lovers in Oklahoma, rejoice!"
- "Get up to speed on a sports marketing career"

 THE STATS

Industry(ies): Sports

Location(s): Oklahoma City, OK

Number of interns: *Annual*: 4-6

Pay: 10 percent commission on sales revenues

Length of internship: 9 months (January-September)

 **THE SCOOP**

The Oklahoma RedHawks are the Triple-A baseball club of the Texas Rangers Franchise. The team plays in the AT&T Bricktown Ballpark, which was built in the early 1980s and seats 13,066 baseball fans. Minor League baseball got its start in 1901 when Minor League executives formed an association (then called the National Association of Professional Baseball Leagues). Oklahoma itself is the hometown of baseball favorites Mickey Mantle and Johnny Bench.

 ON THE JOB

Interns work in sports marketing and commission sales. They sell advertising and arrange for sponsorships and promotions. Interns learn the art of sports selling very quickly and earn commission on their sales.

 GETTING HIRED

Apply by: End of November. Submit a resume, cover letter and recommendation to the address below.

Qualifications:
Open to college sophomores, juniors and seniors and college graduates.

Contact:
Internship Program
Oklahoma RedHawks
P.O. Box 75089
Oklahoma City, OK 73147
Phone: (405) 218-1000
Fax: (405) 218-1001
www.oklahomaredhawks.com

Visit Vault at **www.vault.com** for insider company profiles, expert advice, career message boards, expert resume reviews, the Vault Job Board and more.

VAULT CAREER LIBRARY **327**

Open City Films

 THE BUZZ
- "Indie film lovers, apply here"
- "Learn about film production from the ground up"

THE STATS

Industry(ies): Broadcast & Entertainment; Film

Location(s): New York, NY

Number of interns: *Annual*: 15

Pay: None

Length of internship: 1 college semester (January-April; May-August; September-December)

THE SCOOP

Open City Films is a New York-based independent production company founded in 1989 by producers Jason Kliot and Joana Vicente. Its films have met with critical and commercial accomplishment, including such recent successes as *Coffee & Cigarettes* by Jim Jarmusch, *Three Seasons*, which won three awards at the Sundance Film Festival, and *Down to You*, starring Freddie Prinze Jr. and Julia Stiles. Open City also works with foreign production companies and new directors in "advancing independent vision."

ON THE JOB

Selected interns assist in daily office work in a small but well-established independent production company. Other tasks include research projects, script reading, coverage and runs. Students gain exposure to the complete process of producing a feature, from development to distribution.

GETTING HIRED

Apply by: Rolling. Fax or mail a resume and cover letter to the address below.

Qualifications:
Open to college freshmen, sophomores, juniors and seniors. Reliability, enthusiasm and diligence are required.

Contact:
Internship Coordinator
Open City Films
122 Hudson Street, 5th floor
New York, NY 10013
Fax: (212) 255-0455

Oracle

THE BUZZ
- "Enjoy working at Oracle's amenity-filled office complex"
- "Learn about software development at one of the country's premier tech companies"

THE STATS

Industry(ies): Software; Technology

Location(s): Redwood Shores, CA; various New England locations

Number of interns: *Summer*: 35-40

Pay: Varies by position; stock options

Length of internship: *Summer*: 12-16 weeks

THE SCOOP

For over a quarter of a century, Oracle has been producing software that has shaped the technology of businesses throughout the world. Oracle has the distinction of being the world's largest supplier of information management software and is the second-largest independent software company after Microsoft.

ON THE JOB

Interns work on real projects, mainly in product development. Oracle prides itself on providing a livable work style for its employees. A casual dress code and extensive "campus" replete with cafes, state-of-the-art exercise facilities, and club room are some of the perks, as well as social activities arranged for interns.

GETTING HIRED

Apply by: Rolling. E-mail resume. Applicants are evaluated solely on the basis of their resume.

Qualifications:
Open to college sophomore, junior and senior computer science majors.

Contact:
E-mail: intern_us@oracle.com
www.oracle.com/corporate/employment/college/opportunities

Organization of Chinese Americans

THE BUZZ

- "Advocate for civil rights"
- "Get involved in the Asian-American community"

THE STATS

Industry(ies): Nonprofit

Location(s): Los Angeles, CA; Washington, DC

Number of interns: *Annual*: 15

Pay: $2,000 stipend, paid in two parts

Length of internship: *Spring/summer/fall*: 10 weeks; full-time and overtime

THE SCOOP

The Organization of Chinese Americans was founded in 1973 to advocate for Chinese-American and other Asian-American rights. Forty-four chapters nationwide work to engage Asian Americans in community activities, both on a civic and national level. Other goals are to advocate for legislation securing equal rights and social justice for Asian Americans, break down race barriers through education, and promote a diverse cultural heritage.

ON THE JOB

The OCA looks for interns who have the requisite leadership skills to become actively involved in OCA activities. Interns answer information requests, arrange legislative meetings, write articles, conduct background research for conferences and work on grant projects.

GETTING HIRED

Apply by: *Spring*: November 15; *summer*: March 31; *fall*: July 15. Submit resume, cover letter, transcript, two letters of reference and an application (available for download at www.ocanatl.org/docs/oca/ocaintrnshpapp.doc) to the address below.

Qualifications:
Open to college freshmen, sophomores, juniors and seniors, as well as college graduates and grad students.

Contact:
Washington, DC
Keith McAllister
Organization of Chinese Americans
1001 Connecticut Avenue, NW, Suite 601
Washington, DC 20036
Phone: (202) 223-5500
Fax: (202) 296-0540
www.ocanatl.org/bin/htmlos/0118.2.10358646198900011507?

Los Angeles
Clara Chiu
Organization of Chinese Americans
Phone: (213) 250-9888

Outward Bound–Voyageur School

THE BUZZ

- "Get paid to enjoy the great outdoors"
- "Learn wilderness survival tactics that can also make you stronger in everyday life"

THE STATS

Industry(ies): Education; Environmental

Location(s): Birch Lake, MN; Dillon, MT; Red Lodge, MT

Number of interns: *Summer*: 36

Pay: Paid; $75/week. Free room and board

Length of internship: *Summer*: 8-10 weeks

THE SCOOP

Outward Bound provides challenging adventure/wilderness experiences for teenagers and adults, teaching participants to be self-reliant and to channel their inner strength to respond to challenges. Founded in Great Britain by educator Kurt Hahn in 1941, it is the largest such educational adventure organization in the world. Outward Bound classes last from two days to two months and stress environmental stewardship, experiential learning, group and solo survival, service and wilderness challenge.

ON THE JOB

Interns participate in most programs, learning how and why Outward Bound works, and developing skills needed to be an Outward Bound instructor. Interns work with a senior staff trainer and a group for three weeks. During the courses, interns provide support functions such as driving, logistics, maintenance, rock-climbing and ropes courses. After training, interns become instructors, working with classes of students and adults on outdoor activities designed to teach cooperation and individual growth through team activities.

GETTING HIRED

Apply by: March 1. Send a resume and a completed application form. Download an application at: vobs.com/pdf/vobs_app.pdf.

Qualifications:
Applicants must be over 21, with either teaching or outdoor education experience. Flexibility and sense of humor a must!

Contact:
Human Resources Director
Voyageur Outward Bound School
101 East Chapman Street
Ely, MN 55371
Phone: (218) 365-7790
Fax: (218) 365-7079
E-mail: staffing@vobs.com
vobs.com/jobs-ops.html

Visit Vault at **www.vault.com** for insider company profiles, expert advice, career message boards, expert resume reviews, the Vault Job Board and more.

VAULT CAREER LIBRARY **329**

Overland Entertainment

 THE BUZZ
- "Unusual office work: high-profile clients; glitz, and glam!"
- "Discover the fine art of event managment"

 THE STATS

Industry(ies): Public Relations

Location(s): New York, NY

Number of interns: *Annual*: 2-4

Pay: None. Commuting stipend

Length of internship: *Spring/summer/fall*: 12-16 weeks

THE SCOOP

Overland Entertainment has been in the business of planning major events for the past 15 years. Its diverse accomplishments include award ceremonies, charity galas, conferences and corporate launches. Overland books entertainers and speakers, coordinates activities, designs ambiance, including lighting and set, scouts locations, and does anything else a client needs to make a splash. Overland serves an American and international clientele. Some past clients have included Conde Nast, Grey Advertising, IBM, Louis Vuitton and PepsiCo, to name a few.

ON THE JOB

Interns assist the sales and marketing side of the company's activities, working with staff to plan events and handling clerical duties. Interns are welcome at client events and also have access to free passes to city events, which offer great opportunities to rub elbows with powerful people.

GETTING HIRED

Apply by: Rolling. Send cover letter and resume to the address below.

Qualifications:

Open to high school graduates, college freshmen, sophomores, juniors and seniors, college graduates and grad students

Contact:
Internship Coordinator
Overland Entertainment
257 West 52nd Street
New York, NY 10019
Phone: (212) 262-1270
Fax: (212) 262-5229

Overseas Private Investment Corporation

 THE BUZZ
- "Help U.S. industry invest overseas"
- "Learn all about the high-stakes world of international investing"

 THE STATS

Industry(ies): Financial Services; Government; Venture Capital

Location(s): Washington, DC

Number of interns: *Spring/summer/fall*: 25-40 each

Pay: *Summer*: *undergraduates*: $12.68/hour; *grad students*: $17.57/hour plus transportation subsidy. *Fall/spring*: none; possible academic credit

Length of internship: *Fall/spring*: 3 months (16+ hours/week); *summer*: 3 months (full-time)

THE SCOOP

The Overseas Private Investment Corporation (OPIC) is a self-sustaining U.S. government agency supporting American businesses that want to invest in overseas emerging markets. Selling political risk insurance and loans, OPIC has profited yearly, becoming a self-sustaining agency.

ON THE JOB

Interns work in Congressional affairs, the office of investment policy, economics, environmental, workers' rights, finance, insurance, economic development, investment funds, library, HRM and legal affairs (law students only). Interns conduct risk analyses of overseas investment opportunities, draft press releases, evaluate the economic benefit of overseas investments, keep track of relevant Congressional issues and research workers' rights.

 GETTING HIRED

Apply by: Rolling. Submit an application online at www.opic.gov/internApplication, along with a cover letter, resume and a list of relevant courses. (Legal students follow separate instructions. See www/HRM/internships/interns_ aboutopic.asp for more details.)

Qualifications:
Open to college juniors and seniors and grad students.

Contact:
Overseas Private Investment Corporation
1100 New York Avenue, NW
Washington, DC 20527
Phone: (202) 336-8683
E-mail: internships@opic.gov
www.HRM/internships/interns_aboutopic.asp

Overseas Service Corps of the YMCA

 THE BUZZ
- "Teach English in a far off land"

THE STATS

Industry(ies): Education

Location(s): Taiwan

Number of interns: *Annual*: 25-30

Pay: Paid; $850-$1,010/month. Airfare and health insurance

Length of internship: 1 year, starting in September

THE SCOOP

The Overseas Service Corps of the YMCA provides the Y's Taiwanese branches with native English speakers to teach English language courses. The Overseas Service Corps of the YMCA started in 1974 to help students in need learn English and further their education.

ON THE JOB

Teachers attend an orientation before shipping off to Taiwan together. Upon arrival, participants can expect to spend 80-plus hours per month teaching conversational English. They can also expect to spend an additional 40 hours per month handling administrative duties, including student evaluation, material preparation, meetings, test administration and summer camp staffing.

GETTING HIRED

Apply by: May 15. Contact Patty Schnabel, below, for an application.

Qualifications:
Open to college graduates.

Contact:
Patty Schnabel
10402 Fondren Road
Houston, TX 77096
Phone: (713) 771-8333
E-mail: pattys@ymcahouston.org
www.ymca.net/yworld/taiwan/00recommend.htm

Visit Vault at **www.vault.com** for insider company profiles, expert advice, career message boards, expert resume reviews, the Vault Job Board and more.

VAULT CAREER LIBRARY   331

INTERNSHIP PROFILES:
P

Palo Alto Research Center

 THE BUZZ
- "Affinity for imaging technology a requirement."

 **THE STATS**

Industry(ies): Engineering; Science/Research; Technology

Location(s): Palo Alto, CA

Number of interns: *Summer*: 50

Pay: Paid; $700-$1,000/week. Field trips to local research centers; access to company gym and cafeteria; luncheons with scientists

Length of internship: *Summer/fall*: 13 weeks each

✎ THE SCOOP

The Palo Alto Research Center (PARC) was founded in 1970 as a subsidiary of the Xerox Corporation. PARC conducts innovative scientific research involving the physical and social sciences. Some work includes bit-mapped graphics, ethernet, object-oriented programming and dynamic page description languages.

🏢 ON THE JOB

Interns work on the project they choose with an assigned PARC researcher. Projects typically include bioinformatics, security, ubiquitous computing and vision. Past interns have conducted research on Linux, brain surgery, and 3-D graphics algorithms with applications to brain surgery and DNA sequences. At the end of the summer session, students take part in an intern poster session, participating in a forum to discuss the summer's work.

$ GETTING HIRED

Apply by: *Summer Undergraduate Program*: February 14; *Summer Graduate Program*: beginning in November. Send a resume, transcript and optional letters of reference from relevant summer jobs or significant undergraduate research opportunity programs (UROP) experience while at the university level.

Qualifications:

Open to freshmen, sophomore, junior and senior undergraduates with high academic and technical achievement, a good EECS background or completion of physics core courses, and a research environment interest. Also open to graduates with a bachelor's degree in computer science, mathematics, physics, electrical engineering or related fields, and to MBA students enrolled in a two-year program who have demonstrated interest in technology entrepreneurship or research.

Contact:

Palo Alto Research Center Incorporated
Attention: Undergraduate Internship Program (or Graduate Internship Program or MBA Internship Program)
3333 Coyote Hill Road
Palo Alto, CA 94304

Undergraduate Program
www.parc.com/contact/employment/undergraduate.html

Graduate Program
www.parc.com/contact/employment/graduate.html

MBA Program
www.parc.com/contact/employment/mba.html

Paychex

 THE BUZZ
- "Check into great training and grounding in corporate HR operations"

 **THE STATS**

Industry(ies): Financial Services; Technology

Location(s): Rochester, NY (Corporate HQ); offices in 38 states

Number of interns: *Annual*: 30-40

Pay: Paid; varies by position

Length of internship: *Summer*: 12 weeks; *co-op*: 6 months

 **THE SCOOP**

Paychex is a top provider of payroll, human resources and benefits outsourcing solutions for businesses across the U.S. Started in 1971 with just $3,000 and a good idea, in fiscal 2005 Paychex revenues exceeded $1.4 billion. Paychex has been named one of the Best Companies to Work For by *Fortune* magazine.

🏢 ON THE JOB

Interns are hired into all Paychex corporate operations, including HR, training, accounting, IT, real estate, travel and financial operations. The vast majority of internships are available at the Paychex headquarters in Rochester. In all departments, interns work with a mentor and a supervisor, and also have the ability to train and shadow Paychex employees in areas outside their department. They are not required to do administrative work. Interns are invited to all employee functions and training sessions and also receive lunch vouchers.

$ GETTING HIRED

Apply by: Rolling. Apply through career services or on the Paychex web site, www.paychex.com.

Qualifications:
Open to college juniors and seniors of all majors.

Contact:
www.paychex.com

Peace Corps

THE BUZZ

- "Ask not what you can do for your country, but what you can do for the world"

THE STATS

Industry(ies): Education; Environmental; Government; Health Care; Nonprofit

Location(s): 71 countries around the world

Number of interns: *Annual*: 3,500

Pay: Monthly stipend. Medical and dental insurance; round-trip travel; $6,075 upon completion

Length of internship: 27 months

THE SCOOP

The Peace Corps emerged in 1961 after President John F. Kennedy challenged Americans to serve abroad in the cause of peace and cross-cultural understanding. Since then, tens of thousands of volunteers of all ages and ethnicities have served in 137 countries. Among its many duties, the Peace Corps teaches English, promotes health awareness (particularly for HIV/AIDS), advances an understanding of conservation issues in less economically developed nations, trains entrepreneurs in effective business practices and IT, and works with farmers to prevent soil erosion.

ON THE JOB

Volunteers are placed in countries where their skill sets are most needed. Before starting their assignments, volunteers get three months of in-country training, focusing on language, cross-cultural, and technical skills, as well as on health and safety. The primary focus of work is building the capacity of local communities to meet their own needs through sustainable activities. Volunteers work on projects related to agriculture, business, community development, education and health. Some duties include teaching and setting up schools. The service time expected is just over two years.

GETTING HIRED

Apply by: Rolling. Log on to the organization's web site (www.peacecorps.gov/apply/now/index.cfm) and fill out the online application. The application process will take approximately nine months.

Qualifications:
Open to high school graduates over 18, college freshmen, sophomores, juniors and seniors, college graduates and other people with substantive life experience. Visit www.peacecorps.gov for details. Most programs require work experience and/or a degree.

Contact:
To find the recruitment office nearest you, call:
Phone: (800) 424-8580
Fax: (212) 606-4458
www.peacecorps.gov/wws/students/index.html

Peggy Guggenheim Collection

THE BUZZ

- "Cosmopolitan, artsy and Venetian"
- "A great fit for fine art lovers"

THE STATS

Industry(ies): Art/Museum

Location(s): Venice

Number of interns: *Annual*: 130

Pay: Stipend; 750 EUR/month

Length of internship: 4-12 weeks; available year-round

THE SCOOP

Bordered on the one side by a leafy lane and on the other by the Grand Canal, the Peggy Guggenheim collection is a tranquil haven, housing impressive modern masterpieces. Established in 1949 by Peggy Guggenheim, niece of wealthy industrialist Solomon R. Guggenheim, the museum encompasses four private collections (including Ms. Guggenheim's), and is the most important collection of American and Italian art from the first half of the 20th century in Italy. Among the artists exhibited are Chagall, Giacometti, Morandi, Picasso and Pollock.

ON THE JOB

Interns serve practical functions within the museum, including guarding the galleries, preparing the museum for opening and closing, providing visitors with information, selling tickets and catalogs, and handling administrative tasks. Interns attend weekly seminars to enhance their understanding of museum studies and modern art.

GETTING HIRED

Apply by: *January-April*: October 15; *May-December*: December 1. Contact the address below for an application. Submit a completed form, along with a resume, cover letter, a university transcript and two references.

Qualifications:
Open to college freshmen, sophomores, juniors and seniors, college graduates and grad students. This internship is intended for art, art history or related majors wishing to embark on a museum career.

Contact:
Elena Minarelli
Coordinator for Education and Visitor Services
Peggy Guggenheim Collection
Palazzo Venier dei Leoni
Dorsoduro 701
30123 Venice
Italy
Phone: +39.041.2405.401
Fax: +39.041.2405.426
E-mail: internship@guggenheim-venice.it
www.guggenheim-venice.it

Visit Vault at **www.vault.com** for insider company profiles, expert advice, career message boards, expert resume reviews, the Vault Job Board and more.

VAULT CAREER LIBRARY **335**

Pella Corporation

 THE BUZZ

- "One of the industry's leading innovators in window and door products"
- "Open the door – or the window! – to a top manufacturing and design career"

 STATS

Industry(ies): Manufacturing

Location(s): Pella, IA

Number of interns: Varies with company need

Pay: Paid; 75 percent (sophomores and juniors) – 85 percent (seniors) of entry-level salary plus benefits

Length of internship: *Intern*: summer only; *co-op*: summer plus 1 semester

 THE SCOOP

Founded in 1925 with its patented Rolscreen window screen, Pella manufactures windows and doors for homes and buildings. Pella ranked No. 22 on *Fortune*'s Top 100 Companies to Work For in 2004, making the list for the fifth consecutive year.

 ON THE JOB

Internships and co-ops are available in departments on an as-needed basis. View current openings and requirements, at www.pella.com/careers/college_relations/AboutCoopInternship. asp.

 GETTING HIRED

Apply by: Rolling. Apply online at www.pella.com/careers/ college_relations/AboutCoopInternship.asp.

Qualifications:
Open to college sophomores, juniors and seniors. Check site for positions and their respective requirements.

Contact:
www.pella.com/careers/college_relations/AboutCoopInternship.asp

Penguin Group (USA)

 THE BUZZ

- "The perfect environment for book lovers"
- "Get your foot in the door of the hard-to-crack publishing world"

 THE STATS

Industry(ies): Publishing

Location(s): New York, NY

Number of interns: *Fall/spring*: 25 each; *summer*: 50

Pay: Paid; minimum wage

Length of internship: *Spring/summer/fall*: 10 weeks

 **THE SCOOP**

Penguin Group (USA) Inc. is one of the leading trade book publishers in the United States. The company owns a wide range of imprints and trademarks, including Viking, G.P. Putnam's Sons, Berkley Books, Riverhead Books, Penguin, Dutton, Plume and Signet, among others. It publishes consumer books, in both hardcover and paperback editions, for adults as well as children. It also produces maps, calendars and audiobooks. Penguin Group (USA) Inc. is a division of the internationally renowned Penguin Group, the second-largest English-language trade book publisher in the world. The Penguin Group is owned by Pearson plc, the international media group.

 ON THE JOB

Interns work in art, contracts, editorial, marketing, online, production, publicity, sales and subsidiary rights. Responsibilities vary with department, but may include administrative/clerical tasks, proofreading and fact checking.

 GETTING HIRED

Apply by: *Spring*: January 15; *summer*: February 28; *fall*: August 31. Interested students should submit a resume and cover letter. Be sure to indicate in your cover letter which semester you are applying for and in which business areas you are interested.

Qualifications:
Open to all students with a strong interest in book publishing.

Contact:
Penguin Group (USA)
Human Resources
Internship Coordinator
375 Hudson Street
New York, NY 10014
Fax: (212) 366-2930
E-mail: jobs@us.penguingroup.com

PERA Club

 THE BUZZ
- "Learn to manage a country club"
- "Ramp up a hospitality career in sunny Arizona"

THE STATS

Industry(ies): Hospitality; Sports

Location(s): Phoenix, AZ

Number of interns: *Annual*: 4

Pay: Paid; minimum wage

Length of internship: Flexible

 THE SCOOP

The PERA Club (Project Employees Recreation Association) is the private recreation facility for employees of the Salt River Project, Phoenix's major water and power utility. The center sits on 83 scenic acres and includes outdoor fitness trails, a softball field, a swimming pool and tennis courts. The country club is also the setting for sports leagues and parties, as well as a venue for family, corporate and social events.

 ON THE JOB

Interns work in the recreation department, seeing to the needs of club members including: aquatic fun, the employee store, food and beverage preparation and service, and special events. Interns also oversee and plan social activities and supervise part-time employees. They take part in special customer service and stress management training.

GETTING HIRED

Apply by: Rolling. Write to the address below for an application.

Qualifications:
Open to college freshmen, sophomores, juniors and seniors, as well as graduate students.

Contact:
Internship Coordinator
PERA Club
PER 200
P.O. Box 52025
Phoenix, AZ 85072-2025
Phone: (602) 236-5782

Visit Vault at **www.vault.com** for insider company profiles, expert advice, career message boards, expert resume reviews, the Vault Job Board and more.

VAULT CAREER LIBRARY **337**

Pfizer

 THE BUZZ
- "Help discover the next wonder drug"
- "Jumpstart your research career"

 THE STATS

Industry(ies): Health Care; Pharmaceuticals

Location(s): Ann Arbor, MI; Cambridge, MA; Groton, CT; La Jolla, CA; Morris Plains, NJ; New London, CT; New York, NY; Sandwich, England; Amboise and Fresnes, France; Nagoya and Tokyo, Japan

Number of interns: Varies with department; *finance*: 12-15, annually

Pay: Paid; $1,350/week

Length of internship: *Summer*: 12-15; *co-op*: 6 months

 **THE SCOOP**

Pfizer, the world's largest pharmaceutical company, opened its doors as Charles Pfizer & Company in 1849. It was the first U.S. firm to produce tartaric acid and cream of tartar in 1862. It was all uphill after that as Pfizer sales totaled over $3 million – in 1910! Today, with profits topping $1 billion dollars in 2002, Pfizer is a drug-developing powerhouse with groundbreaking products like Viagra and Zoloft, not to mention everyday standbys such as Benadryl, Listerine, Lubriderm and Neosporin. Medical research continues to play an integral role in its operations.

ON THE JOB

Interns can work in research and development, marketing, finance, human resources, production, sales or legal. Prospective interns and co-ops must apply to the relevant division found on www.pfizer.com/are/careers/mn_campus_internships.html. Other positions may be available in business technology, global manufacturing, and global research and development. Responsibilities vary with department, but may include research, assisting sales staff and administrative functions.

GETTING HIRED

Apply by: Rolling. E-mail a cover letter and resume to Rowe.Resumes@pfizer.com. Reference the name of the internship or co-op you're applying for.

Qualifications:
Open to college freshmen, sophomores, juniors and seniors, as well as grad students. See www.pfizerrdgrad.com/Campus RecruitingExternal/html/internships3.html for qualifications specific to your chosen internship or co-op program.

Contact:
Human Resources
Pfizer Inc.
Pfizer Pharmaceuticals Group
Attn: NAME OF INTERNSHIP
235 East 42nd Street – 13th Floor
New York, NY 10017-5755
E-mail: Rowe.Resumes@pfizer.com
www.pfizer.com/are/careers/mn_campus_internships.html

Manufacturing internship not in Puerto Rico
Global Manufacturing Internship Coordinator
Pfizer Inc.
235 East 42nd Street, MS 13-4
New York, NY 10017-5755

Manufacturing internship in Barceloneta, Puerto Rico
Personnel Associate-Staffing
Pfizer Pharmaceuticals Inc
P.O. Box 628
Barceloneta, Puerto Rico 00617

PGA Tour

 THE BUZZ
- "A stroke above the rest"
- "Get your career on par with the competition"

 THE STATS

Industry(ies): Sports

Location(s): Ponte Vedra Beach, FL (HQ); multiple cities throughout the U.S.

Number of interns: *Summer*: 30-40 (20-23 in Florida)

Pay: Paid; $11/hour. Round-trip travel (up to $500); discounted housing in Vedra Beach, FL

Length of internship: *Summer*: 9-13 weeks

 **THE SCOOP**

The American Professional Golfers Association was established in 1916 when retail entrepreneur Rodman Wanamaker invited some professional and amateur golfers in the New York area to a formal lunch to propose forming a national association. Today, the PGA Tour is a tax-exempt organization of professional golfers. Its aims are to provide professional golfers with competitive earnings, "to protect the intergrity of the game," and to increase the reach of golf nation- and worldwide. The Tour participates in nearly 120 golfing events, including the Champions Tour and the Nationwide Tour, in 38 states and 8 countries outside the U.S., and the organization boasts illustrious players such as Ernie Els, Tom Lehman and Tiger Woods. In addition to providing competitive opportunities for its membership, PGA Tour events also generates significant funds for local charities; last year, the Tours reached the $1 billion mark in charitable contributions.

 ON THE JOB

The PGA Tour offers two internship programs, the Diversity Internship Program and the PGA Tour Internship Program. Both aim to introduce the business side of golf to talented college students. Headquarters hires interns in corporate marketing, communications, human resources, TV producatuin, public relations, golf course operations, and information technology. Positions are also available at the PGA Tour tournament sites in event management and with golf industry partners across the United States.

 GETTING HIRED

Apply by: February 16. Apply online at www.pgatour.com, under "Tour Business."

Qualifications:
Open to full-time college juniors and seniors and grad students who hold a cumulative minimum GPA of 2.6 or better on a 4.0 scale. The Diversity Internship Program is only available to minority college students while the PGA Tour Internship Program is open to all college students, regardless of ethnicity. Candidates must be eligible to work in the U.S.

Contact:
PGA Tour, Inc.
Attn: PGA Tour Internship Program
100 PGA Tour Boulevard
Ponte Vedra Beach, FL 32082
E-mail: mcooney@pgatourhq.com
www.pgatour.com

Visit Vault at **www.vault.com** for insider company profiles, expert advice, career message boards, expert resume reviews, the Vault Job Board and more.

VAULT CAREER LIBRARY **339**

The Philadelphia Center

 THE BUZZ

• "Live in the *real* real world in Philly"

 THE STATS

Industry(ies): Education; internships in all industries

Location(s): Philadelphia, PA

Number of interns: 200

Pay: $10,700/semester tuition; approximately $5,000 for Learning Work (summer)

Length of internship: *Fall* (late August—mid-December), *spring* (mid-January—early May): 16 weeks; *Learning Work: Summer 2007*: 8 weeks (June-July)

 THE SCOOP

The Philadelphia Center is a full-service, experience-based program, managed by Hope College and founded and recognized by the Great Lakes Colleges Association, Inc. The Center is committed to undergraduate education and its connections to field and disciplinary exploration and development; community involvement; experiential learning and critical reflection; graduate school possibilities; career/employment options; and collaborative efforts in programmatic and curricular work. Using a multidisciplinary approach, the Center integrates professional work, academic seminars and independent living experiences in urban communities and offers opportunities in most fields of study.

 ON THE JOB

The Philadelphia Center's connections with over 800 city institutions and businesses allow students to interview for and attain top internships, suiting their fields of study. An advisor and placement supervisor assist students with their internship search and devise a Learning Plan, setting learning objectives for the intern to pursue through the experience. Past interns have worked at the American Red Cross, the Environmental Protection Agency, Merrill Lynch, the Philadelphia 76ers and the Philadelphia Museum of Art.

GETTING HIRED

Apply by: *Fall*: June 15; *spring*: November 15; *Learning Work: Summer 2007*: February 1.

Qualifications:
Open to college sophomores, juniors and seniors enrolled in a U.S. college or university. Complete and send in the application form, downloadable on the web site.

Contact:
The Philadelphia Center
North American Building, Seventh Floor
121 South Broad Street
Philadelphia, PA 19107-4577
Phone: (215) 735-7300
Fax: (215) 735-7373
E-mail: admin@philactr.edu
www.philactr.edu

Phillips Academy

 THE BUZZ

• "Toil amidst the groves of academe"
• "Teach at one of the nation's top prep schools"

THE STATS

Industry(ies): Education

Location(s): Andover, MA

Number of interns: 25 TAs; 3 administrative interns

Pay: Paid; *TA*: $2,600 plus room and board; *AI*: $2,700 plus room and board

Length of internship: *TA*: 6 weeks (June 22-August 3) for TAs; *AI*: 7 weeks

 THE SCOOP

Phillips Academy is a prestigious preparatory school, located north of Boston. Founded in 1778, Phillips Academy (known as Andover) is the oldest incorporated boarding school in the nation. Andover offers a rigorous academic summer program for high school students. The Summer Session enrolls 600 students, who pursue a major and a minor course.

ON THE JOB

Teaching assistants (TAs) experience teaching in a private school setting. During the five-week session, TAs assist skilled teachers with two courses, six days per week, in a discipline related to their major field of study. Tasks include grading assignments, producing study materials, teaching up to 20 percent of the classes, and supervising students both in class and in the dorms. TAs are also expected to coach an extracurricular activity in the afternoon. Administrative interns (AIs) work in the Summer Session office, serving as coordinators for faculty and students, maintaining records and office equipment, and performing clerical tasks.

GETTING HIRED

Apply by: Rolling, but best before February 15.

Qualifications:
TA: open to recent college graduates and grad students. Applications from juniors over 21 years of age will be reviewed. TA applicants must submit a completed application, personal essay, resume, three references and an undergraduate transcript. *AI*: open to college undergraduates. Mandatory background check for all employees.

Contact:
Phillips Academy
Summer Session
180 Main Street
Andover MA 01810-4161
Phone: (978) 749-4406
Fax: (978) 749-4414

For questions regarding either program
Phone: (978) 749-4406
E-mail: employment-summersession@andover.edu
www.andover.edu/summersession

Phillips-Van Heusen

 THE BUZZ
- "Explore fashion and business at this leading clothing company"
- "See what it's like to work behind the scenes at Calvin Klein"

 THE STATS

Industry(ies): Fashion

Location(s): Bridgewater, NJ; Chattanooga, TN; Jonesville, NC; New York, NY; Reading, PA; Wilton, ME; multiple international locations in Bangladesh; China; Hong Kong; Honduras; Indonesia; Malaysia; Mongolia; Philippines; Singapore; Taiwan; Thailand

Number of interns: Varies with company need

Pay: None; academic credit (arranged with your school)

Length of internship: Varies; available year-round

 THE SCOOP

Phillips-Van Heusen can trace its corporate heritage back a long way. Moses Phillips and his wife began sewing shirts by hand in 1881 in Pottsville, Pennsylvania. Shortly after, they moved to New York City and became the first clothiers to place an ad for shirts in the *Saturday Evening Post*. Some time later, John M. Van Heusen developed a comfortable collar in Holland and traveled to the U.S. to find a business partner. He met up with Moses' son, Seymour, and together they established Phillips-Van Heusen. The company is now a huge fashion powerhouse, owning famous labels including Calvin Klein.

 ON THE JOB

Interns work in various departments of the company, including sales, marketing, information technology and finance. Responsibilities vary with department but may include assisting sales and marketing staff with leads, computer systems maintenance or clerical tasks.

GETTING HIRED

Apply by: Rolling. Send a resume and cover letter to the address below.

Qualifications:
Open to college freshmen, sophomores, juniors and seniors, as well as recent college graduates and grad students.

Contact:
Internship Coordinator
Phillips-Van Heusen
200 Madison Avenue
New York, NY 10016
Phone: (212) 381-3500
www.pvh.com/JoinOurTeam_CareerOpps.html

Physicians for Human Rights

 THE BUZZ
- "Work with health professionals and a dedicated staff to fight social ills from genocide to HIV/AIDS to the juvenile death penalty"

 THE STATS

Industry(ies): Health Care; Nonprofit

Location(s): Boston, MA; Washington, DC

Number of interns: *Annual*: 15-18

Pay: None

Length of internship: 3 months-1 year, depending on intern availability and mutual evaluation

 THE SCOOP

Physicians for Human Rights is an organization of over 5,000 health professionals, scientists and concerned citizens that strives to use medical science to investigate and end violations of international human rights. Since 1986, PHR has worked to ban landmines, protect Afghani women, and end the spread of AIDS, and has fought for the rights and freedom of political prisoners, as well as many other issues.

 ON THE JOB

Interns assist supervisors in one of several departments, including Health and Justice for Youth, HealthAction AIDS, Research, Communications, Outreach (includes Colleagues at Risk) and Asylum Network, among others. Interns help research the issues of the specific department, and in some cases help organize (and sometimes attend) conferences, working with dynamic and dedicated human rights professionals.

GETTING HIRED

Apply by: Rolling.

Qualifications:
Open to college undergraduate and graduate students (pre-med, pre-law, public health, nursing, etc.) Medical knowledge is not necessary, but excellent computer and writing skills, as well as an interest in human rights, are.

Contact:
Kathleen M. Carspecken
Executive Assistant/ Intern Coordinator
Physicians for Human Rights
2 Arrow Street
Cambridge, MA 02138
Phone: (617) 301-4223
Fax: (617) 301-4250
E-mail: kcarspecken@phrusa.org
www.phrusa.org

Visit Vault at **www.vault.com** for insider company profiles, expert advice, career message boards, expert resume reviews, the Vault Job Board and more.

VAULT CAREER LIBRARY **341**

Physicians for Social Responsibility

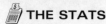 **THE BUZZ**
- "Work to improve public health policies"
- "Educate the community about health care issues"

 THE STATS

Industry(ies): Health Care; Nonprofit

Location(s): Washington, DC; nationwide chapters

Number of interns: *Annual*: 6 (2 per term)

Pay: Paid; $200/week (in DC)

Length of internship: *Spring/summer/fall*: 12-24 weeks; 40 hours/week for a minimum of 3 months

 **THE SCOOP**

Physicians for Social Responsibility has been challenging, informing and instituting legislation regarding public health and safety since its founding in 1961. It has directed the brunt of its efforts toward three major programs: environment and health (educating the public about environmental and health threats due to global warming and pollution), gun violence prevention, and security (advocacy and education about eliminating nuclear arms).

ON THE JOB

Interns work with staff to develop communication and outreach materials, research relevant issues, and attend meetings and Congressional briefings. They may also expect to handle some administrative and clerical tasks. Interns indicate which of PSR's three programs they wish to work on.

GETTING HIRED

Apply by: *Spring*: November 1; *summer*: April 1; *fall*: July 1.

Qualifications:
Open to college juniors and seniors, recent and not-so-recent college graduates and grad students. Submit resume, cover letter and writing samples.

Contact:
Madeline Riley
Internship Coordinator
Physicians for Social Responsibility
1875 Connecticut Avenue, #1012
Washington, DC 20009
Phone: (202) 667-4201
E-mail: mriley@psr.org
www.psr.org

Playhouse on the Square

THE BUZZ
- "Future actors, directors and techies wanted"
- "Interesting opportunity for highly committed theater types"

THE STATS

Industry(ies): Theater/Performing Arts

Location(s): Memphis, TN

Number of interns: *Annual*: 13-16

Pay: $100/week. Free housing, local phone, washer and dryer; health care benefits for a minimal fee; free tickets to performances; departmental training seminars and opportunities to work off-hours with the Memphis Arts Council's Artist in the Schools program

Length of internship: 1 year; work hours are generally from 10:00 a.m.-10:00 p.m., 6 days/week

 THE SCOOP

Founded in 1975 after its sister theater, Circuit Playhouse, Inc., Playhouse on the Square is a nonprofit theater organization. The playhouse is responsible for Teens in Theatre, a summer youth touring group/theater school that services children, teens and adults; and a "Pay What You Can Night" which ensures that patrons who cannot afford ticket prices will not be denied a chance to enjoy shows. Recent productions include, *Guys and Dolls*; *MacBeth*; *Peter Pan*; *I Love You, You're Perfect, Now Change*; *The Philadelphia Story*; *Picnic*; and *Jekyll and Hyde*.

ON THE JOB

Internships at the house are designed to help students develop abilities and future placement for employment. Interns work as interactive assistants in acting, set construction, props, sound, lighting, stage management, costumes and administration.

GETTING HIRED

Apply by: Rolling. Request application materials or send inquires via e-mail to info@playhouseonthesquare.org.

Qualifications:
Open to all college freshmen, sophomores, juniors and seniors, college graduates and grad students that are 21 years of age and over. This is a year-long, full-time commitment.

Contact:
Internship Coordinator
Playhouse on the Square
51 South Cooper
Memphis, TN 38104
Phone: (901) 725-0776
E-mail: info@playhouseonthesquare.org
www.playhouseonthesquare.org/internships.html

PMK/HBH

 THE BUZZ
- "Seeking aspiring PR experts"
- "Create campaigns for the stars"

 THE STATS

Industry(ies): Public Relations

Location(s): New York, NY

Number of interns: *Annual*: 8-10

Pay: None; must receive academic credit. Free passes to film screenings; attend PMK/HBH events; stargazing opportunities

Length of internship: *Spring/summer/fall*: 13-18 weeks each

 THE SCOOP

Founded in 1980, PMK/HBH is a widely recognized leader in entertainment public relations with offices in New York and Los Angeles. PMK/HBH is a division of the Interpublic Sports and Entertainment Group, which deals with an assortment of accounts in the motion picture, television, music and theater industries. Notably, it's been associated with the marketing campaigns (from idea inception to creation) for three of the last four Academy Award winners for Best Picture. PMK/HBH clients include Jennifer Aniston, Nicole Kidman, Matt Damon and Kirsten Dunst.

 ON THE JOB

Interns assist in the day-to-day rigors of clerical duties, serving as staff assistants preparing press releases, sending out mailings and running errands.

 GETTING HIRED

Apply by: Rolling. Submit a resume and cover letter to the address below.

Qualifications:
Open to college freshmen, sophomores, juniors and seniors, recent college graduates and grad students. Open only to students who will receive credit from their college or university.

Contact:
Internship Coordinator
PMK/HBH Public Relations
161 Avenue of the Americas, Suite 10R
New York, NY 10013
Phone: (212) 582-1111

Polo Ralph Lauren

 THE BUZZ
- "Work for the master of casual American fashion"
- "A work experience that's always in style"

 THE STATS

Industry(ies): Fashion

Location(s): New York, NY

Number of interns: *Summer*: 20-25

Pay: None

Length of internship: *Summer*: 10 weeks

 **THE SCOOP**

The Ralph Lauren label has become synonymous with a carefree American lifestyle. The look and the horse-and-rider logo are now famous around the world, allowing the company to branch out with several lines (apparel, home, accessories and fragrances) and philanthropic efforts (mainly involving cancer causes). The majority of the company's sales is in menswear in the U.S.

 ON THE JOB

Interns may be placed in any of the company's 25 departments. However, specific opportunities vary from summer to summer. Duties depend on the department managers' needs and wishes, as they change according to the departments' current projects. Departments range from buying to logistics, and include standards like human resources, public relations and accounting.

 GETTING HIRED

Apply by: *Summer*: January 1. Send resume and cover letter to the address below.

Qualifications:
Open to undergrad sophomores and juniors only.

Contact:
Christopher Vizzone
Polo/Ralph Lauren
625 Madison Avenue, 8th Floor
New York, NY 10022
Fax: (212) 318-7200
E-mail: christopher.vizzone@poloralphlauren.com
www.polo.com

Visit Vault at **www.vault.com** for insider company profiles, expert advice, career message boards, expert resume reviews, the Vault Job Board and more.

VAULT CAREER LIBRARY **343**

Population Institute

THE BUZZ
- "Be a 'Future Leader of the World'"
- "Address overpopulation issues plaguing the globe"

THE STATS
Industry(ies): Education; Government; Health Care; Nonprofit; Public Relations

Location(s): Washington, DC

Number of interns: *Annual:* 5-7

Pay: Paid; $24,000/year. Health, dental and life insurance; vacation and sick days

Length of internship: 1 year

THE SCOOP
The Population Institute, an international nonprofit organization, works to "reduce excess population growth." Established in 1969, the Institute is located in DC and its members work in 172 countries with funding largely derived from charitable foundations, businesses and private individuals. The Institute hopes to reach its goal primarily through education programs that build public awareness for the issue.

ON THE JOB
Future Leaders of the World (FLW) Fellows participate with professionals in all organized activities relating to overpopulation problems. Positions available include public policy coordinators (two to three), media coordinator (one), field coordinators (one to two) and a special programs coordinator (one – who primarily works on planning World Population Awareness Week). The FLW program started in 1980.

GETTING HIRED
Apply by: April 15. Applicants must send a cover letter, resume, three recommendations (two from academic sources) and official transcripts to the address below.

Qualifications:
Open to college juniors and seniors, recent college graduates and grad students between the ages of 21 and 25. International relations, development and nonprofit majors are preferred. Applicants must know one foreign language and have some international experience. Go to population.newc.com/teampublish/71_363_1101.CFM to see the guidelines for applications.

Contact:
Fatou Fall, Education Coordinator
The Population Institute
107 Second Street, NE
Washington, DC 20002
Phone: (202) 544-3300, ext. 121
Fax: (202) 544-0068
E-mail: ffall@populationinstitute.org
www.populationinstitute.org/teampublish/71_363_1029.cfm

PR Communications

THE BUZZ
- "Get into the public relations field"
- "A unique view of Singaporean culture"

THE STATS
Industry(ies): Public Relations

Location(s): Singapore

Number of interns: Varies

Pay: None

Length of internship: 1 month

THE SCOOP
A small public relations firm based in Singapore, PR Communications was founded in 1990 and specializes in communications "that motivates staff to higher productivity levels and loyalty." The company works mostly on corporate reputation, technology and lifestyle/brand marketing projects. PR Communications has worked with Louis Vuitton, Heinz, Dow Chemical, the Eastman Kodak Company, Montblanc, Evian, NorthWest Airlines, Absolut, and some leading local brands in Singapore.

ON THE JOB
Interns work with staff on account servicing and in administrative functions. Duties may include media tracking, writing editorials, and assisting in proposal development.

GETTING HIRED
Apply by: Rolling. E-mail a resume and cover letter to the address below.

Qualifications:
Open to college freshmen, sophomores, juniors and seniors, recent college graduates and grad students. Applicants must have friends or relatives in Singapore, as the company will not be able to arrange temporary work permits for overseas internships. Accomodation must be arranged by the applicants.

Contact:
Fatoma Alladin, Director
Phone: 65-62272135
E-mail: fatoma@prcomm.com.sg
www.prcomm.com.sg

PricewaterhouseCoopers

 THE BUZZ
- "Work on your teamwork and leadership skills"

 THE STATS

Industry(ies): Professional Services

Location(s): New York, NY (HQ); offices across North America and in 148 countries worldwide

Number of interns: Varies

Pay: Paid; competitive salary

Length of internship: Typically 10-12 weeks

 **THE SCOOP**

PricewaterhouseCoopers (PwC) is the world's largest professional services firm, employing over 130,000 people in 148 countries across the globe. It formed in 1998 from a merger between Price Waterhouse and Coopers & Lybrand. PwC maintains 22 industry-specialized practices, from chemicals and technology to real estate and telecommunications. The firm offers specialized service acorss three lines--assurance, advisory and tax, and private company services. In the U.S., PwC operates as PricewaterhouseCoopers LLP, and is the country's sixth-largest privately owned organization. PwC places enormous importance on its internship program since interns represent a significant source of talent for the firm. The majority of interns go on to full-time employment with the firm.

 ON THE JOB

PwC interns begin the program with a comprehensive orientation, followed by a service-specific training program once interns select their line of specialization. This program utilizes case studies, practice exercises, communication modules and technology-enabled study during training. Once training is complete, interns become active members of a client engagement team, serving diverse clients and developing optimal strategies for those clients. Interns are challenged from the start to be active contributors – they provide financial analysis and tax advice to companies of all sizes and industries. Interns are assigned an experienced PwC employee to act as a mentor and to provide career advice, as well as a peer mentor to assist with day-to-day concerns and questions.

At the conclusion of the PwC internship, interns have the opportunity to attend a seminar held at Walt Disney World with hundreds of PwC interns from across the Americas. The seminar supplements the on-the-job training the interns received with the expertise of PwC partners and staff, dynamic external speakers and a world-class curriculum.

 GETTING HIRED

Apply by: Rolling. *Winter internship*: recruitment January-March; *summer internship*: recruitment June-August. Complete an online career profile available at www.pwc.com/ocp, and request an on-campus interview.

Qualifications:
Open to undergraduate sophomores, juniors and seniors.

Contact:
www.pwc.com/internships

Primetime Live

 THE BUZZ
- "Liven up your journalism career"
- "Expose yourself to an experience of a lifetime"
- "Learn all you can from Diane Sawyer and the crew"

 THE STATS

Industry(ies): Broadcast & Entertainment; Journalism

Location(s): New York, NY

Number of interns: *Spring/summer/fall*: 6-10 each

Pay: None

Length of internship: *Spring/summer/fall*: 8-14 weeks

 **THE SCOOP**

Anchored by Sam Donaldson and Diane Sawyer, *Primetime Live* has been a hard-hitting investigative television newsmagazine since it debuted in 1989. Using hidden cameras, the Emmy-award winning show aims to expose corruption. The news show has followed the trail of the zodiac killer, as well as scams involving charity donations and offers celebrity and major political profiles.

 ON THE JOB

Interns get involved in all aspects of broadcast journalism, from the birth of an idea to its presentation on television. Positions are offered in research, production and editing. Interns also have a unique opportunity to work alongside producers, directors, writers, editors and correspondents.

 GETTING HIRED

Apply by: Rolling. Contact the internship program for an application.

Qualifications:
Open to all college freshmen, sophomores, juniors and seniors, recent college graduates and grad students.

Contact:
Internship Program
Primetime Live
ABC News
147 Columbus Avenue, 4th Floor
New York, NY 10023
Phone: (212) 456-1600
www.abcnews.go.com/Sections/Primetime

Visit Vault at **www.vault.com** for insider company profiles, expert advice, career message boards, expert resume reviews, the Vault Job Board and more.

VAULT CAREER LIBRARY **345**

Procter & Gamble

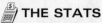 THE BUZZ

- "Spend a Cincinnati summer with Pringles and Pampers"

THE STATS

Industry(ies): Consumer Products

Location(s): Cincinnati, OH

Number of interns/co-ops: *Annual*: 250-350

Pay: Paid

Length of internship: *Spring/summer/fall/winter*: 10-24 weeks

 THE SCOOP

The Procter & Gamble Company got its start in 1837 in Cincinnati, Ohio. Its founders, William Procter, a candle-maker, and James Gamble, who apprenticed for a soap-maker, had married sisters Olivia and Elizabeth Norris. Their father-in-law convinced the two to become business partners selling – what else? – soap and candles. Since then, P&G has evolved into a manufacturing conglomerate of more than 300 well-known, everyday products, including Pampers, Pringles, Tide, Head & Shoulders, Folgers, Crest, Olay, Duracell, Gillette, Braun, and Oral-B. As of 2006, P&G employed almost 140,000 workers in 80 countries.

ON THE JOB

Interns and co-ops work on projects in their area of interest. The company looks for creative candidates with excellent communication skills and problem-solving abilities. Internships are available in customer business development, marketing, consumer market knowledge, research and development, product supply, information and decision solutions, human resources, external relations and finance. Responsibilities vary with position.

GETTING HIRED

Apply by: *Summer*: February 1; *fall/winter/spring*: rolling. Apply online at usjobs.pg.com.

Qualifications:

Open to college sophomores, juniors, seniors and recent graduates. Certain positions require concentrations in specific fields of study. Go to usjobs.pg.com and click on "US Career Advice" for details.

Contact:
Internship Coordinator
Procter & Gamble
1 P & G Plaza
Cincinnati, OH 45202
Phone: (888) 486-7691
www.pg.com/jobs/jobs_us/college_recruiting/internships.jhtml

Pro-Found Software, Inc.

THE BUZZ

- "A rare find: a software company looking for 'elegance'"
- "A nurturing environment for technically literate students"

THE STATS

Industry(ies): Software; Technology

Location(s): Teaneck, NJ

Number of interns: *Annual*: 3-5

Pay: Paid; competitive salary (commensurate with experience and background). Round-trip travel (on an as-needed basis); subsidized housing (on an as-needed basis)

Length of internship: 4 months-1 year

THE SCOOP

Pro-Found Software, Inc., has been creating software for mid-sized and large businesses across several industries since 1989. Founded by its chief technology officer, William Frenkel, the company excels at low-maintenance, integration products, offers fixed-price contracts and boasts a technology demonstration center for its clients. Its founder describes himself as a "compulsive simplifier".

ON THE JOB

The company's official view of internships is a Chinese proverb: "Tell me and I'll forget; show me and I may remember; involve me and I'll understand." Pro-Found Software, Inc., looks for interns who are "elegant" problem solvers to work for the full life cycle of a software program's development.

GETTING HIRED

Apply by: Rolling. Send resume to e-mail address below.

Qualifications:

Open to all college students (including international students) who are proficient in JAVA and/or C/C++ (exposure to Web-based programming is a plus).

Contact:
Internship Coordinator
Pro-Found Software, Inc.
Glenpointe Centre West
500 Frank Burr Boulevard
Teaneck, NJ 07666-6802
Phone: (201) 928-0400
Fax: (201) 928-1122
E-mail: tdare@pro-found.com
www.pro-foundsoftware.com/careers/internships2.html

Public Defender Service for the District of Columbia

 THE BUZZ
- "Investigative internships – assist with legal representation in DC"
- "Wanted: aspiring lawyers with a penchant for public service"

 THE STATS

Industry(ies): Government; Law

Location(s): Washington, DC

Number of interns: *Spring/summer/fall*: 50-70 each

Pay: Generally unpaid, though limited fellowships are available. Travel reimbursement

Length of internship: *Spring/summer/fall*: 3 months each

 THE SCOOP

Started as the Legal Aid Agency in 1960, PDS works to provide high quality legal representation to the many "indigent people facing a loss of liberty in the District of Columbia." The staff attorneys who work as DC public defenders call themselves "Champions of Liberty". PDS is a federally funded independent organization governed by a board of trustees.

 ON THE JOB

The Investigations Division has hired interns for 25 years through its Criminal Law Internship Program. Interns are given extensive training before being paired with an attorney in one of the litigation divisions. Interns are responsible for conducting investigations for the cases to which they are assigned. Approximately 70 percent of the work is conducted in the field. Interns are occasionally hired as full-time staff investigators. Detailed information about internship opportunities can be read on the PDS internships web site, www.pdsdc.org/Internships/ index.asp.

GETTING HIRED

Apply by: Priority deadlines – *spring*: December 1; *summer*: April 1; *fall*: August 1. Online application available at www.pdsdc.org/Internships/Internships/index.asp.

Qualifications:
Open to undergrads, recent college graduates and graduate and law students.

Contact:
Christian Pipe
Internship Coordinator
Public Defender Service for DC
633 Indiana Avenue, NW
Washington, DC 20004
Phone: (202) 824-2310
Fax: (202) 824-2910
E-mail: Internship@pdsdc.org
www.pdsdc.org

Public Interest Research Group

 THE BUZZ
- "Focus on how real problems impact real people"

 THE STATS

Industry(ies): Education; Environmental; Government; Law; Nonprofit; Public Relations

Location(s): Multiple cities in most states of the U.S.

Number of interns: *Annual*: 100-160 undergraduates; 50 graduate and law students

Pay: Varies

Length of internship: Semester, summer, winter break

 **THE SCOOP**

Each U.S. state has its own Public Interest Research Group working with the state capitals to achieve "concrete, practical changes that benefit the public." State PIRGs were introduced in 1971 to address issues affecting the public, from water pollution to consumer privacy. Many state PIRGs are very active on college campuses. In 1983, the individual state PIRGs formed the U.S. PIRG to "act as a watchdog" in the nation's capital and influence national policy debate.

 ON THE JOB

Interns work with PIRG staff members on projects such as creating new policy ideas, devising strategy, researching, drafting legislation, lobbying senators and members of Congress, media outreach and garnering political support for PIRG causes. Supervisors provide ongoing training. Issues and roles vary depending on state agendas and programs.

 GETTING HIRED

Apply by: Rolling. *Undergraduates*: send resume and cover letter to jobs@pirg.org; *graduates*: send resume and cover letter to careers@pirg.org.

Qualifications:
Open to college seniors, recent college graduates and grad and law students. State PIRGs have separate internship programs for undergraduates and graduate students. They offer full-time job openings for recent grads, attorneys and other experienced candidates. See www.pirg.org for details.

Contact:
Amy Perry, Hiring Director
National Association of State PIRGs
29 Temple Place, 2nd Floor
Boston, MA 02111
Phone: (617) 747-4360
Fax: (617) 422-0881
E-mail: jobs@pirg.org (undergraduates)
E-mail: careers@pirg.org (graduate and law students)

Recent graduates
www.pirg.org/jobs/Recentgrads/Index.html

Grad students
www.pirg.org/jobs/internships/graduate/index.html

Visit Vault at **www.vault.com** for insider company profiles, expert advice, career message boards, expert resume reviews, the Vault Job Board and more.

V/\ULT CAREER LIBRARY **347**

The Public Theater

🐝 THE BUZZ

- "To intern, or not to intern? That is the question"
- "All's well that ends well...for your resume"

📟 THE STATS

Industry(ies): Theater/Performing Arts

Location(s): New York, NY

Number of interns: *Annual:* 15-25

Pay: Varies with department

Length of internship: Minimum of 3 months; varies by department

🔍 THE SCOOP

The Public Theater was founded by Joseph Papp as the Shakespeare Workshop in 1954 and is now one of the nation's preeminent cultural institutions. The theater produces new plays, musicals and productions of Shakespeare and other classics in its headquarters on Lafayette Street, and free Shakespeare in Central Park each summer at the Delacorte Theater. Its newest performance space, Joe's Pub, has become a major venue for new work and performances by musicians, spoken-word artists and solo performers.

🏙️ ON THE JOB

Interns work in all departments of The Public Theater, including marketing and audience development, casting, literary, general management, press, producer's office, production and Joe's Pub. Responsibilities vary with department placement.

💰 GETTING HIRED

Apply by: Rolling. Submit a resume and cover letter to the address below.

Qualifications:

Open to college freshmen, sophomores, juniors and seniors, college graduates and grad students.

Contact:
Internship Coordinator
Public Theater
425 Lafayette Street
New York, NY 10003
Phone: (212) 539-8500
Fax: (212) 539-8705
www.publictheater.org
www.joespub.com

Publicis

🐝 THE BUZZ

- "Represent some of the world's largest companies"
- "Learn the art of branding"

📟 THE STATS

Industry(ies): Advertising; Public Relations

Location(s): Dallas, TX; Indianapolis, IN; New York, NY; Seattle, WA

Number of interns: *Summer:* 15-20

Pay: Paid twice monthly; academic credit available

Length of internship: *Summer:* 8 weeks (June-July)

🔍 THE SCOOP

As the fourth-largest communications firm in the world, Publicis represents mega-clients such as Procter & Gamble and L'Oreal. Founder Marcel Bleustein was only 20 years old when he started the company in Paris in 1926. At that point, advertising and marketing were still relatively new fields. The international company is now divided into three businesses: advertising, media buying and consultancy, and SAMS (specialized agencies and marketing services). Publicis Groupe boasts nearly 1,000 agencies in 109 countries under its professional umbrella.

🏙️ ON THE JOB

The program is broken down into three main elements: day-to-day activities, seminars on the advertising business and a project. Interns work in the account service, creative, brand planning and production departments. In their daily activities, interns are given projects to work on no matter which department they work in. Interns are also split into three teams for their project, and each team is assigned a brand to research. Teams study the assigned brand's competition and build a campaign for it, including creative briefs and media plans. Additionally, interns attend weekly seminars to help them learn the different facets of the agency, as well as the advertising industry in general.

💰 GETTING HIRED

Apply by: Rolling. E-mail a resume and cover letter to the address below.

Qualifications:

Open to college freshmen, sophomores, juniors and seniors, recent college graduates and grad students.

Contact:
Internship Coordinator
Publicis New York
4 Herald Square – 950 6th Avenue
New York, NY 10001
Phone: (212) 279 5550
Fax: (212) 279-5560
E-mail: employment@publicis-usa.com
www.publicis-usa.com

INTERNSHIP PROFILES:
Q

Q104.3

🐝 THE BUZZ
- "Be heard at NY's only classic rock radio station"
- "Meet and greet listeners at fun events across the tri-state area"

💹 THE STATS

Industry(ies): Broadcast & Entertainment

Location(s): New York, NY

Number of interns: *Summer*: 4-8; *fall/spring*: 2-5 each

Pay: None; academic credit

Length of internship: *Spring/summer/fall*: 3-4 months

🔑 THE SCOOP

Q104.3 is New York City's only classic rock station. It had previously been a rock station, an "active rock" station and more, until settling on classic rock for the past six years. Most listeners are between 24 and 54 years old. The station employs about 50 people in its Manhattan office. Besides airing classic rock on the radio, Q104.3 also sponsors concerts, events and contests for its listeners.

🏢 ON THE JOB

Interns at Q104.3 work in the programming, promotions and production departments. In the programming department, interns help record commercials, learn how to run the board and may write commercials. Promotions interns spend most of their time in the field interacting with listeners at various events. In production, interns learn more about music and how to program the radio station, and conduct research, as well. Interns are assigned to an employee in the department they are working in, but may work with various station personnel.

💰 GETTING HIRED

Apply by: *Spring*: mid-January; *summer*: mid-April; *fall*: mid-August. Mail resume and cover letter to the address below.

Qualifications:

Open to college freshmen, sophomores, juniors and seniors, but fall and spring interns must receive academic credit. Summer interns do not need to receive credit, but it is preferred.

Contact:
Q104.3
Judy Dillon
1180 Avenue of the Americas
New York, NY 10036
Phone: (212) 819-3177
Fax: (212) 302-7814
E-mail: judydillon@clearchannel.com
www.Q1043.com

Quality Education for Minorities Network

🐝 THE BUZZ
- "Help ensure quality education for all Americans"
- "Represent the under-represented"

💹 THE STATS

Industry(ies): Education; Health Care; Nonprofit; Science/Research

Location(s): Washington, DC; Arlington, VA

Number of interns: *Summer*: 15

Pay: Paid; *undergraduates*: $3,000/summer; *grad students*: $4,000/summer. Round-trip travel; subsidized housing

Length of internship: *Summer*: 10 weeks

🔑 THE SCOOP

Quality Education for Minorities Network (QEM) is a nonprofit focused on improving the education of African Americans, Alaskan Natives, American Indians, Mexican Americans and Puerto Ricans. Its primary programs are centered around community outreach and leadership development and mathematics, science and engineering. The company offers extensive fellowship information and assistance to its members of all ages.

🏢 ON THE JOB

QEM offers two internship programs: Science Student Internships and Health-Focused Internships. For the science program, interns interact with agencies dealing in science policy and develop their research skills. Health interns (who are sponsored by the U.S. Department of Health and Human Services) address the fact that the number of people with HIV/AIDS is disproportionately higher within minority communities. Both programs include an orientation and post-internship evaluation. Interns have an IDP (Individual Development Plan) that outlines training plans and timetables, highlights goals and tracks outcomes.

💰 GETTING HIRED

Apply by: *Summer*: February 2. Download the application at qemnetwork.qem.org/Internship%20folder/Internship%20Description.html.

Qualifications:

Open to college juniors and seniors and enrolled graduate students. Applicants to the science program must have a science background.

Contact:
The Quality Education for Minorities Network
1818 N Street, NW, Suite 350
Washington, DC 20036
Phone: (202) 659-1818
Fax: (202) 659-5408
E-mail: qemnetwork@qem.org
qemnetwork.qem.org

INTERNSHIP PROFILES:
R

RAND Corporation

 THE BUZZ
- "Perfect for budding think tank professionals"
- "A serious academic internship for those who can't get enough of academia"

 THE STATS

Industry(ies): Education; Government; Law; Military; Nonprofit; Science/Research; Technology

Location(s): Arlington, VA; Pittsburgh, PA; Santa Monica, CA

Number of interns: *Summer*: 25

Pay: Stipend, varies with experience; approximately $11,000 for 12 weeks

Length of internship: *Summer*: 12 weeks

 THE SCOOP

The RAND Corporation, a nonprofit research organization, was established in 1945 to explore issues of warfare and technology. Today, RAND has expanded its mission to encompass social and economic issues such as health, education, poverty, crime and the environment.

ON THE JOB

Interns work on ongoing project research, advised by a senior staff member. Each student must present a seminar at the end of the summer. Past topics have ranged from Chinese terrorism to violence among American Latinos.

GETTING HIRED

Apply by: *Summer*: January 1. For application instructions, see: www.rand.org/about/edu_op/fellowships/gsap. Send a resume and cover letter describing research interests. Cover letter should include contact information for three academic references. Submissions must be sent online. Go to the web site after October 1 for instcutions on how to apply. Attach all files in Microsoft Word format.

Qualifications:

Open only to enrolled, full-time graduate students who will not graduate prior to the summer of employment. Applicants must have completed at least two years of graduate work (preferably toward a doctorate). U.S. citizenship is necessary for certain jobs that demand security clearance.

Contact:

Sally Sleeper, PhD
The RAND Corporation
4570 Fifth Avenue, Suite 600
Pittsburgh, PA 15213
Phone: (412) 683-2300, ext. 4914
Fax: (412) 683-2800
E-mail: Summer_director@rand.org
www.rand.org/about/edu_op

Random House, Inc.

 THE BUZZ
- "How to learn book publishing in just one summer"
- "Nothing random about this top publishing internship"

 THE STATS

Industry(ies): Publishing

Location(s): New York, NY

Number of interns: *Summer*: 40

Pay: Paid; $400/week or academic credit. Free books

Length of internship: *Summer*: 10 weeks

 THE SCOOP

Random House is the world's largest general trade book publisher. A division of Bertelsmann AG, RH is also one of the foremost media companies in the world. The company's publishing groups include the Bantam Dell Publishing Group, the Crown Publishing Group, the Doubleday Broadway Publishing Group, the Knopf Publishing Group, the Random House Audio Publishing Group, Random House Children's Books, the Random House Diversified Publishing Group, the Random House Information Group and the Random House Publishing Group. It's also home to many of the world's most popular authors, such as John Grisham, Danielle Steel, Michael Crichton, Anne Rice, Dean Koontz and Dr. Seuss.

 ON THE JOB

Interns are placed in one of the company's publishing groups or in a service group, such as finance, publishing operations, sales, IT or human resources. Random House tries to place interns in their specific areas of interest. Once a week, interns gather for lunch to hear key executives speak about their roles and the work done within their divisions. Speakers may include experts in publishing, publicity, editorial, marketing, finance, production and elsewhere. Interns also travel to RH's operations center in Maryland for a tour of the facilities and to hear talks from key executives there.

GETTING HIRED

Apply by: March 15. Applicants should log on to www.careers.randomhouse.com. Send a resume and cover letter explaining why you want a book publishing internship and what you expect to gain from the program. Note if you have an interest in a specific area. Finalists will be invited to New York (at their own expense) for an interview in the spring.

Qualifications:
Open to rising college seniors.

Contact:
Human Resources
Random House, Inc.
1745 Broadway, MD 19-1
New York, NY 10019
www.careers.randomhouse.com

Raytheon

 THE BUZZ
- "Help defend the homeland"
- "Get ready for your engineering career to take off"

 THE STATS

Industry(ies): Aerospace; Engineering; Military; Science/Research; Technology

Location(s): Nationwide

Number of interns: *Annual*: 400

Pay: Paid; amount varies. Benefits (at some locations); relocation assistance

Length of internship: *Fall/spring/summer*: 3-6 months each

 THE SCOOP

Two former college roommates Laurence K. Marshall and Vannevar Bush, along with scientist Charles G. Smith, founded Raytheon Company in Cambridge, Mass., as the American Appliance Company in 1922. Throughout its more than 80-year history, Raytheon Company has been a leader in developing defense technologies and in converting those technologies for use in commercial markets. From its early days as a maker of radio tubes, its adaptation of World War II radar technology to invent microwave cooking, and its development of the first guided missile, Raytheon has successfully built upon its pioneering tradition to become a global technology leader. Now, Raytheon employs over 80,000 staff and boasted $21.9 billion in 2005 revenues.

ON THE JOB

Most Raytheon locations offer student internships, but specific positions and openings vary depending on the company's needs. Go to www.rayjobs.com/campus for more information. Interns work closely with full-time professionals on a variety of projects, in both the government defense and commercial aviation divisions. The company looks to hire full-time employees from its intern pool.

GETTING HIRED

Apply by: Rolling. Search for open positions and apply online at www.rayjobs.com/campus.

Qualifications:
Open to all enrolled college sophomores, juniors with at least a 3.0 GPA, and majoring in one of the following areas: electrical engineering, computer science, mechanical engineering, industrial engineering, aerospace engineering, finance, human resources or information technology. Due to security clearance requirements, applicants must be U.S. citizens.

Contact:
Raytheon Company
University Programs
870 Winter Street
Waltham, MA 02451
www.rayjobs.com/campus

Reebok

 THE BUZZ
- "Become a top-notch sneaker marketing pro"
- "The twin titan of athletic apparel"

THE STATS

Industry(ies): Consumer Products; Fashion; Retail

Location(s): Stroughton, MA

Number of interns: *Annual*: 32-40

Pay: Paid; *undergraduate*: $500/week; *grad student*: $650/week. Discount on shoes; basketball games and use of gym; enrichment programs

Length of internship: Varies with availability

 THE SCOOP

Reebok International emerged from a company called J.W. Foster and Sons founded in the UK in 1895. Reebok's mission was to help runners improve their performance with specialized athletic footwear. This simple idea has paid off: Reebok currently brings in $3 billion a year and continues to provide shoes and sports equipment for athletes all over the world. The company's other corporate divisions include the Rockport Company, Weebok, Ralph Lauren Footwear and Greg Norman.

 ON THE JOB

Interns work in divisions related to all areas of Reebok's production, including manufacturing, retail, human resources, management, finance and sales. Interns are also "schooled" through Reebok's enrichment programs that focus on career development and possible future placements with Reebok.

GETTING HIRED

Apply by: *Summer*: April 1. Submit a resume and cover letter to the address below.

Qualifications:
Open to all college juniors and seniors, recent college graduates and grad students.

Contact:
Reebok
College Relations Program
100 Technology Center Drive
Stroughton, MA 02072
E-mail: college.recruiting@reebok.com
www.reebok.com

Visit Vault at **www.vault.com** for insider company profiles, expert advice, career message boards, expert resume reviews, the Vault Job Board and more.

V∧ULT CAREER LIBRARY **353**

Regan Books

 THE BUZZ
- "Delve into the elite world of New York book publishing"
- "Learn how books are created"

 THE STATS

Industry(ies): Publishing

Location(s): New York, NY

Number of interns: *Summer*: 8

Pay: None

Length of internship: *Summer*: 10 weeks

 THE SCOOP

Regan Books is an imprint of HarperCollins, publishing a variety of literary genres, from fitness guides to best-selling fiction novels to children's books. Authors published by Regan Books include Wally Lamb, Howard Stern, Jackie Collins, even Eminem and Tony Hawk. Regan prides itself on its political nonfiction titles, evident in its electronic newsletter, *Left, Right & Center*, highlighting books of political commentary.

 ON THE JOB

Interns will assist in several different departments during their 10-week stay at Regan Books. Responsibilities vary with each department, but may include assisting sales staff, proofreading for the editorial department and performing administrative tasks. While learning the various aspects of publishing, interns will develop and pitch a book idea to professional staff at Regan and its parent company, HarperCollins. Interns will also enjoy networking opportunities. It's an ideal internship for students interested in publishing careers.

(\$) GETTING HIRED

Apply by: April 9. Submit a resume with cover letter to the e-mail address below.

Qualifications:
Open to college juniors and seniors. Organized students with related experience, strong written and verbal communication and computer skills preferred.

Contact:
E-mail: collrec@HarperCollins.com
www.harpercollins.com/hc/aboutus/careers.asp#internship

Renew America

 THE BUZZ
- "Help others work toward a better environment"
- "Put your efforts where your heart is"

 THE STATS

Industry(ies): Environmental; Nonprofit

Location(s): Washington, DC

Number of interns: *Spring/summer/fall*: 6 each

Pay: Paid; $7,500/6 months. Access to fitness center

Length of internship: *Spring/summer/fall*: 6 months

 **THE SCOOP**

Renew America has been a nonprofit network since 1989 and is composed of businesses, government leaders and civic activists who empower individuals to improve the environmental quality of their communities. RA maintains the "Environmental Success Index," which chronicles more than 1,400 companies that restore the environment. Each year, RA celebrates 26 outstanding programs from across the country through the National Awards for Sustainability.

 ON THE JOB

Interns generally work with staff members as assistants. Interns are assigned duties that include conducting extensive research on environmental issues and groups, developing and implementing educational programs, designing ideas to improve the network's web site, conducting membership surveys, writing reports and handling general clerical duties.

 GETTING HIRED

Apply by: Rolling. Submit resume, cover letter and writing samples.

Qualifications:
Open to all undergraduates and recent college graduates.

Contact:
Renew America
1200 18th Street, NW
Suite 1100
Washington, DC 20036
Phone: (202) 232-2252
E-mail: renewamerica@ige.org
solstice.crest.org/aboutus_internship.html

The Rhode Island State Government

 THE BUZZ
- "A very structured government internship"
- "Make a big mark on this tiny state"

 THE STATS

Industry(ies): Government; Law

Location(s): Providence, RI

Number of interns: *Spring*: 70; *spring + academic component*: 45-50; *summer*: 200; *fall*: 40

Pay: *Spring*: none; *summer*: $20/day if intern is a Rhode Island resident attending an out-of-state college or university; *fall*: none

Length of internship: *Spring/fall*: 12 weeks each; *summer*: 8 weeks

 **THE SCOOP**

The Rhode Island State Government is Rhode Island's governing body and includes the Department of the Attorney General, the Department of Health and the Public Defender's Office, as well as the legislative, executive and judicial branches of government.

 ON THE JOB

The Rhode Island State Government Intern Program places students in all three of its governing branches, as well as in other departments and agencies, including the Department of the Attorney General and the Department of Administration. One area of the internship program is specifically geared toward law students, who conduct research and even litigation. In addition to its structured spring and summer programs, which require eight to 10 hours per week, a weekly lecture, a paper and an exam, the program also offers several more informal opportunities year-round.

 GETTING HIRED

Apply by: *Spring*: before semester begins; *summer*: May 15; *fall*: before semester begins. For law students, a trial practice or evidence course and a letter from the dean are required.

Qualifications:
Open to college juniors and seniors, as well as graduate and law students. Must have a minimum 2.5 GPA and good academic standing.

Contact:
Robert W. Gemma, Executive Director
The Rhode Island State Government
Internship Program State House, Room 8AA
Providence, RI 02903
Phone: (401) 222-6782
E-mail: intern@rilin.state.ri.us
www.rilin.state.ri.us/studteaguide/intern.html

Rio Grande National Forest

 THE BUZZ
- "If nature is your game, the Rio Grande has a forest for you"
- "Bunk down in the great outdoors"

 THE STATS

Industry(ies): Education; Environmental

Location(s): Monte Vista, CO

Number of interns: *Annual*: 20-30

Pay: $16/day. Free room and board may be available; use of camping supplies may be available; recreational opportunities (e.g., camping, fishing, skiing) depending on type of job

Length of internship: *Spring/summer/fall*: 3-20 weeks and ongoing

 THE SCOOP

In 1908, President Theodore Roosevelt established the Rio Grande National Forest, which combined parts of the former Cochetopah and the present-day San Juan National Forests. The land, now overseen by the United States Forest Service, is one of 11 national forests in Colorado and includes the Sangre de Cristo Mountain Range and glacial canyons of the San Juan Mountains, as well as the headwaters of the Rio Grande River.

 ON THE JOB

Interns are placed in the Student Temporary Employment Program, which provides an opportunity to earn money, train with professionals and combine academic study with hands-on experience. Interns who show strong potential and necessary skills may be recruited as "student trainees" under the Forest Service's Student Creer Experience Program (SCEP). Upon completion of SCEP and degree requirements, interns are eligible for permanent federal employment. SCEP is the primary external recruitment source for entry-level hires in the Forest Service and provides work experience directly related to the student's academic program or career goals.

GETTING HIRED

Apply by: Rolling; *summer*: April 1. Send a resume and cover letter to the address below.

Qualifications:
Open to high school students, college freshmen, sophomores, juniors and seniors, recent college graduates and grad students. International applicants are welcome.

Contact:
Volunteer Program
Rio Grande National Forests
1803 West Highway 160
Monte Vista, CO 81144
Phone: (719) 852-5941

Visit Vault at **www.vault.com** for insider company profiles, expert advice, career message boards, expert resume reviews, the Vault Job Board and more.

VAULT CAREER LIBRARY **355**

Ripon Society

 THE BUZZ
- "Calling all Republicans! Ripon has an opportunity for you"
- "Help moderate the GOP"

 THE STATS

Industry(ies): Government; Nonprofit; Publishing

Location(s): Washington, DC

Number of interns: *Summer*: 2

Pay: Stipend

Length of internship: *Spring/summer/fall*: 8-12 weeks and ongoing

 THE SCOOP

Formed in 1962, the Ripon Society is a nonprofit research and public policy organization promoting the moderate Republican principles of the Republican Party, government and society. Current Ripon Society programs include DC's Breakfast/Dinner Series with members of Congress, national and regional conferences, and publication of *The Ripon Forum*, the Society's bimonthly magazine. The Ripon Society also offers its Rough Rider Award as a tribute to an elected officeholder best exhibiting the ideals of a Teddy Roosevelt-like Republican.

 ON THE JOB

Interns assist staff in all capacities, from conducting research and editing articles for the *Ripon Forum* to organizing conferences. Interns also have the opportunity to participate in Ripon public policy events, interact with members of Congress and attend Congressional hearings.

GETTING HIRED

Apply by: Rolling. Submit a resume and cover letter to the address below.

Qualifications:
Open to all college juniors and seniors, recent college graduates and grad students.

Contact:
Attention: Molly Milliken or Austen Bannan
The Ripon Society
1300 L Street, NW, Suite 900
Washington, DC 20005
Phone: (202) 216-1008
E-mail: info@riponsociety.org
www.riponsociety.org

Roche

 THE BUZZ
- "Get hands-on experience in the pharmaceutical industry"
- "Put the Rx into you resume"

 THE STATS

Industry(ies): Biotech; Health Care; Pharmaceuticals

Location(s): Boulder, CO; Branchburg, NJ; Florence, SC; Indianapolis, IN; Nutley, NJ; Palo Alto, CA; Pleasanton, CA; multiple international locations

Number of interns: Varies depending on internship location and position

Pay: Varies

Length of internship: Varies depending on internship location and position

 THE SCOOP

F. Hoffman-La Roche & Co. (Roche) was founded in 1896. More than a century later, Roche is a health care and biotech leader. The company has three divisions: pharmaceuticals, vitamins and fine chemicals, and diagnostics. The focus of the company is likewise threefold: prevention, diagnosis and drug therapy.

 ON THE JOB

Each Roche location is responsible for its own internship program, if it chooses to offer internships; therefore interns' experiences may vary widely. However, possible internship areas include biology, chemistry, environmental health and engineering. Students interested in working for Roche should search for positions by location at the company's web site, www.roche.com/home/careers/car_opp.htm.

GETTING HIRED

Apply by: Rolling.

Qualifications:
Open to undergraduate and graduate students; additional requirements exist for specific positions.

Contact:
www.roche.com/home/careers/car_opp.htm

Rock Creek Foundation

 THE BUZZ
- "Help those suffering from psychiatric disorders"
- "Work behind the scenes at this medical treatment facility"

 STATS

Industry(ies): Health Care

Location(s): Annapolis, MD; Hyattsville, MD; Lexington Park, MD; Silver Spring, MD; Wheaton, MD; White Marsh, MD

Number of interns: Varies with need

Pay: Varies with position

Length of internship: *Spring*: 4-5 months; *summer*: 3-4 months; *fall*: 3-4 months

 THE SCOOP

The Rock Creek Foundation was established in 1974 to offer better care to patients with psychiatric disorders and developmental disabilities. The Rock Creek Foundation is now one of three Santé Companies. These Maryland-based companies help more than 3,000 patients every year.

 ON THE JOB

Volunteers for the Rock Creek Foundation or the other two Santé Companies (Affiliated Santé Group and Santé Medical Associates) may fill a variety of roles such as tutors, Web managers or fundraisers. Positions offered consider both the skills and aspirations of the individual worker. Students will be exposed to the inner workings of mental health care. One full day of work each week during the semester or summer of volunteering is required. To get more information, see www.thesantegroup.org/DesktopDefault.aspx?tabid=32.

 GETTING HIRED

Apply by: Rolling.

Qualifications:
Open to students who have completed at least two years of college. Send resume and cover letter to the e-mail address below. Interview required.

Contact:
E-mail: balbaneze@santegroup.org
www.thesantegroup.org

Rodale Institute Experimental Farm

 THE BUZZ
- "Cultivate organic farming solutions for tomorrow"
- "Ideal for budding agricultural scientists"

 THE STATS

Industry(ies): Environmental; Science/Research

Location(s): Kutztown, PA

Number of interns: *Annual*: 10

Pay: Paid; $9/hour or unpaid for academic credit

Length of internship: *Spring/summer/fall*: 6-9 months. Spring term generally begins in March or April

 THE SCOOP

The Rodale Institute Experimental Farm (RIEF) is a 333-acre research farm that has been situated in Berks County, Pa., for over 50 years. RIEF focuses its research on problems relating to global food, farming and natural resource management issues to develop farming improvements. The Institute maintains a Demonstration Garden, a scientific research and test facility for regenerative farming on low-input regenerative agriculture, which includes applied weed ecology, nitrogen cycling, soil biology, compost utilization and tree-based cropping systems.

 ON THE JOB

Internships are based around hands-on and "direct work with researchers on short- and long-term trials and experiments covering everything from soil quality indicators to regenerative farming's impact on global warming."

 GETTING HIRED

Apply by: For all terms: December 1. Download application from: www.rodaleinstitute.org/education/internships/home.html. Send application, along with resume, cover letter indicating how the internship will relate to future career goals, transcripts, names and addresses (including telephone numbers and/or e-mail addresses) of three references, and dates of availability, to the address below.

Qualifications:
Open to all recent college graduates, grad students and international students with a background in biology, ecology or agriculture (agronomy/farming systems only).

Contact:
Human Resources Coordinator
The Rodale Institute
611 Siegfriedale Road
Kutztown, PA 19530
Phone: (610) 683-1428
Fax: (610) 683-1431
E-mail: sandra.strausser@rodaleinst.org
www.rodaleinstitute.org/education/internships/home.shtml

Visit Vault at **www.vault.com** for insider company profiles, expert advice, career message boards, expert resume reviews, the Vault Job Board and more.

VAULT CAREER LIBRARY **357**

Roll Call

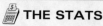 **THE BUZZ**
- "Meet the people and players in Congress."
- "The newspaper of Capitol Hill"

THE STATS

Industry(ies): Government; Journalism

Location(s): Washington, DC

Number of interns: *Spring/summer/fall*: 4-5 each

Pay: None. Stipend for transportation; lunches with members of Congress; attendance welcome at editorial meetings; free copies of newspaper

Length of internship: *Spring/summer/fall*: 10-12 weeks

THE SCOOP

In print since 1955, *Roll Call* is written specifically for members of Congress and their staff as a platform to "communicate with one another across the aisle and between the chambers." *Roll Call* concentrates on editorial opinions, political banter and news around Capitol Hill, and also provides an insightful perspective into the inner workings of Congress.

ON THE JOB

Interns work in the editorial department on various projects ranging from general clerical duties around the office to assisting editors with various assignments and researching and writing their own stories.

GETTING HIRED

Apply by: *Spring*: December 1; *summer*: March 1; *fall*: August 1. Send resume, cover letter and writing samples to the address below.

Qualifications:
Open to college freshmen, sophomores, juniors and seniors, recent college graduates and grad students. International applicants welcome.

Contact:
Internship Coordinator
Roll Call
50 F Street, NW, Suite 700
Washington, DC 20001
Fax: (202) 824-0902
www.rollcall.com

Rolling Stone

 THE BUZZ
- "Fight for your right to rock and write"
- "Edgy music lovers wanted"

THE STATS

Industry(ies): Broadcast & Entertainment; Journalism; Music/Records

Location(s): New York, NY

Number of interns: *Spring/summer/fall*: 10-15 per term, with a higher number in the summer

Pay: None. Academic credit possible but not mandatory. Free promotional merchandise and magazines

Length of internship: *Spring/summer/fall*: 12 weeks

THE SCOOP

Rolling Stone magazine was founded in 1967 by Jann Wenner (then 21), as a grassroots publication in San Francisco embracing the hippie counterculture of the 1960s and 1970s. Over the years, *Rolling Stone* has reinvented the rules of journalism, publishing exclusive interviews, photography and reviews of the music world's hottest performers. Today *Rolling Stone* has become the world's premier music magazine, grossing over $110 million annually and reaching about 1.2 million readers each issue.

ON THE JOB

Interns conduct research for writers/editors, transcribe interviews, compile media packets consisting of the day's top news stories and complete clerical tasks as needed.

GETTING HIRED

Apply by: *Spring*: September 15; *summer*: February 15; *fall*: June 15. Send to the address below a resume, cover letter stating intended start date and the reasons for wanting to work at *Rolling Stone* , three writing samples (preferably published clips), and transcript. No phone or e-mail inquiries.

Qualifications:
Open to all college students and recent college graduates.

Contact:
Editorial Intern Coordinator
c/o Rolling Stone Magazine
1290 Avenue of the Americas, 2nd Floor
New York, NY 10104
www.rollingstone.com

Roy A. Somlyo Productions

 THE BUZZ
- "Work behind the curtain on Broadway"
- "Good start for a career in the theater business"

 THE STATS

Industry(ies): Broadcast & Entertainment; Theater/Performing Arts

Location(s): New York, NY

Number of interns: *Annual*: 4

Pay: None. Free passes to shows

Length of internship: Varies (12-24 weeks); available year-round

 **THE SCOOP**

Roy A. Somlyo currently serves as president of the American Theatre Wing, but he has enjoyed an active career in both theater and television. He produced a number of Broadway and Off-Broadway shows, including *The Man Who*, *Edmund Keen*, *84 Charing Cross Road* and *Anna Christie*. For television, he won three Emmy Awards for his production on the Tony Awards.

 ON THE JOB

Interns assist staff members in all aspects of theater and television production, from readings and auditions to opening night parties.

 GETTING HIRED

Apply by: Rolling. Submit resume and cover letter.

Qualifications:
Open to high school grads, college freshmen, sophomores, juniors and seniors, recent college graduates, college graduates of any age and grad students. International students are eligible.

Contact:
Internship Coordinator
Roy A. Somlyo Productions
234 West 44th Street
New York, NY 10036
Phone: (212) 764-6080
Fax: (212) 764-6363

Visit Vault at **www.vault.com** for insider company profiles, expert advice, career message boards, expert resume reviews, the Vault Job Board and more.

VAULT CAREER LIBRARY **359**

Ruder Finn

 THE BUZZ
- "Be a top flack at this top PR firm"

THE STATS

Industry(ies): Public Relations

Location(s): New York, NY

Number of interns: *Summer/fall/winter*: 7-15 each (varies)

Pay: Paid; *summer interns*: $10/hour; *executive trainees*: based on annual salary of $24,000, pro-rated over 4 months. Field trips to media organizations; social events

Length of internship: *Summer*: June 19-October 20; *fall*: October 23-February 23; *winter*: February 13-June 16

THE SCOOP

In 1948, childhood friends Bill Ruder and David Finn decided to start a firm focusing on the business community within fine arts programs to get corporate PR benefits and provide new sources of support for contemporary artists. Over 50 years later, Ruder Finn has become one of the world's largest independent agencies, creating some of the most successful communications campaigns for start-up companies, Fortune 500 companies, world organizations and cultural institutions.

ON THE JOB

Interns and executive trainees learn fundamental PR skills through writing, media monitoring, media relations, electronic media, special event planning, and new business presentations. The Executive Training Program begins with five days of classes to introduce the fundamental skills of public relations. Participants are then assigned to specific practice areas and weekly classes. Ruder Finn practice areas include Arts & Communications Counselors, Corporate Branding, Corporate Reputation, Corporate Technology Practice, Global Issues Communications, Healthcare, Interactive, Marketing Practice, Planned Television Arts, Travel and Economic Development, and Visual Technology. Not every area accepts an intern each session, but efforts are made to place them in their areas of interest.

GETTING HIRED

Apply by: *Summer*: February 17; *fall*: July 7; *winter*: November 11. Send application, three writing tests, resume, writing sample, official college transcript, and two signed letters of recommendation to the addres below. Visit the Executive Training Program in the career section of the company web site (www.ruderfinn.com) to download the internship/Executive Training Program application and confirm application details and deadlines.

Qualifications:

Executive Training: open to college graduates; *summer intern*: open to college juniors. All applicants must be authorized to work in the U.S.

Contact:
Ms. Ellen Schaplowsky
Executive Vice President,
Director of Training
Ruder Finn, Inc.
301 East 57th Street
New York, NY 10022
Phone: (212) 593-6316
E-mail: schaplowskye@ruderfinn.com
www.ruderfinn.com
www.ruderfinn.com/career_main.asp?career_page=6

INTERNSHIP PROFILES:
S

Saks Fifth Avenue

THE BUZZ

- "Strut your stuff on Fashion Avenue"
- "Passion for fashion? Saks has an internship for you"

THE STATS

Industry(ies): Retail

Location(s): New York, NY

Number of interns: *Summer*: varies

Pay: Paid; $10/hour. Merchandise discount

Length of internship: *Summer*: 10-14 weeks

THE SCOOP

Saks Fifth Avenue was established in 1924 by Horace Saks and Bernard Gimbel, who wanted to construct a specialty retail store that resonated with "fashionable, gracious living". Since opening, Saks Fifth Avenue has become world-renowned for its merchandise, which features such notable designers as Gucci, Ferragamo, Chanel, Prada, Michael Kors, Giorgio Armani, Donna Karan, Jil Sander, St. John, Ralph Lauren, Dolce & Gabbana, Versace, Oscar de la Renta, Ralph Lauren and Calvin Klein, to name a few. The flagship store, located in the heart of midtown Manhattan, is the largest of Saks's locations.

ON THE JOB

Interns gain hands-on experience in a fast-paced retail environment through departments such as communications, finance, human resources, information technology, logistics, merchandising (buyer) and store management. In addition to attending to specific department tasks, interns participate in weekly seminars conducted by the senior management team. Past seminar topics have included overviews of public relations, marketing, direct marketing, understanding merchandising reports, product development, e-commerce, media relations and visual merchandising.

GETTING HIRED

Apply by: *Summer*: Apply in the fall. Recruiting process begins in February. Submit resume and cover letter with request for application to the address below.

Qualifications:
Open to college juniors and seniors and recent college graduates with a cumulative GPA of at least 3.0.

Contact:
Saks Fifth Avenue
Internship Coordinator
12 East 49th Street, 4th Floor
New York, NY 10019
Fax: (212) 940-5424
www.saksfifthavenue.com

San Diego Zoo

THE BUZZ

- "Spend a summer learning about animals"
- "Calling all animal lovers!"

THE STATS

Industry(ies): Science/Research; Tourism/Recreation

Location(s): San Diego, CA

Number of interns: *Summer*: 5-6

Pay: Paid; $360/week. Free passes to the zoo for family and friends; tours of other areas of the zoo

Length of internship: *Summer*: 12 weeks

THE SCOOP

Established in 1916, the San Diego Zoo houses 4,000 rare and endangered birds, mammals and reptiles with 6,500 varieties of exotic plants. Over 3,000 people visit the zoo each year to enjoy its 100-acre tropical garden, Children's Zoo, Botanical Garden and Ituri Forest, which features giant pandas. At the Center for Reproduction of Endangered Species, the zoo applies modern medical and scientific methods to save exotic animal species from extinction.

ON THE JOB

Interns in the Conservation and Research for Endangered Species (CRES) program work on conservation projects as they conduct research in animal behavior, virology/immunology, reproductive physiology, ecology and applied conservation, molecular genetics, cytogenetics, analytical chemistry, pathology and endocrinology. There are also Safari Sleepover student interns, who work weekends with the Zoo's overnight camp program, and Summer Camp student interns, who work at the Wild Animal Park with children from ages 5 to 12. .High school students may also participate in the zoo's Zoo InternQuest and Virtual InternQuest, which allow them to learn from zoo experts either in person or online. Finally, the zoo also offers an exclusive veterinary internship for studetns at the University of California, Davis School of Veterinary Medicine.

GETTING HIRED

Apply by: *Summer*: March 31. Applications for fellowships are available in January. Submit resume and cover letter to the address below.

Qualifications:
Open to high school students, college students and graduate students.

Contact:
Summer Fellowship Committee
Center for Reproduction of Endangered Species
San Diego Zoo
P.O. Box 120551
San Diego, CA 92112-0551
Phone: (619) 231-1515
http://cres.sandiegozoo.org/
www.sandiegozoo.org/employment/general_info.html#fellows

San Francisco 49ers

 THE BUZZ
- "Promote your favorite football team"
- "Get the opportunity to write about one of the country's most popular sports teams"

 THE STATS

Industry(ies): Sports

Location(s): Santa Clara, CA

Number of interns: *Fall*: 6; *fall/winter*: 1 (plus 1 from the training camp internship program)

Pay: Varies with experience

Length of internship: *Fall*: 1-2 months; *fall/winter*: 4-5 months

 **THE SCOOP**

Four years after the team's establishment in 1946, the San Francisco 49ers became a National League franchise and the first team to accomplish this on the West Coast. The 49ers boast five Super Bowl wins and five Vince Lombardi trophies in their illustrious history. In 2005, the team welcomed its 15th head coach, Mike Nolan, son of former 49ers Head Coach Dick Nolan. Players inducted into the NFL Hall of Fame include football greats Joe Montana, Jimmy Johnson and Joe Perry.

ON THE JOB

The San Francisco 49ers offer public relations internships during training camp and the regular season. Students are exposed to various areas of media communications through responsibilities that may include writing stories, assisting players and management with interviews, and helping out with various projects.

 GETTING HIRED

Apply by: Early May. Send resume and cover letter to the address below.

Qualifications:
Open to college freshmen, sophomores, juniors and seniors. Strong writing skills and a major in journalism or public relations preferred.

Contact:
Internship Coordinator
San Francisco 49ers
4949 Centennial Boulevard
Santa Clara, CA 95054
Phone: (408) 562-4933
www.49ers.com

San Francisco Bay Guardian

 **THE BUZZ**
- "Seeking politically and culturally aware student writers"
- "An internship that offers hands-on reporting experience"

THE STATS

Industry(ies): Journalism

Location(s): San Francisco, CA

Number of interns: *Spring/summer/fall*: 8-10 each

Pay: None. Attend parties; free t-shirts and newspapers

Length of internship: *Spring/summer/fall*: 4 months, 2 full days each week

THE SCOOP

Since 1966, the *San Francisco Bay Guardian* has been an independent alternative weekly newspaper with a focus on arts, entertainment and political coverage. The *Guardian* is one of the founding members of the Association of Alternative Newsweeklies and has a strong local focus.

ON THE JOB

Interns begin by writing the *Guardian*'s Superlist (a guide to interesting, often offbeat services and locations in the Bay Area), and progress to more complex research and writing projects, as well as administrative responsibilities. Interns who focus on the news area assist reporters with research and newsgathering and develop their own short *On Guard* articles. Interns interested in arts and entertainment focus on film reviews, music writing and calendar listings. There is also a culture intern position for those who are interested in writing longer, analytical articles. Interns are provided with workshops on city politics, research and writing skills, and freelancing.

GETTING HIRED

Apply by: *Spring*: December 1 for a January start; *summer*: Postmark April 6 for a May start; *fall*: July 30 for a September start. Send resume, cover letter and three writing samples to the address below c/o Intern Coordinator.

Qualifications:
Open to high school students, college freshmen, sophomores, juniors and seniors, recent college graduates and grad students. International applicants welcome.

Contact:
Internship Coordinator
San Francisco Bay Guardian
135 Mississippi Street
San Francisco, CA 94107
Phone: (415) 255-3100
E-mail: deborah@sfbg.com
www.sfbg.com

Visit Vault at **www.vault.com** for insider company profiles, expert advice, career message boards, expert resume reviews, the Vault Job Board and more.

VAULT CAREER LIBRARY **363**

San Francisco Magazine

 THE BUZZ

- "Follow the Golden Gate to your dreams of writing success"
- "Learn sales and marketing at this award-winning regional publication"

 THE STATS

Industry(ies): Advertising; Journalism; Publishing

Location(s): San Francisco, CA

Number of interns: *Annual*: 5-6

Pay: None; possible academic credit

Length of internship: *Summer/fall/winter*: 3-month commitment; 3 days/week

 **THE SCOOP**

San Francisco magazine is a monthly magazine focusing on dining, events, fashion and travel in the Bay Area. The magazine won the 2000 Maggie Award for Best City and Metropolitan Magazine.

 ON THE JOB

Interns work in the editorial or sales/marketing departments. Editorial duties include research and fact checking, with opportunities for reporting and copyediting. Sales and marketing interns support the department's personnel, assisting with sales research, copy and design, and maintaining and distributing media press kits. All interns attend staff meetings where they can propose story ideas.

 GETTING HIRED

Apply by: Rolling. Submit a resume, cover letter and two writing samples to the address below.

Qualifications:

Editorial internship: open to college freshmen, sophomores, juniors and seniors majoring in English or journalism, or grad students with writing and editing experience.

Marketing internship: open to college freshmen, sophomores, juniors and seniors, as well as grad students. A "hardworking yet fun attitude," strong writing ability, ability to multi-task, and familiarity with Word, Excel and Quark X-press (possible training available) are required.

Contact:
Research Editor
San Francisco Magazine
243 Vallejo Street
San Francisco, CA 94111-1553
Phone: (415) 398-2800
Fax: (415) 398-6777
www.sanfran.com/about/jobs.html#Interns

Marketing internship
E-mail: HKulak@sanfranmag.com

San Francisco Opera

 THE BUZZ

- "You could be making beautiful music with SFO"
- "Learn how to put on a show"

 THE STATS

Industry(ies): Music/Records; Theater/Performing Arts

Location(s): San Francisco, CA

Number of interns: *Spring/summer/fall*: 10-12 each

Pay: None

Length of internship: *Spring/summer/fall*: 12 weeks

 THE SCOOP

Founded in 1923 by Gaetano Merola, the San Francisco Opera moved to its home in the War Memorial Opera House in 1932 and is noted for productions that feature the world's foremost opera talent, as well as outstanding new artists. San Francisco Opera is now the second-largest Opera Company in North America. The Opera has featured performances of such works as *Harvey Milk*, *A Streetcar Named Desire* and *Dead Man Walking*.

ON THE JOB

The internship program gives participants experience with the Opera's inner workings, as they become members of their assigned department while establishing professional contacts. The Opera offers experience in artistic and musical administration, finance, information systems, the costume shop, development, guild activities and events, human resources and labor relations, marketing, public relations, the Opera Center, orchestra administration and technical production. At the beginning of each internship, participants establish their learning objectives with supervisors. Toward the conclusion, the supervisor conducts an exit interview, which provides an assessment of the intern's accomplishments, as well as feedback from the intern about the strengths and weaknesses of the program.

GETTING HIRED

Apply by: Rolling. Applications available online at sfopera.com/mi_emp_interns.asp.

Qualifications:
Open to all college freshmen, sophomores, juniors and seniors, recent college graduates and grad students. International applicants welcome.

Contact:
Internship Coordinator
San Francisco Opera
301 Van Ness Avenue
San Francisco, CA 94102
Phone: (415) 861-4008
E-mail: ejohnson@sfopera.com
sfopera.com/mi_emp_interns.asp

Scandinavia House (The American-Scandinavian Foundation)

THE BUZZ
- "Get a little taste of Scandinavia in the middle of New York"
- "Help expose Americans to another culture"

THE STATS

Industry(ies): Nonprofit

Location(s): New York, NY

Number of interns: Varies

Pay: None

Length of internship: Varies; available year-round

THE SCOOP

The American-Scandinavian Foundation is a nonprofit dedicated to promoting Scandinavian culture in the U.S. and improving relations between America and Scandinavian countries. It is headquartered at New York City's Scandinavia House: The Nordic Center in America, which acts as a cultural center for Americans and Scandinavians. The organization was founded in 1910.

ON THE JOB

Interns work on a variety of duties at the Scandinavia House. They can specialize in one of the following areas, or combine interests and roles: ushering, program assistance, library, public relations, information desk, children's programs and administration. Work hours are available during the days, in evenings and on weekends.

GETTING HIRED

Apply by: Rolling. Send resume to the address below.

Qualifications:

Open to high school students; college freshmen, sophomores, juniors and seniors; grad students; and college graduates of all ages.

Contact:
Lynn Carter
Scandinavia House
The Nordic Center in America
58 Park Avenue
New York, NY 10016
Phone: (212) 879-9779
E-mail: lcarter@amscan.org
www.amscan.org

Schlumberger

THE BUZZ
- "Discover a new oil well"
- "Find out what it's like to manage an oil rig"

THE STATS

Industry(ies): Energy/Utilities; Technology

Location(s): Sugarland, TX (HQ)

Number of interns: *Summer*: 500

Pay: Paid; $525-$825/week

Length of internship: *Summer*: 12 weeks

THE SCOOP

Established in 1927, Schlumberger Limited is a global oilfield information services company with major activity in the energy industry. The company employs 57,000 people in over 100 countries around the world. Its services range from oil exploration and offshore drilling to software and hardware development, while its work in measurements and systems focuses on the manufacture of electricity, water and gas meters, which accounts for its recent revenues of $13.2 billion.

ON THE JOB

Schlumberger interns are placed in one of two areas. Interns can work in the oilfield engineering or operations departments. The oilfield department concentrates on programs for students pursuing careers as engineers, scientists and researchers in other areas. Interns in the oilfield department work with crews on an operating base. The operations department offers interns the chance to work on projects outdoors; this sometimes involves challenging weather conditions where real problems may arise.

GETTING HIRED

Apply by: *Summer*: March 31. Submit a resume and cover letter to the address below.

Qualifications:

Open to college seniors, recent college graduates and grad students. International applicants welcome.

Contact:
Recruiting Manager
Schlumberger
300 Schlumberger Drive
Sugarland, TX 77478
Phone: (281) 285-7173
E-mail: recruiting@slb.com
www.careers.slb.com/oncampus/132_internships.cfm

Visit Vault at **www.vault.com** for insider company profiles, expert advice, career message boards, expert resume reviews, the Vault Job Board and more.

VAULT CAREER LIBRARY 365

Science

 THE BUZZ

- "Investigate the latest issues affecting scientific development"
- "Share your thirst for knowledge with leaders in the scientific community"

THE STATS

Industry(ies): Journalism; Publishing; Science/Research

Location(s): Washington, DC

Number of interns: 2 per semester

Pay: Paid; $400/week

Length of internship: *Spring/winter*: January-June; *summer/fall*: July-December

 THE SCOOP

Founded in 1880 by Thomas Edison, *Science* magazine is the premier scientific journal informing the scientific community about science and policy issues. *Science* is now the world's largest circulating weekly of scientific research with over 700,000 subscribers and is published by the American Association for the Advancement of Science. In recent years, *Science* has published landmark papers in fields ranging from molecular genetics to exobiology to condensed matter physics. An August 1996 story on the discovery of possible evidence of primitive life on Mars attracted worldwide attention to the magazine, as well as to current U.S. and international studies using recently launched probes.

 ON THE JOB

Science interns contribute to all facets of the magazine. Working as news writers, they do actual reporting, research, writing and editing under weekly deadlines, and assist with Science Now, the magazine's online database. Interns' duties may include conducting extensive research, writing news stories, assisting in production, filling in for absent staffers and providing help in all areas for staff writers and editors. Past interns have written an average of five to 10 stories with bylines and another 10 or so without.

GETTING HIRED

Apply by: *Winter/spring*: November 1; *smmer/fall*: April 1. Send to the address below a resume, cover letter (indicating the type of internship [volunteer or paid] and the department/program sponsoring the internship), published writing samples and references.

Qualifications:

Open to college seniors with interest, and preferably experience, in writing about science.

Contact:

Dawn Graf, Senior Human Resources Officer
Science Intern Program
1200 New York Avenue, NW, #102
Washington, DC 20005
www.sciencemag.org

Science News

 THE BUZZ

- "Get paid to pursue your passion for science"
- "Test your scientific skills with the big guys"

 **THE STATS**

Industry(ies): Journalism; Science/Research

Location(s): Washington, DC

Number of interns: *Spring/summer/fall*: 1 each

Pay: Paid; $1,800/month

Length of internship: *Spring*: January-April; *summer*: May-August; *fall*: September-December

 THE SCOOP

Science News started in 1922 as a newsletter that covered a weekly summary of science-specific events. It grew into a primary source of science news, eliciting numerous requests from libraries, schools and individuals for direct access to the reports from the early days of atomic energy to the beginnings of modern genetics. *Science News* has since emerged as a National Science Board award-winning publication that remains the only weekly newsmagazine of science published in the United States. *Science News* reaches about 200,000 readers and has covered recent topics such as climate change, dinosaurs, unusual critter behavior, human psychology, planetary studies and cosmology.

 ON THE JOB

Interns are hired as full-time writers under the guidance of editors and experienced science writers. Interns learn about the magazine as they cover scientific publications and meetings. They are also encouraged to conceptualize their own story ideas, while reporting and writing one or two published articles per week, including news stories and longer features.

GETTING HIRED

Apply by: *Spring*: October 15; *summer*: February 1; *fall*: June 15. Send resume, cover letter indicating intended start date, names of three references, and at least three scientific writing samples to the address below.

Qualifications:

Open to grad students studying science writing, but recent college graduates are occasionally hired. Skilled writers working toward an advanced degree in one of the sciences are also considered.

Contact:

Science News Internship
1719 N Street, NW
Washington, DC 20036
www.sciencenews.org

Scott Rudin Productions

 THE BUZZ
- "Entertainment savvy interns wanted"
- "A back door to the world of independent producing"

 THE STATS

Industry(ies): Broadcast & Entertainment; Film; Theater/Performing Arts

Location(s): Los Angeles, CA; New York, NY

Number of interns: *Spring/summer/fall*: 18 each

Pay: None. Breakfast and lunch provided. Occasional free tickets to film screenings

Length of internship: *Spring/summer/fall*: 6-12 weeks each

 THE SCOOP

Operating through Disney Studios, Scott Rudin Productions is a leading independent producer of diverse film and theater productions. The company's first production was the Oscar-winning documentary *He Makes Me Feel Like Dancin'* (1983), followed by *Mrs. Soffel* (1984). Scott Rudin Productions is most recently credited with the films *Sister Act*, *Sabrina*, *Zoolander* and *The Hours*, as well as a Broadway production of *Passion*, which won the Tony Award for Best Musical in 1984.

ON THE JOB

Interns work in the film and production departments. Daily duties include script reading, assisting with castings, general office management, mail sorting and helping to read and analyze manuscripts, screenplays and stage plays.

GETTING HIRED

Apply by: Rolling. Submit a resume and cover letter to the address below.

Qualifications:
Open to all college freshmen, sophomores, juniors and seniors, recent college graduates and grad students.

Contact:
Los Angeles office
Internship Coordinator
Scott Rudin Productions
Walt Disney Studios
500 South Buena Vista Street
Burbank, CA 91521-1759
Phone: (818) 560-4600

New York office
Internship Coordinator
Scott Rudin Productions
120 West 45th Street, 10th Floor
New York, NY 10036

Scripps Institution of Oceanography

 THE BUZZ
- "Help save the ocean's most precious creatures"
- "An in-depth introduction to marine research"

THE STATS

Industry(ies): Education; Environmental; Science/Research

Location(s): La Jolla, CA

Number of interns: *Summer*: 20+

Pay: *Summer*: $2,500 stipend. On-campus housing

Length of internship: *Summer*: June-August

 THE SCOOP

The Scripps Institution was founded in 1903 as an independent biological research laboratory with the mission "to seek, teach, and communicate scientific understanding of the oceans, atmosphere, Earth, and other planets for the benefit of society and the environment." The Institution has been a part of the University of California since 1912 and conducts marine research, graduate training and public service. Scripps staffs about 1,300, including 90 faculty members, 300 other scientists and approximately 200 graduate students. Its annual expenditures total over $140 million. Scripps conducts more than 300 studies, including the "topography of the ocean bottom, the flow and interchange of matter between seawater, earthquakes, the physiology of marine animals, marine chemistry, beach erosion, the marine food chain, the ecology of marine organisms, the geological history of the ocean basins," to name just a few. Scripps also operates a fleet of four ships and the platform FLIP for oceanographic research. Cruises range from local, limited-objective trips to far-reaching expeditions in the world's oceans.

 ON THE JOB

The Summer Training Academy for Research in the Sciences (STARS) Program – available not only to the Scripps Institution but to all departments related to the sciences, including engineering, physics, bioengineering, etc. – is designed to introduce undergraduates to research in the marine and earth sciences. The intensive SURF research training experience prepares students to become research scholars and stimulates serious consideration for graduate study.

GETTING HIRED

Apply by: *Summer*: February 15. Send to the address below a personal statement, a list of three requested UCSD faculty mentors, two letters of reference from faculty members at your school, and a copy of your current transcript. See http://www-ogsr.ucsd.edu/stars/index.htm for further application details.

Qualifications:
Open to college sophomores, juniors and seniors, recent college graduates and master's students with a GPA of at least 3.3 who plan to enroll in a PhD program at a university.

Contact:
Office of Graduate Studies and Research
University of California, San Diego
9500 Gilman Drive – Mail Code 0003
La Jolla, CA 92093-0003
E-mail: stars@ucsd.edu

Visit Vault at **www.vault.com** for insider company profiles, expert advice, career message boards, expert resume reviews, the Vault Job Board and more.

V∧ULT CAREER LIBRARY **367**

The Seattle Times

 THE BUZZ

- "Hone your journalism skills at an award-winning newspaper"
- "Get published and get paid!"

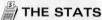 **THE STATS**

Industry(ies): Journalism

Location(s): Seattle, WA

Number of interns: *Summer*: 10

Pay: Paid; $525/week

Length of internship: *Summer*: 12 weeks

THE SCOOP

Owned and operated by the Seattle Times Company, *The Seattle Times* is the largest daily newspaper in Washington State and the largest Sunday circulation newspaper in the Northwest. The *Times* was founded in 1896 and has grown to serve more than 1.5 million readers with a weekly subscription base of 475,000. The newspaper is respected for both its comprehensive local coverage and its national and international reporting. The *Times* has won seven Pulitzer Prizes as well as awards in photojournalism and design.

ON THE JOB

Interns get a hands-on learning experience designed to train future journalists. They work in the reporting, copyediting, photo and graphics departments and focus on personal career development and print journalism. Interns are assigned to work with a staff member who guides them in a variety of projects. Interns are also encouraged to participate in meetings and be as active in the company as possible.

GETTING HIRED

Apply by: *Summer*: November 1. Send to the address below a cover letter, a resume, three references, and a one-page essay describing your reasons for entering journalism and a particular field (i.e., reporting, photography). Also send a duplicate copy of your resume via e-mail to newsinternships@seattletimes.com. *Reporting applicants*: Submit 5 samples of reporting work (photocopies only). *Copy Editing applicants*: Must have strong language skills and some editing experience. *Photojournalism applicants*: Submit 20 samples of your work in the form of CDs, print, slides and/or clips. *Graphics/design applicants*: 20 samples of page designs, illustrations, infographics or clips. Must have strong computer and design skills.

Qualifications:

Open to college sophomores, juniors and seniors and graduate student journalism majors or those who have a demonstrated commitment to print journalism. Previous internship at a daily newspaper is a plus. Applicants must have their own equipment and a car.

Contact:
Newsroom Internship Coordinator
The Seattle Times
P.O. Box 70
Seattle, WA 98111-0070
Phone: (206) 464-2414
Fax: (206) 464-2322
E-mail: newsinternships@seattletimes.com
www.seattletimescompany.com/newsroom/summer.htm

SeaWorld

 **THE BUZZ**
- "Spend a summer with Shamu and the crew"
- "Get wet and wild this summer with the sea folks"

 THE STATS

Industry(ies): Education; Science/Research; Tourism/Recreation

Location(s): Orlando, FL

Number of interns: *Summer*: 25

Pay: Paid; minimum wage. Free passes to SeaWorld, Busch Gardens and Adventure Island; discount on park food and merchandise

Length of internship: *Summer*: May 21-August 3

THE SCOOP

SeaWorld Orlando is the premiere marine adventure park with over 80 million visitors enjoying its 200 acres of shows, rides and animals. Animal adventures include encounters with killer whales, dolphins, sea lions and stingrays. SeaWorld's family programs including swimming with sharks, and sea lion and otter shows.

ON THE JOB

Interns must complete two weeks of training, during which they receive department orientation and information on the animals and camp procedures. Upon completion, interns work through Camp SeaWorld and SeaWorld/Busch Gardens Adventure Camp. Full-time staffers supervise work with campers, including a variety of crafts, games and activities such as snorkeling and canoeing. Intern duties may include preparing for classes, registering campers, teaching classes and assisting camp management with daily operations.

GETTING HIRED

Apply by: *Summer*: April 30. Send cover letter, resume, official college transcript, recommendation form and a completed application (downloadable at www.seaworld.org/career-resources/internship/index.htm) to the address below.

Qualifications:

Open to college students who have completed their sophomore year in good standing at a recognized academic institution and who seek degrees in education, science or recreation. Teaching experience and a basic knowledge of marine life are helpful.

Contact:
Camp SeaWorld Internship Program, Education Department
Sea World of Orlando
7007 Sea World Drive
Orlando, FL 32821
Phone: (800) 406-2244 or (407) 363-2380
Fax: (407) 363-2399
E-mail: SWF-CSWInterns@seaworld.com
www.seaworld.org

Sesame Workshop

 **THE BUZZ**
- "A great place for those who love children and fun"
- "Learn how to spell SUCCESS"

THE STATS

Industry(ies): Broadcast & Entertainment; Education; Nonprofit

Location(s): New York, NY

Number of interns: *Annual*: 60

Pay: None. Possible stipend for lunch and travel

Length of internship: *Summer/fall/winter/spring*: 12 weeks

 THE SCOOP

In operation since 1968, the Sesame Workshop is a nonprofit organization that utilizes the power of television, radio, magazines, books and outreach programs to educate millions of children, parents and teachers worldwide. The workshop produces the groundbreaking *Sesame Street*, as well as children's merchandise, games and software.

ON THE JOB

Interns work in a variety of divisions, including production, research, international, publishing, community education service, new show projects and human resources. Interns also interact with the staff on all levels at meetings and may observe show tapings.

GETTING HIRED

Apply by: Rolling. Mail a resume and cover letter to the address below.

Qualifications:
Open to all college freshmen, sophomores, juniors and seniors, college graduates and grad students. International applicants welcome.

Contact:
Internship Coordinator
Sesame Workshop
One Lincoln Plaza, 4th Floor
New York, NY 10023
Fax: (212) 875-6088
www.sesameworkshop.org/aboutus/involved_jobs.php

Visit Vault at **www.vault.com** for insider company profiles, expert advice, career message boards, expert resume reviews, the Vault Job Board and more.

VAULT CAREER LIBRARY **369**

Seventeen Magazine

 THE BUZZ

- "Express yourself to the youth of America"
- "Be a teen role model"

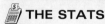 **THE STATS**

Industry(ies): Journalism; Publishing

Location(s): New York, NY

Number of interns: *Spring*: 5-10; *summer* (2 sessions): 12-15 each session; *fall*: 5-10

Pay: None; academic credit. Free magazines and t-shirts; seminars with editors and magazine executives; opportunity to help coordinate fashion shows (marketing interns); "young, hip" office environment

Length of internship: *Fall*: September-January; *spring*: February-May; *summer* sessions (6 weeks each): May-July and July-August

 **THE SCOOP**

Started in 1944, *Seventeen* magazine was the first magazine to target the teen market (girls and young women, ages 12-24). Devoted to fashion and issues relating to teenage girls (as well the latest gossip on the hottest new stars), it has a circulation of 2.3 million.

 **ON THE JOB**

Interns work in the editorial department, which includes fashion, beauty, editorial, public relations, and art and production. Interns function as direct assistants to staff members, performing tasks for the upkeep of the magazine. Duties are divided among departments and vary according to the needs of the magazine, but often include administrative and scheduling tasks.

$ GETTING HIRED

Apply by: Rolling. Send resume, cover letter (detailing applicant's strengths, schedule and level of commitment), and any clips or evidence of work experience (photographs, yearbook layouts, etc.) to the address below.

Qualifications:
Open to college freshmen, sophomores, juniors and seniors who possess a strong interest in journalism, art, production, fashion, PR or entertainment.

Contact:
Contact: Megan Brady
Internship Coordinator
Seventeen Magazine
850 Third Avenue, 9th Floor
New York, NY 10022
Phone: (212) 407-9700
Fax: (212) 204-3977
www.seventeen.com

Shaver's Creek Environmental Center

 THE BUZZ

- "Get a lesson on the environment at Penn State"
- "Do something notable to help the planet"

THE STATS

Industry(ies): Education; Environmental

Location(s): Petersburg, PA

Number of interns: *Annual*: 15

Pay: $150 weekly stipend. Free private rooms; computer access; career development

Length of internship: *Winter/spring*: January-May; *summer*: June-August; *fall*: September-December

THE SCOOP

Founded in 1976, Shaver's Creek Environmental Center is a division of Penn State University, which provides outreach in environmental education through instruction, service and research. Each year, more than 100,000 individuals interact with the Center's environmental education and training programs and follow its mission to "live and interact harmoniously with each other and the natural world."

ON THE JOB

Interns complete a comprehensive two-week training period, after which they become an integral part of the staff and participate in all aspects of the Center's operations. Interns work full-time with the staff as they engage in visitor center operations, animal care, natural history programs for the public, summer camps, residential environment education programs, recreational programs, weekend events and festivals, team building programs, curriculum development and writing articles for the member's newsletter. Staff members serve as mentors and provide interns with evaluation and feedback through observations and videotaping.

$ GETTING HIRED

Apply by: Rolling. Applications are accepted until all positions are filled. Submit resume, cover letter and three references to the address below. Complete the application available at: www.shaverscreek.org/ShaversCreek/joinus/internship.asp.

Qualifications:
Open to all college students and graduates. Experience working with youth desired.

Contact:
Attention: Internship Coordinator
Shaver's Creek Environmental Center
3400 Discovery Road
Petersburg, PA 16669
E-mail: ShaversCreek@outreach.psu.edu
www.shaverscreek.org

Sherwin-Williams

 THE BUZZ
- "Paint a path for your future"
- "Customer service enthusiasts wanted"

THE STATS

Industry(ies): Consumer Products; Manufacturing; Retail

Location(s): Locations throughout the U.S.

Number of interns: *Annual*: 100-200

Pay: Paid; competitive salary based on skills

Length of internship: *Summer*: 9-12 weeks (May-September) and possibly up to 6 months

 THE SCOOP

The Sherwin-Williams Company was founded in 1866 and is currently the largest paint company in the U.S. With over 2,200 stores nationwide, the company provides services and products in painting, chemical coating, color consulting, and tools and supplies. It boasts approximately $5 billion in annual sales and over 25,000 employees. Sherwin-Williams also ranked among the top U.S. Fortune 400 companies.

 ON THE JOB

The Sherwin-Williams Company offers internships at many locations in Ohio and Kentucky. The internship is a nine- to 12-week structured program designed for business students who are interested in learning about the company and its products, and about the retail and manufacturing industries. Duties may involve management, sales and customer service.

GETTING HIRED

Apply by: Rolling. Submit a resume and cover letter to the recruitment contact in your area (see web site).

Qualifications:
Open to college juniors and seniors with a GPA of 2.5 or higher.

Contact:
Stephen Eich — Area Recruitment Specialist
The Sherwin-Williams Company
10740-C Broadway Avenue
Garfield Heights, OH 44125
See the web site for the recruitment contact in your area:
www2.sherwin-williams.com/recruitment/career_paths/MTP/internship.asp

Visit Vault at **www.vault.com** for insider company profiles, expert advice, career message boards, expert resume reviews, the Vault Job Board and more.

VAULT CAREER LIBRARY **371**

Sierra Club

THE BUZZ

- "Environmentally conscious? This internship is for you"
- "Increase awareness about the earth's ecosystem"

THE STATS

Industry(ies): Environmental; Nonprofit

Location(s): Alton, IL; San Diego, CA; San Francisco, CA; Sheridan, WY; Washington, DC

Number of interns: *Annual*: 30-50

Pay: None

Length of internship: *Winter/spring*: January-April; *summer*: May-August; *fall*: September-December

THE SCOOP

The Sierra Club was founded in 1892 with 182 charter members and John Muir as its first elected president. Its mission is to "educate and inspire humanity to be responsible to the earth's ecosystem and its limited resources." The Sierra Club has since grown to over 700,000 members and is one of the foremost conservation organizations today. The Sierra Club has worked with Yosemite and Yellowstone national parks. The organization has also helped get the Clean Water Act and the Endangered Species Act passed, as well as the Alaska National Interest Lands Conservation Act, which will preserve over 100 million acres of wildlife refuges and wilderness.

ON THE JOB

Sierra Club internships can vary by location (there are many chapters) and department. Some notable areas include law, politics and the media. Some interns may be able to "attend meetings related to other fields, monitor hearings, prepare briefing materials and research information on a particular meeting." Political interns assist the director of a particular political system of interest to Sierra Club activities. They may monitor elections, attend political meetings, or research candidates, organizations and related issues. Media interns help prepare "press releases, fact sheets and other materials geared for use by Washington-based reporters, editors and producers." They also write editorials and are often given special projects. Many other internships are available.

GETTING HIRED

Apply by: Various dates. See site internship descriptions for specific dates. Submit resume, cover letter and possibly a two-to five-page writing sample (depending on position). Indicate in the cover letter your specific interest, experience in environmental issues and availability. Search Sierra Club web site (www.sierraclub.org) for "internships" to get a complete list of available positions.

Qualifications:
Open to all college freshmen, sophomores, juniors and seniors, as well as grad students enrolled in a degree program.

Contact:
Washington, DC, chapter
Jeremy Peizer
Sierra Club
408 C Street, NE
Washington, DC 20002
Phone: (202) 675-7905
E-mail: dc-internships@sierraclub.org
www.sierraclub.org
See web site for other chapters

Silicon Graphics, Inc.

 THE BUZZ
- "Make an impact in high-performance computing"

 THE STATS

Industry(ies): Hardware; Software; Technology

Location(s): Chippewa Falls, WI; Eagan, MN; Mountain View, CA (HQ); Silver Spring, MD

Number of interns: *Summer*: 30

Pay: Paid. Salary dependent upon qualifications. BBQ with the CEO; baseball games; brown bag speaker series; paid holidays; relocation and transportation assistance for eligible students

Length of internship: *Summer*: 10-12 weeks (May-August or June-September)

 THE SCOOP

Silicon Graphics, Inc. (SGI) provides high-performance computing, visualization and storage products, services and solutions to scientific, engineering and creative users worldwide. SGI garnered $970 million in revenues for fiscal year 2003, and the company's products, services and mission-are critical to defense and security, science and research, manufacturing, energy and media industries. Whether it be sharing images to aid in brain surgery, finding oil more efficiently, studying the global climate or aiding transition from analog to digital broadcasting, SGI is committed to addressing the next class of challenges for scientific, engineering and creative users.

ON THE JOB

SGI interns work directly with some of the top professionals in the field who push them to challenge themselves. Assignments may include technical support, software development, marketing, human resources and customer service. Interns are also involved in updating software and running QA tests.

GETTING HIRED

Apply by: Rolling. Apply online at www.sgi.com/careers.

Qualifications:
Open to sophomore, junior and senior undergraduates who have completed at least their freshman year, as well as master's, MBA or PhD students pursuing a technical degree or focusing on finance, marketing, human resources, logistics or financial planning.

Contact:
Silicon Graphics, Inc.
Internship Coordinator
100 North Crashman Drive
Chippewa Falls, WI 54729
www.sgi.com/employment/university/interncoop.html

Simon and Goodman Picture Company

 THE BUZZ
- "You could be making beautiful pictures"
- "An independent inroad to the film industry"

 THE STATS

Industry(ies): Broadcast & Entertainment; Film

Location(s): New York, NY

Number of interns: *Spring/summer/fall*: 6 each

Pay: None

Length of internship: *Spring/summer/fall*: 10-16 weeks each

 THE SCOOP

The Simon and Goodman Picture Company was founded in 1987 by independent filmmakers Kirk Simon and Karen Goodman as a film and television production business. It produces programs broadcast on PBS, HBO and National Geographic television. The company received three Academy Award nominations and three Emmy Awards, as well as the DuPont-Columbia Silver Baton Award for Independent Programming. Some joint projects include commercials, corporate and promotional videos and political ads. The firm is currently producing two documentaries for HBO and is in the pre-production phase of a National Geographic special.

ON THE JOB

Interns function as assistants in the production, editing and research departments, implementing a variety of tasks, including general administrative duties, working through the editing process, tracking and engaging in all areas of production. Interns also have direct interaction with the filmmakers and attend film shoots.

GETTING HIRED

Apply by: Rolling. Submit a resume and cover letter to the address below.

Qualifications:
Open to college juniors and seniors, as well as grad students. Film students are preferred.

Contact:
Simon and Goodman Picture Company
Attention: Internship Coordinator
2095 Broadway, Suite 402
New York, NY 10023
Fax: (212) 721-0922
www.sgpic.com

Visit Vault at **www.vault.com** for insider company profiles, expert advice, career message boards, expert resume reviews, the Vault Job Board and more.

 **373**

Skadden, Arps, Slate, Meagher & Flom LLP and Affiliates

 THE BUZZ
- "A high percentage of summer associates are offered full-time positions"
- "Intern at one of the most prominent law firms in the world"

 THE STATS

Industry(ies): Law

Location(s): Multiple U.S. and international cities

Number of interns: *Summer*: around 200

Pay: Paid; $2,800/week

Length of internship: *Summer*: 8-12 weeks

 THE SCOOP

Skadden, Arps, Slate, Meagher & Flom LLP (Skadden) staffs about 1,750 attorneys, all of whom work on a broad variety of legal services. Skadden's clients range from small high-tech start-ups to huge corporations and governmental entities. Marshall Skadden, Les Arps and John Slate opened the firm in 1948 (Bill Meagher and Joe Flom were added to the signage in the 1960s). The firm has always held a strong commitment to public service. Even senior attorneys spend a significant amount of time on pro bono cases. Every year, the firm's Skadden Fellowship Foundation provides two-year fellowships to support 25 young lawyers working full-time on public interest law.

 ON THE JOB

Summer associates often make up Skadden's first hiring pool, and therefore their work is a hardcore, get-your-feet-wet training program. Associates work on cases similar to full-time Skadden attorneys. Though associates work in a variety of areas, over 90 percent of summer associates also work on pro bono cases, as the firm places a strong emphasis on public service law.

(💰) GETTING HIRED

Apply by: Most interns are chosen from on-campus interviews conducted at 50 law schools (a list of which is predetermined by Skadden) every fall and spring, but others are encouraged to apply by contacting the recruitment coordinator of the location where they want to work. Fill out an application at www.skadden.com/recruiting/attorneys_hiring_summer_application.html.

Qualifications:
Generally open to second-year law students only. However, a few first-year students are sometimes hired.

Contact:
Howard L. Ellin
Skadden, Arps, Slate, Meagher & Flom LLP
Four Times Square
New York, NY 10036
Phone: (212) 735-3000
Fax: (212) 735-2000
E-mail: nystuhire@skadden.com
www.skadden.com/recruiting/home.html

Smithsonian Institution

 THE BUZZ
- "The American museumopolis"

 THE STATS

Industry(ies): Art/Museum; Education; Science/Research

Location(s): New York, NY; Washington, DC; Panama

Number of interns: *Annual*: 900

Pay: Paid; varies

Length of internship: Varies

 **THE SCOOP**

The Smithsonian Institution was established in 1846 when English scientist James Smithson left his fortune to the people of the United States for founding an organization to "increase the diffusion of knowledge among men." Millions of sightseers visit the Smithsonian, which is now the world's largest museum complex. The Smithsonian is composed of a group of national museums and research centers that house the U.S. collections in natural history, American history, air and space, the fine arts and the decorative arts, as well as several other fields ranging from postal history to cultural records. The Smithsonian is made up of of 17 museums and galleries, the National Zoo, numerous research facilities in the United States and abroad, the Smithsonian Institution Libraries (a research library system), *Smithsonian* magazine, a traveling exhibition service and an education office.

 ON THE JOB

An internship at the Smithsonian Institute is a structured learning experience that is programmed to the individual's academic and professional goals. Duties are performed under the direct supervision of Smithsonian staff.

 GETTING HIRED

Apply by: Generally, *spring*: October 15; *summer*: February 1; *fall*: June 15. Submit required materials as listed on the web site (varies for different opportunities) to the appropriate internship coordinator at the museum, office or research institute you are interested in, or through the Internship Central Referral Service offered by the Smithsonian Center for Education and Museum Studies. See http://intern.si.edu for further details.

Qualifications:
Open to college seniors, grad students and recent college graduates.

Contact:
Office of Research Training and Services
Smithsonian Institution
MRC 902 P.O. Box 37012
Victor Building, Suite 9300 MRC 902
Washington, DC 20013-7012
Phone: (202) 275-0655
E-mail: siofg@si.edu
www.si.edu/research+study

Sony

 THE BUZZ
- "Learn from one of the world's leading electronics makers"

THE STATS

Industry: Consumer Products; Engineering; Technology

Location(s): Park Ridge, NJ; Tokyo, Japan

Number of interns: *Annual:* 75-80

Pay: Paid; $300-600/week, depending on credentials. Free housing in Tokyo

Length of internship: *Fall/spring:* 10 weeks each; *summer (minority internships):* 10 weeks

THE SCOOP

Sony, not to be confused with Sony Music and Sony Pictures, focuses on electronics. The firm started out making transistor radios for the news-hungry population of war-battered Tokyo in 1945. Workers were paid in raw rice (thus leading to the electric rice cooker). By the end of 1945, Sony had moved on to produce vacuum tube voltmeters and similar gadgets.

ON THE JOB

Interns help Sony develop, test and market new products. Positions are available in engineering, research, marketing and sales, the first two departments requiring applicants to possess technological training and know-how.

GETTING HIRED

Apply by: Rolling. Internships are available year-round.

Qualifications:
Open to college freshmen, sophomores, juniors and seniors. Must be a science/engineering/math major for the engineering and research departments or a finance/business/accounting major for other departments.

Contact:
New Jersey office
Internship Coordinator
Sony Corporation of America
1 Sony Drive
Park, Ridge, NJ 07656
Phone: (201) 930-1000

Japan office
Internship Coordinator
Sony Corporation
6-7-35 Kitashinagawa
Sinagawa-ku, Tokyo, 141 Japan
Phone: 81-3-5448-5770
E-mail: intlgp@jinji.sony.co.jp
www.sony.com/SCA/job.shtml

Visit Vault at **www.vault.com** for insider company profiles, expert advice, career message boards, expert resume reviews, the Vault Job Board and more.

VAULT CAREER LIBRARY **375**

Sony BMG Music Entertainment

 THE BUZZ
- "Celine Dion and Jennifer Lopez will be your co-workers"
- "Get experience at a label with worldwide name recognition"

 **THE STATS**

Industry(ies): Broadcast & Entertainment; Music/Records

Location(s): New York, NY (HQ); Santa Monica, CA; field offices in CA, GA, IL, MA, MD, NY, OH and TX

Number of interns: *Spring/summer/fall (credited internship)*: 100; *summer (minority interns)*: 70

Pay: *Spring/summer/fall (credited)*: none; academic credit; *summer (minority)*: varies with position. Promotional freebies; seminars and trips; invitations to listening parties

Length of internship: *Summer/fall/spring*: 10 weeks each

 THE SCOOP

In 1986, Sony acquired CBS Records, arguably the world's most successful record empire. The resulting division, Sony Music Entertainment, Inc. (SMEI), took over CBS Records' Columbia and Epic record labels and also established new labels such as Chaos Recordings and TriStar Music Group. Now, SMEI has an impossibly rich roster of artists, including the likes of Michael Jackson, Bruce Springsteen and Pearl Jam.

 ON THE JOB

SMEI runs two internship programs. The credited internship is open to undergraduate and graduate students who are able to secure academic credit for their work. The summer minority internship program is a paid experience for minority undergraduate and graduate students that is augmented by a number of seminars and training sessions. Interns are placed in departments including promotions, publicity, retail marketing, artists and repertoire (A&R), A&R Administration, business affairs, finance and MIS.

GETTING HIRED

Apply by: *Credit*: rolling; *minority*: April 1. Submit resume and cover letter.

Qualifications:
Credited internship program: open to college freshmen, sophomores, juniors and seniors, and grad students. Participants in this program must receive academic credit for their work.
Minority internship program: open to minority undergrad and grad students. Applicants must have at least a 3.0 GPA and be returning to school after their internship.

Contact:
Credited internship program
Sony Music Entertainment, Inc.
Credited Internship Program
550 Madison Avenue, 2nd Floor
New York, NY 10022-3211

Minority internship program
Sony Music Entertainment, Inc.
Minority Internship Program
550 Madison Avenue, 13th Floor
New York, NY 10022-3211
Attn: Department 13-5
Internship hotline: (212) 833-7980
www.sonymusic.com/about/jobs.html

Sony Pictures Entertainment

 THE BUZZ
- "Get to the back lot of the film biz"
- "Future production heads wanted"

 THE STATS

Industry(ies): Broadcast & Entertainment; Film

Location(s): Culver City, CA; New York, NY

Number of interns: *Annual*: 60

Pay: None. Free movie passes, promotional materials and admittance to screenings

Length of internship: *Spring/summer/fall*: 10-12 weeks

 THE SCOOP

Established in 1990, Sony Pictures Entertainment is one of the world's largest film and television companies, generating over $3 billion in revenues in 67 countries worldwide. Sony divisions include Columbia TriStar Television, Columbia TriStar Television Distribution, Columbia TriStar Home Video, Sony Theatres and Sony Pictures Classics.

ON THE JOB

Interns work through Sony's College Credit Internship Program or the Diversity Summer Internship Program. Both involve active intern participation in all facets of the inner workings of the business. Interns work on several projects and tasks, depending upon field of interest. Internships are frequently available in production, marketing, publicity and promotions.

GETTING HIRED

Apply by: Rolling. Submit resume and cover letter online at www.sonypicturesjobs.com.

Qualifications:
Open to all college freshmen, sophomores, juniors and seniors and recent college graduates. International applicants are eligible.

Contact:
California office
Sony Pictures Entertainment
Attention: Human Resources
10202 West Washington Blvd., Suite 3900
Culver City, CA 90232-3195
Phone: (310) 244-5158

New York office
Laura Mooney
Internship Coordinator
Sony Pictures Entertainment
550 Madison Avenue, 8th Floor
New York, NY 10022-3109
www.sonypictures.com

Sotheby's

 THE BUZZ
- "Great for fine art lovers"
- "Delve into your passion for the finer (and more expensive) things in life"

THE STATS

Industry(ies): Art/Museum

Location(s): New York, NY

Number of interns: *Annual*: 40-50

Pay: None

Length of internship: *Summer*: 8 weeks

 THE SCOOP

Founded in 1744 by Samuel Baker, Sotheby's is one of the oldest and largest fine art auctioneers in the world. Since then, Baker's original idea has expanded to include book auctions as well as fine and decorative arts that encompass more than 100 Sotheby's offices around the world. In 2000, Sotheby's became the first international art auction house to hold auctions on the Internet. Recent pieces sold through Sotheby's include portions of Sir Elton John's estate, 19th-century European art and furniture, wine, jewelry and fine china.

ON THE JOB

Interns work in business departments such as the press office, graphics or marketing, or in one of 33 expert departments such as American paintings or Chinese works of art. Every Tuesday, interns attend two-hour lectures to learn more about the business side of an auction house and the expert departments. Interns are assigned a mentor outside of the department in which they are interning. Three parties are thrown throughout the summer exclusively for the interns.

GETTING HIRED

Apply by: March 1. Submit a cover letter and resume, along with a request for an application, to the address below.

Qualifications:
Open to all college juniors and seniors, as well as recent college graduates. International applicants welcome.

Contact:
Sotheby's
Internship Coordinator
1334 York Avenue, 8th floor
New York, NY 10021
Phone: (212) 606-7000
www.sothebys.com

Visit Vault at **www.vault.com** for insider company profiles, expert advice, career message boards, expert resume reviews, the Vault Job Board and more.

VAULT CAREER LIBRARY **377**

Source Theatre Company

 THE BUZZ
- "Spend a summer immersed in the theater"
- "Not all the drama in DC is political"

 THE STATS

Industry(ies): Theater/Performing Arts

Location(s): Washington, DC

Number of interns: *Summer*: 20

Pay: None

Length of internship: *Summer*: 8-10 weeks

 **THE SCOOP**

Since its inception in 1977, the Source Theatre Company has been a residence for established and new artists in Washington, DC, that provides the community each season with new plays, contemporary works and reinterpretations of classical pieces. The Source also produces an award-winning annual Washington Theatre Festival that has been credited with developing over 70 new plays through workshops, readings, a Junior Festival and a 10-minute play competition. *The Washington Post* gave Source the Distinguished Community Service Award. The Company also received the Mayor's Arts Award for Excellence in Service to the Arts and has enjoyed over 30 Helen Hayes Award nominations.

ON THE JOB

Interns are responsible for the day-to-day upkeep and operations of the theater and are given clerical and research assignments by the staff. Duties are determined by various departments and include marketing, box office, stage management, technical work and administration.

GETTING HIRED

Apply by: Rolling. Submit resume and cover letter to the address below.

Qualifications:
Open to high school students, all undergraduates, recent college graduates, grad students and international applicants.

Contact:
Internship Coordinator
Source Theatre Company
1835 14th Street, NW
Washington, DC 20009
Phone: (202) 462-1073
Fax: (202) 462-2300
E-mail: Info@sourcetheater.com
www.sourcetheatre.com

The Source

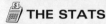 **THE BUZZ**
- "Be among the first to know the latest hip-hop news"
- "Get real, hands-on experience in music journalism"

THE STATS

Industry(ies): Broadcast & Entertainment; Journalism; Publishing

Location(s): New York, NY

Number of interns: *Spring/summer/fall*: 5-8 each

Pay: None

Length of internship: *Spring/summer/fall*: 12 weeks each

THE SCOOP

The Source magazine first hit the scene in 1988 when two of Harvard's radio disc jockeys, Jon Shecter and Dave Mays, used their dorm room to put together a simple newsletter answering their radio listeners' questions about hip-hop. Its first issue went out to 1,000 people in Harvard's listening vicinity. After graduation, Shecter and Mays, now also joined by two more Harvard students, James Bernard and Ed Young, moved the magazine to its New York office in 1991. *The Source* is now considered an established voice for the hip-hop genre.

ON THE JOB

Interns work in the editing or advertising departments. Responsibilities vary with current company needs. For the editorial intern: copyediting, proofreading, research for staff writers and writing short features; for the advertising intern: assisting the staff with leads, calling clients and handling administrative tasks. Interns gain valuable publishing experience and make professional contacts.

GETTING HIRED

Apply by: Rolling. Send a cover letter, resume and a writing sample to the address below.

Qualifications:
Open to high school students, college freshmen, sophomores, juniors and seniors, recent college graduates and grad students. International applicants welcome.

Contact:
Internship Coordinator
The Source
594 Broadway, Suite 510
New York, NY 10012
Phone: (212) 274-0464
Fax: (212) 274-8334
www.thesource.com

South Seas Resort

 THE BUZZ
- "A sunny entree into the hospitality industry"
- "Work and have fun in the Florida sun"

 THE STATS

Industry(ies): Hospitability; Tourism/Recreation

Location(s): Captiva Island, FL

Number of interns: *Annual*: 13-15

Pay: $50/week. Free housing; $20/day for meals; access to all recreational facilities; discounts on water sports and retail shops; free uniform shirts and jackets

Length of internship: *Spring/summer/fall*: 13-15 weeks

 THE SCOOP

Established on Captiva Island in 1990, the South Seas Resort is a 330-acre botanical paradise that boasts miles of sparkling white beaches. Described as "Florida's Tahiti" by *Travel and Leisure* magazine, South Seas offers 21 tennis courts, as well as golfing by the sea, swimming pools, water sports, a marina, and a health and fitness center.

 ON THE JOB

Interns work in the recreation department planning social activities, corporate events and holiday activities. They also assist in coordinating special events such as beach Olympics, golf tournaments and holiday festivities.

GETTING HIRED

Apply by: Rolling. Write to the address below for an application.

Qualifications:
Open to college seniors, recent college graduates and grad students. International applicants welcome.

Contact:
South Seas Resort
5400 Plantation Road
P.O. Box 194
Captiva, FL 33924
Phone: (239) 472-5111
Fax: (239) 472-7541
www.south-seas-resort.com

Visit Vault at **www.vault.com** for insider company profiles, expert advice, career message boards, expert resume reviews, the Vault Job Board and more.

VAULT CAREER LIBRARY **379**

Southern Center for International Studies

 THE BUZZ
- "Help inform the public of U.S. and international policy"

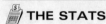 **THE STATS**

Industry(ies): Education; International Relations; Public Relations

Location(s): Atlanta, GA

Number of interns: *Annual*: 10-12

Pay: Paid; *research associate*: $11/hour plus health insurance; *research assistant*: $9/hour plus health insurance; *college-level intern*: stipend of an hourly minimum rate; *high-school intern*: unpaid; *marketing intern*: unpaid. Academic credit available

Length of internship: *High school/college-level/master's intern*: 1 semester, 20-40 hours/week; *research assistant/research associate*: 1 year, 40 hours/week; *marketing intern*: 1 semester, 20-40 hours/week

 THE SCOOP

Founded in 1962, the Southern Center for International Studies (SCIS) is a nonpartisan, nonprofit educational institution based in Atlanta, Georgia, working to internationalize the thinking of the American public by enhancing global awareness and understanding. The Center accomplishes its mission by developing *The World in Transition* series of educational packages, convening a series of educational conferences with national and world leaders, and providing local programs.

 ON THE JOB

The Center has three internship tiers: high school student interns, college-level student-interns and research associates (those with graduate degrees in hand). All interns provide the research support for the Southern Center's various publications and programs. The research team conducts research for and assists in the production of the Center's *World in Transition* series of educational materials and major televised conferences; produces updates on world regions for corporate members and local programs; and provides briefings on current international issues at Center workshops or to local community groups. High school interns are expected to complete a research project on an international policy topic and present their findings at a staff meeting.

The Center also offers internships for college students in the marketing and development department. Student interns will conduct research in the field of international education and assist in finding strategic partners and fundraising opportunities.

 GETTING HIRED

Apply by: Rolling. Submit a resume, cover letter, academic transcripts and letters of recommendation to the address below.

Qualifications:
Open to junior and senior high school students, college juniors and seniors, recent college graduates, grad students and international applicants. Minimum 3.0 GPA required. Marketing internship not open to high school students.

Contact:
Research Center internship
Ms. Bozena Radwanska Zayac, Director, Research Library
The Southern Center for International Studies
320 West Paces Ferry Road NW
Atlanta, GA 30305
Phone: (404) 261-5763, ext. 158
E-mail: bozena@scis.org
www.southerncenter.org
www.southerncenter.org/library.html

Marketing internship
Ms. Ilka Nickolov
Sr. Associate, Marketing and Development Department
The Southern Center for International Studies
320 West Paces Ferry Road
Atlanta, GA 30305
Phone: (404) 261-5763, ext. 140
E-mail: ilka@scis.org

Southern Progress Corporation

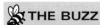 **THE BUZZ**
- "A great publishing internship for those not seeking the Big Apple"
- "One of the largest lifestyle publishers in the country"

 **THE STATS**

Industry(ies): Publishing

Location(s): Birmingham, AL

Number of interns: *Springsummer/fall*: 50 each

Pay: Paid; $10/hour

Length of internship: One summer or 6 months. *Spring*: January-June; *summer:* mid-May through Labor Day; *fall*: July-December. Full-time schedule of 37.5 hours/week

THE SCOOP

Southern Progress Corporation started in 1886 as a simple idea from Colonel Leonidas L. Polk, believing farmers needed a model for their industry. This family-owned company grew into one of the largest lifestyle publishers in the country and operates in 20 U.S. cities with over 1,500 employees. Publications include *Cottage Living*, *Coastal Living*, *Progressive Farmer*, *Southern Living*, *Health*, *Southern Accents*, *Cooking Light* and *Sunset*.

ON THE JOB

Since the internship program began in 1988, over 300 participants have been hired into full-time positions. Interns work in editorial, graphic design, marketing, accounting, advertising, test kitchens, product design, new media and photography. Each intern class participates in several activities, including professional development seminars, service projects, luncheons and after-work socials.

GETTING HIRED

Apply by: *Spring*: October 2; *summer:* February 7; *fall*: March 7.

Download and complete the application on the web site, at http://corp.southernprogress.com/spc/internships. Then e-mail two attachments, the completed application and other in a PDF, to spc_hrinterns@timeinc.com. In the PDF include a one-page cover letter, a resume (two pages maximum), and one to three recommendation letters. If interested in a design, editorial or public relations position, also include five pages maximum of writing or design samples in the PDF.

Qualifications:

Summer: Open to rising college juniors and seniors. *Six month (spring and fall):* Open to college seniors, recent college and master's program graduates (up to a year after graduation) and master's candidates.

Contact:
Meg Dedmon
Student Intern Coordinator
Southern Progress Corporation
2100 Lakeshore Drive
Birmingham, AL 32509
Phone: (205) 445-6000
E-mail: spc_hrinterns@timeinc.com
www.southernprogress.com

Southface Energy Institute

 THE BUZZ
- "Put your energy into improving the environment"

 THE STATS

Industry(ies): Energy/Utilities; Environmental; Nonprofit

Location(s): Atlanta, GA

Number of interns: *Annual*: 6-8

Pay: $335/month stipend. Free housing and utilities; free transportation (cars, bikes, public transportation)

Length of internship: *Spring/summer/fall*: 3-6 months

THE SCOOP

Founded in 1978, the Southface Energy Institute is a nonprofit organization that promotes livable homes, workplaces and communities through education and research, and advocates water and energy conservation, healthy indoor environments and clean air transportation. Southface offers programs on topics such as green building designs, products and practices, as well as livable community planning, sustainable transportation, energy efficiency, water conservation and sustainable landscaping. The Institute promotes over 100 energy-efficient and environmental technologies and concepts, including insulation systems, solar roof shingles, low-emissivity windows, geothermal heat pumps, drought-tolerant landscapes, solar water heaters and an aggressive day lighting strategy.

ON THE JOB

Interns work in areas including sustainable building and community design, energy engineering, resource-efficient landscaping, urban ecology, water quality, wildlife habitats, environmental journalism, environmental policy, public relations and marketing, and computers/graphic design. Interns may also have the opportunity to travel with Institute professionals to home audits and reviews, as well as attend all Southface programs.

GETTING HIRED

Apply by: Rolling. For a detailed description of the program and to apply, visit the Southface internship web site: www.southface.org/web/get_involved/staff_opportunities/sf_internships.htm.

Qualifications:
Open to all college freshmen, sophomores, juniors and seniors, recent college graduates and grad students. International applicants welcome.

Contact:
Southface Energy Institute
241 Pine Street
Atlanta, GA 30308
Phone: (404) 872-3549
Fax: (404) 872-5009
www.southface.org

Visit Vault at **www.vault.com** for insider company profiles, expert advice, career message boards, expert resume reviews, the Vault Job Board and more.

V∧ULT CAREER LIBRARY **381**

Southwest Airlines

 THE BUZZ
- "Ding! You are now free to advance your career"

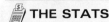 **THE STATS**

Industry(ies): Transportation

Location(s): Dallas, TX

Number of interns: *Annual:* Approximately 40

Pay: Paid; varies by department

Length of internship: *Spring:* 4 months (January start); *summer:* 3 months (June start); *fall:* 4 months (September start)

 **THE SCOOP**

What began as a small Texas airline has grown to become one of the largest airlines in America. Today, Southwest Airlines flies more than 65 million passengers a year to 59 cities across the country, with more than 2,800 flights a day. The focus of the A&E Television show *Airline*, Southwest is a model for other low-cost airlines.

ON THE JOB

The goal of the "No Limits" Internship Program is to provide interns with interactive learning opportunities and hands-on business experience. Each intern will be exposed to practical workplace skills needed for his/her business field. Positions are available in Corporate Communications, Dispatch, Flight Operations, Engineering, Flight Operations Publications, Marketing, Public Relations, Corporate Safety and Maintenance. In addition to a casual work environment, interns may also take advantage of free unlimited space-available flights anywhere the airline flies.

GETTING HIRED

Apply by: Rolling. Applicants must submit a cover letter, resume, copy of transcript (unofficial) and an original essay entitled "Why SWA". Letters of recommendation are optional and should be sent along with the other materials listed above. Public Relations applicants should also include a writing sample. Applicants for the Flight Operations Internship should include a copy of FAA Certificate/Ratings and Medical Certification (if applicable). Applicants for the Flight Operations Publications Internship should include two additional writing samples. Visit www.southwest.com /careers/interns/intern.html for more information.

Qualifications:

Open to college students enrolled in an accredited degree program with a 2.5 GPA. To be eligible, your graduation date must not be before or during the semester in which you apply. Applicants should also be team-oriented, self-motivated and energetic people.

Contact:
Lindsey Lang, College Recruiter
Southwest Airlines
People Department
P.O. Box 36611
HDQ 4HR
Dallas, TX 75235-1611
E-mail: NoLimits@wnco.com
www.southwest.com/careers/interns/intern.html

Southwestern Company

THE BUZZ
- "Learn how to run your own business"
- "Your career begins here!"

THE STATS

Industry(ies): Publishing; Retail

Location(s): Nashville, TN (HQ); Bristol

Number of interns: *Annual:* 3,400

Pay: Paid; varies based on on ability (the average first-year dealer profits $2,928/month or $113/day)

Length of internship: *Annual:* 3-6 months

THE SCOOP

Since 1868, the Southwestern Company has assisted students in financing their education through selling books. The company's mission is to help "students develop the skills and character they need to achieve their goals in life." The company promotes family-friendly reference books and software through a sales force of over 3,400 students each summer.

ON THE JOB

Technically, Southwestern does not "hire" students. Students who are selected are independent contractors – not employees of Southwestern. Students are taught how to run their own business during their summer breaks selling educational material to families in another state. They are not on a time-clock and they make decisions about every facet of their own work. They receive training throughout the school year and for five days in Nashville, Tenn. This is a very challenging program and is not for everyone.

GETTING HIRED

Apply by: Rolling. Apply online at www.southwestern.com/site/students/OnlineApplication.aspx.

Qualifications:

Open to college freshmen, sophomores, juniors and seniors, recent college graduates and grad students. International applicants welcome.

Contact:
International headquarters
The Southwestern Company
2451 Atrium Way
Nashville, TN 37214
Phone: (800) 843-6149
E-mail: sw@southwestern.com
www.southwestern.com

UK office
The Southwestern Company UK, Ltd.
Unit 4, Bakers Park
Cater Road, Bishopworth
Bristol, BS13 7TT
E-mail: sw@southwestern.co.uk

Special Olympics International

 THE BUZZ
- "Help motivate others to succeed"
- "Develop a sense of community spirit"

 THE STATS

Industry(ies): Nonprofit; Sports

Location(s): Washington, DC

Number of interns: *Spring/summer/fall*: 6-10 each

Pay: $35/week stipend. Luncheons with department heads; free t-shirt and merchandise

Length of internship: *Spring/summer/fall*: 8-12 weeks

 **THE SCOOP**

Founded in 1968 by Eunice Kennedy Shriver, Special Olympics International works to empower individuals with mental retardation to become physically fit, productive and respected members of society through sports training and competition. Special Olympics International currently services 1 million individuals in over 150 countries year-round, through training and competition in over 200 varieties of Olympic-type sports.

 ON THE JOB

With over 500,000 volunteers in more than 130 countries, interns work to provide individuals with improved fitness and motor skills, greater self confidence, a more positive self-image, friendships and increased family support. Volunteers work in areas such as sports, public affairs, chapter organizations, marketing, international programs, finance and administration.

 GETTING HIRED

Apply by: Rolling.

Qualifications:
Open to college juniors and seniors, as well as recent college graduates. International applicants welcome.

Contact:
Internship Coordinator
Special Olympics International
1325 G Street, NW, Suite 500
Washington, DC 20005
Phone: (202) 628-3630
www.specialolympics.org

Spin

 THE BUZZ
- "Major contacts in the music and publishing biz"

 **THE STATS**

Industry(ies): Journalism; Music/Records; Publishing

Location(s): New York, NY

Number of interns: *Spring/summer/fall*: 3-4 each

Pay: None. Free magazines, t-shirts and CDs

Length of internship: *Spring/summer/fall*: 16 weeks each

 THE SCOOP

First appearing in 1985, *Spin* is an informational music-focused magazine known for its youthful and opinionated slant. Ninety percent of its readership is in the 18- to 29-year-old age range. The magazine describes itself as "50 percent music news and 50 percent social and political coverage."

ON THE JOB

Interns work in editorial, advertising, marketing, information technology and public relations departments. Duties vary with department but may include fact-checking copy or clerical tasks.

GETTING HIRED

Apply by: *Spring*: November 15; *summer*: March 15; *fall*: July 15. Submit a resume and cover letter to the address below.

Qualifications:
Open to high school graduates, college freshmen, sophomores, juniors and seniors, and recent college graduates.

Contact:
SPIN Editorial Offices
Kyle Anderson
Editorial Intern Coordinator
205 Lexington Avenue, 3rd Floor
New York, NY 10016
Phone: (212) 231-7400
Fax: (212) 231-7312
www.spin.com

Editorial internship
E-mail: editintern@spin.com

IT internship
E-mail: itinterns@vibe.com

All other internships
E-mail: jobs@vibespin.com

Visit Vault at **www.vault.com** for insider company profiles, expert advice, career message boards, expert resume reviews, the Vault Job Board and more.

VAULT CAREER LIBRARY **383**

Spoleto Festival USA

 THE BUZZ
- "Experience European flavor in the heart of South Carolina"

 THE STATS

Industry(ies): Theater/Performing Arts

Location(s): Charleston, SC

Number of interns: Approximately 50

Pay: Paid; $250/week plus $50 travel stipend for out-of-state apprentices. Space-available admission to Festival events; housing at the College of Charleston; use of college gym and facilities

Length of internship: *Spring*: mid-May—mid-June

 THE SCOOP

For 17 days and nights each spring, Spoleto Festival USA fills Charleston, South Carolina's historic theaters, churches and outdoor spaces with over 120 performances by renowned artists, as well as emerging performers in disciplines ranging from opera, theater, music theater, dance and chamber, symphonic, choral, and jazz music and visual arts. Called "one of the best arts festivals in this country" by *The Washington Post*, Spoleto has presented 100 world premieres and 93 American premieres since its inception in 1977.

ON THE JOB

The Apprentice Program is a short-term intensive and exciting opportunity to learn about the world of performing arts and acquire hands-on experience under the guidance of professional arts administrators and technicians in producing an international arts festival. Apprentices work at least a 40-hour week, including long workdays, nights and weekends. Areas include: Artist Services; Box Office; Development; Education; Finance; Media Relations; Merchandising; Office Administration; Orchestra Management; and Production.

 GETTING HIRED

Apply by: February 2. See www.spoletousa.org for apprenticeship descriptions and to download an application.

Qualifications:
Open to recent college graduates and grad students.

Contact:
Apprentice Program
Spoleto Festival USA
P.O. Box 100
Charleston, SC 29402
Phone: (843) 722-2764
www.spoletousa.org

Sponsors for Educational Opportunity (SEO)

 THE BUZZ
- "Top professional internship for students of color"
- "Fast track to the top of the business world"

 THE STATS

Industry(ies): Accounting; Investment Banking; Investment Management; Law; Management & Strategy Consulting; Nonprofit; Technology

Location(s): CT; NJ; NY; San Francisco, CA; Hong Kong

Number of interns: *Summer*: 300

Pay: Paid; $600-1,100/week, depending on industry area

Length of internship: *Summer*: 10 weeks

 THE SCOOP

In 1963, Sponsors for Educational Opportunity, or SEO, was founded as one of New York City's first mentoring programs for high school students of color to give them access to top career and educational opportunities. In 1980, SEO launched the Career Program for talented undergraduates nationwide. The program began with 11 interns working at four investment banks. At the end of the summer, all 11 interns had earned full-time job offers. Today, the Career Program places over 300 interns in different program areas such as accounting, investment banking, law, management consulting and philanthropy. Each year, over 80 percent of the intern class ends the summer with one or more full-time job offers from our partner firms. In addition, SEO interns receive intensive industry training from professional and academic leaders. Interns are assigned mentors from both their industry area as well as the alumni network of over 4,500.

ON THE JOB

SEO interns do real, professional work at their internships, from analyzing balance sheets to assisting corporate lawyers, to interfacing with CFOs and strategy consultants, to evaluating philanthropic programs. The exact nature of the work depends on industry placement.

 GETTING HIRED

Apply by: Apply by November 1 to be considered for the Hong Kong program and Round 1 for all other program areas; December 15 for the San Francisco program, if you are an international applicant, or Round 2 for all other program areas; and January 15 for the final deadline for all program areas. Apply online at www.seo-usa.org.

Qualifications:
Open to outstanding minority college students with a minimum 3.0 GPA. Most program areas are primarily for sophomores and juniors. Seniors are eligible for corporate law and philanthropy programs. Interviews are by invitation only.

Contact:
Career Program
Sponsors for Educational Opportunity
30 West 21st Street, Suite 900
New York, NY 10010
Phone: (212) 979-2040
www.seo-usa.org

Sports Illustrated

 THE BUZZ
- "An invitation to the ultimate pressbox"
- "Mix your passions for sports and entertainment"

THE STATS

Industry(ies): Sports; Public Relations

Location(s): New York, NY

Number of interns: 4-6 per semester

Pay: None. Reimbursement for local travel and $8/day meal money; academic credit; free magazines and promo items; attendance welcome at magazine events (e.g., Swimsuit Party, Sportsman/Sportswoman of the Year); discounts on merchandise in the Time Warner store; contact with sports industry executives and athletes

Length of internship: *Spring/summer/fall*: 12 weeks

 THE SCOOP

In print since 1954, *Sports Illustrated* is the nation's premier sports magazine, admired for its lively in-depth sports reporting, striking photography and vivid design. Owned by Time Warner, *SI* reaches some 22 million readers each week.

ON THE JOB

Interns experience a unique taste of the sports and entertainment industry. According to the internship coordinator, "One week, they may work with the NBA, the next they could be doing background research for an athlete's appearance on *The Tonight Show* [and] the following week they might be working with Major League baseball." Interns typically work in communications. Since 1987, the internship program alumni have landed positions at Nike, the NBA, the NHL, ESPN, Disney and Madison Square Garden and have joined the editorial and photography staff at *SI* and other Time Inc. magazines.

 GETTING HIRED

Apply by: *Spring*: November 1; *summer*: March 1; *fall*: July 15. Interns must receive academic credit. Submit resume, cover letter and relevant writing sample (press release, newspaper article, etc. – no term papers) to the address below.

Qualifications:
Open to college sophomores, juniors and seniors, as well as grad students.

Contact:
Karen Dmochowsky
Sports Illustrated
1271 Avenue of the Americas, 33rd Floor
New York, NY 10020
Phone: (212) 522-8473
Fax: (212) 522-0747
www.si.com

Sprint Nextel

 THE BUZZ
- "The 800-pound gorilla of telecom"
- "Sprint and Nextel have teamed up to form the most complete communications company in the world"

THE STATS

Industry(ies): Communications

Location(s): Mansfield, OH; Orlando, FL; Overland Park, KS; Reston, VA; Tarboro, NC

Number of interns: *Summer*: 100+; *fall*: 10+; *spring*: 10+

Pay: Paid; $10-$25/hour. Housing assistance in specified areas; discounts on Sprint products and services; free calling cards; social activities; educational development; travel to Kansas City for presentations; and more

Length of internship: *Spring*: 1-6 or more months; *summer*: 10-14 weeks; *fall*: 1-6 or more months

 THE SCOOP

Sprint Nextel offers a comprehensive range of wireless and wireline communications services to consumer, business and government customers. Sprint Nextel is widely recognized for developing, engineering and deploying innovative technologies, including two robust wireless networks offering industry leading mobile data services; instant national and international push-to-talk capabilities; and an award-winning and global Tier 1 Internet backbone. For more information, visit www.sprint.com.

ON THE JOB

The Sprint Nextel, Student Employment Program is designed to enhance our recruitment efforts and reinforce the relationships developed through these efforts. The program objectives are to promote meaningful assignments to enhance the student's learning; provide Intern Program orientation materials to students and their supervisors; coordinate opportunities for interaction with Sprint managers, executives and other interns; and to complement existing intern programs to enhance recruiting efforts. We have numerous positions available throughout Sprint Nextel including opportunities in finance, accounting, network engineering and software engineering.

 GETTING HIRED

Apply by: Qualified candidates should apply during the fall semester or early in the spring semester at their universities' Career Services office or at www.sprint.com/hr.

Qualifications:
Open to college freshmen, sophomores, juniors, seniors, and graduate students with a minimum 3.0 GPA.

Contact:
Amanda Boeshart
Sprint Nextel
Internship and Recruiting Program Manager
University Relations and Recruiting
6500 Sprint Parkway
Overland Park, KS
KSOPHL0302-3B604
E-mail: amanda.r.boeshart@sprint.com
www.sprint.com/hr

Visit Vault at **www.vault.com** for insider company profiles, expert advice, career message boards, expert resume reviews, the Vault Job Board and more.

VAULT CAREER LIBRARY **385**

St. Paul's School

 THE BUZZ
- "An apple for the teacher – and that's you!"
- "Help educate today's youth"

 THE STATS

Industry(ies): Education

Location(s): Concord, NH

Number of interns: *Summer*: 38; *fall/spring*: 4

Pay: Paid; $400/week. Free room and board

Length of internship: *Summer*: 5 weeks; *fall/spring*: 10 months

 THE SCOOP

St. Paul's School is considered one of the world's finest boarding schools, known for its illustrious alumni, as well as for its 2,000 wooded acres and top-flight facilities. Established in 1856 by Dr. George Cheyne Shattuck, Jr., the school started with just three pupils who were educated in the doctor's home. Since then, it has grown to house 500 students and 100 faculty members. St. Paul's is a religious school affiliated with the Episcopal Church. The school states, however, that it accepts students from alternate faiths and backgrounds and supports their beliefs.

ON THE JOB

During the summer, interns teach and tutor students in St. Paul's Advanced Studies Program, which offers college-level courses to academically talented juniors from New Hampshire high schools. Interns also supervise recreational activities and dormitories. They enjoy use of libraries and athletic facilities and have access to mentors. Other activities include hiking, skiing and other nearby recreational opportunities.

$ GETTING HIRED

Apply by: *Spring/summer/fall/winter*: January 10.

Qualifications:
Open to college juniors and seniors with a good academic record and an interest in teaching.

Contact:
Apprentice Teaching Program
St. Paul's School
325 Pleasant Street
Concord, NH 03301-2591
Phone: (603) 229-4777
E-mail: asp@sps.edu
asp.sps.edu/today/employment/default.asp?id=3192

© 2006 Vault Inc.

St. Vincent Catholic Medical Centers of New York

 THE BUZZ

- "A pre-med dream in the heart of Greenwich Village"

 **THE STATS**

Industry(ies): Health Care

Location(s): Brooklyn, NY; Elmhurst, NY; Flushing, NY; Harrison, NY; Jamaica, NY; New York, NY; Staten Island, NY

Number of volunteers: *Annual:* 400

Pay: None

Length of volunteer duty: 6 months minimum

 THE SCOOP

Catholic Medical Centers of Brooklyn and Queens, St. Vincent's Hospital and Medical Center of New York, and Sisters of Charity Healthcare in Staten Island merged in 2000 to form St. Vincent Catholic Medical Centers (SVCMC). This nine-hospital organization serves at least 500,000 people each year. Over 3,000 physicians staff its care and research facilities and conduct clinical drug trials for cardiovascular- and cancer-related illnesses, among others.

 ON THE JOB

Volunteer positions are available at all of SVCMC's facilities under "patient contact" or "no patient contact." A higher percentage of volunteers participate in the "patient contact" category and work with nursing staff to tend to the needs of the infirmed. Volunteers who choose "no patient contact" can expect office and administrative work. SVCMC provides non-glamorous but hands-on experiences in departments with immediate need.

GETTING HIRED

Apply by: Rolling. Contact the director of your desired location.

Qualifications:

Open to high school students, college freshmen, sophomores, juniors and seniors, and anyone 16 years of age or older.

Contact:

Audrey Segesdi
Volunteer Cordinator for Bishop Mugavero Center for Geriatric Care
155 Dean Street
Brooklyn, NY 11217
Phone: (718) 694-6707
E-mail: segesdiLUV@aol.com

Betty Susino
Director of Therapeutic Recreation for Holy Family Home
1740 84th Street
Brooklyn, NY 11214
Phone: (718) 232-3666
E-mail: esusino@cmcny.com

Mary Immaculate Hospital/Msrg. Fitzpatrick Skilled Nursing Pavilion
152-11 89th Avenue
Jamaica, NY 11432

Joan Gavigan
Director of Volunteers for St. John's Queens Hospital
90-02 Queens Blvd.
Elmhurst, NY 11373
Phone: (718) 558-1239

Eugenia Daley
Director of Volunteer Services for St. Joseph's
158-40 79th Avenue
Flushing, NY 11366

Arlette Cunningham
Coordinator of Volunteers for St. Mary's Brooklyn Hospital
170 Buffalo Avenue
Brooklyn, NY 11213
Phone: (718) 221-3599
E-mail: acunningham@cmcny.com

Joan M. DeMarco
Administrative Director of Volunteer Services for Bayley Seton Hospital, St. Elizabeth Ann's Health Care & Rehabilitation Center, and St. Vincent's Staten Island Hospital
75 Vanderbilt Avenue
Staten Island, NY 10304
Phone: (718) 818-2111

Patricia Cusack
Manager of Volunteer Services for St. Vincent's Manhattan Hospital
130 West 12th Street
New York, NY 10011
Phone: (212) 604-7268
E-mail: pcusack@saintvincentsnyc.org

Grace Mastoras
Director of Volunteer Services for St. Vincent's Westchester Hospital
275 North Street
Harrison, NY 10528
Phone: (914) 925-5563
www.svcmc.org/portal/waysofgiving/volunteer.asp

Visit Vault at **www.vault.com** for insider company profiles, expert advice, career message boards, expert resume reviews, the Vault Job Board and more.

VAULT CAREER LIBRARY **387**

Starlight Foundation

 THE BUZZ
- "Light the path to a child's heart"

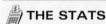 **THE STATS**

Industry(ies): Nonprofit

Location(s): Atlanta, GA; Boston, MA; Chicago, IL; Los Angeles, CA; New York, NY; Redmond, WA; Scarborough, ME; London: Melbourne; Montreal; Sydney; Toronto

Number of interns: *Annual*: 3-6 (New York)

Pay: None. Attendance welcome at events and hospital parties; free promotional items (mugs, t-shirts, etc.)

Length of internship: *Spring/summer/fall*: 12 weeks-1 year

 THE SCOOP

The Starlight Children's Foundation began in 1983 with a wish from a dying boy who befriended actress Emma Samms, who then teamed up with film executive Peter Samuelson to transform that wish into an "international nonprofit organization dedicated to improving the quality of life for seriously ill children and their families." The Starlight Foundation works with more than 1,000 hospitals to help seriously ill children ages four to 18 through "distractive entertainment." The Foundation has granted over 100,000 wishes such as meeting Paul McCartney, visiting Disney World, viewing a taping of Sesame Street and having dinner with Cindy Crawford.

 ON THE JOB

The Foundation staffs over 300 volunteers in its 12 offices. Interns perform a variety of tasks depending on skill and interest. The Foundation tries to utilize interns' unique skills to the best of the organization's benefit. Some volunteers may coordinate special events; others work in wish-granting or assist with fundraising.

(\$) GETTING HIRED

Apply by: Rolling. Call, write, fax or e-mail your interest to your desired chapter's volunteer coordinator. Chapter contact information can be found at www.starlight-newyork.org/about/chapters.htm.

Qualifications:

Open to all college freshmen, sophomores, juniors and seniors, recent college graduates and grad students.

Contact:
Starlight NY*NJ*CT
Attention: Michele Hall
1560 Broadway, Suite 600
New York, NY 10036
Phone: (212) 354-2878, ext.114
Fax: (212) 354-2977
E-mail: Michele@starlightnyc.org
www.starlight-newyork.org/helping/howtov.htm#Internships

Starwood Hotels & Resorts

 THE BUZZ
- "From Albania to Zimbabwe to your hometown"
- "Start a hospitality career at the top of the industry"

THE STATS

Industry(ies): Hospitality; Real Estate; Tourism/Recreation

Location(s): All Starwood hotel locations in the US and many international spots. A complete list of hotels is available at www.starwood.com

Number of interns: *Summer*: 65-150; *winter*: 100-150

Pay: Varies with position and location

Length of internship: *Summer*: 12 weeks; *winter*: 1-2 weeks

 THE SCOOP

Starwood Hotels & Resorts Worldwide, Inc. is one of the largest hotel and leisure companies in the world, with more than 850 properties operating in over 95 countries. Starwood operates eight hotel and resort brands: the St. Regis, Le Meridien, The Luxury Collection, Sheraton, Four Points by Sheraton, Westin, W, and Starwood Vacation Ownership. The company boasts a diverse workforce with more than 145,000 associates worldwide.

 ON THE JOB

Starwood treats each intern as entry-level, full-time professionals in the hospitality field. Students develop guest service and hands-on skills in sales, food and beverage, finance and/or operations. Throughout the summer, students are placed into various roles to develop necessary leadership skills for the hotel industry. The program uses each intern's individual career objectives to create a supervised project the student must complete by the end of internship. The company also features externships during winter and spring breaks during which students are introduced to Starwood and are given networking opportunities, project experience and exposure to needed skills.

(\$) GETTING HIRED

Apply by: Visit a campus recruitment seminar or apply directly to a Starwood hotel.

Qualifications:

Open to college freshmen, sophomores and juniors enrolled in a hotel, hospitality or business program who can demonstrate commitment to the hospitality industry through academic and practical experience.

Contact:
Mary Anne McNulty, Manager of Staffing and College Relations
Starwood Hotels and Resorts Worldwide, North America Division
1111 Westchester Avenue
White Plains, NY 10604
E-mail: maryanne.mcnulty@starwoodhotels.com
www.starwood.jobs

Staten Island Zoo

 THE BUZZ
- "Develop educational programs for kids"
- "Live, learn and play in the zoo"

 THE STATS

Industry(ies): Education; Animal Care

Location(s): Staten Island, NY

Number of interns: 3

Pay: Unpaid

Length of internship: Miminum 1 semester/summer; 5 hours/week; some weekend and holiday hours

 THE SCOOP

Established in 1936, the Staten Island Zoo calls itself the "biggest little zoo" in the New York metropolitan area. With its mission to "help people make a connection to the natural world," the zoo hopes to leave visitors with a more enlightened view and an interest in learning. The zoo features an African Savannah, a tropical forest, an aquarium, a children's center, a serpentarium (for those who like snakes!) and outdoor exhibits. It is the only zoo in the region that offers community outreach programs. Resident animals include a plethora of fish, invertebrates, many reptiles and an amphibian collection. The zoo also offers educational school learning programs.

ON THE JOB

The Staten Island Zoo has 3 professional, hands-on intern positions. The veterinary technician intern assists with daily animal care, routine veterinary work, feeding, cleaning, exhibit maintenance, medical treatments and lab work. The animal care intern assists with daily husbandry and animal care routines. The education intern assists staff with educational programs for children in grades K-9 and zoo guests, develops curriculum and lesson plans, and completes their own project.

GETTING HIRED

Apply by: Rolling, but suggest 1-2 months prior to the the start of each semester. Write for full job descriptions. Send a resume and cover letter to the address below.

Qualifications:

All positions open to college students and graduates; the education position is open to outstanding high school seniors as well. Applicants should be enrolled in a field of study related to the internship, such as veterinary science, biology, zoology, environmental science, or education. Veterinary technician applicants must have prior experience at a veterinary clinic. International applicants are welcome.

Contact:
Dave Johnston
Assistant Director of Education
Staten Island Zoo
614 Broadway
Staten Island, NY 10310
Phone: (718) 442-3174 ext. 37
Fax: (718) 442-8492
E-mail: sizoo4ed@aol.com
www.statenislandzoo.org

Steppenwolf Theatre Company

 THE BUZZ
- "Learn hands on what it takes to be one of the best theaters in the world"

 THE STATS

Industry(ies): Nonprofit; Theater/Performing Arts

Location(s): Chicago, IL

Number of interns: *Summer*: approximately 20; *academic year apprenticeship*: approximately 20

Pay: *Summer internship*: none; academic credit. *Apprenticeship*: paid; monthly catered lunches; free tickets to Steppenwolf productions; free tickets and special offers to art events around Chicago

Length of internship: *Summer*: June-August; *apprenticeship*: September-May. Full-time administrative interns work 28 hours/week; full-time production interns work 40 hours/week

 THE SCOOP

In 1974, the Steppenwolf Theatre Company started performing plays in a church basement in Highland Park, Ill. It has now grown to include 35 ensemble members. Steppenwolf has spawned a generation of America's most gifted artists, such as Joan Allen, John Malkovitch, Martha Plimpton, Amy Morton, Austin Pendleton and founder Gary Sinise, among others.

ON THE JOB

The Steppenwolf Theatre Company Internship Program allows students, graduates and others to experience the inner workings of a professional theater from every angle. All internships at Steppenwolf are hands-on experiences. Through daily assignments and duties with a given department, bi-weekly intern seminars with guest speakers, volunteer opportunities in many areas of the theater, and free tickets to productions, interns are offered the chance to learn from the finest professionals working in theater today.

GETTING HIRED

Apply by: *Summer*: February 15; *apprenticeship*: May 1. Send application, cover letter, a personal statement, resume and two letters of recommendation to the address below. Application available at www.steppenwolf.org, under "Work with Us".

Qualifications:
Open to all college freshmen, sophomores, juniors and seniors, recent college graduates and grad students. Applicants must be at least 18 years of age. International applicants welcome.

Contact:
Steppenwolf Theatre Company
Internship Program
758 West North Avenue, 4th Floor
Chicago, IL 60610
E-mail: internships@steppenwolf.org
www.steppenwolf.org

Visit Vault at **www.vault.com** for insider company profiles, expert advice, career message boards, expert resume reviews, the Vault Job Board and more.

VAULT CAREER LIBRARY **389**

Student Conservation Association

 THE BUZZ

• "Make conservation a way of life"

THE STATS

Industry(ies): Education; Environmental; Nonprofit

Location(s): Charlestown, NH

Number of interns: *Annual:* 1,300 (interns); *Conservation Crews:* 450

Pay: $60/week and round-trip travel; free housing; accident insurance; education awards

Length of internship: *Interns, year-round:* 12 weeks-12 months; *Conservation Crews, summer/fall:* 4-5 weeks

 THE SCOOP

Founded in 1957, the Student Conservation Association, Inc., is a national nonprofit organization that advocates for the environment. SCA leads the nation in providing conservation service opportunities, outdoor skills and leadership training. Every year, in all 50 states, thousands of high school, college, graduate students and others join the association to work for national parks and forests, historic and cultural resources, and urban green spaces.

ON THE JOB

Interns work in national parks, forests, wildlife refuges and conservation centers. Participants are placed in archaeology, American history, backcountry and wilderness management, cave management, environmental education, engineering and surveying, forestry, geology and paleontology, horseback patrol, water resources, land interpretation and visitor services, photography, range management and plant taxonomy, recreation management, trail construction and maintenance, and wildlife and fisheries. Past intern projects have included building trails in the Tetons and tracking desert tortoise in the Mojave Desert.

 GETTING HIRED

Apply by: Rolling.

Qualifications:
Open to high school graduates, college freshmen, sophomores, juniors and seniors, and other adults.

Contact:
Admissions Department
Student Conservation Association
689 River Road
P.O. Box 550
Charlestown, NH 03603-0550
Phone: (603) 543-1700
Fax: (603) 543-1828
E-mail: admissions@thesca.org
www.thesca.org

Student Works Painting

 THE BUZZ
- "Paint the town with your business savvy"

 **THE STATS**

Industry(ies): Management & Strategy Consulting

Location(s): Multiple cities in: AZ; CA; CO; FL; GA; ID; IL; MD; MA; MI; NC; OH; OR; PA; TX; UT; VA; WA; Alberta; British Columbia; Manitoba; Ontario

Number of interns: *Annual*: 750

Pay: Paid; $700/week average

Length of internship: *Spring*: 12 weeks (part-time); *summer*: 12 weeks (full-time)

 **THE SCOOP**

Founded in 1981, the summer management program with Student Works Painting hires high-achieving college students and trains them to manage a business from start to finish. Each selected manager will oversee the marketing, sales, management and customer relations of a house painting business in their hometown. Student Works is the largest residential paint contractor in California. There are many career opportunities available within the company (for above-average performers) and with several affiliated organizations.

ON THE JOB

Interns are provided with the tools and training, the systems and support, and the licenses and insurance necessary to manage a successful business during the summer. The requirements are confidence, leadership skills and motivation. Earnings range from $2,500 to $30,000. Interns go through an intensive training program and are invited to biweekly company events, reward dinners with executives and whitewater rafting. Top performers receive an all-expenses-paid Cabo San Lucas vacation with the company.

GETTING HIRED

Apply by: March 30. Write to one of the addresses below for an application.

Qualifications:
Open to college freshmen, sophomores, juniors and seniors, recent college graduates, college graduates of any age and grad students. International applicants are eligible (undergrads only).

Contact:
United States
Student Works Painting
1505 East 17th Street, Suite 210
Santa Ana, CA 92705
Phone: (888) 450-9675
Fax: (714) 564-8725
www.studentworks.com

Northern California
Student Works Painting
1802 Tice Valley Blvd.
Walnut Creek, CA 94595
Phone: (800) 295-9675
Fax: (925) 937-0434

Alberta and British Columbia
Student Works Painting
Suite 4, 1037 West Broadway
Vancouver
V6H 1E3
Canada
Phone: (800) 665-4992
Fax: (604) 733-6110

Visit Vault at **www.vault.com** for insider company profiles, expert advice, career message boards, expert resume reviews, the Vault Job Board and more.

VAULT CAREER LIBRARY **391**

Supreme Court of the United States

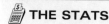 **THE BUZZ**
- "Supreme experience for future politicians"
- "Start your law career at the pinnacle"

 THE STATS

Industry(ies): Government; Law

Location(s): Washington, DC

Number of interns: *Annual*: 6 (2 summer, 2 fall, 2 spring)

Pay: None; $1,000 scholarship may be available

Length of internship: *Spring/summer*: 16 weeks each; *fall*: 10 weeks

 THE SCOOP

The U.S. Supreme Court is America's highest judicial body. The nine justices of the Court meet to discuss and deliver decisions on America's most important jurisprudential issues. The Judicial Internship Program gives college students a chance to work under the administrative assistant, who serves as the Chief Justice's chief of staff.

ON THE JOB

The program was established in 1972 by the Office of the Administrative Assistant to the Chief of Justice. Past interns stress the importance of the applicant's personal statement. Interns also have the chance to attend law-clerk luncheons and special events, and they have access to the cafeteria and gym.

GETTING HIRED

Apply by: *Spring*: October 20; *summer*: March 10; *fall*: June 10. Submit to the address below a resume, transcript, statement explaining your reasons for seeking the internship, short writing sample, three letters of recommendation and an essay of at least two pages on the American constitutional system. Online application available at www.supremecourtus.gov.

Qualifications:

Open to college juniors and seniors and, on occasion, recent college graduates. Constitutional law coursework recommended.

Contact:
Supreme Court of the United States
Judicial Internship Program
Office of the Administrative Assistant to the Chief Justice
Room 5
Washington, DC 20543
Phone: (202) 479-3374
Fax: (202) 479-3484
www.supremecourtus.gov

Surfrider Foundation

 THE BUZZ
- "Help protect America's beaches"

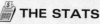 **THE STATS**

Industry(ies): Environmental

Location(s): San Clemente, CA

Number of interns: *Spring/summer/fall*: 4 each

Pay: None

Length of internship: *Spring/summer/fall*: 10-12 weeks each

 **THE SCOOP**

The Surfrider Foundation was established in 1984 when a group of frustrated surfers united to so something about Southern California's increasingly polluted waters. SF has grown into the nonprofit, grassroots organization it is today with over 50,000 members in 63 local chapters across the U.S. Comprised mainly of unpaid volunteers, the staff is dedicated to the "protection and preservation of the world's oceans, waves and beaches through conservation, activism, research and education."

 **ON THE JOB**

SF provides interns with an easygoing environment. Interns are generally involved in a lot of clerical aspects and "busywork," but there are often recreational outings to "hit the beach." The staff works directly with the interns as they execute a variety of research-based, fact-checking and informal projects. The work may be concentrated at the office, but is also often conducted at the library, as well as on the beach.

 **GETTING HIRED**

Apply by: Rolling. Send a resume and cover letter explaining the reasons for wanting to work at Surfrider to the address below.

Qualifications:

Open to high school juniors and seniors, college freshmen, sophomores, juniors and seniors, recent college graduates and grad students.

Contact:
Surfrider Foundation
Internship Program
P.O. Box 6010
San Clemente, CA 92674-6010
Phone: (949) 492-8170
Fax: (949) 492-8142
www.surfrider.org/whoweare5a.asp

Sussex Publishers

 THE BUZZ

- "Improve your psyche and your writing at the same time"

THE STATS

Industry(ies): Journalism; Publishing

Location(s): New York, NY

Number of Interns: *Spring/summer/fall:* 3-4 each

Pay: Small daily stipend

Length of internship: *Spring/summer/fall:* 12-20 weeks. Terms run according to season. *Spring:* January-May; *summer:* June-August; *fall:* September-December)

THE SCOOP

Sussex Publishers is the parent company of the magazine *Psychology Today* and is based in New York, N.Y. The magazine, Sussex's most prominent, prides itself on being "Here to Help". Many contributing writers are expert psychologists, but the tone of the articles is neither clinical nor academic. *Psychology Today* has been growing in popularity outside of its field as well as inside.

ON THE JOB

Psychology Today is Sussex's only publication boasting an internship program. Interns are primarily accepted into the magazine's editorial department (the only one with an organized internship program). Because the office staff is small, hands-on experience is guaranteed. Expect heavy research responsibilities delegated by staff editors. There are also opportunities to write short pieces, predominantly for the news section of the publication.

GETTING HIRED

Apply by: Rolling. Applicants must send a detailed cover letter, resume and three writing samples from published articles or pieces most similar in tone to those in *Psychology Today*.

Qualifications:
Open to college students with strong writing skills, preference given to applicants with college and graduate degrees who intend to pursue journalism.

Contact:
Matthew Hutson
Sussex Publishing
115 East 23rd Street, 9th Floor
New York, NY 10010
Phone: (212) 260-7210
E-mail: matt@psychologytoday.com

Symantec Corporation

THE BUZZ

- "Tech whizzes will love working with a world leader in Internet security"
- "A great opportunity to network (and we don't just mean on computers)"

 THE STATS

Industry(ies): Internet; Software; Technology; Storage

Location(s): Beaverton, OR; Cupertino, CA; Eugene, OR; Santa Monica, CA; Sunnyvale, CA; Mountainville, CA; Waltham, MA; Toronto, ON (Canada)

Number of interns: *Annual:* 100

Pay: Paid; varies

Length of internship: *Summer:* 12 weeks; part-time positions available year-round

THE SCOOP

Symantec Corporation was founded in 1982 by Dr. Gary Hendrix and is now a world leader in Internet security technology. The company develops, markets and supports a complete line of application and system software products designed to enhance individual and workshop productivity, ensure the security, availability and integrity of information, and manage networked computing environments. Headquartered in Cupertino, California, the company has employees in more than 40 countries around the globe.

ON THE JOB

Interns work as members of the following departments: engineering (development & SQA), human resources, finance, marketing, sales and management information services.

GETTING HIRED

Apply by: Rolling. Send resume and cover letter to college_resume@symantec.com.

Qualifications:

Open to college freshmen, sophomores, juniors and seniors, as well as grad students. Students must be currently enrolled in a program of interest to Symantec. International applicants are encouraged to apply.

Contact:
Margo Garcia
Symantec Corporation
350 Ellis Street
Building A
Mountain View, CA 94043
Phone: (650) 527-1014
Fax: (650527-35314
E-mail: college_resume@symantec.com
www.symantec.com

Visit Vault at **www.vault.com** for insider company profiles, expert advice, career message boards, expert resume reviews, the Vault Job Board and more.

VAULT CAREER LIBRARY **393**

VAULT'S
DIVERSITY CENTRAL

INTERNSHIP PROFILES: T

TADA!

 THE BUZZ

- "Have fun with children and theater"
- "Stimulate your passion for theater"

 THE STATS

Industry(ies): Education; Theater/Performing Arts

Location(s): New York, NY

Number of interns: *Annual:* 12

Pay: Stipends for some production interns, as well as training sessions in technical departments and the opportunity to attend all performances and fundraising events (cocktail parties, benefits, etc.)

Length of internship: *Summer/fall/spring:* minimum commitment of 3 months of part-time service or 1 month of full-time service; scheduling is flexible

 THE SCOOP

Founded in 1984, TADA! is a New York-based youth theater company that presents theater and dance performances by children. Each year over 50,000 children are exposed to musical theater through TADA!'s staff of experienced theater professionals. TADA! also sponsors programs that provide workshops and classes for their performers.

 ON THE JOB

An internship through TADA! helps aspiring theater artists advance professionally. Interns work interactively through a variety of administrative, educational, artistic and production tasks. Current internship opportunities include production assistant, student teacher, administrative assistant, literary assistant, development assistant and fundraising assistant.

💲 **GETTING HIRED**

Apply by: Rolling. Send a resume and a cover letter indicating your availability and interests to the address below.

Qualifications:
Open to all college freshmen, sophomores, juniors and seniors, recent college graduates and grad students.

Contact:
Internship Coordinator
TADA!
15 West 28th Street, 3rd floor
New York, NY 10001
Phone: (212) 252-1619
Fax: (212) 252-8763
E-mail: tada@tadatheater.com
www.tadatheater.com/tadacontentpage.asp?sub=ho&pg=intern

Target Corporation

 THE BUZZ

- "See a company like no other, see a new culture, see the rewards, see yourself here"

 THE STATS

Industry(ies): Retail

Location(s): Minneapolis, MN

Number of interns: *Annual: undergraduate:* 200; *MBA:* 29

Pay: Paid

Length of internship: *Summer:* 10 weeks

 THE SCOOP

Target is an upscale discount retailer that provides quality, trend-right merchandise and everyday basics in clean, convenient stores. Target is America's fourth-largest retailer and has more than 1,200 stores in 47 states. The company is 23rd on the Fortune 500 list and has annual revenues of over $41 billion.

 ON THE JOB

During the 10-week summer internship program, students play a significant role in analyzing and developing company strategies. They are assigned to a department and work hands-on with a team to experience the daily activities of their area. Each participant is paired with a mentor who will guide them through the program and provide feedback along the way. Target interns learn through combining classroom training and on-the-job application. Interns are responsible for completing a project and presenting results to Senior Leadership at the end of the program. Interns also participate in roundtable discussions with senior management and meet other interns at various social events.

💲 **GETTING HIRED**

Apply by: Apply through your campus career center. For more information on Target recruitment, visit http://target.com/targetcorp_group/careers/campus_events.jhtml.

Qualifications:
Open to undergraduate students with a 3.0 GPA. MBA positions are open to students who have completed the first year of their MBA program. All interns must have strong analytic, leadership and computer skills. Candidates should also have outstanding verbal and written communication skills, as well as planning and organizational skills.

Contact:
Target Corporation
1000 Nicollet Mall
Minneapolis, MN 55403
Phone: (612) 304-6073
Fax: (612) 696-3731
www.target.com

TBWA/CHIAT/Day

 THE BUZZ
- "Get to pitch real clients at this ad giant"

 THE STATS

Industry(ies): Advertising

Location(s): New York, NY

Number of interns: *Summer*: 12-15

Pay: None

Length of internship: *Summer*: 8 weeks

 THE SCOOP

TBWA/Chiat/Day is owned by the Omnicom Group and is considered one of the leading advertising agencies in New York City. TBWA aspires to create campaigns that enter the popular consciousness and prides itself on "creativity, effectiveness, and disruptive thinking." Other offices are located in San Francisco, Los Angeles and Toronto, but the company's web site indicates that internships are only available in New York. Clients include Absolut and Bayer.

ON THE JOB

The internship program is highly structured. Interns work in accounts, production, interactive, creative, art buying and more. Each intern is assigned an account team and/or department in addition to a mentor. Two speakers a week – usually high-level executives – visit the interns and field questions. The final four weeks of the program are mostly devoted to group projects.

GETTING HIRED

Apply by: *Summer*: March 31. Application includes a print ad write-up. Send the write-up, a resume and cover letter to resumes@tbwachiat.com.

Qualifications:
Open to college juniors and seniors, as well as grad students.

Contact:
Internship Coordinator
TBWA/Chiat/Day, NY
488 Madison Avenue
New York, NY 10022
Phone: (212) 804-1000
Fax: (212) 804-1200
www.tbwachiat.com

Teach for America

 THE BUZZ
- "The fastest route to a career as a teacher"

 THE STATS

Industry(ies): Education; Nonprofit

Location(s): New York, NY; Houston, TX; numerous college campuses throughout the U.S.

Number of interns: *Annual*: 400

Pay: Paid; between $500-$2,250

Length of internship: Varies

THE SCOOP

Teach for America is to trying to level the playing field in public education by recruiting recent college grads for two-year teaching assignments in low-income public school districts across the country. The nonprofit organization was founded by Wendy Kopp, who conceived the idea in her senior thesis at Princeton University in 1989. Teach for America places approximately 2,000 teachers in 18 locations nationwide every year.

ON THE JOB

Although interns do not get hands-on teaching experience, they are able to learn about every other aspect of the organization and how a nonprofit runs. General internships in areas such as marketing or communications are available at the company's headquarters in New York. Interns can also work as operations coordinators at TFA's summer training institutes in New York, Houston and Los Angeles, where they provide administrative and logistical support. Or they can work from their own college campus as campaign coordinators to help raise awareness about TFA and recruit prospective corps members.

GETTING HIRED

Apply by: Rolling. Application procedures depend on the type of internship. The minimum requirements include a resume, cover letter, a completed application (available at www.teachfor america.org/staff.html) and an interview.

Qualifications:
Open to college freshmen, sophomores, juniors and seniors and recent college graduates. Most applicants are interested in teaching or learning about the nonprofit world.

Contact:
Ayanna Heard
Teach for America
315 West 36th Street, 6th Floor
New York, NY 10018
Phone: (800) 832-1230
Fax: (212) 279-2081
www.teachforamerica.org

Visit Vault at **www.vault.com** for insider company profiles, expert advice, career message boards, expert resume reviews, the Vault Job Board and more.

V/ULT CAREER LIBRARY **397**

Texas Instruments

 THE BUZZ

- "Learn about technology from the folks that invented the microchip"

 THE STATS

Industry(ies): Semiconductors; Technology

Location(s): Dallas, TX (HQ)

Number of interns: Varies

Pay: Paid; competitive salary. Travel reimbursement; relocation assistance; benefits

Length of internship: *Annual*: 3-6 months

 **THE SCOOP**

Texas Instruments invented the microchip and Digital Light Processing™ (DLP™) technology, and is the world leader in digital signal processing (DSP) and analog technologies. TI is headquartered in Dallas, Texas, but has job opportunities across the country in cities including San Diego, Tucson and Houston. TI employs nearly 35,000 people worldwide.

 ON THE JOB

Interns step into a real position and are trained on the job to perform real work in a variety of areas. TI jokes that because training is on the job, its internship program is the "best reason on Earth to skip school."

 GETTING HIRED

Apply by: Rolling. E-mail your resume to jobs@ti.com.

Qualifications:
Open to college sophomores, juniors and seniors, as well as grad students. Minimum 3.0 GPA required. Engineering or science majors preferred.

Contact:
Intern Coordinator
Texas Instruments
13350 TI Boulevard, MS 328
Dallas, TX 75243
www.ti.com/recruit/docs/studunioo.shtml

Texas Monthly

 THE BUZZ

- "A Texas-sized opportunity for budding journalists"
- "Learn the magazine business while enjoying sunny Southern hospitality"

 THE STATS

Industry(ies): Journalism; Publishing

Location(s): Austin; TX; Dallas, TX; Houston, TX

Number of interns: *Spring/summer/fall*: 30-35 each

Pay: None. Free subscription to *Texas Monthly*

Length of internship: *Spring/summer/fall*: 10-12 weeks

 **THE SCOOP**

Since 1973, *Texas Monthly* has chronicled life in contemporary Texas, reporting on vital issues such as politics, the environment, industry and education. As a leisure guide, *Texas Monthly* refers to itself as the "indispensable authority" on the Texas scene, covering music, the arts, travel, restaurants, museums and cultural events with its insightful recommendations. *Texas Monthly* has a reputation for providing its readers with a magazine of the highest editorial quality.

 ON THE JOB

Interns work as assistants in all aspects of the magazine's operations. Internships in Austin focus on accounting, advertising, art, circulation, custom publishing, editorial, administration, marketing, new media, production, the publisher's office, research, sales and technology. The Houston/Dallas offices offer internships in advertising and sales.

 GETTING HIRED

Apply by: Rolling. Send a resume and cover letter, stating desired session and department of interest, to the address below.

Qualifications:
Open to college freshmen, sophomores, juniors and seniors, college graduates and grad students.

Contact:
Texas Monthly
Internship Coordinator
P.O. Box 1569
Austin, TX 78767-1569
Phone: (512) 320-6900
Fax: (512) 476-9007
E-mail: humanresources@texasmonthly.com
www.texasmonthly.com/misc/jobs.php

Theatre de la Jeune Lune

 THE BUZZ
- "Don't let the curtain fall on an opportunity like this"
- "Take a play from script to stage"

 THE STATS

Industry: Theater/Performing Arts

Location(s): Minneapolis, MN

Number of interns: *Annual*: 10-40. Varies depending on need of each show

Pay: None. Free tickets to shows and other company shows

Length of internship: Minimum 4.5 month commitment; most are semester-long

 THE SCOOP

Theatre de la Jeune Lune, recipient of the 2005 Regional Tony Award, is a nonprofit company of theater artists founded in France in 1978 by graduates of the renowned theater school Ecole Jacques Lecoq. After seven years of splitting its seasons between France and the United States, Jeune Lune settled permanently in the Minneapolis Warehouse District. With its national reputation for innovative productions and a distinct physical performance style, Jeune Lune made its New York debut with its critically acclaimed production of *Hamlet* in 2004. In addition, its nationally acclaimed production of *The Miser* has been touring the country for the last two seasons. Among the company's other productions are *Children of Paradise: Shooting a Dream*, *The Green Bird* and *Don Juan Giovanni*.

 ON THE JOB

Internships vary based on each department's need, but all offer an experience from the ground up. Internships are available in both the administrative offices (marketing, development, education and patron services, and business) and in production (stage management, directing, and all technical concentrations.)" See the website (www.jeunelune.org/about/intern.html) for details.

GETTING HIRED

Apply by: Rolling (apply as early as possible). Write to the address below to request application.

Qualifications:

Open to high school seniors, college freshmen, sophomores, juniors and seniors, recent college graduates and grad students. International applicants welcome.

Contact:

Theatre de la Jeune Lune
Attention: Internships
105 1st Street
Minneapolis, MN 55401
Phone: (612) 332-3968, ext. 183
Fax: (612) 332-0048
E-mail: internships@jeunelune.org
www.jeunelune.org/about/intern.html

Thirteen/WNET

 THE BUZZ
- "An opportunity to enter the tough-to-crack field of public television"

 THE STATS

Industry(ies): Broadcast & Entertainment; Journalism; New/Interactive Media

Location(s): New York, NY

Number of interns: *Annual*: 100

Pay: None; academic credit may be available (check with your school). Graduates may receive a $10/day stipend

Length of internship: *Spring/summer/fall/winter*: 1 month minimum; 2-3 days/week

 THE SCOOP

Thirteen serves its viewers by providing programming honoring all ethnic backgrounds of the millions that comprise the population of the New York, New Jersey and Connecticut tri-state areas. For about four decades, Thirteen has been asking provocative questions that challenge its audience to grow, think, learn and dream through noncommercial, educational and inspiring programming, including *Charlie Rose*, *BBC World News*, *The Newshour with Jim Lehrer* and *Religion & Ethics Newsweekly*.

 ON THE JOB

Interns gain valuable experience in production, programming, music, technical services, marketing and sales, fundraising and education. Duties vary by position, but all afford participants hands-on training in a field that's "typically difficult to enter." See site for open positions.

GETTING HIRED

Apply by: *Spring*: second Friday in December; *summer*: second Friday in April; *fall*: mid- to late July; *winter*: second Friday in October. Submit a resume and cover letter. If enrolled in a degree program, you must include a statement from your school's registrar proving your registration. State in your cover letter the internship and season for which you are applying, your availability dates, the maximum hours to which you can commit, and what year you expect to graduate.

Qualifications:

Open to all college sophomores, juniors and seniors, as well as grad students.

Contact:
Internship Coordinator
Thirteen/WNET New York
450 West 33rd Street
New York, NY 10001
Fax: (212) 560-6865
E-mail: internships@thirteen.org
www.thirteen.org/homepage/jobs/intern.html

Visit Vault at **www.vault.com** for insider company profiles, expert advice, career message boards, expert resume reviews, the Vault Job Board and more.

VAULT CAREER LIBRARY **399**

TM Advertising

 THE BUZZ
- "A respected Longhorn ad agency"

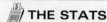 **THE STATS**

Industry(ies): Advertising

Location(s): Dallas, TX

Number of interns: *Summer*: 15 total for creative, account service, media planning and interactive; *spring/fall*: varies based on requests from departments

Pay: Paid; $7.00/hour

Length of internship: *Summer*: June-August; *spring/fall*: varies based on department needs

 THE SCOOP

Formerly known as Temerlin McClain, TM Advertising is a communications agency with divisions in advertising, direct marketing and interactive. Clients include American Airlines, Nationwide Insurance, Verizon SuperPages, Texas Tourism, ExxonMobil and Bell Helicopter.

ON THE JOB

Interns are incorporated into the company's account service, interactive, media planning and creative departments. Responsibilities vary with placement. By the end of their placement, interns will know how an ad agency functions.

GETTING HIRED

Apply by: *Account service/media/general advertising/interactive internship*: March 15. Send to Terri Bauer, at the address listed below. *Interactive/creative internship*: April 15. Submit resumes and nonreturnable creative samples to Beverly Ann Moore, address below.

Qualifications:

Account service/media planning: open to undergraduate sophomores and juniors; *creative*: open to undergraduate sophomores, juniors and seniors.

Contact:
Terri Bauer, Director of Human Resources
TM Advertising
6555 Sierra Drive
Irving, TX 75039
Phone: (927) 830-2589
E-mail: terribauer@tm.com

Beverly Ann Moore, Creative Services
TM Advertising
6555 Sierra Drive
Irving, TX 75039
Phone: (972) 830-2741
E-mail: beverly.moore@tm.com

The Toledo Blade

 THE BUZZ
- "Lots of journalism opportunity in this mid-sized city"

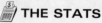 **THE STATS**

Industry(ies): Journalism

Location(s): Toledo, OH

Number of interns: *Summer*: 4; *two-year associate internship*: 3; *photography internship*: 1 each quarter

Pay: Paid; *summer*: $512/week; *two-year position*: $560/week

Length of internship: 13-week commitment preferred; 2 years for associates program

 THE SCOOP

The Toledo Blade is the only daily produced in the Toledo metropolitan area. The city sits on the southwest shore of Lake Erie, just south of Detroit. The daily is known for investigative reports with past cover stories about the Vietnam-era Tiger Force, which brutalized the countryside. The *Buried Secrets, Brutal Truths* series won a 2004 Pulitzer Prize for investigative reporting.

ON THE JOB

Interns work in copyediting or as reporters and photographers. Because *The Blade* is a medium-sized operation with a daily circulation of 146,000, it can't afford a giant staff, so interns get more responsibility than at a larger newspaper.

GETTING HIRED

Apply by: *Summer*: January 15; *two-year associates*: rolling. The paper recommends that interested individuals apply early.

Qualifications:
Summer positions are open to all college juniors and seniors. Must be a communications, journalism, history or English major. Must be at least a junior. Interns must specifically state their area of interest in their application, (reporter, photographer, etc.) and must have the qualifications to back up their aspirations. Two-year positions are available to recent graduates only.

Contact:
Assistant Managing Editor
The Toledo Blade
541 North Superior Street
Toledo, OH 43660
E-mail: luannsharp@theblade.com
www.toledoblade.com

Tommy Boy Music

 THE BUZZ
- "A rarity: a successful independent music business"
- "Tommy Boy did hip-hop before MTV popularized it"

THE STATS

Industry(ies): Music/Records

Location(s): New York, NY

Number of interns: *Summer/fall/spring*: 4-6 each

Pay: *Part-time*: $10/day; *full-time*: $20/day

Length of internship: 3 months-1 year

 THE SCOOP

Tom Silverman started Tommy Boy Music in his crowded NYC apartment in 1981. The company's first hip-hop single (Planet Rock by Afrika Bambaataa and the Soul Sonic Force) soon went gold. Though firmly rooted in hip-hop with stars like Coolio, Tommy Boy soon branched into other genres, including dance music. Seventy-seven Tommy Boy records have gone gold, platinum or multi-platinum. AOL Time Warner purchased half of the company in 1986 and the rest of it in 1989, but Silverman bought the whole thing back in 2002.

ON THE JOB

Interns work on a variety of projects in nearly every department. Available positions vary depending on what's needed, but may include assisting the president, working in the graphics department and dealing with radio promotions. Some duties may involve administrative tasks and computer graphics.

 **GETTING HIRED**

Apply by: Rolling. Send resume and cover letter detailing interests and clerical skills.

Qualifications:
Open to college freshmen, sophomores, juniors and seniors, as well as recent grads and grad students. Computer skills (especially Excel and Word) are required.

Contact:
Linda Williams, Financial Controller
Tommy Boy Entertainment LLC
120 Fifth Avenue, 7th Floor
New York, NY 10011
Phone: (212) 388-8390
Fax: (212) 388-8431
E-mail: Linda.Williams@tommyboy.com
www.tommyboy.com

The Tonight Show with Jay Leno

 THE BUZZ
- "A great way to get your foot in the broadcasting door"
- "Learn from 'the big chin' of late night TV"

THE STATS

Industry(ies): Broadcast & Entertainment

Location(s): Burbank, CA

Number of interns: *Annual*: 1-2 each term

Pay: None; academic credit

Length of internship: *Spring/summer/fall*: varies based on student availability; 3-day/week commitment

THE SCOOP

Jay Leno took up the reins of *The Tonight Show* in 1992, after Johnny Carson retired from his longstanding role as host. (This ruffled a feather or two, particularly those of David Letterman, who took his own late night show off the network soon after and relocated to CBS.) In addition to interviewing some of the hottest stars, Leno also delights his audience with bits like "Jay Walking," where he catches adults saying some of the dumbest things, and "Headlines," where he shares some funny misprints and unfortunate turns of phrase.

ON THE JOB

Tonight Show interns work closely with the show's staff, assisting the producers. They handle general administrative roles, but also have the opportunity to apply some of their studies to their work, and they might even meet the Fruitcake Lady...if they're lucky! NBC often hires successful interns for full-time positions.

GETTING HIRED

Apply by: *Fall*: first week in June; *spring/summer*: first week in September. Apply through the NBC corporate web site, www.nbcjobs.com/Internship_Program.html, or send a resume and cover letter to CAintern@nbc.com. (Indicate which term you are applying for and specify *The Tonight Show* in the body of the e-mail.)

Qualifications:
Open to college sophomores, juniors and seniors. Broadcasting/media majors preferred. Must be able to prove you are enrolled in an accredited institution and can receive academic credit.

Contact
Internship Coordinator
NBC Studios
3000 West Alameda Avenue
Burbank, CA 91523
E-mail: CAintern@nbc.com
www.nbcjobs.com/Internship_Program.html

Visit Vault at **www.vault.com** for insider company profiles, expert advice, career message boards, expert resume reviews, the Vault Job Board and more.

 VAULT CAREER LIBRARY 401

Toyota Motor Sales USA, Inc.

 THE BUZZ

- "Accelerate your business skills at one of the world's leading automotive companies"
- "An opportunity for MBA students that could lead to fulltime employment"

 THE STATS

Industry(ies): Transportation

Location(s): Torrance, CA

Number of interns: *Summer:* 18-20

Pay: Paid

Length of internship: 12 weeks

 **THE SCOOP**

Toyota Motor Sales USA, Inc. (TMS), headquartered in Torrance, Calif., is a wholly owned subsidiary of Toyota Motor Corporation (TMC). Based in Japan, TMC is the second-largest automotive company in the world. TMS is responsible for the marketing, advertising, merchandising, distribution and sales/service activities of Toyota, Lexus, and Scion in the United States. In the U.S., 2004 sales exceeded 2 million vehicles. The Toyota, Lexus, and Scion dealer network numbers nearly 1,400.

 ON THE JOB

TMS hires MBA interns for its marketing/strategy, finance and IS departments. The intern program is the main feeder into the full-time Graduate Management Associate (GMA) position.

 GETTING HIRED

Apply by: Apply through your school's career services office. If TMS does not recruit at your school, log on to www.toyota.com/talentlink to apply. See web site for available internship opportunities. First-year students should apply by December 1.

Qualifications:
GMA applicants should have four to six years of relevant industry experience, and should be enrolled in a top-tier business school.

Contact:
Toyota Motor Sales USA, Inc.
19001 South Western Avenue
A134
Torrance, CA 90501
Attn: MBA Recruiter
www.toyota.com/talentlink

Tracy Watts, Inc.

 THE BUZZ

- "A fashionable internship for hat aficionados"

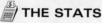 **THE STATS**

Industry(ies): Fashion; Manufacturing

Location(s): New York, NY

Number of interns: *Summer:* 2-4

Pay: None. Free lunch daily; attend fashion shows; free hats

Length of internship: *Summer:* 2 months

 THE SCOOP

Acclaimed hat designer Tracy Watts views millinery as art and problem solving, modernizing classic styles while applying color and fabrication. Her hats and belts continue to be featured in leading fashion magazines, such as *Vogue, Elle, BUST, Jane, Lucky, Glamour, The New York Times Magazine, Mademoiselle, Paper, Marie Claire, Cosmopolitan, Harper's Bazaar, W, Women's Wear Daily* and *Seventeen*. Watts counts several celebrities among her customers, including Winona Ryder, Ben Stiller and Natalie Portman. Madonna sported Tracy's "Cowgirl" on the cover of her album and in the corresponding music video. The Smashing Pumpkins, Total, Janet Jackson and Mary J. Blige have also showcased the designer's work.

ON THE JOB

Interns become involved in all aspects of the garment industry, serving as assistants. Duties range from running errands to construction, making patterns, cutting fabric, blocking felt and making final trimmings.

GETTING HIRED

Apply by: Rolling. Submit a resume, cover letter, and any work samples (e.g., hats or garments) to the address below.

Qualifications:
Open to all college freshmen, sophomores, juniors and seniors, as well as grad students.

Contact:
Internships
Tracy Watts, Inc.
305 West 20th Street
New York, NY 10011
Phone: (212) 727-7349
Fax: (212) 229-0417
E-mail: tracywatts@nyc.rr.com
www.tracywatts.com

Tribeca Film Center

 THE BUZZ
- "Learn the nitty-gritty of producing a film"
- "Work side-by-side with established and up-and-coming producers"

 THE STATS

Industry(ies): Broadcast & Entertainment; Film

Location(s): New York, NY

Number of interns: *Annual*: 18-20

Pay: None; academic credit. Film screenings, potential celebrity gawking

Length of internship: *Spring/summer/fall/winter*: 12-14 weeks each

 THE SCOOP

Jane Rosenthal and Robert De Niro founded Tribeca Entertainment in 1989 with the intent of making it the center of film, television and new media in New York. The company boasts Tribeca Productions, the Tribeca Film Institute and several independent commercial industrial film companies, as well as the 2002 addition of the Tribeca Film Festival, which was attended by more than 150,000 people and generated more than $10.4 million in revenues. Recent movie releases through Tribeca include *About a Boy*, *Analyze That* and *Showtime*.

 ON THE JOB

Interns are assigned a variety of duties based upon their interest and skill. Departments employing interns include executive services, customer relations in greeting clients, administrative and clerical duties, accounting, operations and production.

GETTING HIRED

Apply by: Rolling. Submit a resume and cover letter with availability date and semester for which you are applying.

Qualifications:
Open to college freshmen, sophomores, juniors and seniors, as well as grad students.

Contact:
Internship Coordinator
Tribeca Film Center
375 Greenwich Street
New York, NY 10013
Fax: (212) 941-3898
E-mail: internprogram@tribeca.com
www.tribecafilm.com

Trilogy Software, Inc.

 THE BUZZ
- "Join one of the more innovative software companies"

 THE STATS

Industry(ies): Software; Technology

Location(s): Austin, TX; Bangalore

Number of interns: Varies with company need

Pay: Paid; competitive salary (varies)

Length of internship: *Summer*: 12 weeks

 **THE SCOOP**

Trilogy Software, Inc., creates innovative software solutions for many of the world's top companies. Founded in 1989, it's still privately held and focuses on industry-specific enterprise software for the automotive, communications, computer hardware and insurance industries. The company's methodology has been patented as "Fast Cycle Time".

 ON THE JOB

The Junior Trilogy University (jTU) treats interns like full-time professionals. They work with one of the company's top performers on a real project. Each jTUer learns about one of Trilogy's companies, and by the end of the summer, he or she presents real-value findings. The program includes team lunches and dinners, as well as social activities and mentor sporting events, and is designed to feed into the company's entry-level training program, Trilogy University.

 GETTING HIRED

Apply by: Rolling. Send resume to one of the e-mail addresses below (U.S. if you want to work in the Texas office, India if you want to work in Bangalore).

Qualifications:
Open to college students who have completed their junior year.

Contact:
Trilogy jTU Program
5001 Plaza on the Lake
Austin, TX 78746
Phone: (512) 874-3100
Fax: (512) 874-8900
E-mail: Recruit_india@trilogy.com (India recruiting)
E-mail: Recruit_US@trilogy.com (U.S. recruiting)
www.trilogy.com

Visit Vault at **www.vault.com** for insider company profiles, expert advice, career message boards, expert resume reviews, the Vault Job Board and more.

VAULT CAREER LIBRARY **403**

Turner Broadcasting System

 THE BUZZ
- "Ample opportunities for budding broadcasters"
- "Learn about the business side of entertainment"

 THE STATS

Industry(ies): Broadcast & Entertainment; Journalism; New/Interactive Media; Sports

Location(s): Atlanta, GA; Burbank, CA; Chicago, IL; Los Angeles, CA; New York, NY; North Miami, FL; San Francisco, CA; Washington, DC

Number of interns: *Annual*: 240-300

Pay: None

Length of internship: *Year-round*: 10-16 weeks

 THE SCOOP

Turner Broadcasting System, Inc., was established over two decades ago as a small Atlanta-based UHF station. The company evolved into a major producer of news and entertainment programs around the world, as well as the leading provider for the basic cable industry, which employs 8,000 worldwide. The company belongs to the Time Warner family. Its subdivisions include CNN, TBS, TNT, Cartoon Network, Turner Classic Movies, Court TV, the Atlanta Braves and Turner Sports, among others.

 ON THE JOB

Interns enjoy opportunities in CNN, entertainment networks, sports teams, distribution and the corporate office. Functions include corporate affairs, group services, technology services, sales, customer relations, marketing, production, new media, design, legal and creative services. Interns may also become involved in employee seminar discussions and receive training in broadcast writing and editing.

GETTING HIRED

Apply by: *Fall*: priority date: July 1; deadline: August 24; *Winter/spring*: priority date: October 1; deadline: December 29; *Summer*: priority date: January 31; deadline: April 13. Students should apply online at www.turnerjobs.com. Include a resume and cover letter with the electronic application.

Qualifications:
Open to college juniors, seniors, grad students (students must still be enrolled in school during the internship) and international students with a minimum 3.0 GPA.

Contact:
Internship Coordinator, Human Resources
Turner Broadcasting System
One CNN Center
Atlanta, GA 30303
E-mail: internship.coordinator@turner.com
www.turnerjobs.com

Tyco Toys

 THE BUZZ
- "Work and play at the same time!"
- "Celebrate the art of toy making"

 THE STATS

Industry(ies): Consumer Products; Manufacturing

Location(s): Mt. Laurel, NJ

Number of interns: *Annual*: 2-5

Pay: None

Length of internship: *Spring/summer/fall/winter*: 12 weeks-1 year

 **THE SCOOP**

Tyco Toys, Inc., an international corporation that designs and manufactures children's toys, was founded in 1926. Tyco now grosses nearly $800 million annually and employs over 267,000 people worldwide. In 1997, toy giant Mattel acquired Tyco, whose better-known toys include Jet Turbo Rebound, Matchbox cars, the Magic 8-Ball and Magna Doodle.

 ON THE JOB

Tyco interns work on projects requiring teamwork, ingenuity and creativity, and have tactical responsibilities that give them full-time employee experience. They work in the marketing, advertising, and research and development departments. Interns also learn about their departments as they meet senior-level executives, attend "brown bag" presentations and seminars, and attend social events.

 GETTING HIRED

Apply by: Rolling. Submit a resume and cover letter to the address below.

Qualifications:
Open to all college freshmen, sophomores, juniors and seniors, recent college graduates and grad students. International applicants welcome.

Contact:
Internship Coordinator
Tyco Toys, Inc.
6000 Mid Atlantic Drive
Mt. Laurel, NJ
Phone: (856) 234-7400
www.mattel.com/careers/ca_campusrec.asp

INTERNSHIP PROFILES:
U

UBS Investment Bank

 THE BUZZ
- "Start your financial career at one of the leading fims on the street"

 THE STATS

Industry(ies): Financial Services

Location(s): Stamford, CT (U.S. HQ); Chicago, IL; Houston, TX; Los Angeles, CA; New York, NY; San Francisco, CA

Number of interns: Over 300 during the summer of 2005

Pay: Paid; competitive salary

Length of internship: *Summer*: 10-12 weeks

 THE SCOOP

UBS, one of the world's leading financial firms, combines financial strength with a reputation for innovation and a global culture that embraces change. It is one of the world's largest wealth managers, a premier investment banking and securities firm, and one of the largest global asset managers. As such, UBS provides a full spectrum of services to the world's key institutional investors, intermediaries, banks, insurance companies, corporations, sovereign governments, supranational organizations and private investors. In addition, UBS is a market leader in Switzerland in retail and commercial banking. UBS employs approximately 72,000 people, and operates in over 50 countries and from all major financial centers.

 ON THE JOB

UBS Investment Bank offers summer positions to both undergraduate and MBA students in multiple U.S. office locations. The objective of the internship program is to provide interns with an exceptional learning experience in a demanding and exciting industry. Interns will gain first-hand experience and knowledge of working life within the group they are hired into. Throughout the course of the summer, each business group incorporates business-specific training, development opportunities, networking and social events into its program. Interns are also assigned dedicated mentors to guide and support them throughout the summer.

$ GETTING HIRED

Apply by: Apply for a summer internship through your school's career services office. If UBS Investment Bank does not actively recruit at your school, fill out an online application by January 31, 2006. For more information on the summer internship program, and to access the online application, go to www.ubs.com/graduates.

Qualifications:

Open to undergraduate rising seniors and MBA students who have completed their first year. Applicants should be able to demonstrate outstanding academic and extracurricular achievement, possess strong analytical, quantitative and interpersonal skills, and be enthusiastic about and committed to working in the financial services industry.

Contact:
www.ubs.com/graduates

UCSD Summer Training Academy for Research in the Sciences

 THE BUZZ
- "Training ground for future minority PhDs"

 THE STATS

Industry(ies): Engineering; Science/Research

Location(s): San Diego, CA

Number of interns: *Annual*: 32-40

Pay: Paid; $3,000/summer

Length of internship: *Summer*: 8 weeks

 THE SCOOP

STARS is a federally funded program meant to increase the number of ethnic minorities enrolling in doctoral science programs around the country. The program is connected to the University of California's San Diego campus and faculty. It exposes qualified students to ongoing projects in their fields: physical, life, behavioral, marine and ocean sciences, engineering and math.

 ON THE JOB

Each STARS intern works with a UCSD faculty member on a research project. They also attend Graduate Record Exam (GRE) preparation classes, complete grad school prep work, and go to scientific lectures on current science research. All interns must complete a 10- to 15-page scientific research paper. At the program conference, each intern presents his or her research.

 GETTING HIRED

Apply by: *Summer*: February 16, 2007. For application forms, procedures and updates, go to the UCSD STARS web site starting in November 2006, at www-ogsr.ucsd.edu/stars/program.htm.

Qualifications:

Open to all college sophomores, juniors and seniors, grad students and recent college graduates who are of an underrepresented ethnicity. Must have a 3.3 GPA or higher and be dedicated to enrolling in a PhD program.

Contact:
STARS
Office of Graduate Studies and Research
University of California, San Diego
9500 Gilman Drive, Mail Code 0003
La Jolla, CA 92093-0003
E-mail: stars@ucsd.edu
www-ogsr.ucsd.edu/stars/program.htm

United Nations

 THE BUZZ
- "Work on international harmony in New York City"

 **THE STATS**

Industry(ies): Government; Law

Location(s): New York, NY

Number of interns: *Annual*: 400-500; approximately 120-150 per session

Pay: None. United Nations guided tour

Length of internship: 2-month internships offered 3 times/year; *spring*: mid-January—mid-March; *summer*: early June—early August; *fall*: early September—end of October. Full-time schedule, 5 days/week (9:00 a.m.-5:00 p.m.)

THE SCOOP

Founded in 1945, the United Nations links over 190 countries to promote world peace, literacy, human rights, disease eradication and cordial relations between conflicting nations. The UN pursues these goals with extensive research, meetings, development and programs, which it conducts through its six major divisions: the Security Council, the Economic and Social Council, the Trusteeship Council, the International Court of Justice, the Secretariat and the General Assembly.

ON THE JOB

Interns work in the Secretariat Divisions, where they are assigned to various responsibilities and are exposed to the work of the United Nations. Interns also provide assistance to UN offices through general clerical tasks, organizational duties and research.

GETTING HIRED

Apply by: Application deadlines vary based on the start of each internship session. For specific deadlines and information regarding online application procedures and eligibility critieria, please consult the web site at www.un.org/Depts/OHRM/sds/internsh/index.htm.

Qualifications:
Applicants must be enrolled in a graduate degree program when applying and during the internship.

Contact:
Internship Coordinator
Office of Human Resources Management
Room S-2500 J
United Nations
New York, NY 10017
Fax: (212) 963-9514
E-mail: OHRM_interns@un.org
www.un.org/Depts/OHRM/sds/internsh/index.htm

United Nations Association of the United States of America

 **THE BUZZ**
- "Learn the inner workings of one of the world's leading peace and human rights organizations"

THE STATS

Industry(ies): Government; Law

Location(s): New York, NY

Number of interns: *Summer*: 20-25; *fall/winter*: 7-10

Pay: None. Free books, posters

Length of internship: *Spring/summer/fall*: 10-12 weeks

THE SCOOP

Founded in 1943 by Eleanor Roosevelt, the United Nations Association of the United States of America (UNA-USA) is a nonprofit, nonpartisan organization that supports the work of the United Nations and encourages active civic participation. The UNA-USA encourages Americans to react to issues confronted by the UN, from global health and human rights to the spread of democracy, equitable development and international justice. Today, the UNA-USA has more than 20,000 members spread through 175 local chapters in 43 states.

ON THE JOB

Internships are available in several areas, including business council, communications, development, the UN executive office, education and model UN, media relations, public affairs and national membership. Interns are also included in all aspects of United Nations affairs and can attend "United Nations meetings, briefings, and special UNA-USA events." Interns in the summer program may "organize and direct a weekly 'brown-bag' luncheon program, inviting members of the United Nations, Permanent Missions to the UN, and UNA-USA senior staff to address subjects determined by the interns."

GETTING HIRED

Apply by: *Summer*: March 15. *Fall*: April 22; review process begins July 1. *Spring*: rolling; review process begins November 1. Download the application from www.unausa.org/ aboutus/ internships.asp, and mail it, along with other required materials (see application for details) to the address below.

Qualifications:
Applicants must be enrolled in a degree program in a graduate school at the time of application and during the internship. International applicants where higher education is not divided into undergraduate and graduate stages must have complete at least four years of full-time studies at a university or equivalent institution towards the completion of a degree.

Contact:
United Nations Association of the USA
Internship Coordinator
801 Second Avenue
New York, NY 10017
Phone: (212) 907-1300
Fax: (212) 682-9185
E-mail: gsu@unausa.org
www.unausa.org/aboutus/internships.asp

Visit Vault at **www.vault.com** for insider company profiles, expert advice, career message boards, expert resume reviews, the Vault Job Board and more.

V/\ULT CAREER LIBRARY **407**

United Parcel Service, Inc. (UPS)

THE BUZZ

- "What can brown do for your career?"

THE STATS

Industry(ies): Transportation

Location(s): Atlanta, GA (HQ); worldwide

Number of interns: Varies; based on location and department needs

Pay: Paid; competitive salary

Length of internship: Varies based on intern schedule and department needs

THE SCOOP

United Parcel Service (UPS) began as a domestic messenger service in 1907. Today, UPS employees – known for their brown uniforms – deliver an average of 14.1 million packages and letters per day. Operating in over 200 countries, UPS meets the shipping needs of 1.8 million customers worldwide. UPS also operates one of the world's largest air-cargo airlines, UPS Air Cargo. Its nonpackage subsidiaries include UPS Capital Corporation, Mail Boxes Etc., Inc., UPS Mail Innovations and UPS Professional Services.

ON THE JOB

UPS offers a wide variety of internship and co-op opportunities. Opportunities are available in a wide variety of areas, including marketing, industrial engineering, information services, human resources and communications, to name a few. Openings are posted on the UPS employment web site on an as-needed basis. See www.upsjobs.com for details. UPS also offers separate internships through INROADS and UNCF, programs that enhance educational opportunities for undergraduate students of African American, Hispanic American, Asian American and Native American descent. Contact these organizations for more information.

GETTING HIRED

Apply by: Varies based on position. Go to www.upsjobs.com for application procedures and deadlines for specific internship opportunities.

Qualifications:
Varies by department. See web site for specific needs.

Contact:
United Parcel Service, Inc.
55 Glenlake Parkway, NE
Atlanta, GA 30328
Phone: (404) 828-6000
www.ups.com

United States Chamber of Commerce

THE BUZZ

- "Where the business world and the government intersect"

THE STATS

Industry(ies): Government; Nonprofit

Location(s): Washington, DC, and posts in 69 countries overseas

Number of interns: *Spring/summer/fall*: 25 each

Pay: None. Transportation stipend

Length of internship: *Spring/summer/fall*: 8-12 weeks

THE SCOOP

The United States Chamber of Commerce was created in 1912 to represent the unified interest of U.S. businesses. It maintains the world's largest not-for-profit and includes a staff of lobbyists and lawyers. The Chamber has grown to include more than 3 million businesses and connects nearly 3,000 state and local chambers and 830 associations.

ON THE JOB

At the U.S. Chamber of Commerce, interns obtain hands-on experience in a variety of departments. Internships offer responsibilities such as research, writing, database management, web page maintenance, communications and event preparation. Interns will have the opportunity to network with colleagues and demonstrate their skills and abilities. They will also have the opportunity to attend the Chamber's "Your First Steps to Success" workshop to enhance their resume writing, cover letter writing and interviewing skills.

GETTING HIRED

Apply by: Rolling, but no later than: *winter/spring*: December 20; *summer*: April 20; *fall*: June 20. Download the application from www.uschamber.com/careers/internships/apply.htm. E-mail, mail or fax completed application form, resume, cover letter and brief (one- to two-page) writing sample to the address below. Do not send application materials earlier than one semester prior to when you are interested in interning.

Qualifications:
Open to college juniors and seniors, as well as grad students.

Contact:
Fellowship Coordinator
Human Resources
U.S. Chamber of Commerce
1615 H Street, NW
Washington, DC 20062
Phone: (202) 463-5731
Fax: (202) 463-5328
E-mail: intern@uschamber.com
www.uschamber.com

The United States Commercial Service

 THE BUZZ
- "Help chip away at the American trade deficit"
- "Nirvana for international economists"

 THE STATS

Industry(ies): Government

Location(s): Global (multiple cities in most countries)

Number of interns: *Annual*: 100

Pay: None

Length of internship: *Summer*: 8-12 weeks; *fall*: 8-16 weeks; *spring*: 8-16 weeks

 THE SCOOP

The U.S. Commercial Service works alongside the International Trade Administration (part of the U.S. Department of Commerce) to help American companies increase sales and activity in foreign markets. The group is made up of both American and international employees.

 ON THE JOB

The U.S. Commercial Service's Overseas Work-Study Intern Program places American students interested in economics and business in its worldwide offices. Interns are given "hands-on" responsibilities in the commercial sector of a U.S. embassy. Specific intern duties vary greatly depending on the host office's needs and interns' experience. Check with individual offices (www.export.gov/comm_svc/eac.html) for more details.

GETTING HIRED

Apply by: Rolling. Send a resume and cover letter to the Senior Commercial Officer (SCO) or Principal Commerical Officer (PCO) in the office where you want to work. A complete list of offices and contact information is available at www.export.gov/comm_svc/eac.html.

Qualifications:
Open to all college juniors and seniors and grad students in economics and business administration fields, and related subjects. Students should be planning to continue their ediucation upon completion of the internship, be U.S. citizens in good academic standing, and pass a security assurance check.

Contact:
Phone: (202) 482-3301
www.export.gov/comm_svc/eac.html
www.export.gov

United States Department of Commerce

 THE BUZZ
- "The first step to a business career"

 THE STATS

Industry(ies): Government

Location(s): Washington, DC

Number of interns: Varies

Pay: Varies. Free transportation to and from internship and help with temporary housing

Length of internship: *Spring*: varies; *summer*: 10-12 weeks; *fall*: varies depending on student's schedule

 THE SCOOP

The Department of Commerce and Labor was created in 1903 and renamed simply the Department of Commerce 10 years later. Bureaus of the Department of Commerce include the Bureau of Industry and Security, the Bureau of Economic Analysis, and the National Oceanic and Atmospheric Administration. The Department of Commerce is responsible for examining economic information and export regulations.

ON THE JOB

Each of the 15 bureaus of the Department of Commerce participates in the U.S. Department of Commerce Postsecondary Internship Program. Possible work placements include the National Institute of Standards and Technology, the Census Bureau and the International Trade Administration. All provide networking opportunities.

GETTING HIRED

Apply by: Varies according to bureau. Go to ohrm.doc.gov/intern/internwebsite.htm for a full list of available programs.

Qualifications:
Open to freshman, sophomore, junior and senior undergraduate and graduate students who are United States citizens. Internships obtained through sponsoring organizations (American Indian Science and Engineering, Hispanic Association of Colleges and Universities National Internship Program, Minority Access, Inc., and Oak Ridge Associated Universities) have additional eligibility requirements. Separate requirements are also available for each Department of Commerce bureau.

Contact:
Carin Otero
Intern Program Officer
Department of Commerce
1401 Constitution Avenue, NW, Room 5001
Washington, DC 20230
Phone: (202) 482-1445
E mail: COtero1@doc.gov
ohrm.doc.gov/intern/internwebsite.htm

Visit Vault at **www.vault.com** for insider company profiles, expert advice, career message boards, expert resume reviews, the Vault Job Board and more.

V**A**ULT CAREER LIBRARY **409**

United States Department of Defense

 THE BUZZ
- "Security of the highest order"
- "Students with a passion for justice wanted"

 THE STATS

Industry(ies): Government; Military

Location(s): Washington, DC

Number of interns: *Summer*: 8-10

Pay: Paid; $450-$575/week for grad students

Length of internship: *Summer*: 10 weeks

 THE SCOOP

Established by Congress in 1947, the U.S. Department of Defense oversees U.S. national security. Headquartered at the Pentagon, it manages an annual budget of $260 billion. The DOD is the nation's largest employer, with approximately 1.4 million men and women on active duty, and about 654,000 civilian personnel.

ON THE JOB

Interns work in the Office of General Counsel, as well as in the acquisition and logistics, fiscal, Inspector General, international affairs and intelligence, legal counsel, legislative reference, standards of conduct, and personnel and health policy departments. The program includes training seminars, mentors and specially arranged tours of DOD departments (as well as the U.S. Supreme Court, the Court of Appeals of the Armed Forces, the Senate Armed Services Committee's General Counsel, and the Department of Justice).

GETTING HIRED

Apply by: Rolling. Submit a resume, transcripts, OF 612 (optional application for federal employment), a writing sample and a statement of class rank to the address below.

Qualifications:
Open to college freshmen, sophomores, juniors and seniors, as well as grad students.

Contact:
Honors Legal Internship Program
Office of General Counsel
U.S. Department of Defense
The Pentagon
Room 3E999
Washington, DC 20301-1155
www.defenselink.mil

United States Department of Energy

 THE BUZZ
- "Help develop America's newest energy sources"

 THE STATS

Industry(ies): Energy/Utilities; Government

Location(s): Washington, DC

Number of interns: Varies

Pay: Paid; *GS-5*: $24,701-$27,068; *GS-7*: $30,597-$33,526; *GS-9*: $37,428-$41,010. Participants are eligible for student loan repayment, life insurance, health insurance and thrift savings plan options. Access to fitness centers, child care/personal development and transit subsidy

Length of internship: 2 years

 THE SCOOP

The Department of Energy can be traced as far back as the Manhattan Project and the race to develop the atomic bomb during World War II. The DOE is responsible for U.S. energy security, nuclear stockpile maintenance, environmental cleanup and technological innovations. It's won more R&D awards than any private sector organization, and twice as many as all of the other federal agencies combined. Accolades include awards from *Discover* magazine, energy and water management awards, and several Nobel prizes.

ON THE JOB

Interns in the DOE'S two-year program receive intensive developmental training that focuses on science/engineering and business. After the training, they are hired and assigned to entry-level positions (GS-5 through GS-9) in their respective fields. All interns are trained and placed in site-specific work and developmental projects, which are evaluated and assessed throughout the process.

GETTING HIRED

Apply by: Rolling. Submit a resume and cover letter to the address below.

Qualifications:
GS-5: open to college juniors and seniors working toward a bachelor's degree; *GS-7*: open to graduate students with advanced academic achievement or one year of specialized experience; *GS-9*: open to individuals who have completed their master's or equivalent graduate degree.

Contact:
U.S. Department of Energy
1000 Independence Avenue, SW
Washington, DC 20585
Phone: (800) DIAL-DOE
Fax: (202) 586-4403
www.energy.gov/engine/content.do?BT_CODE=AD_C

United States Department of State

 THE BUZZ
- "Follow in Colin Powell's footsteps"

 THE STATS

Industry(ies): Government

Location(s): Washington, DC

Number of interns: Varies

Pay: Paid and unpaid. For paid positions, applicants must include a Student Aid Report indicating your estimated family contribution number (EFC)

Length of internship: *Summer*: May/July-September; *fall*: September/October-December; *spring*: January/February-April

 THE SCOOP

The Secretary of State is the President's chief foreign policy adviser. The State Department also supports the U.S. foreign affairs activities of other government entities, including the Department of Commerce and the Agency for International Development. It conducts its duties through a smaller workforce than many local governments boast and is comprised of civil service and foreign service employees.

 ON THE JOB

Interns choose to work in Washington, DC, or in an embassy overseas. Duties vary according to office assignment and range from scientific/technical tasks to administrative projects or logistical support. Interns may be assigned research on political, economic, environmental or other issues. They may write reports and correspondence, assist with citizens' services or visa work, or work in information systems, procurement or budget and fiscal operations.

GETTING HIRED

Apply by: *Spring*: July 1; *summer*: November 1; *fall*: March 1. Submit three copies of the following: completed application form (available at www.careers.state.gov/student/ap_intrn.html), a one-page statement of interest detailing why you want to work for the State Department, official transcript and a financial aid transcript for those seeking paid positions. Only online applications will be accepted.

Qualifications:

Open to candidates who possess foreign language ability and are full- or part-time college juniors or seniors, or grad students. Applicants must be U.S. citizens. The department seeks a broad range of academic majors.

Contact:

Intern Coordinator, Recruitment Division
Department of State
2401 E Street, NW, Room 518H
Washington, DC 20522-0108
E mail: careers@state.gov
www.careers.state.gov/student/prog_intrn.html

United States Environmental Protection Agency

 **THE BUZZ**
- "Solid training ground for budding environmental activists"

THE STATS

Industry(ies): Environmental; Government; Science/Research

Location(s): Atlanta, GA; Boston, MA; San Francisco, CA; Washington, DC; offices in every U.S. state

Number of interns: *Annual*: 40

Pay: Paid; $6,000-$10,000/3 months

Length of internship: *Summer*: 3 months; *year-round*: varies

 THE SCOOP

The U.S. Environmental Protection Agency oversees regulations protecting the nation's land and air from pollution, and employs some 18,000 people across the country. For more than 30 years, the EPA has worked to protect the environment and human health by educating citizens and suing companies violating environmental laws.

 ON THE JOB

The National Network for Environmental Management Studies (NNEMS) is a fellowship program where students apply to work on specific projects or environmental problems sponsored by an EPA office. Past topics include environmental policy, regulation and law; environmental service; and computer programming and development.

GETTING HIRED

Apply by: January. Application required. See the organization's web site for up-to-date information (www.epa.gov/enviroed/students.html).

Qualifications:

Open to college freshmen, sophomores, juniors and seniors, as well as grad students. Must be a U.S. citizen or lawfully admitted to the U.S. for permanent residence, enrolled in an accredited educational institution, and pursuing study related to the environment. For undergraduate students, minimum 3.0 GPA and four completed courses related to environmental studies required. For graduate students, enrollment in or acceptance to a graduate program and the completion of one semester of graduate work or four undergraduate courses related to environmental studies is required.

Contact:

Sheri Jojokian
Office of Environmental Education
US EPA (1704A)
1200 Pennsylvania Avenue, NW
Washington, DC 20460
Phone: (800) 358-8769
E-mail: jojokian.sheri@epa.gov
www.epa.gov/epahome/intern.htm

Visit Vault at **www.vault.com** for insider company profiles, expert advice, career message boards, expert resume reviews, the Vault Job Board and more.

VAULT CAREER LIBRARY **411**

United States Holocaust Memorial Museum

 THE BUZZ
- "A serious internship at a top-notch DC museum"

 THE STATS

Industry(ies): Art/Museum; Education

Location(s): Washington, DC

Number of interns: *Summer*: 25; *fall*: 10; *winter*: 10

Pay: Unpaid and paid (paid internships are highly competitive). Field trips; free tickets to museum; attend conferences, lectures, readings, films

Length of internship: *Summer/fall/winter*: 12 weeks each

 THE SCOOP

Established in 1993, the U.S. Holocaust Memorial Museum expands public perception of the Holocaust through exhibitions, lectures, artifacts, first-hand testimonials, films, pictures and educational supplements. The museum aims to give Americans a true piece of a Holocaust victim's life, as visitors are given Identity Cards when they enter the museum. These help the holder learn about the Holocaust through the lives of one of its victims, and toward the end of the exhibit, the visitor learns the victim's fate. The museum details brutal acts committed by the Nazi party and is not recommended for children under age 11.

ON THE JOB

The internship is designed to teach students the history behind the Holocaust and the intricacies of museum operations. Interns assist on several projects at a time while working directly with Holocaust scholars and museum professionals. Positions are available in education, development, communications, exhibitions, collections, survivor affairs, community programs, international education and the Center for Advanced Holocaust Studies.

GETTING HIRED

Apply by: *Summer*: March 15; *fall*: June 15; *winter/spring*: October 15. Send a completed application form (available at www.ushmm.org/museum/volunteer_intern/index.utp?content = intern/right.htm), current resume, certified academic transcript, two letters of recommendation and a cover letter detailing interest in the internship to the address below.

Qualifications:
Open to college sophomores, juniors and seniors, as well as grad students.

Contact:
Office of Volunteer and Intern Services
United States Holocaust Memorial Museum
100 Raoul Wallenberg Place, SW
Washington, DC 20024-2126
Phone: (202) 479-9738
www.ushmm.org/museum/volunteer_intern

United States National Arboretum

 THE BUZZ
- "If you're passionate about plants, this one's for you"
- "Plant the seeds of your career here"

 **THE STATS**

Industry(ies): Environmental; Government; Science/Research

Location(s): Washington, DC

Number of interns: *Annual*: 10-15

Pay: Paid; $10.78/hour (projected)

Length of internship: *Summer/winter/fall*: 3-12 months

THE SCOOP

The National Arboretum is a division of the U.S. Department of Agriculture that is dedicated to improving the environment. The Arboretum concentrates on plant research, educational programs for the public, and cultivating trees, shrubs and flowers. Its collections include the National Herb Garden, Friendship Garden and Fern Valley, as well as the Gotelli Dwarf Conifer, Bonsai and Asian collections. Interns work in plant sciences, the garden unit, research or education.

ON THE JOB

Internships include training in horticulture, botany, research, facilities management and public garden administration. A typical day involves activities including "planting, pruning, weeding, mulching, watering, raking, controlling pests, maintaining plant records and answering public inquiries." Interns also interact with staff through regularly scheduled educational programs and field trips.

GETTING HIRED

Apply by: Rolling. Check web site for details.

Qualifications:
Applicants should have completed course work or have acquired practical experience in horticulture or related fields. Basic gardening or laboratory skills and an interest in plants are beneficial.

Contact
Internship Coordinator
U.S. National Arboretum
3501 New York Avenue, NE
Washington, DC 20002
Phone: (202) 245-4521
www.usna.usda.gov/Education/intern.html

United States Olympic Committee

 THE BUZZ
- "Help oversee the Olympics from a U.S. perspective"

THE STATS

Industry(ies): Sports

Location(s): Chula Vista, CA; Colorado Springs, CO; Lake Placid, NY

Number of interns: *Fall, winter/spring, summer*: 20-24 each in Colorado Springs; 3-5 each in Lake Placid and Chula Vista

Pay: Paid; $8.50/hour; academic credit available. Interns are housed in Olympic Training Center dormitories with meals at the Athletes' Dining Hall. A deduction of $379 will be taken every 2 weeks from intern's wages to cover the cost of room and meals

Length of internship: *Fall*: September 1-December 20; *winter/spring*: January 2-May 25; *summer*: June 1-August 25

THE SCOOP

The United States Olympic Committee (USOC) is America's premier sports organization. Appointed by law, it provides oversight for all Olympic activity in the United States. The USOC supports U.S. sports on the program for the Olympic, Paralympic and Pan American Games, or those who want to be included in the games.

ON THE JOB

Internships are available with USOC divisions or national governing bodies, such as boxing, swimming, volleyball, etc. Interns work in, broadcasting, journalism, marketing, sports administration and sports science (strength, conditioning and testing). Job descriptions and work expectations will be reviewed and explained by the intern's supervisor on the first day of the internship.

GETTING HIRED

Apply by: *Fall*: June 1; *winter/spring*: October 1; *summer*: February 15. E-mail for an official application form. All applicants must submit the USOC application form, along with a resume and official transcripts. Up to three letters of recommendation may also be included. Applications must be received at the manager's office in Colorado Springs, Colorado, by the appropriate application deadline. Incomplete or late applications will not be considered.

Qualifications:
Open to college juniors and seniors, and graduate students currently enrolled in an undergraduate or graduate degree program in an accredited United States college or university. Students who have graduated before the actual starting date of the internship for which they intend to apply are ineligible and will not be considered for an internship position.

Contact:
USOC Student Intern Program
One Olympic Plaza
Colorado Springs, CO 80909-5760
Phone: (719) 866 2597
E-mail: internprog@usoc.org
www.olympic-usa.org/about_us/employment/internship.htm

United States Secret Service

 **THE BUZZ**
- "Tommy Lee Jones would be proud"

THE STATS

Industry(ies): Government; Law

Location(s): Washington, DC (HQ)

Number of interns: *Annual*: 25-50

Pay: None

Length of internship: *Spring/summer/fall*: 10-16 weeks each

THE SCOOP

Following the 1901 assassination of President William McKinley, the Secret Service branched out from its job of suppressing counterfeit currency to ensuring the safety of the President. Since 1984, the service's investigative responsibilities have expanded to include bank fraud, computer and telecom fraud, false IDs, fraudulent access devices, advance fee fraud and money laundering.

ON THE JOB

Interns at the services's DC headquarters work in counterfeit, financial crimes, forensic services, special agent training and employee development, intelligence, technical security, public affairs and administrative operations. Interns in field offices conduct research and do clerical work for the local forgery, counterfeit and fraud units.

GETTING HIRED

Apply by: *Spring*: August 15; *summer*: January 10; *fall*: April 14. Write for application materials.

Qualifications:
Open to all college graduates.

Contact:
Student Volunteer (Intern) Program
Personnel Division
U.S. Secret Service
1800 G Street, NW, Room 912
Washington, DC 20223
Phone: (202) 435-5800
www.secretservice.gov

Visit Vault at **www.vault.com** for insider company profiles, expert advice, career message boards, expert resume reviews, the Vault Job Board and more.

VAULT CAREER LIBRARY **413**

United States Securities and Exchange Commission

THE BUZZ

- "Help fight insider trading"

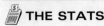 THE STATS

Industry(ies): Financial Services; Government; Law

Location(s): Washington, DC (HQ); Atlanta, GA; Boston, MA; Chicago, IL; Denver, CO; Ft. Worth, TX; Los Angeles, CA; Miami, FL; New York, NY; Philadelphia, PA; Salt Lake City, UT; San Francisco, CA

Number of interns: *Summer*: 186 agencywide

Pay: Varies based on years in school

Length of internship: *Spring/summer/fall*: about 10 weeks

THE SCOOP

Congress created the U.S. Securities and Exchange Commission after a Wall Street stock market crash caused the Great Depression in the 1930s. SEC's mission, according to its web site, is "to enforce the newly-passed securities laws, to promote stability in the markets and, most importantly, to protect investors." Recently, however, some of its leaders have come under fire for their own large compensation packages.

ON THE JOB

Interns gather evidence, help with case files, observe negotiations and prepare trial briefs. They may also participate in weekly brownbag lunches on topics in federal securities laws and attend field trips to NYSE and "mock testimony" workshops. There are also opportunities at the headquarters in the legal offices and fieldwork for investigations.

GETTING HIRED

Apply by: *Fall/spring*: April and November; *summer*: October. Apply online at www.sec.gov by selecting "Employment" and then "Students".

Qualifications:
Open to college sophomores, juniors and seniors.

Contact:
www.sec.gov
www.sec.gov/jobs.shtml#intern

United States Senate Youth Program

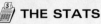 THE BUZZ

- "A not-to-be missed opportunity for aspiring politicos"

THE STATS

Industry(ies): Government

Location(s): Washington, DC

Number of interns: *Spring*: 104

Pay: $5,000 college scholarship. Travel, accommodations and meal expenses provided

Length of internship: 1 week

THE SCOOP

The tradition of the United States Senate Youth Program began in 1962. Two students from each state, the District of Columbia and the Department of Defense Education Activity are sponsored by the William Randolph Hearst Foundation to spend a week in Washington, DC, learning about the United States government. Distinguished alumni include Presidential Advisor Karl Rove, Judge Robert Henry from the U.S. Court of Appeals, and former Lt. Governor of Idaho David LeRoy.

ON THE JOB

During their week sojourn in Washington, DC, students visit Capitol Hill, the White House, the Supreme Court and other notable government establishments. Students network with former United States Senate Youth Program delegates. In addition to their week experience, students are rewarded with a $5,000 scholarship toward their undergraduate study.

GETTING HIRED

Apply by: Varies according to state (see "Selection Contact Page" at www.hearstfdn.org/ussyp). Application, program examination and selection by the office of the chief state or district school required.

Qualifications:
Open to high school juniors and seniors who are student body president, vice president, treasurer or secretary; class president, vice president, treasurer or secretary; student council representative; or a student representative elected to a district, regional or state-level civic or educational organization. Students must also be permanent U.S. residents.

Contact:
Your high school principal or state-level education administrator (see "Selection Contact Page" at www.hearstfdn.org/ussyp).

William Randolph Hearst Foundation
90 New Montgomery Street, Suite 1212
San Francisco, CA 94105-4504
Phone: (415) 543-4057 or (800) 841-7048
Fax: (415) 243-0760
E-mail: USSYP@hearstfdn.org

United Talent Agency

 THE BUZZ

- "Strut your stuff in Hollywood"
- "Discover if you have what it takes to be a top talent agent"

 THE STATS

Industry(ies): Broadcast & Entertainment; Music; Digital Media; Marketing/Lifestyle Branding & Licensing; Philanthropy

Location(s): Beverly Hills, CA

Number of interns: *Annual*: 50-60

Pay: Paid; $350/week plus overtime in mailroom; $400/week plus overtime upon promotion to assistant; $450/week plus overtime after one year of service

Length of internship: *Spring/summer/fall/winter*: 12-16 weeks each

 THE SCOOP

Established in 1991, United Talent Agency represents talent and literary artists, producers, directors, writers and corporations in the entertainment industry. Based in Beverly Hills, UTA clients include Johnny Depp, Harrison Ford, Jim Carrey, Ben Stiller, Vince Vaughn, Martin Lawrence, Jack Black, Owen Wilson, Gwen Steffani, Kate Bosworth, Amazon, directors M. Night Shyamalan, the Coen Brothers, and TV producers David Chase and Dick Wolf, among others.

 ON THE JOB

The UTA training program is an apprenticeship/internship for those focused on becoming agents in the entertainment business. Individuals are first trained in the mailroom as they work their way up the company ladder to eventually assist agents. While working in the mailroom, interns must have excellent organizational skills and the ability to work in a fast-paced environment.

GETTING HIRED

Apply by: Rolling. Submit a resume and cover letter to the address below.

Qualifications:
Open to college juniors and seniors, grad students and international applicants.

Contact:
Human Resources
Agency Training Program
United Talent Agency
9560 Wilshire Blvd., 5th floor
Beverly Hills, CA 90212
Phone: (310) 273-6700
Fax: (310) 247-1111
E-mail: HR@unitedtalent.com
www.united talent.com

Universal Music Group

 THE BUZZ

- "24-karat name in music"

THE STATS

Industry(ies): Broadcast & Entertainment; Music/Records

Location(s): Chicago, IL; Dallas, TX; Greenbelt, MD; Los Angeles, CA; Marietta, GA; Nashville, TN; New York, NY; Queens, NY; San Francisco, CA; Warren, MI; Woburn, MA

Number of interns: *Annual*: 225-400

Pay: None; academic credit. Free promotional merchandise and concert tickets; attendance at most staff meetings

Length of internship: *Spring/summer/fall*: 8-20 weeks each

 THE SCOOP

Universal Music Group develops and markets musical artists such as Ashanti, U2, Beck, Mary J. Blige, Bon Jovi, blink-182, Mariah Carey, Sheryl Crow, DMX, Dr. Dre, Eminem, Eve, Ja Rule, Jay-Z, Limp Bizkit, Nelly, No Doubt, Shaggy, Sting and Weezer. It has "joint ventures and licensees in 63 countries around the world that represents 98 percent of the global music market." The UMG subdivisions include Interscope Geffen A&M, Island Def Jam, Universal/Motown Records Group, Classics and Verve Music Group.

ON THE JOB

Interns are placed in various departments, including marketing, publicity, promotions, A&R, new media, sales, human resources, finance, business and legal, and others.

GETTING HIRED

Apply by: Rolling. Submit a resume, a cover letter that includes your area of interest, an official transcript and a letter on the school's letterhead stating that academic credit will be awarded.

Qualifications:
Open to college freshmen, sophomores, juniors and seniors. Students must receive academic credit from an accredited two- or four-year university and provide documentation from their school on or before their start dates.

Contact:
Internship Coordinator, Human Resources
Universal Music Group
825 Eighth Avenue, 23rd Floor
New York, NY 10019
Phone: (212) 333-8000
www.umusic.com

Visit Vault at **www.vault.com** for insider company profiles, expert advice, career message boards, expert resume reviews, the Vault Job Board and more.

VAULT CAREER LIBRARY **415**

Universal Studios

 THE BUZZ
- "Ride your way to the top"
- "You'll have an entertaining summer"

 THE STATS

Industry(ies): Broadcast & Entertainment; Film

Location(s): Universal City, CA; Santa Monica, CA

Number of interns: *Annual*: 18-20

Pay: Paid and unpaid. Students interested in unpaid positions are required to submit a letter from their school certifying that they will receive academic credit. Those interested in paid positions may earn academic credit as well, but it is not mandatory. Other perks include free promotional items

Length of internship: *Spring/summer/fall/winter*: 10-12 weeks each

 THE SCOOP

For over 85 years, Universal Studios has been providing unique entertainment through motion pictures, home videos, theme parks and attractions, television networks and programming. Universal Studios owns Universal Pictures, Universal TV and Networks Group, and Universal Studios Hollywood.

 ON THE JOB

Internships at Universal Studios are available in the television, pictures, theme parks and corporate groups. Positions relate to marketing, publicity, sales, development, finance, production, food service, information technology, media, Internet, consumer products and human resources.

 GETTING HIRED

Apply by: Rolling. Send resume and cover letter (with availability date and semester for which you are applying) to the address below.

Qualifications:

Open to all college freshmen, sophomores, juniors and seniors, and grad students who are currently registered at an accredited institution.

Contact:
Internship Program
Universal Studios
100 Universal City Plaza
Universal City, CA 91608
Phone: (818) 777-1000
corp.universalstudios.com/college.html

University of California-San Francisco AIDS Health Project

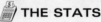 **THE BUZZ**
- "Be on the front lines of the battle against AIDS"

THE STATS

Industry(ies): Health Care; Nonprofit

Location(s): San Francisco, CA

Number of interns: *Annual*: 8-10

Pay: $800 housing stipend payable directly to the intern's landlord

Length of internship: 1 year, starting each July

THE SCOOP

The University of California at San Francisco's AIDS Health Project began in 1984 to provide Bay Area AIDS patients with free psychological support services. Since then, the project has grown to offer counseling to people at risk of infection and caregivers for those afflicted, as well as crisis intervention for those diagnosed with HIV. The program focuses on caring for clients and their families, as well as educating the Bay Area public on AIDS and HIV infection.

ON THE JOB

Tasks vary depending on the type of internship, but can include scheduling patients for HIV tests, assisting in daily research study activity, data entry, clerical duties, fundraising events or even participation in interactive training for the public. Most UCSF AIDS interns will likely have far more contact with clients (and their loved ones) than with test tubes, and those who study humanities (history, art, literature) are encouraged to apply.

GETTING HIRED

Apply by: March 31, but early application is encouraged.

Qualifications:

Open to recent college graduates or grad students. Must complete two essays on 1) why you are applying, and 2) how the program will affect your career. See the web site for detailed job descriptions and application form. See www.ucsf-ahp.org/HTML/internfact.html for details.

Contact:
UCSF AIDS Health Project
Staffing Coordinator
Box 0884
San Francisco, CA 94143-0884
Phone: (415) 476-3890
Fax: (415) 476-3613
E-mail: carol.music@ucsf.edu
www.ucsf-ahp.org/HTML/internfact.html

US-Asia Institute

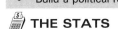 **THE BUZZ**
- "Build amity between the United States and Asian nations"
- "Build a political resume and travel outside the U.S. to boot"

 THE STATS

Industry(ies): Government

Location(s): Washington, DC

Number of interns: *Spring/summer/fall*: 2 each

Pay: None; possible academic credit

Length of internship: *Spring/summer/fall*: 12 weeks each

 **THE SCOOP**

Founded in 1979, the US-Asia Institute promotes greater unity between the governments of Asian countries and Washington, DC, through economic and diplomatic cooperation. The Institute holds conferences and symposiums focusing on relations between America and Asian countries, be it through student exchange or professional staff who travel to each other's countries to experience different cultures.

ON THE JOB

Interns' duties vary but may include researching legal or diplomatic issues specific to U.S. and Asian relations and assisting in presentations regarding those issues. Interns may attend Congressional hearings and conferences held at Asian embassies and at think tanks around Washingto, D.C.

GETTING HIRED

Apply by: *Spring*: November 15; *summer*: March 15; *fall*: July 15. Send a cover letter, letter of recommendation and writing sample.

Qualifications:

Open to all college students, as well as grad students. Applicants must be at least 18 years old.

Contact:
US-Asia Institute
232 East Capitol Street, NE
Washington, DC 20003
Phone: (202) 544-3181
Fax: (202) 543-1748
E-mail: usasiainstitute@verizon.net
www.usaasiainstitute.org

USDA Forest Service

 THE BUZZ
- "Cultivate greenery for tomorrow"

 THE STATS

Industry(ies): Environmental; Government; Tourism/Recreation

Location(s): Various locations in 44 states

Number of interns: *Annual*: 100

Pay: Varies according to the classification of the job and includes sick and annual leave; students in the Student Career Experience Program (SCEP) receive health and life insurance

Length of internship: 1 year

THE SCOOP

With over 30,000 employees ranging from teachers to firefighters to biologists, the USDA Forest Service is able to manage 51,000 square miles of forests and grasslands. The Forest Service has been a leader in conservation since its establishment in 1905. Today, the USDA works in partnership with other government organizations, as well as with universities and landowners.

ON THE JOB

The USDA Forest service offers two student programs: the Student Temporary Employment Program (STEP) and the Student Career Experience Program (SCEP). The primary difference is that STEP does not necessarily relate to a student's academic experience or career aspirations, while SCEP directly relates to these components. SCEP participants must work one to 15 hours per week, while STEP participants may work any agreed-upon hours.

GETTING HIRED

Apply by: Rolling. See your local Forest Service unit (locator available at www.fs.fed.us/recreation/map/finder.shtml) or your college counselor.

Qualifications:

Open to high school students, college freshmen, sophomores, juniors and seniors, graduates and grad students. All must be of legal working age.

Contact:
E-mail: fsjobs@fs.fed.us
www.fs.fed.us/fsjobs/student.html

Visit Vault at **www.vault.com** for insider company profiles, expert advice, career message boards, expert resume reviews, the Vault Job Board and more.

V**AULT** CAREER LIBRARY **417**

The Utah State Legislature

 THE BUZZ

* "Future Utah politicians wanted"

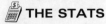 **THE STATS**

Industry(s): Government; Law

Location(s): Salt Lake City, UT

Number of interns: *Annual*: 65

Pay: Paid; $1,800/term. Academic credit available

Length of internship: 45 days (January-March)

THE SCOOP

Established in 1846, the Utah Legislature meets 45 calendar days every year. The state's intern program was formalized in 1971 and has included Rob W. Bishop, the former Speaker of the Utah House. The legislature has 29 senators and 75 representatives, and is largely Republican.

ON THE JOB

Interns are assigned to specific legislators in the House and the Senate, where they handle a variety of duties, including constituent concerns, research and office support.

GETTING HIRED

Apply by: November 15 for the following January. Applicants must submit a transcript and several letters of recommendation to the address below.

Qualifications:

Open to all enrolled college juniors and seniors from the five Utah universities who are at least 18 years old. Applicants must be able to receive college credit for their work.

Contact:

Jerry Howe

The Office of Legislative Research and General Counsel

Student Internship Program

W210 House Building

State Capitol

Salt Lake City, UT 84114

Phone: (801) 538-1032

www.le.state.ut.us/lrgc/internprogram.htm

INTERNSHIP PROFILES: V

Varsity Painters

🐝 THE BUZZ
- "Add a little color to your life"
- "Not suited for those scared of heights"

📅 THE STATS
Industry(ies): Construction/Building Materials

Location(s): Minneapolis, MN

Number of interns: *Summer*: 125

Pay: Paid; $8.50/hour plus bonuses

Length of internship: *Summer*: 16 week

✏️ THE SCOOP
Varsity Painters was established in 1995 by cofounders Joe Perry and Steve Melander who launched their company after graduating from college. The plan was hatched during school when they realized that the sheer mass of college students looking for well-paying summer jobs could easily form a workforce. Varsity, a house-painting company that mostly concentrates on outdoor work, services Minneapolis, St. Paul and the surrounding areas.

🏢 ON THE JOB
Teams of college students are formed to work as a house-painting unit. All interns are thoroughly trained and supervised. It's possible to form your own group if you want to work with friends. Hours are flexible. Equipment is provided.

💰 GETTING HIRED
Apply by: Rolling. Apply online at www.varsitypainters.com /varsitypainters.html.

Qualifications:
Open to all college freshmen, sophomores, juniors and seniors and recent college graduates (some high school students may be hired).

Contact:
Varsity Painters
P.O. Box 24126
Edina, MN 55424-9875
Phone: (612) 938-3886
Fax: (612) 823-2169
www.varsitypainters.com

Vault Inc.

🐝 THE BUZZ
- "Intern for the world's intership experts"
- "Vault loves interns"

📅 THE STATS
Industry(ies): Internet; New/Interactive Media; Publishing

Location(s): New York, NY

Number of interns: *Annual*: 15

Pay: Paid; minimum wage

Length of internship: *Spring/summer/fall*: 12-16 weeks (flexible)

✏️ THE SCOOP
As "The Most Trusted Name in Career Information," Vault has been leading the career publishing field since 1997. Mark Oldman and brothers Hussam and Samer Hamadeh founded the company to "avoid the rat race by writing about it". Vault's site provides invaluable insider information on leaders in a wide range of professional industries such as law, investment banking, consulting, advertising, energy, media and entertainment, biotech and human resources. Vault's printed and online guides reveal continually changing work life for the employees of these companies and organizations around the world.

🏢 ON THE JOB
Though Vault hires interns on an as-needed basis, there are often opportunities in several departments, including editorial and sales. Interns are treated as full-time staff and are exposed to "real" work. In addition to office-based positions, Vault offers campus outreach and campus representative programs, where interns act as Vault agents on their campus to earn extra money and boost their resumes.

💰 GETTING HIRED
Apply by: Rolling. Check the online list of current openings (www.vault.com/admin2/aboutvault/_workvault.jsp?aboutus = 9) for application details. For unlisted positions, send a resume and cover letter to the address below. For campus outreach opportunities, see www.vault.com/admin2/careercenter.jsp; for campus representative positions, see www.vault.com/admin2/ campusrep.jsp.

Qualifications:
Open to high school seniors, all undergraduates, recent college graduates and grad students. See web site for details about current openings and specific requirements.

Contact:
Kandy Black, Human Resources
Vault Inc.
150 West 22nd Street, 5th Floor
New York, NY 10011
Phone: (212) 366-4212
Fax: (212) 366-6117
E-mail: work@vault.com
www.vault.com/admin2/aboutvault/_workvault.jsp?aboutus = 9

Vibe

 THE BUZZ
- "Creative writers with an edge"
- "Hip-hop princesses and princes wanted"

 THE STATS

Industry(ies): Music/Records; Publishing

Location(s): New York, NY

Number of interns: *Annual*: 18-20

Pay: None. Admission to parties and events; free copies of the magazine; CDs and promotional materials; occasional concert tickets

Length of internship: *Spring/summer/fall*: 16 weeks

 THE SCOOP

Founded by Quincy Jones in 1993, *Vibe* is a monthly magazine covering urban music and the hip-hop culture. The magazine goes beyond an entertainment periodical and considers itself a portal for a "growing, young, trend-setting, multicultural audience by covering political issues in the same issue it is profiling the rapper Jay-Z."

ON THE JOB

Interns can work in several areas depending on their interests and skills. Positions are available in editorial, marketing, information technology, advertising and promotions.

GETTING HIRED

Apply by: Rolling. Submit a resume, cover letter and any journalism clips (for the editorial department).

Qualifications:
Open to all college freshmen, sophomores, juniors and seniors, recent college graduates and grad students.

Contact:
Internship Coordinator
Vibe
205 Lexington Avenue, 6th Floor
New York, NY 10016
Phone: (212) 448-7300
Fax: (212) 448-7400
E-mail: interns@vibe.com
E-mail: itinterns@vibe.com (IT department only)
www.vibe.com

Village Voice

 THE BUZZ
- "Make your voice heard at one of the country's largest and most influential alternative papers"

 THE STATS

Industry(ies): Journalism

Location(s): New York, NY

Number of interns: *Annual*: 90 (15 each term)

Pay: None for most positions. A $150/week Mary Wright writing fellowship is offered to minority applicants. Access to *Voice*'s library; free t-shirts, movie passes, CDs and tapes

Length of internship: *Spring*: June-August; *summer*: February-May; *fall*: September-December; *winter*: January- February. 15 hours/week required

 THE SCOOP

In publication since 1955, *The Village Voice* is the largest weekly alternative newspaper in the country. It focuses on features relating to "opinionated arts, culture, music, dance, film and theater reviews, Web dispatches and comprehensive entertainment listings," and reaches over half a million readers weekly. The *Voice* has earned a reputation for its groundbreaking investigations of New York City politics, and is the foremost authority on the NYC downtown vibe. It's also a notable recipient of "three Pulitzer prizes, the George Polk Award, Front Page Awards, Deadline Club Awards and many others."

 ON THE JOB

Interns work as assistants to editors and staff writers in the editorial and photography departments. Past interns have worked alongside writers James Ridgeway and Wayne Barnett, as well as columnists Michael Musto and Toni Schlesinger.

GETTING HIRED

Apply by: *Spring*: December 31; *summer*: March 31; *fall*: July 31; *winter*: November 30. Submit a resume, cover letter, clips of published articles (editorial department) and photography samples (photography department) to the address below.

Qualifications:
Open to some high school students, all college freshmen, sophomores, juniors and seniors, and grad students. International applicants are eligible.

Contact:
Internship Coordinator
The Village Voice
36 Cooper Square
New York, NY 10003
Phone: (212) 475-3300
Fax: (212) 475-8945
www.villagevoice.com/aboutus/jobs.php#intern

Visit Vault at **www.vault.com** for insider company profiles, expert advice, career message boards, expert resume reviews, the Vault Job Board and more.

V\ULT CAREER LIBRARY **421**

Virgin Records

 THE BUZZ
- "One of the world's most irresistible music brands"

THE STATS

Industry(ies): Broadcast & Entertainment; Music/Records

Location(s): Los Angeles, CA; New York, NY; London

Number of interns: *Annual*: 25-45 (U.S.)

Pay: None. Free CDs, concert tickets, t-shirts, invitations to listening parties and promotions

Length of internship: *Spring/summer/fall*: 10-14 weeks each

THE SCOOP

Virgin Records was started by Richard Branson in 1973 as an independent label based in London, and is now part of EMI, the third-largest music company in the world. VR artists include Lenny Kravitz, The Rolling Stones, Smashing Pumpkins, A Perfect Circle, Ben Harper, Blur, Chemical Brothers, Korn, Daft Punk, Daz Dillinger, Dem Franchize Boyz, Dwele, Fatboy Slim, Gorillaz, Janet Jackson, Massive Attack, Jermaine Dupri, RBD, The Red Jumpsuit Apparatus, KT Tunstall and Big Boi.

ON THE JOB

Internships are available in the New York, Los Angeles and London offices in fields related to advertising, artists and repertoire, marketing, tour marketing, promotions, publicity, production, sales and computers. Responsibilities vary with placement.

GETTING HIRED

Apply by: Rolling. Submit a resume and cover letter to the appropriate address below.

Qualifications:

Open to high school students, college freshmen, sophomores, juniors and seniors, recent college graduates, grad students and international students.

Contact:
Melissa Robinson
Internship Coordinator
Human Resources Department
Virgin Records America
150 Fifth Avenue, 7th Floor
New York, NY 10011
Phone: (212) 786-8300

Virginia Symphony

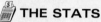 **THE BUZZ**
- "Classical music fans should take note of this opportunity"
- "Make beautiful music for your future"

THE STATS

Industry(ies): Music/Records; Theater/Performing Arts

Location(s): Norfolk, VA

Number of interns: *Annual*: 14-20

Pay: None. Free admission to concerts; mentors

Length of internship: *Spring/summer/fall*: 10-16 weeks

THE SCOOP

Founded in 1920, the Virginia Symphony is a professional ensemble that annually performs more than "140 Classical, Pop, Family, Education and Outreach concerts, including orchestral support of the highly acclaimed Virginia Opera." Recent great achievements include "five compact disc recordings for national release, a performance of Peter and the Wolf which was aired on National Public Radio, performance at the Kennedy Center and an acceptance into the International Conference of Symphony and Opera Musicians."

ON THE JOB

Internships are available in the development, finance, marketing and production departments, and in the executive offices.

GETTING HIRED

Apply by: Rolling. Write to the address below for an application.

Qualifications:

Open to undergraduate students who have completed a minimum of one year of study (or the equivalent), grad students, recent college graduates and career changers currently enrolled in a degree program.

Contact:
Virginia Symphony
Attention: Internship Coordinator
880 North Military Highway, Suite 1064
Norfolk, VA 23502
Phone: (757) 466-3060
www.virginiasymphony.org

Voice of America

 THE BUZZ
- "The news heard 'round the world"
- "A chance to learn about the power of the airwaves up close"

 THE STATS

Industry(ies): Broadcast & Entertainment; Journalism

Location(s): Washington, DC

Number of interns: *Annual*: 45-50

Pay: None. Access to fitness center; interaction with major political players

Length of internship: *Spring/summer/fall*: 6-12 weeks

 THE SCOOP

Established in 1942, the Voice of America is a news organization funded by the U.S. Information Agency to provide insightful data for "Americans and foreigners through short-wave radio transmissions." VOA programming is about 59 percent news and 26 percent reporting on topics related to economics, science, agriculture, medicine, sports, and American history and culture.

 ON THE JOB

Internships are offered in the audience mail, English (newsroom, current affairs and worldwide English), external affairs, affiliate relations and language program divisions.

GETTING HIRED

Apply by: Rolling. Submit a resume and cover letter to the address below.

Qualifications:
Open to high school students, college freshmen, sophomores, juniors and seniors, recent college graduates, grad students and international students.

Contact:
Internship Coordinator: Janice Albritton
Voice of America
Room 1543 HHS-N Building
330 Independence Avenue, SW
Washington, DC 20547
Phone: (202) 619-3117
E-mail: jalbritt@ibb.gov
www.voa.gov/interns

Volkswagen Audi

 THE BUZZ
- "The fast track for go-getters!"
- "Learn from some of the best in the automotive industry"

 THE STATS

Industry(ies): Consumer Products; Engineering; Manufacturing; Technology

Location(s): Auburn Hills, MI; Wolfsburg, Germany

Number of interns: *Annual*: 30-40

Pay: Paid; *Michigan*: $400-$580/week; *Germany*: $150/week plus subsidized housing

Length of internship: 3-6 months

 **THE SCOOP**

In 1932, four vehicle manufacturers merged to create Auto Union AG, the predecessor to today's Audi AG (or Volkswagen Audi). Volkswagen Audi prides itself on a myriad of technological innovations reflected in its products. As the largest European auto manufacturer, Audi is unquestionably a world leader in the automotive industry.

 ON THE JOB

In addition to plenty of hands-on experience in the automotive industry, interns have a lot to gain from Volkswagen Audi's internship program. Perks include a salary, computer training classes, seminars and workshops. Based on interest, interns are assigned to various Audi departments such as marketing, human resources, parts or information technology. Most importantly, interns work on real projects and are treated as equal employees.

GETTING HIRED

Apply by: Rolling. Send resume and cover letter indicating months of availability and career interest to one of the addresses below. An interview is required.

Qualifications:
Open to college juniors and seniors and graduate students. Business majors with a minimum 3.0 GPA preferred.

Contact:
Volkswagen of America, Inc.
Human Resources Group
3800 Hamlin Road
Auburn Hills, MI 48326

Regina Peldszus
Human Resources Group
Volkswagen, A.G.
Berliner Ring 2
38436 Wolfsburg, Germany
Phone: 49-53-6192-1245
Fax: 49-53-6192-2294
www.vw.com

Visit Vault at **www.vault.com** for insider company profiles, expert advice, career message boards, expert resume reviews, the Vault Job Board and more.

V**A**ULT CAREER LIBRARY **423**

Volunteers for Israel

 THE BUZZ
- "Not your average country club internship"

 THE STATS

Industry(ies): Nonprofit

Location(s): Israel

Number of interns: No limit

Pay: None. VFI pays for accommodations and meals during the workweek and helps arrange weekend lodging. Volunteers arrange and pay for their own airfare

Length of internship: Volunteers are encouraged to stay a minimum of 3 weeks, but there are some 2-week and occasional 1-week programs. There may also be specially arranged trips for young adults and singles

 THE SCOOP

A nonprofit, nonsectarian organization, Volunteers for Israel was originally founded in 1982 to provide the small country with volunteer workers during the Lebanon war when Israel's own workers were sent to fight. The program continued after the war and has sent more than 92,000 volunteers from 30 countries to Israel to help the country's economy. VFI works to increase multicultural understanding, intensify Jewish identity and the bonds of solidarity among volunteers and citizens, and to help Israel grow.

 ON THE JOB

Most volunteers are placed on military maintenance bases where they hold noncombative roles. They work side by side with Israelis performing a variety of duties, such as packaging medical supplies or repairing or refurbishing equipment. Others work in nonmilitary areas, such as in a hospital's geriatric, psychiatric or rehabilitation center, functioning in roles similar to that of a candy striper or orderly. VFI provides at least one tour and evening lectures.

GETTING HIRED

Apply by: Rolling. Volunteers can start on specific Sundays or Mondays throughout the year with a few exceptions for holidays. See the web site, www.vfi-usa.org, for schedule details and other information. Download an application from www.vfi-usa.org/application.html. (Application fee: $80.)

Qualifications:
Open to volunteers aged 17 and up – to the young and the young-at-heart.

Contact:
Volunteer Coordinator
Volunteers for Israel
330 West 42nd Street, Suite 1618
New York, NY 10036-6029
Phone: (866) 514-1948
Fax: (215) 473-4473
E-mail: info@vfi-usa.org
www.vfi-usa.org

Volunteers for Peace

 THE BUZZ
- "A short-term Peace Corps"

 THE STATS

Industry(ies): Nonprofit

Location(s): Belmont, VT

Number of interns: *Annual*: 1,400

Pay: None. $200-$400 program fee, approximately

Length of internship: *Spring/summer/fall/winter*: 2-3 weeks each

 THE SCOOP

Over the years, Volunteers for Peace has recruited more than 23,000 volunteers to assist in international workcamps and places about 1,500 annually. Since 1982, VFP has been matching hosts with volunteers to foster cross-cultural understanding and friendship. Currently, VFP offers over 3,000 international voluntary service programs in over 100 countries. Volunteers from various countries can learn about many different cultures at once when placed in the same work camp. VFP allows volunteers to work together to resolve and prevent conflicts and to generally improve the communities' quality of life.

ON THE JOB

Volunteers may go to almost any country including Russia, Mexico, The Netherlands or France. Some projects include teaching local people a new craft they can sell to improve the economy, restoring buildings, entertaining children in orphanages or teaching English to adults or children. Most meals are cooked by the volunteers themselves and accommodations vary for each project. Specific details are available on the web site, www.vfp.org.

GETTING HIRED

Apply by: *Summer*: late March-late May; *fall/spring/winter*: rolling. Write, call or e-mail for application, newsletter and International Workcamp Directory (directory costs $20).

Qualifications:
Open to high school students, college freshmen, sophomores, juniors and seniors, and college graduates.

Contact:
Volunteers for Peace
1034 Tiffany Road
Belmont, VT 05730
Phone: (802) 259-2759
Fax: (802) 259-2922
E-mail: vfp@vfp.org
www.vfp.org

Volunteers in Asia

 THE BUZZ

- "Teach English all over Asia"

 THE STATS

Industry(ies): Education; Nonprofit

Location(s): Stanford, CA (HQ); China; Indonesia; Vietnam

Number of interns: *Annual*: 30-40; *summer*: 12-18

Pay: None. *1- and 2-year*: living stipend based on in-country living expenses; *summer*: $1500-$2000 airfare stipend (long-term participants must fly themselves to Chiang Mai, Thailand). Basic medical insurance; emergency evacuation insurance; training (over 5 weeks for long-term participants and 2-3 weeks for summer participants); visa processing; accommodations; in-country and home office support); other expenses include immunizations and board costs

Length of internship: *Summer*: 6 weeks; *annual*: 1-2 years

 **THE SCOOP**

For the past 40 years Volunteers in Asia's programs have helped to bridge the gap between Asia and the United States. VIA first started at Stanford University, where students spent the summer assisting with various Asian programs. The project was successful and more students joined. During the Vietnam War the program grew substantially, expanding to national recruitment. VIA now sends about 40 volunteers to Asia and brings about 250 Asian students to the United States annually.

 ON THE JOB

VIA volunteers teach English to university and middle school students and work for local nonprofit or nongovernmental organizations in China, Vietnam and Indonesia. During either the long-term or summer programs, there is ample opportunity to study the language, get to know the locals and explore the land. One of VIA's long-term participants assists the summer interns in work preparation and cultural adjustment.

GETTING HIRED

Apply by: February 23. Download the program's application form at www.viaprograms.org/programs_in_asia.

Qualifications:

All programs are open to undergraduate students and college grads who speak English with a native fluency and are excited about cross-cultural exchange.

Contact:
Volunteers In Asia Programs
Haas Center for Public Service, 3rd Floor
P.O. Box 20266
Stanford, CA 94309
Phone: (650) 723-3228
Fax: (650) 725-1805
E-mail: info@viaprograms.org
www.viaprograms.org

Visit Vault at **www.vault.com** for insider company profiles, expert advice, career message boards, expert resume reviews, the Vault Job Board and more.

VAULT CAREER LIBRARY **425**

VΛULT

THE MOST TRUSTED NAME IN CAREER INFORMATION

"Fun reads, edgy details"

– FORBES MAGAZINE

Vault guides and employer profiles have been published since 1997 and are the premier source of insider information on careers.

Each year, Vault surveys and interviews thousands of employees to give readers the inside scoop on industries and specific employers to help them get the jobs they want.

"To get the un-varnished scoop, check out Vault"

– SMARTMONEY MAGAZINE

VΛULT

INTERNSHIP PROFILES:
W

Wadsworth Atheneum Museum of Art

THE BUZZ
- "Start an art career at the creme de la creme of museums"

THE STATS
Industry(ies): Art/Museum

Location(s): Hartford, CT

Number of interns: *Annual*: 1-15

Pay: None

Length of internship: *Spring/summer/fall*: 12-16 weeks each

THE SCOOP
The Wadsworth Atheneum is the oldest continuously operating public art museum in the United States – and one of its more innovative. The Wadsworth Atheneum enjoys a tradition of pioneering new artistic styles and was first to acquire works by renowned artists such as Salvador Dali, Joan Miro and Caravaggio. The museum currently holds 10 different shows yearly.

ON THE JOB
Interns complete projects in administration, archives, curatorial, education, external affairs, design and installation, registrar or collection imaging.

GETTING HIRED
Apply by: *Spring*: October 27; *summer*: March 23; *fall*: July 13. Write or e-mail for application.

Qualifications:
Open to college freshmen and sophomores; preference given to college juniors, seniors, recent graduates and grad students.

Contact:
Wadsworth Atheneum Museum of Art
600 Main Street
Hartford, CT 06103-2990
Phone: (860) 278-2670
Fax: (860) 249-7780
E-mail: susan.carey@wadsworthatheneum.org
www.wadsworthatheneum.org

The Wall Street Journal

 THE BUZZ
- "In the journalism field, it doesn't get much more prestigious than this"
- "A good step toward that Pulitzer"

 THE STATS

Industry(ies): Journalism

Location(s): New York, NY

Number of interns: *Journalism*: 18; *Editorial*: varies

Pay: Paid; $700/week

Length of internship: *Journalism*: 10 weeks (June-August); *Editorial*: 10 weeks (generally June-August, though dates are flexible)

 **THE SCOOP**

With a circulation of 1.8 million, *The Wall Street Journal* is unquestionably one of the top news journals in the United States. Since its establishment in 1889, *The Wall Street Journal* has become one of the most highly respected business newspapers worldwide, with reports on news and political issues that directly affect the American business industry. Currently, the paper employs more than 650 reporters and editors.

 ON THE JOB

The Wall Street Journal offers two separate internship programs. The Journalism Internship allows undergraduate students the opportunity to explore journalism careers in business news and information reporting. Journalism interns work in one of the *Journal*'s many news bureaus located throughout the country.

In the Editorial Page Internship, interns will assist in researching and writing editorials, editing op-ed articles, editing letters to the editor and editing OpinionJournal.com.

 GETTING HIRED

Apply by: *Journalism*: November 1. Send a cover letter, resume and at least 12 of your best bylined clips (clear, unbound photocopies on letter- or legal-sized paper) to Cathy Panagoulias, address below. All submissions become the property of *The Wall Street Journal* and will not be returned.

Editorial: January 15; a decision will be made by February or March. Send or e-mail a cover letter, resume and your best clips to Melanie Kirkpatrick, address below.

Qualifications:

Journalism: open to all currently enrolled undergraduate and graduate students. Prior internships with other newspapers and/or extensive experience on a campus newspaper preferred.

Editorial: open to college seniors. Preference is given to those with reporting, writing and editing experience on a college newspaper or elsewhere.

Contact:
Journalism Internship
Cathy Panagoulias
Assistant Managing Editor
The Wall Street Journal
200 Liberty Street
New York, NY 10281

Editorial Page Internship
Melanie Kirkpatrick
Associate Editor of the Editorial Page
The Wall Street Journal
200 Liberty Street
New York, NY 10281
E-mail: joann.joseph@wsj.com

Visit Vault at **www.vault.com** for insider company profiles, expert advice, career message boards, expert resume reviews, the Vault Job Board and more.

CAREER LIBRARY **429**

Wal-Mart Stores, Inc.

THE BUZZ
- "Roll back the competition"
- "Work alongside mom and pop at the world's largest retailer"

THE STATS
Industry(ies): Retail

Location(s): Bentonville, AR

Number of interns: *Corporate*: 120-170; *MBA*: 10-20

Pay: Paid; *corporate*: $14-$18/hour; *MBA*: competitive salary

Length of internship: *Corporate*: 10 weeks (summer); *MBA*: 12 weeks

 THE SCOOP
Wal-Mart is the world's largest retailer. In business since 1962, it employs approximately 1.5 million at more than 5,170 facilities worldwide. The stores' 138 million customers per week make Wal-Mart one of the world's largest retail conglomerates.

ON THE JOB
Wal-Mart established the Corprate Intern Program to give college students an understanding of its culture and business philosophy. This internship is available only at the home office in Bentonville, Ark. Interns may be assigned to various departments, including merchandising, product development, replenishment, risk control, transportation, logistics, accounting and finance, information systems, benefits/claims, store operations, aviation and human resources. Search the web site for available positions.

The company also offers an MBA internship, in which interns are assigned to a development team and to a specific project within that department. Possible departments include operations, mechandising, marketing, SAM's, finance, global procurement and international. Key leaders in the company serve as mentors to interns, who present their project results at the end of the internship.

GETTING HIRED
Apply by: Rolling. Submit resumes at www.walmartstores.com. Invitations are extended through the end of February.

Qualifications:
Corporate: open to college juniors and seniors. *MBA*: open to first-year MBA students. Relevant field of concentration a plus; heavy emphasis is placed on enthusiasm and a strong work ethic.

Contact:
Amanda Griffin
508 SW Eighth Street
Bentonville, AR 72716-0690
www.walmartstores.com

Walt Disney Corporate Strategy, Business Development, and Technology Group

THE BUZZ
- "A highly competitive, exclusive opportunity for the right MBA"
- "Play a role in planning the direction of this media empire"

THE STATS
Industry(ies): Broadcast & Entertainment; Management & Strategy Consulting

Location(s): Burbank, CA

Number of interns: *Summer*: 1

Pay: Varies

Length of internship: Summer months

THE SCOOP
Walt Disney Corporate Strategy, Business Development, and Technology Group is a sort of secret weapon for the Walt Disney Company. This low-profile organization works exclusively for the Disney corporation and handles strategy assignments in multiple business arenas (almost like Disney's personal consulting company). In addition to corporate strategy, the department covers M&A, strategic alliances, corporate business development, IP management and technology standards. It also aids various business units on their strategy when the issues are large enough to merit corporate attention. The planning group employs only 20 professionals, divided into smaller teams to better handle individual company needs and tasks, which vary depending on the issues the company is facing at the time. The group recently helped tackle the recent hostile takeover bid from Comcast; aided the acquisition of Baby Einstein and the Muppets; and assisted in the incubation of new businesses such as the ESPN and Disney MVNOs.

ON THE JOB
The intern (yes, one and only one) invited to join the Walt Disney Strategic Planning Group team each summer should expect attention and real working responsibility. That chosen MBA student should also be able to handle a bit of pressure and stress. Most importantly, an internship may act as an "in" for this notoriously selective division. Even if it doesn't, though, the prestige it will bring your resume will be priceless.

GETTING HIRED
Apply by: Rolling. Check with your college or university placement office.

Qualifications:
Open to MBA students only. Generally open only to universities chosen by the company.

Contact:
Walt Disney Strategic Planning Group
500 Buena Vista Street
Burbank, CA 91521
www.disney.com

The Walt Disney Studios

 THE BUZZ
- "Be part of the magic!"
- "A leader in producing family entertainment"

 **THE STATS**

Industry(ies): Broadcast & Entertainmnet; Film

Location(s): Burbank, CA

Number of interns: *Summer*: Varies

Pay: Varies

Length of internship: *Summer*: 8-10 weeks

 THE SCOOP

Walt Disney Studios may be best known for introducing Mickey Mouse in 1928; its first full-length animated movie, *Snow White and the Seven Dwarves*, in 1937; or for countless other entertainment milestones. Since the Walt Disney Company's establishment in 1923, the studios have expanded to offer a full range of production and post-production services, including the sound stages of the 1950s and the digital-imaging technologies of the 1990s. Walt Disney Studios remains a leader in the film industry.

 ON THE JOB

This full-time summer opportunity will engage its interns' office and computer skills. Although work will be limited to one area of Walt Disney Studios, a variety of assignments may be expected, depending on skills and placement.

GETTING HIRED

Apply by: *Summer*: January 1-April 15. Send resume and cover letter, outlining professional interests and how you would profit from the internship opportunity, to the e-mail address below.

Qualifications:

Open to sophomore, junior and senior college students who have completed at least their freshman year, as well as graduate students.

Contact:
E-mail: wds.intern@disney.com
www.wdwcollegeprogram.com

Walt Disney World

 THE BUZZ
- "Join the Mickey Mouse Club"
- "Spend a few months at the Happiest Place on Earth"

 THE STATS

Industry(ies): Broadcast & Entertainment; Hospitality; Tourism/Recreation

Location(s): Orlando, FL

Number of interns: Varies

Pay: Varies depending on department and experience

Length of internship: 6 months, beginning in either January or June; *Hilton Head program*: 3 months (May-August)

 THE SCOOP

Through his drawing talent, Walt Disney literally conjured up an empire. One of his most well-known creations, Florida-based theme park Walt Disney World, opened in 1971. Also known as the Magic Kingdom, the park is home to some of Disney's most beloved characters, including Mickey Mouse, Donald Duck and Goofy. The giant resort has grown over the years, now encompassing 47 square miles of land. It includes four theme parks, two water parks and over 20 lodging locations for its visiting guests.

 ON THE JOB

The advanced intern program helps students get experience and make valuable career contacts. Interns work in accounting, the design group, communications, education, industrial engineering, human resources, IT, marketing and sales, merchandising, recreation or science. Most positions go to past college program interns, but there are some that don't require previous Disney experience, such as the animal programs, Living Seas (aquarium), Epcot science center, or positions at Hilton Head (in food and beverage or recreation).

GETTING HIRED

Apply by: Rolling. Online application (available at www.wdwcollegeprogram.com/sap/its/mimes/zh_wdwcp/students/frameset/frameset_apply.html for details) and an interview at a school presentation are required. You can only apply for one advanced internship program, so check the site carefully for the one you want.

Qualifications:

Open to college freshmen, sophomores, juniors and seniors who have completed at least one semester and have previously worked in the Disney College Program. Minimum 2.0 GPA required. Must also have your own transportation and meet the individual requirements of the specific internship applied for. See web site for details.

Contact:
E-mail: wdw.college.recruiting@disney.com
www.wdwcollegeprogram.com

Visit Vault at **www.vault.com** for insider company profiles, expert advice, career message boards, expert resume reviews, the Vault Job Board and more.

CAREER LIBRARY **431**

Warner Music Group

THE BUZZ
- "See the music industry from the inside"

THE STATS

Industry(ies): Music; Sales; Marketing

Location(s): New York, NY; throughout the US

Number of interns: *Annually:* 51; *per term:* 14-17

Pay: Unpaid; $4.00/day stipend. Interns must be able to receive academic credit

Length of internship: *Summer:* 10 weeks; *fall/spring:* 12 weeks. Miminum 2 days or 15 hours/week; maximum 37.5 hours/week.

THE SCOOP

For over thirty years Warner Music Group (WMG) has been the parent company of Warner/Elektra/Atlantic (WEA) Corp., the first major music marketing and distribution company in the United States. In that time WEA has set the standard for sales and marketing in the music industry. In addition to the Warner Brothers, Elektra and Atlantic labels, WEA distributes audio and video releases from Rhino Entertainment, Asylum Records, Word Entertainment, Time-Life Music, Warner Music Latina and Curb Records, as well as several other labels. WEA has approximately 400 employees. In addition to WEA and its labels, WMG also runs Warner/Chappell Music, a leading music publisher.

ON THE JOB

WMG offers students interested in music industry careers a variety of internship opportunities in different departments. Interns work in marketing, sales, e-commerce, creative services and new media. All interns have mentors in their departments, gain hands-on experience about the music industry and are potential candidates for employment with WMG upon graduation.

GETTING HIRED

Apply by: *Summer:* March 15; *fall:* July 15; *spring:* December 15. Applicants interested in working for the New York office should send a resume and cover letter outlining their area of interest to the address below. Students interested in other locations should see the WMG web site. In addition, positions vary from semester to semester; go to www.wmg.com, and follow the link "job opportunities" to view all current and upcoming openings.

Qualifications:
Open to undergraduate and graduate students. Students must be able to receive academic credit for each internship term and interns must commit to an entire season term.

Contact:
Lisa Bertot
Warner Music Group
75 Rockefeller Plaza, 7th Floor
New York, NY 10019
E-mail: lisa.bertot@wmg.com
www.wmg.com

The Washington Center for Internships and Academic Seminars

THE BUZZ
- "Take advantage of unique seminars and lectures"
- "Get a tailored placement--for academic credit!"

THE STATS

Industry(ies): Education; Nonprofit

Location(s): Washington, DC

Number of interns: *Annual:* 1,400

Pay: None guaranteed; participants must receive academic credit. There is an application fee, as well as program and housing fees; 80-85% of students receive financial assistance

Length of internship: *Internship:* 10-15 weeks; *academic seminar:* 1-2 weeks

THE SCOOP

Founded in 1975, the Washington Center for Internships has been providing placements and academic seminars since 1975. The nonprofit organization, which has over 36,.000 alumni from the US and abroad, places college students from more than 850 colleges in DC-based related to their fields. Students are exposed to national and international leaders, and are encouraged to become civically engged. The Center employs over 60 full time staff.

ON THE JOB

Internships are tailored to student interests and placements include non-profits, businesses, international organizations and federal agencies. Students also take an academic course selected from among 30-50 offered each term. They attend large lectures with prominent speakers, participate in small-group meetings with members of Congress, visit embassies and have special briefings and tours related to their fields. At the end of the term, students complete a portfolio consisting of reflective pieces (a learning objective statement and internship defense letter), lecture analyses, an interview summary, a revised resume and work samples. This portfolio is then made available for review by the Center staff and the student's home institution for grade and credit recommendations.

GETTING HIRED

Apply by: Deadlines vary according to internship. See the web site (www.twc.edu) to request an application. Also check the web site for updates on the Center's new 2007 street address.

Qualifications:
Open to undergrads in their sophomore year or beyond, who have a 2.75 GPA or higher and the endorsement of a faculty advisor.

Contact:
Sara Clement
The Washington Center for Internships and Academic Seminars
2301 M Street, NW, 5th Floor
Washington, DC 20037
Phone: (202) 336-7600
Fax: (202) 336-7609
E-mail: info@twc.edu
www.twc.edu

Washington Center for Politics & Journalism

 THE BUZZ
- "Get a front-row seat to national politics"

 **THE STATS**

Industry(ies): Journalism

Location(s): Washington, DC

Number of interns: *Fall/spring*: 13 each

Pay: $3,000 stipend

Length of internship: *Fall/spring*: 16 weeks

 **THE SCOOP**

Founded in 1988, the Washington Center for Politics and Journalism trains political journalism students. The Center runs "The Politics and Journalism Semester," a program providing news bureau internship opportunities combined with seminars on politics.

ON THE JOB

Interns learn about campaign, governance and interest group politics while attending seminars twice weekly. Seminar speakers include political journalists, politicians and political consultants. Each reporter intern is assigned to one of the major Washington news bureaus.

GETTING HIRED

Apply by: *Fall*: first Friday in April; *spring*: first Friday in November. Participating schools may nominate two students per semester. Students from nonparticipating schools may apply directly. Applications can be found on the Center's web site, www.wcpj.org. Published writing samples are required for print-oriented students.

Qualifications:

Open to junior and senior undergrad students (who have completed at least one semester of their junior year), grad students and recent college graduates. Must have serious interest in political journalism as a career. Students with reporting, writing and producing experience are preferred.

Contact:

Terry Michael, Executive Director
Washington Center for Politics & Journalism
P.O. Box 15239
Washington, DC 20003-0239
Phone: (202) 296-8455
Fax: (800) 858-8365
E-mail: terrymichael@wcpj.org
www.wcpj.org

Washington Internships for Students of Engineering

THE BUZZ
- "Love engineering and politics? Here's your internship"

THE STATS

Industry(ies): Engineering

Location(s): Washington, DC

Number of interns: *Summer*: 8-10

Pay: Paid; $2,100/term. Free housing

Length of internship: *Summer*: 9 weeks

THE SCOOP

In 1980, a number of professional engineering societies organized the Washington Internships for Students of Engineering (WISE). The group's mission was, and still is, to produce future leaders in the engineering field by teaching engineering students how to influence the legislative process and help make public policy.

ON THE JOB

Interns are supervised by an engineering professor and work with professionals from their sponsoring societies, such as the American Institute of Chemical Engineers or the American Nuclear Society (ANS). They also meet daily with members of Congress, executive office departments or corporate government affairs offices. Each intern researches, writes and presents a paper on some contemporary engineering-related public policy.

GETTING HIRED

Apply by: *Summer*: December 16. Applicants must include an application (download from www.wise-intern.org/apply.html), two brief essays in response to questions, two faculty references and an official transcript.

Qualifications:

Open to college juniors and seniors, or students entering their last year of engineering or computer science studies, as well as engineering graduates entering a master's program in a policy-related field. ANS, the American Society of Civil Engineering, the American Society of Mechanical Engineers and the Institute of Electrical and Electronics Engineers will only sponsor their society members and have their own qualifications for sponsorship.

Contact:

WISE Program
c/o Erica Wissolik, IEEE-USA
1828 L Street, NW, Suite 1202
Washington, DC 20036-5104
Phone: (202) 785-0017
E-mail: e.wissolik@ieee.org
www.wise-intern.org

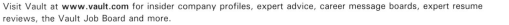 Visit Vault at **www.vault.com** for insider company profiles, expert advice, career message boards, expert resume reviews, the Vault Job Board and more.

VAULT CAREER LIBRARY **433**

Washington Office on Latin America

 THE BUZZ
- "Promote Latin American and Caribbean human rights"

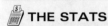 **THE STATS**

Industry(ies): Government; Nonprofit

Location(s): Washington, DC

Number of interns: *Annual*: 21 (7 per session)

Pay: None

Length of internship: *Summer*: 10 weeks; *fall/spring*: 16 weeks

 **THE SCOOP**

The Washington Office on Latin America advocates social justice and human rights in Latin America and the Caribbean. The nonprofit organization has been monitoring the U.S. government's policies on Latin America since 1974. The group reports on the impact of U.S. policies in the region to religious groups, the public and nongovernmental agencies.

ON THE JOB

Interns gain experience in the foreign policy-making process and become familiar with current issues in Latin America by attending meetings with policy-making associates, brown bag lunches with guest speakers and congressional hearings. Interns are assigned to work with a particular staff member on a specific project in order to foster mentoring relationships. In the past, interns have written a background brief on land reform in Nicaragua and documented human rights abuses by the Mexican military, among other topics.

GETTING HIRED

Apply by: *Summer*: March 15; *fall/spring*: rolling. Send to the address below a cover letter, stating availability to work the required hours and area of interest, a resume, a two- to five-page writing sample, and the names and telephone numbers of two references.

Qualifications:
Open to college freshmen, sophomores, juniors and seniors with a proven interest in human rights, democracy and social justice in Latin America. Must be willing to work 24 hours each week, or 32 hours each week for a summer internship.

Contact:
Internship Recruitment Coordinator
Washington Office on Latin America
1630 Connecticut Avenue, NW, Floor 2
Washington, DC 20009
Phone: (202) 797-2171
Fax: (202) 797-2172
E-mail: intern @wola.org
www.wola.org

The Washington Post

THE BUZZ
- "Start the presses!"
- "A first-rate opportunity with one of the nation's most respected newspapers"

THE STATS

Industry(ies): Journalism

Location(s): Washington, DC

Number of interns: *Summer*: 20

Pay: Varies according to education and experience

Length of internship: *Summer*: 3 months

THE SCOOP

With a weekly circulation of more than 5 million, *The Washington Post* is a journalistic powerhouse and employs more than 2,500 people in its business, news/editorial and production branches. Milestones since its 1877 founding include Eugene Meyers' acquisition of the paper in 1933, adding color in 1999 and multiple Pulitzer Prizes. The paper is owned and operated by The Washington Post Company, which also owns *Newsweek*, Kaplan, Inc., and various cable systems.

ON THE JOB

Interns work in several departments of the newspaper, assisting the advertising, accounting or media departments. Although duties will depend on department and need, students may expect clerical, as well as project-based work. Check out www.washington post.com/wp-srv/hr/intern.html?nav=globebot for details.

GETTING HIRED

Apply by: November 1 for editorial positions. Contact the company regarding deadlines for other departments. Send a resume and cover letter indicating experience and area of interest to the e-mail address below.

Qualifications:
Open to college freshmen, sophomores, juniors and seniors. An interest in publishing or media is crucial.

Contact:
Internship Coordinator
Washington Post
1150 15th Street, NW
Washington, DC 20071
E-mail: hr@wpni.com

Washingtonian

 THE BUZZ
- "Become a Beltway insider by working for the magazine that's the buzz of Washington"
- "Gain hands-on experience at this premier regional publication"

 THE STATS

Industry(ies): Publishing

Location(s): Washington, DC

Number of interns: *Annual*: 4-5

Pay: Varies; *editorial*: $7.00/hour; *advertising*: honorarium to cover expenses; *art production*: unpaid

Length of internship: *Spring/summer/fall*: 3-5 months each for editorial, advertising and art ; 40 hours/week

 THE SCOOP

Washingtonian claims to be "the magazine Washington lives by" and covers everything in Washington from schools and education to arts and entertainment, as well as travel, restaurants, health and medicine, real estate, people and, of course, what's hot now in Washington. An online version can be found at www.washingtonian.com. It includes excerpts from the magazine, as well as special online features.

 ON THE JOB

Editorial interns fact check, research and get some writing assignments. They also meet with the heads of each department to learn about the various roles at the magazine. Advertising interns, who act as sales support to the real estate and travel departments, contact advertisers, draft marketing materials and letters, and update advertising files. Art interns scan photos, help design ads and promotional pieces, and call for stock photos. Some interns may be given layout assignments.

 GETTING HIRED

Apply by: *Editorial*: *spring*: November 1; *summer*: March 1; *fall*: July 1. Send a resume, cover letter, three writing samples and references.

Advertising: *spring*: December 15; *summer*: May 15; *fall*: August 15. Submit a resume and cover letter.

Art: *spring*: November 15; *summer*: April 15; *fall*: August 15. Applications should include a resume and cover letter. Applicants may also have to present a portfolio of work created in QuarkXpress and Adobe Photoshop.

Qualifications:
Summer positions are open to all college students and graduates; fall and spring position open only to graduates. Editorial interns must have good reporting, writing and research skills. Advertising and art applicants must be current students or graduates of an arts program.

Contact:
Editorial
Sara Levine
Assistant Editor
Washingtonian
1828 L Street, NW, Suite 200
Washington, DC 20036
E-mail: slevine@washingtonian.com
www.washingtonian.com

Advertising
Carrie Harries
Media Manager
Washingtonian
1828 L Street, NW, Suite 200
Washington, DC 20036
E-mail: charries@washingtonian.com
Phone: (202) 296-1246

Art
Eileen O'Tousa Crowson
Associate Design Director
Washingtonian
1828 L Street, NW, Suite 200
Washington, DC 20036
Phone: (202) 296-3600
E-mail: ecrowson@washingtonian.com

Visit Vault at **www.vault.com** for insider company profiles, expert advice, career message boards, expert resume reviews, the Vault Job Board and more.

CAREER
LIBRARY **435**

WCHS-TV

 THE BUZZ
- "Get behind the scenes at a network affiliate"
- "West Virginians, are you ready for your closeup?"

 THE STATS

Industry(ies): Broadcast & Entertainment; Journalism

Location(s): Charleston, WV

Number of interns: *Annual:* 25

Pay: None; academic credit available

Length of internship: *Spring/summer/fall/winter:* usually 2-3 months each

 THE SCOOP

WCHS-TV reaches 500,000 households and over a million viewers, bringing them news and entertainment since 1954. The ABC affiliate is part of Sinclair Broadcast Group, Inc., which owns or operates more than 60 television stations in 40 markets. The Charleston-Huntington television market, where WCHS operates, is considered geographically the second-largest market east of the Mississippi River, and is ranked 63rd in size in the United States.

ON THE JOB

Interns at WCHS-TV gather news, conduct interviews, research, take in feeds, make calls and more. Interns also assist editors, reporters and camera operators. Top interns may have the opportunity to go out on a shoot with the news crew.

GETTING HIRED

Apply by: Rolling. Send resume, cover letter and recommendations to the address below.

Qualifications:
Open to college freshmen, sophomores, juniors and seniors majoring in a related field and able to earn academic credit for the internship.

Contact:
Paula M. Taylor
New Manager
WCHS-TV
1301 Piedmont Road
Charleston, WV 25301
Phone: (304) 345-4115
Fax: (304) 345-1849
E-mail: ptaylor@sbgnet.com
www.wchstv.com

Wells Fargo & Company

 THE BUZZ
- "Top banking internship on the West Coast"

 **THE STATS**

Industry(ies): Commercial Banking; Financial Services; Investment Management

Location(s): Dallas, TX; Houston, TX; Los Angeles, CA; Minneapolis, MN; San Francisco, CA

Number of interns: *Summer:* 50-70

Pay: Paid; varies. Paid vacation; disability/life insurance; health and dental insurance; flex spending accounts; commuter subsidies; 401(k) matching; tuition reimbursement; discounts on financial products; stock purchase plan

Length of internship: *Summer:* 12 weeks

 THE SCOOP

Created by American Express founder William Fargo in 1850 as a "pony express," Wells Fargo is now one of the banking industry's powerhouses. Today the firm has more than 144,000 employees and controls over $338 billion in assets, providing financial services that range from investments to mortgage finance. Wells Fargo is headquartered in San Francisco, but the firm has 5,900 "stores" around the world and on the Web.

ON THE JOB

Interns work in corporate/wholesale banking or Internet services. Banking interns are assigned to corporate and commercial banking, real estate, or marketing and project management areas and focus on the financial services industry. Internet services interns support current projects, including web site and database developement, online curriculum development, and they may also function as business analysts. Many interns find full-time jobs through the program.

GETTING HIRED

Apply by: *Summer:* January 15. *Banking:* e-mail a resume and cover letter to resume@wellsfargo.com with "Corporate/ Wholesale Banking Undergraduate Summer Intern Program" in subject line. Two rounds of interviews at a Wells Fargo Banking office are required. *Internet services:* apply online at employment.wellsfargo.com/Index.jsp?inc_main=emp_sg_ug_su mmer_isg.html&inc_left_col_1=left_menu_ sg_ug_sip_isg.html.

Qualifications:
Open to college juniors and seniors with good written and verbal skills, analytical aptitude and leadership abilities. Minimum 3.0 GPA required. *Banking:* accounting, finance or business majors preferred. Must be U.S. citizen. *Internet services:* computer science or related coursework/experience and two years of Java experience in a corporate office required. Project management abilities preferred.

Contact:
E-mail: resume@wellsfargo.com
employment.wellsfargo.com/Index.jsp?inc_main=emp_sg_under graduate.html&inc_left_col_1=left_menu_sg_undergraduate.htm

Westwood One Radio Network

 THE BUZZ

- "Go behind the scenes at some of the country's most popular radio shows"
- "Help create what America listens to"

 THE STATS

Industry(ies): Broadcast & Entertainment

Location(s): New York, NY

Number of interns: *Spring/summer/fall*: 6 each

Pay: $50 stipend paid at the end of the term; academic credit

Length of internship: *Summer*: 8 weeks; *fall/spring*: 12-15 weeks

 THE SCOOP

Westwood One is the largest producer of syndicated informational radio programming in the U.S., providing traffic reports, weather updates, news, sports, talk shows, music and special event programs. Consisting of two divisions (Metro/Shadow and Westwood One Radio Network), the network earns its keep selling commercial airtime to advertising clients. Westwood One, which reaches 80 of the largest MSA (metropolitan statistical area) markets, is managed by the Infinity Broadcasting Corporation.

 ON THE JOB

Interns are placed in the programming department or production to work alongside seasoned staff learning the radio business and getting valuable hands-on experience. Responsibilities vary with department, but may include working with artists directly or with studio recording staff. Interns can make great career contacts.

⑤ GETTING HIRED

Apply by: Rolling. (Materials must be in two weeks before start date.) Mail a cover letter, resume, two letters of recommendation (at least one from a faculty member) and proof that your school will give academic credit to the address below.

Qualifications:
Open to college juniors and seniors and grad students. International applicants welcome. Must prove school will accept academic credit.

Contact:
Internship Coordinator
Westwood One
40 West 57th Street
New York, NY 10019
Phone: (212) 641-2000

Weyerhaeuser

 THE BUZZ

- "The fastest way to a job with 'the foremost' in forest products"

 THE STATS

Industry(ies): Manufacturing

Location(s): Federal Way, WA (HQ); Boise, ID; Fort Mill, SC; Hot Springs, AR; many more

Number of interns: *Annual*: 100-150

Pay: Varies

Length of internship: 3-6 months; available year-round. *IT:* starting January, May-June. *Other programs:* Starting January, April, June and September

 THE SCOOP

The Weyerhaeuser Company has been leading the field in international forest products for over a century and has been on the Fortune 200 list for almost 50 years. Currently employing 57,000 people, Weyerhaeuser is based in the state of Washington, but has locations throughout North America and Asia.

 ON THE JOB

Internships are available in sales and marketing, engineering, controllership development (accounting), IT, process optimization, raw materials and forest management. Responbilities vary with department. Most interns are placed near the corporate headquarters in Federal Way, and many go on to full-time employment with the company.

⑤ GETTING HIRED

Apply by: Applications are accepted year-round on a rolling basis, but positions are filled according to quarter and half-year markers (quarter assignments are filled by January, April, June and September and half-year assisgnments by January and late May to early June). Applicants should complete a Taleo profile (applicant tracking software) through the Weyerhauser web site. Most positions take online online applications; see web site for specific contact information and instructions.

Qualifications:
Open to college sophomores, juniors and seniors, as well as grad students. Minimum 3.0 GPA is required in most cases. Potential interns will need to pass a pre-employment drug screen and criminal background check.

Contact:
Weyerhaeuser Company
P.O. Box 9777
Federal Way, WA 98063-9777
E-mail: college@weyerhaeuser.com (U.S.)
www.ywoodu.com

Visit Vault at **www.vault.com** for insider company profiles, expert advice, career message boards, expert resume reviews, the Vault Job Board and more.

CAREER LIBRARY **437**

WGBH

THE BUZZ

- "PBS' legendary affiliate in Boston"
- "You'll gain IQ points just working here"

THE STATS

Industry(ies): Broadcast & Entertainment

Location(s): Boston, MA

Number of interns: 30

Pay: None; academic credit available

Length of internship: Varies; available year-round

THE SCOOP

Starting out as WGBH Radio in 1951 in Boston, the media force now consists of three public radio stations and three public TV stations across the state. And its reach extends far beyond New England since it produces almost one-third of PBS's nationwide primetime TV and online lineups. In fact, its *Antiques Roadshow* program is the highest-rated primetime television show on PBS, with 14 million regular viewers.

ON THE JOB

Internships are available in *American Experience*, *Antiques Roadshow*, *Arthur*, *Basic Black*, *Frontline*, *Greater Boston*, *La Plaza*, National Programming, *Nova*, Pledge Production, Research, WGBH Media Library and *Zoom*. Duties range from office support, to answering viewer mail, to research and production.

GETTING HIRED

Apply by: Rolling. E-mail or mail your resume and a cover letter stating the desired position to the address below. Consult the web site for contact information in various departments, and for their specific application requirements.

Qualifications:
Open to freshman, sophomore, junior and senior undergraduates. Students must be enrolled in college and receiving academic credit for their work. Qualifications vary by department, but basic requirements include strong communication, computer and organizational skills.

Contact:
WGBH
Human Resources Department
125 Western Avenue
Boston, MA 02134
E-mail: human_resources@wgbh.org
www.wgbh.org

WGN-Chicago

THE BUZZ

- "A direct line to a job in radio"
- "The only internship where you can sing along with Harry Carey"

THE STATS

Industry(ies): Broadcast & Entertainment

Location(s): Chicago, IL

Number of interns: *Annual*: 20-30

Pay: $75/week. Travel stipend

Length of internship: *Spring/summer/fall/winter*: 12 weeks each

THE SCOOP

Since 1924, the Tribune Company has owned WGN, the first radio station to broadcast a courtroom case – the Scopes Trial. The microphone from the proceedings is now on display at the Smithsonian. WGN was once voted the most respected and admired radio station in the county by the radio industry. Today, it's one of the top grossing stations in the United States.

ON THE JOB

Internships are available in programming, news, sports and promotions. Responsibilities may include editing, writing, developing show ideas and booking guests. Interns often make the transition to full-time employment.

GETTING HIRED

Apply by: *Spring*: December 1; *summer*: March 1; *fall*: June 1; *winter*: September 1. E-mail a resume and cover letter to the appropriate address below. Regular mail is acceptable, but e-mail submissions are preferred.

Qualifications:
Open to college sophomores, juniors and seniors, as well as grad students and college graduates of any age. Previous media experience preferred.

Contact:
Internship Coordinator
WGN Internship Program
435 North Michigan Avenue
Chicago, IL 60611
wgnradio.com/special/intern.html

Programming
E-mail: programminginternships@wgnradio.com

News writing
E-mail: newsinternships@wgnradio.com

Promotional staff
E-mail: promotionsinternships@wgnradio.com

The White House

 THE BUZZ
- "The world's most famous – and powerful – address"
- "Become part of a huge network of high-achieving alumni"

THE STATS

Industry(ies): Government

Location(s): Washington, DC

Number of interns: *Spring/summer/fall*: 90-100 each

Pay: None

Length of internship: *Spring/summer/fall*: 90 days

 THE SCOOP

While still in its infancy as a nation, in 1792 the U.S. began building the official residence of its leaders, the White House. Construction was overseen by President Washington himself, though he never lived there. Its first occupants were John Adams and his wife, who moved into it in 1800. The White House has been home to presidents and their families ever since, and also serves as the president's office. The house has had a searing past: the British tried to burn it to the ground in 1814, and a fire in the West Wing in 1929 did some serious damage. Today, it holds 23 offices, including Press Secretary, Political Affairs, Cabinet Affairs, Public Liaison and Presidential Correspondence.

 ON THE JOB

Interns may work in any of the 23 offices at the White House. Some duties may include assisting White House staff with administrative tasks. Although the hours can be long and the workload heavy, this internship provides perks like no other. Interns get to meet the President, attend various White House functions and are invited to hear various prominent speakers, including members of the current administration and leading members of Congress.

GETTING HIRED

Apply by: Consult the web site for dates. In addition to a completed application available on the web site, www.whitehouse.gov/government/wh-intern-appl.pdf, prospective interns must include a resume, cover letter and three letters of recommendation. Selected candidates must pass a security clearance before starting.

Qualifications:
Open to college sophomores, juniors and seniors, recent college graduates and grad students. Interns must be at least 18 years of age and citizens of the U.S.

Contact:
The White House Internship Program
1600 Pennsylvania Avenue
Washington, DC 20502
Attention: Ann Gray, Intern Coordinator
Phone: (202) 456-1414
Fax: (202) 456-7966
www.whitehouse.gov/government/wh-intern.html

Whitney Museum of American Art

 THE BUZZ
- "A cutting-edge American art internship"
- "Paint yourself a beautiful future"

THE STATS

Industry(ies): Art/Museum

Location(s): New York, NY

Number of interns: *Annual*: 22-30

Pay: $500 stipend and 2 monthly MetroCards per summer program. Intern's ID card is good for free admission to most New York museums and discounts at museum shops, weekly lectures and exhibition openings

Length of internship: *Summer*: 9 weeks (full-time); *fall/ spring*: 10-16 weeks (part-time)

 THE SCOOP

The Whitney Museum has housed over 13,000 works of modern American art since 1931. It contains a research collection with more than 37,000 books and 500 files pertaining to American art, exhibitions and 12,000 in-house collections that reflect "paintings, sculptures, multimedia installations, drawings, prints and photographs," and more.

 ON THE JOB

Interns are placed in the administration, branch museum, communications and marketing, curatorial, development, education, library, publications and registration departments. Interns work under the supervision of a department head or curator with many departmental duties ranging from research and special projects to routine administrative and clerical tasks.

GETTING HIRED

Apply by: Rolling; *summer*: March 1. Submit a resume, a letter of recommendation, transcript, a list of three museum departments in order of work preference and availability (including intended start date), as well as a one-page statement explaining why you'd like to intern and your prospects and contributions through the program.

Qualifications:
Open to college juniors and seniors who have an interest in American art and museum studies.

Contact:
Whitney Museum of American Art
Internship Program
Human Resources
945 Madison Avenue
New York, NY 10021
E-mail: hr@whitney.org
www.whitney.org

Visit Vault at **www.vault.com** for insider company profiles, expert advice, career message boards, expert resume reviews, the Vault Job Board and more.

CAREER LIBRARY **439**

Widmeyer Communications

 THE BUZZ
- "Communication is key"
- "Learn to love controversy"

 **THE STATS**

Industry(ies): Public Relations

Location(s): Washington, DC (HQ); New York, NY

Number of interns: *Annual*: 5

Pay: Paid; $12/hour. Health benefits and metro subsidy

Length of internship: 12-16 weeks; available year-round

THE SCOOP

Widmeyer Communications is an award-winning independent, full-service public relations agency. For more than 15 years it has delivered successful communications solutions to a diverse array of clients, including industry-leading businesses, local and national associations and nonprofits, as well as a host of public-sector agencies.

ON THE JOB

Interns usually work at the firm's DC headquarters, but opportunities are sometimes available in the New York offices, as well. Known at Widmeyer as "fellows," interns gain hands-on experience through a wide range of real-life projects. Fellows work closely with public relations professionals addressing today's "leading issues, causes, and organizations."

GETTING HIRED

Apply by: Rolling. Submit a resume, cover letter and writing sample to fellowships@widmeyer.com.

Qualifications:
Open to all recent college graduates and grad students.

Contact:
Human Resources Manager
Widmeyer Communications
1825 Connecticut Avenue, NW, 5th floor
Washington, DC 20009
Phone: (202) 667-0901
Fax: (202) 667-0902
E-mail: fellowships@widmeyer.com
www.widmeyer.com

Wildlife Prairie State Park

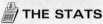 **THE BUZZ**
- "The animals of the prairie are waiting for you"

THE STATS

Industry(ies): Education; Environmental

Location(s): Peoria, IL

Number of interns: *Annual*: 10-14

Pay: Paid; minimum wage. On-site housing may be available; discounts on food and shop merchandise; 2 free guest passes for every month of employment; free admission to the park

Length of internship: *Spring*: March-May; *summer*: mid-May—mid-August; *fall*: September-November

THE SCOOP

Established in 1978, Wildlife Prairie State Park is a nonprofit living heritage experience providing guests with rare recreational and educational opportunities with animals, plants and culture native to Illinois. The 2,000-acre zoological park is home to wolves, bison, waterfowl, black bear, elk, cougar, bobcats, otter, a butterfly garden, wildflowers, lakes, restored prairie and a sightseeing train. The park also features rare, threatened and endangered animals housed in large enclosures replicating their natural habitats.

ON THE JOB

Interns work under a supervisor's direction in the park's education department and must complete a project in addition to daily duties. Common responsibilities include greeting visitors, presenting programs to school groups and the general public (including interpretive programs at special functions such as the Heart of Illinois Fair), monitoring trails, assisting with special events and assisting with other tasks such as opening and closing procedures, animal care and research. Interns are also given the opportunity to write a research-based article for the park's member newsletter.

GETTING HIRED

Apply by: Rolling; *summer*: February 28. Download application (available at www.wildlifeprairiestatepark.org/Educationpages/intern.htm) and send with resume and cover letter to the address below.

Qualifications:
Open to college juniors and seniors, college graduates and grad students. Applicants must have completed at least two years in a degree course in outdoor/environmental education, parks and recreation, biology, education or a related field.

Contact:
Internship Coordinator
Wildlife Prairie State Park
3826 North Taylor Road, R.R. #2, Box 50
Peoria, IL 61615-0998
Phone: (309) 676-0998
www.wildlifeprairiestatepark.org/Educationpages/intern.htm

Wildlife Society

 THE BUZZ
- "A perfect setting for nature lovers"
- "Help save the world through education and science"

 THE STATS

Industry(ies): Education; Environmental; Nonprofit; Science/ Research

Location(s): Bethesda, MD

Number of interns: *Winter/spring*: 1; *summer/fall*: 1

Pay: Paid; $1,200/month. Waived application fee for those interesting in applying for Certified Wildlife Biologist

Length of internship: *Winter/spring*: January-June; *summer/fall*: July-December. Starting and ending dates are flexible

 THE SCOOP

Founded in 1937, the Wildlife Society is an international, nonprofit scientific and educational association working to maintain wildlife with science and education. Society members try to improve wildlife professionals' ability to conserve diversity, sustain productivity and ensure responsible use of wildlife resources. Current Society issues include implementing the 2002 Farm Bill, National Forest System Planning, National Forest System roads management and budgets for federal land management and research agencies, to name a few.

ON THE JOB

Interns work on day-to-day activities. Tasks include researching conservation issues, preparing background information for testimony or comments, writing for and assisting with the preparation of Society publications, and attending hearings. Actual activities depend upon the skills and interest of each intern and The Society's need. Interns also get first-hand experience with the Congressional and administrative processes, as well as networking opportunities with professionals.

GETTING HIRED

Apply by: *Winter/spring*: November 30; *summer/fall*: May 31. Send resume, three references, a college transcript and two writing samples (one general and one technical writing sample are preferred).

Qualifications:
Open to all recent college graduates and grad students. Degrees in wildlife biology/management or other natural resource scientific disciplines are preferred.

Contact:
Laura Bies
The Wildlife Society
5410 Grosvenor Lane, Suite 200
Bethesda, MD 20814-2197
E-mail: laura@wildlife.org
www.wildlife.org

Wilhelmina Models

 THE BUZZ
- "A fashionista's dream come true"
- "See how a first-rate modeling agency works"

THE STATS

Industry(ies): Fashion; Public Relations

Location(s): New York, NY

Number of interns: *Annual*: 5-8

Pay: $35/day stipend. Opportunities to attend fashion events

Length of internship: *Summer*: May-August; flexible hours

 THE SCOOP

Founded by Wilhelmina Cooper in 1967, the Wilhelmina Agency is now one of the leading modeling agencies in the world and represents talent ranging from models to recording artists to other celebrities. Wilhelmina Models operates as a full-service agency representing clients through its New York, Los Angeles and Miami offices. The agency works with hundreds of local model management companies in the U.S. and overseas to scout undiscovered talent and places its talent with companies such as Versace, Donna Karan, Prada, Hugo Boss, Banana Republic, Clinique and Clairol, to name a few. Wilhelmina is also the first fashion company to develop a specific division exclusively representing premier talent in the worlds of music, sports and entertainment.

ON THE JOB

Interns work as assistants to agents, maintaining portfolios and client packages, answering phones and sending models comp card information. They assist with the daily upkeep of the agency. Interns may also help out during the agency's casting calls and events.

 GETTING HIRED

Apply by: Rolling. Submit resume and cover letter to the address below.

Qualifications:
Open to all college freshmen, sophomores, juniors and seniors, grad students and recent college graduates.

Contact:
Wilhelmina Models
300 Park Avenue South
New York, NY 10010
Phone: (212) 473-0700
Fax: (212) 473-3223
www.wilhelmina.com

Visit Vault at **www.vault.com** for insider company profiles, expert advice, career message boards, expert resume reviews, the Vault Job Board and more.

CAREER LIBRARY **441**

Williamstown Theatre Festival

🐝 THE BUZZ
- "Express yourself on stage or off"
- "Off-Off-Off-Broadway never looked so good"

🧮 THE STATS
Industry(ies): Theater/Performing Arts

Location(s): New York, NY; Williamstown, MA

Number of interns: 6-10 per semester; *summer*: 24-30; *spring*: 1 (management)

Pay: None. Free attendance to all performances

Length of internship: *Summer*: 8-14 weeks

🖋 THE SCOOP
Since its founding in 1955, the Williamstown Theatre Festival has produced nearly 500 full productions and myriad workshops. Every summer on the Williams College campus in Massachusetts, WTF presents over 200 performances of classic and new plays, as well as a free outdoor theater series, a cabaret, readings, workshops and events for children.

🏙 ON THE JOB
Interns work in acting, directing, design, tech production, publicity, musical production, box office, general/company management, stage management, production management, house management, photography, literary management and publications management. Interns can create and design their own projects while working with industry professionals.

💰 GETTING HIRED
Apply by: Rolling. Write for an application.

Qualifications:
Open to all college freshmen, sophomores, juniors and seniors, recent college graduates and grad students.

Contact:
Internship Coordinator
Williamstown Theatre Festival
229 West 42nd Street, #801
New York, NY 10036
Phone: (212) 395-9090
Fax: (212) 395-9099
www.wtfestival.org

Williamstown Theatre Foundation
P.O. Box 517
Williamstown, MA 01267
Phone: (413) 458-3200

Wilma Theater

🐝 THE BUZZ
- "Pennsyvlanians who love show business, look here"
- "Great stage theater experience in Philly"

🧮 THE STATS
Industry(ies): Theater/Performing Arts

Location(s): Philadelphia, PA

Number of interns: *Fall, winter/spring, summer*: 6-8 each

Pay: None; academic credit. Attendance welcome at symposia, script readings and preview performances; free tickets to Wilma productions and other local theaters; discounts on studio school classes

Length of internship: Usually, *fall*: August-December; *winter/ spring*: January-May; *summer*: June-August. Start-dates are flexible and can be worked around students' academic schedules

🖋 THE SCOOP
Established in 1973, the Wilma Theater took its name from a feminist collective asserting that Shakespeare's sister was named Wilma(!). The Wilma Theater presents the Philadelphia community with performances like the *Bread & Puppet Theatre*, *Mabou Mines*, *Charles Ludlam's Ridiculous Theatrical Company*, *The Wooster Group*, *Ping Chong & the Fiji Company* and *Spalding Gray*. Recent productions include works by Bertolt Brecht, Athol Fugard, Eugene Ionesco, Joe Orton and Tom Stoppard, as well as new American plays by Tina Howe, Romulus Linney, Quincy Long, Doug Wright, Amy Freed and many others.

🏙 ON THE JOB
Internships are designed to promote maximum growth for adminstrative career paths in the arts and theater. Internships and residencies are available in literary, marketing, public relations, development, special events and education.

💰 GETTING HIRED
Apply by: *Fall*: September 1; *winter/spring*: November 30; *summer*: April 30. Send a resume with a cover letter specifying available dates and preferred position.

Qualifications:
Open to sophomore, junior and senior undergraduate students who have completed a minimum of one year of study, grad students, recent college graduates and career changers currently enrolled in a degree program.

Contact:
Attention: Deborah deCastro Braak
The Wilma Theater
265 South Broad Street
Philadelphia, PA 19107
E-mail: DLB@wilmatheater.org
www.wilmatheater.org

Wilson Quarterly

 THE BUZZ
- "Follow in Wilson's path to greatness"
- "Write your way up Capitol Hill"

 THE STATS

Industry(ies): Publishing

Location(s): Washington, DC

Number of interns: *Spring/summer/fall*: 2 each

Pay: Paid; $6.15/hour

Length of internship: *Spring*: January-May; *summer*: June-August; *fall*: September-December; interns work full-time (32 hours/week). Start- and end-dates are flexible; interns have the option to extend

 THE SCOOP

A division of the Woodrow Wilson International Center for Scholars, *The Wilson Quarterly* is an independent magazine that concentrates on a broad range of issues pertaining to policy, food, culture, religion, science and other fields important to humanity. *The Quarterly* provides scholars, specialists and others with a forum for ideas on the global need for food, ideologies of America and portraits of Mars.

ON THE JOB

Interns work on projects with *Quarterly* editors, researching and fact-checking editorial articles. They use the Library of Congress, the Wilson Center's library, and conduct telephone interviews to gather background information, as well as obtain permission to use art for the magazine. They may write short sidebars appearing within the main articles or contribute to short review sections.

GETTING HIRED

Apply by: Rolling; *spring*: October 15; *summer*: March 15; *fall*: July 15. Online application available at wwics.si.edu/internships/internappform.doc. Send completed application, along with resume, cover letter, three writing samples (500 words each) and three references, to the address below. Faxed or e-mailed applications are not accepted.

Qualifications:
Open to undergraduates who have completed at least their first year, as well as recent college graduates. Applicants can be studying any liberal arts major, but excellent writing skills, attention to detail and the ability to work well under deadline pressures are essential.

Contact:
James Carman, Managing Editor
Wilson Quarterly
One Woodrow Wilson Plaza
1300 Pennsylvania Avenue, NW
Washington, DC 20004-3027
Phone: (202) 691-4023
E-mail: wq@wwic.si.edu
wilsoncenter.org/index.cfm?fuseaction=wq.list

Winant and Clayton Volunteers

 THE BUZZ
- "Beyond tea and scones"

 THE STATS

Industry(ies): Nonprofit; Tourism/Recreation

Location(s): London

Number of interns: *Summer*: 20

Pay: $70/week stipend. Housing and round-trip transportation provided

Length of internship: *Summer*: 9 weeks (7 weeks placement, 2 weeks independent travel)

 THE SCOOP

Winant and Clayton Volunteers was hatched in 1948 by the U.S. Ambassador to Great Britain during WWII (John G. Winant) and church vicar Reverend Phillip "Tubby" Clayton (who was also the private chaplain to the Queen Mother). They believed that a cultural exchange of energetic and caring volunteers would promote personal development and improve U.S.-British relations. Brits volunteering in the U.S. are called Claytons, while Americans volunteering in the UK are called Winants.

ON THE JOB

Winants volunteer for a variety of social service providers, primarily in London's East End, joining other community members in addressing the area's needs concerning playgrounds, rehabilitation programs, neighborhood associations and community health programs, among other things. Winants should be prepared to volunteer independently and in the field. There is not much desk work involved.

GETTING HIRED

Apply by: *Summer*: February 10. Download the application at www.winantclaytonvolunteer.org. Send the completed form with three letters of reference. The application process includes an interview.

Qualifications:
Open to all U.S. citizens over the age of 18.

Contact:
Winant and Clayton Volunteers
109 East 50th Street
New York, NY 10022
Phone: (212) 378-0271
E-mail: info@winantclaytonvolunteer.org
www.winantclaytonvolunteer.org

Visit Vault at **www.vault.com** for insider company profiles, expert advice, career message boards, expert resume reviews, the Vault Job Board and more.

CAREER LIBRARY **443**

Wired

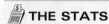 **THE BUZZ**
- "Literate technology lovers needed"

THE STATS

Industry(ies): Journalism; Publishing; Technology

Location(s): San Francisco, CA

Number of interns: *Annual*: 4

Pay: Paid; $12/hour

Length of internship: 6 months; terms run from January to June and from July to December; 40 hours/week

THE SCOOP

Wired is an innovative magazine for technophiles. Founded in 1993, *Wired*'s mission is to "uncover the most surprising and resonant stories about the people, companies, technologies, and ideas that are transforming our lives." Through its authoritative coverage of the digital age, *Wired* helps readers navigate the hot-button issues of the 21st century. Wired was nominated for a National Magazine award for General Excellence in 2004, 2005, and 2006; it won in that category in 2005.

 **ON THE JOB**

Interns work in the editorial department, with the research chief, products editor and senior editors in the Start and Play sections. Their attendance is required at *Wired* staff meetings, and more than welcome at parties and social events. Interns also receive acknowledgement in the magazine's masthead, enjoy a young and casual office culture, and have access to free copies of the magazine.

GETTING HIRED

Apply by: E-mail only. Follow guidelines in the postings on Mediabistro.com and Craigslist.org in spring and fall.

Qualifications:

Open to recent college graduates and grad students. International applicants welcome. Not appropriate for full-time students.

Contact:
E-mail: internships@wiredmag.com
www.wired.com/wired

WISH-TV 8

THE BUZZ
- "One of the Midwest's major news programs"

THE STATS

Industry(ies): Broadcast & Entertainment; Journalism

Location(s): Indianapolis, IN

Number of interns: Varies

Pay: None; academic credit

Length of internship: *Spring*: 15 weeks; *summer*: 10-12 weeks; *fall*: 15 weeks

THE SCOOP

Indianapolis's Channel 8 news went on the air with a 6 p.m. news broadcast on July 1, 1954. That was 13 years after WISH Radio's first broadcast. Initially affiliated with all networks, in 1956 the station primarily allied with CBS. The station is now run by LIN Television, a company that owns or operates 30 stations around the nation.

ON THE JOB

Interns work in news reporting, investigative-team reporting, sports, photography, production, promotion, graphic arts, sales and marketing, public affairs and broadcast engineering. Interns work closely with trained professionals who act as mentors. However, they are given specific projects or stories to work on independently throughout their time at the station.

GETTING HIRED

Apply by: *Spring*: October 15; *summer*: February 15; *fall*: June 15. Send resume and cover letter, specifying the department where in which you want to work, to the address below. Interview required.

Qualifications:

Open to all college juniors and seniors, as well as graduate students. Participants must receive academic credit for the internship.

Contact:
WISH-TV Internship Program
1950 North Meridian Street
Indianapolis, IN 46202
E-mail: Careers@wishtv.com
www.wishtv.com

The Witch House (aka The Corwin House)

THE BUZZ

- "Intern in historic Salem"
- "Crucible enthusiasts welcome"

THE STATS

Industry(ies): Museum; History

Location(s): Salem, MA

Number of interns: *Summer:* 5-7; *fall:* 5-7; *winter:* 1-2; *spring:* 1-2

Pay: Unpaid. *Full-time:* stipend. All interns receive a 20% discount on gift shop purchases, and NEMA (New England Museum Association) membership and benefits (including free admission to NEMA sites).

Length of internship: Varies, average 11-12 weeks. Full-time interns work 40 hours/week during the summer and fall; spring and winter interns must work a minimum of 3 days/week for at least 2 months to qualify for a stipend.

THE SCOOP

Some people think of Nathaniel Hawthorne and the House of the Seven Gables when they hear "Salem," but the Witch House is the real deal. Also known as Corwin House for its owner Jonathan Corwin, it is the only structure with direct ties to the Salem Witch Trials still standing today. Built between 1660-1675, Corwin bought the house in 1675 and lived in it for over forty years. During that time he served as a judge on the Court of Oyer and Terminer in the 1692 trials, which led to the conviction and hanging of nineteen people for witchcraft and inspired writers like Hawthorne and Arthur Miller. Rescued from destruction in 1944 and run as a historic house museum since 1948, the house hosts tours, educational programs, theater festivals, a month-long October festival and its newest program, the Haunted City festival.

ON THE JOB

Interns work in several of the departments that run the house museum, including education, publicity and marketing, collections management, facilities management, and gift shop management. They also assist visitors and are involved in sales. During the busy season from May to early November, interns give 2-3 hour tours to the general public in the house's six interpreted period rooms.

GETTING HIRED

Apply by: *Summer:* April 30; *fall:* August 14; *winter:* November 14; *spring:* February 14. While there are deadlines for specific internship periods, applications are accepted all year long on a rolling basis. Applicants should send a resume and cover letter to the address below. If interested in full-time, stipended internships, schedule an interview or submit a 500-word personal statement.

Qualifications: Open to undergraduates and graduates of BA programs. Applicants with an interest in American history and literature, art history, architectural history and theater are encouraged to apply, but students in all majors are welcome

Contact:
Kelly Gascoine
The Witch House
c/o Park and Recreation
P.O. Box 465
Salem, MA 01970
Fax: (978) 741-0578
E-mail: info@corwinhouse.org
www.salemweb.com/witchhouse

Visit Vault at **www.vault.com** for insider company profiles, expert advice, career message boards, expert resume reviews, the Vault Job Board and more.

CAREER
LIBRARY **445**

WNYC FM 93.9/AM 820 Radio

 THE BUZZ
- "Help spread the word around New York"

 THE STATS

Industry: Broadcast & Entertainment; Journalism

Location(s): New York, NY

Number of interns: Varies

Pay: None; possible academic credit

Length of internship: Varies according to intern schedule and station needs; 3-month commitment preferred

 THE SCOOP

WNYC is the oldest continuously operational radio station in New York – founded in June 1922. As 820 AM, it partnered with the classical music station 93.9 FM 21 years later. The two stations were New York City-owned and -operated until they were purchased by the WNYC foundation in 1995. From news and politics to opinion and comedy, the two public radio stations feature popular shows such as *Fresh Air*, a program about popular culture, and NPR's *All Things Considered*.

ON THE JOB

Volunteers – or interns, if you prefer – have always been in demand at WNYC for financial reasons. There are no departments or even strict walls between interns and volunteers, as neither is paid a salary. Interns and volunteers can be as peripheral or deeply involved as they would like, working as late as they please on projects they choose themselves, or leaving early if they so choose. The flexibility allows interns to learn about many aspects of the radio business, or specialize in just a few.

GETTING HIRED

Apply by: Rolling. Intern applications are filed for six months if there is no immediate availability.

Qualifications:
Open to high school graduates, college freshmen, sophomores, juniors and seniors, and college graduates. Interns are able to get academic credit if enrolled in an accredited program. Otherwise, WNYC welcomes all applicants.

Contact:
Register your interest to volunteer at www.wnyc.org/volunteer/ volunteer_application.html. Interns can apply with a resume and cover letter, sent electronically to:

Traci Jackson
Human Resources
E-mail: employment@wnyc.org
www.wnyc.org/about/volunteer.html

Wolf Trap Foundation for the Performing Arts

 **THE BUZZ**
- "Start an arts management career in the DC area"
- "Help spread a love of the performing arts to children"

THE STATS

Industry(ies): Theater/Performing Arts

Location(s): Vienna, VA

Number of interns: *Annual*: 28-30

Pay: Paid; $2,520 full-time; up to $1,512 part-time. Free concert tickets, discounts at gift shops, guest speaker series, field trips

Length of internship: 12 weeks. *Summer*: May-August, full-time (40-plus hours/week); *fall*: September-December, part-time (maximum 24 hours/week); *spring*: January-April part-time (maximum 24 hours/week)

THE SCOOP

As America's National Park for the Performing Arts, Wolf Trap plays a big part in both the local and national arts communities. Through a wide range of artistic and education programs, Wolf Trap promotes American cultural life and presents the finest in pop, country, folk, classical, opera, jazz and blues, dance and performance art throughout the year at its two venues, the Filene Center and The Barns of Wolf Trap. Some of the most popular artists share the season lineup with rising stars, artists from around the globe and the premieres of specially commissioned works. Additionally, Wolf Trap presents educational programs throughout the Washington, DC, metropolitan area, across the U.S. and abroad. Wolf Trap aims to make the arts accessible and affordable to the broadest possible audience.

ON THE JOB

Interns work in the Wolf Trap Opera Company (in directing, administrative, stage management and technical areas) and in education, development, communications and marketing, human resources, accounting, the box office, group sales, information systems, Internet programs, special events, program and production, and planning and initiatives. Wolf Trap provides its interns with a guest speaker series, field trips, performance facility tours, a mentorship program and professional development training workshops. The Josie A. Bass Internship Program for African-American Students and Los Padres Internship Program for Hispanic/Latino Students expose minority interns to arts administration and prepare them for a career in arts management.

GETTING HIRED

Apply by: *Summer*: March 1; *fall*: July 1; *spring*: November 1. Submit resume, cover letter with a brief personal statement detailing career intentions and department of interest, two references and two contrasting samples of writing no more than three pages each (technical, scenic painting, costuming, stage management, accounting, graphic design, information systems or photography applicants don't need this). Graphic design applicants should include three desktop publishing/design samples.

Qualifications:
Open to sophomore, junior and senior undergraduate students who have completed a minimum of one year of study (or the equivalent), grad students, recent college graduates (up to two years out of school), and career changers currently enrolled in a degree program.

Contact:
Wolf Trap Foundation for the Performing Arts
Intern Coordinator
1645 Trap Road
Vienna, VA 22182
Phone: (703) 255-1933 or (800) 404-8461
Fax: (703) 255-1924
E-mail: internships@wolftrap.org
www.wolf-trap.org/interns/interns.html

Visit Vault at **www.vault.com** for insider company profiles, expert advice, career message boards, expert resume reviews, the Vault Job Board and more.

CAREER LIBRARY **447**

Women Express/Teen Voices

 THE BUZZ
- "Make 'girl power' a reality"

 **THE STATS**

Industr(ies): Journalism; Nonprofit; Publishing

Location(s): Boston, MA

Number of interns: *Annual*: 100

Pay: None; academic credit available

Length of internship: *Summer/fall/winter*: 12 weeks minimum each, ongoing. 10-15 hours/week minimum for most internships; 6-8 hours/week for mentorships

 THE SCOOP

Women Express, founded in 1988, is a nonprofit organization to further social and economic justice by empowering teenage and young adult women. The company uses SHOUT! (Sisters Helping Other Unheard Teens), a journalism mentoring program, and Girls LEAD (Leadership, Empowerment, Activism, Diversity), a critical thinking and enrichment program; and *Teen Voices* magazine and Teen Voices Online to promote positive attitudes and get its social justice message out to young women and girls. The population most directly served is made up of primarily low-income teen girls of color ages 13-18 who live in Boston.

 ON THE JOB

Internship positions are available in the following departments: Teen Program; Fundraising; Marketing; Membership; Technology; Editorial; Mentoring; Art; Photography; Finance; Office Management; and Executive Assistant. Responsibilities vary with placement but may include filing, copying and clerical duties.

GETTING HIRED

Apply by: Rolling. Submit a resume, cover letter and a three- to five-page writing sample to hr@teenvoices.com.

Qualifications:

Open to high school students (ages 18 and over), college students, recent college graduates and grad students. Women of color strongly urged to apply. International applicants welcome.

Contact:

Internship Coordinator
Women Express/Teen Voices
80 Summer Street, Suite 300
Boston, MA 02110
E-mail: hr@teenvoices.com
Phone: (617) 426-5505
www.teenvoices.com

Women Make Movies

 THE BUZZ
- "Learn how to make flicks"
- "Make a beautiful picture behind the scenes"

THE STATS

Industry(ies): Broadcast & Entertainment; Film; Nonprofit

Location(s): New York, NY

Number of interns: *Fall/winter/summer*: 3-5 per department

Pay: None. $4 travel reimbursement/day; free workshops; access to in-house screening room; invitations to events; free movie rentals. Interns volunteering for more than 30 hours/week get $5/day for lunch. An internship stipend of $150 per month is available for web site maintenance assistants with FrontPage skills

Length of internship: *Fall/winter/summer*: 2 months minimum, 3 months is optimal. Interns must work a minimum of 15 hours/week

 THE SCOOP

Women Make Movies was founded in 1972 to address the misrepresentation of women in the media industry through an internationally recognized nonprofit. The organization provides services to both users and makers of film and video programs, with an emphasis on supporting work by women of color. As the leading distributor of women's films and videotapes in North America with over 400 titles, Women Make Movies works with institutions that employ noncommercial, educational media outlets. This includes museums, galleries, colleges and universities, as well as other nonprofit organizations and agencies.

 ON THE JOB

Interns work as assistants in distribution, promotions, the general office, artist services and media workshop, marketing and graphic production/web site maintenance.

GETTING HIRED

Apply by: Rolling. Rolling. Check the website (www.wmm.com) for specific deadlines for the fall/winter/summer intern periods. The application can be downloaded at http://www.wmm.com/about/jobs.shtml#internship. Send a completed application, cover letter, and resume to the address below.

Qualifications:

Open to high school juniors and seniors, college freshmen, sophomores, juniors and seniors, and grad students. International applicants welcome.

Contact:

Women Make Movies
Internship Coordinator
462 Broadway, Suite 500WS
New York, NY 10013
Phone: (212) 925-0606
Fax: (212) 925-2052
E-mail: adminassist@wmm.com or webinfo@wmm.com
www.wmm.com

The Women's Institute for Freedom of the Press

 THE BUZZ

- "Political powerhouses wanted"
- "Affinity for women's rights advocates"

 **THE STATS**

Industry(ies): Education; Journalism; New/Interactive Media; Nonprofit; Publishing

Location(s): Washington, DC

Number of interns: *Annual:* up to 3

Pay: None. Activities and events in DC area

Length of internship: Varies (2-month commitment is required). Part-time schedule – usually 2 days/week in the office, 10 a.m.-2 p.m.; the rest of the part-time internship is independent

 THE SCOOP

The Women's Institute for Freedom of the Press (WIFP) was founded in 1972 by Dr. Donna Allen as a nonprofit research, education and publishing organization operated by a completely voluntary, unpaid staff. It advocates freedom of the press through democratizing media communications. WIFP also publishes the annual *Directory of Women's Media*, available in print and online, as well as an annual print newsletter and a montly online newsletter, both titled *Voices for Media Democracy*.

 **ON THE JOB**

Interns work as part-time assistants focusing on various independent projects, which may include writing and editing articles for the newsletters and publications representing WIFP at meetings with other organizations.

GETTING HIRED

Apply by: Rolling. Submit a resume and cover letter explaining the reason for your interest in an internship with WIFP.

Qualifications:
Open to all college freshmen, sophomores, juniors and seniors, recent college graduates and grad students with a concern for media democracy issues and extending women's voices.

Contact:
Women's Institute for Freedom of the Press
Director: Dr. Martha Leslie Allen
1940 Calvert Street, NW
Washington, DC 20009-1502
Phone: (202) 265-6707
E-mail: martha.allen@wifp.org
www.wifp.org/internship.html

Women's International League for Peace & Freedom

 THE BUZZ

- "Work for world peace in the suffragette tradition"

 THE STATS

Industry(ies): Government; Law; Nonprofit

Location(s): Philadelphia, PA; New York, NY; Geneva

Number of interns: *Annual:* 3-6 (New York); 7-12 (Philadelphia)

Pay: Possible stipend (amount varies)

Length of internship: *Spring/summer/fall:* 12 weeks each

 THE SCOOP

Founded in 1915 by Jane Addams, the first female Nobel Peace Prize winner, along with women from 12 other countries, the Women's International League for Peace & Freedom is the oldest and largest feminist peace group in the world. The organization stemmed from a meeting at the Hague just 10 months before the outbreak of World War I. The secretary general's office is in Geneva, Switzerland, with the U.S. headquarters in Philadelphia and an office in New York.

 ON THE JOB

Interns work with an all-female staff who run the office in a participatory, feminist mode. Positions are usually available in leadership/outreach, development and Internet communications. There is also a Dean Reed Program intern, who works with WILPF branches around the country, as well as a Jeannette Rankin intern who concentrates on legal research. Rankin was the first woman elected to the U.S. House of Representatives.

GETTING HIRED

Apply by: *Spring:* November 15; *summer:* April 1; *fall:* July 15. Send resume, writing sample and letter stating internship goals, dates available and desired position to the address below. An interview will be required.

Qualifications:
Open to all college freshmen, sophomores, juniors and seniors, recent college graduates and grad students.

Contact:
Jody Dodd
WILPF National Office
1213 Race Street
Philadelphia, PA 19107-1691
Phone: (215) 563-7110
Fax: (215) 563-5527
E-mail: jdodd@wilpf.org
www.wilpf.org

Visit Vault at **www.vault.com** for insider company profiles, expert advice, career message boards, expert resume reviews, the Vault Job Board and more.

CAREER LIBRARY **449**

Women's Sports Foundation

 THE BUZZ
- "Strong women wanted"
- "You are women, time to roar"
- "Calling all athletic junkies"

 THE STATS

Industry(ies): Education; Sports

Location(s): East Meadow, NY

Number of interns: *Annual*: 30

Pay: Paid; $450-1000/month (full-time)

Length of internship: 12 weeks minimum-1 year. *Summer*: June-August; *fall*: September-December; *winter/spring*: January-May

 THE SCOOP

Founded in 1974 by Billie Jean King, the Women's Sports Foundation works to ensure equal opportunity in sports and fitness for all females. Through individual and corporate donations, The Foundation reaches out to education, advocacy, research and leadership programs.

 ON THE JOB

The first part of an intern's day deals heavily with activities surrounding The Foundation's Information Referral Service, where the interns answer phones, respond to requests and refer people to other sources for information. The rest of the day is spent working with department supervisors to complete various projects. Past projects have included researching events, writing articles and helping to gather information related to distributing grants. Interns are assigned to education, public relations, advocacy, special events, marketing, publications, Web development and athlete services.

$ **GETTING HIRED**

Apply by: Rolling until positions are filled. Online application available at www.womenssportsfoundation.org/binary-data/WSF_ABOUT_ART/pdf_file/19.pdf. Mail completed application, along with resume and cover letter, to the address below.

Qualifications:

Open to students 18 years of age or older, all college freshmen, sophomores, juniors and seniors, recent college graduates and grad students. International applicants welcome.

Contact:
Internship Coordinator
Women's Sports Foundation
Eisenhower Park East Meadow, NY 11554
Phone: (516) 542-4700 or (800) 227-3988
E-mail: wosport@aol.com
www.womenssportsfoundation.org

Woodrow Wilson International Center for Scholars

 THE BUZZ
- "Ideal for international thinkers"

 THE STATS

Industry(ies): Education; Government

Location(s): Washington, DC

Number of interns: *Spring/summer/fall*: 70 each

Pay: None

Length of internship: *Spring/summer/fall*: 10-16 weeks

 **THE SCOOP**

The Woodrow Wilson International Center for Scholars, established under an act of Congress in 1968, functions as a nonpartisan institute for advanced study. It also allows scholars to interact with policymakers, taking an historical and broad perspective on topics such as America and the global economy, the Cold War, urban studies, preventing conflict, Congress and the environment. The Center also produces *The Wilson Quarterly*.

 ON THE JOB

Interns assist scholars with research and handle related tasks. Interns use online academic databases or other publications to search for necessary information. They are encouraged to participate in "panel discussions, conferences and other meetings, beyond the confines of their particular internship responsibilities as well as join staff and scholars during social events."

 GETTING HIRED

Apply by: *Summer*: March 16; *fall*: July 15; *winter/spring*: November 17. You can download the required application at wwics.si.edu/internships/internappform.doc. Mail completed application, along with resume and cover letter, to the address below. Arrange for an official transcript and two letters of recommendation to be sent to the same address.

Qualifications:

Open to college seniors (though strongly qualified juniors are considered) and international applicants with a valid F-1 or J-1 visa and appropriate work authorization. Applicants must have a GPA of 3.5 or higher.

Contact:
Internships Coordinator, Woodrow Wilson Center
One Woodrow Wilson Plaza
1300 Pennsylvania Avenue, NW
Washington, DC 20004-3027
Phone: (202) 691-4000
Fax: (202) 691-4001
E-mail: internships@wilsoncenter.org
www.wilsoncenter.org

Work Experience Outbound

 THE BUZZ
• "Sunscreen not included"

 THE STATS

Industry(ies): Education; Environmental; Tourism/Recreation

Location(s): Australia; New Zealand; Russia

Number of interns: *Annual*: 650

Pay: Small stipend for the Russian Program (plus a $1,695 program fee); regular pay for the Australian and New Zealand Programs, depending on position

Length of internship: *Russia*: 4-8 weeks; *Australia*: 4 months; *New Zealand*: 4 or 12 months

 **THE SCOOP**

Work Experience Outbound matches U.S. students with employers based in Australia and New Zealand in its Work Experience Down Under (WEDU) program in order to foster a cultural exchange between the U.S. and the two countries. Australian and New Zealand students come to work in the U.S. and Americans head over to Australia and New Zealand. The organization has also been placing American students in Russia with its Camp Counselors Russia program for 13 years.

ON THE JOB

Intern duties vary depending on placement. In Russia, students typically work as camp counselors. In Australia and New Zealand, students travel on a four-month work/travel visa (with WEDU as their sponsoring agency) but are required to find their own living accomodations and position of employment. WEDU provides assistance in the job hunt.

GETTING HIRED

Apply by: Rolling for WEDU; April 15 for Camp Counselors Russia. Download applicantion at www.ccusa.com/applications and submit a $35 fee with form.

Qualifications:
Open high school graduates, college freshmen, sophomores, juniors and seniors, college grads and grad students, and to all American citizens between the ages of 18 and 30 (WEDU) and between 18 and 35 (Camp Counselors Russia).

Contact:
Work Experience, Outbound Program
2330 Marinship Way, Suite 250
Sausalito, CA 94965
Phone: (800) 999-2267
E-mail: ccru@ccusa.com (Camp Counselors – Russia)
E-mail: downunder@ccusa.com (WEDU)
www.ccusa.com/HOME/careers.html

Visit Vault at **www.vault.com** for insider company profiles, expert advice, career message boards, expert resume reviews, the Vault Job Board and more.

CAREER
LIBRARY **451**

World Security Institute

🐝 THE BUZZ

- "Keep your eye on the military"
- "The Pentagon isn't always right"

📟 THE STATS

Industry(ies): Nonprofit

Location(s): Washington, DC

Number of interns: *Spring/summer/fall*: 12-15 each

Pay: Paid; $1,000/month

Length of internship: *Spring*: 5 months; *summer*: 3 months; *fall*: 4 months

🔍 THE SCOOP

The World Security Institute, formerly known as the Center for Defense Information, is a nonprofit, nonpartisan think tank working to bolster national security with international assistance and a reduced reliance on violent (or threatening) solutions. Founded in 1972 by now-retired senior U.S. military officers, CDI has become an independent watchdog of the Pentagon. Committed to independent research and journalism, the Institute provides produces news and policy reports and various publications on such issues as communication, education, and cooperation on the social, economic, environmental, political and military components of international security. An impartial monitor of security issues, the Institute has offices in Washington, DC, Los Angeles, Moscow and Brussels, and provides research and analysis to decision makers from the states to Farsi- and Arabic-speaking countries to China.

🏢 ON THE JOB

WSI hires several full-time interns in foreign affairs research; foreign-language reporting in Farsi, Arabic, Russian and Chinese; television and documentary production; legal analysis; science and technology policy; IT and website administration; and communications. Research interns write for print and online publications on topics such as military policy, media affairs, child soldiers, landmines and missile defense. Television interns assist with the production process in putting together WSI's shows, including Foreign Exchange with Fareed Zakaria. IT interns work on the web site and do some database management and graphic design.

💰 GETTING HIRED

Apply by: *Spring*: October 1; *summer*: March 1; *fall*: June 1. Send resume, cover letter, a three- to five-page writing sample, transcripts (may be unofficial) and two letters of recommendation to the address below. Check the web site for more details.

Qualifications:
Open to all recent college graduates and graduate students, as well as highly qualified undergraduates.

Contact:
Whitney Parker, Internship Coordinator
World Security Institute
1779 Massachusetts Avenue, NW
Washington, DC 20036
Phone: (202) 797-5287
Fax: (202) 462-4559
E-mail: internships@cdi.org
www.worldsecurityinstitute.org

World Wildlife Fund

 THE BUZZ
- "Save more than the whales"
- "Get a jump on science research"

THE STATS

Industry(ies): Environmental; Nonprofit

Location(s): Washington, DC

Number of interns: Varies with organization need

Pay: Stipend for some positions (see web site for details). Weekly brown-bag lectures; contact opportunities with scientists

Length of internship: 3-6 months

THE SCOOP

The World Wildlife Fund began in 1961 when a small but powerful group of European scientists, naturalists, business heads and political leaders banded together in response to a growing need for global conservation. WWF evolved to include over 1 million members worldwide and has helped environmental and conservation efforts in over 13,100 projects across 157 countries. Some of its ongoing ventures include climate change, toxic chemicals in the environment and endangered species preservation.

ON THE JOB

WWF accepts interns into many departments, including environmental education, global forest and trade, and its annual fund drive. Responsibilities and qualifications vary with position, but may include scientific research, writing/editing, developing curricula, database and/or web site maintenance, compiling information sheets and background detail and handling administrative tasks. Many interns are assigned to specific projects and work closely with WWF staff.

GETTING HIRED

Apply by: Rolling. Apply online at www.resourcehire.com/clients/worldwildlifefund/publicjobs.

Qualifications:
Open to recent college grads and graduate students majoring in science education, environmental education, natural history, conservation biology or related fields. (Master's or degree in progress preferred. Program needs vary, so see web site for open positions and and specific qualifications.)

Contact:
World Wildlife Fund
Human Resources
1250 24th Street, NW
Washington, DC 20037
www.resourcehire.com/clients/worldwildlifefund/publicjobs/

WorldTeach

 THE BUZZ
- "For those who love children and learning"

THE STATS

Industry(ies): Education

Location(s): Worldwide

Number of interns: *Annual*: 400

Pay: Host school, community or government provides living allowance (paid in the local currency), to cover day-to-day living expenses (food, local transportation, etc.). It's often equivalent to what a local teacher with the same qualifications would earn. Volunteers pay a program fee to cover international airfare, orientation, ESL training, language classes, health insurance, field support, and placement with a host family and school. Many of the programs are subsidized by the home country.

Length of internship: 1-year and/or summer-long internships available

THE SCOOP

Based at the Center for International Development at Harvard University, WorldTeach is a nonprofit organization that gives interns a chance to make a difference by helping them find positions as volunteer teachers in developing areas of the world. Since its start in 1986, "WorldTeach has placed thousands of volunteer educators in communities throughout Asia, Latin America, Africa, Eastern Europe, and the Pacific Islands."

ON THE JOB

Volunteers become an integral part of their host country, living with a host family or sharing quarters with other volunteer teachers. Beyond their teaching responsibilities, volunteers are encouraged to get involved in community service, such as -- organizing extra-curricular activities and offering classes for parents.

GETTING HIRED

Apply by: Rolling. Send an application form, three essays, a resume, transcript (for year programs only), and two professional or academic references. Interview required for year programs only. Download an application form at www.worldteach.org/apply.

Qualifications:
Open to high school graduates, college undergraduates, and college graduates. Must have a bachelor's degree for year-long programs. Summer programs are open to all applicants 18 years of age and older. Long-term volunteers are required to complete 25 hours of ESL teaching experience (paid or volunteer) prior to their departure.

Contact:
WorldTeach, Center for International Development
79 JFK Street
Cambridge, MA 02138
Phone: (617) 495-5527
E-mail: info@worldteach.org
www.worldteach.org/jobs.html

Visit Vault at **www.vault.com** for insider company profiles, expert advice, career message boards, expert resume reviews, the Vault Job Board and more.

CAREER LIBRARY **453**

Writers Guild of America, West

 THE BUZZ
- "You can work on one your favorite shows"

 THE STATS

Industry(ies): Film; New/Interactive Media; Publishing

Location(s): Los Angeles, CA

Number of interns: *Annual*: 60

Pay: Paid; $672/week

Length of internship: Usually 6-20 weeks; varies with student availability

 **THE SCOOP**

The Writers Guild of America was originally established as the Authors Guild in 1912 to protect the rights of authors of books, short stories and articles. A short time later, drama writers (for the radio medium) formed their own association, then joined forces with the authors, renaming the new entity the Authors League. In 1921, the Screenwriters Guild was born in response to the new motion picture industry, becoming a branch of the Authors League. After more branches merged and the group discovered the art of bargaining, the group renamed itself the Writers Guild of America (with East and West Coast offices) and evolved into the formidable organization the studios haggle with today.

ON THE JOB

Interns work for one of The Guild's member companies in the television-writing field. Interns work closely with seasoned writers, learning how to write dialogue for dramas, sitcoms or other shows. There are great opportunities to make contacts in the field.

GETTING HIRED

Apply by: Rolling. Check the web site for available openings with member companies (www.wga.org and type "internship" into the search box on the left).

Qualifications:
Open to college sophomores, juniors and seniors, recent college graduates and grad students.

Contact:
Internship Coordinator
Writers Guild of America, West
7000 West Third Street
Los Angeles, CA 90048
Phone: (323) 951-4000
Fax: (323) 782-4800
www.wga.org

INTERNSHIP PROFILES:
X

Xerox

 THE BUZZ
- "Advance your career amidst the smell of toner"

THE STATS

Industry(ies): Consumer Products; Hardware; Operations & IT Consulting; Technology

Location(s): Stamford, CT (HQ); El Segundo, CA; Palo Alto, CA; San Diego, CA

Number of interns: *Annual*: 100-250

Pay: Paid; amount varies with position and department. Academic credit available

Length of internship: *Co-op*: 12-24 weeks; available year-round; *summer*: 10-12 weeks; *work-study*: varies; *internship for credit*: varies

 THE SCOOP

How many companies also get to be a verb? Xerox is a $15.7 billion dollar enterprise specializing in document management systems and services that help people deliver the information in a timely manner. Xerox offers one of the widest arrays of printers, copiers, scanners, fax machines and document management software programs in the world. The company also offers consulting services that range from digitizing content to streamline office processes.

ON THE JOB

Xerox's internship programs are known by the somewhat wordy moniker of Xerox College Experiential Learning (XCEL). The paid co-op program is for full-time students who are on leave from school. The summer internship program, also paid, is similar, but only offered during the summer (May-August on the East Coast and June-September on the West Coast). Work-study is a paid internship where students work part-time (20 hours a week) while going to school. The company also offers unpaid internships for which students receive academic credit.

 GETTING HIRED

Apply by: *Summer*: April 1. Submit resume and cover letter (with reference code XHXSTUDENT) online at www.xerox.zcom/employer. For more details on XCEL, go to: www.xerox.com/employment.

Qualifications:
Open to all college freshmen, sophomores, juniors and seniors, college graduates and grad students in the engineering, math sciences, business, economics and information management fields.

Contact:
Garvin Byrd, College Relations
E-mail: d.garvin.byrd@xerox.com
www.xerox.com

© 2006 Vault Inc.

INTERNSHIP PROFILES: Y

Y.E.S. to Jobs

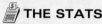 **THE BUZZ**
- "People can't be what they don't know exists"
- "Very professional high school internship"
- "Say yes to this one"

THE STATS

Industry(ies): Broadcast & Entertainment

Location(s): Atlanta, GA; Los Angeles, CA; Miami, FL; Nashville, TN; New York, NY; Washington, DC

Number of interns: Varies, depending on need

Pay: Usually paid; normally minimum wage (amount varies with employer)

Length of internship: 8-10 weeks; available year-round

THE SCOOP

The Y.E.S. (Youth Entertainment Summer) to Jobs program was established when the NAACP, noting a significant lack of diversity in the entertainment industry, called for action. A&M Records founded the nonprofit program in 1987 to give qualified high school students of color a peek inside the professional world of entertainment, providing them early exposure and career guidance. In 2003, the program was expanded to include college students in Los Angeles and New York.

ON THE JOB

Interns work in entry-level positions, often in promotions, sales, merchandising, publicity, accounting and marketing. Arista, Disney, MGM Studios, New Line Cinema, Warner Bros., Fox Sports, Sony Music Entertainment, CNN and DreamWorks are some companies that have sponsored interns in the past. All interns attend a mandatory training program, and most companies have onsite training. Y.E.S. also runs bimonthly career seminars on key aspects of the industry during lunch or after work. Interns are recognized with an awards/culmination event at the end of the summer.

GETTING HIRED

Apply by: *High school/summer*: March 15. Applicants must fill out an application (download from www.yestojobs.org/YESApplication2004.doc) and send it in with a report card, resume, letter of recommendation and statement of interest. Interviews will follow for those in whom Y.E.S. is interested. *College/year-round*: rolling. Send a resume and cover letter to ytjcollegedir@aol.com (no application form necessary).

Qualifications:

The high school program is open to all minority junior and senior high school students, ages 16-18, with a GPA of 2.8 or higher and a 90 percent attendance record. The college program is open to all minority freshmen, sophomores, juniors and seniors, ages 18-25, with a minimum 2.5 GPA.

Contact:

Marsha Cole, High School Program Manager
E-mail: yestojobs@aol.com (cut and paste information; no attachments accepted)

Morgan Fouch, College Program Manager
Y.E.S. to Jobs
P.O. Box 3390
Los Angeles, CA 90078
E-mail: ytcollegedir@aol.com (cut and paste information; no attachments accepted)

YAI/National Institute for People with Disabilities

 THE BUZZ
- "Good social health program"

 THE STATS

Industry(ies): Education; Health Care; Nonprofit

Location(s): New York, NY

Number of interns: Varies with need

Pay: None

Length of internship: Varies with student availability

 THE SCOOP

The YAI/National Institute for People with Disabilities was established in 1957 to provide services, education and training to those who are developmentally disabled and/or have learning disabilities. Services offered include direct care (providing temporary relief for home caregivers), health care, family therapy and professional development, among many others. As a not-for-profit, the network assists over 300 community-based programs in and around the New York City area, as well as some programs in Puerto Rico.

ON THE JOB

Interns can choose to work on the administrative side of operations, doing research, gathering professional information, planning special events, assisting with human resources, fundraising and development, and managing the office. Or, interns can elect to work as educators and supporters of the network's clients, people with developmental disabilities. Since students from all academic backgrounds are invited to apply, the organization works to give interns the support they need to become trained in whatever skills needed to achieve their goals.

GETTING HIRED

Apply by: Rolling. Submit your resume and request an application from careers.hodes.com/yai.

Qualifications:
Open to all college freshmen, sophomores, juniors and seniors, college graduates and grad students of any major.

Contact:
YAI/NIPD Network
Internship Program
460 West 34th Street
New York, NY 10001-2382
Phone: (866) 492-4562
http://yaidreamcareers.org/intern.htm

YMCA

 THE BUZZ
- "Give Y-kids a great summer"
- "Teach swimming and wrangle some horses"

THE STATS

Industry(ies): Education; Nonprofit; Religious

Location(s): Ann Arbor, MI; Augusta, GA; Becket, MA; Boulder, CO; Burlington, KY; Chester, CT; Clearwater, FL; Colorado Springs, CO; Cornwall, CT; Crystal Lake, IL; Denver, CO; Elmdale, KS; Idaho Falls, ID; Imperial Beach, CA; Long Beach, CA; Miami, FL; Oakland, CA; Oracle, AZ; Orlando, FL; Redlands, CA; San Diego, CA; San Francisco, CA; Sarasota, FL; Washington, DC; Woodstock Valley, CT (condensed list)

Number of interns: *Summer*: 100 +

Pay: Paid; minimum wage ($350/week); varies based on position and location

Length of internship: 8-10 weeks

 THE SCOOP

The YMCA (Young Men's Christian Association) was established in London in 1844 by George Williams and a group of friends to counteract the unhealthy social state borne from the industrial revolution. The organization now boasts over 2,500 U.S. locations alone. The YMCA works in 120 other countries, as well, serving over 45 million people with programs that include job training, child care, educational exchange programs and drug abuse prevention, to name a few. YMCA practices Christian principles to help its clientele and maintains that no one is ever turned away if they can't pay for the services.

ON THE JOB

Interns work as camp counselors, activity counselors, site supervisors, program specialists, horse wranglers, administrative support, cooks, mustang riding assistants, trip coordinators, aquatic instructors and lifeguards. Responsibilities vary with position and location, but may include trip supervision, swimming lessons, horseback riding lessons and living in cabins with children. Interns learn supervision and organizational skills.

 GETTING HIRED

Apply by: First week in April; Send letter of interest to appropriate location. See www.ymca.net/employment/ymca_recruiting/pdf/Camp_Vacancy_List.pdf for details.

Qualifications:
Open to high school graduates, college freshmen, sophomores, juniors and seniors, recent college graduates and grad students. Some positions require living with and leading groups of children, so a certification in first aid or adult/child CPR is preferred.

Contact:
Each location has a specific contact name. See web site for details:
www.ymca.net/employment/ymca_recruiting/pdf/Camp_Vacancy_List.pdf

Visit Vault at **www.vault.com** for insider company profiles, expert advice, career message boards, expert resume reviews, the Vault Job Board and more.

VAULT CAREER LIBRARY **459**

Youth For Understanding
International Exchange

 THE BUZZ
- "Bring your lederhosen"

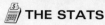 **THE STATS**

Industry(ies): Education; Cultural Immersion

Location(s): Bethesda, MD; Washington, DC metro area

Number of interns: No limit; varies based on program need

Pay: None; mass transportation stipend

Length of internship: Year-round; depends on intern availability

THE SCOOP

Youth For Understanding is one of the world's oldest, largest, and most notable international exchange programs. YFU began in 1951 when minister John Eberly suggested to church leaders that a program be established for German teens to live with U.S. families and attend an American high school. He thought this would help the war-scarred country heal and foster new international relations. Since 1951, YFU offices around the world have exchanged approximately 225,000 high school students. In one year alone, approximately 4,000 students will participate in YFU's programs worldwide.

ON THE JOB

Intern responsibilities include entering data, managing files, preparing mass mailings, making presentations with staff at schools and events, communicating with students and parents, undertaking special projects, and representing YFU at all times.

GETTING HIRED

Apply by: Rolling. E-mail a cover letter and resume to admissions@yfu.org with "Internship" in the subject line.

Qualifications:

Open to college freshmen, sophomores, juniors and seniors, recent college graduates and grad students.

Contact:

Youth for Understanding USA
American Overseas Office
6400 Goldsboro Road, Suite 100
Bethesda, MD 20817
Phone: (240) 235-2100
Fax: (240) 235-2104
E-mail: admissions@yfu.org
www.yfu-usa.org

APPENDIX

Internships by Education Level

Visit Vault at **www.vault.com** for insider company profiles, expert advice, career message boards, expert resume reviews, the Vault Job Board and more.

VAULT CAREER LIBRARY **463**

Visit Vault at **www.vault.com** for insider company profiles, expert advice, career message boards, expert resume reviews, the Vault Job Board and more.

465

Sophomore

Visit Vault at **www.vault.com** for insider company profiles, expert advice, career message boards, expert resume reviews, the Vault Job Board and more.

V**A**ULT CAREER LIBRARY **467**

Visit Vault at **www.vault.com** for insider company profiles, expert advice, career message boards, expert resume reviews, the Vault Job Board and more.

Junior

Visit Vault at **www.vault.com** for insider company profiles, expert advice, career message boards, expert resume reviews, the Vault Job Board and more.

VAULT CAREER LIBRARY **471**

Visit Vault at **www.vault.com** for insider company profiles, expert advice, career message boards, expert resume reviews, the Vault Job Board and more.

VAULT CAREER LIBRARY   **473**

Senior

Visit Vault at **www.vault.com** for insider company profiles, expert advice, career message boards, expert resume reviews, the Vault Job Board and more.

VAULT CAREER LIBRARY **475**

Visit Vault at **www.vault.com** for insider company profiles, expert advice, career message boards, expert resume reviews, the Vault Job Board and more.

V\ULT CAREER LIBRARY **477**

Recent Graduate

Visit Vault at **www.vault.com** for insider company profiles, expert advice, career message boards, expert resume reviews, the Vault Job Board and more.

VAULT CAREER LIBRARY **479**

Visit Vault at **www.vault.com** for insider company profiles, expert advice, career message boards, expert resume reviews, the Vault Job Board and more.

VAULT CAREER LIBRARY **481**

Graduate Student

Visit Vault at **www.vault.com** for insider company profiles, expert advice, career message boards, expert resume reviews, the Vault Job Board and more.

VAULT CAREER LIBRARY **483**

Visit Vault at **www.vault.com** for insider company profiles, expert advice, career message boards, expert resume reviews, the Vault Job Board and more.

VAULT CAREER LIBRARY 485

Internships Accepting International Applications

Visit Vault at **www.vault.com** for insider company profiles, expert advice, career message boards, expert resume reviews, the Vault Job Board and more.

V∧ULT CAREER LIBRARY 487

Internships by State

Visit Vault at **www.vault.com** for insider company profiles, expert advice, career message boards, expert resume reviews, the Vault Job Board and more.

VAULT CAREER LIBRARY 489

Colorado

Connecticut

Delaware

Florida

Georgia

Hawaii

Visit Vault at **www.vault.com** for insider company profiles, expert advice, career message boards, expert resume reviews, the Vault Job Board and more.

VAULT CAREER LIBRARY **491**

Visit Vault at **www.vault.com** for insider company profiles, expert advice, career message boards, expert resume reviews, the Vault Job Board and more.

VAULT CAREER LIBRARY 493

Minnesota

Missouri

Mississippi

Montana

Nebraska

Nevada

New Hampshire

New Jersey

New Mexico

New York

Visit Vault at **www.vault.com** for insider company profiles, expert advice, career message boards, expert resume reviews, the Vault Job Board and more.

VAULT CAREER LIBRARY   **495**

North Carolina

Ohio

Oklahoma

Oregon

Pennsylvania

Rhode Island

South Carolina

Visit Vault at **www.vault.com** for insider company profiles, expert advice, career message boards, expert resume reviews, the Vault Job Board and more.

V VAULT CAREER LIBRARY **497**

South Dakota

Tennessee

Texas

Utah

Vermont

Virginia

Washington

Washington, D.C.

Visit Vault at **www.vault.com** for insider company profiles, expert advice, career message boards, expert resume reviews, the Vault Job Board and more.

V**A**ULT CAREER LIBRARY **499**

West Virginia

Wisconsin

Wyoming

Nationwide

Visit Vault at **www.vault.com** for insider company profiles, expert advice, career message boards, expert resume reviews, the Vault Job Board and more.

VAULT CAREER LIBRARY 501

Internships by Compensation

Paid

Visit Vault at www.vault.com for insider company profiles, expert advice, career message boards, expert resume reviews, the Vault Job Board and more.

VAULT CAREER LIBRARY 503

Visit Vault at **www.vault.com** for insider company profiles, expert advice, career message boards, expert resume reviews, the Vault Job Board and more.

V/\ULT CAREER LIBRARY **505**

Unpaid

Visit Vault at **www.vault.com** for insider company profiles, expert advice, career message boards, expert resume reviews, the Vault Job Board and more.

Stipend

Academic Credit

Visit Vault at **www.vault.com** for insider company profiles, expert advice, career message boards, expert resume reviews, the Vault Job Board and more.

VAULT CAREER LIBRARY **509**

Program Fee

Internships by Industry

Visit Vault at **www.vault.com** for insider company profiles, expert advice, career message boards, expert resume reviews, the Vault Job Board and more.

VAULT CAREER LIBRARY 511

Education

Visit Vault at **www.vault.com** for insider company profiles, expert advice, career message boards, expert resume reviews, the Vault Job Board and more.

VAULT CAREER LIBRARY **513**

Film

Financial Services

Food & Beverage

Government

Visit Vault at **www.vault.com** for insider company profiles, expert advice, career message boards, expert resume reviews, the Vault Job Board and more.

VAULT CAREER LIBRARY **515**

Visit Vault at **www.vault.com** for insider company profiles, expert advice, career message boards, expert resume reviews, the Vault Job Board and more.

VAULT CAREER LIBRARY **517**

Law

Management & Strategy Consulting

Manufacturing

Military

Music/Records

New/Interactive Media

Nonprofit

Visit Vault at **www.vault.com** for insider company profiles, expert advice, career message boards, expert resume reviews, the Vault Job Board and more.

VAULT CAREER LIBRARY **519**

Operations & IT Consulting

Pharmaceuticals

Public Policy

Public Relations

Publishing

Visit Vault at **www.vault.com** for insider company profiles, expert advice, career message boards, expert resume reviews, the Vault Job Board and more.

VAULT CAREER LIBRARY **521**

Sports

Technology

Telecom & Wireless

Theater/Performing Arts

Tourism/Recreation

Transportation

Visit Vault at **www.vault.com** for insider company profiles, expert advice, career message boards, expert resume reviews, the Vault Job Board and more.

V∧ULT CAREER LIBRARY **523**

Alphabetical List of Internships

Visit Vault at www.vault.com for insider company profiles, expert advice, career message boards, expert resume reviews, the Vault Job Board and more.

VAULT CAREER LIBRARY 525

Visit Vault at **www.vault.com** for insider company profiles, expert advice, career message boards, expert resume reviews, the Vault Job Board and more.

VAULT CAREER LIBRARY **527**

Visit Vault at **www.vault.com** for insider company profiles, expert advice, career message boards, expert resume reviews, the Vault Job Board and more.

VAULT CAREER LIBRARY 529

7 187

About the Authors

Samer Hamadeh and Mark Oldman

Samer Hamadeh and Mark Oldman are co-founders of Vault, the leading media company for career information. They are the founders and authors of *The Internship Bible*, and *America's Top Internships*, published by Random House, Inc./The Princeton Review. As the Internship Informants, they are the only nationally recognized experts on the subject of internships.

Visit Vault at **www.vault.com** for insider company profiles, expert advice, career message boards, expert resume reviews, the Vault Job Board and more.

V/\ULT CAREER LIBRARY 531